International Business Transactions

International Business Transactions

Problems, Readings and Materials Relating
to Trade in Goods and Services

SECOND EDITION

Douglas Lee Donoho
NOVA SOUTHEASTERN UNIVERSITY
SHEPARD BROAD COLLEGE OF LAW

CAROLINA ACADEMIC PRESS
Durham, North Carolina

ISBN: 978-1-5310-0636-5
eISBN: 978-1-53100-637-2
LCCN: 2017955183

Carolina Academic Press, LLC
700 Kent Street
Durham, North Carolina 27701
Telephone (919) 489-7486
Fax (919) 493-5668
www.cap-press.com

Printed in the United States of America

Contents

Table of Cases

Foreword

As suggested by its title, this book focuses on legal issues common to business transactions involving more than one nation. International business transactions are, in many respects, similar to domestic transactions that take place strictly within a single country. Like domestic business transactions, international transactions typically involve the exchange of goods, services, knowledge or capital between parties. They are, like domestic transactions, varied and diverse, ranging from a simple sale of goods to complex joint ventures, licensing of intellectual property, franchising, financing, and sale of services.

International business transactions, however, raise a host of legal and practical issues not shared by purely domestic transactions. Some of the complications are primarily practical, caused by distance, international borders, currency exchange, language and culture. Other complications arise because such transactions typically encounter regulatory limitations from multiple governments, which themselves may be the product of international cooperation and agreement. The goal of this course is to examine the legal framework under which these various issues are managed by businesses and the lawyers who counsel them. Rather than attempt a detailed study of the myriad business transactions that cross international boundaries, the materials focus on issues typical to the most common forms of international trade with some emphasis on export of goods and services.

There are essentially four sets of general subject areas presented in the materials. The first subject area focuses on the "private" side of international transactions—that is, the contractual, financial and transportation elements of typical transactions that are controlled by the parties themselves. The international sale of goods transaction provides the primary illustration of such issues. The second general subject area focuses on how government regulation affects international transactions. Here we consider U.S. laws and processes involving customs, export restrictions, boycotts and remedies for alleged unfair trade practices. A third, related subject area surveys the role of international law and institutions in international transactions. This section of the book examines the World Trade Organization (WTO), General Agreement on Tariffs and Trade (GATT), the European Union (EU) and free trade agreements such as the North American Free Trade Agreement (NAFTA). The final general subject area involves the role of intellectual property and licensing in international transactions.

The materials that follow primarily rely on the "problem method" of learning. Each subject presented in the materials is approached from the perspective of a lawyer working through legal issues arising in a hypothetical transaction. Students are provided with excerpts or internet links to relevant primary materials such as statutes, regulations and cases. Frequently, the readings also include links to useful web based resources concerning these primary materials.

In most chapters, secondary academic resources such as treatises and law review articles are deemphasized on the premise that working through primary sources will best prepare students for real practice. Although textual explanation and guidance on basic concepts from the author is always included, the materials are designed to encourage students to think for themselves, use primary sources in a critical and analytical fashion and make practical assessments of possible issues and solutions. *All questions posed in the text are meant to be answered by the students— there are no abstract, obtuse or unanswerable questions set out in the materials.* Students should look for italicized questions along with the assignment that follows each problem. With guidance from their instructor, students are required to examine the material provided not only to learn the relevant law but also to build the essential skills of effective lawyering.

International Business Transactions

Chapter 1

Introduction to International Business Transactions

A. Overview: The Nature of International Business and the Lawyer's Perspective

What are international business transactions? On one level, the answer is simple — they include any business transaction that involves participants in more than one country. Virtually every form of business known in domestic law is also transacted internationally. The most common forms include sales of goods, services and intellectual property; licensing of intellectual property including franchising; and capital investment. What makes these cross-border transactions unique for the lawyer stems from their international character.

The simple fact that international business transactions involve more than one country significantly complicates the practical and legal issues facing the parties and their lawyers. Apart from physical distances, parties to international transactions are separated by jurisdictional, cultural and political boundaries. These characteristics of international transactions create distinct legal issues and concerns warranting specialized study and legal practice. The goal for this introductory chapter is to think broadly about how the international context for a business transaction creates specialized legal concerns. Consider the following simple problem and commentary.

1. Problem One

Professor Don Ho is the creator of a small digital camera and embedded software program that "takes the guess work out of photography." The software not only focuses the camera and frames the picture automatically (without pushing any buttons), but also beeps if the subject is pleasing enough to be recorded in a photograph. The software for the camera is designed for frequent updates which can be delivered electronically through downloading or on a compact disk. The Professor has both United States patent and copyright protection for his product. An on-line distributor of electronics in Spain, Pirates España, has contacted the Professor about commercializing the camera and software for sale in the European Union.

———————

What kinds of legal issues and concerns does the proposed commercialization of the professor's product raise? As an initial matter, one would want to consider the various business arrangements that "commercialization" might involve. Is the Spanish company contemplating manufacturing the cameras in Spain or elsewhere in the European Union? Would it be preferable to manufacture the cameras in a low-cost labor country and then merely assemble or package the product in Spain for distribution in the EU? Are they seeking a joint venture with capital contributions from the Professor or other investors, or instead merely a license to utilize the software and camera design? Perhaps a less complicated arrangement, such as sales in the EU under a distribution or agency agreement, would be preferred? Maybe the Professor would prefer to simply market the camera through Pirates, relying on direct sales of the cameras to consumers? Whatever form the transaction takes, the fact that the parties conduct their business and reside in different countries will cause complications — both practical and legal.

Take the example of a simple direct sale of 100 cameras to Pirates with the software delivered in CD-ROM packaging. Just as in a domestic sale of goods, each party will be concerned, of course, with ensuring the delivery of conforming goods and timely payment of the price. How can these basic goals be accomplished with confidence given that the buyer resides nearly 5000 miles from the seller's place of business, is separated by an ocean, and maintains a bank account denominated solely in Euros? What about the seller's critical interest in maintaining his intellectual property rights embedded in his software creation? Intellectual property rights are territorial. How can the seller's U.S. based interests be protected in Spain from infringement by the buyer or others in the European Union? What if the European Union imposes an unanticipated quota or duty on the goods after contracting, or Spanish customs officials refuse to allow entry based on their perception of public interest, health or safety? What if the goods are lost or damaged in transit, or fail to function? Where would the aggrieved buyer or seller sue in the event of a dispute over alleged contractual breaches? Which nation's laws would control resolution of such disputes?

Note that similar questions might also arise in a purely domestic transaction — after all, California is a distinct legal system and a long way from Florida. There is, however, one important distinction between domestic and international transactions that generates special concerns for the parties in the international context. The resolution of transactional issues in the international context may depend not simply on the relatively familiar and accessible laws of the United States but rather on the application of foreign or international law as well. Similarly, the parties may eventually find themselves before foreign public officials, courts or administrative bodies whose decisions can critically affect their interests or even undermine the transaction. Under these circumstances, a "good deal" can quickly turn sour.

In essence, lawyers involved in international transactions must consider an array of overlapping legal regimes in counseling their clients. For our domestic seller, these may include his home jurisdiction's law (state and federal), foreign domestic law (Spanish), international law (European Union law or applicable treaties), and the "private law" created by his contractual arrangements with the buyer. These contractual terms themselves often reference sets of external standards or commercial practices developed by private organizations, such as the International Chamber of Commerce. Once adopted by the parties, such private "codes" become the law of the contract just as binding as official government regulations. Even if the parties negotiate an agreement over applicable law, all jurisdictions maintain some mandatory legal requirements that cannot be avoided by agreement.

A related complicating feature of international transactions is created through the sometimes competing economic and policy interests of the various governments whose territories are involved. On a most basic level, the transfer of goods, services, or capital across international boundaries necessarily dictates the involvement of governments regulating their national borders. Tariffs or quotas may inhibit or make importation more costly, while embargos or export controls may prevent the shipment of certain goods to particular countries for reasons of national security or foreign policy.

Similarly, while parties are typically free to contract on whatever terms they deem advantageous, most governments impose certain restrictions and requirements on transactions grounded in perceived public interest. Environmental controls placed on automobiles manufactured in the United States, for example, are fully applicable to imported German cars regardless of private contractual arrangements. Capital investments and transfers of technology are often subject to national regulations and restrictions. Domestic law may, for instance, restrict foreign ownership of sensitive industries such as those involving telecommunications, financial services, or media. Taxes, safety regulations, labor laws, currency exchange limits, and even politically based trade restrictions, must be considered.

Many of these government imposed restrictions and requirements, including those involving the customs border, are themselves derived from international agreements or processes such as free trade agreements, the GATT rules or WTO decisions. Thus, although national health and safety laws may prevent entry of certain goods, such restrictions generally must not discriminate against imports under international trade law. The result is a complex matrix of private contract, national regulations, and international rules on fair trade that must be evaluated and understood by counsel.

International traders and their counsel have developed a series of legal responses and practices that help manage the risks inherent in international transactions. In the following materials, we will examine such practices and the legal framework under which international business and trade takes place, focusing on the United States as an example. An excellent and important illustration of this legal framework involves the basic international sale of goods and use of documentary collections, which is the subject of the next several chapters.

Chapter 2

Sale of Goods: Introduction to Transaction Risks and the Documentary Sale

A. Overview

Our goal for this chapter is to identify the most common major risks associated with international sales of goods, and to learn how to alleviate or lessen such risks by using the sales contract, transport documents, and intermediaries. We will start with a simple, single transaction involving the sale of tangible goods.

This chapter focuses on a traditional sales arrangement aptly described as a "documentary sale" (also called "documents against payment" or by the bank process known as "documentary collections"). You will discover that a documentary sale includes several critical components, including the sales contract, transportation and transport documents (e.g., bills of lading), and payment. Sometimes it includes payment through letters of credit. Each of these component parts of a documentary sales transaction deserve a more detailed examination than that given in this introductory lesson. In subsequent chapters, we will take a closer look at the legal issues surrounding each part of the typical documentary sale. The focus of this chapter is on the big picture—gaining a general understanding of the primary risks involved in an international sale of goods and how a documentary sale transaction works to ease them. Analyze the following problem with this goal in mind.

B. Problem Two: Guano from Nauru

1. Facts

Bobby is an organic farmer who lives in Fort Lauderdale, Florida. He wants to buy some guano. Guano is a natural organic fertilizer consisting primarily of bird or bat droppings. Guano is the real thing, according to Bobby, not to be confused with Guano Apes.[1]

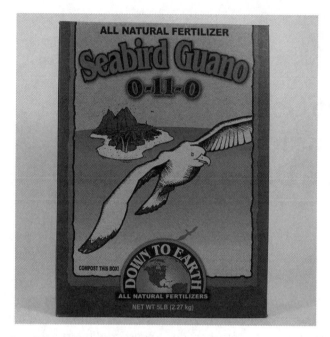

Bobby has found a seller of high quality, inexpensive guano in Nauru,[2] a small (8.1 sq. miles) island nation in the South Pacific. Her name is Sue. Here is where Sue lives and works, more than 7000 miles away from Bobby:

Courtesy: U.S. Department of Energy's Atmospheric Radiation Measurement Program.

Sue is offering to sell Bobby one (1) ton of guano, grade A quality, for ten (10) Australian dollars (AUD is the currency of Nauru) per ten (10) pound bag. Bobby likes

---

1. https://www.youtube.com/user/gapesofficial.
2. http://wikitravel.org/en/Nauru.

the price and wants the goods but is understandably nervous. What if Bobby pays $2000 AUD to Sue and gets bad guano, or none at all? What about the cost of transportation? Would Sue accept U.S. dollars in payment? In any case, how would he get the money to Sue and in what form? Bob would love to wait until he receives and inspects the guano before paying Sue with a personal check. But why would Sue accept this arrangement with the risk that the check might "bounce" or Bob simply won't pay?

2. Assignment

(1) Based upon the resources below, *make a list of the issues and risks that Bob and Sue should consider before entering into this transaction.* Also use common sense and your legal training to date, to think it through. Focus on both general categories of risk (e.g., transportation) as well as specific practical issues (e.g., who has to arrange and pay for shipping, what if the goods are lost). The resources on transaction risks provided below aren't intended to provide a comprehensive picture but rather to facilitate your thinking.

(2) *After compiling your list of issues and risks, explain how Bob and Sue might resolve them based on the resources provided below.* Your evaluation should focus on how using a "documentary sale" arrangement might help reduce or eliminate such risks. *You should, at minimum, be able to explain how a documentary sale works, what risks it addresses, and what it requires.*

C. Resources & Materials

1. Identifying Buyer & Seller Risks

a. General Commercial Transactional Risks

There are many helpful descriptions on the web of the general commercial risks associated with international sales of goods. Consider, for example, lists and descriptions of such risks offered by The Encyclopedia of Credit.[3] You will find that the primary risks to the seller and buyer correspond to basic contractual performance. An exporter fears the risk of non-payment or rejection of goods after delivery to the buyer. Correspondingly, the importer fears paying for goods that never arrive or fail to conform to the contract. There are, however, many other potential risks involved that one should consider, ranging from general economic, cultural and political factors, to concerns that are more specific to the transaction itself. *Review the referenced web site, or others that you may find, to identify what these various risks might include.* The following subsections take a closer look at critical risks relating to payment.

---

3. http://www.encyclopediaofcredit.com/International-Commercial-Risk.

b. Payment Alternatives and Corresponding Risks

Getting paid is obviously a central consideration for any seller. As noted in the excerpt below, "to exporters, any sale is a gift until payment is received." The risk of non-payment despite delivery of goods is a particularly critical risk in international transactions. The following excerpt from the U.S. Department of Commerce, International Trade Administration publication Trade Finance Guide[4] reviews common payment arrangements in trade. In subsequent chapters, we will take a closer look at some of these options. For now, simply take note of basic distinctions between the various options and corresponding risks for the seller.

ITA Trade Finance Guide

Methods of Payment in International Trade

To succeed in today's global marketplace, exporters must offer their customers attractive sales terms supported by the appropriate payment method to win sales against foreign competitors. As getting paid in full and on time is the primary goal for each export sale, an appropriate payment method must be chosen carefully to minimize the payment risk while also accommodating the needs of the buyer. As shown below, there are four primary methods of payment for international transactions. During or before contract negotiations, it is advisable to consider which method in the diagram below is mutually desirable for you and your customer.

Key Points

- International trade presents a spectrum of risk, causing uncertainty over the timing of payments between the exporter (seller) and importer (foreign buyer).

- To exporters, any sale is a gift until payment is received.

- Therefore, the exporter wants payment as soon as possible, preferably as soon as an order is placed or before the goods are sent to the importer.

- To importers, any payment is a donation until the goods are received.

- Therefore, the importer wants to receive the goods as soon as possible, but to delay payment as long as possible, preferably until after the goods are resold to generate enough income to make payment to the exporter

Cash-in-Advance

With this payment method, the exporter can avoid credit risk, since payment is received prior to the transfer of ownership of the goods. Wire transfers and credit cards are the most commonly used cash-in-advance options available to exporters. However, requiring payment in advance is the least attractive option for the buyer, as this method creates cash flow problems. Foreign buyers are also concerned that the goods may not be sent if payment is made

---

4. trade.gov/media/publications/pdf/trade_finance_guide2007.pdf.

in advance. Thus, exporters that insist on this method of payment as their sole method of doing business may find themselves losing out to competitors who may be willing to offer more attractive payment terms.

Letters of Credit

Letters of credit (LCs) are among the most secure instruments available to international traders. An LC is a commitment by a bank on behalf of the buyer that payment will be made to the exporter provided that the terms and conditions have been met, as verified through the presentation of all required documents. The buyer pays its bank to render this service. An LC is useful when reliable credit information about a foreign buyer is difficult to obtain, but you are satisfied with the creditworthiness of your buyer's foreign bank. An LC also protects the buyer since no payment obligation arises until the goods have been shipped or delivered as promised.

Documentary Collections

A documentary collection is a transaction whereby the exporter entrusts the collection of a payment to the remitting bank (exporter's bank), which sends documents to a collecting bank (importer's bank), along with instructions for payment. Funds are received from the importer and remitted to the exporter through the banks involved in the collection in exchange for those documents. . . .

Open Account

An open account transaction means that the goods are shipped and delivered before payment is due, usually in 30 to 90 days. Obviously, this is the most advantageous option to the importer in cash flow and cost terms, but it is consequently the highest risk option for an exporter. Due to the intense competition for export markets, foreign buyers often press exporters for open account terms since the extension of credit by the seller to the buyer is more common abroad. Therefore, exporters who are reluctant to extend credit may face the possibility of the loss of the sale to their competitors. However, with the use of one or more of the appropriate trade finance techniques, such as export credit insurance, the exporter can offer open competitive account terms in the global market while substantially mitigating the risk of nonpayment by the foreign buyer.

. . . .

When to Use Cash-in-Advance Terms

- The importer is a new customer and/or has a less-established operating history.
- The importer's creditworthiness is doubtful, unsatisfactory, or unverifiable.
- The political and commercial risks of the importer's home country are very high.

- The exporter's product is unique, not available elsewhere, or in heavy demand.
- The exporter operates an Internet-based business where the acceptance of credit card payments is a must to remain competitive.

. . . .

When to Use Documentary Collections

With D/Cs, the exporter has little recourse against the importer in case of non-payment. Thus, D/Cs should be used only under the following conditions:

- The exporter and importer have a well-established relationship.
- The exporter is confident that the importing country is politically and economically stable.
- An open account sale is considered too risky, and an LC is unacceptable to the importer.

. . . .

How to Offer Open Account Terms in Competitive Markets

Open account terms may be offered in competitive markets with the use of one or more of the following trade finance techniques: (1) Export Working Capital Financing, (2) Government-Guaranteed Export Working Capital Programs, (3) Export Credit Insurance, (4) Export Factoring, and (5) Forfaiting. More detailed information on each trade finance technique is provided in provided in other sections of the *Trade Finance Guide*.

A somewhat more simple description of "how to get paid"[5] in an export sale is provided by the Australian Trade Commission. The Encyclopedia of Credit website offers a similar description of payment methods with some additional commentary[6] on risks.

c. Foreign Exchange or Currency Risks

Currency or foreign exchange risks (sometimes called "transaction risks") arise from the simple fact that parties to an international transaction are doing business in countries utilizing different currencies. In general, the seller of goods will want payment in the currency of his home jurisdiction or a readily convertible alternative. Thus, if a Romanian electronics store wishes to buy and stock Apple computers, it will either have to persuade Apple to accept Leu or buy U.S. Dollars. One party or the other must exchange currencies, typically through its bank, but ultimately on the Foreign Exchange Market (ForEx). The need to exchange one currency for another obviously requires some method for establishing their relative values—precisely

---

5. https://www.austrade.gov.au/Australian/Export/Guide-to-exporting/Getting-paid.
6. http://www.encyclopediaofcredit.com/Methods-of-Payment-for-International-Sales.

how many Leu are equivalent to one Dollar? These currency values are in constant flux, determined primarily by market forces including basic principles of supply and demand for those currencies. Watch this Common Craft <u>video on ForEx</u>[7] which explains the process in simple terms.

Why is currency a risk factor for international sales of goods? Put simply, the relative value of the currencies involved will undoubtedly change during the course of the transaction. If our Romanian buyer agreed to pay $10,000 for the shipment of computers, and one Leu is valued at that time at twenty (.20) cents (5 Leu per Dollar), the buyer expects the purchase to cost him 50,000 Leu. If, however, the Leu drops in value before actual payment, such that one Leu is worth only fifteen (.15) cents, the buyer must spend 66,666 Leu for the same computers (in order to give the seller the agreed $10,000). That's a lot of Leu.

This risk can play out in reverse against the seller's expectations as well, particularly if the seller has agreed to payment in a foreign currency. Holding receivables owed in foreign currency will result in lost revenue if those currencies appreciate relative to the Dollar (when converted, the payment will return fewer Dollars than originally hoped). If a seller has sufficient leverage, it may insist on payment in its own currency. However, accepting the buyer's currency may be attractive to increase competitiveness.

Buyers and sellers may hedge currency risks in various ways, including "forward" or "future" exchange contracts (agreeing to a rate for a certain currency exchange at a future date) or foreign currency options (buying an option to buy foreign currency at a certain rate). If interested in further reading, there are many useful sources on the web such as: <u>6 Ways to Control Foreign Exchange Risk</u>[8] and the Wikipedia entry on <u>Foreign Exchange Hedge</u>.[9]

2. Addressing the Issues & Risks

a. The Sales Contract

Resolving transaction issues and allocating risks starts with the sales contract. An important feature of private contracting is that, in most jurisdictions, the parties are relatively free to allocate risks and responsibilities as they see fit. The parties can agree on, for example, how and when payment will be made, whether the buyer will inspect the goods prior to payment, the currency of payment, and applicable law. As described in detail below, one possible contractual choice that addresses basic issues regarding payment and delivery involves an arrangement often called a documentary sale (or more generally "documentary collections"). Subsequent lessons will more closely examine the sales contract, its role in international transactions and

---

7. https://www.youtube.com/watch?v=-qvrRRTBYAk&feature=related.

8. http://accounting-financial-tax.com/2009/07/6-ways-to-control-foreign-exchange-risk/.

9. https://en.wikipedia.org/wiki/Foreign_exchange_hedge.

common legal issues arising from it. *For now, simply review the following sample contracts and check lists (or others that you find on-line). Find general illustrations of the subjects and terms parties commonly include in the sales contract to address various transaction issues and risks.* Look for clauses that specifically address the issues you identified in assignment one. After perusing these documents, turn your attention to the specifics of the documentary sale.

i. Model International Sales Contracts

International Chamber of Commerce Version[10]

International Trade Center Version[11]

ii. Check Lists for Drafting

CON-TRACTS.com[12]

IE Business Daily (John Tulac), Part One,[13] Part Two,[14] Part Three[15]

GlobalNegotiator.com International Sales Template[16]

Many other alternative contract models, samples, and checklists are available on the web. A particularly useful source, with a variety of commercial contracts derived from SEC filings, is located at: http://www.onecle.com/.

b. Negotiable Bills of Lading & Documents of Title

If our parties agree to the proposed transaction, the seller will eventually have to "deliver"[17] the agreed upon one ton of grade A guano to the buyer. Unless this delivery takes place at the seller's business premises, it will always involve at least one "carrier" who will take responsibility for transporting the goods to an agreed upon location.

---

10. www.giur.uniroma3.it/materiale/didattico/business_contract/ICC%20-%20Interna tional%20Sale%20Contract.pdf.

11. www.intracen.org/uploadedFiles/intracenorg/Content/Exporters/Exporting_Better /Templates_of_contracts/3%20International%20Commercial%20Sale%20of%20Goods.pdf.

12. http://www.con-tracts.com/id72.html.

13. http://iebusinessdaily.com/contract-checklist-international-sale-goods-commentary-part -one/.

14. http://iebusinessdaily.com/contract-checklist-for-international-sale-of-goods-with -commentary-part-two/.

15. http://iebusinessdaily.com/contract-checklist-for-international-sale-of-goods-part-three/.

16. https://www.google.com/url?sa=t&rct=j&q=&esrc=s&source=web&cd=7&ved=0ahUKEwi 8otCuwsHNAhWmz4MKHWtIBIoQFghSMAY&url=http%3A%2F%2Fwww.globalnegotiator .com%2Ffiles%2Finternational-sale-contract-template-sample.pdf&usg=AFQjCNGSBOnWVhBF jkEyOu_qod2QQEfhXA&sig2=xeK9IoUJEIVnl6lb7sCHUw&cad=rja.

17. Note that the term "delivery" in sales law has a meaning distinct from its common English usage. Delivery in this context signifies the seller's compliance with the contractual requirement that he make the goods available to the buyer at a specified place. Under a common contractual arrangement, delivery in this sense takes place when the goods are turned over to a carrier for transportation, regardless of who arranged and paid for that transportation. Thus, delivery may or may not coincide with transportation responsibilities associated with the goods and does not necessarily imply that the buyer has actually taken physical possession.

You will discover in subsequent chapters that responsibility for transportation can be on either the buyer or seller, depending upon the sales contract.[18] For ease of explanation, let's assume that our seller is responsible for transportation in this transaction, as would be common in a documentary sale. Approximately ninety percent of international commerce still travels by sea. Given Nauru's location, our problem transaction would undoubtedly prove no exception. Sue the seller will, therefore, find and arrange for transportation of the Guano by ocean shipping, to a U.S. port near the buyer.

The seller, who is now also the "shipper," will want at least three things from the carrier. First, she will want confirmation of her contractual arrangements with the carrier—the terms by which the carrier has agreed to transport the goods. Second, the seller/shipper will want some proof of what she has delivered to the carrier, showing that the goods have been turned over and are safely on board the vessel—a receipt for the goods. Third, the seller/shipper will want to retain the right to control, and even retake possession of her goods, until she eventually gets paid—a form of title. The negotiable ocean bill of lading serves each of these functions. Later chapters will more closely examine the legal responsibilities of the carrier relating to the contract for carriage. For present purposes, it is important to understand that the negotiable bill of lading serves two critical functions relating to the documentary sales arrangement: (1) a confirmation that certain goods have been shipped and (2) a document of title giving its holder a right to possession of the goods.

Consider those functions carefully in light of the following description of "documentary collections." Your goal, for now, is not to decipher the various legal intricacies of the bill of lading or documentary sale transaction. Rather, focus on understanding how this arrangement works to lessen buyer's and seller's risks. *Why would parties to an international sale of goods choose a documentary sale? How does this arrangement alleviate certain risks in the international transaction?*

c. The Documentary Collections Process

A documentary sale is, in essence, an arrangement under which the buyer agrees to pay upon presentment of specified documentation regarding the goods. These documents must, at minimum, indicate that the goods have been shipped, and give the buyer ownership rights to them. As described above, a negotiable ocean bill of lading is a critical document in this regard. The buyer is, in a sense, literally buying the documents that represent the goods or, put differently, making payment "against" the documents—hence the alternative general terminology "documentary sale" or "documents against payment." The parties may also, under such arrangements, create an obligation to pay in the future. Here the buyer would receive the documents of title upon signing ("accepting") a bill of exchange or time draft requiring payment at a later date ("documents against acceptance").

---

18. The various possibilities are further explored in Chapter 4, which focuses on terms of trade.

There are many helpful descriptions of the documentary sale on the web. Consider the <u>description by Export.gov</u>,[19] and the practical advice posted on the web by practitioners and export companies such as <u>ABC-Amega.com</u>[20] (with further explanations and an easy to follow <u>flow chart</u>).[21]

Since the actual payment and movement of the documents is typically handled by intermediaries such as banks, this arrangement is often referred to by the banking term for the process—"documentary collections." Review the following descriptions of the process and role of banks. Take special note of how the documentary sale alleviates some, but not all, of the risks associated with the transaction. It is easy to find useful descriptions and illustrations of the documentary sale and collection process on the internet. Try, for example, the <u>Trade Facilitation Implementation Guide</u>[22] provided by <u>UNECE</u>[23] (with diagram).

You should also find the following U.S. Department of Commerce description of the process, taken from its <u>Trade Finance Guide</u>[24] helpful:

Typical Simplified D/C Transaction Flow

1. The exporter ships the goods to the importer and receives the documents in exchange. 2. The exporter presents the documents with instructions for obtaining payment to his bank. 3. The exporter's remitting bank sends the documents to the importer's collecting bank. 4. The collecting bank releases the documents to the importer on receipt of payment or acceptance of the draft. 5. The importer uses the documents to obtain the goods and to clear them at customs. 6. Once the collecting bank receives payment, it forwards the proceeds to the remitting bank. 7. The remitting bank then credits the exporter's account.

Documents against Payment Collection

With a D/P collection, the exporter ships the goods and then gives the documents to his bank, which will forward the documents to the importer's collecting bank, along with instructions on how to collect the money from the importer. In this arrangement, the collecting bank releases the documents to the importer only on payment for the goods. Once payment is received, the collecting bank transmits the funds to the remitting bank for payment to the exporter.

---

19. https://www.export.gov/article?id=Trade-Finance-Guide-Chapter-4-Documentary
-Collections.

20. http://www.abc-amega.com/articles/credit-management/d-p-d-a-and-their-use-in
-international-sales-transactions.

21. www.abc-amega.com/DA-DP_Process_Map.pdf.

22. http://tfig.unece.org/contents/collections.htm.

23. http://tfig.unece.org/about.html.

24. trade.gov/publications/pdfs/tfg2008ch4.pdf.

3. Lingering Risks

The arrangement described above goes a long way toward reducing the primary concerns of the buyer and seller. After all, the seller can retain a legal right of possession for her guano until the buyer pays, and the buyer can be relatively confident that goods described as guano are being shipped by an independent party. But some significant risks for both parties remain. For the seller, it is still possible that the buyer might eventually refuse, or become unable, to pay when presented with the required documents. How can the seller be assured that the buyer won't change his mind or become insolvent? If this happens, the seller will still have control over the goods but will be forced to attempt resale in a foreign jurisdiction, or ship the goods back at great expense.

Similarly, the documentary sale arrangement does not completely protect the buyer from some important transaction risks. Hopefully you noticed that an agreement to pay upon presentment of documentation generally means that the buyer must pay before first inspecting the goods. His obligation to pay is upon presentment of documents, not upon acceptance of the goods as conforming to the contract. In essence, the buyer purchases the documents that entitle him to possession of the goods when discharged from the carrier. Isn't it possible that the goods will prove to be non-conforming once they are delivered? How can our buyer, Bobby, ensure that he will receive the grade A guano that he has paid for?

a. Buyer's Risk: Payment for Non-Conforming Goods

A documentary sale does not guarantee the buyer that the seller has lived up to her contract by delivering conforming goods. One answer for the buyer, we will see, might be as simple as negotiating with the seller over which documents must be presented before payment is made. If the seller agrees, the buyer may require that the seller produce documentary evidence of an inspection by an independent source certifying that the goods provided to the carrier conform to the contract. By naming this inspection certificate as one of the documents required for payment, the buyer now has solid assurance that conforming goods have been shipped. The buyer, of course, must be willing to pay for this luxury.

b. Seller's Payment Risk: Financing Sales Through Documentary Credits

For the seller, the most common answer to the lingering risk of non-payment or buyer insolvency is somewhat more complicated and expensive. One very common alternative is to use bank financing in the form of a documentary letter of credit. A documentary letter of credit is essentially a method of financing which can be added, for a price, to the documentary sales transaction. In later chapters, we examine a variety of common legal issues related to letters of credit, including the responsibilities of banks. For now, your goal should only be to understand the basic function and purpose for letter of credit financing in documentary sales. *Who is obligated to pay the seller under the letter of credit and under what circumstances? How does this arrangement help alleviate the seller's risk of non-payment?*

Consider the following three basic features of a documentary letter of credit. First, the letter of credit is essentially a promise made by the buyer's bank ("issuing bank") that it will pay the designated seller the contract price, upon the seller's presentment of specified documentation. Second, this documentation will correspond to whatever the buyer needs to take possession of the goods — this should include documents of title (bill of lading), customs documents (e.g., certificate of origin), a commercial invoice for the goods, proof of insurance and, if agreed, an inspection certificate. Third, the issuing bank's promise to pay is irrevocable and completely independent of the parties' performance in the underlying sales contract.

If the seller performs by presenting the documents called for in the credit, the bank will pay regardless of the buyer's desires. The bank's obligation to pay is not secondary or conditioned on the buyer's performance or solvency. In essence, the seller has substituted the credit-worthy bank for the buyer. Critically, the bank's obligation to pay is completely independent from the underlying sales transaction and disputes over its performance. If the seller prefers, it can add an additional promise to pay from a bank in its locality by paying a fee for "confirmation" of the credit. If confirmed, the credit documentation will be first presented to the local confirming bank, which will pay and send the documents to the issuing bank.

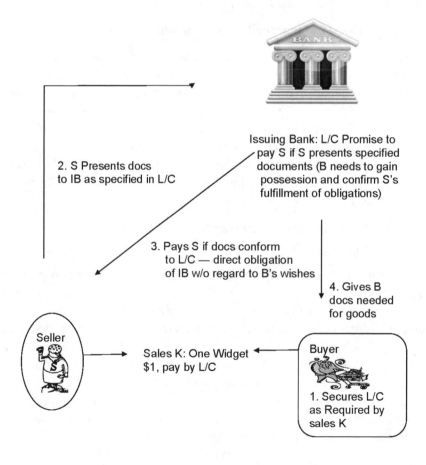

There are many reasonable alternative descriptions of documentary credits on the web including: Creditguru.com;[25] Export.gov;[26] and even Wikipedia.[27] There are, of course, many sophisticated and colorful charts and diagrams[28] of the letter of credit transaction, and images or samples,[29] available on the web, but none with a salt shaker seller.

In subsequent chapters, we examine the letter of credit arrangement in far more detail, with a focus on the bank's legal obligations and liabilities. You will discover that there are also alternatives to the L/C. We will also review the role of other potential participants in such transactions, including advising banks, confirming banks, nominated banks, freight forwarders and carriers. For now, your goal should be limited to answering the following question.

How does the letter of credit alleviate the seller's fears that the buyer might refuse or be unable to pay after shipment has been made?

---

25. http://www.creditguru.com/index.php/credit-management/international-trade-credit-mana gement/articles-letter-of-credit/81-what-is-a-letter-of-credit.

26. https://www.export.gov/article?id=Chapter-3-Letters-of-Credit.

27. https://en.wikipedia.org/wiki/Letter_of_credit.

28. https://www.google.com/search?q=documentary+credit+diagram&hl=en&lr=&as_qdr=all &as_rights=1&prmd=imvns&tbm=isch&tbo=u&source=univ&sa=X&ei=bovjT-DAGJGi8QT -r5yGCA&ved=0CFAQsAQ&biw=1140&bih=544.

29. https://www.google.com/search?q=sample+letter+of+credit&tbm=isch&tbo=u&source =univ&sa=X&ved=0ahUKEwipjpf_uOLQAhUFrlQKHY0SA_cQsAQIKA&biw=1366&bih=633.

Chapter 3

Contract Fundamentals in the International Sale of Goods

A. Overview

Your goal for the next several chapters is to learn some legal basics about the sales contract and its role in the international sale of goods. Chapter Three focuses on contract formation issues and introduces the International Convention on the Sale of Goods (CISG). We will also consider "choice of law" issues and some selected drafting concerns. After completing this chapter, you should know the general prerequisites to forming a binding contract, and how the CISG and UCC would resolve differences between the parties' contractual communications (often called the "battle of the forms"). You should also develop a general understanding of the choice of law problem and its importance. Chapter Four continues our focus on the sales contract by examining allocation of contractual obligations and risks through shorthand references called "terms of trade." Chapter Five completes our survey of basic contractual issues by examining breach and remedies under the CISG. It also briefly reviews sales organized through distribution or agency arrangements. Electronic communication in contracting is considered in our review of e-commerce in Chapter Eight.

B. Problem Three: Inorganic Squid

1. Facts

Barney, a Florida based wholesale supplier of seafood to organic restaurants, often buys frozen squid, or "calamari," for his customers. To be marketable for organic restaurants, the squid must be of a certain size, weight and maturity, and be free of preservatives. By searching the internet, Barney located a seller of frozen squid, Sibyl Industries, whose business is located on the Greek island of Santorini. Sibyl's website displayed an advertisement promoting a special sale price of $10 per ten-pound bag of "grade A" squid. The site presented the following picture of "all natural squid" as the product on sale:

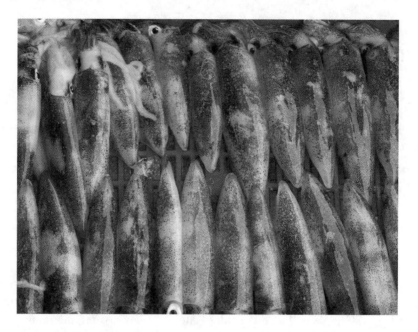

Believing that the product would satisfy his needs, Barney responded to this posting by sending Sibyl an email which stated:

> "I hereby order two hundred bags of grade A frozen Greek squid, $10 per bag, U.S. currency, payment against documents, CIF Fort Lauderdale; product for resale to organic restaurants."

Sibyl responded to Barney's email by sending him, via return email, an "order confirmation" which stated:

> "We agree to sell you two hundred bags of grade A frozen squid, $2000 CIF Fort Lauderdale, goods sold AS IS with no warranties express or implied."

One day later, Sibyl shipped the squid and, through an intermediary, presented Barney with documentation relating to that shipment including an on-board bill of lading describing the promised goods. Barney promptly paid the $2000 in exchange for the documents. When the squid arrived two weeks later, Barney discovered that the squid was of various sizes, about one half being too small for restaurant sales. More problematic, the package labels revealed that the squid contained several commonly used preservatives rendering it useless for his intended resale to organic restaurants.

2. Assignment

Analyze the following questions, not necessarily in the order presented. *Do Barney and Sibyl have a binding contract? If so, what are its terms? What law will control the legal issues involved? If Barney sues Sibyl, who will win and why?* You should assume that both the United States and Greece are parties to the Convention on the International Sale of Goods, which is described further below.

C. Resources

Consider the following resources in analyzing the problem, starting with the issue of controlling law.

1. Choice of Law

Barney and Sibyl appear headed for a dispute. Their respective rights and obligations will turn upon whether they have entered into a valid, binding contract and, if so, what that contract provides about the quality and condition of the goods. These issues, in turn, will depend on what the applicable law provides about contract formation, particularly when parties fail to confirm their intentions in a single, signed document but instead, as here, simply exchange communications.

What is the applicable law? In most jurisdictions, the parties to a contract may choose the applicable law as a term of their contract. Under most circumstances, courts will honor the parties' agreement over choice of law unless that choice somehow violates public policy or circumvents mandatory law.[1] What happens if the parties, as here, fail to specify the applicable law? The existence of an "international aspect," a connection to more than one national jurisdiction, suggests that more than one nation's laws could be viewed as controlling. Would the national laws of Greece apply given that the Seller resides, and delivery of the goods took place, in that jurisdiction? Since Greece is a member of the European Union, perhaps there is relevant EU law that would apply instead. Another obvious alternative is that U.S. law, federal or state, should control the issues.

The question will not turn simply on who sues first and where. Rather, especially given an international dispute, the courts in most countries will consider a set of rules that will determine which jurisdiction's law should control, an issue commonly known as "Conflicts of Law" (or in civil law systems, "Private International Law"). In resolving conflicts of law issues, courts typically apply their own jurisdiction's body of rules for determining the applicable law.

---

1. Such limits on party autonomy appear in most conflicts rules. The application of such mandatory law may come as a rude surprise to parties who may find their selection of law usurped by the forum's decision that such a rule must be applied to their dispute. The EU Regulation on conflicts in contractual obligations (Rome I) distinguishes between rules that may not be derogated from by agreement from those which are "overriding mandatory provisions." The latter is meant to represent a narrower category involving "provisions the respect for which is regarded as crucial by a country for safeguarding its public interests, such as its political, social or economic organization. . . ."

Consider the following two examples of conflict principles, the U.S. Restatement (Second) of Conflicts and the European Union Rome Convention and subsequent regulations. *How would these two different sets of conflicts principles resolve the choice of law issue in the dispute between our potential litigants?*

a. Restatement (Second) of Conflicts[2]

§ 6. CHOICE OF LAW PRINCIPLES

(1) A court, subject to constitutional restrictions, will follow a statutory directive of its own state on choice of law.

(2) When there is no such directive, the factors relevant to the choice of the applicable rule of law include

> (a) the needs of the interstate and international systems,

> (b) the relevant policies of the forum,

> (c) the relevant policies of other interested states and the relative interests of those states in the determination of the particular issue,

> (d) the protection of justified expectation,

> (e) the basic policies underlying the particular field of law,

> (f) certainty, predictability and uniformity of result, and

> (g) ease in the determination and application of the law to be applied.

§ 188. LAW GOVERNING IN ABSENCE OF EFFECTIVE CHOICE BY THE PARTIES

(1) The rights and duties of the parties with respect to an issue in contract are determined by the local law of the state which, with respect to that issue, has the most significant relationship to the transaction and the parties under the principles stated in § 6.

(2) In the absence of an effective choice of law by the parties (see § 187), the contacts to be taken into account in applying the principles of § 6 to determine the law applicable to an issue include:

> (a) the place of contracting,

> (b) the place of negotiation of the contract,

> (c) the place of performance,

> (d) the location of the subject matter of the contract, and

> (e) the domicile, residence, nationality, place of incorporation and place of business of the parties.

These contacts are to be evaluated according to their relative importance with respect to the particular issue.

---

2. Copyright (c) 1971 The American Law Institute.

(3) If the place of negotiating the contract and the place of performance are in the same state, the local law of this state will usually be applied, except as otherwise provided in §§ 189–199 and 203.

If you are interested in further guidance, the full text of the Restatement, along with official commentary, is available from a variety of <u>on-line sources</u>.[3] According to Professor Weintraub, "the Second Restatement, which guides courts and lawyers, is incoherent . . . . Suffice it here to state that the Second Restatement's bizarre mixture of territorial bias and focus on the substance of conflicting laws has mislead many courts into exchanging simple territorial rules for mind-numbing lists of territorial contacts 'to be taken into account.'"[4] Sounds like fun. Let's do it. The following case provides an illustration of the Restatement in action.

b. Case Law Applying the Restatement

i. Kristinus v. H. Stern Com. E Ind. S.A., 463 F. Supp. 1263 (1979)

LASKER, District Judge.

While visiting Rio de Janeiro in December, 1974, Rainer Kristinus, a Pennsylvania resident, purchased three gems from H. Stern Com. E Ind. S.A. (H. Stern) for $30,467.43. According to Kristinus, a flyer advertising H. Stern's wares had been slipped under the door of his hotel room in Brazil. The flyer contained the following statement (in English) in red type:

> "Every sale carries Stern's one-year guarantee for refund, credit or exchange either here or in your own country. H. Stern Jewelers New York, (681 Fifth Avenue) are at your disposal for help and service."

Kristinus asserts that when he purchased the gems, a vice-president of H. Stern assured him that he would be able to return them for a complete refund in New York. In January, 1975, Kristinus tendered the gems to H. Stern Jewelers, Inc. in New York City and requested a refund. His request was denied, and this suit for specific performance of the alleged oral promise to refund the purchase price followed.

H. Stern moves to dismiss the complaint on the ground that the alleged oral promise is unenforceable under the laws of Brazil, which H. Stern contends govern the transaction in question.

The provisions of Brazilian law on which H. Stern relies are Articles 141 and 142 of the Brazilian Civil Code, which provide:

> "Article 141. Except in cases specifically provided for to the contrary, evidence which is solely by testimony is only admitted as to Contracts whose value does not exceed Cr $10.000,00 (ten thousand cruzeiros).
>
> Sole Paragraph. Whatever the amount of the Contract, evidence by testimony is admissible as a subsidiary to or complement of evidence in writing.

---

3. http://www.kentlaw.edu/perritt/conflicts/rest188.html.

4. Russell Weintraub, <u>The Restatement Third of Conflicts of Laws: An Idea Whose Time Has Not Come,</u> 75 Indiana L.J. 679 (2000).

Article 142. There cannot be admitted as witnesses:

IV. The person interested in the object of the litigation, as well as the ancestor and the descendant, or collateral relative, through the third degree of one of the parties, whether by blood or by affiliation."[1]

The question presented at this juncture is not whether H. Stern has properly stated Brazilian law, but whether a New York court would apply that law or the law of the state of New York in the circumstances of this case. . . . We conclude that a New York court would apply the law of New York, and accordingly we deny H. Stern's motion to dismiss.

In deciding choice of law questions, the rule in New York is that "the law of the jurisdiction having the greatest interest in the litigation will be applied and that the facts or contacts which obtain significance in defining State interests are those which relate to the purpose of the particular law in conflict." . . . In short, New York courts balance New York's interest in having New York law apply against a foreign state's interest in having foreign law apply.

An examination of the provisions of the Brazilian Civil Code on which H. Stern relies suggests that those provisions promote two interests. First, they protect the integrity of the judicial process in Brazil against the taints of perjured and biased testimony, by 1) requiring that testimony regarding a contract be corroborated by written evidence (Article 141), and 2) barring testimony from interested parties (Article 142). This interest is not implicated in the present case, since the integrity of the Brazilian judicial process is not threatened in a suit in the United States District Court for the Southern District of New York.

Second, Article 141 protects persons who transact business in Brazil from unfounded contractual claims by requiring that such claims, to be enforceable, be supported by a writing. This interest of Brazil does have a bearing on this case, since presumably Brazil seeks to provide this protection to anyone who transacts business there, regardless of where suit on the transaction is brought. The question, then, is whether this interest is greater than any interest that New York may have in applying its own law (which we assume, for the purposes of this motion, would permit enforcement of the contract alleged by Kristinus) to the transaction involved here.

Although Kristinus is not a New York resident, New York may nonetheless assert an interest on his behalf. . . . New York's contacts with this case are 1) that H. Stern transacts business in New York through its franchisee and agent, H. Stern Jewelers, Inc., and 2) that the alleged promise that Kristinus seeks to enforce was to refund the purchase price of the gems in New York through that franchisee. New York has some interest in ensuring that persons who transact business within its borders (and

---

1. H. Stern's expert on Brazilian law states that the statement in the flyer that Kristinus received in Brazil would not "be sufficient under Brazilian law to constitute a written contract or even a writing sufficient to enable plaintiff, or his wife, to testify as to the Contract." Affidavit of Paul Griffith Garland, Exhibit B to Defendant's Notice of Motion, P 4.

thus subject themselves to some extent at least to the authority of the state) honor obligations, including contracts made elsewhere. Usually, of course, this interest must bow to the paramount interest of the state or country where the contract is made in regulating the conduct of those within its territory. When the contract is to be performed in New York, however, New York's interest is heightened, since its ability to regulate business affairs and the rights and obligations of those within its territory is then directly implicated. In such circumstances, we conclude that a New York court would decline to apply foreign law where, as here, that law would foreclose enforcement of a contract valid under New York law. In short, a New York court would not permit H. Stern of Brazil to contract in Brazil to refund Kristinus' purchase price in New York, and then rely on the laws of Brazil to avoid its obligation under the contract. . . . . Accordingly, New York law should be applied. This is an equitable result, since it simply preserves the dispute between the parties for resolution on the merits.

For the reasons stated, H. Stern's motion to dismiss is denied.

c. European Union Law on Conflicts[5]

Regulation (EC) No 593/2008[6] of the European Parliament and of the Council of 17 June 2008 on the law applicable to contractual obligations (Rome I).[7]

Article 1

Material scope

1. This Regulation shall apply, in situations involving a conflict of laws, to contractual obligations in civil and commercial matters.

It shall not apply, in particular, to revenue, customs or administrative matters.

2. The following shall be excluded from the scope of this Regulation:

. . . . [e.g., legal status of individuals, family law disputes, certain negotiable instruments, trusts]

Article 3

Freedom of choice

1. A contract shall be governed by the law chosen by the parties. The choice shall be made expressly or clearly demonstrated by the terms of the contract or the circumstances of the case. By their choice the parties can select the law applicable to the whole or to part only of the contract.

. . . .

---

5. The Regulation supplants the prior "Rome Convention 80/934/ECC, http://eur-lex.europa.eu /legal-content/EN/ALL/?uri=CELEX:41980A0934, on the Law Applicable to Contractual Obligations" (opened for signature in Rome on 19 June 1980, effective 1991) for most EU countries except the United Kingdom and Denmark. Note that subject matters other than contractual disputes are subject to other EU Regulations specific to such topics, such as non-contractual obligations and matrimonial disputes.

6. http://eur-lex.europa.eu/legal-content/EN/ALL/?uri=CELEX:32008R0593.

7. © European Union, http://eur-lex.europa.eu/. Only European Union legislation printed in the paper edition of the *Official Journal of the European Union* is deemed authentic.

3. Where all other elements relevant to the situation at the time of the choice are located in a country other than the country whose law has been chosen, the choice of the parties shall not prejudice the application of provisions of the law of that other country which cannot be derogated from by agreement.

. . . .

Article 4

Applicable law in the absence of choice

1. To the extent that the law applicable to the contract has not been chosen in accordance with Article 3 and without prejudice to Articles 5 to 8, the law governing the contract shall be determined as follows:

(a) a contract for the sale of goods shall be governed by the law of the country where the seller has his habitual residence;

(b) a contract for the provision of services shall be governed by the law of the country where the service provider has his habitual residence;

. . . .

(e) a franchise contract shall be governed by the law of the country where the franchisee has his habitual residence;

(f) a distribution contract shall be governed by the law of the country where the distributor has his habitual residence;

. . . .

2. Where the contract is not covered by paragraph 1 or where the elements of the contract would be covered by more than one of points (a) to (h) of paragraph 1, the contract shall be governed by the law of the country where the party required to effect the characteristic performance of the contract has his habitual residence.

3. Where it is clear from all the circumstances of the case that the contract is manifestly more closely connected with a country other than that indicated in paragraphs 1 or 2, the law of that other country shall apply.

4. Where the law applicable cannot be determined pursuant to paragraphs 1 or 2, the contract shall be governed by the law of the country with which it is most closely connected.

Article 5

Contracts of carriage

. . . .

Article 6

Consumer contracts

1. Without prejudice to Articles 5 and 7, a contract concluded by a natural person for a purpose which can be regarded as being outside his trade or profession (the consumer) with another person acting in the exercise of his trade or profession (the

professional) shall be governed by the law of the country where the consumer has his habitual residence, provided that the professional:

(a) pursues his commercial or professional activities in the country where the consumer has his habitual residence, or

(b) by any means, directs such activities to that country or to several countries including that country, and the contract falls within the scope of such activities.

Article 7

Insurance contracts

. . . .

Article 9

Overriding mandatory provisions

1. Overriding mandatory provisions are provisions the respect for which is regarded as crucial by a country for safeguarding its public interests, such as its political, social or economic organization, to such an extent that they are applicable to any situation falling within their scope, irrespective of the law otherwise applicable to the contract under this Regulation.

2. Nothing in this Regulation shall restrict the application of the overriding mandatory provisions of the law of the forum.

. . . .

Article 19

Habitual residence

1. For the purposes of this Regulation, the habitual residence of companies and other bodies, corporate or unincorporated, shall be the place of central administration. The habitual residence of a natural person acting in the course of his business activity shall be his principal place of business.

2. Where the contract is concluded in the course of the operations of a branch, agency or any other establishment, or if, under the contract, performance is the responsibility of such a branch, agency or establishment, the place where the branch, agency or any other establishment is located shall be treated as the place of habitual residence.

. . . .

It is helpful to consider the following summary of the EU approach (although it specifically relates to the prior Rome Convention), and compare it to the approach taken by the Restatement.[8] Focus on the description of presumptions regarding "closest connection," and the notion of "characteristic performance." These offer elements of certainty that appear absent from the Restatement approach. Also note the special protections offered to non-business consumers.

---

8. The EU also maintains rules regarding where a person may be sued. *See* Council Regulation (EC) No 44/2001, 22 December 2000, On Jurisdiction and the Recognition and Enforcement of Judgments in Civil and Commercial Matters (Brussels I).

Summary taken from "<u>European Judicial Network</u>":[9]

- By ensuring that the courts in all the European Union countries apply the same law to the same international contract, unification of the conflict of law rules reduces the risk of *forum shopping* within the Community.

- The rules of the Rome Convention are in force in all Member States, including Denmark. . . .

- Where the parties have not determined which law shall be applicable to their contract, the contract will be governed by the law of the country with which it has the closest connection. The contract is presumed to be connected with the country where the party who is to provide the characteristic performance is habitually resident, which in general in practice means that a sales contract is governed by the law of the country where the seller is established and a contract for services is governed by the law of the country place where the service provider is established. But these are only presumptions and the court can choose to apply a different law if it finds that such law is more closely connected with the contract in question.

- Like the Brussels I Regulation, the Rome Convention contains special rules to protect the weaker parties, such as consumers and employees. The mere fact that a contract specifies that a particular law is to be applicable shall not deprive a consumer or an employee of the protection of mandatory rules of the law normally applicable to them. . . .

How do you think a court would resolve the choice of law question facing Barney and Sibyl if their brewing dispute ends up in litigation in the United States? Would the result be different under the EU (Rome I) Regulations?[10] What are the key points of contention under the two approaches?

2. Introduction to the Convention on Contracts for the International Sale of Goods

a. Overview

It should be clear to you, after reviewing the material provided above, that it is difficult to predict what law will control a contract dispute if the parties fail to agree on that term in their contract. One obvious lesson to draw from an examination of conflicts principles is that parties to a contract should not leave this issue to chance and uncertainty. The material below, which concerns the substance of our parties' contract

---

9. http://ec.europa.eu/civiljustice/applicable_law/applicable_law_ec_en.htm.

10. Note that we have not directly addressed the issue of which conflicts principles would be applied if the suit were brought before a national Greek tribunal. Would a Greek court apply national law concerning conflicts (given that the dispute involves a non-EU member) or resolve the dispute under the EU Regulation? The EU Regulation itself is not clear on this question and, adding to the issue's complexity, Greece is party to a bilateral agreement with the United States regarding conflicts. *See* <u>Europa Civil Justice</u>, http://ec.europa.eu/civiljustice/applicable_law/applicable _law_gre_en.htm. The Rome I Regulation specifically defers to such treaties in Article 25.

dispute, should also demonstrate that the consequences of a court's choice of law may sometimes have a dramatic effect on the parties' rights and obligations. Given such uncertainty, prudent traders negotiate an agreement regarding both choice of law and forum. This may not always be simple, of course, since all parties to an international sales contract may prefer that their own jurisdiction's laws apply to any disputes.

We will see that an important alternative to ordinary domestic law is for the parties to select a more neutral set of rules such as those found in the <u>Convention on Contracts for the International Sale of Goods</u> (CISG).[11] The CISG, created and promoted by the United Nations Commission on International Trade Law (<u>UNCITRAL</u>),[12] is an international treaty designed to provide a jurisdictionally neutral set of "default" rules for international sale of goods contracts. The rules are "default" both because parties may opt out of any or all of the CISG provisions,[13] and because many CISG provisions are drafted to serve a gap-filling role when contracting parties are silent on some aspects of performance. When applicable, the CISG supplants local domestic law including, in the case of the United States, the UCC. The treaty is divided into four "parts" and various "Chapters" which reflect the general scope of its provisions.

PART I Sphere of Application and General Provisions (Arts. 1–13)

These provisions define when the CISG applies to a transaction, exclude certain transactions, and provide general rules on interpretation, trade usage, contract formalities, and modification.

PART II Formation of the Contract (Arts. 14–24)

These provisions define basic rules on contract formation involving offer and acceptance.

PART III Sale of Goods

This part of the convention covers the essential substantive rules regarding the basic obligations and rights of buyers and sellers, including delivery, inspection, risk of loss, warranties, provision of documents, acceptance or rejection of goods, payment, breach of contract, notice, remedies and damages.

---

11. <u>http://www.uncitral.org/uncitral/en/uncitral texts/sale goods/1980CISG.html</u>. Other alternatives could include the choice of a third country's laws, or model laws or international conventions created by international organizations such as <u>UNIDROIT</u> (International Institute for the Unification of Private Law), www.unidroit.org/about-unidroit/overview. UNIDROIT's "Principles of International Commercial Contracts" is a good example. The 2010 version of the Principles purports to: "Set forth general rules for international commercial contracts" which "shall be applied when the parties have agreed that their contract be governed by them . . . may be applied when the parties have agreed that their contract be governed by general principles of law, the *lex mercatoria* or the like . . . may be applied when the parties have not chosen any law to govern their contract . . . may be used to interpret or supplement international uniform law instruments . . . may be used to interpret or supplement domestic law . . . may serve as a model for national and international legislators." Some have suggested that the UNIDROIT model is best seen as serving a complimentary or "gap filling" role. *See, e.g.,* H. Kronke, *The UN Sales Convention, The UNIDROIT Contract Principles and the Way Beyond,* 25 Journal of Law and Commerce 451 (2005).

12. http://www.uncitral.org/uncitral/en/about_us.html.

13. CISG Article 6.

As of 2017, eighty-five nations have adopted the CISG, including the United States and most of its important trading partners (not including the U.K.).[14]

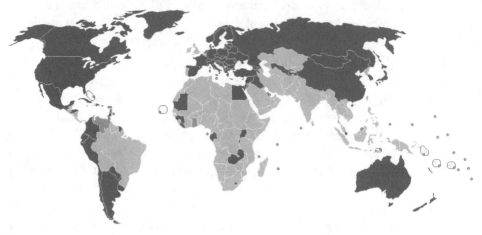

Map Image from: Alinor at en.wikipedia, Wikimedia Commons.

An alternative map with dates of adoption is available from UNCITRAL.[15]

This Chapter essentially focuses upon Parts I and II of the CISG. After reviewing commonly used trade terms in Chapter Four, we will return to Part III of the treaty, concentrating on CISG approaches to basic contractual rights and obligations, breaches and remedies.

In reviewing the following material, focusing on issues presented in the problem, you should:

(1) First, determine when the CISG applies (rather than local domestic commercial law).

(2) Next, identify and evaluate relevant provisions of the CISG relating to contract formation to determine whether Barney and Sue have a binding contract.

(3) Third, identify the parties' likely arguments under the CISG regarding what terms, critical to their dispute, would be included in their contract.

(4) Finally, analyze the issues under relevant provisions of the UCC, which are provided here in the form of Florida statutes. Would application of the UCC produce a different outcome than the CISG under these facts?

Review the treaty text to find pertinent provisions relating to the applicability of the CISG and its approach to contract formation. Given the questions above, you should also, obviously, look for provisions that address disputes over conflicting terms in the parties' communications. While you will find that Article 19 is most critical to our parties' dispute, a complete analysis will also require consideration of the other

---

14. *See* Uncitral.org/uncitral/en/uncitral_texts/sale_goods/1980CISG_status.html.
15. http://www.uncitral.org/uncitral/en/uncitral_texts/sale_goods/1980CISG_status_map.html.

provisions relating to contract formation. After scrutinizing the Convention text, consider the case excerpts provided below.

b. CISG Scope of Application

Since the United States has ratified the CISG, its provisions will potentially apply to many international sales contracts involving American businesses. By its terms, the CISG applies to most sales contracts[16] in which the parties have their principle places of business in a CISG member country, and have not expressly opted out.[17] In this regard, it is important to note that American parties who expressly select state law to govern a contract may have inadvertently chosen the CISG. Under the Supremacy Clause of the Constitution (Article IV), state law includes applicable federal law, which is both superior to state law and may include international treaties.[18] The federal courts have found that the CISG forms part of this superior federal law. As the case below suggests, parties might not effectively opt out of the CISG by simply specifying that a certain state's laws will govern the contract.

i. BP Oil International, LTD. v. Empresa Estatal Pertroleos De Ecuador (PetroEcuador), 332 F.3d 333 (5th Cir. 2003)

Before Smith and Barksdale, Circuit Judges,
and Fitzwater, District Judge.

Jerry E. Smith, Circuit Judge:

Empresa Estatal Petroleos de Ecuador ("PetroEcuador") contracted with BP Oil International, Ltd. ("BP"), for the purchase and transport of gasoline from Texas to Ecuador. PetroEcuador refused to accept delivery, so BP sold the gasoline at a loss. BP appeals a summary judgment dismissing PetroEcuador and Saybolt, Inc. ("Saybolt"), the company responsible for testing the gasoline at the port of departure. We affirm in part, reverse in part, and remand.

---

16. The CISG expressly excludes its application to certain contracts including sales:
   (a) of goods bought for personal, family or household use, unless the seller, at any time before or at the conclusion of the contract, neither knew nor ought to have known that the goods were bought for any such use;
   (b) by auction;
   (c) on execution or otherwise by authority of law;
   (d) of stocks, shares, investment securities, negotiable instruments or money;
   (e) of ships, vessels, hovercraft or aircraft;
   (f) of electricity.

17. It is possible that the CISG could be applied to a party who is not located in a CISG member state under Article 1(b) if conflict principles point to application of a CISG member state's laws. The United States has expressly opted out of this provision. Thus, U.S. based contractual parties are only subject to the CISG if the other contractual party has its principle place of business in another CISG member state.

18. Not all U.S. treaties, even if approved by the Senate and ratified by the President, automatically become operative domestic law. Under the doctrine of "self-execution," only those treaties that were intended to directly create domestic legal obligations become part of our law. The CISG is such a treaty and is a binding source of federal law. Additional discussion of this topic appears in Chapter 9.

I.

PetroEcuador sent BP an invitation to bid for supplying 140,000 barrels of unleaded gasoline deliverable "CFR" to Ecuador. "CFR," which stands for "Cost and FReight," is one of thirteen International Commercial Terms ("Incoterms") designed to "provide a set of international rules for the interpretation of the most commonly used trade terms in foreign trade." . . .

BP responded favorably to the invitation, and PetroEcuador confirmed the sale on its contract form. The final agreement required that the oil be sent "CFR La Libertad-Ecuador." A separate provision, paragraph 10, states, "Jurisdiction: Laws of the Republic of Ecuador." The contract further specifies that the gasoline have a gum content of less than three milligrams per one hundred milliliters, to be determined at the port of departure. PetroEcuador appointed Saybolt, a company specializing in quality control services, to ensure this requirement was met.

To fulfill the contract, BP purchased gasoline from Shell Oil Company and, following testing by Saybolt, loaded it on board the M/T TIBER at Shell's Deer Park, Texas, refinery. The TIBER sailed to La Libertad, Ecuador, where the gasoline was again tested for gum content. On learning that the gum content now exceeded the contractual limit, PetroEcuador refused to accept delivery. Eventually, BP resold the gasoline to Shell at a loss of approximately two million dollars.

BP sued PetroEcuador for breach of contract and wrongful draw of a letter of guarantee. After PetroEcuador filed a notice of intent to apply foreign law pursuant to Fed.R.Civ.P. 44.1, the district court applied Texas choice of law rules and determined that Ecuadorian law governed. BP argued that the term "CFR" demonstrated the parties' intent to pass the risk of loss to PetroEcuador once the goods were delivered on board the TIBER. The district court disagreed and held that under Ecuadorian law, the seller must deliver conforming goods to the agreed destination, in this case Ecuador. The court granted summary judgment for PetroEcuador . . . .

II

. . . .

III

BP and PetroEcuador dispute whether the domestic law of Ecuador or the CISG applies. After recognizing that federal courts sitting in diversity apply the choice of law rules of the state in which they sit, *Coghlan v. Wellcraft Marine Corp.*, 240 F.3d 449, 452 n. 2 (5th Cir.2001) (citation omitted), the district court applied Texas law, which enforces unambiguous choice of law provisions. *DeSantis v. Wackenhut Corp.*, 793 S.W.2d 670, 678 (Tex.1990). Paragraph 10, which states "Jurisdiction: Laws of the Republic of Ecuador," purports to apply Ecuadorian law. Based on an affidavit submitted by PetroEcuador's expert, Dr. Gustavo Romero, the court held that Ecuadorian law requires the seller to deliver conforming goods at the agreed destination, making summary judgment inappropriate for BP.

A.

Though the court correctly recognized that federal courts apply the choice of law rules of the state in which they sit, it overlooked its concurrent federal question jurisdiction that makes a conflict of laws analysis unnecessary. The general federal question jurisdiction statute grants subject matter jurisdiction over every civil action that arises, *inter alia,* under a treaty of the United States. 28 U.S.C. § 1331(a). The CISG, ratified by the Senate in 1986, creates a private right of action in federal court. *Delchi Carrier v. Rotorex Corp.,* 71 F.3d 1024, 1027–28 (2d Cir.1995). The treaty applies to "contracts of sale of goods between parties whose places of business are in different States . . . [w]hen the States are Contracting States." CISG art. 1(1)(a). BP, an American corporation, and PetroEcuador, an Ecuadorian company, contracted for the sale of gasoline; the United States and Ecuador have ratified the CISG.

As incorporated federal law, the CISG governs the dispute so long as the parties have not elected to exclude its application. CISG art. 6. PetroEcuador argues that the choice of law provision demonstrates the parties' intent to apply Ecuadorian domestic law instead of the CISG. We disagree.

A signatory's assent to the CISG necessarily incorporates the treaty as part of that nation's domestic law. BP's expert witness as to Ecuadorian law, Xavier Rosales-Kuri, observed that "the following source of *Ecuadorian law* would be applicable to the present case: (i) United Nations Convention on the International Sale of Goods. . . ." PetroEcuador's expert did not disagree with this assessment. Given that the CISG *is* Ecuadorian law, a choice of law provision designating Ecuadorian law merely confirms that the treaty governs the transaction.

Where parties seek to apply a signatory's domestic law in lieu of the CISG, they must affirmatively opt-out of the CISG. In *Asante Techs., Inc. v. PMC-Sierra, Inc.,* 164 F.Supp.2d 1142, 1150 (N.D.Cal. 2001), the court held that a choice-of-law provision selecting British Columbia law did not, without more, "evince a clear intent to opt out of the CISG. . . . Defendant's choice of applicable law adopts the law of British Columbia, and it is undisputed that the CISG *is* the law of British Columbia."

Similarly, because the CISG is the law of Ecuador, it governs this dispute. "[I]f the parties decide to exclude the Convention, it should be expressly excluded by language which states that it does not apply and also states what law shall govern the contract." An affirmative opt-out requirement promotes uniformity and the observance of good faith in international trade, two principles that guide interpretation of the CISG. CISG art. 7(1).

B.

The CISG incorporates Incoterms through article 9(2), which provides:

> "The parties are considered, unless otherwise agreed, to have impliedly made applicable to their contract or its formation a usage of which the parties knew or ought to have known and which in international trade is widely known

to, and regularly observed by, parties to contracts of the type involved in the particular trade concerned." CISG art. 9(2).

Even if the usage of Incoterms is not global, the fact that they are well known in international trade means that they are incorporated through article 9(2).

... Shipments designated "CFR" require the seller to pay the costs and freight to transport the goods to the delivery port, but pass title and risk of loss to the buyer once the goods "pass the ship's rail" at the port of shipment. The goods should be tested for conformity before the risk of loss passes to the buyer. In the event of subsequent damage or loss, the buyer generally must seek a remedy against the carrier or insurer. *In re Daewoo Int'l (Am.) Corp.,* 2001 WL 1537687, 2001 U.S. Dist. LEXIS 19796, at *8 (S.D.N.Y. Dec. 3, 2001).

In light of the parties' unambiguous use of the Incoterm "CFR," [seller] fulfilled its contractual obligations if the gasoline met the contract's qualitative specifications when it passed the ship's rail and risk transferred to [buyer]. CISG art. 36(1). Indeed, Saybolt's testing confirmed that the gasoline's gum content was adequate before departure from Texas. Nevertheless, in its opposition to [seller]'s motion for summary judgment, [buyer] contends that [seller] purchased the gasoline from Shell on an "as is" basis and thereafter failed to add sufficient gum inhibitor as a way to "cut corners." In other words, the cargo contained a hidden defect.

... Nevertheless, [seller] could have breached the agreement if it provided goods that it "knew or could not have been unaware" were defective when they "passed over the ship's rail" and risk shifted to [buyer]. CISG art. 40.

Therefore, there is a fact issue as to whether [seller] knowingly provided gasoline with an excessive gum content. The district court should permit the parties to conduct discovery as to this issue only.

————

In the BP Oil case, above, the court confirms a point that commentators had suspected—to avoid application of the CISG, parties must affirmatively opt out with explicit language. Since both parties had their "places of business" in nations that had adopted the CISG (Article 1), and the treaty formed part of each nation's domestic law, choosing Ecuadorian law did not avoid the CISG.

What happens when a business has multi-national operations and multiple places of business? Article 10 provides: "... a) if a party has more than one place of business, the place of business is that which has the closest relationship to the contract and its performance, having regard to the circumstances known to or contemplated by the parties at any time before or at the conclusion of the contract...." In *Asante Technologies, Inc. v. PMC Sierra, Inc.,*164 F. Supp. 2d 1142 (N.D. Cal. 2001), the defendant Delaware Corporation managed its contractual relationship with a California based plaintiff through a Californian distributor. The defendant seller also maintained an office in Oregon where many of its engineers were based. Nevertheless, the court found that, since the contractual dispute centered around technical representations made by the defendant through its Canadian corporate headquarters, the defendant's "place of business" for these purposes was in Canada. Hence, the CISG applied.

3. CISG Contract Formation

a. *Magellan International Corporation v. Salzgitter Handel GmbH, 76 F. Supp. 2d 919 (N.D. Ill. 1999)*

MILTON I. SHADUR, Senior United States District Judge.

OPINION: MEMORANDUM OPINION AND ORDER

Salzgitter Handel GmbH ("Salzgitter") has filed a motion pursuant to Fed.R.Civ.P. ("Rule") 12(b)(6) ("Motion"), seeking to dismiss this action brought against it by Magellan International Corporation ("Magellan"). Because the allegations in Complaint Counts I and II state claims that are sufficient under Rule 8(a), Salzgitter's Motion must be and is denied as to those claims. Count III, however, is deficient and is therefore dismissed without prejudice.

Facts

In considering a Rule 12(b)(6) motion to dismiss for failure to state a claim, this Court accepts all of Magellan's well-pleaded factual allegations as true, as well as drawing all reasonable inferences from those facts in Magellan's favor (*Travel All Over the World, Inc. v. Kingdom of Saudi Arabia*, 73 F.3d 1423, 1429 (7th Cir. 1996)). What follows is the version of events set out in the Complaint, when read in that light.

Offers, Counter-offers and Acceptance

Magellan [buyer] is an Illinois-based distributor of steel products. Salzgitter [seller] is a steel trader that is headquartered in Düsseldorf, Germany and maintains an Illinois sales office. In January 1999. Magellan's Robert Arthur ("Arthur") and Salzgitter's Thomas Riess ("Riess") commenced negotiations on a potential deal under which Salzgitter would begin to act as middleman in Magellan's purchase of steel bars — manufactured according to Magellan's specifications — from a Ukrainian steel mill, Dneprospetsstal of Ukraine ("DSS"). By letter dated January 28, Magellan provided Salzgitter with written specifications for 5,585 metric tons of steel bars, with proposed pricing, and with an agreement to issue a letter of credit ("LC") to Salzgitter as Magellan's method of payment. Salzgitter responded two weeks later (on February 12 and 13) by proposing prices $5 to $20 per ton higher than those Magellan had specified.

On February 15 Magellan accepted Salzgitter's price increases, agreed on 4,000 tons as the quantity being purchased, and added $5 per ton over Salzgitter's numbers to effect shipping from Magellan's preferred port (Ventspills, Latvia). Magellan memorialized those terms, as well as the other material terms previously discussed by the parties,[2] in two February 15 purchase orders.

---

2. Price, quantity, delivery date, delivery method and payment method had all been negotiated and agreed to by the parties.

Salzgitter then responded on February 17, apparently accepting Magellan's memorialized terms except for two "amendments" as to prices. Riess asked for Magellan's "acceptance" of those two price increases by return fax and promised to send its already-drawn-up order confirmations as soon as they were countersigned by DSS. Arthur consented, signing and returning the approved price amendments to Riess the same day.

On February 19 Salzgitter sent its pro forma order confirmations to Magellan. But the general terms and conditions that were attached to those confirmations differed in some respects from those that had been attached to Magellan's purchase orders, mainly with respect to vessel loading conditions, dispute resolution and choice of law.

Contemplating an ongoing business relationship, Magellan and Salzgitter continued to negotiate in an effort to resolve the remaining conflicts between their respective forms. While those fine-tuning negotiations were under way, Salzgitter began to press Magellan to open its LC for the transaction in Salzgitter's favor. On March 4 Magellan sent Salzgitter a draft LC for review.[3]

Salzgitter wrote back on March 8 proposing minor amendments to the LC and stating that "all other terms are acceptable." Although Magellan preferred to wait until all of the minor details (the remaining conflicting terms) were ironed out before issuing the LC, Salzgitter continued to press for its immediate issuance.

On March 22 Salzgitter sent amended order confirmations to Magellan. Riess visited Arthur four days later on March 26 and threatened to cancel the steel orders if Magellan did not open the LC in Salzgitter's favor that day. They then came to agreement as to the remaining contractual issues.[4]

Accordingly, relying on Riess's assurances that all remaining details of the deal were settled, Arthur had the $1.2 million LC issued later that same day.

Post-Acceptance Events

Three days later (on March 29) Arthur and Riess engaged in an extended game of "fax tag" initiated by the latter. Essentially Salzgitter demanded that the LC be amended to permit the unconditional substitution of FCRs for bills of lading—even for partial orders—and Magellan refused to amend the LC, also pointing out the need to conform Salzgitter's March 22 amended order confirmations to the terms of the parties' ultimate March 26 agreement. At the same time, Magellan requested minor modifications in some of the steel specifications. Salzgitter replied that it was too late to modify the specifications: DSS had already manufactured 60% of the order, and the rest was under production.

---

3. One of the LC terms—also included in Magellan's purchase orders—required ocean bills of lading to be presented as a condition precedent to Salzgitter's right to draw on the LC. But Salzgitter was permitted to substitute forwarder's Certificates of Receipt ("FCR") for bills of lading as to the full order if Magellan were to be more than 20 days late in providing a vessel for shipment.

4. For example, the parties agreed that the contract would be governed by the United Nations Convention on the International Sale of Goods (the "Convention").

Perhaps unsurprisingly in light of what has been recited up to now, on the very next day (March 30) Magellan's and Salzgitter's friendly fine-tuning went flat. Salzgitter screeched an ultimatum to Magellan: Amend the LC by noon the following day or Salzgitter would "no longer feel obligated" to perform and would "sell the material elsewhere." On April 1 Magellan requested that the LC be canceled because of what it considered to be Saltzgitter's breach. Salzgitter returned the LC and has since been attempting to sell the manufactured steel to Magellan's customers in the United States.

Magellan's Claims

Complaint Count I posits that—pursuant to the Convention—a valid contract existed between Magellan and Salzgitter before Salzgitter's March 30 ultimatum. Hence that attempted ukase is said to have amounted to an anticipatory repudiation of that contract, entitling Magellan to relief for its breach.

Count II seeks specific performance of the contract or replevin of the manufactured steel. That relief is invoked under the Illinois version of the Uniform Commercial Code ("UCC," specifically 810 ILCS 5/2-716) because Magellan is "unable to 'cover' its delivery commitments to its customers without unreasonable delay" (Complaint p.42).

Finally, Count III asserts that specifications given to Salzgitter for transmittal to DSS constitute "trade secrets" pursuant to the Illinois Trade Secrets Act ("Secrets Act," which defines the term "trade secret" at 765 ILCS 1065/2(d)). Salzgitter is charged with misappropriation of those trade secrets in attempting to sell the manufactured steel embodying those secrets to Magellan's customers (Complaint pp.9, 45–47). Magellan relatedly claims that the threat of future disclosure and use of those asserted trade secrets by Salzgitter causes Magellan irreparable harm (Complaint p.49).

. . . .

Rule 12(b)(6) Standard

. . . .

"Federal notice pleading requires the plaintiff to set out in her complaint a short and plain statement of the claim that will provide the defendant with fair notice of the claim. However, a complaint need not spell out every element of a legal theory to provide notice. . . . A pleading need contain only enough to allow the defendant to understand the gravamen of the plaintiff's complaint."

Thus no claim will be dismissed unless "it is clear that no relief could be granted under any set of facts that could be proved consistent with the allegations" (*Hishon v. King & Spalding,* 467 U.S. 69, 73, 81 L. Ed. 2d 59, 104 S. Ct. 2229 (1984), quoting *Conley v. Gibson,* 355 U.S. 41, 45–46, 2 L. Ed. 2d 80, 78 S. Ct. 99 (1957)).

Count I: Breach of Contract

Choice of Law

As stated earlier, Magellan first claims entitlement to relief for breach of contract. Because the transaction involves the sale and purchase of steel—"goods"—the parties acknowledge that the governing law is either the Convention or the UCC.

Under the facts alleged by Magellan, the parties agreed that Convention law would apply to the transaction, and Salzgitter does not now dispute that contention. That being the case, this opinion looks to Convention law.

Pleading Requirements

. . . [T]he specification of the pleading requirements to state a claim for breach of contract under the Convention truly poses a question of first impression. Despite that clean slate, even a brief glance at the Convention's structure confirms what common sense (and the common law) dictate as the universal elements of any such action: formation, performance, breach and damages. Hence under the Convention, as under Illinois law (or the common law generally), the components essential to a cause of action for breach of contract are (1) the existence of a valid and enforceable contract containing both definite and certain terms, (2) performance by plaintiff, (3) breach by defendant and (4) resultant injury to plaintiff. In those terms it is equally clear that Magellan's allegations provide adequate notice to Salzgitter that such an action is being asserted (Complaint pp.7–15).

Formation of a contract under either UCC or the Convention requires an offer followed by an acceptance (see Convention Pt. II). Although analysis of offer and acceptance typically involves complicated factual issues of intent—issues not appropriately addressed on a motion to dismiss—this Court need not engage in such mental gymnastics here. It is enough that Magellan has alleged facts that a factfinder could call an offer on the one hand and an acceptance on the other.

Under Convention Art. 14(1) a "proposal for concluding a contract addressed to one or more specific persons constitutes an offer if it is sufficiently definite and indicates the intention of the offeror to be bound in case of acceptance." So, if the indications of the proposer are sufficiently definite and justify the addressee in understanding that its acceptance will form a contract, the proposal constitutes an offer (*id*. Art. 8(2)). For that purpose "[a] proposal is sufficiently definite if it indicates the goods and expressly or implicitly makes provision for determining the quantity and the price" (*id*. Art. 14(1)).

In this instance Magellan alleges that it sent purchase orders to Salzgitter on February 15 that contained the material terms upon which the parties had agreed. Those terms included identification of the goods, quantity and price. Certainly an offer could be found consistently with those facts.

But Convention Art. 19(1) goes on to state that "[a] reply to an offer which purports to be an acceptance but contains additions, limitations or other modifications is a rejection of the offer and constitutes a counter-offer." That provision reflects the common law's "mirror image" rule that the UCC has rejected (see *Filanto,* 789 F. Supp. at 1238). And Salzgitter's February 17 response to the purchase orders did propose price changes. Hence that response can be seen as a counter-offer that justified Magellan's belief that its acceptance of those new prices would form a contract.

Although that expectation was then frustrated by the later events in February and then in March, which in contract terms equated to further offers and counter-offers, the requisite contractual joinder could reasonably be viewed by a factfinder as having jelled on March 26. In that respect Convention Art. 18(a) requires an indication of assent to an offer (or counter-offer) to constitute its acceptance. Such an "indication" may occur through "a statement made by or other conduct of the offeree" (*id*.). And at the very least, a jury could find consistently with Magellan's allegations that the required indication of complete (mirrored) assent occurred when Magellan issued its LC on March 26. So much, then, for the first element of a contract: offer and acceptance.

Next, the second pleading requirement for a breach of contract claim — performance by plaintiff — was not only specifically addressed by Magellan (Complaint p.39) but can also be inferred from the facts alleged in Complaint p.43 and from Magellan's prayer for specific performance. Magellan's performance obligation as the buyer is simple: payment of the price for the goods. Magellan issued its LC in satisfaction of that obligation, later requesting the LC's cancellation only after Salzgitter's alleged breach (Complaint pp.24, 31). Moreover, Magellan's request for specific performance implicitly confirms that it remains ready and willing to pay the price if such relief were granted.

As for the third pleading element — Salzgitter's breach — Complaint p.38 alleges:

"Salzgitter's March 30 letter (Exhibit G) demanding that the bill of lading provision be removed from the letter of credit and threatening to cancel the contract constitutes an anticipatory repudiation and fundamental breach of the contract."

It would be difficult to imagine an allegation that more clearly fulfills the notice function of pleading. Convention Art. 72 addresses the concept of anticipatory breach:

"(1) If prior to the date for performance of the contract it is clear that one of the parties will commit a fundamental breach of contract, the other party may declare the contract avoided.

"(2) If time allows, the party intending to declare the contract avoided must give reasonable notice to the other party in order to permit him to provide adequate assurance of his performance.

"(3) The requirements of the preceding paragraph do not apply if the other party has declared that he will not perform his obligations."

And Convention Art. 25 states in relevant part:

"A breach of contract committed by one of the parties is fundamental if it results in such detriment to the other party as substantially to deprive him of what he is entitled to expect under the contract . . ."

That plain language reveals that under the Convention an anticipatory repudiation pleader need simply allege (1) that the defendant intended to breach the contract before the contract's performance date and (2) that such breach was fundamental. Here Magellan has pleaded that Salzgitter's March 29 letter indicated its pre-performance intention not to perform the contract, coupled with Magellan's allegation that the bill of lading requirement was an essential part of the parties' bargain. That being the case, Salzgitter's insistence upon an amendment of that requirement would indeed be a fundamental breach.

Lastly, Magellan has easily jumped the fourth pleading hurdle—resultant injury. Complaint p.40 alleges that the breach "has caused damages to Magellan."

Count II: Specific Performance or Replevin

. . . .

Count III: Trade Secret Misappropriation

. . . .

Conclusion

It may perhaps be that when the facts are further fleshed out through discovery, Magellan's claims against Salzgitter will indeed succumb either for lack of proof or as the consequence of some legal deficiency. But in the current Rule 12(b)(6) context, Salzgitter's motion as to Counts I and II is denied, and it is ordered to file its Answer to the Complaint on or before December 20, 1999. As to the Count III trade secret claim, however, Salzgitter's motion to dismiss is granted without prejudice.

4. Disputes Over Conflicting Terms

The "battle of the forms" appears de rigueur in first year contracts classes. The battle occurs when the buyer and seller enter into a contract, not through an agreement memorialized in a single document, but rather through the exchange of various, often divergent, communications. In some cases, of course, the divergent terms come to light prior to contractual performance. Here, the question is whether the parties have entered into a binding contract at all. More typically, the parties perform as expected, oblivious to lurking contractual problems, and the consequence of divergent terms is never tested. If a squabble develops after performance, however, the dispute may turn upon which terms control.

A dispute over conflicting terms seems to be brewing between the parties in our problem. Focus first on what the CISG provides regarding this "international battle of the forms." Start with the text. *How would the dispute between Barney and Sybil turn out under these provisions?* Subsequently, we will compare the CISG approach with U.S. domestic law in the form of the Uniform Commercial Code. *How might the outcome be different under the UCC?*

a. CISG and the International Battle of Forms

Start your analysis by closely examining those provisions of the treaty text[19] (alternative source here[20]) that focus on contract formation. Examining the rules, you should discover critical terms whose meaning is subject to interpretation. Two extremely use-

---

19. www.uncitral.org/pdf/english/texts/sales/cisg/V1056997-CISG-e-book.pdf.
20. http://www.cisg.law.pace.edu/cisg/text/treaty.html.

ful resources in this regard are the websites provided by <u>UNCITRAL</u>[21] (UN Commission on International Trade Law—the organization that drafted the CISG) and the <u>Pace Institute</u>[22] for International Commercial Law. Each provides research materials and annotations by CISG article. The Pace site also provides <u>links to the UNCITRAL case digest organized by CISG article</u>.[23] The Pace site compiles cases and arbitral decisions <u>by national jurisdictions</u>.[24] The <u>UNCITRAL digest and commentary, "CLOUT"</u>[25] (Case Law on UNCITRAL Texts), essentially a summary of case law world-wide, is especially helpful in deciphering some key provisions, and in describing how courts have interpreted them. Examine the digest entries for those CISG articles that you believe will control our dispute before reading the cases set out below.

b. The Last Shot Approach

i. Norfolk Southern Railway Company v. Power Source Supply, Inc.

Civil Action No. 06-58 J, 2008 U.S. Dist. LEXIS 56942,
also available at <u>Pace CISG Cases</u>[26]

MEMORANDUM OPINION AND ORDER

BACKGROUND

Power Source Supply (hereinafter Defendant) is a Canadian corporation whose principal place of business is Calgary, Alberta, Canada. It supplies used and rebuilt equipment to the railroad, oil, and gas industries. Norfolk Southern Railway Company (hereinafter Plaintiff) is a Virginia corporation with its principal place of business in Virginia; it also operates a locomotive repair facility in Altoona, Pennsylvania.

On July 29, 2004, Defendant faxed to Plaintiff in Altoona purchase order #222147 for twelve SD40 type locomotives and twenty-four B23-7 type locomotives at a total price of $1,000,000. . . . Reflecting [a later] phase in the Parties' negotiations, on September 13, 2004 Defendant faxed a new purchase order, #222258, to Plaintiff in "Altuna" (sic), in which it offered to pay $1.3 million for the same 36 locomotives described in the previous purchase order provided that ten of the 12 SD40 locomotives had blue cards.[3] There was no firm delivery date, although Plaintiff's representative told Defendant that Plaintiff would "shoot for January 15, [2005]."

In November of 2004 Defendant offered to sell WATCO, a start-up railroad company, the 10 blue-carded SD-40s for $140,000 each and the two remaining SD-40s,

---

21. http://www.uncitral.org/uncitral/en/about_us.html.
22. http://www.cisg.law.pace.edu/.
23. http://cisgw3.law.pace.edu/cisg/text/digest-2012-toc.html.
24. http://www.cisg.law.pace.edu/cisg/text/casecit.html.
25. http://www.uncitral.org/uncitral/en/case_law.html.
26. http://cisgw3.law.pace.edu/cases/080725u1.html.
3. The term "blue card" refers to the Federal Railroad Administration's Form FRA 6180-49A, which documents various inspections and tests performed on the locomotives. Document No. 52 p.2. A locomotive must have a blue card before it may legally be used to haul freight.

which were to be used for parts, for $25,000 apiece. On January 13, 2005 Plaintiff mailed Defendant a bill of sale reflecting the terms agreed upon in September, 2004, which was then executed by Jamie Crowshaw, President of PSS.

WATCO subsequently relaxed several of its requirements, including that ten of the locomotives be blue-carded . . . . On February 6, 2005, after further negotiations between Plaintiff and Defendant, Defendant sent Plaintiff in Altoona "Purchase Order #222258, Revision 1," which reduced the number of blue-carded locomotives from ten to three and reduced the sale price from $1,300,000 to $1,097,500. The text of the "Revision 1" order, although not the price, had been "cut and pasted" from the WATCO invoice.

On February 9, 2005, Defendant faxed Plaintiff in Altoona "Purchase Order #222258, Final Revision," in which Plaintiff further reduced the final purchase price to $1,073,315 to reflect Defendant's provision of additional equipment to be used with the locomotives and in compensation for Defendant's claim that Plaintiff had not met an allegedly agreed-upon delivery deadline. WATCO paid Defendant in full on February 11, 2005 and Crowshaw [defendant's President] executed Plaintiff's final Bills of Sale on February 14, 2005. Plaintiff avers that at the time of delivery, all locomotives delivered to WATCO "were in compliance with the requirements set forth in the Final [Revision] Purchase Order." . . .

To date Defendant has paid Plaintiff $289,000. Plaintiff filed the instant action on March 13, 2006, pleading breach of contract and in the alternative unjust enrichment and seeking recovery of the remainder of the agreed-upon price. In its answer Defendant denied liability and made counterclaims for breach of contract, justifiable reliance, breach of express warranty, breach of implied warranty of fitness for particular purpose, and breach of implied warranty of merchantability. Plaintiff filed its motion for summary judgment on October 24, 2007 . . . . Defendant has filed no response to date.

JURISDICTION AND VENUE

The Parties' documents are silent as to choice of law. This action is therefore governed by the United Nations Convention on Contracts for the International Sale of Goods (hereinafter CISG), *Delchi Carrier SpA v. Rotorex Corp.*, 71 F.3d 1024, 1027 n.1 (2d Cir. 1995) (citing CISG art. 1); *see also Chateau des Charmes Wines, Ltd. v. Satiate USA, Inc.*, 328 F.3d 528, 530 (9th Cir. 2003) (noting that both the United States and Canada are "contracting states to the C.I.S.G.") . . . .

DISCUSSION

Summary judgment

A "principal purpose[] of the summary judgment rule is to isolate and dispose of factually unsupported claims or defenses . . . and it should be interpreted in a way that allows it to accomplish [that] purpose." *Celotex Corp. v. Catrett*, 477 U.S. 317, 322, 106 S.Ct. 2548, 2553, 91 L.Ed.2d. 265, 275 (1986). . . . There is no issue of material fact "[w]here the record taken as a whole could not lead a rational trier of fact to find for the non-moving party," *Matsushita Elec. Indus. Co., Ltd., v. Zenith Radio Corp,* 475 U.S. 574, 587, 106 S.Ct. 1348, 1356, 89 L.Ed.2d 538, 552 (1986) . . . .

As noted above, Defendant has made no response to Plaintiff's motion.

The contract

a. Delivery

The Parties' agreement went through numerous iterations prior to delivery of the locomotives and equipment. Although not required by the CISG, *see* CISG art. 29(1), each of these changes was supported by consideration: when Defendant required ten locomotives to be blue-carded Plaintiff's price went up; when Defendant required that only three locomotives be blue-carded Plaintiff's price went down; when Defendant claimed that Plaintiff was dilatory in its delivery Plaintiff further reduced its price.

It is apparent to the Court that each agreement between the parties superseded the previous agreement. *See Valero Mktg. & Supply Co. v. Greeni Oy,* 242 Fed.Appx. 840, 844–45 (3d Cir. 2007) (finding permissible contract modification under the CISG where a delivery date extension accompanied by a price reduction was agreed to by the parties). None of the agreements included a written delivery date. Under the CISG, delivery is therefore to be "within a reasonable time after the conclusion of the contract." CISG art. 33(c). Defendant, based on Plaintiff's representation on September 10, 2004, that Plaintiff would "shoot for January 15th" as a delivery date, argues that Plaintiff's failure to meet that deadline constituted a breach of the Parties' agreement and therefore Defendant owes Plaintiff nothing and, in fact, Defendant is entitled to recover damages from Plaintiff.

Even assuming that the words "shoot for" could create a binding obligation, Plaintiff's final purchase order is dated February 6, 2005, over three weeks after the alleged January 15, 2005 deadline. The CISG requires delivery within a reasonable time after the conclusion of the contract, not before. Since the contract could not have been concluded before the final purchase order was sent, Plaintiff could not have breached by its failure to deliver on January 15, 2005.

b. Warranties

Defendant has alleged that Plaintiff breached both express warranties and the implied warranties of fitness for a particular purpose and merchantability and argues that it is therefore not only not liable for further payments to Plaintiff but that Plaintiff is liable for damages to Defendant. Whether Defendant's assertions are treated as defenses or counterclaims, Defendant has the burden of showing that the goods Plaintiff delivered did not conform to the terms of the Parties' agreement. *See Chicago Prime Packers, Inc. v. Northam Food Trading Co.,* 408 F.3d 894, 897–98 (7th Cir. 2005). . . .

Regarding the matter of implied warranties, Plaintiff concedes that although the CISG does not specifically include the implied warranties of fitness and merchantability, CISG art. 35 may properly be read to suggest them. The CISG also allows, however, for their disclaimer. CISG art. 35(2); John Edward Murray, Jr., Murray on Contracts § 100, at 633 (41, ed. 2001). The last documents to be executed in the Parties' transaction were Plaintiff's bills of sale, which were executed by Defendant on February 14, 2005. They expressly disclaimed all warranties except that of marketable title to the enumerated items with the following language:

> THE EQUIPMENT BEING SOLD ON AN "AS, WHERE IS" BASIS AND WITH ALL FAULTS. EXCEPT AS SET FORTH HEREIN, THE SELLER MAKES NO REPRESENTATION OR WARRANTY, EITHER EXPRESS OR IMPLIED, AS TO THE CONDITION OF THE EQUIPMENT, INCLUDING WITHOUT LIMITATION ANY IMPLIED WARRANTY OF MERCHANT-ABILITY OR FITNESS FOR A PARTICULAR PURPOSE, AND EX-PRESSLY DISCLAIMS LIABILITY AND SHALL NOT BE LIABLE FOR LOST PROFITS OR FOR INDIRECT, INCIDENTAL CONSEQUENTIAL OR COMMERCIAL LOSSES OF ANY KIND.

The disclaimer was on the second page of each of the two-page documents, in capital letters as above, and in the same font size as the rest of the text.

The validity of the disclaimer cannot be determined by reference to the CISG itself. CISG art 4(a). It is therefore necessary to turn to the forum's choice of law rules. . . . *Zapata Hermanos Sucesores, S.A. v. Hearthside Baking Co., Inc.,* 313 F.3d 385 390 (7th Cir. 2002) (using, in a CISG case involving an Illinois firm, "choice of law principles" to determine that the common law of Illinois applied "to any issues . . . not covered in express terms by the Convention") . . . .

Under Pennsylvania law, the first step in a choice of laws analysis is to determine whether "there is an actual or real conflict between the potentially applicable laws." *Hammersmith v. TIG Ins. Co.,* 480 F.3d 220, 230 (3d Cir. 2007). . . .

After examining the final, executed bills of sale, under the standards set forth above, the Court finds the disclaimer to be valid under either the laws of Pennsylvania or Alberta. There is no conflict, and hence no need for a conflict of laws analysis.

There remains, however, the question of whether the Final Revision of the purchase order, which does not exclude any warranties for six of the SD 40 locomotives, or the final bill of sale, which excludes implied warranties for all items, is the final manifestation of the Parties' agreement. This battle of the forms must be resolved by reference to CISG art. 19, which reads as follows:

> (1) A reply to an offer which purports to be an acceptance but contains additions, limitations or other modifications is a rejection of the offer and constitutes a counter-offer.

> (2) However, a reply to an offer which purports to be an acceptance but contains additional or different terms which do not materially alter the terms of the offer constitutes an acceptance, unless the offeror, without undue delay, objects orally to the discrepancy or dispatches a notice to that effect. If he does not so object, the terms of the contract are the terms of the offer with the modifications contained in the acceptance.

(3) Additional or different terms relating, among other things, to the price, payment, quality and quantity of the goods, place and time of delivery, extent of one party's liability to the other or the settlement of disputes are considered to alter the terms of the offer materially.

Since the disclaimer in the bill of sale related to both the quality of the goods and Plaintiff's liability to Defendant, the Court finds that the bills of sale materially altered the terms of the purchase order and that therefore the bills of sale constituted a rejection its terms. The bills of sale instead constituted a counter-offer by Plaintiff which Defendant accepted by its execution of the bills of sale on February 14, 2005. As such, the final agreement between the parties included no implied warranties of any sort.

Damages

There is no outstanding issue of material fact in this case. The Court finds as a matter of law that Plaintiff fully performed the final iteration of the Parties' agreement and is entitled to Defendant's full performance in turn. Pursuant to CISG art. 74, which is "designed to place the aggrieved party in as good a position as if the other party had properly performed the contract," *Delchi,* 71 F.3d at 1029 (citation omitted), Plaintiff is therefore due the outstanding balance on the contract of $784,315. Plaintiff is not, however, allowed attorneys' fees under Article 74 or any other part of the CISG. *Zapata,* 313 F.3d at 388–89.

. . . .

---

c. The Standard Terms Variation

A variant of the battle of forms problem occurs when parties attempt to incorporate "standard terms" into their agreements by reference (or even in small print on the back of invoices written in a foreign language). You will discover below that such practices raise additional issues regarding intent and fair notice.

The UNCITRAL Digest summarizes the cases this way:

Conflicting standard terms

6. The Convention does not have special rules to address the issues raised when a potential seller and buyer both use standard contract terms prepared in advance for general and repeated use (the so-called "battle of the forms"). A conflict exists when the two sets of terms differ partially, and also when one of the standard terms does not contain provisions on an issue expressly included in the other's set of standard terms. Several decisions conclude that the parties' performance notwithstanding partial contradiction between their standard terms established an enforceable contract. As for the terms of these contracts, several decisions would include those terms on which the parties substantially agreed, and replace those standard terms that (after appraisal of all the terms) conflict with the default rules of the Convention

(knock-out rule); several other decisions give effect to the standard terms of the last person to make an offer or counter-offer that is then deemed accepted by subsequent performance by the other party (last-shot rule). Another decision refused to give effect to the standard terms of either party: the seller was not bound by the buyer's terms on the back of the order form in the absence of a reference to them on the front of the form, while the seller's terms—included in a confirmation letter sent after the contract was concluded—were not accepted by the buyer's silence.

i. *Roser Technologies, Inc. v. Carl Schreiber GmbH d/b/a CSN Metals, 2013 U.S. Dist. LEXIS 129242 (W.D. Pa., Sept. 10, 2013), available at Pace CISG Cases*[27]

Memorandum Opinion

I. Introduction

This is a breach of contract action involving a contract for the manufacture and sale of copper molding plates. Plaintiff Roser Technologies, Inc. ("RTI") alleges that Defendant Carl Schreiber GmbH d/b/a CSN Metals ("CSN") breached its supply contract when CSN insisted that RTI expedite payment or secure a letter of credit. CSN filed a Second Amended Counterclaim alleging that RTI breached the contract by repudiation . . . .

II. Factual Background

This case revolves around two exchanges of documents for the manufacture and sale of copper mold plates. The first document exchange began on May 11, 2011, when CSN provided quotation 714257 to RTI. On August 9, 2011, RTI sent purchase order 6676, which was "per CSN quote 714257," to CSN. On October 8, 2011, CSN sent order confirmation 17507 to RTI. The order confirmation listed RTIs order number as 6676.

The second document exchange began on August 11, 2011, when CSN provided quotation 714576 to RTI. On August 23, 2011, RTI sent purchase order 6761, which was "per CSN quote 414576," to CSN. On August 25, 2011, CSN sent order confirmation 17579 to RTI, which listed the order number as "6761."

The first page of CSN quotations 714257 and 714576 included the following language, "According to our standard conditions of sale to be found under www.csnmetals.de, we have pleasure in quoting without engagement as follows [.]" The second page of both quotations included the following language, "If we have offered a payment target, a sufficient coverage by our credit insurance company is assumed. In case this cannot obtained we have to ask for equivalent guarantees or payment in advance."

The first page of CSN order confirmations 17507 and 17579 stated, "We thank you for your purchase order. This order confirmation is subject to our standard conditions of sale as known (www.csnmetals.de)." CSN's standard conditions of sale pro-

---

27. http://cisgw3.law.pace.edu/cases/130910u1.html.

vide, among other things, that "supplies and benefits shall exclusively be governed by German law. The application of laws on international sales of moveable objects and on international purchase contracts on moveable objects is excluded."

On October 4, 2011, CSN emailed RTI. CSN informed RTI that "Cofoaca USA cut the credit line complete." CSN informed RTI that "the best options are to change into 'payment in advance' or L/C (letter of credit)." On October 17, 2011, CSN emailed RTI offering a third option: "[I]n order to minimize our risk we can also offer you to change the delivery to partial shipments. The second shipment would leave as soon as the payment for the first shipment has been transferred to us etc." RTI sent CSN a letter dated October 24, 2011, advising that because of CSN's refusal to perform, RTI would procure the requested copper from an alternate supplier. . . .

IV. Discussion

A. Choice-of-Law

1. Applicable Standard

For the reasons discussed *infra,* this Court has jurisdiction pursuant to 28 U.S.C. §§ 1331 and 1332. The Court must apply the choice-of-law rules of the forum state, Pennsylvania. . . .

"The first step in the analysis is to identify the . . . laws [that] might apply." *Id.* The parties agree that the choice is between the Uniform Commercial Code ("UCC"), and the United Nations Convention for the International Sale of Goods ("CISG"). Next, the Court must "determine whether or not an actual conflict exists. . . .

The main issue before the Court is which, if any, of CSN's standard conditions are included as part of the contracts that are the subject of this litigation. RTI argues that there is no choice-of-law issue because the UCC and CISG do not differ with respect to the issue before the Court. CSN argues that there is a difference and that the CISG applies. Thus, the Court will discuss the approaches of the UCC and the CISG with respect to this situation, commonly referred to as a battle of the forms, to determine if there is a conflict that needs to be resolved.

2. Uniform Commercial Code

"The UCC addresses the sad fact that many sales contracts are not fully bargained, not carefully drafted, and not understandingly signed by both parties. In these cases, [the Court] appl[ies] UCC section 2-207 to ascertain the terms of an agreement."

In this case, the standard conditions that CSN seeks to have included as part of the contract are merely referenced in the documents that were exchanged. "Under the UCC, a provision will not be incorporated by reference if it would result in surprise or hardship to the party against whom enforcement is sought." *Standard Bent Glass,* 333 F.3d at 448. Furthermore, "[u]nder UCC section 2-207(2)(b), absent objection, additional terms become part of the contract unless they materially alter it.

A material alteration is one that would result in surprise or hardship if incorporated without express awareness by the other party." *Id.* at 448 n. 12 (internal quotation marks and citation omitted). Thus, under the UCC, whether the standard conditions are incorporated into the contract between the parties depends upon whether incorporation would result in surprise or hardship to RTI.

3. Convention for the International Sale of Goods

a. Additional Terms

Additional terms are governed by Article 19 of the CISG . . . .

i. American Court Decisions

Few American courts, either state or federal, have interpreted Article 19. In *Claudia v. Olivieri Footwear Ltd.*, 1998 WL 164824 (S.D.N.Y. Apr.7, 1998), the United States District Court for the Southern District of New York held that Article 19 embodies the mirror image rule. *Id.* at *7 n. 6 . . . . In *Travelers Prop. Cas. Co. of Am. v. Saint-Gobain Technical Fabrics Canada Ltd.*, 474 F.Supp.2d 1075 (D.Minn.2007), the United States District Court for the District of Minnesota noted that "Article 19 embodies a mirror image rule." *Id.* at 1082. . . .

ii. Other Authorities

"When [American Courts] interpret treaties, [they] consider the interpretations of the courts of other nations." . . . German Courts have interpreted Article 19 as embodying a mirror image rule. *See* Bundesgerichtshof [BGH] [Federal Supreme Court] Jan. 9, 2002 (*Powdered milk case*), 2002 BGHReport 265, English translation available at (Pace CISG Cases[28]); Oberlandesgericht [OLG] [Appellate Court Frankfurt am Main] June 26, 2006 (*Printed goods case*), English translation available at (Pace CISG Cases[29]) (last accessed Sept. 10, 2013) (noting that "the silence of [Buyer] to [Seller]'s order confirmations is not to be considered as an affirmation of [Seller's standard terms referred to."); Amtsgericht Kehl [AG Kehl] [Petty District Court] Oct. 6, 1995 (*Knitware case*), English translation available at (Pace CISG Cases[30]) (last accessed Sept. 10, 2013) ("Assuming that [seller] had sent its General Conditions to the [buyer], this would have constituted a counteroffer in the sense of CISG Article 19(1)."

. . . .

Thus, with respect to the battle of the forms, the determinative factor under the CISG is when the contract was formed. The terms of the contract are those embodied in the last offer (or counteroffer) made prior to a contract being formed. Once the contents of the original contract are determined, both parties must affirmatively assent to any amendment to the terms of the contract for such amendment to become part of the contract. *See Chateau des Charmes Wines Ltd. v. Sabate USA Inc.*, 328 F.3d

---

28. http://cisgw3.law.pace.edu/cases/020109g1.html.
29. http://cisgw3.law.pace.edu/cases/060626g1.html.
30. http://cisgw3.law.pace.edu/cases/951006g1.html.

528, 531 (9th Cir.2003). Furthermore, standard conditions are only incorporated into an offer if the other party had proper notice.

"[N]o provision of the [CISG] creates such diametrical opposition to the [UCC] rule as does Article 19 in its clear adoption of the 'mirror image' rule. . . ." Ronald A. Brand, *Fundamentals of International Business Transactions: Volume I*, 75 (2013). Under the UCC, standard conditions in an acceptance that materially alter the terms of the agreement are disregarded. Under the CISG, an acceptance with different standard conditions is not actually an acceptance, but rather is a rejection and counteroffer.

b. Incorporation of Standard Conditions

i. American Court Decisions

The United States District Court for the District of Maryland addressed the incorporation of standard conditions in *CSS Antenna*. The Court considered the fact that there was "no evidence on the record to show that [buyer] had actual knowledge of [seller's] General Conditions." *CSS Antenna*, 764 F.Supp.2d at 754. The Court also considered that the parties had never previously discussed the standard conditions in negotiations as weighing heavily against inclusions of the general conditions in the contract. *Id.*

Former Chief Judge Lancaster also addressed the incorporation of standard conditions under the CISG in *Tyco Valves & Controls Distribution GmbH v. Tippins, Inc.*, 2006 WL 2924814 (W.D.Pa. Oct.10, 2006). He found factors to be considered when determining if standard conditions have been properly incorporated include whether the other party actually received the standard conditions and whether there is evidence that the other party read the standard conditions (such as initials next to the standard conditions). *Id.* at *5.

ii. Other Authorities

Under the CISG, "[i]t is . . . required that the recipient of a contract offer that is supposed to be based on general terms and conditions have the possibility to become aware of them in a reasonable manner." Bundesgerichtshof [BGH] [Federal Supreme Court] Oct. 31, 2001 (*Machinery case*), 2001 BGHZ No. 149, English translation available at (Pace CISG Cases[31]) (last accessed Sept. 10, 2013). As the German Supreme Court stated:

> [I]t is easily possible to attach to his offer the general terms and conditions, which generally favor him. It would, therefore, contradict the principle of good faith in international trade as well as the general obligations of cooperation and information of the parties to impose on the other party an obligation to inquire concerning the clauses that have not been transmitted and to burden him with the risks and disadvantages of the unknown general terms and conditions of the other party.

---

31. http://cisgw3.law.pace.edu/cases/011031g1.html.

Id. (internal citations omitted). In other words, "[i]t is accepted by legal practice that the other party must have the possibility to easily take note of the General Terms and Conditions." Oberlandesgericht [OLG] [Appellate Court Dusseldorf] Apr. 21, 2004 (*Mobile car phones case*), English translation available at (Pace CISG Cases[32]) (last accessed Sept. 10, 2013).

Thus, UCC Section 2-207 also differs in a significant manner from CISG Articles 8 and 14 with respect to the incorporation of standard conditions. Under the UCC, standard conditions are incorporated unless they would cause surprise or hardship to the other party. Under the CISG standard conditions are only incorporated if one party attempts to incorporate the standard conditions and the other party had reasonable notice of this attempted incorporation. Accordingly, a conflict exists between the UCC and CISG, and the Court must determine which law applies to the instant case.

4. Applicability of CISG

As mandated by Article VI of the United States Constitution, Pennsylvania's choice-of-law principles recognize that international treaties to which the United States is a contracting state, when applicable, are controlling. *See Sinha v. Sinha*, 834 A.2d 600, 603 (Pa.Super.2003). The CISG "applies to contracts of sale of goods between parties whose places of business are in different States . . . when the States are Contracting States." . . . The parties' places of business were in different states, as is required by Article 1(2) of the CISG. E.g. doc. no. 3-1, 12 (listing RTI's place of business as Titusville, PA and CSN's place of business as Neunkirchen, Germany).

"Because both the United States [and Germany] are signatories to the CISG and the alleged contract at issue involves the sale of goods . . . the CISG governs." *Forestal Guarani*, 613 F.3d at 397. However, just because the CISG governs does not necessarily mean that it applies in this case. Under Article 6 of the CISG, the parties may choose to exclude application of the CISG. In order for the contract to exclude the CISG it must include language which affirmatively states that the CISG does not apply. *BP Oil Int'l, Ltd., v. Empresa Estatal Petroleos de Ecuador*, 332 F.3d 333, 337 (5th Cir.2003) . . . .

In this case, CSN attempted to exclude the CISG in its standard conditions, which stated, "Supplies and benefits shall exclusively be governed by German law. The application of laws on international sales of moveable objects and on international purchase contracts on moveable objects is excluded." Even if the standard conditions are incorporated into the parties' contract, this attempted exclusion is ineffective. It does not explicitly reference the CISG. Furthermore, CSN's standard conditions attempt to exclude international law on the sale of "moveable objects." The CISG does not use the term "moveable objects." The only use of the word "objects" is as a synonym for the word "protests" not as a synonym for the word "goods."

Furthermore, the parties' positions in this litigation demonstrate that they believe exclusion was ineffective. Neither party argues that German law is applicable. Instead, they argue for either the CISG or the UCC. The papers that were exchanged between

---

32. http://cisgw3.law.pace.edu/cases/040421g3.html.

the two parties do not mention the UCC, or Pennsylvania law. . . . The attempted exclusion is ineffective, and the CISG is the applicable law with respect to the instant contract dispute.

B. Contract Formation

Having determined that the CISG is the applicable law, the Court turns to the formation of a contract between RTI and CSN. CSN argues that RTIs purchase orders were offers and that CSN's order confirmations were rejections and counteroffers under the CISG. Alternatively, CSN argues that if it's order confirmations are considered acceptances, that the purchase orders (the offers) included CSN's standard conditions via reference to CSN's quotations. RTI on the other hand, argues that its purchase orders were offers that did not include by reference CSN's standard conditions and that CSN's order confirmations were in fact acceptances of the offers.

1. RTIs Purchase Orders

CSN's standard conditions are part of the contract under any theory being advanced by the parties if RTI's purchase orders incorporated by reference CSN's standard conditions. CSN's quotations included the following language, "According to our standard conditions of sale to be found under www.csnmetals.de, we have pleasure in quoting without engagement as follows." RTIs purchase orders were "per CSN quote" followed by the respective quotation numbers.

. . . The parties do not cite, and the Court is not aware of, any decisions from courts in the United States addressing whether, under the CISG, an offer that references a document, which references standard conditions, incorporates those standard conditions in the offer. However, the Court finds instructive a decision from the Austrian Supreme Court. Oberster Gerichtshof [OGH] [Supreme Court] (*Tantalum powder case*), Dec. 17, 2003, English translation available at (Pace CISG Cases[33]) (last accessed Sept. 10, 2013) (citing CISG Articles 8 & 14). The Court held that "standard terms, in order to be applicable to a contract, must be included in the proposal of the party relying on them as intended to govern the contract in a way that the other party under the given circumstances knew or could not have been reasonably unaware of this intent."

In this case, RTI did not intend the standard conditions to apply to the contract. This fact is plain from the face of the purchase orders. The purchase orders included terms that were different from those included in CSN's standard conditions. For example, the purchase orders state that the orders are FOB destination while CSN's standard conditions state that the orders are FOB origin. Furthermore, the quotations state that payment is due within 90 days (with important exceptions discussed *infra*), while the purchase orders state that payment would be due within 60 days. Thus, RTI did not have the requisite intent to incorporate the standard terms that were referenced in CSN's quotations. *See Tantalum powder case* ("It requires an un-

---

33. http://cisgw3.law.pace.edu/cases/031217a3.html.

ambiguous declaration of the provider's intent."). Accordingly, the Court finds that RTI's purchase orders did not incorporate CSN's quotations.

2. CSN's Order Confirmations

a. Standard Conditions

Having determined that RTI's purchase orders did not incorporate CSN's standard conditions referenced in its quotations, the Court must determine whether CSN's order confirmations constituted acceptances under the CISG or constituted rejections and counteroffers. The Court has detailed the manner in which the CISG treats the battle of the forms, *supra*.

The first page of CSN's order confirmations stated, "We thank you for your purchase order. This order confirmation is subject to our standard conditions of sale as known (www.csnmetals.de)." Doc. No. 3-1, 17, 32. As discussed *supra*, CSN's standard conditions were not incorporated into the RTI purchase orders. Therefore, if the standard conditions were properly incorporated into the order confirmations, the order confirmations would constitute counteroffers and not acceptances.

The Court finds persuasive *CSS Antenna*. In that case, an order confirmation included the following language: "According to our general conditions . . . [which] can be viewed at . . . our homepage. . . ." *CSS Antenna*, 764 F.Supp.2d at 754. The Court held that language to be "ambiguous at best." *Id.*

In the case at bar, all of the factors that weigh against a finding that CSN's standard conditions were properly incorporated into the contract are present while none of the factors that weigh in favor of incorporation are present. The language included on the order confirmations was ambiguous at best, as the language merely directs the other party to a website which needs to be navigated in order for the standard conditions to be located. *See CSS Antenna*, 764 F.Supp.2d at 754. There is no evidence that RTI had actual knowledge of the attempted inclusion of CSN's standard conditions. *See id.* There is no evidence that the parties had discussed incorporation of the standard conditions during contract negotiations. *See id.* There is no evidence that RTI actually received CSN's standard conditions. *Tyco*, 2006 WL 2924814 at *5. Further, no employee of RTI initialed next to the statement attempting to incorporate the standard conditions. *Id.*

. . . Thus, the Court finds that, when considering all of the evidence, CSN's reference to its standard conditions did not suffice to incorporate those terms into the order confirmations. Therefore, CSN's standard conditions are not part of the contract as they were not a part of either the purchase orders or order confirmations.

b. Payment Target Language

As former Chief Judge McLaughlin stated, "there is one sub issue [relating to the incorporation of CSN's standard conditions.]" The order confirmations stated that, "If we have offered a payment target, a sufficient coverage by our credit insurance company is assumed. In case this cannot obtained we have to ask for equivalent guarantees or payment in advance."

The Court finds that this language was properly incorporated into both order confirmations. It was in regular print on the front of both order confirmations. *Id.* The language did not reference any other document but rather was an independent additional term under Article 19 of the CISG. Furthermore, the additional term was material under CISG Article 19(3), as it related to payment terms for the goods.

RTI's sole argument against this additional term under the CISG is that the additional term did not impose any duty on RTI but merely gave CSN the ability to ask for equivalent guarantees or advance payment. This argument is without merit. . . . Any reasonable businessperson reading such a statement would have recognized that this term was a requirement if CSN did not obtain sufficient coverage from its insurance carrier.

The additional term that was properly incorporated into CSN's order confirmations was material under Article 19. Thus, the order confirmations were not in fact acceptances but rather constituted counteroffers.

3. RTI's Acceptance

The final step in determining if a contract was formed between RTI and CSN is consideration of the emails that were exchanged between the parties in August 2011. CSN argues that these emails were acceptances by RTI and therefore a valid contract was formed between the parties.

On August 9, 2011, RTI emailed CSN **purchase order 6676** (*emphasis added*). On August 10, 2011, CSN replied, stating:

> [T]hanks again for the new purchase order. . . . * * *VERY IMPORTANT: * * * As you know we need "FULLY APPROVED DRAWINGS", original format. Please provide to us ASAP. . . .

CSN then followed-up on August 15, 2011, asking for an approximate date that it would receive the drawing from RTI. RTI responded that same day stating that "The approved drawings went out UPS today, and you should receive them Wednesday, 8/17/11." CSN then acknowledged receipt of those drawings on August 17, 2011.

On August 23, 2011, RTI emailed CSN **purchase order 6761** (*emphasis added*). On August 25, 2011, CSN replied, stating:

> [T]hanks for being a little sort [sic], but today's almost same crazy as yesterday. Please find our order confirmation attached. To play safe, let's have the usual crosscheck: In case you would realize anything wrong or feel something important is missing on it, please let us know as it's most important for us to make sure about best customer service and support. If there's any question about it from your side, please feel welcome to contract any time you need. Please send the fully approved, original format drawings over to us ASAP, so that we proceed on our end.

Later on August 25, 2011, RTI replied stating that "After reviewing your order confirmation, please proceed with the manufacture of these plates." *Id.*, 2. On August 26,

2011, CSN sent an email that stated "ok . . . thanks for the quick reply. Still make sure to the the [sic] order drawings to us. (fully approved, original format.)" *Id.*

Article 18(1) of the CISG provides that "A statement made by or other conduct of the offeree indicating assent to an offer is an acceptance." RTI's acceptance of CSN's counteroffer with respect to purchase **order 6761** (emphasis added) is evident from the email exchange. RTI stated that it had reviewed CSN's order confirmation and that CSN could "proceed with the manufacture of these plates." This was an affirmative statement indicating assent to the counteroffer, the order confirmation, without any reservation or attempted alteration. Thus, with respect to purchase order 6761, a contract was formed by RTI's email to CSN that stated manufacture could go forward. The terms of the contract were those set forth in CSN's order confirmation, including the term relating to advance payment. However, CSN's standard conditions were not incorporated into the contract that was entered into between the parties for the reasons set forth *supra*.

Although not as explicit as the conduct relating to purchase order 6761, RTI also accepted CSN's counteroffer with respect to purchase **order 6676** (emphasis added). CSN's emails of August 10, 2011, and August 15, 2011, made clear that they needed RTI's drawings in order to proceed with the order. RTI then took affirmative action and followed the directions that were set forth in CSN's emails by sending via UPS the drawings for CSN's use. RTI then made an affirmative statement to CSN regarding the mailing of the drawings to CSN. Thus, RTI accepted CSN's counteroffer, at the very latest, on August 17, 2011, when CSN received the drawings. RTI made no statement in any email to CSN that it was not accepting the additional term that CSN included in its counteroffer, the order confirmation. Thus, a valid contract under the CISG was also formed with respect to purchase order 6676. The terms of the contract were those set forth in CSN's order confirmation, including the term relating to advance payment. However, CSN's standard conditions were not incorporated into the contract that was entered into between the parties for the reasons set forth *supra*.

C. Breach of Contract

Having determined the parties' obligations under the contract, the Court now turns to whether either party breached its obligations under the contract. CSN argues that RTI repudiated the contract and therefore was in material breach. Article 71 of the CISG provides that: "A party may suspend the performance of his obligations if, after the conclusion of the contract, it becomes apparent that the other party will not perform a substantial part of his obligations as a result of . . . his conduct in preparing to perform or in performing the contract." In this case, there is no dispute that RTI refused to perform on the contract. RTI sent a letter to CSN on October 24, 2011, stating that it would procure the requested copper from an alternate supplier. On October 25, 2011, RTI sent an email to CSN stating that "P.O.'s 6676 and 6761 are cancelled immediately due to CSN's inability to conform to RTIs terms listed on the P.O.'s." *Id.*, 37. CSN responded stating that "please be informed the cancellation of the order is NOT ACCEPTED by CSN." . . .

It is hard to imagine a clearer repudiation. RTI sent repeated notices to CSN over an 11 day period setting forth its reasons for not performing the contract. In short, RTI believed that the terms of the contract were different than they actually were. Thus, RTI breached its contractual obligations to CSN.

V. Conclusion

This contract dispute demonstrates the confusion that can arise in a battle of the forms, particularly when the applicable law is disputed. For the reasons set forth above, the CISG governs this contract dispute. RTIs purchase orders did not incorporate CSN's standard conditions via reference to CSN's quotations. CSN's order confirmations did not incorporate its standard conditions. However, CSN did include within its counteroffer a term relating to payment if CSN's insurer refused to cover the transaction. Thereafter, CSN affirmatively invoked that term. After its invocation by CSN, RTI breached its contractual obligations by repudiating the contract. Therefore, RTI's Motion for Judgment on the Pleadings (doc. no. 40) will be DENIED and CSN's Cross-Motion for Judgment on the Pleadings (doc. no. 44) will be GRANTED.

———————

c. Uniform Commercial Code (UCC)

The UCC provides somewhat different "rules of engagement" for the "battle of the forms" than the approach taken under the CISG. Examine the text of §672.207 of the Florida Commercial Code below. What are the critical differences in language and to what effect? The UCC is designed to avoid the pitfalls of the common law "mirror image rule" which allowed parties to easily escape their commitments based on discrepancies in contractual terms. While UCC §207 tends to keep parties in their sales contracts despite discrepant terms, the CISG largely reflects the mirror image approach, purportedly to better adhere to actual intent. Do the increased risks involved with international transactions explain this difference in priorities? *How might the outcome of the dispute in our problem turn out differently under the UCC approach rather than under the CISG?*

i. *Florida Commercial Code*[34]

672.207 Additional terms in acceptance or confirmation.

(1) A definite and seasonable expression of acceptance or a written confirmation which is sent within a reasonable time operates as an acceptance even though it states terms additional to or different from those offered or agreed upon, unless acceptance is expressly made conditional on assent to the additional or different terms.

(2) The additional terms are to be construed as proposals for addition to the contract. Between merchants such terms become part of the contract unless:

(a) The offer expressly limits acceptance to the terms of the offer;

———————

34. http://www.leg.state.fl.us/Statutes/index.cfm?App_mode=Display_Statute&URL=0600
-0699/0671/0671ContentsIndex.html&StatuteYear=2010&Title=%2D%3E2010%2D%3EChapter
%20671.

(b) They materially alter it; or

(c) Notification of objection to them has already been given or is given within a reasonable time after notice of them is received.

(3) Conduct by both parties which recognizes the existence of a contract is sufficient to establish a contract for sale although the writings of the parties do not otherwise establish a contract. In such case the terms of the particular contract consist of those terms on which the writings of the parties agree, together with any supplementary terms incorporated under any other provisions of this code.

ii. Additional, Material Terms: Paul Gottlieb & Co., Inc. v. Alps South Corporation

985 So. 2d 1 (Fla. Ct. App. 2007)

CASANUEVA, Judge.

. . . .

I. FACTUAL BACKGROUND

Gottlieb is a fabric converter based in New York City. Gottlieb supplies its customers specialty knitted fabrics that are shipped directly from third-party knitting and finishing mills. Alps is a manufacturer of medical devices located in St. Petersburg, Florida. Alps produces various types of liners that amputees use to attach prosthetic devices. In January 2000, Alps used liners that consisted of a specially designed gel material covered in spandex fabric that stretched to allow the liner to be placed over the appendage and then compressed to provide stability.

[Alps contracted with Gottlieb to supply the specialty fabric "Coolmax." Gottlieb was not aware of Alps' specific intended use of the fabric or potential substantial costs that Alps might incur if the fabric failed to meet specifications. When Gottlieb later substituted alternative yarn to create the fabric, Alps began receiving customer complaints and eventually recalled the product from the market at great expense.]

The business relationship ended when Gottlieb failed to receive payment for a submitted bill. Gottlieb then brought an action to collect damages due to the nonpayment. In turn, Alps counterclaimed for damages it asserted were caused by Gottlieb's breach of warranty. Of importance to the damage claim is the language set forth on the back of Gottlieb's finished goods contract which purports to limit its liability. The trial court ultimately considered this language to be an affirmative defense to the counterclaim.

Following a nonjury trial, the trial court awarded damages to Gottlieb on its claim totaling $28,846.29; awarded damages to Alps on its counterclaim of $694,640.04; and determined that under Florida's U.C.C. provisions, the limitation of liability clause was a material alteration of the parties' contract. The trial court declined to enforce the provision concluding that by operation of law, it was not a part of the contract.

II. LIMITATION OF LIABILITY CLAUSE

This dispute arises from the common, but risky, commercial practice where the seller and buyer negotiate a contract involving goods by exchanging each others' standardized forms. The transactions of this type involved here are governed by section 2-207 of the U.C.C., codified in section 672.207, Florida Statutes (2000).

Here, Gottlieb first contends that the trial court erred by failing to enforce the limitation of liabilities clause found on the back of its finished goods contract. The clause in contention reads:

> BUYER SHALL NOT IN ANY EVENT BE ENTITLED TO, AND SELLER SHALL NOT BE LIABLE FOR INDIRECT OR CONSEQUENTIAL DAMAGES OF ANY NATURE, INCLUDING, WITHOUT BEING LIMITED TO, LOSS OF PROFIT, PROMOTIONAL OR MANUFACTURING EXPENSES, INJURY TO REPUTATION OR LOSS OF CUSTOMER.

In its analysis, the trial court determined the clause constituted a material alteration under section 672.207(2) and as such it did not become part of the contract. . . . Since this is a pure question of law, we review the trial court's conclusion de novo.

A. Preservation

. . . .

B. The Battle of the Forms

We next determine whether the trial court erred by failing to enforce the limitation of liability clause. For the following reasons, we conclude the trial court erred.

"[T]he rules of engagement for the 'battle of the forms' are set out in the Uniform Commercial Code ('U.C.C.'), s. 2-207." *Bayway Ref. Co. v. Oxygenated Mktg. & Trading*, 215 F.3d 219, 223 (2d Cir. 2000). The same rules of engagement apply in Florida and are codified in section 672.207. Subsections (1) and (2) of the statute are intended, according to the Florida Code Comments provided with the 1965 Enactment, to end the battle by eliminating the uncertainty that often results from the exchange of conflicting purchase order forms and acknowledgement and acceptance forms. . . .

These statutory provisions allow the formation of a contract where an acceptance contains additional or different terms than the original offer. While such an acceptance ordinarily would not meet the strict requirements of the common law mirror image rule, the U.C.C. provides a more flexible approach. Under section 672.207(2), additional terms included in an acceptance are construed as proposals for addition to the contract. *See A & M Eng'g Plastics, Inc. v. Energy Saving Tech. Co.*, 455 So.2d 1124 (Fla. 4th DCA 1984). Between merchants, the terms become part of the contract unless they fall into an exception. § 672.207(2). Within the context of section 672.207(2), the parties do not dispute that they are merchants, that Gottlieb's offer did not expressly limit acceptance to its terms, and that Alps did not object to the additional terms within a reasonable amount of time. The remaining issue is whether the limitation of damages clause, as an additional term, materially altered the contract. If the additional term materially alters the contract, it is excluded.

Procedurally, in determining whether a term constitutes a material alteration, other courts have placed the burden of proof upon the party seeking the term's exclusion. . . . We conclude that this rule is appropriate and hold that a party seeking the exclusion of a contractual term or provision pursuant to setion 672.207 (2), as constituting a material alteration, has the burden of proof. . . .

C. Surprise or Hardship

Having determined which party appropriately bears the burden of proof, we next address the nature of proof that a party must offer to meet its burden. Unfortunately, the law in this area is not yet clearly developed. For example, Official Comment 4 to U.C.C. § 2-207 offers examples of "typical clauses which would normally 'materially alter' the contract" and that would "result in surprise or hardship if incorporated without express awareness by the other party." . . .

In contrast, Official Comment 5 to U.C.C. § 2-207 offers "[e]xamples of clauses which involve no element of *unreasonable surprise* and which therefore are to be incorporated in the contract unless notice of objection is seasonably given." (Emphasis added.) Relying on this language and common law principles, some courts have removed hardship from the analysis and look solely for surprise. *See Union Carbide Corp. v. Oscar Mayer Foods Corp.*, 947 F.2d 1333 (7th Cir. 1991); *Suzy Phillips Originals, Inc. v. Coville, Inc.*, 939 F. Supp. 1012 (E.D. N.Y. 1996). Previously, this court considered whether a term was a material alteration under section 672.207 in *Advanced Mobilehome Systems of Tampa, Inc. v. Alumax Fabricated Products, Inc.*, 666 So. 2d 166 (Fla. 2d DCA 1995), and approved of the rationale of *Union Carbide* to reach its decision (observing that a change is material if agreement to it cannot be presumed). There, Judge Posner explained:

> What is expectable, hence unsurprising, is okay; what is unexpected, hence surprising, is not. Not infrequently the test is said to be "surprise or hardship," but this appears to be a misreading of Official Comment 4 to UCC § 2-207. . . .

Union Carbide, 947 F.2d at 1336. Today, we continue to follow this rationale.

Turning first to the surprise prong, Alps must prove "that, under the circumstances, it cannot be presumed that a reasonable merchant would have consented to the additional term." *See Bayway Refining, 215 F.3d at 224.* The finished goods contract at issue was the sixth in a series between the two parties and each contract included the limitation of liability term. Each proposed contract contained the terms which were visible on its face. The sole evidence presented at trial to establish surprise was that Alps had not read the contract before the dispute arose. Florida law has never excused a party from a contract simply because it failed to read the contract terms. Additionally, Official Comment 5 to U.C.C. § 2-207 includes clauses which limit remedies in a reasonable manner among the examples of terms which do not involve unreasonable surprise. The record in this case does not allow a conclusion that Gottlieb's limitation of liability clause was an unreasonable surprise to Alps.

The record is similarly lacking with respect to hardship as a result of surprise. Courts that consider hardship look to whether the term would "impose substantial economic hardship on the non-assenting party." *Horning*, 730 F.Supp. at 962. . . .

Here, the facts do not permit a result identical to that of *Horning*. Gottlieb never represented that, in the event of a breach, it would reimburse Alps for any or all consequential damages it sustained resulting from the breach. Instead, the evidence showed that Alps previously had returned a sample of nonconforming fabric to Gottlieb with a letter insisting on conforming goods. This letter did not mention or make claim for additional costs or damages resulting from Gottlieb's prior breach of performance. The evidence shows that Alps never informed Gottlieb of any consequences other than discontinuing their relationship. Alps did not inform Gottlieb of the specific manner in which the subject fabric would be used or what product would be crafted. Thus, Gottlieb could not foresee the *greater extent* of its potential liability, should a subsequent breach occur. Because Alps neglected to inform Gottlieb of the larger consequences of the breach, we conclude that Alps cannot maintain that incorporating the limitation of liability clause would result in a severe economic hardship. Thus, Alps failed to carry the burden of proof on hardship.

For these reasons, we conclude that the trial court erred by not enforcing the limitation of consequential damages clause. The award of consequential damages must be stricken.

Finally, we note that enforcing of the clause at issue only bars consequential damages. The limitation in this clause does not exclude other damages available under the law. . . .

. . . .

iii. Different, Material Terms & the Knock Out Rule: Richardson v. Union Carbide Industrial Gases, Inc., and Rage Engineering, Inc., v. Hoeganaes Corp.

790 A.2d 962 (N.J. App. Div. 2002)

Worker injured in furnace explosion brought action against employer, equipment supplier, and other defendants, alleging products liability, negligence, and breach of express and implied warranty. Supplier cross-claimed against employer for indemnity.

. . . .

Affirmed.

The opinion of the court was delivered by BRAITHWAITE, J.A.D.

In this appeal, we are required to address whether the "knock-out" rule applies in New Jersey when there are conflicting terms in a contract governed by the Uniform Commercial Code ("UCC"), codified at N.J.S.A. 12A:1-101 to 11-108. The effect of applying the "knock-out" rule is that the conflicting terms do not become part of the parties' contract and the contract "consists of those terms on which the writings of the parties agree, together with any supplementary terms incorporated under any other provisions of this act." N.J.S.A. 12:2-207 (3). We conclude that the "knock-out" rule applies in New Jersey and affirm the summary judgment granted to defendant Hoeganaes Corporation ("Hoeganaes"), dismissing defendant Rage Engineering Inc.'s ("Rage") cross-claim for indemnification.

Because this appeal arises from the grant of summary judgment, we must view the facts, and all favorable inferences from those facts, in the light most favorable to Rage. These are the facts.

Prior to 1988, Hoeganaes operated furnace 2S, which was used for annealing iron powders. In 1988, Hoeganaes undertook the conversion of furnace 2S to a distalloy furnace. Part of the conversion process required the purchase of a powder transporter system or a "dense phase system" to transport iron powder to the input end of the furnace. Hoeganaes purchased the system from Rage after inquiring from two other possible sellers.

. . . .

The proposals issued by Rage were typed in a letter format addressing the items desired by Hoeganaes. At the base of each page of each proposal, the following language in capital letters was typed: "ANY PURCHASE ORDER ISSUED AS A RESULT OF THIS QUOTE IS MADE EXPRESSLY SUBJECT TO THE TERMS AND CONDITIONS ATTACHED HERETO IN LIEU OF ANY CONFLICTING TERMS PROPOSED BY PURCHASER." The terms and conditions attached to Rage's proposals were standard terms that were sent with every proposal and appeared in standard boilerplate format. The terms and conditions were not discussed during Rage's meetings with Hoeganaes.

At the top of the terms and conditions was a Limitation of Acceptance which stated:

> LIMITATION OF ACCEPTANCE. This sale (including all services) is limited to and expressly made conditional on Purchaser's assent to these Terms and Conditions as well as all other provisions contained in any other document to which these Terms and Conditions are attached. Purchaser agrees: (a) These Terms and Conditions . . . shall be deemed to supercede and take precedence over all prior writings, representations or agreements regarding this sale; (b) These Terms and Conditions . . . shall represent our complete agreement; (c) Any inconsistent, conflicting or additional terms or conditions proposed by Purchaser in any order, acceptance or other document or form shall be void and without effect unless Seller shall specifically and expressly accept same in writing; (d) No modification of these Terms and Conditions . . . will be affected by Seller's shipment of goods/equipment or the provision of services following receipt of Purchaser's order, acceptance or other document or form containing terms which are inconsistent, conflicting or in addition to these Terms and Conditions . . . ; and (e) Any acceptance of goods/equipment or services, or payment constitutes an acceptance by Purchaser of these Terms and Conditions. . . .

The Rage terms and conditions also had an indemnity clause, which stated:

INDEMNITY. Purchaser shall indemnify and hold Seller harmless against and in respect of any loss, claim or damage (including costs of suit and attorneys' fees) or other expense incident to or in connection with: the goods/equipment; the furnishing of design, installation (including site preparation) or other services; processing or use by any person of any goods/equipment or system (including personal injury to the employees of Seller and Purchaser); . . . .

At the bottom of the purchase orders issued by Hoeganaes the following language in bold face type appeared: "THIS ORDER IS ALSO SUBJECT TO THE TERMS AND CONDITIONS ON THE REVERSE SIDE OF THIS PAGE[.]" The reverse side of the purchase orders included the following section at the top of the boilerplate terms and conditions section:

1. Compliance with Terms and Conditions of Order—The terms and conditions set forth below, along with the provisions set forth on the front page hereof, constitute the entire contract of purchase and sale between Buyer and Seller. Any provisions in the Seller's acceptance, acknowledgment or other response to this Order which are different from or in addition to any of the terms and conditions and other provisions of this Order are hereby objected to by Buyer and such different or additional provisions shall not become a part of Buyer's contract of purchase and sale.

Furthermore, the reverse side also contained the following indemnity clause and a clause stating that the purchase order constituted the entire agreement:

14. Indemnification—Seller agrees to indemnify and hold harmless and protect Buyer, its affiliated and subsidiary companies, successors, assigns, customers and users of its products from and against all losses, damages, liabilities, claims, demands (including attorneys fees'), and suits at law or equity that arise out of, or are alleged to have arisen out of, directly or indirectly, any act of omission or commission, negligent or otherwise, of Seller, its sub-contractors, their employees, workmen, servants or agents, or otherwise out of the performance or attempted performance by Seller of this purchase order.

16. This purchase order contains the entire agreement between the parties and the provisions hereof or rights hereunder may be modified or waived only in writing by Buyer's authorized officials. All matters in connection herewith shall be determined under the laws of New Jersey.

Thus, both Rage and Hoeganaes exchanged documents, pertinent here, with conflicting indemnity clauses. Other than as expressed in the boilerplate language, neither side objected to the language in the documents and the contract was performed.

Plaintiff Jeffrey Richardson was an employee of Hoeganaes when he was injured by the explosion of furnace 2S on May 13, 1992. On September 15, 1994, plaintiff filed suit against numerous defendants including Hoeganaes and Rage. Plaintiff alleged that Rage "did design, manufacture, maintain, assemble, inspect, test, sell and/or distribute the systems and facilities design and/or its component parts" for the furnace which caused his injuries. Plaintiff alleged breaches of the Products Liability Act, N.J.S.A. 2A:58-1 to -11, implied and express warranties and negligence. In its answer, Rage cross-claimed against Hoeganaes seeking contractual indemnification. Hoeganaes, in its answer to the cross-claim, denied any right to indemnification arising out of the contract.

On May 15, 1997, Rage filed a motion for summary judgment seeking contractual indemnification from Hoeganaes. Hoeganaes cross-moved for summary judgment seeking dismissal of Rage's cross-claim for contractual indemnity. On August 15, 1997, the motion judge granted Hoeganaes' motion and dismissed Rage's claim for indemnification.

Rage's subsequent motion for reconsideration was denied. Thereafter, plaintiff settled his claims. Rage now appeals from the summary judgment granted to Hoeganaes, dismissing Rage's contractual indemnification claim.

On appeal, Rage contends that the motion judge erred when he applied N.J.S.A.12A:2-207(3) and found that the parties' contract did not include Rage's indemnity provision. We reject Rage's contention, concluding that the "knock-out" rule applies and that Rage's indemnity clause did not become part of the contract.

. . . .

We address first, Rage's second point, which asserts that the "knock-out" rule should not have been applied to its indemnity clause. This issue has not been addressed previously by our courts in a published opinion.

We note that N.J.S.A. 12A:2-207 addresses "additional terms in acceptance" and also uses the language "different" terms. In N.J.S.A. 12A:2-207(2), however, where the standard to determine whether additional terms become part of the parties' contract, the word "different" is not employed.

N.J.S.A. 12A:2-207 is silent on the question of whether "additional or different terms" mean the same thing. There is seemingly no agreement on that question. *Northrop v. Litronic Indus.*, 29 F.3d 1173, 1175 (7th Cir. 1994). It is unclear whether the reference to "different" terms in the acceptance, N.J.S.A. 12A:2-207 (1), means that the drafters intended "different" to be treated like "additional" terms under N.J.S.A. 12A:2-207(2).

Comment three of N.J.S.A. 12A:2-207, suggests that both additional and different terms, are governed by N.J.S.A. 12A:2-207(2). However, comment six . . . advances the proposition that conflicting terms in exchanged writing must be assumed to be mutually objected to by each party with the result of a mutual "knock-out" of the conflicting terms.[4]

---

4. The relevant portion of comment six states:

    Where clauses on confirming forms sent by both parties' conflict each party must be assumed to object to a clause of the other conflicting with one on the confirmation sent by himself. As a result the requirement that there be notice of objection which is found in subsection (2) is satisfied and the conflicting terms do not become a part of the contract. The contract then

Scholars differ on this subject. . . .

There are, however, three recognized approaches by the courts to the issue of conflicting terms in contracts under circumstances such as here. The majority view is that the conflicting terms fall out and, if necessary, are replaced by suitable UCC gap-filler provisions. . . .

The minority view is that the offeror's terms control because the offeree's different terms cannot be saved by N.J.S.A. 12A:2-207(2), because that section applies only to additional terms. . . .

The third view assimilates "different" to "additional" so that the terms of the offer prevail over the different terms in the acceptance only if the latter are materially different. This is the least adopted approach. . . .

We conclude that the majority approach, the "knock-out" rule, is preferable and should be adopted in New Jersey. We reach this conclusion because the other approaches are inequitable and unjust and run counter to the policy behind N.J.S.A. 12A:2-207, which addresses a concern that existed at common law.

. . . Our adoption of the "knock-out" rule advances the goal of reformation of the common law mirror-image rule.

. . . .

In granting the motion for summary judgment, the judge implicitly adopted the "knock-out" rule. An approach other than the knock-out rule for conflicting terms would result in Rage, or any offeror, always prevailing on its terms solely because it sent the first form. That is not a desirable result, particularly when the parties have not negotiated for the challenged clause.

II

Now we address Rage's first point. Rage asserts that the motion judge erred in analyzing the matter under N.J.S.A. 12A:2-207 (3) rather than N.J.S.A. 12A:2-207 (2). We are satisfied that under either analysis the result is the same and, therefore, summary judgment was properly granted to Hoeganaes.

N.J.S.A. 12A:2-207(2) sets forth the standard to determine if additional terms of an acceptance become part of the contract. The additional terms between merchants become part of the contract unless:

(a) the offer expressly limits acceptance to the terms of the offer;

(b) they materially alter it; or

(c) notification of objection to them has already been given or is given within a reasonable time after notice of them is received.

---

consists of the terms originally expressly agreed to, terms on which the confirmations agree, and terms supplied by this Act, including subsection (2).

Applying this section here leads inescapably to the conclusion that Rage's indemnity clause did not become part of the contract. Although Rage's offer specifically limited acceptance to the terms of its offer, Hoeganaes' acceptance materially altered Rage's offer with respect to the issue of indemnification. Additionally, Hoeganaes' acceptance objected to any terms or conditions of the Rage offer that were different from or in addition to any of the terms of its own acceptance.

Moreover, comment six to N.J.S.A. 12A:2-207, which expresses the "knock-out" rule that we addressed earlier in this opinion, supports the conclusion that Rage's indemnity clause did not become part of the contract. Thus, N.J.S.A. 12A:2-207(2) offers no support for Rage's position.

Applying N.J.S.A. 12A:2-207(3) leads to the same result. Here, the contested provision addressed indemnity and only became relevant after plaintiff was injured, some three years after the conversion of the furnace was completed. Pursuant to N.J.S.A. 12A:2-207(3), the conduct of the parties recognizes the existence of a contract and the "terms of the particular contract consist of those terms on which the writings of the parties *agree,* together with any supplementary terms incorporated under any other provisions of this Act." (Emphasis added). Because the parties' writings disagree on indemnity, that term did not become part of the contract.

Chapter 4

Terms of Trade

A. Overview

"Terms of Trade" are abbreviations that are commonly incorporated into sales and shipping documents as short hand references that define certain rights and obligations of the parties. Such terms, originally developed by private traders as a part of mercantile custom, not only define basic shipping and delivery obligations but may also determine risk of loss, payment arrangements, insurance obligations, inspection rights, and other issues. In this fashion, a term of trade may also implicitly define what is included in a particular price.

There are a variety of trade term definitions derived from both commercial codes, like the UCC, and from private sources, like "Incoterms," published by the International Chamber of Commerce [1] ("ICC"). As a consequence, the meaning of any particular term, such as "free on board" ("FOB"), may vary depending on its source definition. Thus, FOB under Incoterms may have a somewhat different meaning than FOB under the UCC, or under definitions prevailing in the United Kingdom or elsewhere. The ICC's Incoterms were created, at least in part, to provide a more consistent and uniform understanding of commonly used terms in international trade.

Use of trade terms is, however, completely voluntary. Contractual parties are free to incorporate whatever terms and source definitions that best suit their interests. Thus, a contract calling for CIF Incoterms 2010 will be controlled by the definition of that term set by the ICC, even if the UCC would otherwise apply to the transaction. In international trade, Incoterms now dominate.[2] Some courts have even suggested that contractual silence implies default to Incoterms for international sales transactions, under trade usage rules, such as CISG Article 9.[3]

---

1. https://iccwbo.org/

2. INCOTERMS 2010 officially acknowledged, for the first time, that such terms may also be utilized in domestic transactions.

3. *See St. Paul Guardian Ins. v. Neuromed Med. Sys.,* No. 00 CIV. 9344, 2002 WL 465312, at *2, at *9–*10 (S.D.N.Y. March 26, 2002) (stating that "INCOTERMS are incorporated into the CISG through Article 9(2)").

Our goal for this chapter is to learn how trade terms function in allocating risks and responsibilities in international sale of goods transactions. As illustrations, we will closely examine several of the most commonly used Incoterms, such as FOB, FCA, CIF, and CIP. After this chapter you should know the specific contractual significance of designating a price in such terms. You should also understand the general differences between categories of Incoterms, including those associated with only "port to port" ocean transportation versus those designed for "multi-modal" transportation. The following problem raises some of the basic issues regarding international trade terms and will facilitate our study.

B. Problem Four: Chinese Rods & Reels

1. Facts

Barney owns a fishing equipment shop in Fort Lauderdale, Florida. He recently contacted a manufacturer of fishing equipment located in the People's Republic of China about supplying Barney's retail shop with fishing rods and reels. This Chinese seller, Real Big Fish PRC, gave Barney a price sheet with four price options described in this way: "1. $10 per rod & reel combo delivered at our factory, Beijing; 2. $11 per rod & reel delivered onto your vessel in Port of Shanghai; 3. $13 per rod & reel shipped to you at Port Everglades, Florida via our carrier Big Chinese Ships; or 4. $15 per rod & reel delivered to your address in Fort Lauderdale." Barney needs advice regarding the legal implications of each of these alternatives. He is concerned, among other things, about (1) how payment will be made under these options, (2) whether he can trust the seller to send him what he wants, (3) whether he can inspect the goods prior to payment, (4) who will be responsible for customs, and (5) which party will bear the risks of damage or loss of the goods during shipment.

2. Assignment

(1) Advise Barney about his rights and obligations assuming that Incoterms 2010 will apply to his transaction. What are the differences in obligations and risks between the various arrangements offered by the Seller and why should Barney choose one over the others? What Incoterm would be most appropriate to each arrangement?

(2) Fill in the blanks on the chart which appears at the end of the materials referenced below.

C. Resources

1. General Overview

In general, Incoterms define the seller's and buyer's obligations as they relate to transportation, delivery, and cost obligations. In so doing, the terms often also resolve related issues such as risk of loss, payment, insurance, customs clearance and inspection. The terms are organized, as of 2010, in two categories: those designed for ocean transportation of goods and those suited for "any mode" of transport, particularly "multimodal" container traffic in which ocean shipping is only one part. The most common example of multimodal traffic involves the transfer of containers of freight, consolidated at a point inland, from truck or rail transportation (or both) to an ocean bound vessel, all under the same transport documents and responsibility of a single transportation service ("multimodal transport operator").[4] This is <u>distinguishable from "intermodal"</u>[5] transport, which may utilize more than one form of transportation but each pursuant to a distinct shipping contract and carrier. The two categories of terms are generally similar but accommodate the fact that, for practical reasons, delivery of the goods to a carrier under multi-modal container arrangements will take place somewhere other than at the ship's rail. Differences in types of transportation and transport documentation are described in more detail in Chapter Six.

Both categories of terms follow a pattern under which the seller's obligations increase from simply delivering the goods to the buyer at seller's own place of business ("EXW"—out the back door, so to speak) to delivery to the buyer at his place of business with all costs, from inland transportation to customs tariffs, included ("DDP"—delivery duty paid). Remember, in this regard, that "delivery" is a term of art signifying that the seller has made the goods available to the buyer—an event that commonly takes place when the goods are handed over to the carrier.

In between these "EX" terms and "D" terms, of which there are several, Incoterms define two other major sets of terms that similarly vary by increasing seller obligations. Here, under the "F" and "C" terms, Incoterms offer parallel sets of terms which account for the mode of transportation. Under traditional "F" ocean shipping terms, the seller will deliver the goods either "free alongside" ("FAS") or "free on board" ("FOB") a vessel arranged and paid for by the buyer at a named port of shipment. This may be contrasted to alternative domestic definitions of FOB, such as UCC § 2-319, which may distinguish between "FOB Origin" and "FOB Destination" contracts. Under Incoterms, FOB New York is understood to mean that the place of delivery and shipment is the Port of New York. This point of delivery also determines related issues such as passing the risk of loss, transportation, loading cost allocations, and

---

4. In practice, more than one carrier may actually be involved in the shipment but responsibility and organization is that of a single entity, the multimodal transport operator, which issues the "multimodal" or "combined" bill of lading.

5. http://www.cratexgroup.com/intermodal-vs-multimodal-what-is-the-difference/.

export clearance (the actual details of which may be altered by the parties as they choose). If the parties utilize multi-modal container transport, these terms must be adjusted since the seller will deliver the goods to a carrier, for consolidation or "containerization," at a place other than a vessel at the port of shipment. Hence the term "free carrier" ("FCA") is used, under which delivery takes place when the seller places the goods in the custody of the first carrier at some place other than a port.

The "C" terms increase the seller's obligations regarding transportation and insurance. Under the "CIF" term (Cost, Insurance, Freight), for example, the seller must not only deliver the goods on board a vessel, where the risk of loss again passes, but must also insure the goods, and arrange and pay for that transportation to the named port of destination. In contrast to Incoterm FOB, the place named under a "C" term is, therefore, understood to be the port of destination rather than the port of origin. These expenses will, of course, be reflected in the price of the goods and, in this sense, "C" terms can also be thought of as a "price terms."

Note again that, contrary to your likely intuition, "delivery" of the goods, per the parties' sales contract, will still take place when the goods are loaded. Although the seller must arrange and pay for transportation to the destination port named, it fulfills its contractual obligation to deliver goods when the carrier takes them on board.

Importantly, the CIF term also impliedly defines the method of payment, requiring the buyer to "pay against documents" without any right of inspection. In contrast, "F" terms are not impliedly payment terms and allow any form of payment that the parties choose. Thus, parties choosing FOB terms may also specify payment against documents, or any other payment method to their liking.

If the transport is other than port to port via ocean or inland waterway, Incoterms require the use of alternative "C" terms such as "CPT" ("Cost Paid To") or "CIP" ("Cost, Insurance Paid To"). These terms, like FCA, can be used for any mode of transport, including multi-modal transport with partial shipment by sea, and account for delivery of the goods at a place other than an ocean port of shipment.

Here is a complete list of the terms currently defined under Incoterms 2010:

RULES FOR ANY MODE OR MODES OF TRANSPORT

EXW	EX WORKS
FCA	FREE CARRIER
CPT	CARRIAGE PAID TO
CIP	CARRIAGE AND INSURANCE PAID TO
DAT	DELIVERED AT TERMINAL
DAP	DELIVERED AT PLACE
DDP	DELIVERED DUTY PAID

RULES FOR SEA AND INLAND WATERWAY TRANSPORT

FAS	FREE ALONGSIDE SHIP
FOB	FREE ON BOARD

CFR	COST AND FREIGHT
CIF	COST INSURANCE AND FREIGHT

2. Description of Specific Terms

There are many general explanations of trade terms on the internet,[6] including a very clear and accurate general description found on Wikipedia.[7] Below is a simple version offered by U.S. Government export promotion agency, Export.gov.[8] For the genuine Inco-enthusiast, or those suffering from insomnia, they also offer an hour long webinar.[9]

a. Incoterms 2010

RULES FOR ANY MODE OF TRANSPORT:

ExWorks (EXW): the seller fulfills his obligations by having the goods available for the buyer to pick up at his premises or another named place (i.e. factory, warehouse, etc.). Buyer bears all risk and costs starting when he picks up the products at the seller's location until the products are delivered to his location. Seller has no obligation to load the goods or clear them for export.

Free Carrier (FCA): the seller delivers the goods export cleared to the carrier stipulated by the buyer or another party authorized to pick up goods at the seller's premises or another named place. Buyer assumes all risks and costs associated with delivery of goods to final destination including transportation after delivery to carrier and any customs fees to import the product into a foreign country.

Carriage Paid To (CPT): seller clears the goods for export and delivers them to the carrier or another person stipulated by the seller at a named place of shipment. Seller is responsible for the transportation costs associated with delivering goods to the named place of destination but is not responsible for procuring insurance.

Carriage and Insurance Paid To (CIP): seller clears the goods for export and delivers them to the carrier or another person stipulated by the seller at a named place of shipment. Seller is responsible for the transportation costs associated with delivering goods and procuring minimum insurance coverage to the named place of destination.

Delivered at Terminal (DAT): seller clears the goods for export and bears all risks and costs associated with delivering the goods and unloading them

---

6. http://blog.oxforddictionaries.com/2016/04/should-you-capitalize-internet/.

7. https://en.wikipedia.org/wiki/Incoterms.

8. https://www.export.gov/welcome.

9. http://2016.export.gov/webinars/eg_main_039891.asp.

at the terminal at the named port or place of destination. Buyer is responsible for all costs and risks from this point forward including clearing the goods for import at the named country of destination.

Delivered at Place (DAP): seller clears the goods for export and bears all risks and costs associated with delivering the goods to the named place of destination not unloaded. Buyer is responsible for all costs and risks associated with unloading the goods and clearing customs to import the goods into the named country of destination.

Delivered Duty Paid (DDP): seller bears all risks and costs associated with delivering the goods to the named place of destination ready for unloading and cleared for import.

RULES FOR SEA AND INLAND WATERWAY TRANSPORT:

Free Alongside Ship (FAS): seller clears the goods for export and delivers them when they are placed alongside the vessel at the named port of shipment. Buyer assumes all risks/costs for goods from this point forward.

Free on Board (FOB): seller clears the goods for export and delivers them when they are onboard the vessel at the named port of shipment. Buyer assumes all risks/cost for goods from this moment forward.

Cost and Freight (CFR): seller clears the goods for export and delivers them when they are onboard the vessel at the port of shipment. Seller bears the cost of freight to the named port of destination. Buyer assumes all risks for goods from the time goods have been delivered on board the vessel at the port of shipment.

Cost, Insurance, and Freight (CIF): seller clears the goods for export and delivers them when they are onboard the vessel at the port of shipment. Seller bears the cost of freight and insurance to the named port of destination. Seller's insurance requirement is only for minimum cover. Buyer is responsible for all costs associated with unloading the goods at the named port of destination and clearing goods for import. Risk passes from seller to buyer once the goods are onboard the vessel at the port of shipment.

The website IncotermsExplained.com[10] (not making that up) provides an explanation of each term, complete with diagrams outlining various responsibilities of the buyer and seller. There are also many charts and diagrams available on the internet. One of the better charts is presented by Export.gov (authored by John S. James, Co.[11]):

---

10. https://www.incotermsexplained.com/the-incoterms-rules/incoterms-2010-rules/.
11. http://johnsjames.com/.

INCOTERMS® 2010 REFERENCE CHART

John S. James Co.

SERVICES	Rules for any mode or modes of transport							Rules for sea and inland waterway transport			
	EXW	FCA	CPT	CIP	DAT	DAP	DDP	FAS	FOB	CFR	CIF
	Ex Works	Free Carrier	Carriage Paid To	Carriage & Insurance Paid To	Delivered at Terminal	Delivered at Place	Delivered Duty Paid	Free Alongside Ship	Free on Board	Cost & Freight	Cost, Insurance & Freight
	Who Pays	Who Pays	Who Pays	Who Pays	Who Pays	Who Pays	Who Pays	Who Pays	Who Pays	Who Pays	Who Pays
Export Packing	Seller	Seller	Seller	Seller	Seller	Seller	Seller	Seller	Seller	Seller	Seller
Marking & Labeling	Seller	Seller	Seller	Seller	Seller	Seller	Seller	Seller	Seller	Seller	Seller
Block and Brace	1	1	1	1	1	1	1	1	1	1	1
Export Formalities	Buyer	Seller	Seller	Seller	Seller	Seller	Seller	Seller	Seller	Seller	Seller
Freight Forwarder Fees	Buyer	Buyer	Seller	Seller	Seller	Seller	Seller	Buyer	Buyer	Seller	Seller
Inland Freight to Main Carrier	Buyer	2	Seller	Seller	Seller	Seller	Seller	Seller	Seller	Seller	Seller
Origin Port/Terminal Fees	Buyer	Buyer	Seller	Seller	Seller	Seller	Seller	Buyer	Seller	Seller	Seller
Vessel Loading Fees	Buyer	Buyer	Seller	Seller	Seller	Seller	Seller	Buyer	Seller	Seller	Seller
Ocean or Airfreight	Buyer	Buyer	Seller	Seller	Seller	Seller	Seller	Buyer	Buyer	Seller	Seller
Nomination of US Freight Forwarder	Buyer	Buyer	Seller	Seller	Seller	Seller	Seller	Buyer	Buyer	Seller	Seller
Marine Insurance	3	3	3	Seller	3	3	3	3	3	3	Seller
Unload Main Carrier Charges	Buyer	Buyer	4	4	Seller	Seller	Seller	Buyer	Buyer	4	4
Destination Terminal/Port Fees	Buyer	Buyer	4	4	4	Seller	Seller	Buyer	Buyer	4	4
Nomination of On-Carriage	Buyer	Buyer	5	5	5	5	Seller	Buyer	Buyer	Buyer	Buyer
Security Information Requirements	Buyer	Buyer	Buyer	Buyer	Buyer	Buyer	Buyer	Buyer	Buyer	Buyer	Buyer
Customs Entry Service Fees	Buyer	Buyer	Buyer	Buyer	Buyer	Buyer	Seller	Buyer	Buyer	Buyer	Buyer
Duties, Taxes, Customs Fees	Buyer	Buyer	Buyer	Buyer	Buyer	Buyer	Seller	Buyer	Buyer	Buyer	Buyer
Deliver to Buyer	Buyer	Buyer	5	5	5	5	Seller	Buyer	Buyer	Buyer	Buyer
Deliverying Carrier Unloading	Buyer	Buyer	Buyer	Buyer	Buyer	Buyer	Buyer	Buyer	Buyer	Buyer	Buyer

Notes:

1 - Incoterms® 2010 do not deal with the parties' obligations for stowage within a container and therefore, where relevant, the parties should deal with this in the sales contract.

2 - FCA Seller's Facility – Buyer pays inland freight; other FCA qualifiers. Seller arranges and loads pre-carriage carrier and pays inland freight to the "F" delivery place

3 - Incoterms® 2010 does not obligate the buyer nor must the seller to insure the goods, therefore this issue be addressed elsewhere in the sales contract.

4 - Charges paid by Buyer or Seller depending on contract of carriage.

5 - Charges paid by Seller if through Bill of Lading or door-to-door rate to Buyer's destination

INCOTERMS® IS A REGISTERED TRADEMARK OF THE INTERNATIONAL CHAMBER OF COMMERCE. THIS DOCUMENT IS NOT INTENDED AS LEGAL ADVICE BUT IS BEING PROVIDED FOR REFERENCEPURPOSES ONLY. USERS SHOULD SEEK SPECIFIC GUIDANCE FROM INCOTERMS® 2010 AVAILABLE THROUGH THE INTERNATIONAL CHAMBER OF COMMERCE AT WWW.ICCBOOKS.COM

The following simple chart from Wikipedia is also helpful:

Duties of seller according to Incoterms 2010

	Loading on truck (carrier)	Export-Customs declaration	Carriage to port of export	Unloading of truck in port of export	Loading charges in port of export	Carriage to port of import	Unloading charges in port of import	Loading on truck in port of import	Carriage to place of destination	Insurance	Import customs clearance	Import taxes
EXW	No	No	No	No	No	No	No	No	No	No	No	No
FCA	Yes	Yes	No	No	No	No	No	No	No	No	No	No
FAS	Yes	Yes	Yes	Yes	No	No	No	No	No	No	No	No
FOB	Yes	Yes	Yes	Yes	Yes	No	No	No	No	No	No	No
CFR	Yes	Yes	Yes	Yes	Yes	Yes	No	No	No	No	No	No
CIF	Yes	Yes	Yes	Yes	Yes	Yes	No	No	No	Yes	No	No
DAT	Yes	Yes	Yes	Yes	Yes	Yes	Yes	No	No	No	No	No
DAP	Yes	Yes	Yes	Yes	Yes	Yes	Yes	Yes	Yes	No	No	No
CPT	Yes	Yes	Yes	Yes	Yes	Yes	Yes	Yes	Yes	No	No	No
CIP	Yes	Yes	Yes	Yes	Yes	Yes	Yes	Yes	Yes	Yes	No	No
DDP	Yes	Yes	Yes	Yes	Yes	Yes	Yes	Yes	Yes	No	Yes	Yes

Export.gov, in a shorter alternative web video on IncoTerms, also provides the following chart in Pdf.

Many commercial freight companies also provide visual aids and general definitions of the terms derived from ICC materials (sometimes for the older Incoterms 2000). Far too many, yet helpful, visual aids[12] are available on the web.

Based upon what you have learned, you should be able to fill in the simple chart that appears below.

Obligations of Buyer & Seller

Issues/ risks	FCA	FOB	CIF	CIP	DDP
Transportation/shipping (arranging & paying)					
"Delivery" (place)					
Risk of loss passes					
Insurance					
Payment (when & how)					
Inspection (when?)					
Customs/formalities (responsibility)					
Other costs					

---

12. https://www.google.com/search?q=incoterms+2010&hl=en&client=firefox-a&hs=E6k&rls=org.mozilla:en-US:official&channel=fflb&prmd=imvns&tbm=isch&tbo=u&source=univ&sa=X&ei=buJHUMLUIIH89QTH-4HoDw&ved=0CEkQsAQ&biw=1680&bih=946.

Although probably not self-evident to you now, using the incorrect Incoterm in an international sale of goods carries serious practical and legal risks. Consider blog postings by Roy Becker[13] and Jim Trubits,[14] and IncotermsExplained.com's "Ten Common Mistakes,"[15] each of which illustrates some of the dangers. One prominent risk highlighted by Export.gov involves use of EX-W terms. Under U.S. export regulations, a U.S. based seller remains the "U.S. principle party of interest" for purposes of export licensing compliance. Thus, even though the seller has released the goods to the buyer's possession and the buyer must clear customs under the EX-W term, the seller could be held responsible for subsequent violations of U.S. export restrictions (if, for example, the buyer diverts the goods to North Korea). You will learn in Chapter 11 that a violation of U.S. export and licensing restrictions can have devastating consequences for exporters, not the least of which is the luxurious accommodations of federal prison.

How would you advise Barney regarding use of trade terms in his proposed transaction with Really Big Fish, PRC? What trade terms would be most appropriate under the four options offered? Are there any reasons that Barney might prefer, as a practical matter, one arrangement over another?

---

13. http://www.shippingsolutions.com/blog/incoterms-lesson-the-danger-of-using-ex-works-for-your-exports.

14. http://mohawkglobal.com/global-news/potential-pitfalls-for-exporters-using-ex-works/.

15. https://www.incotermsexplained.com/the-incoterms-rules/common-mistakes/.

Chapter 5

Contractual Breach & Remedies Under the CISG

A. Overview

This chapter focuses on remedies for breaches of contract under the CISG. Some important comparisons to the UCC will also be addressed. An important side benefit of focusing on breach and remedies is that it requires consideration of the most primary aspects of sales and contracting. Your goal should be to understand the essential obligations of a buyer and seller, how breach is defined under the CISG, the role of notice, and the remedy options available to a non-breaching party. For each remedy option, you should also consider practical implications and the feasibility of the remedy under the circumstances. After completing this chapter, you should be able to give sound basic advice about the general rights, responsibilities, and remedies of contractual parties relating to an alleged breach of a sales contract governed by the CISG.

Culminating our examination of the basic sale of goods contract, the final section of this chapter includes a review of other common sales arrangements, such as agency and sales distribution agreements.

In order to examine remedies available to both buyers and sellers, there are three related problems presented. Problems 5A and 5B address buyer's remedies for a seller's breach, addressing two distinct but common scenarios. Problem 5C focuses on the seller's remedies for the most common forms of buyer's breach—refusal to take delivery or to pay.

Part One: Buyer's Remedies

A. Problem Five A: Buyer's CISG Remedies

1. Facts

On January 10, 2017, Sport Rags Inc., of Fort Lauderdale, Florida, sent a "purchase order" to the Chavez Jersey Company, located in Cartagena, Columbia. The order offered to purchase "2000 first quality, all cotton, 3/4 sleeve length football jerseys imprinted with the words: 'Blockbuster Proud Sponsor of Super Bowl LI, NRG Stadium, Houston, February 5, 2017.'" The order form quoted a price of "$5.00 per jersey, United States currency, FOB Cartagena, delivery January 25, 2017; Incoterms 2010." The Chavez Company quickly accepted this offer the next day by sending a confirming "order acknowledgment" letter stating identical terms.

Sport Rags intended to use the jerseys to fulfill a contract it had with Blockbuster Video Corporation. Under this contract, Sport Rags had promised to distribute 2000 jerseys with the Blockbuster logo to football fans attending the Super Bowl on February 5, 2017. Blockbuster agreed to pay Sport Rags $10 per jersey distributed cost free to the first 2000 fans entering the stadium.

Assume that it is January 27, 2017. Mr. Rags of Sport Rags has called your office for advice. He has yet to receive notice that the merchandise promised by Chavez has been received by the carrier and he is worried that it will not arrive in time, or at all, to fulfill the Blockbuster contract. He tells you that it takes at least 5 days to ship merchandise from Cartagena to the Houston, Texas, seaport. He also indicates that a local company is willing to produce the required jerseys for $20 per jersey on a rush basis.

2. Assignment

Please advise the buyer, Sport Rags, about its options under the CISG given the circumstances described above. Start with and focus on the text of the treaty. As you study the text, you should identify critical words, phrases, and concepts that seem to require interpretation. References to annotations and excerpts from a few helpful cases are provided to assist you. *You should, at minimum, answer each of the following questions:*

- *What are the essential obligations of the buyer and seller with regard to critical issues, such as delivery and payment?*
- *What constitutes a fundamental breach under the CISG?*
- *What remedy options are available to the buyer in case of breach (fundamental or otherwise)?*
- *What are the requirements for the buyer to invoke such remedies?*
- *What are the practical implications of these various remedies under the buyer's current circumstances?*
- *What damages are available to the buyer and when?*

B. Resources

1. Overview of CISG Remedies

Any examination of remedies for breach of contract should begin, of course, with consideration of the parties' basic contractual obligations, rights and responsibilities. Most actionable breaches, after all, involve a failure to fulfill such basic obligations. Typically, at least where a properly drawn contract is involved, the contract itself will define such matters with provisions relating to delivery of the bargained for goods, acceptance, payment, inspection, necessary documentation, warranties and transfer of title. Inclusion of trade terms such as those examined in Chapter Four is one way parties commonly define some of those rights and obligations.

Even if certain terms are omitted, both the UCC and CISG provide default rules that apply when the parties fail to define such basic issues in their agreement. For example, the seller's most basic obligation is defined by Article 30 of the CISG:

Article 30

The seller must deliver the goods, hand over any documents relating to them and transfer the property in the goods, as required by the contract and this Convention.

A breach is obviously the failure by one party to fulfill its contractual obligations. You will find, however, that not all breaches are treated the same way under the CISG. Indeed, the remedies available to the buyer often turn upon whether the breach at issue is considered "fundamental." This contrasts sharply with the UCC's "perfect tender" approach under which a buyer may reject goods ". . . if the goods or the tender of delivery fail in any respect to conform to the contract."[1]

There are also generally applicable prerequisites and limitations on the available remedies. Two important examples are notice requirements and mitigation. In this regard, you may find it useful to make a list of the various remedy options available to the buyer (and later the seller) and their corresponding prerequisites or limitations. Note that the term "remedies" reasonably includes the question of damages. You should, however, recognize that the CISG has distinct provisions that define what damages are available for breaches and under what conditions. As you consider these remedy options, you should also examine the distinct issue of available damages.

It is also important to consider the practical implications of the various remedies provided. For example, if your client has immediate need for what is a fungible good,

---

1. The so-called perfect tender rule derives from UCC § 2-601, https://www.law.cornell.edu/ucc, which provides that a buyer of a single installment of goods (that is, delivery of the goods contracted for in one installment) may reject the goods in whole or part, "if the goods or the tender of delivery fail in any respect to conform to the contract . . . ." This approach greatly favors buyers who may reject goods even if there is substantial compliance (minor non-conformities). The potential harsh results of perfect tender are, however, tempered by the right to cure under 2-508 and, at least for some courts, the requirement of good faith dealing in 1-304. The rule is also different for sales involving delivery in installments under 2-612 ("substantially impairs . . . and cannot be cured"); when the buyer attempts to revoke an acceptance 2-608 ("substantially impairs"); when events require a change in carrier/method of delivery 2-614; in cases of commercial impracticability 2-615; and when the parties agree otherwise.

seeking specific performance (even if available legally) might not be practically feasible. Similarly, if the client can make use of non-conforming goods, through resale or otherwise, then avoidance of the contract might not be his best option given the obligations to mitigate, return rejected goods, and the financial and litigation risks associated with avoidance. Other options, such as a reduction in the price, might prove more practical and less risky. Choice of remedy must also, of course, consider the client's ultimate objectives and long term interests.

As in previous chapters, you should start by closely examining the CISG text[2] to identify basic rules and critical terms that require further interpretation (an annotated version of the text[3] is available at the Pace CISG website). You should first examine "General Provisions," articles 25–29, which provide critical definitions and set out certain prerequisites for the later defined remedies. Prior to examining those remedies, review "Section II," articles 30–44, which describe the essential obligations of a seller, including default rules on delivery of conforming goods, provision of necessary documentation and warranties. (In problem 5C, below, you will follow the same pattern and review parallel articles (53–65) that describe the primary obligations of buyers.) Has the seller in Problem 5A breached the contract and, if so, in what way? Is there a failure to deliver or simply a delayed or "late" delivery?

Precisely defining the alleged breach and its nature will ultimately determine which, if any, remedies the buyer is entitled to seek. You should now, after reviewing the CISG articles that define the seller's essential obligations and breach, carefully examine the list of buyer's remedies set out in articles 45–52, paying close attention to any prerequisites or limitations. Here's an important tip. Viewed in broad strokes, a non-breaching party's remedy options derive from, essentially, three possible choices regarding the sale: (1) affirm the contract as performed and seek damages; (2) seek substitute or "specific" performance of the contract; or (3) avoid the contract based on fundamental breach and seek damages. In the mix of remedy options falling within these categories, one must also consider the right or option to "cure" defects, the obligation to mitigate damages, and the practical consequences of avoidance.

You will undoubtedly find the UNCITRAL Digest and commentary (the same one that you were introduced to in Chapter Three) very useful in understanding the CISG approach to remedies. Some short excerpts from the Digest's "overviews" sections are included here along with links to the full annotation of case law worldwide. You should first read the excerpted "overviews," both to gain a general understanding of the CISG's approach and to identify which provisions are critical to your analysis of Problem 5A. Thereafter, consult the case digest references as needed.

---

2. www.uncitral.org/pdf/english/texts/sales/cisg/V1056997-CISG-e-book.pdf.
3. http://www.cisg.law.pace.edu/cisg/text/cisg-toc.html.

2. The <u>UNCITRAL Digest</u>[4] Overviews

Chapter I General provisions (articles 25–29)

OVERVIEW

1. Chapter I of Part III of the Convention, entitled "General Provisions," encompasses four articles — articles 25–29. The first two of those articles deal with matters relating to avoidance of contract: article 25 defines a "fundamental breach," which is a prerequisite for avoidance of contract under articles 49(1)(*a*), 51(2), 64(1)(*a*), 72(1), and 73(1) and (2) (as well as a prerequisite for a buyer to require delivery of substitute goods under article 46(2)); article 26 states that effective avoidance of contract requires notice to the other party. . . .

Chapter II Obligations of the seller (articles 30–52)

OVERVIEW

1. The provisions in Chapter II of Part III of the Convention, entitled "Obligations of the seller," contain a comprehensive treatment of the Convention's rules on the seller's duties under an international sales contract governed by the CISG. The chapter begins with a single provision describing in broad strokes the seller's obligations (article 30), followed by three sections that elaborate on the constituent elements of those obligations: Section I, "Delivery of the goods and handing over of documents" (articles 31–34); Section II, "Conformity of the goods and third party claims" (articles 35–44); and Section III, "Remedies for breach of contract by the seller" (articles 45–52). Chapter II of Part III generally parallels Chapter III ("Obligations of the buyer," articles 53–65) of Part III in both structure and focus.

. . . .

Section I of Part III, Chapter II Delivery of the goods and handing over of documents (articles 31–34)

OVERVIEW

1. Section I of Chapter II ("Obligations of the seller") in Part III ("Sale of goods") of the Convention contains provisions elaborating on two of the seller's primary obligations described in article 30 of the CISG: the obligation to deliver the goods, and the obligation to hand over documents relating to the goods. . . . Provisions dealing with conformity of delivered goods (as well as with the effect of third party claims to delivered goods) are contained in a different division —

. . . .

Section II. Conformity of the goods and third party claims

OVERVIEW

1. The second section of Chapter II of Part III of the Convention contains provisions addressing some of the most important seller obligations under a contract for

---

4. http://www.uncitral.org/uncitral/en/case_law/digests.html.

sale—in particular, the obligation to deliver goods that conform to the requirements of the contract and of the Convention in terms of quantity, quality, description and packaging (article 35), as well as the duty to ensure that the goods are free from third party claims to ownership rights (article 41) and to intellectual property rights (article 42). Other provisions connected to the question of conformity are included in the section, including an article governing the relation between the timing of a defect's occurrence and the division of responsibility therefore between the seller and the buyer (article 36), and a provision addressing the seller's right to cure a lack of conformity if goods are delivered before the date required for delivery.

2. The section also includes provisions regulating the procedure that a buyer must follow in order to preserve claims that the seller has violated the obligation to deliver conforming goods or to deliver goods free from third party claims. These include a provision governing the buyer's duty to examine the goods following delivery (article 38) and provisions requiring the buyer to give notice of alleged violations of the seller's obligations (articles 39 and 43(1)), as well as provisions excusing or relaxing the consequences of a buyer's failure to give the required notice (articles 40, 43(2), and 44). Articles 38 and 39 have proven to be among the most frequently-invoked (and most controversial) provisions in litigation under the Convention.

Section III. Remedies for breach of contract by the seller

OVERVIEW

1. The provisions in Section III of Part III, Chapter II of the Convention address various aspects of the remedies available to a buyer that has suffered a breach of contract by the seller: they catalogue those remedies and authorize their use (article 45(1)); they define their availability and operation (articles 45(2) and (3), 46, 48, and 50); they provide for an aggrieved buyer's right to avoid the contract (articles 47 and 49), thereby regulating the buyer's choice between alternative sets of remedies; and they define the operation of the buyer's remedies in certain special circumstances (articles 51 and 52).

RELATION TO OTHER PARTS OF THE CONVENTION

2. The current section on buyer's remedies is paralleled by the Convention's section on seller's remedies (Section III of Part III, Chapter III, articles 61–65). Many of the individual provisions in these sections parallel each other. Thus article 45, which catalogues the buyer's remedies, parallels article 61, which catalogues the seller's remedies; article 46, which authorizes the buyer to require performance by the seller, parallels article 62, which authorizes the seller to require the buyer's performance; article 47, which permits the buyer to fix an additional period of time for the seller to perform, parallels article 63, which permits the seller to fix an additional period of time for the buyer to perform; and article 49, which governs the buyer's right to avoid the contract, parallels article 64, which governs the seller's right to avoid.

3. Given that remedies play a central role in any system of legal rules for transactions, it is not surprising that the provisions in Section III have important connections to a variety of other parts and individual articles of the Convention. For example, the buyer's right to require performance under article 46 is subject to the rule in article 28 relieving a court of the obligation to order specific performance in circumstances in which it would not do so under its own law. Article 48, which establishes the seller's right to cure a breach after the required time for delivery has passed, is closely related to the rule in article 37, permitting the seller to cure up to the required time for delivery. The Section III provisions on the buyer's right to avoid the contract have close connections to many provisions elsewhere in the CISG, including, inter alia, the definition of fundamental breach (article 25), the requirement that avoidance be effected by notice (article 26), the rules authorizing avoidance of contract in certain special circumstances (articles 72 and 73), the articles providing for damages conditioned upon avoidance (articles 75 and 76), the provisions dealing with a buyer's obligation to preserve goods in its possession if it intends to "reject" them (articles 86–88), and, of course, the provisions of Section V of Part III, Chapter V on "effects of avoidance." There is a particularly close connection between article 45(1) *(a)*, which authorizes an aggrieved buyer to recover damages, and the provisions defining how damages are to be calculated, which are found in Section II of Part III, Chapter V (articles 74–77).

Provisions Common to the Obligations of the Seller and of the Buyer (articles 71–88)

OVERVIEW

1. Chapter V, which contains provisions applicable with respect to both the seller's obligations and the buyer's obligations, is the final chapter of Part III ("Sale of Goods"), and thus is the last chapter of the Convention containing substantive rules for international sales.1 It's six constituent sections are: Section I—"Anticipatory breach and instalment contracts"; Section II—"Damages"; Section III—"Interest"; Section IV—"Exemption"; Section V—"Effects of avoidance"; and Section VI—"Preservation of the goods."

Damages (articles 74–77)

OVERVIEW

1. Articles 45(1)*(b)* and 61(1)*(b)* of the CISG provide that an aggrieved buyer and an aggrieved seller, respectively, may claim damages as provided in articles 74 to 77 if the other party "fails to perform any of his obligations under the contract or this Convention." Articles 74 to 77, which comprise Section II of Chapter V of Part III, set out the damage formulas that apply to the claims of both aggrieved sellers and aggrieved buyers. These damage provisions are exhaustive and exclude recourse to domestic law.

2. Article 74 establishes the general formula applicable in all cases where an aggrieved party is entitled to recover damages. It provides that "damages for breach of

contract" comprise all losses, including loss of profits, caused by the breach, to the extent that these losses were foreseeable by the breaching party at the time the contract was concluded. An aggrieved party may claim under article 74 even if entitled to claim under article 75 or 76. The latter articles explicitly provide that an aggrieved party may recover additional damages under article 74.

3. Articles 75 and 76 apply only in cases where the contract has been avoided. Article 75 measures damages concretely by reference to the price in a substitute transaction, while article 76 measures damages abstractly by reference to the current market price. Article 76(1) provides that an aggrieved party may not calculate damages under article 76 if it has concluded a substitute transaction under article 75. If, however, an aggrieved party concludes a substitute transaction for less than the contract quantity, both articles 75 and 76 may apply.

4. Pursuant to article 77, damages recoverable under articles 74, 75 or 76 are reduced if it is established that the aggrieved party failed to mitigate losses. The reduction is the amount by which the loss should have been mitigated.

. . . .

3. Case Digest by Article

You can follow the links below for case annotations summarizing judicial interpretations of the CISG text — look for what you need to respond to the problem and questions.

Article 25[5]

Article 46[6]

Article 47[7]

Article 48[8]

Article 49[9]

Article 50[10]

Article 51[11]

Article 71[12]

5. http://www.uncitral.org/pdf/english/clout/digest2008/article025.pdf.
6. http://www.uncitral.org/pdf/english/clout/digest2008/article046.pdf.
7. http://www.uncitral.org/pdf/english/clout/digest2008/article047.pdf.
8. http://www.uncitral.org/pdf/english/clout/digest2008/article048.pdf.
9. http://www.uncitral.org/pdf/english/clout/digest2008/article049.pdf.
10. http://www.uncitral.org/pdf/english/clout/digest2008/article050.pdf.
11. http://www.uncitral.org/pdf/english/clout/digest2008/article051.pdf.
12. http://www.uncitral.org/pdf/english/clout/digest2008/article071.pdf.

An alternative and useful manner to access the UNICTRAL database of case law is found at the Pace CISG website general portal,[19] which also organizes the cases by country. This website also provides annotations with links[20] to cases by CISG article, and academic commentary (if you are having trouble sleeping).

C. Problem Five B (Buyer's Remedies Continued)

Problem 5A above addresses just one of the many circumstances under which the issue of fundamental breach might arise — late or non-delivery of goods. Problem 5B shifts to an even more common form of breach involving delivery of non-conforming goods. Once again, fundamental breach plays a central role. *How would the CISG address the following factual variation on Problem 5A?*

Assume all of the facts provided in Problem 5A above, except that on January 30, 2012, Chavez delivered jerseys to the carrier in Cartagena. When they arrived in Ft. Lauderdale three days later, Sports Rags discovered that there were only 1,500 jerseys in the shipment, one half of which incorrectly read "Backbuster" instead of "Blockbuster." The jerseys were also made of 20% polyester rather than 100% cotton.

Utilize the sources referenced above in Part One to respond to this question. It will be helpful to remember the differences between "delivery" of goods, payment, and their "acceptance" as conforming to the contract. Hopefully you will recall that, depending upon the contract (term of trade), delivery often takes place when the seller places the goods at buyer's disposal. This may be accomplished, in many cases, by handing the goods over to the designated carrier. Remember also that risk of loss

---

13. http://www.uncitral.org/pdf/english/clout/digest2008/article072.pdf.
14. http://www.uncitral.org/pdf/english/clout/digest2008/article073.pdf.
15. http://www.uncitral.org/pdf/english/clout/digest2008/article074.pdf.
16. http://www.uncitral.org/pdf/english/clout/digest2008/article075.pdf.
17. http://www.uncitral.org/pdf/english/clout/digest2008/article076.pdf.
18. http://www.uncitral.org/pdf/english/clout/digest2008/article077.pdf.
19. http://iicl.law.pace.edu/cisg/cisg.
20. http://www.cisg.law.pace.edu/cisg/text/cisg-toc.html.

often transfers to the buyer at this point. Buyer might not, however, be obligated to pay at delivery. For example, under a documents against payment arrangement, buyer pays when presented with the documents that entitle him to possession from the carrier. He has no right to inspect the goods prior to payment under such terms but, instead, has agreed to rely upon the documentation. Under alternative payment terms, the buyer might not have to pay until some later date, including after inspection. Delivery and payment are not, therefore, synonymous.

Similarly, "acceptance" of the goods is not necessarily tied to either delivery or the payment obligation. It signifies that the buyer has had an opportunity to inspect the goods for conformity to the contract. This might occur sometime after both delivery and payment. Even if the buyer has paid for goods under a documentary sale, he may still later reject those goods for non-conformity upon inspection. In Part Two below, you will should see how these obligations and rights also directly relate to the seller's remedies for buyer's breach.

Part Two: Seller's Remedies

A. Overview

In a general sense, the CISG remedies available to sellers closely parallel those available to buyers. Not surprisingly, the buyer's basic obligations form the "flip side" of the seller's Article 30 obligation to deliver conforming goods:

Article 53

The buyer must pay the price for the goods and take delivery of them as required by the contract and this Convention.

Precisely how and when payment must be made, and delivery should occur, is controlled by the parties' contract. However, just as with seller's obligations, the CISG also provides default rules. Note how articles 57(1)(b) and 58 accommodate the documentary sale arrangement we studied in Chapter Two.

Article 57

(1) If the buyer is not bound to pay the price at any other particular place, he must pay it to the seller:

(a) at the seller's place of business; or

(b) if the payment is to be made against the handing over of the goods or of documents, at the place where the handing over takes place.

. . . .

Article 58

(1) If the buyer is not bound to pay the price at any other specific time, he must pay it when the seller places either the goods or documents control-

ling their disposition at the buyer's disposal in accordance with the contract and this Convention. The seller may make such payment a condition for handing over the goods or documents.

(2) If the contract involves carriage of the goods, the seller may dispatch the goods on terms whereby the goods, or documents controlling their disposition, will not be handed over to the buyer except against payment of the price.

(3) The buyer is not bound to pay the price until he has had an opportunity to examine the goods, unless the procedures for delivery or payment agreed upon by the parties are inconsistent with his having such an opportunity.

. . . .

As a result of the buyer's distinct obligations, the most common forms of buyer breaches are different in nature from those of a seller. A buyer's failure to take delivery or pay the price for goods has very different practical implications that distinguish such breaches from a seller's failure to deliver conforming goods. As a result, seller's remedies under the CISG include features distinct from buyers' remedies. If, for example, the seller is contemplating an action seeking payment of the contract price, he should remember that delivery of the goods must also then be made—even sellers cannot have their cake and eat it too. This particular remedy is then most commonly sought when the buyer has already taken possession of the goods. Similarly, before attempting to force a buyer to take delivery, a seller must first attempt resale in order to mitigate any damages. Think carefully about such differences between the buyer's and seller's obligations as you evaluate problem 5C below, which focuses on the seller's CISG remedies.

B. Problem Five C: Seller's Remedies

1. Facts

Assume that the 2000 jerseys identified above in problem 5A are all delivered to Sport Rags in exact conformance to the parties' contract. However, Sport Rags' deal with Blockbuster has fallen through (perhaps Blockbuster's bankruptcy ten years ago was to blame) and Sport Rags now refuses to pay.

2. Assignment

Evaluate the seller's remedies under the CISG for buyer's breach.

- *What remedy options are available to the seller in case of buyer's breach (fundamental or otherwise)?*
- *What are the requirements for the seller to invoke such remedies?*

- *What are the practical implications of these various remedies under the seller's current circumstances?*

- *What damages are available to the seller and when?*

C. Resources

1. Excerpt from <u>UNCITRAL: Overview</u>[21]

Part III, Chapter III Obligations of the buyer (articles 53–65)

OVERVIEW

1. Chapter III of Part III of the Convention contains provisions addressing the buyer's obligations under an international sales contract governed by the CISG. Both the structure and the focus of the chapter parallel Chapter II ("Obligations of the seller," articles 30–52) of Part III. . . .

Taking delivery (article 60)

. . . .

RELATION TO OTHER PARTS OF THE CONVENTION

2. Several aspects of the buyer's obligation to take delivery are not addressed in Section II and instead are controlled by provisions governing the seller's obligation to make delivery. Thus article 31, which regulates the place for seller to make delivery, and article 33, which governs the time for seller to deliver, presumably apply also to the buyer's obligation to take delivery.

Remedies for breach of contract by the buyer (articles 61–65)

OVERVIEW

1. The remedies available to a seller that has suffered a breach of contract by the buyer are addressed in Section III of Chapter III of Part III. The first provision in the section, article 61, catalogues those remedies and authorizes an aggrieved seller to resort to them. The remaining provisions of the section address particular remedies or prerequisites to remedies: the seller's right to require the buyer to perform (article 62), the seller's right to set an additional period for the buyer's performance (article 63), the seller's right to avoid the contract (article 64), and the seller's right to set specifications if the buyer fails to do so in timely fashion (article 65).

RELATION TO OTHER PARTS OF THE CONVENTION

2. The subject matter of the current section—"Remedies for breach of contract by the buyer"—obviously parallels that of Section III of Chapter II of Part III—

---

21. http://www.uncitral.org/pdf/english/clout/CISG_Digest_2016.pdf.

"Remedies for breach of contract by the seller" (articles 45–52). Many individual provisions within these sections form matched pairs. Thus article 61, which catalogs the seller's remedies, closely parallels article 45, which catalogs the buyer's remedies. Other provisions in the current section that have analogues in the section on buyer's remedies include article 62, seller's right to require buyer's performance (parallel to article 46); article 63, seller's right to fix an additional period for buyer to perform (parallel to article 47); and article 64, seller right to avoid the contract (parallel to article 49).

3. As was the case with the provisions on buyers' remedies, the articles governing sellers' remedies operate in conjunction with a variety of provisions outside the current section. Thus the seller's right to require performance by the buyer is subject to the rule in article 28 relieving a court from the obligation to order specific performance in circumstances in which it would not do so under its own law. The authorization in article 61(1)(b) for a seller to claim damages for a buyer's breach operates in connection with (and, indeed, expressly refers to) articles 74–76, which specify how damages are to be measured. Article 49, stating when an aggrieved seller can avoid the contract, is part of a network of provisions that address avoidance, including the definition of fundamental breach (article 25), the requirement of notice of avoidance (article 26), provisions governing avoidance in certain special circumstances (articles 72 and 73), measures of damages available only if the contract has been avoided (articles 75 and 76), and the provisions of Section V of Part III, Chapter V on "effects of avoidance."

2. UNCITRAL Case Digest

You can follow the links below for case annotations summarizing judicial interpretations of the CISG text — look for what you need to respond to the problem and questions).

- Article 61[22]
- Article 62[23]
- Article 63[24]
- Article 64[25]
- Article 65[26]

---

22. http://www.uncitral.org/pdf/english/clout/digest2008/article061.pdf.
23. http://www.uncitral.org/pdf/english/clout/digest2008/article062.pdf.
24. http://www.uncitral.org/pdf/english/clout/digest2008/article063.pdf.
25. http://www.uncitral.org/pdf/english/clout/digest2008/article064.pdf.
26. http://www.uncitral.org/pdf/english/clout/digest2008/article065.pdf.

3. Chart of CISG Remedy Options

B's Remedies	*Give Notice*	*S's remedies*
S's breach	↓	B's Breach
- non-delivery		- nonpayment
- non-conformity		- refuse delivery

Art. 26 (FB avoidance)
& 39 (specify non-conformity)

34 → S cure documents
37 → S cure prior to performance date

Art. 45 lists alternatives:		Art. 61 lists alternatives:
• 46 > compel		62 > compel
(S.P.—deliver conforming/		(action on price: pay/take
or substitute goods if FB)		delivery)
• 47 > set additional time		63 > added time
(deliver conforming goods)		(for payment/take delivery)

(notice/avoidance creates FB → late delivery or payment)

48 → cure after performance date
if not unreasonable burden, etc.

• 49 > Avoid	(Art. 25 f.b.)	64 > Avoid
• 50 > Reduce Price		

All breaches → damages & mitigation (74–77) / restitution & preservation of goods

Three Essential Options (with adequate notice)

- compel performance (includes "substitute goods")

    OR

- avoid K (FB)

    OR

- accept (may include price reduction)

    + Seek Damages (which depends on the option chosen)

Part Three: Alternative Sales Methods: Agency, Distribution Agreements, Export Intermediaries and Sales Representatives

Most of the material presented thus far in this book have focused on what might be best described as simple "direct sales." That is, transactions involving the sale of goods flowing directly from a seller to a buyer under a single contract. Although important and helpful as a learning tool, such transactions are far from the only or most common way to sell goods internationally. Frequently, exporters rely on more comprehensive and complicated forms of distribution utilizing agents and other intermediaries. The following somewhat lengthy excerpt from Export.gov provides a good summary of these alternatives, and all we need for present purposes. It also surveys some basic approaches and alternatives in seeking export sales and advice on contracting.

From export.gov[27]

Approaches to Exporting

The way you choose to export your products can have a significant effect on your export plan and specific marketing strategies. The various approaches to exporting relate to your company's level of involvement in the export process. There are at least four approaches that may be used alone or in combination:

1. Passively filling orders from domestic buyers, who then export the product. These sales are indistinguishable from other domestic sales as far as the original seller is concerned. . . .

2. Seeking out domestic buyers who represent foreign end users or customers. Many U.S. and foreign corporations, general contractors, foreign trading companies, foreign government agencies, foreign distributors, retailers, and others in the United States purchase for export. These buyers constitute a large market for a wide variety of goods and services. In this approach, your company may know that its product is being exported, but the domestic buyer still assumes the risks and handles the details of exporting.

3. Exporting indirectly through intermediaries. With this approach, your company engages the services of an intermediary firm that is capable of finding foreign markets and buyers for your products. EMCs, ETCs, [see below] international trade consultants, and other intermediaries can give you access to well-established expertise and trade contacts, but you retain considerable control over the process and can realize some of the other benefits of exporting, such as learning more about foreign competitors, new technologies, and other market opportunities.

4. Exporting directly. This approach is the most ambitious and challenging because your company handles every aspect of the exporting process from market research and planning to foreign distribution and payment collections. A significant commitment of management time and attention is required to achieve good results. However, this approach may also be the best way to achieve maximum profits and long-term growth. . . .

Before making those kinds of decisions, you may want to consult trade specialists such as those at the U.S. Commercial Service. They can be helpful in determining the best approach or mix of approaches for you and your company.

---

27. https://www.export.gov/article?id=Approaches-to-Exporting.

Once your company is organized to handle exporting, a proper channel of distribution needs to be carefully chosen for each market. These channels include sales representatives, agents, distributors, retailers, and end users.

Indirect Exporting

The principal advantage of indirect exporting for a smaller U.S. company is that an indirect approach provides a way to enter foreign markets without the potential complexities and risks of direct exporting. Several kinds of intermediary firms provide a range of export services, and each type of firm can offer distinct advantages to your company.

Confirming Houses

Confirming houses or buying agents represent foreign firms that want to purchase your products. They seek to obtain the desired items at the lowest possible price and are paid a commission by their foreign clients. In some cases, they may be foreign government agencies or quasi-governmental firms empowered to locate and purchase desired goods. An example is a foreign government purchasing mission.

A good place to find these agents is through foreign government embassies and embassy Web sites or through the U.S. Commercial Service.

Export Management Companies

An export management company can act as the export department for producers of goods and services. It solicits and transacts business in the names of the producers it represents or in its own name for a commission, salary, or retainer plus commission. . . .

EMCs usually specialize by product or by foreign market, or sometimes by both. . . .

One disadvantage of using an EMC is that you may lose control over foreign sales. . . .

Export Trading Companies

An export trading company can facilitate the export of U.S. goods and services. Like an EMC, an ETC can either act as the export department for producers or take title to the product. A special kind of ETC is a group organized and operated by producers. These ETCs can be organized along multiple- or single-industry lines and can also represent producers of competing products.

Exporters may consider applying for an Export Trade Certificate of Review under the Export Trading Company Act of 1982. A certificate of review provides limited antitrust immunity for specified export activities. For more information, see http://www.trade.gov/mas/ian/etca/index.asp or call (202) 482-5131.

Export Agents, Merchants, or Remarketers

Export agents, merchants, or remarketers purchase products directly from the manufacturer, packing and labeling the products according to their own specifications. They then sell these products overseas through their contacts in their own names and assume all risks.

In transactions with export agents, merchants, or remarketers, your firm relinquishes control over the marketing and promotion of your product. . . .

Direct Exporting

The advantages of direct exporting for your company include more control over the export process, potentially higher profits, and a closer relationship to the overseas buyer and marketplace, as well as the opportunity to learn what you can do to boost overall competitiveness. However, those advantages come at a price; your company needs to devote more time, personnel, and resources to direct exporting than it would to indirect exporting.

Sales Representatives

An overseas sales representative is the equivalent of a manufacturer's representative in the United States. The representative uses your company's product literature and samples to present the product to potential buyers. Ordinarily, a representative handles many complementary lines that do not conflict. The sales representative usually works for a commission, assumes no risk or responsibility, and is under contract for a definite period of time (renewable by mutual agreement). The contract defines territory, terms of sale, method of compensation, reasons and procedures for terminating the agreement, and other details. The sales representative may operate on either an exclusive or a non-exclusive basis.

Agents or Representatives

The widely misunderstood term agent means a representative who normally has authority—perhaps even a power of attorney—to make commitments on behalf of the firm that he or she represents. Firms in the United States and other developed countries have stopped using that term because agent can imply a power of attorney. They rely instead on the term representative. It is important that the contract state whether the representative or agent has the legal authority to obligate your firm.

Distributors

The foreign distributor is a merchant who purchases goods from a U.S. exporter (often at a discount) and resells them for a profit. The foreign distributor generally provides support and service for the product, relieving the U.S. exporter of those responsibilities. The distributor usually carries an inventory of products and a sufficient supply of spare parts and also maintains adequate facilities and personnel for normal servicing operations. Distributors typically handle a range of non-competing, complementary products. End users do not usually buy from a distributor; they buy from retailers or dealers.

The terms and length of association between your company and the foreign distributor are established by contract. Some U.S. companies prefer to begin with a relatively short trial period and then extend the contract if the relationship proves satisfactory to both parties. The U.S. Commercial Service can help you identify and select distributors and can provide general advice on structuring agreements.

Foreign Retailers

You may also sell directly to foreign retailers, although in such transactions products are generally limited to consumer lines. The growth of major retail chains in markets such as Canada and Japan has created new opportunities for this type of direct sale. The approach relies mainly on traveling sales representatives who directly contact foreign retailers, although results might also be achieved by mailing catalogs, brochures, or other literature.

. . . .

Contacting and Evaluating Foreign Representatives

Once your company has identified a number of potential representatives or distributors in the selected market, you should write, e-mail, or fax each one directly. Just as your firm is seeking information on the foreign representative, the representative is interested in corporate and product information on your firm. The prospective representative may want more information than your company normally provides to a casual buyer. . . .

Your firm should investigate potential representatives or distributors carefully before entering into an agreement with them. (See Box 5.2 for an extensive checklist of factors to consider in such evaluations.) . . .

You should also ask for the prospective representative or distributor's assessment of the in-country market potential for your firm's products. Such information is useful in gauging how much the representative knows about your industry; it provides valuable market research as well.

Negotiating an Agreement with a Foreign Representative

When your company has found a prospective representative that meets its requirements, the next step is to negotiate a foreign sales agreement. Export Assistance Centers provide advice to firms contemplating that step. The International Chamber of Commerce also provides useful guidelines and can be reached at (212) 703-5065 or www.iccwbo.org.

Most representatives are interested in your company's pricing structure and product profit potential. They are also concerned with the terms of payment; product regulation; competitors and their market shares; the amount of support provided by your firm, such as sales aids, promotional material, and advertising; training for the sales and service staff; and your company's ability to deliver on schedule.

The agreement may contain provisions that specify the actions of the foreign representative, including the following:

- Not having business dealings with competing firms (because of antitrust laws, this provision may cause problems in some European countries)

- Not revealing any confidential information in a way that would prove injurious, detrimental, or competitive to your firm

- Not entering into agreements with other parties that would be binding to your firm

- Referring all inquiries received from outside the designated sales territory to your firm for action

. . . It may be appropriate to include performance requirements, such as a minimum sales volume and an expected rate of increase.

In drafting the agreement, you must pay special attention to safeguarding your company's interests in case the representative proves less than satisfactory. (See Chapter 10 for recommendations on specifying terms of law and arbitration.) It is vital to include an escape clause in the agreement that allows you to end the relationship safely and cleanly if the representative does not fulfill expectations. . . .

In all cases, escape clauses and other provisions to safeguard your company may be limited by the laws of the country in which the representative is located. For this reason, you should learn as much as you can about the legal requirements of the representative's country and obtain qualified legal counsel in preparing the contract. These are some of the legal questions to consider:

- How far in advance must the representative be notified of your intention to terminate the agreement? Three months satisfy the requirements of many countries, but a registered letter may be needed to establish when the notice was served.

- What is "just cause" for terminating a representative? Specifying causes for termination in the written contract usually strengthens your position.

- Which country's laws (or which international conventions) govern a contract dispute? Laws in the representative's country may forbid the representative company from waiving its nation's legal jurisdiction.

- What compensation is due to the representative on dismissal? Depending on the length of the relationship, the added value of the market that the representative created for you, and whether termination is for just cause as defined by the foreign country, you may be required to compensate the representative for losses.

- What must the representative give up if dismissed? The contract should specify the return of property, including patents, trademarks, name registrations, and customer records.

- Should the representative be referred to as an agent? In some countries, the word agent implies power of attorney. The contract needs to specify whether the representative is a legal agent with power of attorney.

- In what language should the contract be drafted? In most cases, the contract should be in both English and the official language of the foreign country. Foreign representatives often request exclusivity for marketing in a country or region. It is recommended that you not grant exclusivity until the foreign representative has proven his or her capabilities or that it be granted for a limited, defined period of time, such as one year, with the possibility of renewal. The territory covered by exclusivity may also need to be defined, although some countries' laws may prohibit that type of limitation.

The agreement with the foreign representative should define what laws apply to the agreement. Even if you choose U.S. law or that of a third country, the laws of the representative's country may take precedence. Many suppliers define the United Nations Convention on Contracts for the International Sale of Goods (CISG, or the Vienna Convention) as the source of resolution for contract disputes, or they defer to a ruling by the International Court of Arbitration of the International Chamber of Commerce. For more information, refer to the International Chamber of Commerce arbitration page, which is accessible at www.iccwbo.org.

International Trade Center Model Sales distribution agreement[28]

Part Four: Observations about International Dispute Resolution

A. Overview

Resolution of disputes is, of course, a key function of the law and potentially on the horizon of any transaction. As discussed in Chapter Three, the potential for disputes must be considered in planning out, and drafting documentation for any international transaction. In this chapter, we examined remedies available under the CISG for contractual breach, including damages. These choices are, in reality, often limited by practical concerns based upon the likely costs, risks, efficiency, and potential success of any legal action required to seek them. The importance of these considerations is greatly amplified when the dispute involves an international transaction. Uncertainty regarding applicable law, differences in legal approaches (common law versus civil, for example), proceedings in foreign languages, biased decision-makers, securing competent local counsel, and the inconvenience of distance, are just some of the potential complications.

A detailed exposition of international dispute resolution is far outside the scope of this book. The subject is not infrequently addressed in stand-alone law school courses, and enjoys its own practice group committee[29] at the ABA. There are, however, some fundamental considerations about international dispute resolution that should be helpful to your practical understanding of the subjects we have covered, including structuring a sales transaction, contracting terms, and pursuing remedies for breach. What follows is a brief review of these considerations.

---

28. http://www.intracen.org/WorkArea/DownloadAsset.aspx?id=37603.
29. https://apps.americanbar.org/litigation/committees/international/about.html.

B. Choice of Law

As Chapters Three and Five make clear, the potential for disputes makes negotiation over choice of law an essential component of any transaction. In most instances, other than attempts to avoid mandatory local law, courts will recognize and enforce the parties' selection of the law governing their relationship.[30] Occasionally, some jurisdictions insist on some relationship between the parties and the law chosen. Note that most jurisdictions will apply their own procedural rules (process, discovery, evidence, motions and so on) to a dispute, even when the parties have selected an alternative source of substantive law. It is also possible that the subject matter of the dispute may be viewed as falling outside of the scope of a selection clause, if not drafted carefully. For example, a number of U.S. courts have found[31] that tort-related claims, even fraud in the inducement, fall outside of a dispute "under" the contract.[32]

Failure to reach agreement on the issue will undoubtedly haunt some unhappy participant, who finds his rights determined under unfamiliar and unfavorable foreign law. Chapter Three included two cases in which the outcome of the parties' dispute turned on the court's choice of applicable law. In *Kristinus*, the parties' silence on the issue of applicable law required the court to engage in the uncertain process of weighing jurisdictional interests, ultimately selecting New York law, even though neither party resided there. Under the alternative, Brazilian law, the defendant's alleged promises to the plaintiff were unenforceable, but not under New York law. In *BP Oil v. Empresa*, the parties unwittingly selected the CISG by choosing the law of Ecuador. While Ecuadorian domestic law provided that goods must conform to the contract when received and inspected by the buyer, the CISG provided that risk of loss to the goods passed upon delivery to the carrier. Choice of law may very much matter.

C. Forum Selection

Distinct from choosing the substantive rules governing a potential dispute, a critical choice confronting transactional parties involves selecting a forum. The selection

---

30. In a variation that only a law professor could love, it is possible for a court, applying the selected law, to disallow the parties' choice, through application of the relevant choice of law or conflicts principles. In other words, the application of Florida law may include the Florida rules on conflicts which may dictate that the dispute be governed by some other jurisdiction's law. Accordingly, it is common to exclude conflicts of laws principles from the law selected.

31. *Krock v. Lipsay*, 97 F.3d 640 (2d Cir. 1996), https://scholar.google.com/scholar_case?case=17699596013869626522&q=Krock+v.+Lipsay&hl=en&as_sdt=40006&as_vis=1.

32. In an article in Corporate Counsel, lawyers Eric Fishman and Amada Freye suggest the following contractual language to avoid these problems: "This contract shall be governed and construed in accordance with the laws of [selected State], excluding that State's choice of law principles, and all claims relating to or arising out of this contract, or the breach thereof, whether sounding in contract, tort or otherwise, shall likewise be governed by the laws of [selected State], excluding that State's choice-of-law principles." Eric Fishman & Amada Freye, *Drafting a better choice-of-law clause*, Corporate Counsel, April 19, 2013.

of dispute forum and type (courts, arbitration, conciliation, mini-trial, mediation, or coin-toss) may create significant advantages or disadvantages to the parties. Not surprisingly, most litigants are reluctant to find themselves in the courts of a foreign, and often geographically distant, state. A U.S. company is likely to prefer a familiar and trustworthy court system, with proceedings conducted in English, not too far from home. A foreign litigant suffers obvious disadvantages, including increased costs, inconvenience, and perhaps subtle hostility. On the other hand, sometimes a defendant company would prefer a foreign forum with weak enforcement mechanisms, lower damage awards, limited discovery rules, or other obstacles to a plaintiff's claims.

Failure to select a forum also poses the prospect of forum shopping, a race to the courthouse, and multiple, conflicting litigations. In many such cases, one litigant may seek orders from their favored forum to halt foreign proceedings, or request removal of the action under doctrines like forum non conveniens.[33]

There is an overlap here with issues of jurisdiction, both substantive and personal. In the United States, the exercise of jurisdiction over a claim and defendant must comport with due process standards—minimum contacts such as purposefully availing oneself of state resources. What about maintaining a website that can be accessed by a consumer over the internet?[34] French nationality of a litigant is sufficient to exercise jurisdiction in France, even if the transaction is completely foreign. In one controversial case, a French court fined Yahoo! for posting the web page of a U.S. based seller of Nazi paraphernalia, on its U.S. based servers. Yahoo! Challenged the French proceeding the U.S. courts, which subsequently found that they had personal jurisdiction over the French plaintiffs, in an action aimed at preventing enforcement

---

33. In _Gulf Oil Corp. v. Gilbert_, 330 U.S. 501, 507 (1947), the U.S. Supreme Court summarized the doctrine: "The principle of forum non conveniens is simply that a court may resist imposition upon its jurisdiction even when jurisdiction is authorized by the letter of a general venue statute." Thus, using a set of discretionary factors, a federal court may dismiss a transnational dispute in favor of a foreign, more convenient, forum. "If the combination and weight of factors requisite to given results are difficult to forecast or state, those to be considered are not difficult to name. An interest to be considered, and the one likely to be most pressed, is the private interest of the litigant. Important considerations are the relative ease of access to sources of proof; availability of compulsory process for attendance of unwilling, and the cost of obtaining attendance of willing, witnesses; possibility of view of premises, if view would be appropriate to the action, and all other practical problems that make trial of a case easy, expeditious, and inexpensive. There may also be questions as to the enforceability of a judgment if one is obtained. The court will weigh relative advantages and obstacles to fair trial." The seminal case elaborating these rules is _Piper Aircraft Co. v. Reyno_, 454 U.S.235 (1981).

34. In a widely followed opinion, _Zippo Mfr. Co. v. Zippo Dot Com, Inc._, 952 F. Supp. 1119 (W.D. Pa. 1997), a Pennsylvania federal court ruled that jurisdiction would depend the degree to which the site was passive or interactive and commercial (there finding jurisdiction was proper since the defendant maintained 3000 customers in the state). _See also McBee v. Delica Co._, 417 F.3d 107 (1st Cir. 2005) (declining a trademark infringement case against a Japanese language website hosted in Japan, but accessible from the United States, based on lack of substantive jurisdiction for extraterritorial application of the Lanham Act).

of the French court's orders.[35] In a similar vein, the Australian high court allowed jurisdiction over a defamation claim against Dow Jones relating to a Barron's article, posted in the United States, but downloaded by Australians.[36] If a state maintains excessively liberal rules for finding substantive and personal jurisdiction, companies face the daunting prospect of being hauled into court in unexpected places, and a race to the courthouse. A contractual forum selection clause may prevent these undesirable consequences.

There have been some significant efforts to reinforce recognition of a contractual forum selection clauses. Since the case of _M/S Bremen v. Zapata Off-Shore Co._, 407 U.S. 1 (1972), U.S. courts will routinely uphold forum selection clauses, unless doing so would violate "strong public policy," or is shown to be "unreasonable or unjust," or the result of "fraud or overreaching." In 2009, the United States signed the Hague Convention on Choice of Court Agreements.[37] Chapter II of this agreement, which was adopted by the EU and entered into force in 2015, obligates a chosen court to exercise its jurisdiction (and other, non-chosen courts to refrain from hearing the dispute), in business to business commercial contracts. The U.S. has yet to ratify the agreement, apparently conflicted over federalism issues.[38]

International Alternative Dispute Resolution

Dispute resolution through national courts is typically protracted, expensive, inflexible, public, and highly adversarial. Judges, and juries when available, may often lack expertise regarding complex commercial issues. At least one party to the dispute may have deep reservations about potential bias. Considering these disadvantages, alternative forms of dispute resolution have become an increasingly popular option for international transactions. The most commonly cited advantages include lower costs, neutrality, finality, confidentiality, expertise, flexibility and party control, choice of language and location, and certainty of enforcement.

The two most common forms of alternative dispute resolution share similar advantages but are quite distinct. Mediation essentially involves the facilitation of a negotiated settlement by an independent party and is not, typically, binding unless an agreement is reached. Arbitration, in contrast, involves a binding determination of rights through an agreed upon, private mechanism, typically relying on independent

---

35. See _Yahoo! Inc. v. La Ligue Contre le Racisme et L'Antisemitisme_, 433 F.3d 1199 (9th Cir. 2006). Interestingly, within the EU, excessive exercises of jurisdiction are curtailed by the Brussels Convention (Convention on Jurisdiction and the Enforcement of Judgements, https://curia.europa.eu/common/recdoc/convention/en/c-textes/brux-idx.htm) and by Regulation 44/2001 (http://eur-lex.europa.eu/LexUriServ/LexUriServ.do?uri=CELEX:32001R0044:en:HTML), but not with regard to suits involving non-EU litigants.

36. See _Dow Jones and Co. v. Gutnick_ (2002) V.S.C. 305, HCA 56; 210 CLR 575, 77 ALJR 255, http://www.5rb.com/case/gutnick-v-dow-jones-co-inc/.

37. https://en.wikipedia.org/wiki/Hague_Choice_of_Court_Convention.

38. See Glen P. Hendrix, et al, _Memorandum of the American Bar Association Section of the International Law Working Group on the Implementation of the Hague Convention on Choice of Court Agreements_, 49 International Lawyer 255 (ABA, 20116).

experts. The parties must agree to arbitrate and, typically in a contractual clause, may dictate the methodology, time and place of any proceedings involved. The parties may choose their own arbitral process on an ad hoc basis, or may rely on an institutional arbitration service with pre-existing rules and procedures. A commonly relied upon set of rules for both institutional and ad hoc arbitration proceedings are the United Nations Commission on International Trade Law ("UNCITRAL") Arbitration Rules.[39] UNICITRAL provides this description of these rules:

> The UNCITRAL Arbitration Rules provide a comprehensive set of procedural rules upon which parties may agree for the conduct of arbitral proceedings arising out of their commercial relationship and are widely used in ad hoc arbitrations as well as administered arbitrations. The Rules cover all aspects of the arbitral process, providing a model arbitration clause, setting out procedural rules regarding the appointment of arbitrators and the conduct of arbitral proceedings, and establishing rules in relation to the form, effect and interpretation of the award. At present, there exist three different versions of the Arbitration Rules: (i) the 1976 version; (ii) the 2010 revised version; and (iii) the 2013 version which incorporates the UNCITRAL Rules on Transparency for Treaty-based Investor-State Arbitration.[40]

> The UNCITRAL Arbitration Rules were initially adopted in 1976 and have been used for the settlement of a broad range of disputes, including disputes between private commercial parties where no arbitral institution is involved, investor-State disputes, State-to-State disputes and commercial disputes administered by arbitral institutions. . . .

> The UNCITRAL Arbitration Rules (as revised in 2010) have been effective since 15 August 2010. They include provisions dealing with, amongst others, multiple-party arbitration and joinder, liability, and a procedure to object to experts appointed by the arbitral tribunal. A number of innovative features contained in the Rules aim to enhance procedural efficiency, including revised procedures for the replacement of an arbitrator, the requirement for reasonableness of costs, and a review mechanism regarding the costs of arbitration. They also include more detailed provisions on interim measures.

International arbitral institutions provide an organized structure and management of the arbitration process. There are dozens of these institutions (*see* ABA List of International Arbitration Institutions[41] and International Trade Center's on-line ADR resource guide[42]). Some of the more prominent and busy international arbitral institutions include the: International Chamber of Commerce;[43] London Court of

---

39. http://www.uncitral.org/uncitral/en/uncitral_texts/arbitration/2010Arbitration_rules.html.
40. http://www.uncitral.org/uncitral/en/uncitral_texts/arbitration/2014Transparency.html.
41. http://apps.americanbar.org/dch/comadd.cfm?com=IC730000&pg=1.
42. http://www.intracen.org/itc/trade-support/arbitration-and-mediation/.
43. https://iccwbo.org/dispute-resolution-services/.

International Arbitration;[44] and American Arbitration Association International Centre for Dispute Resolution.[45] Also note the existence of specialized processes for state-investor disputes, such as the Word Banks' International Center for Settlement of Investment Disputes (ICSID[46]).

These institutions have their own suggested rules of procedure, and model contractual clauses. The ICC suggests the following contractual language:

> For contracting parties who wish to have future disputes referred to arbitration under the LCIA Rules, the following clause is recommended. Words/spaces in square brackets should be deleted/completed as appropriate.

>> "Any dispute arising out of or in connection with this contract, including any question regarding its existence, validity or termination, shall be referred to and finally resolved by arbitration under the LCIA Rules, which Rules are deemed to be incorporated by reference into this clause.

>> The number of arbitrators shall be [one/three].

>> The seat, or legal place, of arbitration shall be [City and/or Country].

>> The language to be used in the arbitral proceedings shall be [ ].

>> The governing law of the contract shall be the substantive law of [ ]."

Enforcement and Recognition

A critical issue in dispute, whether litigated in court or resolved through arbitration, is enforcement and collection of damages. Even if the dispute is litigated on home turf, the victorious party may be forced to seek recognition and enforcement of that judgment in a foreign state where the defendant has assets. International law does not itself require mutual recognition of foreign court judgments. An obligation to recognize and enforce, however, is frequently created by treaty or unilaterally adopted under domestic law. In the EU, for example, judgments of the courts of one member state are readily recognized by all other EU members under EC Judgment Regulation 44/2001,[47] and subject to challenge only on limited grounds. The 2005 Hague Convention on Choice of Court Agreements, described above, would also create uniform rules of recognition and enforcement of foreign judgments. The Convention would generally require recognition and enforcement among the courts of all member states, with no review of the merits or findings of fact, and with limited grounds for challenge including lack of notice, fraud, public policy, or a failure to "compensate a party for actual loss or harm suffered."

---

44. http://www.lcia.org/Dispute_Resolution_Services/LCIA_Arbitration.aspx.

45. https://www.icdr.org/icdr/faces/home;jsessionid=sMQW9Fme1HfjEa6yfO9v6vxomDyKb vehj-eu7-XfJwaz5ZP3jVho!1343119801?_afrWindowId=null&_afrLoop=998519487217324& _afrWindowMode=0&_adf.ctrl-state=8i9oegbe_4#%40%3F_afrWindowId%3Dnull%26 _afrLoop%3D998519487217324%26_afrWindowMode%3D0%26_adf.ctrl-state%3D26z7zipr8_4.

46. https://icsid.worldbank.org/en/

47. http://eur-lex.europa.eu/LexUriServ/LexUriServ.do?uri=OJ:L:2001:012:0001:0023:en:PDF.

For countries not party to a treaty, recognition and enforcement is a matter for local domestic law, which may erect substantial obstacles. In the United States, most states have adopted a form of the 1963 Uniform Foreign Money-Judgments Recognition Act (*see also Hilton v. Guyot*, 159 U.S. 113 (1895),[48] in which the Supreme Court set out standards of comity favoring recognition of foreign judgments). The Florida version, which requires reciprocity in the foreign judgment country, is 55.601, Uniform Out-of-Country Foreign Money-Judgment Recognition Act.[49] The statute makes the process simple but also includes defenses:

55.605   Grounds for nonrecognition. —

(1) An out-of-country foreign judgment is not conclusive if:

(a) The judgment was rendered under a system which does not provide impartial tribunals or procedures compatible with the requirements of due process of law.

(b) The foreign court did not have personal jurisdiction over the defendant.

(c) The foreign court did not have jurisdiction over the subject matter.

(2) An out-of-country foreign judgment need not be recognized if:

(a) The defendant in the proceedings in the foreign court did not receive notice of the proceedings in sufficient time to enable him or her to defend.

(b) The judgment was obtained by fraud.

(c) The cause of action or claim for relief on which the judgment is based is repugnant to the public policy of this state.

(d) The judgment conflicts with another final and conclusive order.

(e) The proceeding in the foreign court was contrary to an agreement between the parties under which the dispute in question was to be settled otherwise than by proceedings in that court.

(f) In the case of jurisdiction based only on personal service, the foreign court was a seriously inconvenient forum for the trial of the action.

(g) The foreign jurisdiction where judgment was rendered would not give recognition to a similar judgment rendered in this state.

---

48. "When an action is brought in a court of this country, by a citizen of a foreign country against one of our own citizens, to recover a sum of money adjudged by a court of that country to be due from the defendant to the plaintiff, and the foreign judgment appears to have been rendered by a competent court, having jurisdiction of the cause and of the parties, and upon due allegations and proofs, and opportunity to defend against them, and its proceedings are according to the course of a civilized jurisprudence, and are stated in a clear and formal record, the judgment is prima facie evidence, at least, of the truth of the matter adjudged; and it should be held conclusive upon the merits tried in the foreign court, unless some special ground is shown for impeaching the judgment, as by showing that it was affected by fraud or prejudice, or that by the principles of international law, and by the comity of our own country, it should not be given full credit and effect." *Id*. at 205–206.

49. http://www.leg.state.fl.us/Statutes/index.cfm?App_mode=Display_Statute&URL=0000-0099/0055/0055.html.

(h) The cause of action resulted in a defamation judgment obtained in a jurisdiction outside the United States, unless the court sitting in this state before which the matter is brought first determines that the defamation law applied in the foreign court's adjudication provided at least as much protection for freedom of speech and press in that case as would be provided by the United States Constitution and the State Constitution.

The effectiveness of arbitration as an alternative to the courts depends significantly on its exclusivity, and eventual recognition and enforcement of the arbitral award. If a contractual clause requiring arbitration is not fully enforceable (or the dispute falls outside its scope), the benefits of ADR can easily be circumvented by filing a competing lawsuit. Similarly, an award will be meaningless unless courts in the place where the defendant has assets will enforce it. These two critical prerequisites to effective use of arbitration have been enormously enhanced by the widespread adoption of the UNCITRAL Convention on the Recognition and Enforcement of Foreign Arbitral Awards, commonly called the New York Convention.[50] Under the Convention, the United States and 155 other countries have committed to enforce both commercial arbitration clauses (precluding court jurisdiction), and resulting awards, among the member states. The United States has implemented the Convention in the Federal Arbitration Act.[51] The U.S. Supreme Court has also endorsed a strong policy of recognition and enforcement in a series of cases. The relative certainty of enforcement created by the NY Convention is one factor leading to the current popularity of the arbitration alternative for international commercial disputes.

---

50. http://www.uncitral.org/uncitral/en/uncitral_texts/arbitration/NYConvention.html.
51. https://www.law.cornell.edu/uscode/text/9.

Chapter 6

Transportation of Goods, Bills of Lading and Carriers

A. Overview

This chapter focuses on legal issues commonly encountered in the international transportation of goods. Our focus is on the role, obligations, and liabilities of carriers, with emphasis on the ocean bill of lading and its role in the documentary sale.

You should recall from Chapter One that transport documents and, in particular, the negotiable bill of lading, play an essential role in international sales. Since the buyer and seller are in different countries, they will typically rely on intermediaries, such as banks and carriers, to successfully transfer the goods and ensure payment. There are a wide variety of transport documents that may be used to complete this process depending upon the mode of transport and the parties' needs. Because the parties commonly transfer ownership through the exchange of transport documents, a key distinction between various types of transport documents involves their suitability for this function. In essence, negotiability allows the seller to transfer title to the goods by delivering the endorsed transport document over to the buyer. This role is particularly critical in the traditional documentary sales transaction.

A negotiable ocean bill of lading is the classic example, and most commonly used method, of fulfilling these functions of transportation, transfer of title, and payment. Among other things, the bill of lading incorporates two critical features that facilitate international sales in this regard. First, since the bill should indicate what the carrier has received and loaded on the vessel, it serves not only as a receipt for goods (for the seller) but also as confirmation that the seller has delivered certain goods, as described in the bill, to the carrier onto a vessel for shipment. Second, because the carrier will issue the bill made out "to order of," the bill serves as a negotiable document of title allowing its holder the legal right of ownership and possession, which can be transferred to others through endorsement.

Possession of the properly endorsed negotiable bill is, in essence, ownership and constructive possession of the goods themselves. In a documentary sale, the carrier will first issue the bill to the order of the shipper (seller) who thereby retains rights to the goods until the buyer pays for them upon presentment of the bill and other documents. Once the buyer pays, the seller will endorse the bill to the buyer who, now with title, may collect the goods upon their arrival or sell them by endorsing the bill to another party. These two features of the negotiable ocean bill of lading facilitate the documentary sale since the buyer will pay the seller in exchange for the bill because the bill describes what has been shipped and gives the buyer title and the right of possession.

The bill of lading also serves another important function, in that it reflects the terms that control the carrier's contract to transport the goods. These terms must be consistent with federal law, the Carriage of Goods by Sea Act (COGSA), as described further below. Persons with legal interests in the cargo will be, of course, vitally interested in such terms if the goods are lost or damaged during shipment and a claim against the carrier is contemplated.

The role of a bill of lading in a documentary sale is directly related to the relevant legal obligations of the carrier when receiving and transporting goods. These obligations also determine the potential liability of carriers for lost or damaged goods and the role of the bill of lading in such claims. There are two primary rule sets relevant to these issues. The first is COGSA, which generally controls carriers' responsibilities in shipping and, in turn, some important aspects of the bill of lading. COGSA also establishes the basic rules relating to carrier liability for mishandled or damaged goods. The second important statute is the Federal Bills of Lading Act (commonly referred to as the "Pomerene Act"). The Pomerene Act creates rules that protect the negotiability and use of bills of lading, as well as some aspects of carrier liability when things go wrong.

Do things ever go wrong when a carrier transports goods across the oceans? Monterey Bay Aquarium Research Institute[1] estimates that thousands of containers go missing[2] overboard every year. Why? If interested, look at videos and photos of container ships on the open ocean.[3] The Institute discovered this container off Monterey Bay at a depth of 1,300 meters (4,200 feet), one of 15 that fell off a ship near the Monterey Bay Marine Sanctuary.

The following problem requires application of the basic rules, created in COGSA and the Pomerene Act, with regard to issues common to carriers and bills of lading — improperly delivered, lost, or damaged goods. The facts diverge somewhat from the actual circumstances of modern shipping (most prominently, using boxes rather than consolidated container traffic) in order to clearly illustrate the underlying legal issues. Examine these statutory provisions carefully before reading the provided case illustrations and applying the law to the problem.

---

1. http://www.mbari.org/.
2. http://www.mbari.org/benthic-biology-winter-2013-dec-12/.
3. https://www.youtube.com/watch?v=Vx9FmEq5D6A.

© 2004 MBARI.

B. Problem Six: Alligator Boots, Looking Good in Nauru

1. Facts

Sam Seller, a producer of alligator skin boots located in Fort Lauderdale, Florida, entered into a contract with Billy Buyer. Billy is located, of course, on the South Pacific Island of Nauru. Under the terms of their contract, Sam agreed to sell Billy 4,000 pairs of "genuine Alligator Skin Boots," $100 per pair, CIF Port of Nauru, Republic of Nauru. The parties agreed to ship the boots in two installments. Sam organized Billy's order and, through the services of a <u>freight forwarder</u>[4] (licensed as an "<u>Ocean Transportation Intermediary</u>"[5] by the Federal Maritime Commission),[6] loaded the first installment of 100 boxes marked "10 gator boots," on board Big Boat Carrier's biggest boat. The carrier issued Sam an ocean freight bill of lading stating: "To Order of Sam

---

4. https://www.export.gov/article?id=Freight-Forwarder-What-is-a-FF.

5. http://www.ncbfaa.org/Scripts/4Disapi.dll/4DCGI/cms/review.html?Action=CMS_Document&DocID=8624&MenuKey=about.

6. Traditionally, a freight forwarder primarily offers a logistical service through which it arranges carriage and export of goods as an agent of the seller. In the United States, federal law regulates such services, and distinguishes among different types of providers including "<u>Ocean Freight Forwarders</u>" and "<u>Non-Vessel Operating Common Carriers (NVOCCs)</u>," https://www.fmc.gov/resources/ocean_transportation_intermediaries.aspx. NVOCCs take on responsibility as a carrier for the actual shipment of the goods and issue their own bills of lading for transportation arranged with a common carrier. In recent years, both carriers and freight forwarders have expanded their services, crossing over into so-called "third party logistics providers" (3pl's) whose legal status is not always clear. *See, e.g.*, William J. Augello, *Freight Transport Free For All*, Inbound Logistics (March 2006), http://www.inboundlogistics.com/cms/article/freight-transport-free-for-all/.

Seller . . . on board, 100 cardboard boxes said to contain 10 gator boots, in apparent good order, SWLC." Using the bank collection system, Sam presented this bill of lading and other documents to Billy. Billy then paid Sam, who endorsed the bill of lading to Billy. Billy promptly sold his interest in the boots and endorsed the bill of lading to his buyer, Always Sad Sally's Boot Emporium, on Main Street in Nauru.

One week later, Sam brought the second installment of boots to the Big Boats' dock. This time, Big Boats workers loaded 300 boxes on board its second biggest boat and gave Sam an ocean freight bill of lading stating: "To Order of Sam Seller . . . on board, 300 cardboard boxes said to contain 10 gator boots, in apparent good order, SWLC."

Two weeks later, the first big boat arrived in Nauru. Billy presented the sales contract and a photocopy of the first bill of lading to the carrier at its port warehouse who then allowed Billy to take away this first installment of the boots. Within a week, the second big boat arrived in Nauru. However, only 200 boxes of boots were disgorged from the vessel. Seventy-five of these boxes contained only sawdust, 25 of the boxes (and the boots inside) were soaked with seawater, and the remaining 100 boxes contained cheap, imitation alligator skin boots.

2. Assignment

Identify and evaluate potential claims that Sad Sally and Billy may have against the carrier Big Boats based on the resources provided or referenced below. You will find it necessary to answer the following questions.

(1) What basic obligations does COGSA impose on carriers, particularly regarding information that must be included when issuing bills of lading?

(2) What, if anything, does COGSA provide regarding carrier liability based upon these obligations?

(3) What does the Pomerene Act provide regarding a carrier's delivery obligations and potential liabilities under a bill of lading and how are these distinct from COGSA?

(4) What damages are available to the cargo interests under COGSA and the Pomerene Act?

C. Resources

1. COGSA

a. Overview

COGSA is a federal statute that generally governs the legal relationship between shippers and carriers for ocean transportation to and from the United States. It reflects the United States' commitment to a 1924 treaty (officially titled "International Convention for the Unification of Certain Rules of Law Relating to Bills of Lading," commonly referred to as the "Hague Rules"). The act provides rules regarding the carrier's primary obligations and liabilities both with regard to the handling of the goods and issuance of bills of lading. It is mandatory law that parties may not avoid through contractual agreement. Shippers and carriers may, however, extend the act's coverage to include the carrier's agents, and beyond the "tackle to tackle" ocean shipment. This is important to some modern shipping arrangements, such as "through carriage," and multimodal transport, including inland components.

The Hague Rules were revised in 1968 and 1979. The revised set of rules are now commonly called the "Hague-Visby" rules. Although many of its trading partners adopted these newer rules, the United States has not.

An attempt to revise the Hague Rules, which arguably favor carriers and industrialized nations, took the form of a 1978 U.N. Convention known as the "Hamburg Rules." The United States and other industrialized nations have not adopted these revisions. In 2009, the United States joined twenty-three other nations in signing a new "United Nations Convention on Contracts for the International Carriage of Goods Wholly or Partly by Sea," known as the "Rotterdam Rules." This convention has not yet been ratified by the United States and is not yet in effect.

b. Selected COGSA Provisions

COGSA is codified in the United States Code as part of the historical and revision notes to the re-codification of the Harter Act, at 46 U.S.C. § 30701.

46 U.S.C. App. § 1300. Bills of lading subject to chapter

Every bill of lading or similar document of title which is evidence of a contract for the carriage of goods by sea to or from ports of the United States, in foreign trade, shall have effect subject to the provisions of this chapter.

46 U.S.C. App. § 1301. Definitions

When used in this chapter—

(a) The term "carrier" includes the owner or the charterer who enters into a contract of carriage with a shipper.

(b) The term "contract of carriage" applies only to contracts of carriage covered by a bill of lading or any similar document of title, insofar as such document relates to the carriage of goods by sea, including any bill of lading or any similar document as aforesaid issued under or pursuant to a charter party from the moment at which such bill of lading or similar document of title regulates the relations between a carrier and a holder of the same.

(c) The term "goods" includes goods, wares, merchandise, and articles of every kind whatsoever, except live animals and cargo which by the contract of carriage is stated as being carried on deck and is so carried.

(d) The term "ship" means any vessel used for the carriage of goods by sea.

(e) The term "carriage of goods" covers the period from the time when the goods are loaded on to the time when they are discharged from the ship.

46 U.S.C. App. § 1302. Duties and rights of carrier

Subject to the provisions of section 1306 of this Appendix, under every contract of carriage of goods by sea, the carrier in relation to the loading, handling, stowage, carriage, custody, care, and discharge of such goods, shall be subject to the responsibilities and liabilities and entitled to the rights and immunities set forth in sections 1303 and 1304 of this Appendix.

46 U.S.C. App. § 1303. Responsibilities and liabilities of carrier and ship

(1) Seaworthiness

The carrier shall be bound, before and at the beginning of the voyage, to exercise due diligence to—

(a) Make the ship seaworthy;

(b) Properly man, equip, and supply the ship;

(c) Make the holds, refrigerating and cooling chambers, and all other parts of the ship in which goods are carried, fit and safe for their reception, carriage, and preservation.

(2) Cargo

The carrier shall properly and carefully load, handle, stow, carry, keep, care for, and discharge the goods carried.

(3) Contents of bill

After receiving the goods into his charge the carrier, or the master or agent of the carrier, shall, on demand of the shipper, issue to the shipper a bill of lading showing among other things—

(a) The leading marks necessary for identification of the goods as the same are furnished in writing by the shipper before the loading of such goods starts, provided such marks are stamped or otherwise shown clearly upon the goods if uncovered, or on the cases or coverings in which such goods are contained, in such a manner as should ordinarily remain legible until the end of the voyage.

(b) Either the number of packages or pieces, or the quantity or weight, as the case may be, as furnished in writing by the shipper.

(c) The apparent order and condition of the goods: Provided, That no carrier, master, or agent of the carrier, shall be bound to state or show in the bill of lading any marks, number, quantity, or weight which he has reasonable ground for suspecting not accurately to represent the goods actually received, or which he has had no reasonable means of checking.

(4) Bill as prima facie evidence

Such a bill of lading shall be prima facie evidence of the receipt by the carrier of the goods as therein described in accordance with paragraphs (3)(a), (b), and (c), of this section: Provided, That nothing in this chapter shall be construed as repealing or limiting the application of any part of chapter 801 of title 49.

(5) Guaranty of statements

The shipper shall be deemed to have guaranteed to the carrier the accuracy at the time of shipment of the marks, number, quantity, and weight, as furnished by him; and the shipper shall indemnify the carrier against all loss, damages, and expenses arising or resulting from inaccuracies in such particulars. The right of the carrier to such indemnity shall in no way limit his responsibility and liability under the contract of carriage to any person other than the shipper.

. . . .

(6) Notice of loss or damage; limitation of actions

Unless notice of loss or damage and the general nature of such loss or damage be given in writing to the carrier or his agent at the port of discharge before or at the time of the removal of the goods into the custody of the person entitled to delivery thereof under the contract of carriage, such removal shall be prima facie evidence of the delivery by the carrier of the goods as described in the bill of lading. If the loss or damage is not apparent, the notice must be given within three days of the delivery.

. . . .

RIGHTS AND IMMUNITIES OF CARRIER AND SHIP

46 U.S.C. App. § 1304.

(1) Neither the carrier nor the ship shall be liable for loss or damage arising or resulting from unseaworthiness unless caused by want of due diligence on the part of the carrier to make the ship seaworthy, and to secure that the ship is properly manned, equipped, and supplied, and to make the holds, refrigerating and cool chambers, and all other parts of the ship in which goods are carried fit and safe for their reception, carriage, and preservation in accordance with the provisions of paragraph (1) of section 3. Whenever loss or damage has resulted from unseaworthiness, the burden of proving the exercise of due diligence shall be on the carrier or other persons claiming exemption under this section.

(2) Uncontrollable causes of loss

Neither the carrier nor the ship shall be responsible for loss or damage arising or resulting from—

(a) Act, neglect, or default of the master, mariner, pilot, or the servants of the carrier in the navigation or in the management of the ship;

(b) Fire, unless caused by the actual fault or privity of the carrier;

(c) Perils, dangers, and accidents of the sea or other navigable waters;

(d) Act of God;

(e) Act of war;

(f) Act of public enemies;

(g) Arrest or restraint of princes, rulers, or people, or seizure under legal process;

(h) Quarantine restrictions;

(i) Act or omission of the shipper or owner of the goods, his agent or representative;

(j) Strikes or lockouts or stoppage or restraint of labor from whatever cause, whether partial or general: Provided, That nothing herein contained shall be construed to relieve a carrier from responsibility for the carrier's own acts;

(k) Riots and civil commotions;

(l) Saving or attempting to save life or property at sea;

(m) Wastage in bulk or weight or any other loss or damage arising from inherent defect, quality, or vice of the goods;

(n) Insufficiency of packing;

(o) Insufficiency or inadequacy of marks;

(p) Latent defects not discoverable by due diligence; and

(q) Any other cause arising without the actual fault and privity of the carrier and without the fault or neglect of the agents or servants of the carrier, but the burden of proof shall be on the person claiming the benefit of this exception to show that neither the actual fault or privity of the carrier nor the fault or neglect of the agents or servants of the carrier contributed to the loss or damage.

(3) Freedom from negligence

The shipper shall not be responsible for loss or damage sustained by the carrier or the ship arising or resulting from any cause without the act, fault, or neglect of the shipper, his agents, or his servants.

(4) Deviations

Any deviation in saving or attempting to save life or property at sea, or any reasonable deviation shall not be deemed to be an infringement or breach of this Act or of the contract of carriage, and the carrier shall not be liable for any loss or damage resulting therefrom: Provided, however, That if the deviation is for the purpose of loading or unloading cargo or passengers it shall, prima facie, be regarded as unreasonable.

(5) Amount of liability; valuation of cargo

Neither the carrier nor the ship shall in any event be or become liable for any loss or damage to or in connection with the transportation of goods in an amount exceeding $500 per package lawful money of the United States, or in case of goods not shipped in packages, per customary freight unit, or the equivalent of that sum in other currency, unless the nature and value of such goods have been declared by the shipper before shipment and inserted in the bill of lading. This declaration, if embodied in the bill of lading, shall be prima facie evidence, but shall not be conclusive on the carrier.

By agreement between the carrier, master, or agent of the carrier, and the shipper another maximum amount than that mentioned in this paragraph may be fixed: Provided, that such maximum shall not be less than the figure above named. In no event shall the carrier be liable for more than the amount of damage actually sustained.

. . . .

46 U.S.C. App. § 1307. Agreement as to liability prior to loading or after discharge

Nothing contained in this chapter shall prevent a carrier or a shipper from entering into any agreement, stipulation, condition, reservation, or exemption as to the responsibility and liability of the carrier or the ship for the loss or damage to or in connection with the custody and care and handling of goods prior to the loading on and subsequent to the discharge from the ship on which the goods are carried by sea.

For reference, here is the entire COGSA text.[7]

c. Case Law Interpreting & Applying COGSA

In reading the following case, pay attention to the court's application of COGSA to the facts, particularly the role of the bill of lading, the prima facie case for loss, the "Q defense," and the package limitation on damages. Also take note of the practices and procedures deployed by the parties during the transaction to protect their interests.

i. American Nat. Fire Ins. v. M/V Seaboard Victory, No. 08-21811-CIV, 2009 WL 6465299 (S.D. Fla., Oct. 9, 2009)

Patricia A. Seitz, District Judge.

THIS MATTER is before the Court on Plaintiffs' Motion for Summary Judgment and Defendant Seaboard's Motion for Partial Summary Judgment. This is an action governed by the Carriage of Goods By Sea Act, in which the subrogee of a distributor seeks to recover damages for lost cargo against Defendants, who were responsible for shipping the distributor's goods from Miami to Panama. The distributor, Motta Internacional S.A. ("Motta"), engaged Defendant, Seaboard Marine, Ltd. ("Seaboard"), to transport cargo from a warehouse in Miami, operated by Motta's affiliate, to a Motta warehouse in Panama. After Motta unloaded Seaboard's container, it claimed that some of that cargo, namely 1 box of Canon cameras and 252

---

7. https://www.law.cornell.edu/uscode/html/uscode46a/usc_sup_05_46_10_28.html.

cartons of Nintendo Wiis, was missing. Motta's subrogees, Plaintiffs, American National Fire Insurance Company and Great American Insurance Company of New York, then brought this action against Seaboard and its agent Newport Trucking Company ("Newport") pursuant to Seaboard's bill of lading, which is governed by COGSA.

... Seaboard's attempts to undermine Plaintiff's prima facie case do not raise a genuine issue of material fact and Seaboard presents no evidence to establish it was not at fault. As a result, Plaintiffs are entitled to summary judgment. Furthermore, under the limitation-of-liability provision in Seaboard's bill of lading, Plaintiffs are entitled to damages of $126,500 for the loss of 253 packages of cargo, plus prejudgment interest and costs.

I. Statement of Facts

Plaintiffs filed this action to recover damages for lost cargo on June 25, 2008. In their instant Motion for Summary Judgment, they maintain that as a matter of law they are entitled to a judgment of $126,500.00 per the bill of lading's limitation-of-liability provision for loss of 1 box of Canon cameras and 252 cartons of Wii consoles, plus prejudgment interest and costs. Seaboard has filed a cross-motion for Partial Summary Judgment on damages, asserting that Plaintiffs can only be entitled to $3,500 in damages under the limitation-of-liability provision, calculated based on a loss of 1 box of Canon cameras and 6 pallets of Wii consoles. The following facts are undisputed unless otherwise noted.

A. Order of Wiis and Initial Attempt to Transport Cargo

Pursuant to a purchase order from Motta, Nintendo delivered 803 cartons of Wii consoles to a warehouse in Miami operated by Crossroads Inc. ("Crossroads").... Crossroads is an affiliate of Motta and warehouses merchandise that Motta purchases. According to the delivery receipt, those 803 cartons collectively weighed 20,467 pounds, or approximately 25.49 pounds a carton.

Crossroads then removed some of the Wiis from inventory to prepare them for shipment to Motta's warehouse in Panama. To initiate the transfer, Crossroads generated an internal invoice bearing a purchase order number of 896377 reflecting Crossroads' intent to send to Panama 467 cartons in 11 pallets (42 cartons to a pallet) and 5 separate cartons. The weight of a shrink-wrapped pallet with 42 cartons is 1,042 pounds. A corresponding "pick slip" generated on July 16, 2009 indicates that 11 pallets and 5 extra cartons of Wiis were selected from inventory pursuant to the purchase order identified on Crossroads' internal invoice (number 896377).... A checkmark on the pick slip reflects that these cartons were removed from inventory and staged to be loaded. A Crossroads warehouse receipt dated July 17, 2007 (W.R.12180) reflects the processing of purchase order 896377 consisting of 11 pallets of Wiis.

Crossroads then attempted to ship these Wiis and other cargo to Panama on an American President Line ("APL") container. Though Crossroads had customarily used Seaboard to ship cargo to Panama, Motta asked Crossroads in May of 2007 to use Eagle Global Logistics ("Eagle") as a logistics provider and Eagle wanted to use

APL for a shipment to Panama at that time. On June 13, 2007, empty APL Container No. TGHU 7486648 ("APL Container") arrived at Crossroads' warehouse. . . . On July 9, 2007, Eagle supplied Crossroads with booking information for an APL vessel scheduled to depart on July 18, 2007.

Accordingly, on July 17, 2007, Crossroads personnel loaded the APL Container. The loading list for the APL Container that itemizes each item of cargo loaded indicates that Crossroads loaded the APL Container with cargo weighing a total 18,530 pounds. This cargo included the 467 Nintendo Wii cartons, consisting of 11 pallets of Wii cartons and an additional 5 cartons that were either added to the Wii pallets or to other pallets in the APL Container. It also included a box of Canon cameras weighing 314 pounds. All of the weights on the packing list were derived from either measurement at Crossroads' warehouse or shipping documents.

Crossroads personnel then closed and sealed the APL Container and sent it to the Port of Miami. Guillermo Ortega, Crossroads' warehouse supervisor, had the doors of the APL Container closed in his presence and had seals placed on the inner door closing mechanisms on both the right and left doors. Additionally, he had a bar seal installed between the two inner door closing mechanisms and secured in place with a locking pin. Once the APL Container was closed and sealed, a driver from Salom Transportation picked up the container to take to the Port of Miami. However, the APL Container could not be loaded on the APL vessel that was scheduled to leave on July 18, 2007.

B. Delivery of Cargo to Seaboard

As a result, Crossroads ordered an empty container from Seaboard to transport the cargo and had Eagle return the loaded APL Container to the Crossroads warehouse. (Blandon Dec. ¶ 23). Crossroads booked a "House/House" move with Seaboard, meaning that Seaboard was to pick up the loaded container from Crossroads and deliver it to Motta's warehouse in Panama. On July 19, 2007, Seaboard received empty Seaboard Container SMLU 780661–2 ("Seaboard Container").

On July 20, 2007, Crossroads employees transloaded cargo from the APL Container into the Seaboard Container. Salom brought the APL Container back to Crossroads at approximately 11:10 a.m. Crossroads personnel then broke the three seals on the APL container, removed all of the cargo therein, and, with the exception of cargos of cigarettes, perfumes and ORM-D ("Other Regulated Materials — Domestic") materials, loaded the cargo into the Seaboard Container.

Crossroads generated a new packing list to reflect the cargo transloaded into the Seaboard Container. With the cigarettes, perfume and ORM–D materials omitted, this new loading list reflected a total cargo weight of 12,211 pounds. Crossroads also created a load list identifying the contents of the Seaboard Container and sent it to Motta's warehouse in Panama. The load list reflected the number of Wii cartons being shipped, but not the number of Wii pallets.

Seaboard subsequently issued a bill of lading for the shipment providing for "house-to-house" transport of Motta's cargo such that the provisions of COGSA were to govern "before loading on and after discharge from the vessel and throughout the entire time the Goods or Containers . . . are in the care, custody and/or control of [Seaboard and its] agents." The bill of lading identified the "No. of Pkgs." as "1." However, the cargo was described as "140′ DRY HIGH CUBE CNTR S.L.W.C. 487 PCS CONTG ELECTRONICS—VIDEO GAMES PHOTO CAMERA." The bill of lading also confirmed Crossroads' packing list weight of 12,211 pounds, but contained the limiting language "Particulars Furnished By Shipper."

Additionally, the bill of lading contained a provision limiting Seaboard's liability in the event of loss or damage to the cargo:

20. LIMITATION OF LIABILITY.

Except as otherwise provided in this Clause or elsewhere in this Bill of Lading, in case of any loss or damage to or in connection with cargo exceeding in actual value the equivalent of $500 lawful money of the United States, per package, or in case of cargo not shipped in packages, per shipping unit, the value of the cargo shall be deemed to be $500 per package or per shipping unit. . . . The words "shipping unit" shall mean each physical unit or piece of cargo not shipped in a package, including articles of things of any description whatsoever, except cargo shipped in bulk, and irrespective of the weight or measurement unit employed in calculating freight and related charges.

Once the transloading was completed and the doors closed, Ortega placed yellow bullet seals 355476 and 35477 on the inner closing mechanisms of the right and left hand closed doors. He also placed a bar seal, with seal No. 16007, between the two inner closing mechanisms, which was secured with a locking pin that was also numbered 16007. At the time that he placed the locking pin into the bar seal bracket affixed to the right-hand door (the "Locking Bracket"), there was no hole drilled into the back side of the Locking Bracket. (*Id.*). Ortega then took photographs of the closed and sealed doors, which indicate the Container was closed and sealed by 12:15 p.m. A driver from Seaboard's agent, Defendant Newport Trucking Company ("Newport"), left Crossroads' warehouse in Northwest Miami with the Container at about 1 p.m.

However, the Newport truck carrying the Seaboard Container did not weigh in at the Port of Miami until three hours later and its cargo weighed substantially less than the 12,211 pounds reflected on the bill of lading. At 3:59 p.m., a weight ticket generated at the Port indicates the Container only contained 5,600 to 6,700 pounds of cargo, after taking into account the weights of the empty truck, empty container and chassis. . . . A Seaboard checker at the Port of Miami affixed a seal on the right door, but did not check behind the bar lock seal or look for evidence of tampering with the rivets or bolts in the rear doors.

C. Outturn in Panama

On July 26, 2007, the Seaboard Container arrived at Motta's warehouse in Panama at about 12:25 p.m. Before moving the Container to a staging area for unloading, Motta personnel put the Container in an enclosed hangar with metal doors that could only be accessed through a locked gate. Security guards monitored the hangar at all times.

Motta personnel opened the Container at about four o'clock the afternoon of Friday, July 27, 2007. A warehouse supervisor who managed the unloading, Gerardo Lan, used a delivery document he received from Motta's import department titled, "Declaracion de Movimento," to verify the container number and seal numbers. He also used the load list Crossroads had sent to Panama in order to verify the contents of the Container. Lan briefly examined the Container to verify the numbers on the seals matched those on the delivery document. He observed that the seals were intact and without the appearance of tampering. . . . The bullet seals and bar seal were then cut with pliers so the Container could be opened and unloaded.

Upon opening the Container, Motta personnel found only 5 Wii pallets and an empty box that was supposed to have contained 116 Canon cameras. Lan immediately noticed that the box for Canon cameras was empty. As a result, he notified Ricardo Williams, Motta's import and claims manager, of the missing Canon cameras just after the Container was unloaded. Motta sent Seaboard a claim letter for the missing Canon cameras on July 30, 2007.

The Locking Bracket was not removed at the time of unloading because the personnel unloading the truck did not have an electric saw to cut the bar seal. However, Lan had a welder remove it at a later time with a torch because he knew the seals would be needed to investigate the shortage of Canon cameras. A photograph of the seals was taken, but it only depicts the front side of the Locking Bracket showing the number of the seal.

While Motta personnel immediately realized the Container was missing Canon cameras, they did not know that 6 pallets of Wiis were missing from the Container at the time it was opened. Lan observed the removal of five pallets and a single carton of Nintendo Wiis, but did not notice that six pallets of Wiis were missing because the load list only identified the number of cartons of Wiis that were loaded, not the number of pallets. Also, Lan's job was to verify the identity and condition of the Container, not the quantity of the goods contained therein. However, Lan later confirmed for an electronics warehouse manager, Fulvio Trolla, that only five pallets were unloaded from the container. Trolla then informed Motta's import and claim manager Ricardo Williams on August 1, 2007 that six pallets of Wiis were missing from the Container. As a result, Motta sent a second claim letter to Seaboard on August 1, 2007 stating that "at the time of unloading on July 27, 2007 we found ourselves with a shortage of 6 pallets of Nintendo Wiis . . . and 116 pieces of Canon Cameras."

A surveyor came to Motta's warehouse on Tuesday July 31, 2007 to follow up on the claim for the missing Canon cameras. Williams informed the surveyor of the missing Wiis on August 1, 2007 and they then watched a video of the unloading of the Container to confirm only five pallets were unloaded. The surveyor examined the bar seal and corroborated the number on the seal, but his report does not note whether a hole was drilled into the back of the Locking Bracket. Williams also handled the seals sometime after they were removed, but did not look for or observe a hole drilled into the back of the Locking Bracket.

After Motta paid Nintendo for the Wiis and presented a claim to Plaintiffs, Plaintiffs hired a marine surveyor, Brian Mahoney Jr., to investigate the cause of the loss of cargo. Mahoney examined the seals at an unspecified date and examined the Seaboard Container on November 13, 2007. Mahoney found that a hole had been drilled into the back of the Locking Bracket and opines that the hole would enable removal of the locking pin and opening of the bar seal. Furthermore, Mahoney found evidence of tampering with the right door inner locking device that would enable bypass of a seal on the door. Specifically, he observed that the unusual shape of one of the rivets on the locking device, rust patterns on that rivet and fresh gouge in the paint on the door surface suggested that the original rivet had been removed and replaced with a secondary rivet. He opines that the right-hand door of the Container could have been opened by removing the original rivet to bypass the door lock.

II. Summary Judgment Standard

Summary judgment under Fed.R.Civ.P. 56(c) is appropriate when "the pleadings, depositions, answers to interrogatories, and admissions on file, together with the affidavits, if any, show that there is no genuine issue as to any material fact and that the moving party is entitled to a judgment as a matter of law." . . .

Despite the unique burden shifting provisions in COGSA, "the treatment of a summary judgment motion under COGSA is no different from the way similar motions are dealt with in any other litigation." *Transatlantic Marine Claims Agency, Inc. v. M/V "OOCL Inspiration,"* 137 F.3d 94, 101 (2d Cir. 1998).

III. Analysis

"To hold a carrier liable for missing or damaged goods under COGSA, a shipper must prove that the goods were damaged or lost while in the carrier's custody." *Plastique Tags, Inc. v. Asia Trans Line, Inc.,* 83 F.3d 1367, 1369 (11th Cir. 1996). The shipper meets this burden and establishes a prima facie case by showing (1) full delivery of the goods in good condition to the carrier, and (2) outturn by the carrier of the cargo with damages or missing goods. *Id.* However, "[a]plaintiff shipper is not required to prove that the carrier was at fault, or how the damage might have occurred." *M.Goldetz Export Corp. v. S/S Lake Anja,* 751 F.2d 1103, 1109 (2d Cir. 1985).

Once a shipper establishes a prima facie case, the burden of proof shifts to the carrier to demonstrate either (1) it exercised due diligence to prevent the cargo damage, or (2) the damage was caused by an "excepted cause" listed in COGSA's Section 4(2). *Banana Servs., Inc. v. M/V Fleetwave,* 911 F.2d 519, 521 (11th Cir. 1990). As a result, "COGSA's framework . . . places the risk of non-explanation for mysterious maritime damage squarely on defendants." . . . "While it is true that the burden is on the plaintiff to establish a prima facie case under COGSA, a defendant must offer more than blanket assertions about mysterious possible causes if it is to survive a motion for summary judgment." "[I]f the defendant's evidence is so weak that it inflicts no meaningful damage to the plaintiff's prima facie case, the defendant will have judgment entered against it." [*Transatlantic* at 101-102].

1. Delivery of Goods

First, the Court must address whether Plaintiffs have established Seaboard's receipt of the Canon cameras and Wii pallets in good condition.[6] COGSA plaintiffs often use the carrier's bill of lading to establish the first element of a prima facie case. "A clean bill of lading is prima facie evidence that the carrier received the goods it describes. It creates a rebuttable presumption the goods were delivered to the carrier in good condition and thus satisfies that element of the plaintiff's prima facie case." *Terman Foods, Inc. v. Omega Lines*, 707 F.2d 1225, 1226 (11th Cir. 1983) (citations omitted). However, in order for a bill of lading to constitute prima facie proof that the carrier received cargo in a sealed container, the bill of lading "must either be without limiting language such as 'shipper's load and count' or it must contain terms that the carrier can verify." *Plastique* at 1369–70. If the carrier cannot verify terms in the bill of lading, the shipper can still satisfy its prima facie case by submitting eyewitness testimony or other evidence to establish the condition of the goods upon delivery and outturn. . . .

Here, Plaintiffs have submitted both the Seaboard bill of lading and eyewitness testimony to establish the first element of their prima facie case. While the bill of lading contains the limiting language, "Particulars Furnished By Shipper," it also states that the gross weight of the cargo is 12,211 pounds. Cargo weight in a bill of lading is easy to verify and can establish the first element of a prima facie case. *See, e.g., Westway Coffee Corp. v. M.V. Netuno*, 675 F.2d 30, 33 (2d. Cir. 1982); *PT Indonesia Epson Ind. v. Orient Overseas Container Line, Inc.*, 219 F. Supp. 2d 1265, 1270-71 (S.D. Fla. 2002). Plaintiffs also offer Crossroads' warehouse supervisor Guillermo Ortega's eyewitness testimony that he saw Crossroads employees transload 11 pallets and 5 cartons from the APL Container into the Seaboard Container. . . . Unrebutted, either method of proof satisfies the first element of a prima facie case.

Seaboard attempts to refute this evidence by claiming the cargo weights listed in the Declaracion de Movimento (Ex. 21) contradict the weights listed on Crossroads' packing documents, . . . but the document is not admissible as to the weight of the cargo. Seaboard has not put forth any "evidence sufficient to support a finding that the [document] in question is what its proponent claims," i.e., a record reflecting an accurate assessment of the weight of the cargo. . . . As Seaboard has no evidence to rebut either the weight listed in the bill of lading or eyewitness testimony that 11 pallets of Wiis and 1 box of Canon cameras were loaded into the Container, Plaintiffs have proven as a matter of law that Motta delivered 11 pallets and 1 box of Canon cameras to Seaboard.

---

6. While COGSA only covers transport from the port of receipt to the port of discharge, a carrier and a shipper can extend COGSA so that it applies prior to loading and subsequent to discharge of goods from a ship. . . . Motta and Seaboard did just that by executing a bill of lading expressly stating that the provisions of COGSA shall govern "before loading on and after discharge from the vessel and throughout the entire time the Goods or Containers . . . are in the care, custody and/or control of [Seaboard and its] agents. . . ." In this case, the cargo was delivered to Seaboard at the Crossroads warehouse in Miami and outturned at Motta's warehouse in Panama.

2. Missing Goods at Outturn

Having established the first element of its prima facie case with two methods of proof, the weight in the bill of lading and eyewitness testimony, Plaintiffs can satisfy the second element by showing either missing weight or missing containers at outturn. *See, e.g., Westway,* 675 F.2d at 33 (shortfall in number of cartons in sealed container satisfied second element of prima facie case when first element was established through weight in bill of lading). Plaintiffs offer evidence supporting both methods of proof.

Motta's failure to submit a claim for the missing Wiis within three days of outturn triggers a weak legal presumption that Seaboard delivered them in good condition. Section 1306(6) COGSA states as follows:

> Unless loss of notice or damage and the general nature of such loss or damage be given in writing to the carrier or his agent at the port of discharge before or at the time of the removal of the goods into the custody of the person entitled to delivery thereof under the contract of carriage, such removal shall be prima facie evidence of the delivery by the carrier of the goods as described in the bill of lading. *If the loss or damage is not apparent, the notice must be given within three days of delivery.*

(emphasis added). When the shipper fails to give timely notice, this provision creates a presumption that the carrier delivered the cargo in good order. . . . However, this presumption is "normally not conclusive" and "disappears from the case once the [plaintiff] comes forward with sufficient evidence that the cargo was damaged or short prior to delivery." . . .

Plaintiffs' evidence easily rebuts this presumption. First, the fact that the Container was missing 5,500 to 6,600 pounds of cargo at the Port of Miami, during Seaboard's possession of the Container, is compelling evidence that 6 pallets of Wiis were missing at outturn. *See Transatlantic,* 137 F.3d at 99 (plaintiff need not produce evidence directly pertaining to delivery and outturn to establish prima facie case). Plaintiffs have bolstered this proof with eyewitness testimony and video evidence . . . that only five pallets were in the Container when it was opened, as well as evidence that the Container was kept under tight security between outturn and opening. . . . Given the weakness of the resulting legal presumption and Plaintiffs' convincing evidence of loss at outturn, Motta's failure to give notice until 6 days after outturn is immaterial. *See, e.g., Transatlantic* (affirming summary judgment for plaintiff despite carrier's claim that notice of damage was belated).

. . . .

In this case, Plaintiffs present evidence of tampering with the Locking Bracket on the bar seal and the locking mechanism on the right-hand door. Plaintiffs' expert surveyor, Brian Mahoney, found that a hole had been drilled into the back of the Locking Bracket of the bar seal and asserts that the hole would enable the removal of the locking pin and opening of the bar seal. Furthermore, Mahoney found evidence suggesting the backside of a rivet of a locking device on the right-hand door had been removed. . . .

Having provided undisputed evidence of missing weight at outturn, and supplemental undisputed evidence of constant security of the Container following Seaboard's delivery, missing cargo at opening and tampering with the Container's locking mechanisms, Plaintiffs' are entitled to summary judgment on the second element of their prima facie case. While Seaboard raises hypotheticals as to what may have happened to the goods prior to or after delivery, the Court need not "engage in fanciful assumptions that the harm might possibly have occurred outside the defendants' control." *Transatlantic* at 99.

3. "Q Clause" Defense

Since Plaintiffs have established their prima facie case as a matter of law, Seaboard must come forward with some evidence of due diligence or a statutory exemption to survive Plaintiffs' motion for summary judgment. "Once the shipper establishes a prima facie case, the burden of proof shifts to the carrier to prove either it exercised due diligence to prevent the damage . . . or that the harm resulted from one of the excepted causes" listed in the statute. . . . If a plaintiff has established its prima facie case, "the carrier must 'explain what took place or suffer the consequences. . . .'"

Seaboard claims that it has evidence to support a defense under COGSA's "Q Clause," which absolves a carrier from liability for losses that are not attributable to the carrier's fault or negligence. A carrier is not responsible for loss "arising without the actual fault and privity of the carrier and without the fault or neglect of the agents or servants of the carrier." 46 U.S.C. § 30701, Sec. 4(2)(q). In asserting a defense under the Q Clause, "the burden of proof shall be on the person claiming the benefit of this exception to show that neither the actual fault or privity of the carrier contributed to the loss or damage." *Id.*

However, Seaboard does not provide an "expl[anation of] what took place" such that it can raise a defense under Section 4(2)(q). Seaboard offers no evidence from Newport's truck driver or any other Seaboard witness that proffers an explanation as to how the goods went missing during Seaboard's custody of the Container without fault on the part of Seaboard or its agents. . . .

4. Damages

Next, the Court must address the Parties' cross-motions for summary judgment on damages. The Parties ground their respective arguments on differing interpretations of the limitation of liability provision in the Seaboard bill of lading. This provision limits Plaintiffs' recovery to "$500 per package or per shipping unit." Plaintiffs request $126,500.00 based on a loss of 252 cartons of Wiis and 1 box of Canon cameras. Seaboard's Motion for Partial Summary Judgment claims that Plaintiffs are entitled to only $3,500 in damages based on a loss of 6 Wii pallets and 1 box of Canon cameras.

COGSA has a limitation-of-liability provision, but parties are free to amend that provision in their bill of lading as long as the amendment is in favor of the shipper. 46 U.S.C. § 30701, Notes Sec. 7 . . . . Here, the Parties have amended the limitation of liability provision by setting a limit for liability "per package or per shipping unit" and defining each "shipping unit" as "each physical unit or *piece of cargo not shipped in a package,* including articles or things of any description whatsoever. . . ." In addressing the competing motions for summary judgment on damages, the Court must address whether the lost cargo was shipped in "packages" or some other "shipping unit" and then ascertain the number of packages or shipping units for which Plaintiffs can assert damages.

Unfortunately, the term 'package' is not defined in COGSA. . . . However, in the Eleventh Circuit, a "package" is considered to be "a class of cargo, irrespective of size, shape or weight, to which some packaging preparation for transportation has been made, which facilitates handling but which does not necessarily conceal or completely enclose the goods." . . .

The "touchstone" and analysis as to whether the goods in a container are enclosed in "packages" is "the contractual agreement between the parties as set forth in the bill of lading." *Fireman's Fund Ins. Co. v. Tropical Shipping and Construction Co.,* 254 F.3d 987, 997 (11th Cir. 2001). When a shipper places goods in packages "as used in the ordinary sense of the word" and the number of the packages within the container is disclosed to the carrier in the bill of lading or otherwise, each described package or unit within the container constitutes a package. . . . If, however, "a bill of lading lists the number of containers as the number of packages, and fails to disclose the number of COGSA packages within each container," the container itself is the "package" under COGSA's limitation of liability provision. . . . "[A]n ambiguity on a bill of lading regarding the number of COGSA packages should be resolved in favor of the shipper." *Sony Magnetic Prods. v. Merivienti O/Y,* 863 F.2d 1537, 1542 (11th Cir. 1989).

Here, Seaboard's bill of lading identified the "No. of Pkgs." as "1" while describing the cargo as "140′ DRY HIGH CUBE CNTR S.L.W.C. 487 PCS [pieces] CONTG ELECTRONICS—VIDEO GAMES PHOTO CAMERA." Because the bill of lading lists the number of containers (1) as the number of packages, the Court must determine whether the description adequately identifies the number of packages or whether the Seaboard bill of lading describes the cargo such that it must be "classified as 'goods not shipped in packages.'" . . .

"The fact that the term 'pieces' is used to describe plaintiff's cargo can cut either way" on this issue. *Transatlantic Marine Claims Agency, Inc.,* 1993 U.S. Dist. LEXIS 4555, (S.D.N.Y. Apr. 9, 1993). In *Hayes-Leger,* the Eleventh Circuit held that use of the term "pieces" in the description, "1 CONTAINER SAID TO CONTAIN: 3,542 PCS. WOVEN BASKETS AND RATTAN FURNITURES," was "insufficient to indicate to the carrier that the goods were 'packaged.'" 765 F.2d at 1081, n. 9. In doing so, the Court cited to the Second Circuit case, *Binladen BSB Landscaping v. M.V. "Nedlloyd Rotterdam,"* 759 F.2d 1006 (2d Cir. 1985), which stated that a shipper intending to rely on the description portion of the bill of lading to disclose the number of "packages" must indicate "the number of items qualifying as packages (i.e., connoting preparation in some way for transport), such as 'bundles,' 'cartons,' or the like." *Id.* at 1013–14.

However, a district court in the Second Circuit has since held that containers of printing presses and spare parts contained "packages" under COGSA when the description of the cargo in the bill of lading used the term "pieces." *Transatlantic,* 1993 U.S. Dist. LEXIS 4555 (S.D.N.Y. Apr. 9, 1993). The Court held that use of that term complied with *Binladen*'s requirement that the bill of lading "'describe objects that can reasonably be understood from the description as being packages' or that it 'indicate an alternative number of packages'" apart from the container itself. *Id.* at *13. Undisputed evidence that the machinery was packed and wrapped in clear plastic prior to transport supported this holding because it established preparation of the cargo that could facilitate its transport. *Id.* at *12.

In this case, the bill of lading's description of cargo constituted by "pieces" of electronics, cameras and video games indicated to Seaboard that it was shipping "packages" of electronics equipment. The undisputed evidence reflects that the "pieces" referenced in the bill of lading were actually cartons of Wiis that each contained 3 Wii consoles. Cartons are unquestionably "packages" "as used in the ordinary sense of the word," . . . and is a form of package expressly recognized in *Binladin.* . . . Additionally, electronics equipment is a form cargo that one would assume to be shipped overseas in packaged form.

Furthermore, Plaintiffs are entitled to damages based on the packages identified in the bill of lading, even if those packages were loaded on pallets before being placed in the container. . . . Here, there is no ambiguity in the bill of lading to suggest that pallets could be the relevant packaging unit. As a result, under the terms of the bill of lading, Plaintiffs are entitled to $500 for each of the lost packages identified therein, not for each lost pallet. . . .

Here, Plaintiffs have proven the loss of 252 packages of Wii consoles and 1 package of Canon cameras. As a result, they are entitled to $126,500 in damages, per the bill of lading's limit of $500 in damages for each lost package. . . .

ii. Berisford Metals v. S/S Salvador, 779 F.2d 841 (2d Cir. 1985)

Before FRIENDLY, MANSFIELD and WINTER, Circuit Judges.

MANSFIELD, Circuit Judge.

Berisford Metals Corporation (Berisford), plaintiff in this cargo-loss action, appeals from an order and judgment of the Southern District of New York, Gerard L. Goettel, Judge, granting its motion for summary judgment against the ship S/S Salvador and A/S Ivarans Rederi (Ivarans), its owner and operator, for loss of 70 bundles of tin ingots valued at $483,214.90 but applying the limitation of liability provision of §4(5) of the Carriage of Goods by Sea Act, 46 U.S.C. §1304(5)[1] (COGSA), to limit the

---

1. Section 4(5) of COGSA, 46 U.S.C. §1304(5) provides:

"Neither the carrier nor the ship shall in any event be or become liable for any loss or damage to or in connection with the transportation of goods in an amount exceeding $500 per package lawful money of the United States, or in case of goods not shipped in packages, per customary freight unit, or the equivalent of that sum in other currency, unless the nature and value of such goods have been declared by the shipper before shipment and inserted in the bill of lading. This declaration, if embodied in the bill of lading, shall be prima facie evidence, but shall not be conclusive on the carrier."

defendants' liability to $500 per bundle, or a total of $35,000. Defendants cross-appeal from the district court's denial of their motion for dismissal of the action. We reverse the judgment to the extent that it limits defendants' liability to $500 per bundle and remand the case with directions to enter judgment in Berisford's favor for the full value of the lost cargo. We affirm the district court's denial of defendants' motion to dismiss the complaint.

The material facts are not in dispute. On June 23, 1983, Berisford contracted to purchase from Paranapanema International Ltd. (Paranapanema), located in Sao Paolo, Brazil, 50 metric tons of grade A tin ingots in bundles at a price of $13,140 per metric ton (a price later changed by the parties of $13,300 per metric ton). The terms were F.O.B. vessel at Santos, Brazil, for shipment to New York in January 1984.[2] Payment was to be made net cash 45 days after ocean bill of lading date against presentation of a "full set of shipping documents," which, in conjunction with the F.O.B. vessel term, was understood by the parties as requiring a clean on board bill of lading.

Pursuant to the contract Paranapanema delivered 100 bundles, each containing 30 tin ingots and steel-strapped onto wooden pallets, to Ivarans' agent at Santos, Agencia de Vapores Grieg, S.A. (Grieg), which maintains a terminal located about 5 kilometers from the dock where cargo would be loaded onto Ivarans' ship. Grieg acknowledged receipt of the bundles on December 29, 1983. Grieg stuffed the 100 bundles into four 20-foot containers at its terminal, as follows:

Container No. NICU 901692 35 bundles

Container No. NICU 703002 35 bundles

Container No. IVLU 904540 9 bundles

Container No. IVLU 902420 21 bundles

The containerization was carried out "at ship's convenience", to which Berisford did not object. Clause 6 of the bill of lading later issued by Ivarans authorized the carrier to stow goods "as received or, at Carrier's option, by means of containers or similar articles of transport used to consolidate goods".

After stuffing of each container its doors were closed, locked and sealed. On January 3, 1984, the containers were transported by Grieg to a Brazilian government-controlled storage yard located near the loading dock. Upon delivery of the containers to that yard they appeared, from the sound and handling of the trucks used to transport them, to be loaded, not empty. The government storage yard issued receipts indicating weights approximately equaling those listed on the shipping documents. At that point the seals and locks appeared unchanged.

On January 4, 1984, the containers were removed from the yard and loaded by stevedores aboard the vessel. On the same date Grieg, acting on behalf of Ivarans and

---

2. F.O.B. or Free on Board "means that title to property passes from the seller to buyer at the designated FOB point." 10 *Williston on Contracts*, § 1079A, at 94 n. 6 (3d ed. 1967). Since the vessel was designated as the FOB point in this case title to the goods was to pass when the goods were loaded on board the ship. *See id.*, § 1080A, at 109-10 (Standard American Foreign Trade Definitions).

the Master of the S/S Salvador, issued a clean on board bill of lading stating that the ship had received "100 bundles steel strapped on wooden skids containing 3000 refined tin ingots, 'Mamore' brand, with a minimum purity of 99.9%". The gross weight was stated on the bill to be "50,647" kilos and the net weight as "49,845" kilos. Par. 3 of the conditions on the back side of the bill of lading provided that the provisions of COGSA would apply throughout "the entire time the goods [would be] in the carrier's custody, including the period of carrier's custody before loading on and after discharge from the ship". The bill further stated that unless a higher value had been declared in writing prior to delivery and inserted in the bill, the $500 limit per package specified by COGSA would govern the carrier's liability. *See* note 1, *supra*.

Upon the loading of the four containers aboard the ship, neither Ivarans nor its agent Grieg verified the contents or made a tally of the 100 bundles represented by the bill of lading to be in the containers. After being loaded aboard the ship, the containers were not shifted from their place of stowage until the ship arrived in New York on January 19, 1984, at the Red Hook Terminal in Brooklyn. There the four containers were discharged on January 20, 1984, and placed on the ground outside Pier 11 to await stripping. On January 24, 1984, Universal Maritime Services, Ivarans' stevedore, opened the four containers by using a bolt cutter or pliers to cut the seals and found that two of them supposed to contain 70 bundles were empty. Before being broken the seals of the containers appeared to be intact, with no evidence of tampering; in fact, the seals were pitted and rusted. Neither the floors of the two containers nor the snow-covered ground around them near Pier 11 revealed any evidence of recent removal of any cargo from the containers. Each bundle would have weighed approximately 1100 lbs.

On January 27, 1984, Berisford wrote U.S. Navigation, Ivarans' New York agent, charging Ivarans with responsibility for the loss of the 70 bundles. On February 7th Mr. K.W. Hansen, a marine surveyor retained by U.S. Navigation to investigate the loss, rendered a written report which stated that in his opinion the "70 missing bundles of tin ingots were never loaded in the two containers."

In the meantime the Mellon Bank in New York, representing Paranapanema, the seller and shipper of the tin ingots, presented to Berisford in accordance with the purchase contract a full set of shipping documents with respect to the 100 bundles of tin ingots purchased by Berisford, including three original on board bills of lading issued by the carrier (Ivarans), Paranapanema's invoice, weight and analysis certificates, and a draft in the amount of $662,938.50, payable 45 days after the bill of lading date. Since the papers were in order and complied with the parties' purchase contract Berisford accepted the draft and on February 17, 1984, paid the full amount of the purchase price to the Mellon Bank as collection agent for Paranapanema. In addition, Berisford paid Ivarans' freight charges amounting to $10,101.67.

On August 31, 1984, Berisford commenced the present action, seeking $525,000 damages for the missing cargo. Defendants' answer admitted receipt of the shipment of bundles of tin ingots but denied liability, asserting its rights under COGSA and its bill of lading with respect to the shipment, including COGSA's $500 per package limitation on its liability, and alleging that it acted without any fault or neglect. On February 5, 1985, after the parties had conducted pre-trial discovery, including the taking of depositions Berisford moved for summary judgment, contending that it had paid the purchase price in reliance on Ivarans' representation in its on board bill of lading that the 70 missing bundles had been loaded aboard its ship, that it was committed by its purchase contract to pay the purchase price upon the seller's presentation of the shipping documents, and that the defendant carrier's issuance of a clean on board bill of lading when in fact the ship had not received the 70 bundles constituted a "quasi-deviation," depriving the carrier of the benefits of the bill of lading, including its per package limitation on liability. Berisford sought damages in the amount of $483,214.90 plus interest.

Ivarans did not seriously question the probability that the loss of the 70 bundles occurred prior to its loading of the containers aboard its ship in Santos. Indeed, the evidence that the two containers had not been opened after loading and prior to their being found empty upon their arrival in New York (while still in Ivarans' custody) was overwhelming. Ivarans offered no evidence to the contrary. . . . In opposing plaintiff's motion the defendants, in an affidavit of their attorney, Chester D. Hooper, asked that the complaint be dismissed or in the alternative that Ivarans' liability be limited to $500 per bundle.

In an oral bench opinion Judge Goettel . . . granted plaintiff's motion to the extent of awarding it judgment in the sum of $35,000, from which both parties appeal.

DISCUSSION

The central question raised by this appeal is whether a carrier that issues a clean on board bill of lading erroneously stating that certain goods have been received on board when they have not been so loaded should be precluded from limiting its liability pursuant to an agreement binding the parties to the terms of §4(5) of COGSA, 46 U.S.C. §1304(5). For the purpose of resolving this issue a brief review of pertinent admiralty law principles is helpful.

As we recently reaffirmed in *Allied Chemical International Corp. v. Companhia de Navegocao Lloyd Brasileiro*, 775 F.2d 476, 478, 481–82 (1985), a negotiable or order bill of lading is a fundamental and vital pillar of international trade and commerce, indispensable to the conduct and financing of business involving the sale and transportation of goods between parties located at a distance from one another. It constitutes an acknowledgement by a carrier that it has received the described goods for shipment. It is also a contract of carriage. As a document of title it controls the possession of the goods themselves. It has been said that the bill and the goods become one and the same, with the goods being "locked up in the bill." *Id.* 96. As the court stated in *Pollard v. Reardon*, 65 F. 848, 852 (1st Cir. 1895),

> "In the developments of commerce and commercial credits the bill of lading has come to represent the property, but with greater facility of negotiation, transfer, and delivery than the property itself. . . . And it has become so universal and necessary a factor in mercantile credits that the law should

make good what the bill of lading thus holds out. There is every reason found in the law of equitable estoppel and in sound public policy for holding, and no injustice is involved in holding, that, if one of two must suffer, it should be he who voluntarily puts out of his hands an assignable bill of lading, rather than he who innocently advances value thereon."

. . . .

The carrier's responsibility for issuance of false bills of lading was thoroughly considered by this court in *Olivier Straw Goods Corporation v. Osaka Shosen Kaisha*, which was the subject of two appeals over a period of four years, 27 F.2d 129 (2d Cir. 1928) (*Olivier I*), aff'd after remand, 47 F.2d 878 (2d Cir.) (*Olivier II*). In that case, which was remarkably similar to the present one, the shipper delivered 18 cases of hemp to the carrier at its Yokohama dock for shipment by steamer to New York. The carrier issued and delivered to the shipper a bill of lading representing that the cases had been loaded on the ship Alaska Maru when in fact they had not been loaded because that ship had been diverted elsewhere due to an earthquake. The cases of hemp, which had been placed by the carrier in an unprotected dockside shed, were lost as a result of looting. Relying on the bill of lading and other shipping papers forwarded to it by the shipper, the purchaser's bank accepted and paid the shipper's invoice. The purchaser then sued the carrier for the value of the hemp. In an opinion by Judge Augustus Hand, concurred in by Judges Learned Hand and Swan, the court held the carrier liable for the full value of the goods described in the bill of lading, stating:

> "The bill of lading recited that the goods were shipped in apparent good order and condition. That statement was a warranty that they were so shipped, and the libelant, as indorsee of the bill of lading, acquired the direct obligation of the carrier and with it the right to sue. . . .

> "The warranty that the goods were on board was broken by the failure to ship them, and that breach . . . deprived the carrier of the right to invoke the clauses limiting liability. In *The Sarnia*, 278 F.459 (1921), where the cargo had been improperly stowed on deck, we held that the valuation clauses in the bill of lading did not serve to limit damages. We said, at page 461 of 278 F.: 'The general rule undoubtedly is that, if the shipowner commits a breach of the contract of affreightment which goes to the essence of the contract, he is not entitled after such breach to invoke the provisions of the contract which are in his favor.'

> "Certainly a breach like the one here, which arose from a failure to ship the cargo at all, with its consequent loss or destruction on land, was no less fundamental than a deviation in the voyage, or than stowage of cargo on deck contrary to agreement, or than misdelivery of goods. In all such circumstances valuation clauses in the bill of lading have been held inoperative to relieve the shipowner. . . ." *Olivier II, supra*, at 879–80.

Although we have declined to extend full liability in some contexts that have been likened to deviations or "quasi-deviations" in a voyage, . . . we have steadfastly adhered to the result reached in *Olivier II* and have cited the case with approval for the proposition that the $500 per package limitation of liability may not be invoked by a carrier that has issued an on board bill of lading erroneously representing that goods were loaded aboard its ship, regardless whether or not the carrier acted fraudulently. *Elgie & Co. v. SS "S.A. Nederburg"*, 599 F.2d 1177, 1181 (2d Cir. 1979). It is true that *Elgie & Co.* involved a shipment from the United States governed by the Pomerene Act, 49 U.S.C. § 81 *et seq.*, which does not contain limitation of liability provisions. However, the court took pains to point out that it did not base its holding on that distinction but on what it conceived to be "established doctrines of admiralty law", citing *Olivier II.* Similarly we recognized that it was "the common law rule" that such a fundamental misstatement in a bill of lading need not be fraudulent or intentional for liability to ensue. 599 F.2d at 1180.

The *Olivier II* ruling represents just as sound public policy today as it did in 1931. Whether one likens the carrier's issuance of a false bill of lading with respect to its loading of cargo to a "deviation," a "breach of warranty" or a representation which it must be "estopped" to deny, its adverse impact on trade and on reliance on bills as an essential method of facilitating trade is serious. Title to the goods usually passes from the seller to the buyer when the seller delivers the goods to the carrier and the carrier or its agent issues a bill. In the past, on board bills, signifying that the goods had been loaded on board the ship, were generally required. More recently, "received for shipment" bills, which indicate merely that the carrier has received the goods, are sometimes used. *See* 10 *Williston, supra,* at § 1078A, pp. 83–87.

In this case, an on board bill was clearly required by the parties. When the proper bill issues, the seller then ceases to assume any risk of loss or damage. The carrier, by issuing the bill, enables the seller to collect full payment of the purchase price from the buyer since presentation of the bill to the buyer assures it that the seller has fulfilled its commitment to ship the goods and obligates the buyer to pay for them. Presentation of an on board bill also serves to satisfy the buyer that the goods have not been stolen or lost while in the custody of the carrier prior to loading, an interval during which the seller bears the risk of any loss in any transaction requiring such a bill. If, instead, the buyer were free to question the accuracy of the bill upon presentation, the entire structure would be weakened as a method of carrying out commercial transactions.

. . . .

When a carrier, on the other hand, makes a representation in a bill of lading with respect to *its own conduct* it is properly held to a higher standard since it is reasonably expected to be aware of *its own actions,* including whether or not it has loaded cargo, *Olivier II, supra;* . . . or has loaded the cargo below or above decks. . . . As we stated in *Nichimen Company v. M.V. Farland*, 462 F.2d 319, 330 (2d Cir. 1972), "the duty to load, stow, and discharge cargo-and the consequences for failing to do so properly-fall upon the ship and her owners." 46 U.S.C. § 1303(2) specifically provides, "The carrier shall properly and carefully *load*, handle, stow, carry, keep, care for, and discharge the goods carried." (Emphasis supplied).

Applying the foregoing principles to the present case, we conclude that the defendants must be held responsible for the full value of the lost cargo at the time of shipment in Santos and cannot invoke the $500 per package limitation of liability provision of § 4(5) of COGSA, 46 U.S.C. § 1304(5). The carrier here, having received 100 bundles of tin ingots from the shipper in Santos, issued a false F.O.B. bill of lading with respect to its own conduct, warranting that on January 4, 1984, it had loaded 100 bundles on its ship when in fact it had loaded only 30. The bill of lading, whether or not intentionally false, enabled the shipper to collect from Berisford, the buyer, the full purchase price for 100 bundles. If the carrier had disclosed that 70 bundles had not been loaded, Berisford would have been entitled to refuse payment and the loss would have fallen on the seller of the goods as required by the conditions of the sales contract. The carrier's misrepresentation therefore amounted to a fundamental breach going to the very essence of its contract and precluding it from invoking those provisions extending the limitation of liability terms of § 4(5) of COGSA to the period when the goods were on shore.

Defendants cannot escape responsibility on the ground that the four containers into which it claims that it had placed the bundles after receipt from the shipper were locked and sealed at the time when the containers were loaded aboard its ship, the S.S. Salvador. It is undisputed that the defendant received from the shipper the 100 separate bundles and that for its own convenience it placed them in the four containers. It was thereafter responsible for verifying the contents before loading the containers and issuing a clean on board bill of lading. The weight of the missing 70 bundles of tin ingots was approximately 78,885 lbs. Even if opening of the containers posed difficulties, at the very least the carrier owed a duty to verify the weight of the containers at shipside before they were placed aboard its ship and before it stated that they contained 100 bundles of tin ingots weighing the equivalent of 50,647 kilos or 111,656 lbs., which would have been 78,885 lbs. in excess of the weight of the containers actually loaded.

. . . .

Lastly, Ivarans contends that since the theft of the ingots occurred while the property was in the temporary custody of the Brazilian government it is exempted from liability by § 4(2)(q) of COGSA, 46 U.S.C. § 1304(2)(q), which was incorporated in the parties' contract. Section 4(2)(q) exempts the carrier from liability for damage or loss "arising without the actual fault and privity of the carrier and without the fault or neglect of the agents or servants of the carrier, but the burden of proof shall be on the person claiming the benefit of this exception. . . ." The argument misconceives the nature of Berisford's claim. Its suit is not based on the theft of the ingots or on Ivarans' negligence but on the carrier's false representation that it loaded the 70 bundles on its ship. Regardless whether some third party stole the ingots, the carrier here was obligated to state truthfully what it had loaded. If the carrier had truthfully stated what it had loaded on the ship, Berisford would not have been required to pay the purchase price for the 70 bundles of unloaded ingots which it had contracted to purchase. As between the purchaser, which could not have verified the accuracy of the carrier's representation as to the number of bundles loaded, and the carrier, the carrier is the party that must be held responsible for loss resulting from the falsity of its warranty that the goods had been loaded when in fact it had not put them aboard its ship.

Our holding leaves intact the principle that, once goods are aboard the ship as represented, a carrier may be responsible for misdescription of the apparent condition of the goods loaded by it only upon proof of knowledge or intent. *The Carso, supra.* We hold simply that when a carrier misrepresents its own conduct in loading goods aboard ship it is responsible for the misrepresentation and may not invoke contract provisions incorporating COGSA's limitations on liability.

The order and judgment of the district court are reversed and the case is remanded to the district court with directions to enter judgment in favor of Berisford in the sum of its full damages, plus that portion of freight and handling charges attributable to the lost bundles, and costs and interest from January 20, 1984.

2. The Pomerene Act (Federal Uniform Bills of Lading Act)

a. Overview

This 1916 federal statute prescribes the basic rights and duties that arise from bills of lading used in interstate commerce, including international shipments from the United States. The act provides rules for both non-negotiable ("straight") and negotiable bills of lading but focuses upon ensuring the negotiability of order bills by detailing the rights and obligations that arise from their issuance, transfer and possession. The potential liabilities of carriers issuing order bills are also addressed. Pay particular attention to provisions creating carrier disclaimers and estoppel.

b. Selected Provisions of the Pomerene Act (49 U.S.C. Ch. 801[8])

§ 80101. Definitions

In this chapter—

(1) "consignee" means the person named in a bill of lading as the person to whom the goods are to be delivered.

(2) "consignor" means the person named in a bill of lading as the person from whom the goods have been received for shipment.

(3) "goods" means merchandise or personal property that has been, is being, or will be transported.

(4) "holder" means a person having possession of, and a property right in, a bill of lading.

---

8. https://www.gpo.gov/fdsys/pkg/USCODE-2010-title49/html/USCODE-2010-title49 -subtitleX-chap801.htm.

(5) "order" means an order by indorsement on a bill of lading.

(6) "purchase" includes taking by mortgage or pledge.

§ 80102. Application

This chapter applies to a bill of lading when the bill is issued by a common carrier for the transportation of goods—

(1) between a place in the District of Columbia and another place in the District of Columbia;

(2) between a place in a territory or possession of the United States and another place in the same territory or possession;

(3) between a place in a State and a place in another State;

(4) between a place in a State and a place in the same State through another State or a foreign country; or

(5) from a place in a State to a place in a foreign country.

§ 80103. Negotiable and nonnegotiable bills

(a) Negotiable bills.—

(1) A bill of lading is negotiable if the bill—

(A) states that the goods are to be delivered to the order of a consignee; and

(B) does not contain on its face an agreement with the shipper that the bill is not negotiable.

(2) Inserting in a negotiable bill of lading the name of a person to be notified of the arrival of the goods—

(A) does not limit its negotiability; and

(B) is not notice to the purchaser of the goods of a right the named person has to the goods.

(b) Nonnegotiable bills.—

(1) A bill of lading is nonnegotiable if the bill states that the goods are to be delivered to a consignee. The indorsement of a nonnegotiable bill does not—

(A) make the bill negotiable; or

(B) give the transferee any additional right.

(2) A common carrier issuing a nonnegotiable bill of lading must put "nonnegotiable" or "not negotiable" on the bill. This paragraph does not apply to an informal memorandum or acknowledgment.

§ 80104. Form and requirements for negotiation

(a) General rules.—

(1) A negotiable bill of lading may be negotiated by indorsement. An indorsement may be made in blank or to a specified person. If the goods are

deliverable to the order of a specified person, then the bill must be indorsed by that person.

(2) A negotiable bill of lading may be negotiated by delivery when the common carrier, under the terms of the bill, undertakes to deliver the goods to the order of a specified person and that person or a subsequent indorsee has indorsed the bill in blank.

§ 80105. Title and rights affected by negotiation

(a) Title. — When a negotiable bill of lading is negotiated —

(1) the person to whom it is negotiated acquires the title to the goods that —

(A) the person negotiating the bill had the ability to convey to a purchaser in good faith for value; and

(B) the consignor and consignee had the ability to convey to such a purchaser; and

(2) the common carrier issuing the bill becomes obligated directly to the person to whom the bill is negotiated to hold possession of the goods under the terms of the bill the same as if the carrier had issued the bill to that person.

§ 80110. Duty to deliver goods

(a) General rules. — Except to the extent a common carrier establishes an excuse provided by law, the carrier must deliver goods covered by a bill of lading on demand of the consignee named in a nonnegotiable bill or the holder of a negotiable bill for the goods when the consignee or holder —

(1) offers in good faith to satisfy the lien of the carrier on the goods;

(2) has possession of the bill and, if a negotiable bill, offers to indorse and give the bill to the carrier; and

(3) agrees to sign, on delivery of the goods, a receipt for delivery if requested by the carrier.

(b) Persons to whom goods may be delivered. — Subject to section 80111 of this title, a common carrier may deliver the goods covered by a bill of lading to —

(1) a person entitled to their possession;

(2) the consignee named in a nonnegotiable bill; or

(3) a person in possession of a negotiable bill if —

(A) the goods are deliverable to the order of that person; or

(B) the bill has been indorsed to that person or in blank by the consignee or another indorsee.

§ 80111. Liability for delivery of goods

(a) General rules. — A common carrier is liable for damages to a person having title to, or right to possession of, goods when —

(1) the carrier delivers the goods to a person not entitled to their possession unless the delivery is authorized under section 80110(b)(2) or (3) of this title;

(2) the carrier makes a delivery under section 80110(b)(2) or (3) of this title after being requested by or for a person having title to, or right to possession of, the goods not to make the delivery; or

(3) at the time of delivery under section 80110(b)(2) or (3) of this title, the carrier has information it is delivering the goods to a person not entitled to their possession.

§ 80113. Liability for nonreceipt, misdescription, and improper loading

(a) Liability for nonreceipt and misdescription. — Except as provided in this section, a common carrier issuing a bill of lading is liable for damages caused by nonreceipt by the carrier of any part of the goods by the date shown in the bill or by failure of the goods to correspond with the description contained in the bill. The carrier is liable to the owner of goods transported under a nonnegotiable bill (subject to the right of stoppage in transit) or to the holder of a negotiable bill if the owner or holder gave value in good faith relying on the description of the goods in the bill or on the shipment being made on the date shown in the bill.

(b) Nonliability of carriers. — A common carrier issuing a bill of lading is not liable under subsection (a) of this section —

(1) when the goods are loaded by the shipper;

(2) when the bill —

(A) describes the goods in terms of marks or labels, or in a statement about kind, quantity, or condition; or

(B) is qualified by "contents or condition of contents of packages unknown", "said to contain", "shipper's weight, load, and count", or words of the same meaning; and

(3) to the extent the carrier does not know whether any part of the goods were received or conform to the description.

(c) Liability for improper loading. — A common carrier issuing a bill of lading is not liable for damages caused by improper loading if —

(1) the shipper loads the goods; and

(2) the bill contains the words "shipper's weight, load, and count", or words of the same meaning indicating the shipper loaded the goods.

(d) Carrier's duty to determine kind, quantity, and number. —

(1) When bulk freight is loaded by a shipper that makes available to the common carrier adequate facilities for weighing the freight, the carrier must determine the kind and quantity of the freight within a reasonable time after

receiving the written request of the shipper to make the determination. In that situation, inserting the words "shipper's weight" or words of the same meaning in the bill of lading has no effect.

(2) When goods are loaded by a common carrier, the carrier must count the packages of goods, if package freight, and determine the kind and quantity, if bulk freight. In that situation, inserting in the bill of lading or in a notice, receipt, contract, rule, or tariff, the words "shipper's weight, load, and count" or words indicating that the shipper described and loaded the goods, has no effect except for freight concealed by packages.

For additional information consult the entire text of the Pomerene Act.[9]

c. Case Law Interpreting the Pomerene Act & COGSA: Estoppel

i. Industria Nacional Del Papel v. M/V "Albert F," 730 F.2d 622 (11th Cir. 1984)

Buyer of goods brought in rem action against vessel to recover for nondelivery of goods. The United States District Court for the Southern District of Florida, Joe Eaton, Chief Judge, entered judgment in favor of buyer, and vessel appealed. The Court of Appeals, Hatchett, Circuit Judge, held that: (1) vessel was "carrier" within meaning of Carriage of Goods by Sea Act and Pomerene Act; (2) vessel was liable for nondelivery of goods under Pomerene Act; (3) statements in bill of lading were insufficient to escape liability for nondelivery of goods under Pomerene Act; (4) loading of cargo on vessel created maritime lien enforceable in rem; (5) mistake concerning parties' opinions concerning duration of litigation was insufficient to compel vessel owner to post additional security; and (6) buyer could not obtain in personam judgment against vessel owner in excess of amount of security posted by vessel owner to secure vessel's release from arrest.

Affirmed.

HATCHETT, Circuit Judge:

In this action, we must determine whether a vessel may be held liable in rem for non-delivery of its cargo described in a clean on board bill of lading. We affirm the district court which held the vessel liable in rem because it was estopped from impeaching the bill of lading.

On January 9, 1979, the appellee, Industria Nacional Del Papel (Induspapel), ordered 1,500 metric tons of soft wood kraft pulp from Sanca Steel Corporation (Sanca), costing $569,790. In February, 1979, the cargo was loaded aboard the appellant vessel, the M/V ALBERT F, in southern Florida, and the vessel sailed for the Dominican Republic. On the same date, Induspapel paid Sanca.

---

9. http://www.csb.uncw.edu/people/eversp/classes/BLA361/Intl%20Law/Additional%20Research/Federal%20Bill%20of%20Lading%20Act.pdf.

The M/V ALBERT F arrived in Port Haina, Dominican Republic, on February 19, 1979, without the cargo specified in the bill of lading. Instead, it outturned 505 bales of wastepaper. Induspapel received practically worthless cargo, and sued the vessel and its claimant owner, Fairwind Container Express (Fairwind) to recover the amount it paid.

Claiming to be acting on behalf of Induspapel, Sanca originally arrested the M/V "ALBERT F." Subsequently, the vessel was released upon Fairwind's posting of $344,500 as security, and Induspapel was substituted for Sanca as the proper plaintiff. The district court ruled for Induspapel holding that the vessel was estopped from impeaching the clean bill of lading, and therefore, was liable in rem for the nondelivery of the cargo specified in the bill of lading. The M/V ALBERT F contends the district court erred in holding that it was estopped from impeaching the bill of lading and in finding it liable in rem. Induspapel cross-appeals claiming that the district court erred in reducing Induspapel's prejudgment interest award and in denying it an increase in the amount of security posted by Fairwind.

A. Estoppel

The Pomerene Act, 49 U.S.C.A. § 81-124 (West 1951), applies to all "[b]ills of lading issued by any common carrier for the transportation of goods . . . from a place in a State to a place in a foreign country . . . ." 49 U.S.C.A. § 81. The Pomerene Act fails to define "carrier," but the Carriage of Goods By Sea Act (COGSA), 46 U.S.C.A. § 1300-1315 (West 1975), defines "carrier" as, "the owner or the charterer who enters into a contract of carriage with a shipper." 46 U.S.C.A. § 1301 (West 1975). "Since COGSA was enacted against the backdrop of the Pomerene Act," we will utilize COGSA's definition of "carrier" to determine whether the M/V ALBERT F is a "carrier" within the meaning of the Pomerene Act.

The Fifth Circuit has held that a vessel is a "carrier" as defined in section 1301 of COGSA where (a) the ship transported and discharged cargo; (b) the bill of lading was issued for the master; and (c) no contractual relationship existed absolving the ship and its owner from liability for the cargo. These factual circumstances exist in this case, and the M/V ALBERT F is a "carrier" within the meaning of COGSA and the Pomerene Act. Since the vessel was a common carrier transporting cargo from the United States to a foreign country, the Pomerene Act applies to this case. 49 U.S.C.A. § 81.

Section 22 of the Pomerene Act provides that a carrier issuing a bill of lading will be liable "[to] the holder of an order bill, who has given value in good faith, relying upon the description therein of the goods, . . . for damages caused by the nonreceipt by the carrier of all or part of the goods upon or prior to the date therein shown, or their failure to correspond to their description thereof in the bill at the time of its issue." [49 U.S.C.A.§ 102]. This provision codified the estoppel principal which held "carriers liable to consignees and good faith assignees for value for misrepresentations in their bill of lading." *Elgie & Co. v. SS "S.A. Nederburg,"* 599 F.2d 1177, 1179 (2d Cir. 1979).

Title 49 U.S.C. § 102 holds the carrier liable for goods receipted for by him but not actually received. *Elgie*, 599 F.2d at 1179 . . . . The M/V ALBERT F received certain goods and issued a bill of lading describing 854 tons of soft wood kraft pulp, but the goods received did not conform to the goods described in the bill of lading. The vessel, therefore, is liable for the non-delivery of the goods pursuant to 49 U.S.C. § 102.[2]

The M/V ALBERT F contends, however, that the exculpatory provision of the Pomerene Act, 49 U.S.C. § 101, exempts it from liability.[3] The vessel claims that certain words contained in the bill of lading free them from liability.[4] The bill of lading declares that "particulars [are] furnished by shipper;" the bill also states:

> "The shipper, consignee and owner of the goods and the holder of this bill of lading agree to be bound by all the stipulations, exceptions, and conditions stated herein whether written, printed, stamped, or incorporated on the front or reverse side hereof, as fully as if they were all signed by such shipper, consignee, owner, or holder."

These statements are insufficient to escape liability under 49 U.S.C. § 101. The words "particulars furnished by shipper" fail to relieve the carrier of liability under COGSA, and therefore, they do not exempt the M/V ALBERT F from liability under the Pomerene Act. . . . Since COGSA and the Pomerene Act protect the holder in due course from misleading bills of lading, statements insufficient to avoid liability under COGSA should not be permitted to avoid liability under the Pomerene Act. Moreover, the words "particulars furnished by shipper" fail to indicate that the shipper loaded the cargo, because COGSA presumes the shipper will furnish the particulars placed in the bill of lading by the carrier. 46 U.S.C.A. § 1303(3) (West 1975).

The preprinted paragraph in the bill of lading also fails to satisfy the standard in 49 U.S.C.§ 101. The paragraph does not indicate that the shipper loaded the cargo, and therefore, such an attempted disclaimer of liability is ineffective. . . .

ii. Portland Fish v. States Steamship Company, 510 F.2d 628 (9th Cir. 1974)

Pursuant to its agreement to purchase frozen tuna from a seller in the Philippines, Portland Fish Company, the plaintiff, deposited an irrevocable letter of credit with

---

2. A holder in due course cannot recover from a carrier under [§ 102], unless he has relied on the bill of lading. . . . Induspapel relied on the bill of lading. Only after receiving the bill of lading did it pay Sanca. *See also, T.J. Stevenson & Co. v. 81,193 Bags of Flour*, 629 F.2d 338, 373-74 (5th Cir. 1980).

3. Title 49 U.S.C.§ 101 states in pertinent part:
The carrier may also by inserting in the bill of lading the words 'Shippers weight, load, and count,' or other words of like purport, [to] indicate that the goods were loaded by the shipper and their description of them made by him; and if such statement be true, the carrier shall not be liable for damages caused by the improper loading or by the nonreceipt or by the misdescription of the goods described in the bill of lading . . . .

4. While the words "shippers weight, load, and count" are absent from the bill of lading, the statute provides for the inclusion of "other words of like purport" to avoid liability for the nonreceipt of goods. 49 U.S.C. § 101.

a Manila bank, authorizing payment to seller of $562.50 per short ton of fish upon presentation of a bill of lading.

Thereafter, seller delivered some fish to States Steamship Company, the defendant (hereafter Carrier), for carriage and received from the latter its bill of lading. Carrier verified by piece count the number of fish received, but, having no facilities for weighing them, accepted seller's weight. This information was reflected in the bill as follows:

"SAID TO BE:	SAID TO WEIGH:
IN BULK 30 SHORT TONS	60000
CLIPPER YELLOW	Lbs.
FIN TUNA GILLED & GUTTED	
SAID TO CONTAIN:	519 PIECES"

Immediately underneath appeared this endorsement:

"One Lot frozen fish said to contain 519 pieces said to weigh 60,000 lbs., freight charges to be adjusted on basis of properly certified outturn weights when such outturn weights are found to be three (3%) percent or more in excess of or under Bill of Lading weights."

Seller then presented its sight draft with bill of lading and supporting documents to the Manila bank, which paid him for 30 short tons of tuna. However, Carrier, upon reaching its destination, outturned 580 fish, which weighed only 12.825 short tons.

Plaintiff commenced this suit in admiralty to recover from Carrier the amount of the difference between the sum paid to Seller against the letter of credit and the value of the cargo outturned. Plaintiff's theory was that Carrier was estopped to impeach the weight shown in its bill of lading. The district court rejected plaintiff's contention and ruled that, since the Carrier had outturned all of the fish received from shipper, plaintiff should take nothing on its claim against Carrier and that Carrier should recover (on its counterclaim) against plaintiff the value of the 61 fish delivered plaintiff by mistake. Plaintiff appeals from the ensuing judgment. We reverse.

Ocean bills of lading in foreign trade are given effect subject to the provisions of the Carriage of Goods by Sea Act (COGSA), 46 U.S.C. §§ 1300-1315. Carrier's primary contention, upheld by the district court, is that the provision in Section 3, subsection 4, of COGSA, making a carrier's bill of lading "prima facie evidence" of the receipt of the goods, connotes a rebuttable presumption merely, and thus precludes estoppel. We disagree.

This circuit, as well as others, has consistently held the doctrine of estoppel applicable in cases arising under COGSA and its predecessor, the Harter Act. *Daido Line v. Thomas P. Gonzalez Corp.*, 299 F.2d 669, 673 n. 9 (9th Cir. 1962); *Demsey &*

Associates v. S.S. Sea Star, 461 F.2d 1009, 1015 (2d Cir. 1972); *Cummins Sales & Service, Inc. v. London & Overseas Insurance Co.*, 476 F.2d 498, 500, 501 (5th Cir. 1973). A good discussion of the early development of the estoppel doctrine as it pertains to bills of lading is contained in District Judge Woolsey's opinion in *The Carso*, 43 F.2d 736 (S.D.N.Y.1930).

COGSA was enacted against the backdrop of the Federal Bill of Lading (Pomerene) Act of 1916, 49 U.S.C. §§ 81–124. Section 22 of the Pomerene Act, 49 U.S.C. § 102, amounts to a codification of the estoppel principle and would be dispositive here, were it not for the inapplicability of the Pomerene Act to bills of lading issued in foreign ports. Nevertheless, the proviso contained in section 3(4) of COGSA, 46 U.S.C. § 1303(4), expressly prohibits a construction of COGSA which would limit or repeal the effect of the Pomerene Act, and the legislative history of COGSA evidences a congressional concern for the continued prevention of such abuses as the Pomerene Act was designed to eliminate.

We consider it highly unlikely that Congress intended that carriers be held to different standards of care in the issuance of bills of lading covered by the Act, depending solely on the location of the port of issuance, particularly where one of the primary purposes of COGSA was the establishment of uniformity in bills of lading and the definition by law of the rights and duties of water carriers in foreign trade.

Moreover, it is well recognized that one of Congress' objectives in enacting COGSA was generally to enhance the currency and negotiability of ocean bills of lading. *See, e.g., Daido Line v. Thomas P. Gonzalez Corp.*, supra, at 673 n. 9; *Spanish American Skin Co. v. The Ferngulf*, 242 F.2d 551, 553 (2d Cir. 1957); *Kupfermann v. United States*, 227 F.2d 348, 350 (2d Cir. 1955); *George F. Pettinos, Inc. v. American Export Lines*, 68 F.Supp. 759, 764 (E.D.Pa.1947), *aff'd*, 159 F.2d 247 (3d Cir. 1947). As stated in Gilmore & Black, The Law of Admiralty (1957), at 125-126:

> "COGSA allows a freedom of contracting out of its terms, but only in the direction of *increasing* the shipowner's liabilities, and never in the direction of diminishing them. This apparent onesidedness is a commonsense recognition of the inequality in bargaining power which both Harter and COGSA were designed to redress, and of the fact that one of the great objectives of both Acts is to prevent the impairment of the value and negotiability of the ocean bill of lading. Obviously, the latter result can never ensue from the increase of the carrier's duties." (Emphasis in original.)

The continued vitality of the estoppel doctrine clearly serves this significant congressional objective.

It should perhaps be noted that COGSA expressly provides the means by which carriers, in case of doubt concerning the goods, may protect themselves and avoid liability if they choose to do so. Thus (to reiterate) section 3 contains the provision "[t]hat no carrier, master, or agent of the carrier, shall be bound to state or show in the bill of lading any marks, number, quantity, or weight which he has reasonable ground for suspecting not accurately to represent the goods actually received, or which he has had no reasonable means of checking." Accordingly, under the Pomerene Act or, in the case of inbound bills, under the doctrine of estoppel, such statements as the carrier does make become conclusive as against a holder in due course.

Of course we recognize that the party urging estoppel against the carrier must demonstrate that he has relied on the description that appears in the bill, for it is elementary that, absent reliance, there can be no estoppel. Thus the doctrine is not applicable in a suit by a shipper against a carrier, or where reliance on the description by a holder for value is not reasonable, or where the holder does not rely on the description at all. But here plaintiff's reliance is manifest and was fully justified. The bill was "clean"—the qualification "said to weigh" did not befoul it.

The judgment is reversed, and the cause is remanded with directions to enter judgment for plaintiff.

ORDER ON REHEARING

On rehearing, several ocean carriers have moved for leave to file briefs amicus curiae. However, it appears that the issues sought to be raised in such briefs concern the possible effect of our decision on the ocean transportation of containerized cargoes—those in sealed "packages" not normally opened and inspected by the carrier at the time he issues a bill of lading. The motions are denied. Since the case before us involves solely a bulk shipment subject to piece count, the questions thus raised will have to wait another day for decision. We intimate no opinion on them. Appellee's petition contains nothing new; the points reiterated have all been covered—in our opinion, correctly—in our earlier opinion.

The petition for rehearing is denied.

Chapter 7

Letters of Credit

A. Overview

This chapter, in two parts, focuses on legal issues surrounding letter of credit financing in documentary sales transactions. Our goal is to understand the legal rights and obligations of the various parties involved in letter of credit financing, particularly the banks. After completing this chapter, you should understand how the documentary letter of credit works and why it is used in international sales of goods. You should understand the primary obligations of the banks that issue or confirm credits and be able to work through the most common legal problems associated with such financing, including potential liabilities when events go wrong.

The chapter is organized around two principles central to these issues. The first, commonly referred to as the doctrine of strict compliance, involves the standard under which banks examine documents required by the letter of credit. This doctrine, and related bank obligations, is addressed in Part One below. Part Two examines the "independence principle," which provides that the bank's obligations under the letter of credit are distinct from, and independent of, the underlying sales transaction. The standard aphorism is that banks deal in documents, not in goods.

Part One: The Bank's Obligations and the Doctrine of Strict Compliance

A. Overview

Among other purposes, letters of credit are frequently used as a means for financing international sales of goods, ensuring payment by a credit-worthy party. A letter of credit works well within a documentary sales transaction and operates in a similar fashion. Indeed, since letters of credit used in international sales of goods function strictly through the exchange of documents, they are often called "documentary credits." However, while a letter of credit may be used in documentary sales, letter of credit financing is not required for such transactions. Rather, use of a letter of credit adds costs (banks must be paid) and must be agreed upon as the method of payment in the parties' sales contract. Alternative means for secure financing are explored briefly at the end of the chapter.

In a documentary export credit, a bank has essentially promised the *buyer/importer ("customer" or "account party")* that *the bank ("issuing bank")* will pay the *seller/exporter ("beneficiary")* upon the presentment of specified documents. If the seller presents documents that conform precisely to those specified under the credit, then the bank will pay the contract price, typically by honoring a <u>draft</u>[1] (also known as a <u>bill of exchange</u>[2] — sample included in link) drawn up by the seller. The bank's obligation to pay is primary and does not depend upon the wishes of the buyer or conformity of the goods. It is a promise to pay independent of the party's performance of contractual obligations, except as to the presentment of the required documents themselves.

Payment can be immediate (sight draft) or at a specified later date. Since the seller is relying upon the bank's promise to pay, the seller has essentially replaced the buyer with a well-known, credit-worthy source for payment, the bank. Under standard practices typically required, the credit is "irrevocable." Thus, the buyer will be unable to stop the bank from paying even if the buyer changes its mind or becomes insolvent. (Unless the buyer is a known credit-worthy customer of the bank, the bank will typically only issue the credit once buyer has deposited sufficient funds under the bank's control.) In essence, the buyer arranges in a letter of credit for the bank's independent and irrevocable promise to pay the seller, if the seller produces the documents required by the credit. Because documentation is so critical, international banking standards require that the documents "strictly comply" with the letter of credit. This standard, which is more fully explored below, also makes the bank's role relatively ministerial, efficient and unambiguous.

The documents typically required by a credit, at least on their face, tend to demonstrate the seller's performance of the sales contract. The bill of lading, for example, gives the buyer some assurance that the seller has shipped goods without apparent damage roughly corresponding to the contract (recall the limited information contained in bill of lading descriptions of goods, as reviewed in Chapter 6). The bank's promise to pay the seller, however, is not dependent in any way upon actual performance of the underlying sales contract. Disputes over performance, including delivery of non-conforming goods, are not grounds for the bank to dishonor the credit. The

---

1. http://www.creditmanagementworld.com/letterofcredit/lcinternationaldrafts.html.

2. http://www.shareyouressays.com/112069/9-essential-elements-of-a-bill-of-exchange-with-specimens.

bank pays based on the presentation of documents, not upon the fact or proof of actual contractual performance.

This separation of the bank's obligations from the sales contract, often described as the "independence principle," facilitates trade not only by easing the seller's risk of an insolvent buyer (since the seller now has the bank's independent promise to pay) but also by rendering the bank's obligation to pay independent of any disputes about the underlying sales contract. Cost effective and efficient financing through banks would be nearly impossible if made contingent upon proof that the seller had performed to buyer's satisfaction. The independence principle and exceptions to it are explored in Part Two of this chapter.

If the seller distrusts the buyer's bank, or prefers to avoid potential disputes in a foreign jurisdiction (in case the issuing bank fails to pay), she may seek to add another payment obligation from a "confirming" bank. A confirming bank, which normally would be known to the seller and located in the seller's jurisdiction, adds its own independent promise to pay the seller upon presentment of the documents called for in the credit. Now the seller can be assured of payment by a credit-worthy and reliable source located in his own jurisdiction, as well as the independent payment obligations of the issuing bank and buyer.

Since the bank's obligation to pay is independent from actual performance of the sales contract, the letter of credit arrangement leaves the buyer still facing the prospect of contractual breach by the seller, particularly delivery of non-conforming goods. The buyer's protection here, just as in a documentary sales transaction, lies in the choice of documentation required for payment under the credit. A clean, "shipped on-board" bill of lading assures the buyer that cargo has been loaded on the carrier's vessel for shipment. As explored in Chapter Six, however, representations about the goods in the bill of lading are typically limited and ultimately derived from the seller. The buyer cannot generally know from the bill of lading that the goods shipped actually conform to the sales contract specifications. Given these limits, the buyer would prefer more definitive assurances that the seller has performed. Other documents, such as commercial invoices, packing lists, proof of insurance, export documentation and inspection certificates, can provide these additional performance assurances. Such documents are, therefore, commonly called for by the letter of credit terms. Similarly, documents required for clearing customs,[3] such as a certificate of origin, export license, destination control statement or other specialized certifications, must also be supplied. (Chapter Eleven provides further detail regarding such documentation.)

There are many visual aids on the web tracing out the typical steps required in a simple documentary credit. The following diagram, complete with an explanation

---

3. https://www.export.gov/article?id=U-S-Compliance-related-Documents.

of the various stages, was formerly found at the website of <u>Express Trade Capital</u> (expresstradecapital.com):

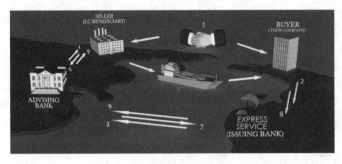

(diagram by Dasha Burns)

Transaction Structure:

1. Your company enters into a purchase agreement with your supplier.

2. Your company completes an Application for an Irrevocable letter of credit with information pertaining to your transaction and then submits it to Express Service for processing.

3. The letter of credit is usually issued within 24 hours of the time we receive your completed application. Upon issuance, the Issuing Bank sends the letter of credit to the Advising Bank electronically.

4. The Advising bank establishes the authenticity of the letter of credit and informs the Beneficiary (i.e., your supplier) that it has been received.

5. Your supplier produces and ships goods to your company against the letter of credit.

6. The Supplier / Beneficiary presents the Documents to the Advising Bank for payment under the letter of credit.

[Author's note: the Advising Bank does not examine the documents nor pay—it acts merely as a conduit.]

7. The Advising bank sends the Documents to the Issuing bank which checks to make sure they conform to the terms of the letter of credit.

8. Your company pays Express Service for the amount drawn under the letter of credit or has previously made arrangements for extended credit terms.

9. Express Service through the Issuing Bank releases the Documents to your company and the Issuing Bank wires the funds to your Supplier through its Advising Bank.

The "advising bank" described above serves precisely the function implied by its label—it notifies the seller/beneficiary of the credit and facilitates the process. An advising bank does not, however, incur any obligation to pay under the letter of credit.

This bank might, for a fee, take on such an obligation by adding its confirmation and thereupon become a "confirming bank."

It is also common to find the term "nominated" bank in this mix. The nominated bank is one authorized in the credit to examine the documents and pay — "the bank with which the credit is available or any bank in the case of a credit available with any bank."[4] The credit is "available" at this nominated bank, meaning that the seller may present the documents at that bank. This nominated bank could be the confirming bank, but could also be any bank designated, such as a correspondent bank of the issuer located in the seller's jurisdiction. The nominated bank does not necessarily confirm the credit, since confirmation creates an independent obligation to pay the beneficiary. Note that these various roles are distinct from the question of "negotiation" of the draft, which may involve the bank purchasing the draft at a discount. (*See* Availability and Negotiation: How to Avoid Confusion[5] for a detailed explanation of this distinction.)

For alternative general descriptions of the documentary export credit, you might read one of the following (the first one being somewhat more informative): Export. gov,[6] Crfonline.org,[7] and the ever handy and reliably accurate Wikipedia.[8] You can find sample L/Cs at many websites, including Export.gov[9] (same link as above with accompanying explanations), Letter of Credit.biz,[10] Open World of Learning.com,[11] and GT Risk.com.[12]

The following problem requires you to evaluate bank performance under a typical letter of credit arrangement, focusing on the doctrine of strict compliance.

B. Problem Seven A: Ruff's Bone

1. Facts

On April 1, Kid's Rom, a computer software company located in Atlanta Georgia, sent the following email to the home office of Copykats Inc. in Buenos Aires, Argentina: "We hereby order 20,000 copies of the CD Rom 'Ruff's Bone', Windows 8

---

4. http://www.letterofcredit.biz/Nominated-Bank.html.

5. http://www.tradefinanceconsulting.com/press — articles/availability-and-negotiation -how-to-avoid-confusion.

6. https://www.export.gov/article?id=Letters-of-Credit-and-Documentary-Collection.

7. http://www.crfonline.org/orc/cro/cro-9-1.html.

8. https://en.wikipedia.org/wiki/Letter_of_credit.

9. https://www.export.gov/article?id=Letters-of-Credit-and-Documentary-Collection.

10. http://www.letterofcredit.biz/at_sight_letter_of_credit_sample.html.

11. https://www.google.com/url?sa=t&rct=j&q=&esrc=s&source=web&cd=2&ved =0ahUKEwj7v9C5_7nOAhWFeCYKHb5aBeAQFggiMAE&url=http%3A%2F%2Fwww.openlearn-ingworld.com%2FInternational_Business_Course%2FSection_4%2FSampleLC_6-12-07.pdf&usg =AFQjCNFjlaTNYQxWSpg7zF-KPmAybEYeng&sig2=jdsFORpUGAt9Haa6NC3a1g&cad=rja.

12. http://www.gtrisk.com/Sample_Export_LC.html

compatible, $10.00 each, CIF Savannah Georgia, for delivery about April 15." Co-pykats responded the next day in a return email that stated: "We acknowledge and agree; payment by confirmed, irrevocable letter of credit."

Finding these terms acceptable, Kid's Rom contacted the First Farmers Bank in Atlanta to secure the required letter of credit. Farmers issued an irrevocable letter of credit on April 5, which called for payment of $200,000 to Copykats upon present-ment of "a clean, shipped on-board bill of lading; certificates of origin, inspection and insurance; and, a commercial invoice for '20,000 CD Rom, Windows 8 Edition of Ruff's Bone'." The credit stated that its provisions were "governed by the UCP 600." On April 10, the Banco de Argentina added its confirmation and advised Copykats that the documentary credit had been opened on its behalf.

On April 15, Copykats took 20 cardboard boxes, each containing 1000 CDs, to Big Ships Inc. in Buenos Aires. Big Ships provided Copykats a negotiable ocean bill of lading which stated: "received for shipment — 20 cardboard boxes stamped and said to contain '1000 cds ruff's bone' . . . ." Big Ships then promptly loaded the boxes on board its only vessel, which set sail that same day for Georgia.

On Thursday April 16, Copykats presented this bill of lading, a commercial invoice for "20,000 Compact Disks, Windows Version of 'Ruff's Bone'" and cer-tificates of origin, inspection and insurance to Banco de Argentina which paid Copykats immediately and forwarded the documents to First Farmers Bank in Atlanta.

On Thursday, April 23, before Farmers Bank had taken any action regarding the letter of credit, Kid's Rom received a telex from its agent in Caracas asserting that the goods shipped by Copykats were probably illegal counterfeits. He also noted that Copykats had permanently closed its office in Buenos Aires after receiving payment on the letter of credit. Its owner was last seen drinking tropical fruit punch on a beach in Aruba.

2. Assignment

It is 3 p.m. on Thursday, April 23. The purchasing manager of Kid's Rom now sits in your office biting his fingernails, sobbing softly and whimpering about how un-certain life is. Please advise him regarding his company's best course of action, in-cluding an analysis of the potential liabilities of the various parties, relating to the letter of credit transaction described above.

Base your analysis on the text of the UCP and other resources provided or linked below. Start by tracing through the standard process for such letters of credit. You should be able to answer the following questions.

(1) How should export letter of credit financing work in a perfect world?

(2) How and when must confirming and issuing banks make the decision to pay and under what standards?

(3) What happens if a bank rejects the documents?

(4) Can the banks be held liable for either wrongfully rejecting or accepting the documents?

C. Resources

1. Uniform Customs & Practices

International letters of credit (also called "export credits" or "trade credits") are almost universally made subject to a set of rules created by the International Chamber of Commerce called the Uniform Customs and Practice (UCP).[13] Much in the same way that the ICC's Incoterms created a unifying body of rules regarding terms of trade, the UCP has become the standard set of rules governing banking practices, obligations and liabilities for international letters of credit. The latest revision of these rules, UCP 600, was adopted in 2007. Your focus in evaluating the facts described above should be on these rules.

a. Selected Provisions of the UCP 600

Article 1 Application of UCP

The Uniform Customs and Practice for Documentary Credits, 2007 Revision, ICC Publication no. 600 ("UCP") are rules that apply to any documentary credit ("credit") (including, to the extent to which they may be applicable, any standby letter of credit) when the text of the credit expressly indicates that it is subject to these rules. They are binding on all parties thereto unless expressly modified or excluded by the credit.

Article 2 Definitions

For the purpose of these rules:

Advising bank means the bank that advises the credit at the request of the issuing bank.

Applicant means the party on whose request the credit is issued.

Banking day means a day on which a bank is regularly open at the place at which an act subject to these rules is to be performed.

Beneficiary means the party in whose favour a credit is issued.

Complying presentation means a presentation that is in accordance with the terms and conditions of the credit, the applicable provisions of these rules and international standard banking practice.

---

13. In the United States, state law versions of the UCC Article 5 control domestic letters of credit. Parties to a domestic credit may, however, supplant most of Article 5 by providing that the UCP controls the credit.

Confirmation means a definite undertaking of the confirming bank, in addition to that of the issuing bank, to honour or negotiate a complying presentation.

Confirming bank means the bank that adds its confirmation to a credit upon the issuing bank's authorization or request.

Credit means any arrangement, however named or described, that is irrevocable and thereby constitutes a definite undertaking of the issuing bank to honour a complying presentation.

Honour means:

a. to pay at sight if the credit is available by sight payment.

b. to incur a deferred payment undertaking and pay at maturity if the credit is available by deferred payment.

c. to accept a bill of exchange ("draft") drawn by the beneficiary and pay at maturity if the credit is available by acceptance.

Issuing bank means the bank that issues a credit at the request of an applicant or on its own behalf.

Negotiation means the purchase by the nominated bank of drafts (drawn on a bank other than the nominated bank) and/or documents under a complying presentation, by advancing or agreeing to advance funds to the beneficiary on or before the banking day on which reimbursement is due to the nominated bank.

Nominated bank means the bank with which the credit is available or any bank in the case of a credit available with any bank.

Presentation means either the delivery of documents under a credit to the issuing bank or nominated bank or the documents so delivered.

Presenter means a beneficiary, bank or other party that makes a presentation.

. . . .

Article 4 Credits v. Contracts

a. A credit by its nature is a separate transaction from the sale or other contract on which it may be based. Banks are in no way concerned with or bound by such contract, even if any reference whatsoever to it is included in the credit. Consequently, the undertaking of a bank to honour, to negotiate or to fulfil any other obligation under the credit is not subject to claims or defences by the applicant resulting from its relationships with the issuing bank or the beneficiary.

A beneficiary can in no case avail itself of the contractual relationships existing between banks or between the applicant and the issuing bank.

b. An issuing bank should discourage any attempt by the applicant to include, as an integral part of the credit, copies of the underlying contract, proforma invoice and the like.

Article 5 Documents v. Goods, Services or Performance

Banks deal with documents and not with goods, services or performance to which the documents may relate.

. . . .

Article 7 Issuing Bank Undertaking

Provided that the stipulated documents are presented to the nominated bank or to the issuing bank and that they constitute a complying presentation, the issuing bank must honour if the credit is available by:

i. sight payment, deferred payment or acceptance with the issuing bank;

. . . .

Article 8 Confirming Bank Undertaking

Provided that the stipulated documents are presented to the confirming bank or to any other nominated bank and that they constitute a complying presentation, the confirming bank must: honour, if the credit is available by

a. sight payment, deferred payment or acceptance with the confirming bank;

. . . .

Article 9 Advising of Credits and Amendments

a. A credit and any amendment may be advised to a beneficiary through an advising bank. An advising bank that is not a confirming bank advises the credit and any amendment without any undertaking to honour or negotiate.

. . . .

Article 10 Amendments

a. Except as otherwise provided by article 38, a credit can neither be amended nor cancelled without the agreement of the issuing bank, the confirming bank, if any, and the beneficiary.

. . . .

Article 14 Standard for Examination of Documents

a. A nominated bank acting on its nomination, a confirming bank, if any, and the issuing bank must examine a presentation to determine, on the basis of the documents alone, whether or not the documents appear on their face to constitute a complying presentation.

b. A nominated bank acting on its nomination, a confirming bank, if any, and the issuing bank shall each have a maximum of five banking days following the day of presentation to determine if a presentation is complying. This period is not curtailed or otherwise affected by the occurrence on or after the date of presentation of any expiry date or last day for presentation.

c. A presentation including one or more original transport documents subject to articles 19, 20, 21, 22, 23, 24 or 25 must be made by or on behalf of the beneficiary not later than 21 calendar days after the date of shipment as described in these rules, but in any event not later than the expiry date of the credit.

d. Data in a document, when read in context with the credit, the document itself and international standard banking practice, need not be identical to, but must not conflict with, data in that document, any other stipulated document or the credit.

e. In documents other than the commercial invoice, the description of the goods, services or performance, if stated, may be in general terms not conflicting with their description in the credit.

. . . .

j. When the addresses of the beneficiary and the applicant appear in any stipulated document, they need not be the same as those stated in the credit or in any other stipulated document, but must be within the same country as the respective addresses mentioned in the credit. Contact details (telefax, telephone, email and the like) stated as part of the beneficiary's and the applicant's address will be disregarded. However, when the address and contact details of the applicant appear as part of the consignee or notify party details on a transport document subject to articles 19, 20, 21, 22, 23, 24 or 25, they must be as stated in the credit.

k. The shipper or consignor of the goods indicated on any document need not be the beneficiary of the credit.

l. A transport document may be issued by any party other than a carrier, owner, master or charterer provided that the transport document meets the requirements of articles 19, 20, 21, 22, 23 or 24 of these rules.

Article 15 Complying Presentation

a. When an issuing bank determines that a presentation is complying, it must honour.

b. When a confirming bank determines that a presentation is complying, it must honour or negotiate and forward the documents to the issuing bank.

c. When a nominated bank determines that a presentation is complying and honours or negotiates, it must forward the documents to the confirming bank or issuing bank.

Article 16 Discrepant Documents, Waiver and Notice

a. When a nominated bank acting on its nomination, a confirming bank, if any, or the issuing bank determines that a presentation does not comply, it may refuse to honour or negotiate.

b. When an issuing bank determines that a presentation does not comply, it may in its sole judgment approach the applicant for a waiver of the discrepancies. This does not, however, extend the period mentioned in sub-article 14(b).

c. When a nominated bank acting on its nomination, a confirming bank, if any, or the issuing bank decides to refuse to honour or negotiate, it must give a single notice to that effect to the presenter.

The notice must state:

i. that the bank is refusing to honour or negotiate; and

ii. each discrepancy in respect of which the bank refuses to honour or negotiate; and

iii. a) that the bank is holding the documents pending further instructions from the presenter; or

b) that the issuing bank is holding the documents until it receives a waiver from the applicant and agrees to accept it, or receives further instructions from the presenter prior to agreeing to accept a waiver; or

c) that the bank is returning the documents; or

d) that the bank is acting in accordance with instructions previously received from the presenter.

d. The notice required in sub-article 16(c) must be given by telecommunication or, if that is not possible, by other expeditious means no later than the close of the fifth banking day following the day of presentation.

e. A nominated bank acting on its nomination, a confirming bank, if any, or the issuing bank may, after providing notice required by sub-article 16(c)(iii)(a) or (b), return the documents to the presenter at any time.

f. If an issuing bank or a confirming bank fails to act in accordance with the provisions of this article, it shall be precluded from claiming that the documents do not constitute a complying presentation.

g. When an issuing bank refuses to honour or a confirming bank refuses to honour or negotiate and has given notice to that effect in accordance with this article, it shall then be entitled to claim a refund, with interest, of any reimbursement made.

Article 17 Original Documents and Copies

a. At least one original of each document stipulated in the credit must be presented.

b. A bank shall treat as an original any document bearing an apparently original signature, mark, stamp, or label of the issuer of the document, unless the document itself indicates that it is not an original.

c. Unless a document indicates otherwise, a bank will also accept a document as original if it:

i. appears to be written, typed, perforated or stamped by the document issuer's hand; or

ii. appears to be on the document issuer's original stationery; or

iii. states that it is original, unless the statement appears not to apply to the document presented.

d. If a credit requires presentation of copies of documents, presentation of either originals or copies is permitted.

e. If a credit requires presentation of multiple documents by using terms such as "in duplicate", "in two fold" or "in two copies", this will be satisfied by the presentation of at least one original and the remaining number in copies, except when the document itself indicates otherwise.

Article 18 Commercial Invoice

a. A commercial invoice:

i. must appear to have been issued by the beneficiary (except as provided in article 38);

ii. must be made out in the name of the applicant (except as provided in sub-article 38(g));

iii. must be made out in the same currency as the credit; and

iv. need not be signed.

b. A nominated bank acting on its nomination, a confirming bank, if any, or the issuing bank may accept a commercial invoice issued for an amount in excess of the amount permitted by the credit, and its decision will be binding upon all parties, provided the bank in question has not honoured or negotiated for an amount in excess of that permitted by the credit.

c. The description of the goods, services or performance in a commercial invoice must correspond with that appearing in the credit.

. . . .

Article 20 Bill of Lading

a. A bill of lading, however named, must appear to:

i. indicate the name of the carrier and be signed by:

• the carrier or a named agent for or on behalf of the carrier, or

• the master or a named agent for or on behalf of the master.

. . . .

ii. indicate that the goods have been shipped on board a named vessel at the port of loading stated in the credit by: pre-printed wording, or an on board notation indicating the date on which the goods have been shipped on board.

The date of issuance of the bill of lading will be deemed to be the date of shipment unless the bill of lading contains an on board notation indicating the date of shipment, in which case the date stated in the on board notation will be deemed to be the date of shipment.

If the bill of lading contains the indication "intended vessel" or similar qualification in relation to the name of the vessel, an on board notation indicating the date of shipment and the name of the actual vessel is required.

iii. indicate shipment from the port of loading to the port of discharge stated in the credit.

. . . .

iv. be the sole original bill of lading or, if issued in more than one original, be the full set as indicated on the bill of lading.

. . . .

Article 26 "On Deck", "Shipper's Load and Count", "Said by Shipper to Contain" and Charges Additional to Freight

a. A transport document must not indicate that the goods are or will be loaded on deck. A clause on a transport document stating that the goods may be loaded on deck is acceptable.

b. A transport document bearing a clause such as "shipper's load and count" and "said by shipper to contain" is acceptable.

c. A transport document may bear a reference, by stamp or otherwise, to charges additional to the freight.

Article 27 Clean Transport Document

A bank will only accept a clean transport document. A clean transport document is one bearing no clause or notation expressly declaring a defective condition of the goods or their packaging. The word "clean" need not appear on a transport document, even if a credit has a requirement for that transport document to be "clean on board."

Article 34 Disclaimer on Effectiveness of Documents

A bank assumes no liability or responsibility for the form, sufficiency, accuracy, genuineness, falsification or legal effect of any document, or for the general or particular conditions stipulated in a document or superimposed thereon; nor does it assume any liability or responsibility for the description, quantity, weight, quality, condition, packing, delivery, value or existence of the goods, services or other performance represented by any document, or for the good faith or acts or omissions, solvency, performance or standing of the consignor, the carrier, the forwarder, the consignee or the insurer of the goods or any other person.

Article 35 Disclaimer on Transmission and Translation

A bank assumes no liability or responsibility for the consequences arising out of delay, loss in transit, mutilation or other errors arising in the transmission of any messages or delivery of letters or documents, when such messages, letters or documents are transmitted or sent according to the requirements stated in the credit, or when the bank may have taken the initiative in the choice of the delivery service in the absence of such instructions in the credit.

. . . .

A bank assumes no liability or responsibility for errors in translation or interpretation of technical terms and may transmit credit terms without translating them.

. . . .

2. Illustrative Case Law: Doctrine of Strict Compliance

a. Eximetals Corporation v. Pinheiro Guimaraes, S.A., 73 A.D.2d 526 (1979)

MEMORANDUM DECISION.

Order, Supreme Court, New York County, entered June 29, 1979, denying motion of Bank Leumi Trust Company of New York for summary judgment, is unanimously reversed, on the law, and said motion for summary judgment is granted and the cross-claim of Banco do Nordeste do Brasil, S.A. against Bank Leumi Trust Company of New York is dismissed on the merits, with costs to appellant Bank Leumi Trust Company of New York.

These motions for summary judgment in companion cases present the question of liability on letters of credit issued respectively by Israel Discount Bank and Bank Leumi Trust Company of New York where the letters of credit were not honored for the reason that the documents presented to the issuing banks do not meet the requirements of the letters of credit. We hold that the issuing banks are not liable on the letters of credit.

Both letters of credit were issued to finance an import transaction involving some steel flanges being purchased apparently by Eximetals Corporation, a New York corporation, from defendant Pinheiro Guimaraes, S.A., a Brazilian corporation. Pinheiro Guimaraes apparently negotiated these letters of credit with Banco do Nordeste do Brasil, S.A. and Banco Mercantil do Brasil ("Brazilian banks"). In each case the letter of credit called for payment on presentation of certain documents including an "inspection certificate verified by and countersigned by Mr. Gang," apparently the president of plaintiff corporation.

The Israel Discount Bank's letter of credit required that the inspection certificate "must now certify that the material shipped is 7124 units Ribbet Flange in accordance with sample and buyers drawing No. 17865 @ $210.00 each." The document presented as an inspection certificate omitted completely the phrase "Ribbet Flange in accordance with sample and buyers drawing No. 17865," but did say "as per shippers proforma invoice of November 9th, 1977." Israel Discount Bank refused to pay on the letter of credit because of this omission. Thereafter the Brazilian banks presented a pro forma invoice which did include the omitted phrase. In our view this was not a sufficient compliance with the requirements of the letter of credit.

The documents presented against the letter of credit must comply precisely with the requirements of the letter of credit. The New York Court of Appeals thus stated the rule:

> "We have heretofore held that these letters of credit are to be strictly complied with, which means that the papers, documents, and shipping descriptions must be followed as stated in the letter. There is no discretion in the bank or trust company to waive any of these requirements." *Anglo-South American Trust Co. v. Uhe*, 261 N.Y. 150, 156-57, 184 N.E. 741, 743.

Again in *Courtaulds North America, Inc. v. North Carolina National Bank*, 528 F.2d 802, 806 (4th Cir.), the Court said:

> "No substitution and no equivalent, through interpretation or logic, will serve. Harfield, Bank Credits and Acceptances (5th Ed. 1974), at p. 73, commends and quotes aptly from an English case: 'There is no room for documents which are almost the same, or which will do just as well.' *Equitable Trust Co. of N.Y. v. Dawson Partners, Ltd.*, 27 Lloyd's List Law Rpts. 49, 52 (1926). Although no pertinent North Carolina decision has been laid before us, in many cases elsewhere, especially in New York, we find the tenet of Harfield to be unshaken."

Here the letter of credit stated that the inspection certificate "must now certify" that the goods are "Ribbet Flange in accordance with sample and buyers drawing No. 17865." It did not do so.

Nor does the reference to a later supplied pro forma invoice meet this requirement. The bank's function in the comparison of documents with the letter of credit is quite ministerial. Further in this case, the letter of credit expressly stipulated that the inspection certificate be countersigned by Mr. Gang. There is nothing signed or countersigned by Mr. Gang which says that the pro forma invoice subsequently furnished by the Brazilian banks, presumably obtained from the sellers, was in fact the pro forma invoice to which Mr. Gang referred in the purported inspection certificate.

While a similar objection is urged with respect to the Bank Leumi letter of credit, we think that as to this particular objection there may well be a question of fact whether the Bank Leumi waived the objection by making its original objection on other grounds and not on this ground. However, the Bank Leumi did promptly object on the ground that the inspection certificate was "not signed although countersigned," and shortly amplified this by saying that the certificate was "not signed by issuer." We think this was a valid objection. The requirement that the inspection certificate be "countersigned" by Mr. Gang means that his signature should be added to someone else's signature, presumably the person making the inspection. Thus Webster's Third New International Dictionary at 520 (1971 ed.) defines the verb "counter-sign" as meaning "to add one's signature to (a document) after another's to attest authenticity." We do not think that the fact that the certificate was on the letterhead of a "Hepco Trading Co." means that Hepco was signing or certifying to anything. Indeed, the purported inspection certificate states that the specifications and quantities are verified and certified "by me." And the only signature is the purported signature of Mr. Gang. Nor may the defect be ignored because of the fact that Mr. Gang was the president of the buyer corporation. The obligation of the letter of credit is the obligation of the Bank Leumi and its terms are spelled out in the letter of credit. Those terms may not be varied except by consent of the issuer bank, nor is it for the bank to decide in this case whether one signature is as good as two.

For the purpose of this motion, we have of course assumed that the signature of Mr. Gang is not a forgery although Mr. Gang claims it is. Furthermore, the charges of fraud made by the Brazilian banks against the importer and exporter do not make enforcible a letter of credit which is not otherwise enforcible. In some cases, fraud may be a reason why a letter of credit otherwise enforcible should not be enforced. But in general, fraud does not give rise to a cause of action on a letter of credit.

There is no showing of any fact which should estop the banks from making any defenses they have to the letters of credit.

b. Beyene v. Irving Trust Company, 596 F. Supp. 438 (S.D.N.Y. 1984), aff'd, 762 F.2d 4 (2d Cir. 1985)

LASKER, District Judge.

The issue presented is whether Irving Trust Company ("Irving") acted properly in refusing to honor a letter of credit issued on behalf of plaintiff Dessaleng Beyene. Irving moves for summary judgment to dismiss the complaint against it on the grounds that it complied with the obligations which apply under the Uniform Customs and Practice for Documentary Credits ("UCP") of the International Chamber of Commerce, and that plaintiff Jean Hanson lacks standing to maintain this action. Beyene and Hanson oppose the motion on the grounds that there exist material questions of fact which cannot be resolved on a motion for summary judgment. For the reasons set forth below, Irving's motion is granted.

I.

In March of 1978 Beyene, executive director of the Lynx International Group, Inc., a general merchandising and exchange corporation located in Arlington, Virginia, agreed to sell and to export to Mohammed Sofan, a resident of the Yemen Arab Republic, two prefabricated houses known as "O'Domes." Sofan attempted to finance the purchase through the use of a letter of credit in the amount of $62,400 which was issued by the Yemen Bank for Reconstruction and Development ("YBRD") in August of 1978 in favor of Beyene. YBRD designated Irving as the confirming bank for the letter of credit and Irving subsequently notified Beyene of the letter's terms and conditions. The letter's expiration date was initially set as October 19, 1978, but it was ultimately extended until May 31, 1979. During the intervening period, Beyene designated the National Bank of Washington ("NBW") as the collecting bank and he notified Irving that he had made assignments to NBW from the letter's proceeds totaling $50,000. The complaint alleges that Irving was also aware that Hanson was entitled to receive $40,000 of the credit, although Irving disputes this proposition and contends that it was unaware until July of 1979, that Hanson played a role in any of these transactions after the letter had expired.

On May 4, 1979 NBW mailed to Irving all of the documents required under the terms of the letter of credit. According to a summary of events prepared in October 1979 by Paul D. Shaffer, the NBW official responsible for submitting these documents, Ragai S. Nasser, an employee in Irving's letter of credit section, telephoned Shaffer on May 10, 1979 to inform him of five discrepancies in the submitted documents. The two which are relevant in resolution of the issues presented here were (1) that the bill of lading for the O'Domes issued on April 16, 1979 was not presented to

Irving within 21 days from that date as required under UCP Article 42 and (2) that the bill of lading listed the party to be notified as Mohammed Soran instead of Mohammed Sofan.[2]

Shaffer's summary states that Nasser agreed to waive the late presentment of the bill of lading discrepancy because he could not confirm the actual date of the bill's receipt by Irving. However, Nasser's affidavit in support of the summary judgment motion makes no mention of any waiver.

Shaffer also testified at his deposition that both he and Nasser discussed the fact that the Soran-Sofan misspelling was "an extremely minor discrepancy," that Nasser was going to look into the possibility that Irving might honor the credit in spite of the discrepancy but that Irving never waived the discrepancy and continued to maintain that one existed, and that Irving would send to YBRD a cable noting the single misspelling discrepancy and requesting authorization to pay the letter of credit.[5]

As to three remaining discrepancies noted by Irving, NBW mailed to Irving corrected documents on May 25, which Irving claims it did not receive until June 4, after the letter of credit had expired. On June 5, 1979, Irving cabled YBRD for authorization after noting the late presentation of the bill of lading, a discrepancy which Shaffer claims Irving waived, and the misspelling of Sofan's name. Irving subsequently sent three follow up cables to the Yemen bank on June 8, 13, and 21.

According to Shaffer's prepared summary, he spoke with Irving's Nasser on June 25 and was told, in effect, that Sofan had refused to pay due to the discrepancies in the documents presented by NBW to Irving. In an effort to cure the misspelling discrepancy, NBW sent to Irving a corrected bill of lading—identifying Sofan as the party to be notified—on July 25, although the buyer continued to refuse to authorize payment. Subsequent efforts by Beyene to obtain payment proved unrewarding. Beyene and Hanson then filed suit against Irving and NBW for wrongful dishonor of the letter of credit . . . .

II.

Irving argues that it is entitled to summary judgment on the grounds that, *inter alia,* it complied with its obligations under the UCP as a confirming bank and that it was under a duty to pay the proceeds of the letter of credit only if Beyene fully complied with the credit's terms and conditions. Irving contends that three discrepan-

---

2. Article 41 provides:
   Notwithstanding the requirement of Article 37 that every credit must stipulate an expiry date for presentation of documents, credits must also stipulate a specified period of time after the date of issuance of the Bills of Lading or other shipping documents during which presentation of documents for payment, acceptance or negotiation must be made. If no such period of time is stipulated in the credit, banks will refuse documents presented to them later than 21 days after the date of issuance of the Bills of Lading or other shipping documents.
   5. This procedure was required under UCP Article 3(c) which provides in relevant part: "[U]ndertakings [by an advising or confirming bank, Irving in this instance,] can neither be amended or cancelled without the agreement of all parties thereto."

cies in the documents presented by NBW each support its decision not to honor the letter of credit: (1) some corrected documents were received by Irving after the May 31, 1979 expiration date for the letter of credit; (2) NBW presented documents to Irving more than 21 days after the bill of lading was issued on April 16, 1979, contrary to UCP Article 41; and (3) the misspelling of Sofan's name in the bill of lading was a material discrepancy. Plaintiffs respond that the deposition testimony of Paul Shaffer establishes material facts in dispute, as to whether documents were timely presented to Irving and concerning the misspelling of Sofan's name, and that the disputed facts bar an award of summary judgment in Irving's favor.

Plaintiffs are correct that Shaffer's deposition and summary of events differ sharply from Irving's statement of facts and raise questions of fact with regard to whether Irving waived the timeliness discrepancies and whether it is estopped from raising the untimely presentment of the documents in support of its motion. . . . However, review of the Shaffer deposition does not reveal any factual dispute between the parties as to whether the Sofan-Soran misspelling was a material discrepancy. Inasmuch as this discrepancy alone supports granting Irving's motion, plaintiffs' arguments pertaining to this issue are examined in detail.

III.

The plaintiffs contend that Irving implicitly waived the misspelling discrepancy because Shaffer testified at his deposition that he expected Irving to honor the letter of credit because he considered the misspelling to be "an extremely minor discrepancy." . . . Plaintiffs also dispute the materiality of the misspelling discrepancy by relying upon Beyene's affidavit which states that the error could have had no practical effect because an Arab name like Sofan's is not translatable into English in a meaningful way and that in Yemen it would not be possible to locate and notify Sofan of delivery of the goods in question based upon his name alone.

Review of the transcript of Shaffer's deposition reveals that Irving did not implicitly waive the misspelling discrepancy. At the outset, Shaffer's testimony regarding his view of the spelling error does not affect Irving's position. Although both Nasser and Shaffer did discuss the fact that the error was a minor one, it is clear that Nasser continued to maintain that a discrepancy existed and that at no time did he waive the mistake.

The law is clear that a single discrepancy, including one involving the misspelling of a party's last name, is sufficient to excuse a confirming bank from paying the proceeds of a letter of credit. . . .

> "[T]he essential requirements of a letter of credit must be strictly complied with by the party entitled to draw against the letter of credit, which means that the papers, documents and shipping descriptions must be as stated in the letter." *Venizelos, S.A. v. Chase Manhattan Bank*, 425 F.2d 461, 465 (2d Cir. 1970); *accord, Courtaulds North America, Inc. v. North Carolina National Bank*, 528 F.2d 802, 805-06 (4th Cir. 1975) . . . .

The *Courtaulds* case illustrates the operation of the rule. There a bank was held properly to have refused payment under a letter of credit because, although the letter required that the draft be accompanied by an invoice stating that it covered "100% acrylic yarn," the invoice stated only that the goods were "Imported Acrylic Yarn." 528 F.2d at 803.

The rule of strict compliance reflects the fact that a letter of credit is a contract between the bank and the beneficiary of the letter that is separate and distinct from the commercial contract between the beneficiary (usually the seller) and the bank's customer (usually the buyer). The letter of credit is not tied to or dependent upon the underlying commercial transaction. . . . In determining whether to pay, the bank looks solely at the letter and the documentation the beneficiary presents, to determine whether the documentation meets the requirements in the letter.

It is the complete separation between the underlying commercial transaction and the letter of credit that gives the letter its utility in financing transactions. The parties to the commercial contract bring in a third party—the bank—to finance the transaction for them. The bank's sole function is the financing; it is not concerned with or involved in the commercial transaction. This restriction simplifies the bank's role and enables it to act quickly and surely. Because the bank is not involved in the commercial transaction, however, all its rights and duties are set out in and defined by the letter of credit. The bank is not expected or required to be familiar with or to consider the customs of, or the special meaning or effect given to particular terms in, the trade.

Here, the Soran-Sofan misspelling in the bill of lading meant that the documents submitted by NBW did not strictly comply with the terms of the letter of credit. As a result, assuming Irving acted improperly when it made note of an additional discrepancy, the fact remains that the undisputed spelling mistake alone was sufficient to excuse Irving's obligation to pay the letter of credit's proceeds to Beyene.

Moreover, the quotation above from *Marino* highlights the fact that a confirming bank need not ascertain the magnitude of each discrepancy before its obligation to pay is relieved. Under the rule of "strict compliance," Irving did not have to scrutinize the underlying transaction between Beyene and Sofan, nor did it have to establish whether the misspelling of an Arab name was a meaningful mistake or find that it was a major error before it could claim that a discrepancy in the documents existed.[8] Irving was therefore under no duty to honor the letter of credit.

Defendant's motion for summary judgment is accordingly granted. The complaint is dismissed.

It is so ordered.

---

8. Even if a compliance rule of arguably greater liberality applied in this case, *see, e.g., Flagship Cruises Ltd. v. New England Merchants National Bank*, 569 F.2d 699, 705 (1st Cir. 1978). ("variance between documents specified and documents submitted is not fatal if there is *no* possibility that the documents could mislead the paying bank to its detriment."), plaintiffs have not established with sufficient certainty that there was no possibility that Irving could have been misled to its detriment by paying Beyene. For example, it is conceivable that the spelling error could have led to the non-delivery or mis-delivery of the O'Domes. To support this theory Irving points out that a June 28, 1979 cable from Beyene to Irving noted that Sofan had not been alerted to the goods' arrival.

Part Two: Fraud & The Independence Principle

A. Overview

Your goal for this part of the chapter is to understand the relationship between the letter of credit transaction and the underlying sales transaction, particularly when there is fraud. You should already recognize from the last module that the bank's obligation to pay under a letter of credit is not dependent upon either buyer or seller performance in the underlying sale. Under the "independence principle," breach of the sales contract is simply not grounds for a bank to refuse to pay under a letter of credit. Thus, when the seller presents documents that comply with the requirements of the credit, the bank will pay regardless of whether the seller adequately performs his obligations in the underlying sale.

While the independence principle may make perfect sense in the context of contractual breaches—after all, the letter of credit could not efficiently serve its basic functions if banks were required to evaluate the seller's performance in the sales transaction—what about situations involving outright fraud and deceit? The UCP is silent on the matter. The UCC, however, recognizes a limited exception to deal with certain kinds of fraud. The problem below focuses on this limited fraud exception to the independence principle. We will also briefly look at other types of credits, particularly "standby" letters of credit or demand guarantees.

B. Problem Seven B: The Secrets of Life

1. Facts

Professor Don Ho has developed a unique computer program on CD-ROM that he claims will reveal all of life's little secrets to its users, including the reason for our existence. Professor Ho produces the CDs in his Davie, Florida garage. On April 1, Professor Ho received a telegram from Micro Sales Brazil, Inc. (MSB) offering to purchase 10,000 of his CD-ROMs. MSB is located in Rio de Janeiro. MSB's telegram set forth the following terms: "10,000 'Ho's Secrets of Life' CD-ROMs, Windows 8 format, $100,000 CIF Rio de Janeiro, Brazil, delivery by April 30."

The next day, Ho sent a return telegram to MSB that stated "I accept your offer to purchase 10,000 Secrets of Life CD's, $100,000 CIF Rio, delivery by April 30, payment by irrevocable L/C."

On April 5, MSB opened an irrevocable letter of credit on Ho's behalf with Big Bucks Bank promising to honor a draft for $100,000 to "Professor Ho," 10 days after presentment of "a commercial invoice for 10,000 'Ho's Secrets of Life, Windows 8 formatted, CD-ROMs,' a certificate of origin and a clean, shipped on-board ocean bill of lading." The letter of credit was made explicitly subject to the UCP 600.

On April 15, Ho delivered 20 boxes marked "500 Ho's Secrets of Life CDs" to the Dawn Treader steamship line. Dawn Treader personnel loaded the boxes on board the MS Dawn Treader and promptly issued a bill of lading to Ho that stated: "20 boxes said to contain 500 'Ho's Secrets of Life', in apparent good order," and "shipped on board." That same day Ho presented this bill of lading, along with a certificate of origin and a commercial invoice for "10,000 'Ho's Secrets of Life', Windows 8 formatted, CD-ROMs" to Big Bucks Bank.

MSB now believes, based on information from "its sources in Davie," that the boxes aboard the Dawn Treader actually contain only outdated, Apple formatted, word processing programs and some blank "floppy" disks.

2. Assignment

Assume that Big Bucks Bank is still examining the documents presented by the alleged shyster Ho under the letter of credit but must accept or reject them within the next two business days. Utilizing the resources provided below, please advise MSB about its legal rights and options to prevent payment under the letter of credit. *You should begin by "dissecting" the relevant UCC provision—what precisely triggers its application, what does it allow or require the banks to do (if anything), and what standards are used?* You must also consider what constitutes fraud as opposed to a plain vanilla breach of contract.

C. Resources

1. UCC (Florida Version)

675.108. Issuer's rights and obligations

(1) Except as otherwise provided in s. 675.109, an issuer shall honor a presentation that, as determined by the standard practice referred to in subsection (5), appears on its face strictly to comply with the terms and conditions of the letter of credit. Except as otherwise provided in s. 675.113 and unless otherwise agreed with the applicant, an issuer shall dishonor a presentation that does not appear so to comply.

(2) An issuer has a reasonable time after presentation, but not beyond the end of the seventh business day of the issuer after the day of its receipt of documents:

(a) To honor;

(b) If the letter of credit provides for honor to be completed more than 7 business days after presentation, to accept a draft or incur a deferred obligation; or

(c) To give notice to the presenter of discrepancies in the presentation.

(3) Except as otherwise provided in subsection (4), an issuer is precluded from asserting as a basis for dishonor any discrepancy if timely notice is not given, or any discrepancy not stated in the notice if timely notice is given.

(4) Failure to give the notice specified in subsection (2) or to mention fraud, forgery, or expiration in the notice does not preclude the issuer from asserting as a basis for dishonor fraud or forgery as described in s. 675.109(1) or expiration of the letter of credit before presentation.

675.109. Fraud and forgery

(1) If a presentation is made that appears on its face strictly to comply with the terms and conditions of the letter of credit, but a required document is forged or materially fraudulent, or honor of the presentation would facilitate a material fraud by the beneficiary on the issuer or applicant:

(a) The issuer shall honor the presentation, if honor is demanded by:

1. A nominated person who has given value in good faith and without notice of forgery or material fraud;

2. A confirmer who has honored its confirmation in good faith;

3. A holder in due course of a draft drawn under the letter of credit which was taken after acceptance by the issuer or nominated person; or

4. An assignee of the issuer's or nominated person's deferred obligation that was taken for value and without notice of forgery or material fraud after the obligation was incurred by the issuer or nominated person.

(b) The issuer, acting in good faith, may honor or dishonor the presentation in any other case.

(2) If an applicant claims that a required document is forged or materially fraudulent or that honor of the presentation would facilitate a material fraud by the beneficiary on the issuer or applicant, a court of competent jurisdiction may temporarily or permanently enjoin the issuer from honoring a presentation or grant similar relief against the issuer or other persons only if the court finds that:

(a) The relief is not prohibited under the law applicable to an accepted draft or deferred obligation incurred by the issuer;

(b) A beneficiary, issuer, or nominated person who may be adversely affected is adequately protected against loss that it may suffer because the relief is granted;

(c) All of the conditions to entitle a person to the relief under the laws of this state have been met; and

(d) On the basis of the information submitted to the court, the applicant is more likely than not to succeed under its claim of forgery or material fraud and the person demanding honor does not qualify for protection under paragraph (1)(a).

2. Uniform Commercial Code Official Comments, § 5-114

The Official Comments to UCC § 5-114 provide helpful guidance on the meaning of several critical concepts central to the fraud exception, including what constitutes "material fraud." The Comment points out that not just any fraudulent act will trigger the exception and references court decisions for the proposition that "[m]aterial fraud by the beneficiary occurs only when the beneficiary has no colorable right to expect honor and where there is no basis in fact to support such a right to honor." In a similar vein, the Comment cites cases suggesting that the fraud must be "so serious as to make it obviously pointless and unjust to permit the beneficiary to obtain the money." Stating it differently, "the beneficiary's conduct has 'so vitiated the entire transaction that the legitimate purposes of the independence of the issuer's obligation would no longer be served.'" Importantly, the Comment also notes that, even in the absence of specified parties that must be paid, the banks have no duty to dishonor when presented with evidence of material fraud so long as there is any doubt about the facts.

3. Illustrative Case Law: UCC Fraud Exception

a. *United Bank Limited v. Cambridge Sporting Goods,* *41 N.Y.2d 254 (1976)*

GABRIELLI, Justice.

On this appeal, we must decide whether fraud on the part of a seller-beneficiary of an irrevocable letter of credit may be successfully . . . asserted as a defense against holders of drafts drawn by the seller pursuant to the credit. If we conclude that this defense may be interposed by the buyer who procured the letter of credit, we must also determine whether the courts below improperly imposed upon appellant buyer the burden of proving that respondent banks to whom the drafts were made payable by the seller-beneficiary of the letter of credit, were not holders in due course. The issues presented raise important questions concerning the application of the law of letters of credit and the rules governing proof of holder in due course status set forth in article 3 of the Uniform Commercial Code. . . .

In April, 1971 appellant Cambridge Sporting Goods Corporation (Cambridge) entered into a contract for the manufacture and sale of boxing gloves with Duke Sports (Duke), a Pakistani corporation. Duke committed itself to the manufacture of 27,936 pairs of boxing gloves at a sale price of $42,576.80; and arranged with its Pakistani bankers, United Bank Limited (United) and The Muslim Commercial Bank (Muslim), for the financing of the sale. Cambridge was requested by these banks to cover payment of the purchase price by opening an irrevocable letter of credit with its bank in New York, Manufacturers Hanover Trust Company (Manufacturers). Manufacturers issued an irrevocable letter of credit obligating it, upon the receipt of certain documents indicating shipment of the merchandise pursuant to the contract, to accept and pay, 90 days after acceptance, drafts drawn upon Manufacturers for the purchase price of the gloves.

Following confirmation of the opening of the letter of credit, Duke informed Cambridge that it would be impossible to manufacture and deliver the merchandise within the time period required by the contract, and sought an extension of time for performance until September 15, 1971 and a continuation of the letter of credit, which was due to expire on August 11. Cambridge replied on June 18 that it would not agree to a postponement of the manufacture and delivery of the gloves because of its re-sale commitments and, hence, it promptly advised Duke that the contract was can-celed and the letter of credit should be returned. Cambridge simultaneously notified United of the contract cancellation.

Despite the cancellation of the contract, Cambridge was informed on July 17, 1971 that documents had been received at Manufacturers from United purporting to evi-dence a shipment of the boxing gloves under the terms of the canceled contract. The documents were accompanied by a draft, dated July 16, 1971, drawn by Duke upon Manufacturers and made payable to United, for the amount of $21,288.40, one half of the contract price of the boxing gloves. A second set of documents was received by Manufacturers from Muslim, also accompanied by a draft, dated August 20, and drawn upon Manufacturers by Duke for the remaining amount of the contract price.

An inspection of the shipments upon their arrival revealed that Duke had shipped old, unpadded, ripped and mildewed gloves rather than the new gloves to be manu-factured as agreed upon. Cambridge then commenced an action against Duke in Supreme Court, New York County, joining Manufacturers as a party, and obtained a preliminary injunction prohibiting the latter from paying drafts drawn under the letter of credit; subsequently, in November, 1971 Cambridge levied on the funds subject to the letter of credit and the draft, which were delivered by Manufacturers to the Sheriff in compliance therewith. Duke ultimately defaulted in the action and judgment against it was entered in the amount of the drafts, in March, 1972.

... The present proceeding was instituted by the Pakistani banks to vacate the levy made by Cambridge and to obtain payment of the ... drafts on the letter of credit. The banks asserted that they were holders in due course of the drafts which had been made payable to them by Duke and, thus, were entitled to the proceeds thereof irrespective of any defenses which Cambridge had established against their transferor, Duke, in the prior action which had terminated in a default judgment. The banks' motion for summary judgment on this claim was denied and the request by Cambridge for a jury trial was granted. Cambridge sought to depose the petitioning banks, but its request was denied and, as an alternative, written interrogatories were served on the Pakistani banks to learn the circumstances surrounding the transfer of the drafts to them. At trial, the banks introduced no evidence other than answers to several of the written interrogatories which were received over objection by Cam-bridge to the effect that the answers were conclusory, self-serving and otherwise in-admissible. Cambridge presented evidence of its dealings with Duke including the cancellation of the contract and uncontested proof of the subsequent shipment of essentially worthless merchandise.

The trial court concluded that the burden of proving that the banks were not hold-ers in due course lay with Cambridge, and directed a verdict in favor of the banks on the ground that Cambridge had not met that burden; the court stated that Cambridge failed to demonstrate that the banks themselves had participated in the seller's acts of fraud, proof of which was concededly present in the record. The Appellate Division affirmed, agreeing that while there was proof tending to establish the defenses against the seller, Cambridge had not shown that the seller's acts were "connected to the petitioners (banks) in any manner." The Appellate Division also held that CPLR 3117 "seemingly" authorized the introduction of the challenged interrogatories into evidence.

We reverse and hold that it was improper to direct a verdict in favor of the petitioning Pakistani banks. We conclude that the defense of fraud in the transaction was established and in that circumstance the burden shifted to petitioners to prove that they were holders in due course and took the drafts for value, in good faith and without notice of any fraud on the part of Duke (Uniform Commercial Code, s 3-302). Additionally, we think it was improper for the trial court to permit petitioners to introduce into evidence answers to Cambridge's interrogatories to demonstrate their holder in due course status.

This case does not come before us in the typical posture of a lawsuit between the bank issuing the letter of credit and presenters of drafts drawn under the credit seeking payment (see, generally, White and Summers, Uniform Commercial Code, s 18-6, pp. 619–628). Because Cambridge obtained an injunction against payment of the drafts and has levied against the proceeds of the drafts, it stands in the same position as the issuer, and, thus, the law of letters of credit governs the liability of Cambridge to the Pakistani banks. Article 5 of the Uniform Commercial Code, dealing with letters of credit, and the Uniform Customs and Practice for Documentary Credits promulgated by the International Chamber of Commerce set forth the duties and obligations of the issuer of a letter of credit. [2] . . . A letter of credit is a commitment on the part of the issuing bank that it will pay a draft presented to it under the terms of the credit, and if it is a documentary draft, upon presentation of the required documents of title (see Uniform Commercial Code, s 5-103). Banks issuing letters of credit deal in documents and not in goods and are not responsible for any breach of warranty or nonconformity of the goods involved in the underlying sales contract (see Uniform Commercial Code, s 5-114, subd. (1); Uniform Customs and Practice, General Provisions and Definitions (c) and article 9; *O'Meara Co. v. National Park Bank of N.Y.*, 239 N.Y. 386, 146 N.E. 636 . . . . Subdivision (2) of section 5-114, however indicates certain limited circumstances in which an issuer May properly refuse to honor a draft drawn under a letter of credit or a customer may enjoin an issuer from honoring such a draft. . . . Thus, where "fraud in the transaction" has been shown and the holder has not taken the draft in circumstances that would make it a

---

2. It should be noted that the Uniform Customs and Practice controls, in lieu of article 5 of the code, where, unless otherwise agreed by the parties, a letter of credit is made subject to the provisions of the Uniform Customs and Practice by its terms or by agreement, course of dealing or usage of trade (Uniform Commercial Code, s 5-102, subd. (4)). . . . Moreover, the Uniform Customs and Practice provisions are not in conflict nor do they treat with the subject matter of section 5-114 which is dispositive of the issues presented on this appeal . . . . Thus, we are of the opinion that the Uniform Customs and Practice, where applicable, does not bar the relief provided for in section 5-114 of the code.

holder in due course, the customer may apply to enjoin the issuer from paying drafts drawn under the letter of credit (see 1955 Report of N.Y. Law Rev.Comm., vol. 3, pp. 1654–1559). This rule represents a codification of precode case law most eminently articulated in the landmark case of *Sztejn v. Schroder Banking Corp.*, 177 Misc. 719, 31 N.Y.S. 2d 631, Shientag, J., where it was held that the shipment of cowhair in place of bristles amounted to more than mere breach of warranty but fraud sufficient to constitute grounds for enjoining payment of drafts to one not a holder in due course . . . . Even prior to the *Sztejn* case, forged or fraudulently procured documents were proper grounds for . . . avoidance of payment of drafts drawn under a letter of credit (Finkelstein, Legal Aspects of Commercial Letters of Credit, pp. 231–236, 247); and cases decided after the enactment of the code have cited *Sztejn* with approval . . .

The history of the dispute between the various parties involved in this case reveals that Cambridge had in a prior, separate proceeding successfully enjoined Manufacturers from paying the drafts and has attached the proceeds of the drafts. It should be noted that the question of the availability and the propriety of this relief is not before us on this appeal. The petitioning banks do not dispute the validity of the prior injunction nor do they dispute the delivery of worthless merchandise. Rather, on this appeal they contend that as holders in due course they are entitled to the proceeds of the drafts irrespective of any fraud on the part of Duke (see Uniform Commercial Code, § 5-114, subd. (2), par. (b)). Although precisely speaking there was no specific finding of fraud in the transaction by either of the courts below, their determinations were based on that assumption. The evidentiary facts are not disputed and we hold upon the facts as established, that the shipment of old, unpadded, ripped and mildewed gloves rather than the new boxing gloves as ordered by Cambridge, constituted fraud in the transaction within the meaning of subdivision (2) of section 5-114. It should be noted that the drafters of section 5-114, in their attempt to codify the *Sztejn* case and in utilizing the term "fraud in the transaction," have eschewed a dogmatic approach and adopted a flexible standard to be applied as the circumstances of a particular situation mandate. It can be difficult to draw a precise line between cases involving breach of warranty (or a difference of opinion as to the quality of goods) and outright fraudulent practice on the part of the seller. To the extent, however, that Cambridge established that Duke was guilty of fraud in shipping, not merely nonconforming merchandise, but worthless fragments of boxing gloves, this case is similar to *Sztejn*.

If the petitioning banks are holders in due course they are entitled to recover the proceeds of the drafts but if such status cannot be demonstrated their petition must fail.[6] The parties are in agreement that section 3-307 of the code governs the pleading and proof of holder in due course status . . . .

---

6. Although several commentators have expressed a contrary view, the weight of authority supports the proposition that fraud on the part of the seller-beneficiary may not be interposed as a defense to payment against a holder in due course to whom a draft has been negotiated . . . . This approach represents the better view that as against two innocent parties (the buyer and the holder in due course) the former, having chosen to deal with the fraudulent seller, should bear the risk of loss . . . .

Even though section 3-307 is contained in article 3 of the code dealing with negotiable instruments rather than letters of credit, we agree that its provisions should control in the instant case. Section 5-114 (subd. (2), par. (a)) utilizes the holder in due course criteria of section 3-302 of the code to determine whether a presenter may recover on drafts despite fraud in the sale of goods transaction. It is logical, therefore, to apply the pleading and practice rules of section 3-307 in the situation where a presenter of drafts under a letter of credit claims to be a holder in due course. In the context of section 5-114 and the law of letters of credit, however, the "defense" referred to in section 3-307 should be deemed to include only those defenses available under subdivision (2) of section 5-114, i.e., noncompliance of required documents, forged or fraudulent documents or fraud in the transaction. In the context of a letter of credit transaction and, specifically subdivision (2) of section 5-114, it is these defenses which operate to shift the burden of proof of holder in due course status upon one asserting such status . . . .

Thus, a presenter of drafts drawn under a letter of credit must prove that it took the drafts for value, in good faith and without notice of the underlying fraud in the transaction (Uniform Commercial Code, § 3-302).

Turning to the rules of section 3-307 as they apply to this case, Cambridge failed to deny the effectiveness of the signatures on the draft in its answer and, thus, these are deemed admitted and their effectiveness is not an issue in the case. However, this does not entitle the banks as holders to payment of the drafts since Cambridge has established "fraud in the transaction." The courts below erroneously concluded that Cambridge was required to show that the banks had participated in or were themselves guilty of the seller's fraud in order to establish a defense to payment. But, it was not necessary that Cambridge prove that United and Muslim actually participated in the fraud, since merely notice of the fraud would have deprived the Pakistani banks of holder in due course status.

In order to qualify as a holder in due course, a holder must have taken the instrument "without notice * * * of any defense against * * * it on the part of any person" (Uniform Commercial Code, s 3-302, subd. (1), par. (c)). . . . It was error for the trial court to direct a verdict in favor of the Pakistani banks because . . . this determination rested upon a misallocation of the burden of proof; and we conclude that the banks have not satisfied the burden of proving that they qualified in all respects as holders in due course, by any affirmative proof. The only evidence introduced by the banks consisted of conclusory answers to the interrogatories which were improperly admitted by the Trial Judge (see discussion, Infra). The failure of the banks to meet their burden is fatal to their claim for recovery of the proceeds of the drafts and their petition must therefore be dismissed.

. . . .

Accordingly, the order of the Appellate Division should be reversed, with costs, and the petition dismissed.

D. Standby Letters of Credit & Demand Guarantees

Thus far, we have focused on the widely used "commercial" or "documentary" letter of credit typically used for financing in a standard export sales transaction. There are, however, other types of credits that serve distinct purposes, or are designed for the special needs of the particular transaction. One of the most common of these credits is the "standby" letter of credit. This form of documentary credit arose in the United States as a result of regulations that prevent U.S. banks from issuing direct guarantees of third party performance. A similar arrangement often issued outside of the United States, where such restrictions on banks do not apply, is called a "demand guarantee." Both standby credits and demand guarantees differ from standard commercial letters of credit, particularly in that both are essentially conditional or secondary obligations triggered by a principle party's default. In other words, they are essentially a "fail-safe" device that require the bank to pay only when a party to the underlying transaction has failed to perform.

Standby credits can guarantee either financial or non-financial contractual obligations. One common use of a standby letter of credit is to assure performance by the *seller* of services. This purpose contrasts sharply with a commercial export credit, which is designed to ensure payment by the *buyer* of the contract price. The respective roles of the buyer and seller in a performance standby credit are essentially reversed from the traditional commercial letter of credit. The applicant is now the seller and the beneficiary the buyer. The financial standby credit, in contrast, is used to guarantee payment of a financial obligation. If the buyer has promised to pay for goods in 90 days, the financial standby credit will allow the seller recourse if the buyer fails to do so.

Standby credits and demand guarantees are, like commercial credits, documentary in nature and, counterintuitively, the independence principle still applies. Even though the bank's obligation to pay under a standby credit relates to performance of the underlying contract, this obligation is triggered by presentation of specified documentation. The bank itself does not investigate, nor is it concerned with actual performance under the sale or services contract. The issuing bank essentially promises to pay the buyer upon notification of a specified condition. This may come in the form of documentation from an independent party certifying breach by the seller or, in the case of a "clean" or "suicide" credit, simply a demand by the buyer.

Consider a simple example. If a U.S. construction firm contracts to build a shopping center in Saudi Arabia, the Saudi buyer may want some form of guarantee or assurance that the work will be done in an adequate and timely fashion. One way to do this is to require that the construction firm secure a standby letter of credit or demand guarantee under which the Saudi buyer would be paid a specified amount in the case of performance breach by the seller. The parties might reasonably condition payment under the credit upon presentment of specified documents demonstrating the seller's failure to perform. If the Saudi buyer presents these documents to the bank demanding payment, the bank will pay if the documents comply with the credit.

Although the UCP 600 could control a standby credit, the ICC has published two sets of rules designed specifically for standby credits and demand guarantees—the International Standby Practices 1998 ("ISP 98"; <u>ICC Publication No. 590</u>[14]) and <u>Uniform Rules For Demand Guarantees</u>,[15] 2010 Revision (ICC Publication No. 758, updating Publication No. 458).

Review this linked <u>description of the standby letter of credit</u>[16] provided by a practitioner, and then read the case that follows. Note that the case is also instructive regarding the typical pattern for international disputes—consider particularly the role of arbitration, the existence of multiple lawsuits in various jurisdictions and choice of law issues.

1. Case Law Illustration: *American Express Bank v. Banco Español de Crédito*, 597 F. Supp. 2d 394 (S.D.N.Y. 2009)

RICHARD J. HOLWELL, District Judge:

This case is about international demand guaranties, a form of commercial credit used to secure the performance of international construction contracts. In particular, it involves a bank's attempts to enforce another bank's counterguaranties, despite the fact that it has refused to pay the primary guaranties on the ground that demand was made in bad faith.

The banks' dispute originates in two contracts to build power substations in Pakistan. The contractor, a Spanish company, claims that it fully performed the contracts. The purchaser, a semi-autonomous agency of the government of Pakistan, thinks otherwise. A panel of arbitrators appointed by the International Chamber of Commerce ("ICC") sided with the contractor and directed the Pakistani purchaser to cancel guaranties securing the contractor's performance. Instead of abiding by the arbitrators' decision, the purchaser continued to demand payment of the guaranties and initiated an action in Pakistan to set aside the award and enforce the guaranties. Neither the contractor nor the purchaser is a party to this action.

---

14. http://store.iccwbo.org/isp-98-international-standby-practices.

15. https://iccwbo.org/global-issues-trends/banking-finance/global-rules/

16. http://www.letterofcredit.biz/difference_between_standby_letter_of_credit_vs_commercial_letter_of_credit.html.

In this dispute between the banks, the Court holds that: (1) the guaranties and counterguaranties are governed by letter-of-credit law; (2) in light of the final, binding ICC award, the guarantor, plaintiff American Express Bank ("AEB"), has no obligation to pay under its guaranties and, therefore, no good faith basis to demand payment of the counterguaranties issued by Banco Español de Crédito ("Banesto"); and (3) AEB's request for a declaration that it will be entitled to payment in the event that it is compelled at some future date to pay in Pakistan is not presently justiciable. AEB's complaint is therefore dismissed without prejudice to the filing of a new action following further developments in Pakistan.

I. BACKGROUND

The history of this case is long and spans four jurisdictions. The Court recounts only enough of it to explain the basis for the current decision. In doing so, the Court accepts as true the factual allegations of the complaint, and makes additional findings of fact necessary to determine whether the Court has subject matter jurisdiction.

A. The Underlying Contracts

In April and July 1995, Isolux Wat S.A. ("Isolux") and the Pakistan Water and Power Development Authority ("WAPDA") entered into two contracts for the construction of electrical substations in Pakistan. . . . Isolux is a Spanish engineering and construction company. (ICC Award 2.) WAPDA is a semi-autonomous agency of the government of Pakistan, which is responsible for coordinating infrastructure development schemes in the water and power sectors.

The contracts required Isolux to install two 220/132 KV substations (the numbers refer to voltage), and to supply and install telecommunication equipment for twenty lower voltage peripheral grid stations. (ICC Award 2.) In exchange, WAPDA apparently agreed to pay Isolux about $35 million. (*See* ICC Award 11.) In the event of a dispute, the parties agreed to submit their claims to arbitration at the ICC. (*See* ICC Award 2.) . . . The clause further provided that "[t]he award of the majority of the [arbitrators] shall be final and binding on both parties." (*Id.*)

B. The Guaranties and Counterguaranties

To secure Isolux's performance, WAPDA required Isolux to obtain two demand guaranties. Such guaranties, which are common in international construction contracts, provide a simple way for a buyer to obtain cash for substitute performance if a contractor defaults. (*See generally* David J. Barru, How to Guarantee Contractor Performance on International Construction Projects: Comparing Surety Bonds With Bank Guarantees and Standby Letters of Credit, 37 Geo. Wash. Int'l L. Rev. 51 (2005)). Isolux asked defendant Banesto to arrange the guaranties. (*See* Compl. Ex. 1.) Banesto in turn asked AEB, the plaintiff here, to execute guaranties in favor of WAPDA in Lahore, Pakistan. (*See id.*) . . . The AEB branch in Pakistan agreed to issue guaranties to WAPDA, provided that Banesto issue counterguaranties in its favor.

The following diagram summarizes the legal relationships between WAPDA, Isolux, and the banks. The instruments at issue in this action appear in bold:

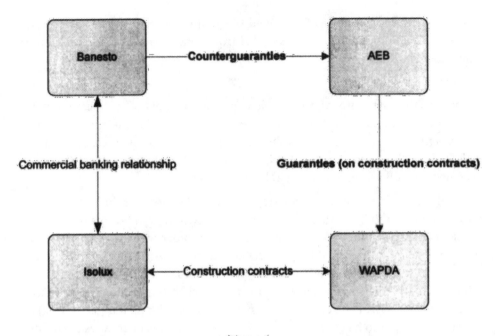

Figure 1

Banesto and AEB made arrangements for the guaranties in a series of SWIFT messages sent in November 1995.[2] On November 16, Banesto sent AEB a message asking that it issue two guaranties in WAPDA's favor, both for a total of U.S. $1,778,571.50 and 5,486,500 Pakistani rupees. (Compl. Ex. 1.) The critical undertakings in the guaranties provided:

> the surety [i.e., AEB] waiving all objections and defences under the aforesaid contract, hereby irrevocably and independently guarantee[s] to pay to WAPDA without delay upon WAPDA's first written demand any amount claimed by WAPDA upto [sic] the sum named herein, against WAPDA's written declaration that the principal [Isolux] has refused or failed to perform the aforementioned contract. (Compl. Ex. 1 (capitalization normalized).)

AEB, in other words, agreed to pay WAPDA under the guaranties based on a written certification that Isolux had failed to perform. For its part, Banesto agreed to repay any liabilities AEB incurred under the guaranties. Specifically, Banesto's messages to AEB promised, in banker's pidgin, that "Our counterguarantee irrevocable unconditional in your favour is valid to receive your eventual claims made under your guarantee that we undertake to pay to you on your first demand notwithstanding any contestation from us or our applicants part [sic] or third party." (*Id.* (capitalization normalized).)

---

2. The acronym stands for "Society for Worldwide Interbank Financial Telecommunication," a cooperative society organized under Belgian law. SWIFT operates a secure, worldwide financial messaging network that banks use to do business with one another. (*See* SWIFT, About SWIFT, http:// www. swift. com/ index. cfm? item_ id=41322 (last visited Nov. 7, 2008).)

On November 30, 1995, AEB executed the guaranties. At Banesto's request, the guaranties' expiration dates were extended from time to time, most recently until September 30, 2004.

C. Contract Disputes

By 2004, disputes arose regarding Isolux's performance of the contracts and WAPDA's concomitant payment obligations, the details of which are unimportant here. (*See generally* ICC Award 2, 11–16.) The disputes provoked legal proceedings in four jurisdictions: Switzerland, Spain, Pakistan, and the United States. Since 2004, however, neither AEB nor Banesto has paid anyone a cent. . . .

Legal proceedings began on February 11, 2004, when Isolux submitted a request for arbitration to the ICC International Court of Arbitration. (Terms of Reference 2.) Isolux's request sought money damages and an order requiring WAPDA to return all the guaranties issued in connection with the construction contracts. (ICC Award 13.) At the same time that Isolux submitted a request for arbitration, it obtained an injunction from a Spanish court to freeze the status quo. The injunction (1) enjoined WAPDA from demanding payment on the AEB guaranties, and (2) directed Banesto not to honor any requests for payment of any guaranties or counterguaranties related to the construction contracts. (*See* Auto [Court Order], Juzgado de 1° Instancia N° 42, Madrid (Feb. 2004), Walker Decl. Ex. H, at 4).

Five months later, WAPDA informed AEB that Isolux had failed to perform the underlying contracts and demanded payment of AEB's guaranties. Without having paid the guaranties, AEB on July 15 and July 16, 2004 sent Banesto SWIFT messages demanding payment of the counterguaranties. . . . Banesto refused, citing the Spanish injunction. . . .

In February 2005, WAPDA filed a lawsuit against AEB in Lahore, Pakistan to recover on the guaranties. (*See* Summons and Compl., *Pakistan Water & Power Development Authority v. American Express Bank, Ltd.,* Civil Suit No. 30 of 2005 (Lahore High Court Feb. 10, 2005)) . . . . The complaint alleged that Isolux failed to perform the construction contracts, . . . that WAPDA had made demand on the guaranties . . . and that AEB had wrongfully refused to honor them . . . . As relief, WAPDA demanded damages in the amount of the guaranties, plus the costs of suit.

In March 2006, an arbitral hearing was held in Geneva, Switzerland. . . . .

Before the arbitral panel issued its decision, AEB on May 8, 2006 filed suit against Banesto in the Southern District of New York. In its complaint, AEB alleged that Banesto breached its agreement to pay AEB under its counterguaranties, and that Banesto breached the terms and conditions of an account agreement governing a U.S. dollar account Banesto maintained with AEB. AEB demanded damages in the amount of the counterguaranties, plus the costs of enforcement. . . .

D. The Arbitral Decision and Subsequent Proceedings in Pakistan

While not communicated to this Court in a timely fashion, the ICC tribunal had issued its decision on February 6, 2007. The decision ordered that (1) Isolux pay

WAPDA U.S. $196,116.92 and 892,589 rupees; (2) WAPDA pay Isolux 60,632,495.86 rupees; and (3) WAPDA cancel a large number of guaranties and performance bonds, among them the guaranties at issue here. (ICC Award 92–93 & annex 1, at 4.). Under the decision, which called for setoffs to be calculated at the exchange rate prevailing on the date of the award, WAPDA owed Isolux approximately $788,066. Isolux owed WAPDA nothing. According to a report submitted by Banesto and not contested by AEB, the award became final and binding as a matter of Swiss law upon notification to the parties. (Letter from Dr. Michael Schöll to Álvaro López de Argumedo & Dorieta Vicente, at 2–3 (Mar. 5, 2007), Cadarso Decl., Ex. C.)

Undeterred by the arbitral decision, WAPDA continued its efforts to enforce the guaranties in Pakistan. By letter dated May 29, 2007, AEB informed this Court that "WAPDA . . . is not abiding by the award, including the direction to release the guaranties of American Express Bank, and has filed a proceeding in Pakistan to have the award set aside." (Letter from David Rabinowitz to Hon. Richard J. Holwell (May 29, 2007).) In its defense of that action, AEB specifically claims that (1) WAPDA's demands for payment of the guaranties are *mala fide* (in bad faith), and (2) AEB has no obligation to pay WAPDA. . . .

. . . .

II. DISCUSSION

The Court holds that AEB is not entitled to immediate payment of the counterguaranties or a declaration of its future rights. Before considering the merits of AEB's claims, however, two threshold issues must be addressed.

A. Choice of Forum Law

First, the parties dispute which forum's law governs AEB's claims to payment under the counterguaranties. Citing an account agreement executed in New York and evidence that Banesto and AEB have an "integrated global relationship," AEB argues that New York law should apply. . . . Banesto thinks that Spanish law applies, or that if New York law applies, it is not subject to any liabilities here that it would not also be subject to in Spain.

In light of the conclusions the Court reaches below, there is no need to resolve this issue now. . . . For the purposes of the pending motions, the Court will therefore assume that New York law applies.

B. Choice of Substantive Law

Next, the parties dispute whether AEB's guaranties and Banesto's counterguaranties, assuming New York law applies, are subject to letter-of-credit law, particularly Article 5 of the New York Uniform Commercial Code. Banesto contends that AEB's guaranties are "functionally and legally equivalent" to international letters of credit, and thus subject to letter-of-credit law. (Def.'s First Mem. 15.) AEB counters that the instruments are simple contracts, not subject to Article 5. (*See* Pl.'s First Mem. 5.) The practical significance of the dispute is that if letter-of-credit law applies, Banesto can take advantage of the "material fraud" exception recognized in Article 5. . . . The

Court agrees with Banesto, and holds that both the guaranties and the counter-guaranties are governed by letter-of-credit law.

By way of background, the typical letter-of-credit transaction involves three legal relationships: (1) an underlying contractual relationship between the party that obtains the letter of credit (the "applicant") and the party entitled to draw on it (the "beneficiary"); (2) a relationship between the party that issues the letter of credit (the "issuer") and the applicant concerning the terms and amount of the credit; and (3) a relationship between the issuer and the beneficiary, which "embod[ies] the issuer's commitment to 'honor drafts or other demands for payment presented by the beneficiary or a transfer beneficiary upon compliance with the terms and conditions specified in the credit.'" . . .

In a standard "commercial" letter of credit, the issuer undertakes to pay the purchase price of goods upon receiving the seller's invoice and other documents evidencing a right to payment. *See* Dolan, ¶¶ 3.04–3.05, at 3-18 to 3-22. A "standby" letter of credit differs with respect to the documents necessary to draw on the credit. Unlike a commercial letter, a standby typically does not require the presentation of a negotiable bill of lading or other transport document; instead, the beneficiary may collect simply by certifying that the applicant failed to perform its underlying contractual obligations. *See* Dolan ¶ 3.06, at 3-23.

Both standby and commercial letters of credit create "an obligation wholly independent of the underlying commercial transaction." *3 Com*, 171 F.3d at 744. This feature of letters of credit, known as the "independence principle," has been termed a "fundamental principle" of the law of credits. *Id*. Because of this principle, it is ordinarily enough to present documents that strictly comply with the terms of a letter of credit to draw on it.

The guaranties and counterguaranties at issue in this case share this essential feature of independence from the underlying contractual relationships, and, therefore, are governed by letter-of-credit law. In the guaranties, AEB "irrevocably and independently guarantee[d] to pay to WAPDA without delay upon WAPDA's first written demand any amount claim by WAPDA." (Compl. Ex. 1.) In the counterguaranties, Banesto undertook to pay AEB "on [its] first simple demand which shall be final and conclusive." (*Id*.) These provisions plainly reflect the parties' expectation that WAPDA would receive money promptly if it submitted a facially valid certification that Isolux failed to perform its obligations—a defining characteristic of standby letters of credit.

Beyond this, a leading treatise on the law of credits favors treating instruments such as the ones at issue here as letters of credit. *See* Dolan, ¶ 1.05[2], at 1-31. As the treatise explains, "foreign banks and foreign branches of domestic banks have introduced a product that they call a 'guarantee' (sic) and to which letter of credit law is quite congenial. 'First-demand guarantees,' 'performance guarantees,' and 'simple-demand guarantees' are the foreign bank equivalents of the standby." *Id*.

. . . .

C. Merits

Turning to the merits, AEB contends that it is entitled to immediately enforce the counterguaranties, and to a declaration setting out Banesto's liabilities in the event that it pays WAPDA pursuant to a Pakistani court order. Neither contention has merit.

1. AEB Has No Basis to Immediately Enforce the Counterguaranties

Taking a somewhat extreme view of the independence principle, AEB first maintains that it is entitled to draw on the counterguaranties regardless of its obligation to pay WAPDA. (*See* Pl.'s Third Mem. 1; Pl.'s First Mem. 6.) The flaw in this argument is obvious: In view of the ICC award—and as a question of basic contract law, international law, and New York law—WAPDA's continued demands for payment of the guaranties lack any basis in law or fact. Thus, until the award is modified or vacated, neither WAPDA nor AEB has a "colorable right" to demand honor of the guaranties or counterguaranties. *See* N.Y.U.C.C. § 5-109 official cmt. 1.

First, as for contract: The construction contracts' arbitration clause provides that "[t]he award of the majority of the [arbitrators] shall be final and binding on both parties." (ICC Award 2.) . . . WAPDA participated fully in the ICC arbitration, and lost. And the parties here have made no suggestion that there is a colorable ground for vacating the award. In short, on the record before the Court, WAPDA's continued demands for payment are flatly inconsistent with its contractual obligations.

Second, as for international law: In 2005, Pakistan ratified the New York Convention on the Recognition and Enforcement Arbitral Awards, 21 U.S.T. 2517, 330 U.N.T.S. 38 ("N.Y. Conv."). . . . Though the convention does not expressly speak to the res judicata effect of an international arbitral award, . . . it reflects the principle that until it is successfully challenged, an arbitral award presumptively establishes the rights and liabilities of the parties to the arbitration. Specifically, the convention provides that subject to its enforcement provisions, "[e]ach Contracting State shall recognize arbitral awards as binding and enforce them in accordance with the rules of procedure of the territory where the award is relied upon." N.Y. Conv. Art. 3. WAPDA's continued demands for payment of AEB's guaranties are inconsistent these international law obligations as well.

Finally, as for New York law: Since at least 1980, New York courts have recognized that a final and conclusive international arbitral award is res judicata as to a party that fully participated in the proceeding. *See Guard-Life Corp. v. S. Parker Hardware Mfg. Corp.*, 50 N.Y.2d 183, 428 N.Y.S. 2d 628, 406 N.E.2d 445, 452 (1980). To the extent that the bona fides of WAPDA's and AEB's demands for payment are judged under New York law, the ICC award precludes WAPDA's continuing demands for payment.

Thus, under multiple bodies of law, the ICC award presumptively establishes the rights and liabilities of WAPDA and AEB until such time as WAPDA succeeds in having the award modified or vacated by a court. AEB, moreover, recognizes this. In Pakistan, it has argued that all disputes arising out of the construction contracts are to be settled in arbitration; that WAPDA's demands for payment under the guaranties were made in bad faith; and that it has no obligation to pay WAPDA anything. . . .

Whether or not AEB is estopped from taking an inconsistent position here, its position in Pakistan better reflects the legal relationships at the heart of this case. AEB has no obligation to pay under its guaranties and, therefore, no good faith basis to demand payment of the counterguaranties issued by Banesto. It follows that, on the current record, Banesto's refusal to honor AEB's demands for honor is proper.

. . . .

Undeniably, this decision leaves AEB in a difficult position. If Pakistan's courts order that AEB honor the principal guaranties, AEB honors the guaranties, and Banesto refuses to honor the counterguaranties or otherwise reimburse AEB, AEB will be required to initiate a new action to recoup payment from Banesto. As the Court has already indicated, a demand for honor in the event that AEB was ordered to pay the guaranties would almost certainly be made in good faith. Moreover, Banesto would likely have an independent obligation to repay AEB if AEB paid WAPDA in reliance on a Pakistani court judgment. But this is not the scenario before the Court. And until Pakistan's courts act, this Court cannot, consistent with the Constitution's limits on federal jurisdiction, issue a binding declaration of the future rights of AEB and Banesto.

III. CONCLUSION

Banesto's motion to dismiss is granted without prejudice to the filing of a new action following entry of judgment in Pakistan. AEB's motion for summary judgment is denied. The Clerk is directed to close this case.

SO ORDERED.

E. Alternative Forms of Export Financing

The International Trade Administration of the U.S. Department of Commerce publishes a useful "Trade Finance Guide,"[17] which is available for viewing or download from the US.Gov website. The guide includes sections on various alternative financing methods including letters of credit, forfaiting, factoring and export credit insurance. Consider the following short excerpt from the guide regarding export credit insurance.

1. Trade Finance Guide: Export Credit Insurance

Chapter 8 Export Credit Insurance

Export credit insurance (ECI) protects an exporter of products and/or services against the risk of nonpayment by a foreign buyer. In other words, ECI significantly

---

17. trade.gov/media/publications/pdf/trade_finance_guide2007.pdf.

reduces the payment risks associated with doing business internationally by giving the exporter conditional assurance that payment will be made in the event that the foreign buyer is unable to pay. Simply put, with an ECI policy, exporters can protect their foreign receivables against a variety of risks, which could result in nonpayment by foreign buyers. The policy generally covers commercial risks—insolvency of the buyer, bankruptcy or protracted defaults (slow payment), and certain political risks—war, terrorism, riots, and revolution, as well as currency inconvertibility, expropriation, and changes in import or export regulations. The insurance is offered either on a single-buyer or portfolio multi-buyer basis for short-term (up to one year) and medium-term (one to five years) repayment periods.

Key Points

- ECI allows you to offer competitive open account terms to foreign buyers while minimizing the risk of nonpayment.

- Creditworthy buyers could default on payment due to circumstances beyond their control.

- With reduced nonpayment risk, you can increase your export sales, establish market share in emerging and developing countries, and compete more vigorously in the global market.

- With insured foreign account receivables, banks are more willing to increase your borrowing capacity and offer attractive financing terms.

Coverage

Short-term ECI, which provides 90 to 95 percent coverage against buyer payment defaults, typically covers (1) consumer goods, materials, and services up to 180 days, and (2) small capital goods, consumer durables and bulk commodities up to 360 days. Medium-term ECI, which provides 85 percent coverage of the net contract value, usually covers large capital equipment up to five years.

How Much Does It Cost?

Premiums are individually determined on the basis of risk factors such as country, buyer's creditworthiness, sales volume, seller's previous export experience, etc. Most multi-buyer policies cost less than 1 percent of insured sales while the prices of single-buyer policies vary widely due to presumed higher risk. However, the cost in most cases is significantly less than the fees charged for letters of credit. ECI, which is often incorporated into the selling price, should be a proactive purchase, in that you have coverage in place before a customer becomes a problem.

Where Can I Get Export Credit Insurance?

ECI policies are offered by many private commercial risk insurance companies as well as the Export-Import Bank of the United States (Ex-Im Bank), the government agency that assists in financing the export of U.S. goods and services to international markets. U.S. exporters are strongly encouraged to shop for a good specialty insurance broker who can help them select the most cost-effective solution for their needs. Reputable, well-established companies that sell commercial ECI policies can be easily found on the Internet. You may also buy ECI policies directly from Ex-Im Bank. In addition, a list of active insurance brokers registered with Ex-Im Bank is available at *www.exim.gov* or you may call **1-800-565-EXIM** for more information.

Pros and Cons of Ex-Im Bank's Export Credit Insurance

- Offers coverage in emerging foreign markets where private insurers may not operate.

- Exporters electing an Ex-Im Bank Working Capital Guarantee may receive a 25 percent premium discount on Multi-buyer Insurance Policies.

- Ex-Im Bank insurance policies are backed by the full faith and credit of the U.S. government.

- Offers enhanced support for environmentally beneficial exports.

- The products must be shipped from the United States and have at least 50 percent U.S. content.

- Unable to support military products or purchases made by foreign military entities.

- Support for exports may be closed or restricted in certain countries per U.S. foreign policy.

Chapter 8

E-Commerce & Electronic Data Exchanges

A. Overview

This chapter provides an introduction to the emerging role of electronic communications and documentation in international business transactions. "E-Commerce" is a term commonly used to describe a wide variety of transactions that are conducted by using digital, electronic communications, typically through computer networks. With the emergence of "e-tailers" such as Amazon, and electronic marketplaces like e-Bay, it is now common for consumers to purchase goods and even services through e-mail or websites. One can buy a television, purchase software to run it, and rent streamed media to watch on it, all by simply clicking a computer mouse (and, more recently, by voice command). Literally millions of consumers all over the world now regularly purchase goods on-line, creating enormous opportunities for large and small businesses alike to reach distant customers.[1] Access to the global marketplace requires only the internet and a credit card. The importance of electronic commerce to international trade has prompted the U.S. government to provide

---

1. Forrester Research predicts that business to consumer ("B2C") e-commerce in the United States will approach $410 billion by 2018, representing over 10% of all retail sales. Allison Enright, *U.S. online retail sales will grow 57% by 2018*, May 12, 2014, https://www.digitalcommerce360.com /2014/05/12/us-online-retail-sales-will-grow-57-2018/. (The U.S. Census reported $97 billion in B2C e-commerce sales during the second quarter of 2016. https://www.google.com/url?sa=t&rct =j&q=&esrc=s&source=web&cd=4&cad=rja&uact=8&ved=0ahUKEwiZ4tXYmerOAhWC1h4 KHd23ClkQFghAMAM&url=https%3A%2F%2Fwww.census.gov%2Fretail%2Fmrts%2Fwww% 2Fdata%2Fpdf%2Fec_current.pdf&usg=AFQjCNHWM4L1triClUQO01wp-2pa1AtMVg&sig2 =OYzixLOIXkOeZRZe8llrGw) Regarding the EU, Forrester reported that: "In the coming five years, the number of Europeans shopping online will grow from 100 million to 174 million." On a similar note, it has been reported that Chinese consumers purchased more than 40 billion dollars in "cross border" e-commerce in 2015. Chenan Xia, *Cross-border e-commerce is luring Chinese shoppers*, http://www.mckinsey.com/industries/high-tech/our-insights/crossborder-ecommerce-is-luring -chinese-shoppers.

significant training and assistance for U.S. exporters (*see* export.gov: "Preparing Your Business for Global eCommerce,"[2] and "eCommerce Plan Checklist/Video"[3]).

This consumer oriented trade, commonly called "B2C" (business to consumer), is dwarfed by the volume of electronic transactions between businesses.[4] The high volume of business to business electronic transactions, commonly called "B2B," reflects the fact that companies increasingly use electronic mechanisms for inventory management[5] and supply chains.[6] For related businesses or long-term contracting partners, use of electronic transactions is often controlled through master agreements (here is a sample[7]), which are focused only on the exchange of documentation through electronic means, or "EDI," and private networks. Such transactions are sometimes conducted through automated systems in which computers ("electronic agents") place and confirm orders. These transactions may even be directed by automated inventory systems, such as a grocery store's price scanner used during checkout. When the store's computer indicates low inventory of Coco Puffs based on the scanner information, it automatically sends a resupply order to a similarly automated warehouse system. Humans need not apply.

In this chapter, we focus on two related but distinct aspects of this digital commercial revolution—creation of contractual obligations through electronic, digitized communications (e.g., sales conducted via email and the internet) and use of electronic data interchange rather than paper bound documentation (e.g., electronic bills of lading and letters of credit). We will also introduce additional commercial considerations raised by electronic transactions involving consumer protection and privacy.

Your goal for this chapter should be to identify the central legal issues raised by international electronic transactions, and understand the legal system's developing legislative responses to these new ways of doing business. Part One, and the following problem, raises many of the basic issues and concerns involving electronic contracting. Part Two reviews developing legal responses to electronic documentation in international transactions, including use of electronic bills of lading and letters of credit.

---

2. https://www.export.gov/article?id=1-Guide-Overview.

3. https://www.youtube.com/watch?v=ot49c7fIUco&feature=youtu.be.

4. As to B2B on-line transactions the website ecommerce&b2b reports: "Frost & Sullivan projects that B2B e-commerce will hit $12 trillion in sales worldwide by 2020, up from $5.5 trillion in 2012. This number is inclusive of EDI, by the way. However, with over $600B in non-EDI B2B e-commerce transactions in 2013, we can expect major growth into the trillions over the next couple years." https://www.digitalcommerce360.com/2014/12/08/b2b-e-commerce-tops-list-emerging-industries/.

5. https://en.wikipedia.org/wiki/Inventory_management_software.

6. https://www.researchgate.net/publication/267247300_INTEGRATION_OF_E-COMMERCE_AND_SUPPLY_CHAIN_A_NEW_BUSINESS_MODEL.

7. https://www.google.com/url?sa=t&rct=j&q=&esrc=s&source=web&cd=3&ved=0ahUKEwjztO_ZjfHOAhUU3WMKHf0-CEoQFggyMAI&url=http%3A%2F%2Fwww.nscorp.com%2Fcontent%2Fdam%2Fnscorp%2Fsuppliers%2Felectronic-data-interchange-agreement.pdf&usg=AFQjCNHH0pr6-VLdcDwezrXeJU1At2r5-A&sig2=VB92UchH_KXpdS9SyvlMyw&cad=rja.

Part One: Contracting in E-Commerce

A. Overview

Many of the legal issues familiar to traditional contracting are complicated by the nature of an electronic transaction. Consider, for example, the role of paper documentation in a traditional sale of goods. Basic rules regarding offer and acceptance, and the requirement that certain transactions be confirmed in a "signed writing," must be adapted to the electronic environment. Choice of law, consumer protection, and dispute settlement issues become even more complicated when an e-tailer from one country sells goods to consumers in a wide variety of distant jurisdictions through the web. Similarly, when traders choose to utilize electronic documents rather than traditional paper bills of lading and letters of credit, authentication and security issues may become problematic.

There have been legislative responses to the special legal problems created by the advent of efficient electronic sales transactions. In 1999, the <u>Uniform Law Commission</u>[8] (creator, along with the American Law Institute, of the UCC) adopted a model act on electronic transactions called the Uniform Electronic Transactions Act ("UETA"). This model act, which essentially equates electronic signatures and records with their traditional pen and paper counterparts, was designed to create a uniform approach to electronic contracting. It was followed on the federal level by the Electronic Signatures in Global and National Commerce Act ("E-Sign") in 2000. This federal statute, closely modeled after UETA but less comprehensive,[9] applies to most interstate and foreign trade but provides that any state may "modify, limit or supersede" its provisions by adopting UETA. As of 2017, 47 states have adopted UETA, excerpts of which are provided below. The three outlier states, Illinois, New York and Washington, have their own statutes governing electronic transactions in ways similar to UETA.

B. Problem Eight: Rotten Dutch Bulbs

1. Facts

Raymond Dumont, the owner of Hillbilly Dirt Farms (a Florida corporation), arrived in your office this morning and related the following tale of woe. Sometime in early February, Dumont visited the website of the world famous Dutch Boy Farm's

---

8. http://www.uniformlaws.org/.

9. Unlike UETA, E-SIGN does not address some important issues such as the attribution of electronic signatures, mistakes, admissibility of electronic records as evidence, and setting the time at which electronic communications are deemed sent and received. *See generally*, Robert A. Wittie & Jane K. Winn, *Electronic Records and Signatures under the Federal E-SIGN Legislation and the UETA*, 56 Bus. Law. 293-340 (2000).

"Bulb Supercenter." Dutch Boy Farms is physically located in Rotterdam, Netherlands. While visiting the website, Dumont was impressed by pictures of a new variety of tulip bulb, called the "tropics master." This bulb variety was, the website proclaimed, "the tropics residing tulip lover's dream, specially bred to withstand the heat and humidity of sub-tropical climates such as that of South Florida." Dumont found a price list on the website listing the "tropics master" at "$1 per bulb," and clicked on a link labeled "orders." This action generated a form asking for quantities, colors, and personal information such as the buyer's address and credit card information. Dumont clicked a box designating "Tropic Master Tulip Bulbs," entered "1000" as the quantity desired, and typed in his address and credit card information. He then clicked a small box indicating that he agreed to Dutch Boy's "terms and conditions" and then on another button that asked if he wanted to confirm and finalize his order.

The next day, Dumont received an automated e-mail reply with the Dutch Boys' address at the bottom. The e-mail stated:

> Order Confirmation: Your goods have been shipped, air freight pre-paid, total billed: $1250, including handling and shipping. All disputes are to be settled exclusively before the Dutch Bulb Farmers Benevolent Association and Arbitration Board in Rotterdam, Netherlands, under the laws of the Netherlands. Goods supplied outside Europe, sold "as is."

This e-mail response surprised Dumont, who did not want bulbs without a guarantee and thought that shipping costs were included in the website price list. His concern was compounded by a review of the "tropics master" bulbs that he found that morning on the website "Bulber's Review." The review described the new bulb variety as "wimpy" and "often ridden with parasites that could prevent importation." Dumont attempted to cancel the order via return e-mail but has not received a reply other than "this e-mail has been automatically generated, reply e-mails cannot be answered." He was also miffed about suddenly receiving dozens of e-mail solicitations from gardening companies, as well as a few "adult content" websites with a gardening theme. He wants to know what to do and whether he is stuck with some "rotten Dutch bulbs."

2. Assignment

1. *Please make a list of potential legal issues that might arise in the transaction described above by virtue of the parties' use of electronic communications.* Use the references provided below and your knowledge of basic contract law, as well as what you have already learned in this class about international contracting. You should consider, among other things, contract formalities, statute of frauds, conflicts of law, and dispute resolution. Do not, however, limit yourself to these categories. Also, think about the consumer protection and privacy concerns raised by a purely digital transaction. *What would a lawyer want to know and find out when*

advising a client about an international sale conducted exclusively through electronic means?

2. Using the references below (or others that you find on your own), identify common approaches used to accommodate the legal issues that you have identified in assignment one above. Reviewing these sources should also help you identify what kinds of issues electronic transactions might create more generally.

3. Formulate a response to Raymond's questions — is he bound by a contract, and if so, what are its terms?

C. Resources

1. Jurisdiction & Conflicts of Law

Electronic contracting, particularly over the internet, raises a number of sticky jurisdictional and choice of law issues. In our problem, for example, a foreign website offered merchandise for sale that reached a consumer in the United States. Do U.S. laws regarding electronic contracting even apply to this transaction? Do U.S. consumer protection and privacy laws apply? Can the seller demand choice of law and forum terms that avoid application of such laws? Can U.S. courts or administrative bodies legitimately exercise personal jurisdiction over the seller? Where does the sale take place — in cyberspace? Since buyers can access a website storefront from across the globe, these questions raise the troubling possibility for e-tailers of "jurisdiction anywhere." Peruse one of these linked papers, by either the Berkman Center for Internet & Society[10] or the law firm Pepper Hamilton,[11] regarding the jurisdictional dilemmas of e-commerce. Both identify some critical issues raised by B2C internet transactions, and describe the business perspective on such problems. What are the central issues addressed in these position papers?

2. Contract Formalities

In first year contracts, every law student learns that the essence of contractual obligations involves the exchange of promises — an offer, an acceptance and consideration — for which there exists mutual assent. Certain formalities and rules on how and when contracts are formed help determine if an agreement has been reached, what its terms are, and its authenticity. With a bar exam presumably looming, hopefully you will remember the "mailbox"[12] rules on the effective timing of offers, acceptances, and rejections. (If need be, you can review such rules in this video,[13] which

---

10. https://cyber.harvard.edu/olds/ecommerce/disputes.html.

11. http://www.pepperlaw.com/publications/controlling-chaos-frameworks-for-governing-virtual-relationships-2005-12-28/.

12. https://en.wikipedia.org/wiki/Posting_rule.

13. https://www.youtube.com/watch?v=uaG2MqjG7GY.

conclusively demonstrates that some people have too much time on their hands.) You should also recall that under the "statute of frauds,"[14] certain contracts must be sufficiently memorialized by a "writing," and be "signed" by the party against whom enforcement is sought (see, e.g., UCC § 2-201).[15] How do such rules play out in the context of electronic contracting? How is mutual assent determined? How is the authenticity of a signature established? Review the following legislative responses to these and related questions.

a. Federal "E-Sign" Act, Selected Provisions[16]

TITLE I — ELECTRONIC RECORDS AND SIGNATURES IN COMMERCE

SEC. 101. GENERAL RULE OF VALIDITY.

(a) IN GENERAL. — Notwithstanding any statute, regulation, or other rule of law (other than this title and title II), with respect to any transaction in or affecting interstate or foreign commerce —

(1) a signature, contract, or other record relating to such transaction may not be denied legal effect, validity, or enforceability solely because it is in electronic form; and

(2) a contract relating to such transaction may not be denied legal effect, validity, or enforceability solely because an electronic signature or electronic record was used in its formation.

. . . .

(c) CONSUMER DISCLOSURES. —

(1) CONSENT TO ELECTRONIC RECORDS. — Notwithstanding subsection (a), if a statute, regulation, or other rule of law requires that information relating to a transaction or transactions in or affecting interstate or foreign commerce be provided or made available to a consumer in writing, the use of an electronic record to provide or make available (whichever is required) such information satisfies the requirement that such information be in writing if —

(A) the consumer has affirmatively consented to such use and has not withdrawn such consent;

(B) the consumer, prior to consenting, is provided with a clear and conspicuous statement —

(i) informing the consumer of (I) any right or option of the consumer to have the record provided or made available on paper or in nonelectronic form, and (II) the right of the consumer to withdraw the consent . . .

---

14. https://en.wikipedia.org/wiki/Statute_of_frauds.

15. https://www.law.cornell.edu/ucc/2/2-201.

16. Full text: frwebgate.access.gpo.gov/cgi-bin/getdoc.cgi?dbname=106_cong_bills&docid =f:s761enr.txt.pdf.

. . . .

SEC. 102. Exemption from Preemption

(a) IN GENERAL. — A State statute, regulation, or other rule of law may modify, limit, or supersede the provisions of section 101 with respect to State law only if such statute, regulation, or rule of law —

(1) constitutes an enactment or adoption of the Uniform Electronic Transactions Act as approved and recommended for enactment in all the States by the National Conference of Commissioners on Uniform State Laws in 1999 . . .

. . . .

b. *Uniform Electronic Transactions Act* (UETA)[17] — *Selected Provisions, Florida*

FS § 668.50

DEFINITIONS. — As used in this section:

(a) "Agreement" means the bargain of the parties in fact, as found in their language or inferred from other circumstances and from rules, regulations, and procedures given the effect of agreements under provisions of law otherwise applicable to a particular transaction.

(b) "Automated transaction" means a transaction conducted or performed, in whole or in part, by electronic means or electronic records, in which the acts or records of one or both parties are not reviewed by an individual in the ordinary course in forming a contract, performing under an existing contract, or fulfilling an obligation required by the transaction.

(c) "Computer program" means a set of statements or instructions to be used directly or indirectly in an information processing system in order to bring about a certain result.

(d) "Contract" means the total legal obligation resulting from the parties' agreement as affected by this act and other applicable provisions of law.

(e) "Electronic" means relating to technology having electrical, digital, magnetic, wireless, optical, electromagnetic, or similar capabilities.

(f) "Electronic agent" means a computer program or an electronic or other automated means used independently to initiate an action or respond to electronic records or performances in whole or in part, without review or action by an individual.

(g) "Electronic record" means a record created, generated, sent, communicated, received, or stored by electronic means.

---

17. http://www.leg.state.fl.us/statutes/index.cfm?mode=View%20Statutes&SubMenu=1&App _mode=Display_Statute&Search_String=uniform+electronic+transactions&URL=0600-0699 /0668/Sections/0668.50.html.

(h) "Electronic signature" means an electronic sound, symbol, or process attached to or logically associated with a record and executed or adopted by a person with the intent to sign the record.

. . . .

(m) "Record" means information that is inscribed on a tangible medium or that is stored in an electronic or other medium and is retrievable in perceivable form, including public records as defined in s. 119.011.

(n) "Security procedure" means a procedure employed for the purpose of verifying that an electronic signature, record, or performance is that of a specific person or for detecting changes or errors in the information in an electronic record. The term includes a procedure that requires the use of algorithms or other codes, identifying words or numbers, encryption, or callback or other acknowledgment procedures.

(3) SCOPE.—

(a) Except as otherwise provided in paragraph (b), this section applies to electronic records and electronic signatures relating to a transaction.

(b) This section does not apply to a transaction to the extent the transaction is governed by:

1. A provision of law governing the creation and execution of wills, codicils, or testamentary trusts;

2. The Uniform Commercial Code other than s. 671.107 and chapters 672 and 680; [Author note: Ch. 672 is the enactment of Article 2, Sales, of the UCC; Ch. 680 covers leases]

3. The Uniform Computer Information Transactions Act [Author note: This Model Law on technology licensing and software sales has not been adopted]; or

4. Rules relating to judicial procedure.

. . . .

(5) USE OF ELECTRONIC RECORDS AND ELECTRONIC SIGNATURES; VARIATION BY AGREEMENT.—

. . . .

(b) This section applies only to transactions between parties each of which has agreed to conduct transactions by electronic means. Whether the parties agree to conduct a transaction by electronic means is determined from the context and surrounding circumstances, including the parties' conduct.

. . . .

(d) Except as otherwise provided in this section, the effect of any provision of this section may be varied by agreement. The presence in certain provisions of this section of the words "unless otherwise agreed," or words of similar import, does not imply that the effect of other provisions may not be varied by agreement.

. . . .

(7) LEGAL RECOGNITION OF ELECTRONIC RECORDS, ELECTRONIC SIGNA-TURES, AND ELECTRONIC CONTRACTS.—

(a) A record or signature may not be denied legal effect or enforceability solely because the record or signature is in electronic form.

(b) A contract may not be denied legal effect or enforceability solely because an electronic record was used in the formation of the contract.

(c) If a provision of law requires a record to be in writing, an electronic record satisfies such provision.

(d) If a provision of law requires a signature, an electronic signature satisfies such provision.

(8) PROVISION OF INFORMATION IN WRITING; PRESENTATION OF RECORDS.—

(a) If parties have agreed to conduct a transaction by electronic means and a pro-vision of law requires a person to provide, send, or deliver information in writing to another person, the requirement is satisfied if the information is provided, sent, or delivered, as the case may be, in an electronic record capable of retention by the re-cipient at the time of receipt. An electronic record is not capable of retention by the recipient if the sender or the sender's information processing system inhibits the ability of the recipient to print or store the electronic record.

. . . .

(c) If a sender inhibits the ability of a recipient to store or print an electronic rec-ord, the electronic record is not enforceable against the recipient.

(d) The requirements of this section may not be varied by agreement, pro-vided: . . .

(9) ATTRIBUTION AND EFFECT OF electronic RECORD AND electronic SIGNATURE.—

(a) An electronic record or electronic signature is attributable to a person if the record or signature was the act of the person. The act of the person may be shown in any manner, including a showing of the efficacy of any security procedure applied to determine the person to which the electronic record or electronic signature was attributable.

(b) The effect of an electronic record or electronic signature attributed to a person under paragraph (a) is determined from the context and surrounding circumstances at the time of its creation, execution, or adoption, including the parties' agreement, if any, and otherwise as provided by law.

(10) EFFECT OF CHANGE OR ERROR.—If a change or error in an electronic record occurs in a transmission between parties to a transaction, the following rules apply:

(a) If the parties have agreed to use a security procedure to detect changes or er-rors and one party has conformed to the procedure, but the other party has not, and the nonconforming party would have detected the change or error had that party also conformed, the conforming party may avoid the effect of the changed or erroneous electronic record.

(b) In an automated transaction involving an individual, the individual may avoid the effect of an electronic record that resulted from an error made by the individual in dealing with the electronic agent of another person if the electronic agent did not provide an opportunity for the prevention or correction of the error and, at the time the individual learns of the error, the individual:

1. Promptly notifies the other person of the error and that the individual did not intend to be bound by the electronic record received by the other person.

2. Takes reasonable steps, including steps that conform to the other person's reasonable instructions, to return to the other person or, if instructed by the other person, to destroy the consideration received, if any, as a result of the erroneous electronic record.

3. Has not used or received any benefit or value from the consideration, if any, received from the other person.

(c) If paragraphs (a) and (b) do not apply, the change or error has the effect provided by the other provision of law, including the law of mistake, and the parties' contract, if any.

(d) Paragraphs (b) and (c) may not be varied by agreement.

(11) NOTARIZATION AND ACKNOWLEDGMENT.—

(a) If a law requires a signature or record to be notarized, acknowledged, verified, or made under oath, the requirement is satisfied if the electronic signature of the person authorized by applicable law to perform those acts, together with all other information required to be included by other applicable law, is attached to or logically associated with the signature or record. Neither a rubber stamp nor an impression type seal is required for an electronic notarization.

. . . .

(12) RETENTION OF ELECTRONIC RECORDS; ORIGINALS.—

(a) If a law requires that a record be retained, the requirement is satisfied by retaining an electronic record of the information in the record which:

1. Accurately reflects the information set forth in the record after the record was first generated in final form as an electronic record or otherwise.

2. Remains accessible for later reference.

(b) A requirement to retain a record in accordance with paragraph (a) does not apply to any information the sole purpose of which is to enable the record to be sent, communicated, or received.

(c) A person may satisfy paragraph (a) by using the services of another person if the requirements of paragraph (a) are satisfied.

(d) If a provision of law requires a record to be presented or retained in its original form, or provides consequences if the record is not presented or retained in its original form, that law is satisfied by an electronic record retained in accordance with paragraph (a).

(e) If a provision of law requires retention of a check, that requirement is satisfied by retention of an electronic record of the information on the front and back of the check in accordance with paragraph (a).

. . . .

(13) ADMISSIBILITY IN EVIDENCE.—In a proceeding, evidence of a record or signature may not be excluded solely because the record or signature is in electronic form.

(14) AUTOMATED TRANSACTIONS.—In an automated transaction, the following rules apply:

(a) A contract may be formed by the interaction of electronic agents of the parties, even if no individual was aware of or reviewed the electronic agents' actions or the resulting terms and agreements.

(b) A contract may be formed by the interaction of an electronic agent and an individual, acting on the individual's own behalf or for another person, including by an interaction in which the individual performs actions that the individual is free to refuse to perform and which the individual knows or has reason to know will cause the electronic agent to complete the transaction or performance.

(c) The terms of the contract are determined by the substantive law applicable to the contract.

(15) TIME AND PLACE OF SENDING AND RECEIVING.—

(a) Unless otherwise agreed between the sender and the recipient, an electronic record is sent when the record:

1. Is addressed properly or otherwise directed properly to an information processing system that the recipient has designated or uses for the purpose of receiving electronic records or information of the type sent and from which the recipient is able to retrieve the electronic record.

2. Is in a form capable of being processed by that system.

. . . .

(b) Unless otherwise agreed between a sender and the recipient, an electronic record is received when the record enters an information processing system that the recipient has designated or uses for the purpose of receiving electronic records or information of the type sent and from which the recipient is able to retrieve the electronic record; and is in a form capable of being processed by that system.

(c) Paragraph (b) applies even if the place the information processing system is located is different from the place the electronic record is deemed to be received under paragraph (d).

(d) Unless otherwise expressly provided in the electronic record or agreed between the sender and the recipient, an electronic record is deemed to be sent from the sender's place of business and to be received at the recipient's place of business. For purposes of this paragraph, the following rules apply:

1. If the sender or recipient has more than one place of business, the place of business of that person is the place having the closest relationship to the underlying transaction.

2. If the sender or the recipient does not have a place of business, the place of business is the sender's or recipient's residence, as the case may be.

(e) An electronic record is received under paragraph (b) even if no individual is aware of its receipt.

(f) Receipt of an electronic acknowledgment from an information processing system described in paragraph (b) establishes that a record was received but, by itself, does not establish that the content sent corresponds to the content received.

(g) If a person is aware that an electronic record purportedly sent under paragraph (a), or purportedly received under paragraph (b), was not actually sent or received, the legal effect of the sending or receipt is determined by other applicable provisions of law. Except to the extent permitted by the other provisions of law, the requirements of this paragraph may not be varied by agreement.

(h) An automated transaction does not establish the acceptability of an electronic record for recording purposes.

The follow brief summary of UETA[18] by the Uniform Law Commission provides helpful insights about what you should look for in its text.

The basic rules are in Section 7 of UETA. The most fundamental rule in Section 7 provides that a "record or signature may not be denied legal effect or enforceability solely because it is in electronic form." The second most fundamental rule says that "a contract may not be denied legal effect or enforceability solely because an electronic record was used in its formation." The third most fundamental rule states that any law that requires a writing will be satisfied by an electronic record. And the fourth basic rule provides that any signature requirement in the law will be met if there is an electronic signature.

Almost all of the other rules in UETA serve the fundamental principles set out in Section 7, and tend to answer basic legal questions about the use of electronic records and signatures. Thus, Section 15 determines when information is legally sent or delivered in electronic form. It establishes when electronic delivery occurs — when an electronic record capable of retention by the recipient is legally sent and received ....

Another rule that supports the general validity of electronic records and signatures in transactions is the rule on attribution in Section 9 .... UETA

---

18. http://www.uniformlaws.org/ActSummary.aspx?title=Electronic%20Transactions%20Act.

states that a signature is attributable to a person if it is an act of that person, and that act may be shown in any manner. If a security procedure is used, its efficacy in establishing the attribution may be shown . . . .

Section 10 provides some rules on errors and changes in messages. It favors the party who conforms to the security procedure used in the specific transaction against the party who does not, in the event there is a dispute over the content of the message.

Under the provisions of UETA, would the exchange of electronic communications between Raymond and Dutch Boy satisfy the statute of frauds requirements? Did Raymond assent to the transaction with a "signature" and assent to all of Dutch Boy's terms by "clicking" the box provided? A case excerpt relating to this question appears below. If there was an agreement, did Raymond engage in an "automated transaction" with an electronic agent during which Raymond made an "error" without adequate means for correction? After considering these questions, evaluate Raymond's situation from the perspective of EU law as described in the sections that follow the case, particularly those relating to privacy and consumer protection.

c. Clicking & Wrapping: Consent in the Electronic Environment: Lawrence Feldman v. Google, Inc. 513 F. Supp. 2d 229 (E.D. Pa. 2007)

GILES, District Judge.

I. Introduction

. . . .

Defendant's motion seeks to enforce the forum selection clause in an online "click-wrap" agreement, which provides for venue in Santa Clara County, California, which is within the San Jose Division. In his original complaint, Plaintiff based his claims on a theory of express contract. In his Amended Complaint, however, Plaintiff offers a wholly new legal theory. He argues that no express contract existed because the agreement was not valid. Withdrawing his express contract allegations, Plaintiff advanced the theory of implied contract because he argues he did not have notice of and did not assent to the terms of the agreement and therefore there was no "meeting of the minds." Plaintiff also argues that, even if the agreement were controlling, it is a contract of adhesion and unconscionable, and that the forum selection clause is unenforceable.

. . . .

II. Factual Background . . .

On or about January 2003, Plaintiff, a lawyer with his own law firm, Lawrence E. Feldman & Associates, purchased advertising from Defendant Google, Inc.'s "Ad-Words" Program, to attract potential clients who may have been harmed by drugs under scrutiny by the U.S. Food and Drug Administration. In the AdWords program, whenever an internet user searched on the internet search engine, Google.com, for keywords or "Adwords" purchased by Plaintiff, such as "Vioxx," "Bextra," and "Celebrex," Plaintiff's ad would appear. If the searcher clicked on Plaintiff's ad, Defendant would charge Plaintiff for each click made on the ad. This procedure is known as "pay per click" advertising. . . .

Plaintiff claims that he was the victim of "click fraud." Click fraud occurs when entities or persons, such as competitors or pranksters, without any interest in Plaintiff's services, click repeatedly on Plaintiff's ad, the result of which drives up his advertising cost and discourages him from advertising. Click fraud also may be referred to as "improper clicks" or, to coin a phrase, "trick clicks." Plaintiff alleges that twenty to thirty percent of all clicks for which he was charged were fraudulent. He claims that Google required him to pay for all clicks on his ads, including those which were fraudulent.

Plaintiff does not contend that Google actually knew that there were fraudulent clicks, but alleges . . . that Google had the capacity to determine which clicks were fraudulent, but did nothing to prevent the click fraud, and did not adequately warn him about click fraud or investigate his complaints about click fraud.

. . . .

The Online Agreement and Forum Selection Clause . . .

The type of contract at issue here is commonly referred to as a "clickwrap" agreement. A clickwrap agreement appears on an internet webpage and requires that a user consent to any terms or conditions by clicking on a dialog box on the screen in order to proceed with the internet transaction. *Specht v. Netscape Comms. Corp.*, 306 F.3d 17, 22 (2d Cir.2002); Kevin W. Grierson, Enforceability of "Clickwrap" or "Shrinkwrap" Agreements Common in Computer Software, Hardware, and Internet Transactions, 106 A.L.R. 5th 309, § 1.a n. 3 (2004); 4-GL Computer Contracts C (2006). Even though they are electronic, clickwrap agreements are considered to be writings because they are printable and storable. See, e.g., *In re RealNetworks, Inc., Privacy Litigation*, No. 00–c–1366, 2000 U.S. Dist. LEXIS 6584, at *8–11, 2000 WL 631341, at *3–4 (N.D.Ill. May 11, 2000).

To determine whether a clickwrap agreement is enforceable, courts presented with the issue apply traditional principles of contract law and focus on whether the plaintiffs had reasonable notice of and manifested assent to the clickwrap agreement. See, e.g., *Specht*, 306 F.3d at 28–30; . . . John M. Norwood, A Summary of Statutory and Case Law Associated With Contracting in the Electronic Universe, 4 DePaul Bus. & Comm. L.J. 415, 439–49 (2006) (discussing clickwrap cases) . . . . Absent a showing of fraud, failure to read an enforceable clickwrap agreement, as with any binding contract, will not excuse compliance with its terms.

. . . .

Plaintiff claims he did not have notice or knowledge of the forum selection clause, and therefore that there was no "meeting of the minds" required for contract formation. In support of this argument, Plaintiff cites *Specht v. Netscape Comms. Corp.*, in which the Second Circuit held that internet users did not have reasonable notice of the terms in an online agreement and therefore did not assent to the agreement under the facts of that case. 306 F.3d at 20, 31.

The facts in *Specht*, however, are easily distinguishable from this case. There, the internet users were urged to click on a button to download free software. *Id.* at 23, 32. There was no visible indication that clicking on the button meant that the user agreed to the terms and conditions of a proposed contract that contained an arbitration clause. *Id.* The only reference to terms was located in text visible if the users scrolled down to the next screen, which was "submerged." *Id.* at 23, 31–32. Even if a user did scroll down, the terms were not immediately displayed. *Id.* at 23. Users would have had to click onto a hyperlink, which would take the user to a separate webpage entitled "License & Support Agreements." *Id.* at 23–24. Only on that webpage was a user informed that the user must agree to the license terms before downloading a product. *Id.* at 24. The user would have to choose from a list of license agreements and again click on yet another hyperlink in order to see the terms and conditions for the downloading of that particular software. *Id.*

The Second Circuit concluded on those facts that there was not sufficient or reasonably conspicuous notice of the terms and that the plaintiffs could not have manifested assent to the terms under these conditions. *Id.* at 32, 35. The Second Circuit was careful to differentiate the method just described from clickwrap agreements which do provide sufficient notice. *Id.* at 22 n. 4, 32–33. . . .

Through a similar process, the AdWords Agreement gave reasonable notice of its terms. In order to activate an AdWords account, the user had to visit a webpage which displayed the Agreement in a scrollable text box. Unlike the impermissible agreement in *Specht*, the user did not have to scroll down to a submerged screen or click on a series of hyperlinks to view the Agreement. Instead, text of the AdWords Agreement was immediately visible to the user, as was a prominent admonition in boldface to read the terms and conditions carefully, and with instruction to indicate assent if the user agreed to the terms.

That the user would have to scroll through the text box of the Agreement to read it in its entirety does not defeat notice because there was sufficient notice of the Agreement itself and clicking "Yes" constituted assent to all of the terms. The preamble, which was immediately visible, also made clear that assent to the terms was binding. The Agreement was presented in readable 12-point font. It was only seven paragraphs long—not so long so as to render scrolling down to view all of the terms inconvenient or impossible. A printer-friendly, full-screen version was made readily available. The user had ample time to review the document.

Unlike the impermissible agreement in *Specht*, the user here had to take affirmative action and click the "Yes, I agree to the above terms and conditions" button in order to proceed to the next step. Clicking "Continue" without clicking the "Yes" button would have returned the user to the same webpage. If the user did not agree to all of the terms, he could not have activated his account, placed ads, or incurred charges.

The AdWords Agreement here is very similar to clickwrap agreements that courts have found to have provided reasonable notice. See, e.g., *Forrest v. Verizon Communications, Inc.*, 805 A.2d 1007, 1010–11 (D.C.2002) (holding that adequate notice was provided of clickwrap agreement terms where users had to click "Accept" to agree to the terms in order to subscribe, an admonition in capital letters was presented at the top of the agreement to read the agreement carefully, the thirteen-page agreement appeared in a scroll box with only portions visible at a time, and the forum selection clause was located in the final section and presented in lower case font) . . . .

A reasonably prudent internet user would have known of the existence of terms in the AdWords Agreement. Plaintiff had to have had reasonable notice of the terms. By clicking on "Yes, I agree to the above terms and conditions" button, Plaintiff indicated assent to the terms. Therefore, the requirements of an express contract for reasonable notice of terms and mutual assent are satisfied.

3. International Responses to E-Commerce Generally

a. European Union General Directives on E-Commerce[19]

Not surprisingly, the European Union has promulgated legislation with a focus on e-commerce generally, similar to UETA. A 1999 directive required recognition of qualified electronic signatures.[20] In 2000, the EU adopted its Directive on Electronic Commerce (2000/31/EC).[21] Like UETA, the Directive essentially requires EU member states to create legislation recognizing the validity of electronic contracts.[22] The Directive is, however, broader than UETA in that it addresses issues such as transparency of commercial communications, unsolicited communications, regulation of professional service providers, placing of orders and correction of error, provision of essential information (e.g., prices must include taxes and delivery costs) and regulation of internet based sellers. The EU summary[23] of the Directive describes it this way:

---

19. A "directive" is a form of indirect legislation that requires EU member states to achieve stated goals, or impose stated requirements and limitations through national legislative action ("take measures to ensure that . . ."). A directive essentially requires member states to achieve particular results without dictating the precise means. Directives may be distinguished from "regulations" which create an EU rule of direct applicability throughout the Union. See this EU Guide: http://ec.europa.eu/info/law/law-making-process/types-eu-law_en.

20. According to the EU summary of the "legal effects" of "Directive 1999/93/EC": "An advanced eSignature based on a qualified certificate satisfies the legal requirements of a signature in relation to data in electronic form in the same way as a handwritten signature satisfies those requirements in relation to paper-based data. [For convenience, this type of signature can be called a 'qualified eSignature'. Although the Directive describes it, it does not actually define it.] It is also admissible as evidence in legal proceedings. An eSignature may not legally be refused as evidence in legal proceedings simply because it is: in electronic form; not based on a qualified certificate; not created by a secure signature-creation device." http://eur-lex.europa.eu/legal-content/EN/ALL /?uri=CELEX:31999L0093.

21. eur-lex.europa.eu/LexUriServ/LexUriServ.do?uri=OJ:L:2000:178:0001:0016:EN:PDF.

22. EU Directive 2000/31/EC, Article 9.

23. http://ec.europa.eu/internal_market/e-commerce/directive/index_en.htm.

The Electronic Commerce Directive, adopted in 2000, sets up an Internal Market framework for electronic commerce, which provides legal certainty for business and consumers alike. It establishes harmonised rules on issues such as the transparency and information requirements for online service providers, commercial communications, electronic contracts and limitations of liability of intermediary service providers. The proper functioning of the Internal Market in electronic commerce is ensured by the Internal Market clause, which means that information society services are, in principle, subject to the law of the Member State in which the service provider is established. In turn, the Member State in which the information society service is received cannot restrict incoming services.

b. Other International Responses to E-Commerce

International electronic commerce clearly creates the significant potential, if not inevitability, of incompatible legal and technological approaches to basic commercial issues. The potential for overlapping and inconsistent regimes calls out for international cooperation and the development of international frameworks. Beyond controlling issues such as contract formalities, international agreements over dispute resolution, personal jurisdiction, application of health and safety laws, and consumer protection and privacy, would reduce uncertainty and greatly promote international ecommerce. Apart from the EU's efforts referenced above, a number of international organizations, including the WTO,[24] have begun concentrated work in this area. The United Nations Commission on International Trade Law, UNCITRAL,[25] has produced the earliest and most advanced of these efforts toward harmonization, promulgating several model laws on electronic commerce, which come in the form of proposed treaties. The UN encourages nations to adopt the model laws, enhancing harmonization and more uniform approaches to electronic commerce. Excerpts from these model laws are available at the UNCITRAL website linked above. Peruse the text of the Model Law on Electronic Commerce (1996)[26] to identify articles that you believe would be relevant to the issues presented in the problem. There is no need to analyze the text generally, which is similar to the rules created in E-Sign and UETA. Rather, simply note the subjects covered and general approaches taken.

UNCITRAL's description of the purposes for this 1996 Model Law on Electronic Commerce, as provided in its "Guide To Enactment,"[27] is generally instructive regarding the legal challenges posed by international electronic commerce:

> 16. The Model Law thus relies on a new approach, sometimes referred to as the "functional equivalent approach", which is based on an analysis of the purposes and functions of the traditional paper-based requirement with a

---

24. https://www.wto.org/english/tratop_e/ecom_e/ecom_e.htm.
25. http://www.uncitral.org/uncitral/en/about_us.html.
26. www.uncitral.org/pdf/english/texts/electcom/05-89450_Ebook.pdf.
27. www.uncitral.org/pdf/english/texts/electcom/05-89450_Ebook.pdf.

view to determining how those purposes or functions could be fulfilled through electronic-commerce techniques. For example, among the functions served by a paper document are the following: to provide that a document would be legible by all; to provide that a document would remain unaltered over time; to allow for the reproduction of a document so that each party would hold a copy of the same data; to allow for the authentication of data by means of a signature; and to provide that a document would be in a form acceptable to public authorities and courts. It should be noted that in respect of all of the above-mentioned functions of paper, electronic records can provide the same level of security as paper and, in most cases, a much higher degree of reliability and speed, especially with respect to the identification of the source and content of the data, provided that a number of technical and legal requirements are met. However, the adoption of the functional-equivalent approach should not result in imposing on users of electronic commerce more stringent standards of security (and the related costs) than in a paper-based environment.

UNCITRAL has also created several other more specific model laws and conventions relating to international electronic commerce including the <u>2005 — United Nations Convention on the Use of Electronic Communications in International Contracts</u>.[28] UNCITRAL describes this convention as follows:

> Adopted by the General Assembly on 23 November 2005, the Convention aims to enhance legal certainty and commercial predictability where electronic communications are used in relation to international contracts. It addresses the determination of a party's location in an electronic environment; the time and place of dispatch and receipt of electronic communications; the use of automated message systems for contract formation; and the criteria to be used for establishing functional equivalence between electronic communications and paper documents — including "original" paper documents — as well as between electronic authentication methods and hand-written signatures.

In a similar vein, UNICITRAL also developed the <u>2001 — UNCITRAL Model Law on Electronic Signatures with Guide to Enactment</u>.[29] It describes the model law this way:

> Adopted by UNCITRAL on 5 July 2001, the Model Law aims at bringing additional legal certainty to the use of electronic signatures. Building on the flexible principle contained in article 7 of the UNCITRAL Model Law on Electronic Commerce, it establishes criteria of technical reliability for the equivalence between electronic and hand-written signatures. The Model Law

---

28. http://www.uncitral.org/uncitral/en/uncitral_texts/electronic_commerce/2005Convention.html.

29. http://www.uncitral.org/uncitral/en/uncitral_texts/electronic_commerce/2001Model_signatures.html.

follows a technology-neutral approach, which avoids favouring the use of any specific technical product. The Model Law further establishes basic rules of conduct that may serve as guidelines for assessing possible responsibilities and liabilities for the signatory, the relying party and trusted third parties intervening in the signature process.

c. E-Commerce & the CISG

As you learned in earlier chapters, the CISG will govern many international sales transactions involving U.S. interests. Since the CISG's creation in 1980, prior to the internet, the world has obviously changed. It should not be surprising that the CISG does not directly address electronic contracting. At least with respect to contract formalities, however, the convention might appear more accommodating to electronic transactions than the UCC, since there is no requirement that a contract be in writing.[30] On the other hand, the convention's treatment of other critical issues, such as notice or defining when an offer, acceptance or rejection has "reached" a relevant party, is less clear in the context of electronic communications. Browse the "opinion" of the non-official CISG Advisory Council[31] on the subject.

4. Issues of Security and Authentication

An obvious issue in electronic commerce involves the authenticity of communications. This is particularly true for international transactions that are likely to encounter varied approaches to such issues among different national jurisdictions, causing both legal and technical incompatibilities. The 2006 UNCITRAL report on electronic commerce describes the problems and various international responses to these issues.

2006 UNCITRAL Report on Electronic Commerce:

I. Definition and methods of electronic signature and authentication

A. General remarks on terminology

15. The terms "electronic authentication" and "electronic signature" are used to refer to various techniques currently available on the market or still under development for the purpose of replicating in an electronic environment some or all of the functions identified as characteristic of handwritten signatures or other traditional authentication methods.

16. A number of different electronic signature techniques have been developed over the years. Each technique aims at satisfying different needs and providing different levels of security, and entails different technical requirements. Electronic authentication and signature methods may be classified in three categories: those based on the knowledge of the user or the recipient (e.g. passwords, personal identification numbers (PINs)), those based on

---

30. CISG Article 11.
31. http://www.cisgac.com/cisgac-opinion-no1/.

the physical features of the user (e.g. biometrics) and those based on the possession of an object by the user (e.g. codes or other information stored on a magnetic card). . . . Technologies currently in use include digital signatures within a public key infrastructure (PKI), biometric devices, PINs, user-defined or assigned passwords, scanned handwritten signatures, signature by means of a digital pen, and clickable "OK" or "I accept" boxes . . . .

18. In some cases, the expression "electronic authentication" is used to refer to techniques that, depending on the context in which they are used, may involve various elements, such as identification of individuals, confirmation of a person's authority (typically to act on behalf of another person or entity) or prerogatives (for example, membership in an institution or subscription to a service) or assurance as to the integrity of information. In some cases, the focus is on identity only, but sometimes it extends to authority, or a combination of any or all of those elements . . . .

Part one. Electronic signature and authentication methods

20. In keeping with the distinction made in most legal systems between signature (or seals, where they are used instead) as a means of "authentication", on the one hand, and "authenticity" as the quality of a document or record on the other, both model laws complement the notion of "originality" with the notion of "signature". Article 2, subparagraph (*a*), of the UNCITRAL Model Law on Electronic Signatures defines electronic signature as data in electronic form in, affixed to or logically associated with, a data message, which may be used to "identify the signatory" in relation to the data message and to "indicate the signatory's approval of the information contained in the data message".

107. In some countries, the courts have been inclined to interpret signature requirements liberally. . . . Thus, where the parties had regularly used e-mail in their negotiations, the courts have found that the originator's typed name in an e-mail message satisfied statutory signature requirements. A person's deliberate choice to type his name at the conclusion of all e-mails messages has been considered to be valid authentication. The readiness of the United States courts to accept that e-mail messages and names typed therein are capable of satisfying writing requirements follows a liberal interpretation of the notion of "signature", which is understood as encompassing "any symbol executed or adopted by a party with present intention to authenticate a writing" so that, in some instances, "a typed name or letterhead on a document is sufficient to satisfy the signature requirement".

Legal recognition of foreign electronic authentication
and signature methods

137. Legal and technical incompatibilities are the two principal sources of difficulties in the cross-border use of electronic signature and authentication

methods, in particular where they are intended to substitute for a legally valid signature. Technical incompatibilities affect the interopera-
bility of authentication systems. Legal incompatibilities may arise because
the laws of different jurisdictions impose different requirements in relation to the use and validity of electronic signature and authentication
methods.

Criteria for recognition of foreign electronic
authentication and signature methods

156. It is not common for domestic laws expressly to deny legal recognition
to foreign signatures or certificates, ... the European Union directive on
electronic signatures effectively requires foreign certification services providers to comply both with their original and with the European Union regime, which is a higher standard than is required from certification services
providers accredited in a State member of the European Union.

. . . .

5. Consumer Protection & Privacy

E-commerce poses clear risks for consumers, ranging from fraud and identity theft
to unwanted collection of personal data and buying preferences. Legislative responses
to such threats, in turn, affect business practices. Does UETA or E-SIGN provide any
protections for consumers engaged in paperless electronic sales? Consult the statutory provisions set out above.

a. The EU Approach

The EU is developing a uniform and demanding approach to consumer protection and privacy relating to e-commerce and data mining. The general E-Commerce
Directive, referenced above, instituted some of the groundwork for these protections.
A number of additional early directives, expressly focused on consumers, expanded
on these protections as described below.

i. Distance Selling

Consider the following EU summary of the "Distance Selling Directive[32] (Directive 97/7/EC)":[33]

The aim of EU legislation in the field of distance selling is to put consumers who purchase goods or services through distance communication
means in a similar position to consumers who buy goods or services in shops.
"Distance communication means" include traditional means of distance of
communication, such as press adverts accompanied by order forms, cata-

---

32. http://ec.europa.eu/consumers/archive/cons_int/safe_shop/dist_sell/index_en.htm.
33. http://eur-lex.europa.eu/legal-content/EN/ALL/?uri=CELEX:31997L0007.

logue sales, telephone. It also covers more technologically advanced means of distance communication such as teleshopping, mobile phone commerce (m-commerce), and the use of the internet (e-commerce).

. . . .

According to the Directive, the following consumer rights, among others, need to be respected:

- Provision of comprehensive information before the purchase
- Confirmation of that information in a durable medium (such as written confirmation)
- Consumer's right to cancel the contract within a minimum of 7 working days without giving any reason and without penalty, except the cost of returning the goods (right of withdrawal)
- Where the consumer has cancelled the contract, the right to a refund within 30 days of cancellation
- Delivery of the goods or performance of the service within 30 days of the day after the consumer placed his order
- Protection from unsolicited selling
- Protection from fraudulent use of payment cards

ii. Processing and Transfer of Personal Data

In addition to the Distance Selling Directive, the EU also adopted a number of directives requiring national governments to erect certain protections for individuals regarding the processing and transfer of personal data.

The most important of these, Directive 95/46/EC ("Data Protection Directive"),[34] requires, among other things, that "data subjects" (i.e., people) have a right of access and correction of data collected. It also includes the right to be informed and object before such data is disclosed to others for marketing. Importantly for international businesses, the Directive prohibits the transfer of personal data from an EU member state to any third country that does not maintain adequate levels of data protection. This led to the creation of "safe harbor" arrangements under which U.S. companies could agree to specified rules on transfers of personal data, through the U.S. Department of Commerce, and thereby establish compliance with EU law. This approach was upended, at least temporarily, by the revelations of Edward Snowden about NSA spying. Since it did not protect Europeans' personal data from U.S. government spying, the European Court of Justice essentially rejected the safe harbor arrangement in Schrems v. Data Protection Commissioner.[35]

---

34. http://eur-lex.europa.eu/legal-content/EN/TXT/?uri=celex:31995L0046.
35. https://www.lawfareblog.com/safe-harbor-framework-dead.

Moreover, because the Directive (like all directives) allows each EU member state to comply with its general requirements in its own specific ways, e-businesses currently face differing national compliance rules. In essence, an e-tailer or internet provider operating throughout the EU would have to ensure compliance with 28 potentially distinct sets of rules on data protection. (*See also* 2002/58/EC Directive on Privacy and Electronic Communications.[36])

In 2016, the EU adopted a new regulation (directly binding legislation distinct from directives) which will replace Directive 95/46 and be fully applicable from May 25, 2018. Regulation (EU) 2016/679[37] will create uniform and consistent rules binding throughout the EU for the protection of natural persons with regard to the processing of personal data and the transfer of such data. These rules include consent requirements, notification of data breaches, and a "right to be forgotten."

According to the EU, the Regulation simplifies data protection rules through harmonization, creates a single EU data protection authority, simplifies international transfers of data out of the EU to "facilitate global trade," and makes it easier for citizens to protect their on-line data—saving "€2.3 billion per year" in compliance costs. For foreign sellers offering goods and services to EU individuals (or monitoring their preferences), the Regulation provides for "adequacy decisions" relating to the adequacy of protections in that foreign jurisdiction, and allows for the use of "binding corporate rules" establishing required protections. Pursuant to these rules, the EU and U.S. trade authorities have established a "Privacy Shield"[38] mechanism in 2016, under which U.S. businesses may seek certification of compliance with EU standards. (For examples, see U.S. Department of Commerce list of certified companies.[39])

The European Commission has provided a "guide for citizens"[40] that "explains how individuals' data protection rights are guaranteed under the Privacy Shield." A summary and set of "fact sheets" on the new Regulation is available on the Europa webpages Reform of EU Data Protection Rules.[41] These developing rules on personal privacy dovetail with guarantees found[42] in the EU Charter of Fundamental Rights[43] (Articles 7, 8, 47) protecting personal data.

---

36. http://eur-lex.europa.eu/legal-content/EN/TXT/?uri=CELEX:32001R0045.

37. http://eur-lex.europa.eu/legal-content/EN/TXT/?uri=uriserv:OJ.L_.2016.119.01.0001.01.ENG&toc=OJ:L:2016:119:TOC.

38. https://www.privacyshield.gov/welcome.

39. https://www.privacyshield.gov/list.

40. https://www.google.com/url?sa=t&rct=j&q=&esrc=s&source=web&cd=1&cad=rja&uact=8&ved=0ahUKEwiqnNfjipDSAhWK4iYKHaNcDRQQFggcMAA&url=http%3A%2F%2Fec.europa.eu%2Fjustice%2Fdata-protection%2Fdocument%2Fcitizens-guide_en.pdf&usg=AFQjCNGrTjRMOR-hSaQq33LSU6SyXpBeGw&sig2=M8QVee7Z_qg5Z60PfPPkgw.

41. http://ec.europa.eu/justice/data-protection/reform/index_en.htm.

42. http://ec.europa.eu/justice/data-protection/individuals/index_en.htm.

43. http://ec.europa.eu/justice/fundamental-rights/charter/index_en.htm.

iii. The EU and the Cookie: E-Privacy <u>Directives 2002/58/EC</u>[44] & <u>2009/136/</u> <u>EC</u>[45]) on Personal Data Collection & Tracking

© Jonathunder, *Peanut butter cookie with a chocolate chip smiley face*, 17 October 2010[46]

Internet shoppers now commonly experience the somewhat "creepy" modern phenomenon of targeted advertisements that track individual internet searches and purchases. (Distinguish this from regulation of the processing, transfer and use of such data described above.) Someone in the shadows is clearly watching. "Don't worry, we've just left you some cookies." Data collection through computer <u>tracking cookies</u>[47] (and other spyware) is an important tool for internet sellers and marketers but poses significant privacy concerns that have increasingly prompted regulatory responses. The EU has developed privacy protections that include an "opt-in" requirement that consumers be informed of, and affirmatively consent to, most types of cookies. Review the EU's guidance to sellers, information service providers and marketers about such policies in the <u>EU Internet Handbook</u>.[48] Recall that an EU directive sets policies that national governments must implement, but in potentially diverse, specific ways. This raises a critical, lingering question for internet providers

---

44. http://eur-lex.europa.eu/LexUriServ/LexUriServ.do?uri=CELEX:32002L0058:en:HTML.

45. http://eur-lex.europa.eu/legal-content/EN/ALL/?uri=CELEX:32009L0136.

46. By Jonathunder (Own work) [CC BY-SA 3.0 (http://creativecommons.org/licenses/by-sa/3.0) or GFDL (http://www.gnu.org/copyleft/fdl.html)], via Wikimedia, Commonshttps://commons .wikimedia.org/wiki/File:ChocolateChipSmile.jpg.

47. http://www.allaboutcookies.org/.

48. http://ec.europa.eu/ipg/basics/legal/cookies/index_en.htm.

and other "cookie dispensers" as to whether compliance with the privacy regulations is based on the nation of origin (where the business is established) or destination (where the consumers are located).

Part Two: Electronic Data Interchange, Documentary Credits and Transport Documents

A. Overview

Electronic Data Interchange (EDI) is a term that describes the replacement of traditional flows of paper documentation with electronic communications. The National Institute of Standards and Technology, an agency of the U.S. federal government that developed early standards, describes EDI this way:

Federal Information Processing Standards Publications[49]

1. Name of Standard. Electronic Data Interchange (EDI) (FIPS PUB 161-2).

2. Category of Standard. Electronic Data Interchange.

3. Explanation.

3.1. Definition and Use of EDI. EDI is the computer-to-computer interchange of strictly formatted messages that represent documents other than monetary instruments. EDI implies a sequence of messages between two parties, either of whom may serve as originator or recipient. The formatted data representing the documents may be transmitted from originator to recipient via telecommunications or physically transported on electronic storage media. . . .

An example of EDI is a set of interchanges between a buyer and a seller. Messages from buyer to seller could include, for example, request for quotation (RFQ), purchase order, receiving advice and payment advice; messages from seller to buyer could include, similarly, bid in response to RFQ, purchase order acknowledgment, shipping notice and invoice. These messages may simply provide information, e.g., receiving advice or shipping notice, or they may include data that may be interpreted as a legally binding obligation, e.g., bid in response to RFQ or purchase order.

Problem 8 above is an example of a typical electronic B2C transaction that did not involve a documentary sale or letter of credit financing. But what if the parties chose instead to require payment against documents and letter of credit financing as is common in B2B transactions? From prior chapters, you already know that such arrangements are "awash" in a sea of documents, heavily dependent upon physical exchanges. Apart from the credit itself, the transaction typically involves many other

---

49. https://www.nist.gov/itl.

documents including, critically, the negotiable bill of lading. Similarly, the traditional commercial letter of credit transaction depends upon the preparation, presentation and acceptance of documents, some of which must be authenticated and negotiated through signature.

The advantages of using electronic alternatives to physical document transfers are obvious. It's much cheaper, much faster, and easier to exchange, maintain, store and retrieve electronic records. Despite such advantages, significant obstacles, relating to function and security, have hindered this potential transition to electronic formats. How can a bill of lading be "endorsed" and transferred to another party, securely and with confidence, when in an electronic form? How can the many documents required by a letter of credit be authenticated and kept secure? What constitutes an "original" when a document is in electronic form? In case of dispute, will a court accept print outs of electronic documentation under applicable rules of evidence? Consider the following materials that explore these basic issues, which involve not only legal, but also practical and technological questions.

B. Developing Legal Regimes for Electronic Paperless International Transactions

1. Electronic Letters of Credit

Letters of credit and bills of lading are expressly excluded from UETA since they may fall under UCC Articles 5 and 7 respectively. The ICC published the "eUCP" in 2002, apparently based on a perception that the market was poised for widespread adoption of electronic credits and recognition that the UCP was premised on a paper based environment. A revised version 1.1 was published in 2007. The eUCP provides a limited set of rules and definitions that may be used to supplement and adapt the UCP to electronic documentary credits. As illustrations consider eArt. 3 and 8.

a. eUCP

Article 3: Definitions

a. Where the following terms are used in the UCP, for the purposes of applying the UCP to an electronic record presented under an eUCP credit, the term:

i. appear on their face and the like shall apply to examination of the data content of an electronic record.

ii. document shall include an electronic record.

iii. place for presentation of electronic records means an electronic address.

iv. sign and the like shall include an electronic signature.

v. superimposed, notation or stamped means data content, whose supplementary character is apparent in an electronic record.

b. The following terms used in the eUCP shall have the following meanings:

i. electronic record means

- data created, generated, sent, communicated, received or stored by electronic means

- that is capable of being authenticated as to the apparent identity of a sender and the apparent source of the data contained in it, and as to whether it has remained complete and unaltered, and

- is capable of being examined for compliance with the terms and conditions of the eUCP credit.

ii. electronic signature means a data process attached to or logically associated with an electronic record and executed or adopted by a person in order to identify that person and to indicate that person's authentication of the electronic record.

iii. format means the data organization in which the electronic record is expressed or to which it refers.

iv. paper document means a document in a traditional paper form.

v. received means the time when an electronic record enters the information system of the applicable recipient in a form capable of being accepted by that system. Any acknowledgement of receipt does not imply acceptance or refusal of the electronic record under an eUCP credit.

Article 8: Originals and Copies

Any requirement of the UCP or an eUCP credit for presentation of one or more originals or copies of an electronic record is satisfied by the presentation of one electronic record.

2. Bills of Lading Transmitted Via EDI

a. _Incoterms 2010_[50]

Electronic communication

Previous versions of Incoterms® rules have specified those documents that could be replaced by EDI messages. Articles A1/B1 of the Incoterms® 2010 rules, however, now give electronic means of communication the same effect as paper communication, as long as the parties so agree or where customary. This formulation facilitates the evolution of new electronic procedures throughout the lifetime of the Incoterms® 2010 rules.

---

50. https://iccwbo.org/resources-for-business/incoterms-rules/incoterms-rules-2010/.

3. 2008 UN Convention on Carriage of Goods (Rotterdam Rules)

The "Rotterdam Rules" are the latest version of the treaty which was the original sources for COGSA. These new rules, which have not been adopted by the United States, make direct reference to electronic communications in bills of lading. As one source[51] puts it:

> Another highly appreciated feature of Rotterdam rules is they advocate the prevalence of negotiable electronic transport document or the Electronic Bill of Lading. The Electronic BL can be transferred and holds the same liability as the paper form. The rights incorporated in it can be transferred by the holder to the other person by transferring the electronic transport record. It is issued only if the parties agree to issue a negotiable electronic transport document and thus it consequently replaces negotiable transport document.

Chief Officer Abhishek Bhanawat, *Rotterdam Rules — Redefining and Introducing the Electronic Bill of Lading*, Maritime Law.

Here are a few key provisions. (The full text[52] is available from UNCITRAL.)

Article 3

Form requirements

The notices, confirmation, consent, agreement, declaration and other communications referred to in articles 19, paragraph 2; 23, paragraphs 1 to 4; 36, subparagraphs 1(*b*), (*c*) and (*d*); 40, subparagraph 4(*b*); 44; 48, paragraph 3; 51, subparagraph 1(*b*); 59, paragraph 1; 63; 66; 67, paragraph 2; 75, paragraph 4; and 80, paragraphs 2 and 5, shall be in writing.

Electronic communications may be used for these purposes, provided that the use of such means is with the consent of the person by which it is communicated and of the person to which it is communicated.

. . . .

Chapter 3

Electronic transport records

Article 8

Use and effect of electronic transport records

---

51. http://www.marineinsight.com/maritime-law/rotterdam-rules-redefining-and-introducing-the-electronic-bill-of-lading/.

52. https://www.google.com/url?sa=t&rct=j&q=&esrc=s&source=web&cd=4&ved=0ahUKEwir-cu_oMLPAhUEwiYKHd1BAAQQFgg0MAM&url=http%3A%2F%2Fwww.uncitral.org%2Fpdf%2Fenglish%2Ftexts%2Ftransport%2Frotterdam_rules%2FRotterdam-Rules-E.pdf&usg=AFQjCNExSR3kbzcQWpQhFoJKguTKzoJz_w&sig2=8428wcXl9qoymZLLst7UKA&cad=rja.

Subject to the requirements set out in this Convention:

> (*a*) Anything that is to be in or on a transport document under this Convention may be recorded in an electronic transport record, provided the issuance and subsequent use of an electronic transport record is with the consent of the carrier and the shipper; and

> (*b*) The issuance, exclusive control, or transfer of an electronic transport record has the same effect as the issuance, possession, or transfer of a transport document.

C. Services Facilitating Electronic Credits, Bills of Lading & Alternative Payment Systems

Paperless international trade transactions have obvious benefits in terms of potential cost savings, efficiency, speed and centralization of processing. A leading approach to facilitating paperless transactions (solving problems of authentication, security and replication of function) has been to create independent services that provide a secure technological platform, or "digital infrastructure," for the exchange of documents. Participants in an international paperless transaction often rely upon an intermediary with a secure technological platform and a set of rules that enable the paperless transactions. Several such services are briefly described below.

The potential for reliance on electronic documentation and such services was significantly enhanced in 2010 when leading Protection & Indemnity ("P & I") insurance groups agreed to cover losses associated with purely electronic transactions. A P & I group or "club" is an "independent, non-profit making mutual insurance association, providing cover for its shipowner and charterer members against third party liabilities relating to the use and operation of ships."[53]

1. BOLERO[54] (Bill of Lading Electronic Registry Organization)

Bolero is a private commercial provider of a digital infrastructure for international electronic transactions. It describes itself as a central registry system for trade related documents that "would ensure that any documents sent over Bolero would have the same legal meaning as the paper document it replaced, irrespective of legal jurisdiction." Its website further asserts:

> Bolero provides a unique and highly secure multi-bank trade messaging infrastructure enabling standardised multi-bank communication for a

---

53. *See* International Group of Protection and Indemnity Clubs, http://www.igpandi.org/about.
54. http://www.bolero.net/.

corporate with all its partner banks whilst at the same time providing a standardised multi-bank communication channel for a bank to its corporate customers. In addition, Bolero provides comprehensive "on-demand" web-based applications in support of the end-to-end trade finance processes to automate Export Letter of Credit, Import Letter of Credit, Guarantee Applications, Beneficiary-side Guarantees and Documentary Collections. Bolero has also deployed, in partnership with a significant global bank, a substantial supply chain finance solution for a large US retailer and its major suppliers across Asia. Bolero acts as an independent intermediary and trusted third party bringing together corporates and banks to deliver multi-bank standardisation and to enable trade finance collaboration.

2. SWIFT[55] (Society for Worldwide Interbank Financial Telecommunications)

SWIFT is an organization (primarily a member-owned banking cooperative) that provides network and communication protocols that allow financial institutions to exchange messages in a standardized, technologically secure fashion. These standards and mechanisms can be used, among other things, to facilitate electronic message exchanges for documentary credits. Its website describes some alternatives:

MT 798: the 'Trade Envelope'

A comprehensive solution for corporate trade, FIN MT 798 caters for the following instruments:

- Import letters of credit
- Export letters of credit
- Guarantees/standby letters of credit.

Using MT 798, you can apply to your bank for a letter of credit or guarantee, and receive an Advice of L/C back from your bank. Your bank can then notify the Issuance of an L/C or Guarantee, or notify an amendment.

For more detail (including diagrams), see SWIFT's Trade for Corporates factsheet.[56]

A fairly recent innovation involving SWIFT and the ICC is called the "Bank Payment Obligation." SWIFT describes it this way:

The Bank Payment Obligation (BPO)

Trade finance has long been characterised by paper-based processes, which are often time-consuming and inefficient. This is now changing and SWIFT is playing a key role in driving the digitisation of trade flows.

---

55. https://www.swift.com/.
56. https://www.swift.com/node/34661.

The Bank Payment Obligation

Launched in 2013, the Bank Payment Obligation (BPO) is a standardised, irrevocable payment instruction which uses ISO 20022 data structures. The BPO offers buyers and sellers a way to secure and finance their trade transactions, regardless of size, geography or industry.

The BPO sits alongside payment terms such as letters of credit, advanced payment or open account. Unlike traditional instruments, however, the BPO combines legally binding rules with electronic messaging and matching capabilities.

3. essDOCS

Started in 2005, essDOCS[57] (pronounced "S docs") describes itself as "the world's leading enabler of paperless trade, providing customer-led solutions that automate and accelerate trade operations & finance." It utilizes a platform called "CargoDocs," which is, apparently, customized for different trade functions ranging from "liner" traffic (container shipping) to "trade finance." For example, the company's promotional blurb regarding liner traffic states:[58]

> CargoDocs for Liner provides eDoc solutions for container shipments, covering both Ocean (Master) and House eB/Ls. It enables Ship Owners, NVOCCs, their Agents and/or remote Documentation Centres to collaboratively draft B/Ls with Shippers/Exporters, and to electronically sign and issue Bills of Lading.

Note: Ocean or Master Bills are issued by shipping companies/ carriers, typically to freight forwarders; "house" bills[59] are issued to shippers by agents, such as a freight forwarders or non-vessel operating common carriers, known as NVOCCs,[60] and relate to the specific goods being transported.

Regarding electronic trade finance[61] (such as letters of credit), essDOCS promises that:

> CargoDocs acts as a multi-bank electronic Presentation platform, allowing eUCP Presentation — under a Documentary Credit — of title documents such as original CargoDocs electronic Bills of Lading plus relevant supporting electronic documents: Commercial Invoices, Independent Inspectors' Certificates, Vessel Reports, Government Certificates such as Phytosanitary Certificates, Chamber of Commerce signed Certificates of Origin and so forth.

---

57. https://www.essdocs.com/.
58. https://www.essdocs.com/solutions.
59. http://www.businessdictionary.com/definition/house-bill-of-lading-B-L.html.
60. http://howtoexportimport.com/Difference-between-NVOCC-and-Freight-Forwarder-466.aspx.
61. https://www.essdocs.com/solutions/banks/epresentation.

essDOCS also provides a <u>slick video explanation</u>[62] of its services on its website. Its services can be <u>coordinated with the SWIFT</u>[63] system of bank messaging.

4. e-title<u>^{TM}</u>[64]

The P & I insurance groups (noted above, these industry "clubs" self-insure a wide variety of risks associated with international cargo) have also agreed to cover transactions utilizing a relatively new mechanism that facilitates use of EDI called "e-title." Unlike essDOCS and BOLERO, the technology is designed not for use through an intermediary but rather as a means for trade participants to directly transfer documents of title, such as bills of lading, through electronic means. Its backers describe the product this way (note the term "peer-to-peer"):

> e-title™ is patented, peer-to-peer technology that enables the creation and transfer of title and negotiable documents, such as the bill of lading . . . . e-title™ complements existing Supply Chain, Trade Documentation and Financial Supply Chain applications by focusing exclusively on the electronic title creation and negotiation. This fills the gap in current trade documentation services — enabling full electronic trading, documentary credits and collections, and release of goods — without overlapping with functionality already available in the market.
>
> The e-title™ solution combines title document functionality with digital signatures that enable secure transfer during negotiation. These components run on tamper-proof hardware, known as a Hardware Security Modules or HSMs that prevents alterations or forgery of a title document when it is in the possession of the shipper, bank or importer . . . . The e-title™ software provides the full functionality required to create, transfer and surrender bills of lading electronically. . . . e-title™ uses industry-standard digital signature technology as the means to secure electronic titles transferred between e-title™ peers. The use of digital signatures ensures that e-title™ manages the transfer of titles to the appropriate party and that the bill of lading data is immune from forgery or changes.

Click <u>here</u>[65] for more information on digital signatures.

---

62. https://www.youtube.com/watch?v=FSgZyj4tY3o&feature=youtu.be.
63. https://www.essdocs.com/press-room/essdocs-announces-electronic-presentation-trade-documents-over-swift-and-extension.
64. http://www.e-title.net/index.php/the-solution/what-is-e-title.
65. https://en.wikipedia.org/wiki/Digital_signature.

Chapter 9

Introduction to Government Regulation of International Business Transactions

A. Overview

Thus far, this course has focused on the legal obligations and rights of private (non-governmental) participants in international transactions, examining the traditional sale of goods as an illustration. You should at this point know and understand the following general topics — that is, be able to spot the relevant issues, articulate the applicable rules with precision and apply those rules in a reasoned explanation of likely outcomes:

1. **Documentary Sales** — What the documentary sale is, how it works and why it is used (including which documents are critical to such sales and why);

2. **Terms of Trade** — The rights and obligations of buyers and sellers inferred from use of INCOTERMS CIF & FOB, FCA and CIP, as well as a general understanding of the difference among the categories of INCOTERMS;

3. **Contract Formation** — The basic rules regarding contract formation under the CISG, including the "battle of the forms," and how those rules are distinct from the UCC;

4. **Contractual Breach & Remedies** — Remedies under CISG, including fundamental breach, notice avoidance, damages and practical issues regarding return of goods and mitigation;

5. **Bills of Lading & Carriers** — The functions of the bill of lading, carrier's obligations, and potential liability for wrongful delivery or lost or damaged goods under COGSA & the Pomerene Act, as well as disclaimers and damage limitations;

6. **Commercial Letters of Credit** — The functions of commercial export credits, legal obligations of issuing and confirming banks under the UCP 600, application

of the strict compliance doctrine, timing and notice requirements for dishonor, and the UCC fraud exception to the independence principle;

7. **E-Commerce and Electronic Data Interchange**—How UETA and EU law have responded to the various legal issues created by paperless electronic commerce, and current practices regarding electronic credits and bills of lading.

Our study of international business transactions will now shift focus to the regulation of such transactions by national governments and international intergovernmental organizations. Among other things, we will examine the World Trade Organization, free trade areas and customs unions, customs and tariffs, export regulations, and trade remedy law directed at "unfair" trade practices. The goal is to survey the ways in which both national governments and international institutions affect international business transactions, and trade generally. In many cases, these forms of government regulation determine the ultimate feasibility and costs of a transaction. They are, therefore, critical considerations for businesses, and the lawyers who represent them.

We will begin by reviewing the role of international law and institutions, focusing in Part One of the chapter on an introduction to the World Trade Organization (WTO), the General Agreement on Tariffs and Trade 1994 (GATT 94), and the relationship between international regulation of trade and domestic law. In a subsequent chapter, we will examine other international institutions associated with free trade agreements and customs unions, including the EU. Part Two of the chapter examines the inherent tension between international regulation of trade and competing domestic priorities, focusing on the WTO's treatment of domestic health and safety measures that restrict international trade. In particular, Part Two focuses on application of GATT Article XX exceptions, and the Sanitary & Phytosanitary Agreement, in the GATT dispute settlement process, raising important questions about the role of international governance of trade issues.

Part One: Introduction to GATT, the WTO and International Trade Disciplines

A. Overview

The focus of this chapter is on the ways in which the WTO affects international business transactions. At the outset, however, it is important to recognize that the WTO does not directly regulate or control such transactions. Rather, the effects of WTO regulation of trade are almost exclusively applied strictly through domestic law. We have already seen in the sale of goods context, that both the sending state (exporting seller) and the receiving state (importing buyer) will inevitably impose legal obligations or restrictions that affect the transaction. COGSA rules on carriers, and the Pomerene Act rules on bills of lading, are familiar examples from our prior classes.[1] Customs regulations, tariffs, and export controls are examples we will soon study. You will now discover that international institutions and law play an important part in the formation and content of such domestic regulation. COGSA, for example, is directly derived from, and fulfills, U.S. obligations relating to the 1924 Hague Convention[2] on shipping and bills of lading. United States customs rates and practices, and rules on trade remedies, directly reflect obligations created under the WTO system and other international agreements.

Thus, in the background of national regulation of trade, there lies an important relationship between domestic law and international law, and institutions. This part of the chapter focuses on this relationship, exploring both how the WTO works, and how international legal obligations associated with the WTO become part of the domestic law affecting private transactions. We will also examine the most basic legal obligations created in GATT 94 — obligations which are (often imperfectly) incorporated or reflected in domestic trade law.

Your goals for this part of the chapter should include understanding:

(1) The purposes of the WTO and GATT 94;

(2) The organizational structure, powers and authority of the WTO;

(3) The four foundational legal principles of GATT;

(4) The substantive scope of rules under the WTO (that is, what subjects fall within its jurisdiction);

(5) How the dispute settlement process of the WTO works; and

(6) The relationship between the law of GATT, the WTO dispute settlement processes, and domestic law.

We will address each of these topics in the context of evaluating the following problem.

B. Problem Nine A: Don't Eat the Fish

1. Facts

In 1975, Australia committed itself in a GATT tariff binding[3] to reduce its former 20 percent ad valorem tariff on "salmon" to 10 percent. In 2015, approximately 36,000 tons of fresh or frozen, wild salmon (caught live in North West Pacific Ocean) was

---

1. The CISG obviously will also frequently have an important effect on a sales transaction. The treaty's legal status and effect, at least in the United States, derives from its incorporation into domestic law as a "self-executing" treaty. In contrast to COGSA and the Pomerene Act, however, the CISG is "optional" law in the sense that parties can freely exclude its application in whole or part.

2. http://www.admiraltylawguide.com/conven/haguerules1924.html.

3. The General Agreement on Tariffs and Trade provides the central legal principles of the WTO system regarding trade in goods. Article 2 of the GATT requires that member states honor their agreements with other members regarding applicable tariff rates over specified periods.

imported into Australia from Canada and the United States. Another 1.5 tons of wild salmon caught in the Atlantic Ocean was imported from European Union countries. While Australia has no native wild salmon of its own, it does have an ocean fishing industry that focuses on tuna, herring, and swordfish. It also has a growing fish farming industry that produces "farm-raised" salmon, as well as other species of fish for human consumption.

On June 1, 2016, the Australian Minister of Natural Resources announced the adoption of two measures directed at the importation of salmon. The Government has asserted that the measures are necessary to avoid the spread of parasites that could potentially harm native fish populations, and the health of consumers. It is well established that about 10% of live salmon caught in the wild carry certain parasites. The incidence of infestation is approximately the same for fish harvested in the Atlantic and Pacific fishing grounds.

First, Australia imposed a ban on the importation of uncooked, fresh or frozen, wild salmon from the Northern Pacific Ocean region. All of the affected salmon is harvested by Canadian, Russian and U.S. based fishing industries. Second, all imported farm raised salmon is required to undergo heat treatment prior to retail sale in Australia. Australia's burgeoning fish farming industry currently faces stiff competition from a number of other nations. Australian fish farmers are exempted from the heat treatment requirements.

2. Assignment

The learning goals set out above are broken down here into a series of questions falling into three general categories. *Your specific assignment for Part One is, then, to develop a response to each of the questions based upon information provided on the WTO website (follow links below or "google" it) and the readings that follow.*

a. The WTO as an Intergovernmental Organization

Answer the following basic questions about the WTO as an organization:

(i) What are the WTO's powers and purposes?

(ii) Whose interests does the WTO serve?

(iii) How is the WTO's institutional structure organized?

(iv) What subject matters fall within the jurisdiction of the WTO?

(v) What legal authority does the WTO have (can it make legally binding decisions, create new rules, or sanction non-compliance)?

(vi) What is the legal status of the GATT (and related WTO treaties) under United States law — is it binding, supreme, or actionable by individuals?

b. GATT Legal Pillars

Analyze the fact pattern above to identify and articulate claims that the United States, Canada, and Russia might raise before a GATT dispute settlement panel. You should focus on Articles I, II, III and XI of GATT (GATT 47 text). Also consider Article XXIII in formulating these claims.

c. Dispute Settlement & Enforcement

How does the WTO resolve disputes between member states concerning their various legal obligations? Assume that a WTO dispute settlement panel finds that Australia's measures violate the GATT agreement. *What remedies are available to the complaining states? How are GATT obligations and dispute settlement decisions enforced?*

C. Resources

1. History of the GATT and Evolution of the WTO

Browse through the web pages provided by the WTO regarding its history and evolution[4] (at minimum, follow the narrative through the description of the "Uruguay Round").

Also peruse the BBC's useful chronology[5] of GATT events. This chronology demonstrates the organization's success in liberalizing trade through reduction of tariffs and other barriers, as well as its transformation into the more fully formed international legal regime now known as the WTO.

2. WTO as an International Organization

Visit http://www.wto.org/ and, at minimum, peruse links under the menu tab "About WTO" (such as "Who We Are," "What We Do," "Overview," "Understanding the WTO," and "WTO in Brief/Organization"). Your purpose is in reviewing this material is to answer the basic questions about the WTO assigned above.

3. The Legal Framework and Scope of Legal Obligations (Subjects within WTO Legal Regime)

The WTO webpage, "Understanding the WTO: The Agreements . . . Overview: A Navigational Guide,"[6] is helpful in understanding the substantive scope of the WTO legal regime. The WTO organizational chart[7] is also useful in that it visually displays the trading system's overarching legal structure organized by topics, and links corresponding treaty obligations falling within the organization's jurisdiction. For example, under the "Council on Trade in Goods," you will find a series of committees on different subjects such as "market access," "agriculture," and "technical bar-

---

4. https://www.wto.org/english/thewto_e/whatis_e/tif_e/fact4_e.htm.
5. http://news.bbc.co.uk/2/hi/europe/country_profiles/2430089.stm.
6. https://www.wto.org/english/thewto_e/whatis_e/tif_e/agrm1_e.htm.
7. https://www.wto.org/english/thewto_e/whatis_e/tif_e/org2_e.htm.

riers." Each of these corresponds to various legal obligations and agreements contained within the WTO system. Similarly, the menu "Trade Topics,"[8] organizes various subjects within the WTO's jurisdiction into topical headings.

What precisely is "GATT 94" and how does it relate to "GATT 47"? What are GATS, TRIPS, and the Dispute Settlement Understanding? How do the TBT and SPS agreements fit within this legal framework?

Next, peruse the WTO "Legal Texts"[9] page (linked to "documents and resources" tab on the top of most WTO webpages). The long list of treaties, decisions and protocols provide a convenient overview of the various subjects that fall within the WTO legal regime. The text of the various treaties can be easily accessed through the links provided.

On the right side of each treaty listed, there is also a link labeled "interpretation" which will take you the WTO "Analytical Index."[10] The on-line Analytical Index is an excellent resource for finding critical interpretations of WTO-related legal obligations as developed through the dispute settlement process. The Index, which is organized by article and key words, provides pertinent excerpts from cases decided by the WTO dispute settlement process (panels and appellate body).

Part "b" of the assignment above, asks you to evaluate possible claims in Problem 9 on behalf of the United States, Canada and Russia. *It is necessary to examine some of these excerpts for interpretations of key words and phrases from the treaty text that are critical to answering that part of the assignment.*

4. Dispute Settlement Processes

Dispute settlement has become a vital part of the WTO's work, providing both resolution of trade disputes, and important jurisprudence about the meaning of the WTO body of rules. Review the following links to understand how that process works.

• "Dispute Settlement"[11] Gateway (also linked under the "Trade Topics" tab).
  This webpage provides links to various general descriptions, videos, "courses," and explanations of the process, such as "Introduction to Dispute Settlement" and "Legal Basis." It also provides links to pending and decided disputes ("The Disputes"). The link "Legal texts: the WTO Agreements"[12] provides a useful alternative introduction and general description of the process (and many other parts of the WTO legal regime).

• Chart[13] outlining stages of dispute settlement.

---

8. https://www.wto.org/english/tratop_e/tratop_e.htm.
9. https://www.wto.org/english/docs_e/legal_e/legal_e.htm.
10. https://www.wto.org/english/res_e/booksp_e/analytic_index_e/gatt1994_e.htm.
11. https://www.wto.org/english/tratop_e/dispu_e/dispu_e.htm.
12. https://www.wto.org/english/docs_e/legal_e/ursum_e.htm#Understanding.
13. https://www.wto.org/english/thewto_e/whatis_e/tif_e/disp2_e.htm.

- WTO's "<u>Map of Disputes</u>."[14] It is always fun to see who is suing who, and why. Are there any discernable patterns?

5. Enforcement

To rule violators: "Go directly to jail. Do not pass Go, do not collect . . . ." Well, not so much. Read the description of remedies provided by the WTO (near the bottom of the page) under "The Dispute Has Been Decided: <u>What Next</u>?"[15] Then review Articles 19–22 of the <u>Dispute Settlement Agreement</u>.[16] What is the preferred remedy for violations of WTO legal obligations? What are the legal consequences for member states that violate trade rules? How does the WTO enforce dispute settlement decisions?

When examining WTO remedies, it is important to distinguish between the binding nature of an international obligation and its enforceability. Consider the following brief excerpt, which involves a scholarly exchange on this distinction with regard to the WTO.

John Jackson, *International Law Status of WTO Dispute Settlement Reports: Obligation to Comply or Option to "Buy Out"?* 98 Am. J. Int'l L. 109–125 (2004)[17]

In a stimulating Editorial Comment in the July 1996 issue of the *American Journal of International Law,* Judith Bello articulated a view regarding the rules of the World Trade Organization (WTO) as follows:

> [T] he WTO rules are simply not "binding" in the traditional sense. When a panel established under the WTO Dispute Settlement Understanding issues a ruling adverse to a member, there is no prospect of incarceration, injunctive relief, damages for harm inflicted or police enforcement. The WTO has no jailhouse, no bail bondsmen, no blue helmets, no truncheons or tear gas. Rather, the WTO essentially a confederation of sovereign national governments—relies upon voluntary compliance.

As a critique of and response to Bello's argument, . . . I acknowledged the ambiguity of the treaty text (Dispute Settlement Understanding, or DSU) but argued that an adopted dispute settlement report establishes an international law obligation upon the member in question to change its practice to make it consistent with the rules of the WTO Agreement and its annexes. In this view, the "compensation" (or retaliation) approach is only a fallback in the event of noncompliance.

> . . . Later, Judith Bello graciously clarified her view in a book review:

> . . . In this *Journal,* I authored a 1996 editorial supporting the WTO and future "fast track" (now called trade promotion) authority for new trade

---

14. https://www.wto.org/english/tratop_e/dispu_e/dispu_maps_e.htm.
15. https://www.wto.org/english/thewto_e/whatis_e/tif_e/disp1_e.htm.
16. https://www.wto.org/english/docs_e/legal_e/28-dsu_e.htm.
17. http://scholarship.law.georgetown.edu/facpub/111/

negotiations. For this purpose, I sought to counter the complaint by some nongovernmental organizations that U.S. sovereignty and decision making authority would thereby be delegated wholesale to "faceless bureaucrats" in Geneva, not accountable to the American people. Jackson courteously and fairly wrote a reply . . . to clarify that the previous GATT and now WTO obligations are binding as a matter of law, even when they cannot be enforced. That is, while a WTO member may choose not to come into compliance with a panel decision—preferring, instead, to provide compensation or suffer WTO-authorized retaliation—that member is not satisfying its legal obligation but, in a WTO-prescribed manner, is mitigating the effects of the imbalance in WTO rights and obligations resulting from noncompliance. In fact, I share Jackson's view that the WTO establishes binding obligations, although I continue to regard favorably the GATT/WTO's realistic recognition that it cannot enforce specific compliance.

Although academics may argue, then kiss and make up over whether dispute settlement rulings are technically binding, it is clear that the WTO does not directly enforce such decisions in any meaningful way. Rather, compliance is encouraged through authorization of self-help measures, and the long term reciprocal benefits associated with participation in the system.

Can such a system be effective for small nations that successfully challenge the action of large trading partners such as the United States, China or the EU? This question is captured by the old joke about where 800 pound guerillas sleep. The answer is, wherever they want to. Do the 800 pound guerillas of world trade care if Barbados retaliates with compensatory trade sanctions for violations of GATT 94?

6. Domestic Legal Status of WTO International Obligations

The various treaties that constitute the WTO system (often referred to as the "Uruguay Round agreements") are international treaty obligations of the United States.[18]

---

18. Under Article III of the U.S. Constitution, a treaty is created when the President ratifies it after receiving the advice and consent of the Senate by a 2/3 majority. Another form of international obligation, called an executive agreement, is also recognized under U.S. law. An executive agreement is created by the President directly without Senate approval. Although such agreements may derive from the executive's own authority over foreign affairs, they are often supported by authority delegated by the Congress. The original GATT 47 agreement was never consented to by the Senate but rather adopted by the President as an executive agreement. A hybrid type of arrangement frequently used in international trade is commonly called "fast track" (see https://www.brookings.edu/research/fast-track-trade-promotion-authority/). Under fast track procedures, the President negotiates a treaty and presents its text to the entire Congress for an "up or down" vote, without possible amendment. The treaty becomes binding internationally as an executive agreement, and congressional approval takes the form of domestic legislation implementing the treaty obligation as Congress deems fit. The Uruguay Round agreements that now form the WTO, as well as the North American Free Trade Agreement, were created under fast track procedures.

In simplest terms, an international treaty forms a "contract-like" mutual promise between nations. This means that the United States has promised the other members of the WTO that it will honor the legal commitments set forth in the various WTO agreements. It has similarly promised to abide by decisions of the dispute settlement process, in the manner reflected in the links provided above.

What is the domestic legal status and effect of these commitments? Like most countries, the United States' approach to this question should be characterized, in international law parlance, as "dualist." This means that our legal system maintains a distinction between international law obligations and binding domestic law. International obligations and rules only become operative (sometimes referred to as having "direct effect") within the domestic legal system when they are purposefully incorporated into that system. In U.S. practice, this means either Congress has implemented the international obligations through legislation or, in relatively rare instances, the treaty is "self-executing." A self-executing treaty is one that was intended to create domestic rules without further action by the Congress.[19] The CISG is an important example of a self-executing treaty, which now forms part of the American legal system although it was never enacted into federal statutory law. (Additional explanations on treaty basics under U.S. law, including "fast track" authority, appear in the notes for these pages.)

Once incorporated and given direct effect, international rules and obligations generally have the same legal status as other federal law—superior to inconsistent state law. In cases of conflict with other federal law, the last in time prevails.[20] However, if not self-executing or implemented through legislation, the treaty obligation is simply not domestic law, even though it nevertheless creates an international obligation.

Distinct but related issues regarding domestic legal status involve the questions of standing and causes of action. It is entirely possible that an international treaty may be incorporated into domestic law and yet not be enforceable by private claimants. In other words, private parties may lack standing[21] to assert the treaty as grounds for a court's decision. Nor could they sue for damages allegedly caused by a government breach of the treaty. In such circumstances, it is typical that the treaty is only actionable in the courts at the behest of the federal government.

---

19. The doctrine of self-executing treaties, which appears facially inconsistent with the text of Article II and the Supremacy Clause of Article VI, was first established by Chief Judge John Marshal in *Foster v. Neilson*, 27 U.S. 253 (1829). An important recent application of the doctrine outside the trade context appears in *Medellin v. Texas*, 129 S. Ct. 360 (2008).

20. The courts will always interpret the treaty to avoid conflict with existing federal law if possible. Similarly, even when a treaty obligation has not been incorporated into domestic law, courts may use the treaty for interpretive purposes when construing the meaning of other ambiguous federal law. *See Murray v. The Charming Betsey*, 6 U.S. 2 Cranch 64 (1804) ("An act of Congress ought never to be construed to violate the law of nations if any other possible construction remains . . . .").

21. The term "standing" is not used here in the sense of Article III constitutional standing of a litigant to bring cases before federal courts but rather in the more general meaning of authorization or entitlement.

What about the WTO Uruguay Round agreements? What is the domestic legal status of the various WTO treaty obligations, the institutional output of its institutions (interpretations and decisions of the WTO itself), and dispute settlement rulings?

Although these agreements constitute binding international obligations of the United States, it is clear that they have no domestic legal effect, except to the extent that the federal government chooses to rely on them. In 1994, Congress passed the Uruguay Round Agreements Act (URAA). This 650-page statute implements the WTO agreements into domestic law and gives final authority for U.S. participation in the WTO. The URAA,[22] however, explicitly limits domestic application of the agreements and dispute settlement rulings. Section 102[23] provides:

SEC. 102. RELATIONSHIP OF THE AGREEMENTS TO
UNITED STATES LAW AND STATE LAW.

(a) RELATIONSHIP OF AGREEMENTS TO UNITED STATES LAW.—

(1) UNITED STATES LAW TO PREVAIL IN CONFLICT.—No provision of any of the Uruguay Round Agreements, nor the application of any such provision to any person or circumstance, that is inconsistent with any law of the United States shall have effect.

(2) CONSTRUCTION.—Nothing in this Act shall be construed—

(A) to amend or modify any law of the United States, including any law relating to—

(i) the protection of human, animal, or plant life or health,

(ii) the protection of the environment, or (iii) worker safety, or

(B) to limit any authority conferred under any law of the United States, including section 301 of the Trade Act of 1974, unless specifically provided for in this Act.

(b) RELATIONSHIP OF AGREEMENTS TO STATE LAW.—

. . . .

(2) LEGAL CHALLENGE.—

(A) IN GENERAL.—No State law, or the application of such a State law, may be declared invalid as to any person or circumstance on the ground that the provision or application is inconsistent with any of the Uruguay Round Agreements, except in an action brought by the United States for the purpose of declaring such law or application invalid.

. . . .

---

22. www.gpo.gov/fdsys/pkg/BILLS-103hr5110enr/pdf/BILLS-103hr5110enr.pdf.
23. 19 U.S.C. § 3512(a)(1).

(c) EFFECT OF AGREEMENT WITH RESPECT TO PRIVATE REMEDIES.—

(1) LIMITATIONS.—No person other than the United States—

(A) shall have any cause of action or defense under any of the Uruguay Round Agreements or by virtue of congressional approval of such an agreement, or

(B) may challenge, in any action brought under any provision of law, any action or inaction by any department, agency, or other instrumentality of the United States, any State, or any political subdivision of a State on the ground that such action or inaction is inconsistent with such agreement.

Thus, although the WTO agreements prevail over inconsistent state law, only the federal government may seek a judicial order to that effect. If the government violates one of the agreements to an international trader's detriment, there is no recourse. (Recall also that only governments can invoke the WTO dispute settlement processes.) Similarly, the URAA rejects application of dispute settlement rulings. Section 123(g) of the act essentially ensures that only Congress can change domestic law in response to a dispute settlement ruling, and prevents federal agencies from automatically altering related regulations.[24] Not surprisingly given the clear dictates of the URAA, U.S. courts have consistently rejected attempts to use WTO treaties, and dispute settlement rulings, to challenge or interpret domestic law.[25]

The approach of the European Union is very similar to that of the United States in regard to the legal effect of WTO law.[26] Thus, WTO provisions do not confer legal rights on private parties, and have no direct effect within the Union. The European

---

24. The URAA's "Statement of Administrative Action," which is an authoritative interpretation of the act, Section 102(d), 19 U.S.C. § 3511(a)(2) (2003), similarly provides that: "Reports issued by panels or the [AB] . . . have no binding effect under the law of the United States. . . ." Uruguay Round Agreements Act, Statement of Administrative Action, H.R. Doc. No. 103-826, at 822 (1994), reprinted in 1994 U.S.C.C.A.N. 4040 ("SAA").

25. *See, e.g.,Timken Co. v. United States*, 354 F.3d 1334 (Fed. Cir. 2004); *Gilda Indus., Inc. v. United States*, 446 F.3d 1271 (Fed. Cir. 2006). In *Corus Staal BV v. Dep't of Commerce*, 395 F.3d 1343 (Fed. Cir. 2005) the court declared:

"Neither the GATT nor any enabling international agreement outlining compliance therewith . . . trumps domestic legislation; if U.S. statutory provisions are inconsistent with the GATT or an enabling agreement, it is strictly a matter for Congress. Congress has enacted legislation to deal with the conflict presented here. It has authorized the USTR . . . to determine whether or not to implement WTO reports and determinations and, if so implemented, the extent of implementation."

However, several bi-national panels under the NAFTA dispute settlement system have used the *Charming Betsey* doctrine, *see* footnote 20 *supra*, to rely on WTO appellate body decisions. *See In the Matter of Certain Softwood Lumber Products from Canada: Final Affirmative Antidumping Determination*, USA-CDA-2002-1904-02 (N. Am. Free Trade Agreement Binat'l Panel 2005) (Decision of the Panel Following Remand) at 25, 42-44.

26. The European Union (for legal reasons referred to as the "European Communities" in WTO matters) joined the WTO in 1995. All 27 EU member states are also WTO members in their own right. The EU Commission speaks for all EU members at most meetings. WTO, *The European*

Court of Justice has also applied this limitation to member states seeking to challenge EU law.[27]

7. The Legal Pillars of GATT: MFN, National Treatment, Tariff Concessions & Quantitative Restrictions

Analyze the following articles of GATT 47,[28] which represent foundational legal principles for the system. (These obligations are now legally subsumed with the much larger umbrella of GATT 94.) What limitation on governmental interference with the market does each article provide? Which terms and phrases in the text seem critical and in need of interpretation? Consult the WTO "Analytical Index"[29] and review the Appellate Body and Panel interpretations of these critical terms.

How might the United States, Canada, and Russia rely on these articles to challenge Australia's measures on imported salmon described in the problem above?

Article I: General Most-Favoured-Nation Treatment

1. With respect to customs duties and charges of any kind imposed on or in connection with importation or exportation or imposed on the international transfer of payments for imports or exports, and with respect to the method of levying such duties and charges, and with respect to all rules and formalities in connection with importation and exportation, and with respect to all matters referred to in paragraphs 2 and 4 of Article III, any advantage, favour, privilege or immunity granted by any contracting party to any product originating in or destined for any other country shall be accorded immediately and unconditionally to the like product originating in or destined for the territories of all other contracting parties.

. . . .

Article II: Schedules of Concessions

1. (*a*) Each contracting party shall accord to the commerce of the other contracting parties treatment no less favourable than that provided for in the appropriate Part of the appropriate Schedule annexed to this Agreement.

. . . .

Article III: National Treatment on Internal Taxation and Regulation

1. The contracting parties recognize that internal taxes and other internal charges, and laws, regulations and requirements affecting the internal sale, offering for sale, purchase, transportation, distribution or use of products, and internal quantitative

---

Union and the WTO, https://www.wto.org/english/thewto_e/countries_e/european_communities _e.htm.

27. *See Portugal v. Council*, 23 November 1999, Case C-149/96.; *Van Parys v. Belgische Interventie en Restitutiebureau* (C-377/02). *See also* Case C-69/89, *Nakajima v. Council*, 1991 E.C.R. I-2069.

28. https://www.wto.org/english/docs_e/legal_e/gatt47_01_e.htm.

29. https://www.wto.org/english/res_e/booksp_e/analytic_index_e/gatt1994_e.htm.

regulations requiring the mixture, processing or use of products in specified amounts or proportions, should not be applied to imported or domestic products so as to afford protection to domestic production.

2. The products of the territory of any contracting party imported into the territory of any other contracting party shall not be subject, directly or indirectly, to internal taxes or other internal charges of any kind in excess of those applied, directly or indirectly, to like domestic products. Moreover, no contracting party shall otherwise apply internal taxes or other internal charges to imported or domestic products in a manner contrary to the principles set forth in paragraph 1.

. . . .

4. The products of the territory of any contracting party imported into the territory of any other contracting party shall be accorded treatment no less favourable than that accorded to like products of national origin in respect of all laws, regulations and requirements affecting their internal sale, offering for sale, purchase, transportation, distribution or use. The provisions of this paragraph shall not prevent the application of differential internal transportation charges which are based exclusively on the economic operation of the means of transport and not on the nationality of the product.

. . . .

8. (*a*) The provisions of this Article shall not apply to laws, regulations or requirements governing the procurement by governmental agencies of products purchased for governmental purposes and not with a view to commercial resale or with a view to use in the production of goods for commercial sale.

(*b*) The provisions of this Article shall not prevent the payment of subsidies exclusively to domestic producers, including payments to domestic producers derived from the proceeds of internal taxes or charges applied consistently with the provisions of this Article and subsidies effected through governmental purchases of domestic products.

. . . .

Ad Article III

Any internal tax or other internal charge, or any law, regulation or requirement of the kind referred to in paragraph 1 which applies to an imported product and to the like domestic product and is collected or enforced in the case of the imported product at the time or point of importation, is nevertheless to be regarded as an internal tax or other internal charge, or a law, regulation or requirement of the kind referred to in paragraph 1, and is accordingly subject to the provisions of Article III.

. . . .

Paragraph 2

A tax conforming to the requirements of the first sentence of paragraph 2 would be considered to be inconsistent with the provisions of the second sentence only in cases where competition was involved between, on the one hand, the taxed product and, on the other hand, a directly competitive or substitutable product which was not similarly taxed.

Article XI: General Elimination of Quantitative Restrictions

1. No prohibitions or restrictions other than duties, taxes or other charges, whether made effective through quotas, import or export licences or other measures, shall be instituted or maintained by any contracting party on the importation of any product of the territory of any other contracting party or on the exportation or sale for export of any product destined for the territory of any other contracting party. . . .

Article XXIII: Nullification or Impairment

1. If any contracting party should consider that any benefit accruing to it directly or indirectly under this Agreement is being nullified or impaired or that the attainment of any objective of the Agreement is being impeded as the result of

> (*a*) the failure of another contracting party to carry out its obligations under this Agreement, or

> (*b*) the application by another contracting party of any measure, whether or not it conflicts with the provisions of this Agreement, or

> (*c*) the existence of any other situation,

> the contracting party may, with a view to the satisfactory adjustment of the matter, make written representations or proposals to the other contracting party or parties which it considers to be concerned. Any contracting party thus approached shall give sympathetic consideration to the representations or proposals made to it.

> . . . .

Part Two: International Trade Disciplines, National Priorities & the Accommodation of Sovereignty

A. Overview

Promotion of free trade is the core function and founding premise of the WTO and the original GATT. The application of international rules which regulate how and when governments can impose restrictions on trade is central to this mission. The WTO describes itself this way: "The World Trade Organization (WTO) deals with the global rules of trade between nations. Its main function is to ensure that trade flows as smoothly, predictably and freely as possible."

The WTO system has placed significant emphasis on its dispute settlement process in order to make these "global rules of trade," or "disciplines," effective. Although states often resolve their trade disputes through negotiation, WTO panels are frequently called upon to declare whether the domestic law of a member state violates its international obligations. A decision that domestic law violates these international obligations necessarily challenges the domestic policy choices that underlie a state's trade restrictive practices. It is, therefore, not surprising that the WTO dispute settlement process is often accused of invading national sovereignty—in some senses it clearly does. The resulting controversies are particularly acute when the domestic laws being challenged involve health, safety, conservation, or environmental priorities.

There is, in this sense, a built-in tension between a state's legitimate concerns regarding its domestic priorities and the overarching goal of free trade promoted by the WTO system. Large anti-globalism protests at WTO meetings are, in part, a reflection of this tension and the fear that "faceless" international decision makers are usurping domestic priorities in the name of free trade. One could reasonably argue that unelected and unaccountable decision makers at the WTO, who lack domestic democratic legitimacy, have a built-in institutional bias favoring free trade over other values. On the other hand, nations might easily evade their international commitments to free and fair trade under the pretense of pursuing domestic health and safety. It is sometimes difficult to discern between legitimate domestic concerns and basic economic protectionism.

Anti-globalism protesters pepper sprayed at WTO meeting in Seattle, Washington. Photo by Steve Kaiser,[30] Wikimedia Commons[31]

---

30. https://www.flickr.com/people/41267996@N00?rb=1.

31. https://commons.wikimedia.org/wiki/File:WTO_protests_in_Seattle_November_30 _1999.jpg.

Historically, the GATT attempted to accommodate such concerns by creating exceptions to its basic obligations (such as the "legal pillars" described above) that apply under specified conditions. These exceptions, which include important limitations designed to protect free trade, appear primarily in Article XX of the GATT 47.

The 1994 expansion and restructuring of the GATT took these accommodations an important step further by creating two new sets of treaty-based rules focused on trade barriers justified by public health and safety. The Agreement on Technical Barriers to Trade[32] (TBT) focuses on product specifications and technical requirements — such as physical characteristics, methods of production, and quality control. For example, a domestic legal requirement that all bicycle chains possess a certain tensile strength, be tested in specified ways, and bear labelling information, would all be technical standards, and potential barriers to free trade. Such technical standards for products may also be imposed for reasons of national security, prevention of deceptive practices, and environmental protection. The TBT generally encourages countries to use international standards, and prohibits particular types of discriminatory regulations. According to the WTO:

> Technical regulations and standards are important, but they vary from country to country. Having too many different standards makes life difficult for producers and exporters. If the standards are set arbitrarily, they could be used as an excuse for protectionism. Standards can become obstacles to trade. But they are also necessary for a range of reasons, from environmental protection, safety, national security to consumer information. And they can help trade. Therefore the same basic question arises again: how to ensure that standards are genuinely useful, and not arbitrary or an excuse for protectionism.
>
> The **Technical Barriers to Trade Agreement (TBT)** tries to ensure that regulations, standards, testing and certification procedures do not create unnecessary obstacles.

Within recent years, WTO Dispute Settlement Panels have declared U.S. rules (a) requiring labelling of tuna products[33] as "dolphin safe," (b) prohibiting clove flavored[34] but not menthol favored cigarettes, and (c) requiring country of origin labelling[35] of certain meat products all to be in violation of the TBT. In each case, the U.S. regulations were found to lack "even-handedness" and have discriminatory effects (essentially failed to provide national treatment to foreign products).

The Sanitary and Phytosanitary Agreement[36] (SPS) sets out rules for domestic restrictions justified by the safety of food, agricultural and animal resources—

---

32. https://www.wto.org/english/tratop_e/tbt_e/tbt_e.htm.
33. https://www.wto.org/english/tratop_e/dispu_e/cases_e/ds381_e.htm.
34. https://www.wto.org/english/tratop_e/dispu_e/cases_e/ds406_e.htm.
35. https://www.wto.org/english/tratop_e/dispu_e/cases_e/ds386_e.htm.
36. https://www.wto.org/english/tratop_e/sps_e/spsagr_e.htm.

such as the risks of chemical or biological contaminations of food sources, or the effects of toxic substances on people. It follows a framework of legal obligations and restrictions very similar to the TBT. That framework is examined in greater detail below.

This part of Chapter 9 exposes the on-going battle over domestic health, safety and environmental measures that are alleged to unfairly restrict international trade. The problem focuses on application of the Article XX exceptions, and provisions of the more recent SPS agreement, as illustrations of the underlying tensions.

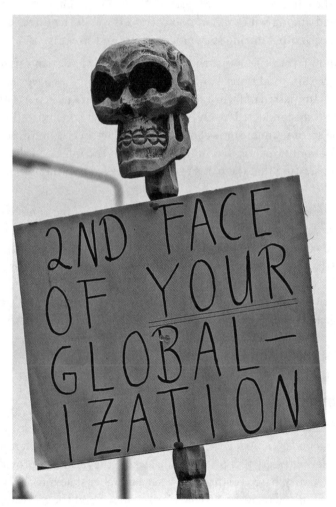

Photo by <u>Herder3</u>,[37] <u>Wikimedia Commons</u>[38]

---

37. https://commons.wikimedia.org/wiki/User:Herder3.

38. https://commons.wikimedia.org/wiki/File:Antiglob_rostock_2_6_07.jpg.

B. Problem Nine B: More Sick Fish

1. Facts

In addition to the facts presented in Part A above, assume the following facts.

It is well established that about 10% of live salmon caught in the wild carry parasites. The incidence of infestation is approximately the same for fish harvested in the Atlantic and Pacific fishing grounds. It is also well established from several scientific studies that the parasites, which are easily detectible through a visual inspection of the fish, spread among wild salmon populations through the direct contact of the live fish with each other during spawning in rivers and streams.

Most salmon farmers fear that the parasites could infest farm-raised fish, if exposed under certain conditions. However, no empirical studies have been conducted regarding contamination of farm-raised fish, and there are no reports of such infestations. One study conducted by an Australian scientist concluded that such parasites could be spread, under some conditions, to other species of fish such as catfish and tilapia, but only when raised in fish tanks with the infested fish. There are no studies demonstrating that the parasite can migrate from salmon to other fish species in the wild.

Available studies regarding the effect on humans of these parasites have not found any long-term serious illnesses associated with consumption of infested fish. However, one study by a respected Norwegian university has concluded that consumption of more than 2 pounds of infested fish in a serving may cause fever and stomach distress, when the fish is improperly prepared. The author of the study concluded his report with the observation that "then again, eating two pounds of even clean fish in one sitting might give anyone a stomach ache." Relevant international standards relating to such parasites place no limitations on the harvesting, sale, or consumption of salmon which are infested.

2. Assignment

a. *Given the additional facts provided above, evaluate Australia's "fishy" health and safety measures under (1) Article XX of GATT 47; and (2) the SPS Agreement.* Focus first on the relevant treaty text prior to considering the decisions provided or referenced below. Identify, based on that text, what a member state must show in order to gain the benefit of the relevant Article XX exceptions and the SPS agreement. The appellate body decisions excerpted below will provide important interpretive guidance on critical portions of the treaty texts.

b. Evaluate whether the SPS agreement, Article XX, and the WTO dispute settlement process itself, is a sound way to approach resolution of the tension between free trade and domestic priorities involving health, safety, environmental concerns, and human rights. *Does the process lack democratic legitimacy and accountability? Do such decisions represent a "free trade biased" interference with domestic self-*

governance? Are claims that the WTO processes infringe on national sovereignty valid in light of the organization's limited enforcement mechanisms? Is there an alternative other than unilateralism dominated by 800 pound guerillas?

C. Resources

1. Article XX Exceptions

Look through the dispute resolution annotations found at the WTO website for interpretations critical to resolution of the problem under Article XX. Start with the questions posed just above. **Yes,** *research the issues!* The WTO's "Analytical index"[39] provides links that you can follow for interpretations of the relevant treaty language.

2. Sanitary and Phytosanitary Agreement

a. SPS Agreement Text

Read over the WTO's general introduction[40] of the Sanitary and Phytosanitary Agreement. Then, scrutinize the treaty text set out below to determine the critical issues regarding the agreement's application to the problem. What terms must be interpreted, and how do those terms relate to each other? Consider, for example, differences in the language used in the three sections of Article 3. How do these provisions relate to Articles 2 and 5? You will find an appellate body ruling interpreting the agreement and these provisions below. The ruling is a good illustration of the sophisticated and subtle characteristics of the WTO's evolving legal jurisprudence. You might also again consult the analytical index webpage.

Agreement on the Application of Sanitary
and Phytosanitary Measures

. . . *Desiring* therefore to elaborate rules for the application of the provisions of GATT 1994 which relate to the use of sanitary or phytosanitary measures, in particular the provisions of Article XX(b);[1]

Article 1: General Provisions

1. This Agreement applies to all sanitary and phytosanitary measures which may, directly or indirectly, affect international trade. Such measures shall be developed and applied in accordance with the provisions of this Agreement.

. . . .

---

39. https://www.wto.org/english/res_e/booksp_e/analytic_index_e/gatt1994_e.htm.

40. https://www.wto.org/english/tratop_e/sps_e/spsund_e.htm.

1. In this Agreement, reference to Article XX(b) includes also the chapeau of that Article.

Article 2: Basic Rights and Obligations

1. Members have the right to take sanitary and phytosanitary measures necessary for the protection of human, animal or plant life or health, provided that such measures are not inconsistent with the provisions of this Agreement.

2. Members shall ensure that any sanitary or phytosanitary measure is applied only to the extent necessary to protect human, animal or plant life or health, is based on scientific principles and is not maintained without sufficient scientific evidence, except as provided for in paragraph 7 of Article 5.

3. Members shall ensure that their sanitary and phytosanitary measures do not arbitrarily or unjustifiably discriminate between Members where identical or similar conditions prevail, including between their own territory and that of other Members. Sanitary and phytosanitary measures shall not be applied in a manner which would constitute a disguised restriction on international trade.

4. Sanitary or phytosanitary measures which conform to the relevant provisions of this Agreement shall be presumed to be in accordance with the obligations of the Members under the provisions of GATT 1994 which relate to the use of sanitary or phytosanitary measures, in particular the provisions of Article XX(b).

Article 3: Harmonization

1. To harmonize sanitary and phytosanitary measures on as wide a basis as possible, Members shall base their sanitary or phytosanitary measures on international standards, guidelines or recommendations, where they exist, except as otherwise provided for in this Agreement, and in particular in paragraph 3.

2. Sanitary or phytosanitary measures which conform to international standards, guidelines or recommendations shall be deemed to be necessary to protect human, animal or plant life or health, and presumed to be consistent with the relevant provisions of this Agreement and of GATT 1994.

3. Members may introduce or maintain sanitary or phytosanitary measures which result in a higher level of sanitary or phytosanitary protection than would be achieved by measures based on the relevant international standards, guidelines or recommendations, if there is a scientific justification, or as a consequence of the level of sanitary or phytosanitary protection a Member determines to be appropriate in accordance with the relevant provisions of paragraphs 1 through 8 of Article 5.[2] Notwithstanding the above, all measures which result in a level of sanitary or phytosanitary protection different from that which would be achieved by measures based on international standards, guidelines or recommendations shall not be inconsistent with any other provision of this Agreement.

---

2. For the purposes of paragraph 3 of Article 3, there is a scientific justification if, on the basis of an examination and evaluation of available scientific information in conformity with the relevant provisions of this Agreement, a Member determines that the relevant international standards, guidelines or recommendations are not sufficient to achieve its appropriate level of sanitary or phytosanitary protection.

4. Members shall play a full part, within the limits of their resources, in the relevant international organizations and their subsidiary bodies, in particular the Codex Alimentarius Commission, the International Office of Epizootics, and the international and regional organizations operating within the framework of the International Plant Protection Convention, to promote within these organizations the development and periodic review of standards, guidelines and recommendations with respect to all aspects of sanitary and phytosanitary measures.

5. The Committee on Sanitary and Phytosanitary Measures provided for in paragraphs 1 and 4 of Article 12 (referred to in this Agreement as the "Committee") shall develop a procedure to monitor the process of international harmonization and coordinate efforts in this regard with the relevant international organizations.

Article 4: Equivalence

1. Members shall accept the sanitary or phytosanitary measures of other Members as equivalent, even if these measures differ from their own or from those used by other Members trading in the same product, if the exporting Member objectively demonstrates to the importing Member that its measures achieve the importing Member's appropriate level of sanitary or phytosanitary protection. For this purpose, reasonable access shall be given, upon request, to the importing Member for inspection, testing and other relevant procedures.

. . . .

Article 5: Assessment of Risk and Determination of the Appropriate Level of Sanitary or Phytosanitary Protection

1. Members shall ensure that their sanitary or phytosanitary measures are based on an assessment, as appropriate to the circumstances, of the risks to human, animal or plant life or health, taking into account risk assessment techniques developed by the relevant international organizations.

2. In the assessment of risks, Members shall take into account available scientific evidence; relevant processes and production methods; relevant inspection, sampling and testing methods; prevalence of specific diseases or pests; existence of pest- or disease-free areas; relevant ecological and environmental conditions; and quarantine or other treatment.

3. In assessing the risk to animal or plant life or health and determining the measure to be applied for achieving the appropriate level of sanitary or phytosanitary protection from such risk, Members shall take into account as relevant economic factors: the potential damage in terms of loss of production or sales in the event of the entry, establishment or spread of a pest or disease; the costs of control or eradication in the territory of the importing Member; and the relative cost-effectiveness of alternative approaches to limiting risks.

4. Members should, when determining the appropriate level of sanitary or phytosanitary protection, take into account the objective of minimizing negative trade effects.

5. With the objective of achieving consistency in the application of the concept of appropriate level of sanitary or phytosanitary protection against risks to human life or health, or to animal and plant life or health, each Member shall avoid arbitrary or unjustifiable distinctions in the <u>levels</u> it considers to be appropriate in different situations, if such distinctions result in discrimination or a disguised restriction on international trade. Members shall cooperate in the Committee, in accordance with paragraphs 1, 2 and 3 of Article 12, to develop guidelines to further the practical implementation of this provision. In developing the guidelines, the Committee shall take into account all relevant factors, including the exceptional character of human health risks to which people voluntarily expose themselves.

6. Without prejudice to paragraph 2 of Article 3, when establishing or maintaining sanitary or phytosanitary measures to achieve the appropriate level of sanitary or phytosanitary protection, Members shall ensure that such measures are not more trade-restrictive than required to achieve their appropriate level of sanitary or phytosanitary protection, taking into account technical and economic feasibility.[3]

7. In cases where relevant scientific evidence is insufficient, a Member may provisionally adopt sanitary or phytosanitary measures on the basis of available pertinent information, including that from the relevant international organizations as well as from sanitary or phytosanitary measures applied by other Members. In such circumstances, Members shall seek to obtain the additional information necessary for a more objective assessment of risk and review the sanitary or phytosanitary measure accordingly within a reasonable period of time.

. . . .

Annex A: Definitions

1. *Sanitary or phytosanitary measure*—Any measure applied:

   (a) to protect animal or plant life or health within the territory of the Member from risks arising from the entry, establishment or spread of pests, diseases, disease-carrying organisms or disease-causing organisms;

   (b) to protect human or animal life or health within the territory of the Member from risks arising from additives, contaminants, toxins or disease-causing organisms in foods, beverages or feedstuffs;

   (c) to protect human life or health within the territory of the Member from risks arising from diseases carried by animals, plants or products thereof, or from the entry, establishment or spread of pests; or

   (d) to prevent or limit other damage within the territory of the Member from the entry, establishment or spread of pests.

---

3. For purposes of paragraph 6 of Article 5, a measure is not more trade-restrictive than required unless there is another measure, reasonably available taking into account technical and economic feasibility, that achieves the appropriate level of sanitary or phytosanitary protection and is significantly less restrictive to trade.

Sanitary or phytosanitary measures include all relevant laws, decrees, regulations, requirements and procedures including, *inter alia*, end product criteria; processes and production methods; testing, inspection, certification and approval procedures; quarantine treatments including relevant requirements associated with the transport of animals or plants, or with the materials necessary for their survival during transport; provisions on relevant statistical methods, sampling procedures and methods of risk assessment; and packaging and labelling requirements directly related to food safety.

. . . .

4. *Risk assessment*—The evaluation of the likelihood of entry, establishment or spread of a pest or disease within the territory of an importing Member according to the sanitary or phytosanitary measures which might be applied, and of the associated potential biological and economic consequences; or the evaluation of the potential for adverse effects on human or animal health arising from the presence of additives, contaminants, toxins or disease-causing organisms in food, beverages or feedstuffs.

5. *Appropriate level of sanitary or phytosanitary protection*—The level of protection deemed appropriate by the Member establishing a sanitary or phytosanitary measure to protect human, animal or plant life or health within its territory.

NOTE: Many Members otherwise refer to this concept as the "acceptable level of risk".

b. SPS Dispute Settlement Case Law

i. United States v. European Communities

January 1998 (98-0099), EC Measures Concerning Meat
and Meat Products (Hormones), AB-1997-4,
Report of the Appellate Body

I. Introduction: Statement of the Appeal

The European Communities, the United States and Canada appeal from certain issues of law and legal interpretations in the Panel Reports, EC Measures Concerning Meat and Meat Products (Hormones) . . . .

The Panel dealt with a complaint against the European Communities relating to an EC prohibition of imports of meat and meat products derived from cattle to which either the natural hormones: . . . administered for growth promotion purposes. This import prohibition was set forth in a series of Directives of the Council of Ministers that were enacted before 1 January 1995.

. . . As under the previously applicable Directives, it is prohibited to place on the market, or to import from third countries, meat and meat products from animals to which such substances, including the six hormones at issue in this dispute, were administered. This Directive also continues to allow Member States to authorize the administration, for therapeutic and zootechnical purposes, of certain substances having a hormonal or thyrostatic action. Under certain conditions, Directive 96/22 allows the placing on the market, and the importation from third countries, of meat and meat products from animals to which these substances have been administered for therapeutic and zootechnical purposes.

The Panel circulated its Reports to the Members of the WTO on 18 August 1997. The US Panel Report and the Canada Panel Report reached the same conclusions in paragraph 9.1:

> (i) The European Communities, by maintaining sanitary measures which are not based on a risk assessment, has acted inconsistently with the requirements contained in Article 5.1 of the Agreement on the Application of Sanitary and Phytosanitary Measures.

> (ii) The European Communities, by adopting arbitrary or unjustifiable distinctions in the levels of sanitary protection it considers to be appropriate in different situations which result in discrimination or a disguised restriction on international trade, has acted inconsistently with the requirement contained in Article 5.5 of the Agreement on the Application of Sanitary and Phytosanitary Measures.

> (iii) The European Communities, by maintaining sanitary measures which are not based on existing international standards without justification under Article 3.3 of the Agreement on the Application of Sanitary and Phytosanitary Measures, has acted inconsistently with the requirements of Article 3.1 of that Agreement.

In both Reports, the Panel recommended in paragraph 9.2:

> . . . that the Dispute Settlement Body requests the European Communities to bring its measures in dispute into conformity with its obligations under the Agreement on the Application of Sanitary and Phytosanitary Measures.

. . . .

2. Standard of Review

The European Communities claims that the Panel erred in law by not according deference to the following aspects of the EC measures: first, the decision of the European Communities to set and apply a level of sanitary protection higher than that recommended by the Codex Alimentarius (the "Codex") for the risks arising from the use for growth promotion of the hormones in dispute; second, the EC's scientific assessment and management of the risk from the hormones at issue, and third, the EC's adherence to the precautionary principle and its aversion to accepting any increased carcinogenic risk.

It is submitted by the European Communities that WTO panels should adopt a deferential "reasonableness" standard when reviewing a Member's decision to adopt a particular science policy or a Member's determination that a particular inference from the available data is scientifically plausible. To the European Communities, the Panel in this case imposed its own assessment of the scientific evidence.

. . . .

IV. Allocating the Burden of Proof in Proceedings Under the SPS Agreement

The first general issue that we must address relates to the allocation of the burden of proof in proceedings under the SPS Agreement. . . .

The Panel begins its analysis by setting out the general allocation of the burden of proof between the contending parties in any proceedings under the SPS Agreement. The initial burden lies on the complaining party, which must establish a prima facie case of inconsistency with a particular provision of the SPS Agreement on the part of the defending party, or more precisely, of its SPS measure or measures complained about. When that prima facie case is made, the burden of proof moves to the defending party, which must in turn counter or refute the claimed inconsistency. This seems straightforward enough and is in conformity with our ruling in United States — Shirts and Blouses, which the Panel invokes and which embodies a rule applicable in any adversarial proceedings.

. . . .

So far as fact-finding by panels is concerned, their activities are always constrained by the mandate of Article 11 of the DSU: the applicable standard is neither de novo review as such, nor "total deference", but rather the "objective assessment of the facts". . . .

VI. The Relevance of the Precautionary Principle in the Interpretation of the SPS Agreement

. . . .

It appears to us important, nevertheless, to note some aspects of the relationship of the precautionary principle to the SPS Agreement. First, the principle has not been written into the SPS Agreement as a ground for justifying SPS measures that are otherwise inconsistent with the obligations of Members set out in particular provisions of that Agreement. Secondly, . . . These explicitly recognize the right of Members to establish their own appropriate level of sanitary protection, which level may be higher (i.e., more cautious) than that implied in existing international standards, guidelines and recommendations. Thirdly, a panel charged with determining, for instance, whether "sufficient scientific evidence" exists to warrant the maintenance by a Member of a particular SPS measure may, of course, and should, bear in mind that responsible, representative governments commonly act from perspectives of prudence and precaution where risks of irreversible, e.g. life-terminating, damage to human health are concerned. . . .

We accordingly agree with the finding of the Panel that the precautionary principle does not override the provisions of Articles 5.1 and 5.2 of the SPS Agreement.

. . . .

X. The Interpretation of Articles 3.1 and 3.3 of the SPS Agreement

. . . [T]he Panel developed three legal interpretations, which have all been appealed by the European Communities . . . . As may be expected, the Panel's three interpretations are intertwined.

A. The Meaning of "Based On" as Used in Article 3.1 of the SPS Agreement

Article 3.1 provides:

> To harmonize sanitary and phytosanitary measures on as wide a basis as possible, Members shall base their sanitary or phytosanitary measures on international standards, guidelines or recommendations, where they exist, except as otherwise provided for in this Agreement, and in particular in paragraph 3.

. . . .

We find, therefore, that for a sanitary measure to be based on an international standard in accordance with Article 3.1, that measure needs to reflect the same level of sanitary protection as the standard. In this dispute a comparison thus needs to be made between the level of protection reflected in the EC measures in dispute and that reflected in the Codex standards for each of the five hormones at issue.

We read the Panel's interpretation that Article 3.2 "equates" measures "based on" international standards with measures which "conform to" such standards, as signifying that "based on" and "conform to" are identical in meaning. The Panel is thus saying that, henceforth, SPS measures of Members must "conform to" Codex standards, guidelines and recommendations.

We are unable to accept this interpretation of the Panel. In the first place, the ordinary meaning of "based on" is quite different from the plain or natural import of "conform to". . . . A measure that "conforms to" and incorporates a Codex standard is, of course, "based on" that standard. A measure, however, based on the same standard might not conform to that standard, as where only some, not all, of the elements of the standard are incorporated into the measure.

In the second place, "based on" and "conform to" are used in different articles, as well as in differing paragraphs of the same article. . . . The implication arises that the choice and use of different words in different places in the SPS Agreement are deliberate, and that the different words are designed to convey different meanings. . . .

Accordingly, we disagree with the Panel's interpretation that "based on" means the same thing as "conform to".

. . . .

B. Relationship Between Articles 3.1, 3.2 and 3.3 of the SPS Agreement

. . . .

Under Article 3.2 of the SPS Agreement, a Member may decide to promulgate an SPS measure that conforms to an international standard. Such a measure would embody the international standard completely and, for practical purposes, converts it into a municipal standard. Such a measure enjoys the benefit of a presumption (albeit a rebuttable one) that it is consistent with the relevant provisions of the SPS Agreement and of the GATT 1994.

Under Article 3.1 of the SPS Agreement, a Member may choose to establish an SPS measure that is based on the existing relevant international standard, guideline or recommendation. Such a measure may adopt some, not necessarily all, of the elements of the international standard. The Member imposing this measure does not benefit from the presumption of consistency set up in Article 3.2; but, as earlier observed, the Member is not penalized by exemption of a complaining Member from the normal burden of showing a prima facie case of inconsistency with Article 3.1 or any other relevant article of the SPS Agreement or of the GATT 1994.

Under Article 3.3 of the SPS Agreement, a Member may decide to set for itself a level of protection different from that implicit in the international standard, and to implement or embody that level of protection in a measure not "based on" the international standard. The Member's appropriate level of protection may be higher than that implied in the international standard. The right of a Member to determine its own appropriate level of sanitary protection is an important right. . . .

C. The Requirements of Article 3.3 of the SPS Agreement

The right of a Member to define its appropriate level of protection is not, however, an absolute or unqualified right. Article 3.3 also makes this clear:

    . . . .

For the purposes of paragraph 3 of Article 3, there is a scientific justification if, on the basis of an examination and evaluation of available scientific information in conformity with the relevant provisions of this Agreement, a Member determines that the relevant international standards, guidelines or recommendations are not sufficient to achieve its appropriate level of sanitary or phytosanitary protection.

    . . . .

Article 3.3 is evidently not a model of clarity in drafting and communication. The use of the disjunctive "or" does indicate that two situations are intended to be covered. These are the introduction or maintenance of SPS measures which result in a higher level of protection:

(a) "if there is a scientific justification"; or

(b) "as a consequence of the level of . . . protection a Member determines to be appropriate in accordance with the relevant provisions of paragraphs 1 through 8 of Article 5".

. . . On balance, we agree with the Panel's finding that although the European Communities has established for itself a level of protection higher, or more exacting, than the level of protection implied in the relevant Codex standards, guidelines or recommendations, the European Communities was bound to comply with the requirements established in Article 5.1. We are not unaware that this finding tends to suggest that the distinction made in Article 3.3 between two situations may have very limited effects and may, to that extent, be more apparent than real. Its involved and layered language actually leaves us with no choice.

Consideration of the object and purpose of Article 3 and of the SPS Agreement as a whole reinforces our belief that compliance with Article 5.1 was intended as a countervailing factor in respect of the right of Members to set their appropriate level of protection. . . .

The requirements of a risk assessment under Article 5.1, as well as of "sufficient scientific evidence" under Article 2.2, are essential for the maintenance of the delicate and carefully negotiated balance in the SPS Agreement between the shared, but sometimes competing, interests of promoting international trade and of protecting the life and health of human beings. We conclude that the Panel's finding that the European Communities is required by Article 3.3 to comply with the requirements of Article 5.1 is correct and, accordingly, dismiss the appeal of the European Communities from that ruling of the Panel.

XI. The Reading of Articles 5.1 and 5.2 of the SPS Agreement:
Basing SPS Measures on a Risk Assessment

We turn to the appeal of European Communities from the Panel's conclusion that, by maintaining SPS measures which are not based on a risk assessment, the European Communities acted inconsistently with the requirements contained in Article 5.1 of the SPS Agreement.

Article 5.1 of the SPS Agreement provides:

> Members shall ensure that their sanitary or phytosanitary measures are based on an assessment, as appropriate to the circumstances, of the risks to human, animal or plant life or health, taking into account risk assessment techniques developed by the relevant international organizations.

A. The Interpretation of "Risk Assessment"

At the outset, two preliminary considerations need to be brought out. The first is that the Panel considered that Article 5.1 may be viewed as a specific application of the basic obligations contained in Article 2.2 of the SPS Agreement, which reads as follows:

> Members shall ensure that any sanitary or phytosanitary measure is applied only to the extent necessary to protect human, animal or plant life or health, is based on scientific principles and is not maintained without sufficient scientific evidence, except as provided for in paragraph 7 of Article 5. (underlining added)

We agree with this general consideration and would also stress that Articles 2.2 and 5.1 should constantly be read together. Article 2.2 informs Article 5.1: the elements that define the basic obligation set out in Article 2.2 impart meaning to Article 5.1.

. . . .

1. Risk Assessment and the Notion of "Risk"

Paragraph 4 of Annex A of the SPS Agreement sets out the treaty definition of risk assessment: This definition, to the extent pertinent to the present appeal, speaks of:

> ... the evaluation of the potential for adverse effects on human or animal health arising from the presence of additives, contaminants, toxins or disease-causing organisms in food, beverages or feedstuffs.

Interpreting the above definition, the Panel elaborates risk assessment as a two-step process that "should (i) identify the adverse effects on human health (if any) arising from the presence of the hormones at issue when used as growth promoters in meat . . . , and (ii) if any such adverse effects exist, evaluate the potential or probability of occurrence of such effects".

... What needs to be pointed out at this stage is that the Panel's use of "probability" as an alternative term for "potential" creates a significant concern. The ordinary meaning of "potential" relates to "possibility" and is different from the ordinary meaning of "probability". "Probability" implies a higher degree or a threshold of potentiality or possibility. It thus appears that here the Panel introduces a quantitative dimension to the notion of risk.

. . . .

2. Factors to be Considered in Carrying Out a Risk Assessment

. . . .

The listing in Article 5.2 begins with "available scientific evidence"; this, however, is only the beginning. We note in this connection that the Panel states that, for purposes of the EC measures in dispute, a risk assessment required by Article 5.1 is "a scientific process aimed at establishing the scientific basis for the sanitary measure a Member intends to take". . . . It is essential to bear in mind that the risk that is to be evaluated in a risk assessment under Article 5.1 is not only risk ascertainable in a science laboratory operating under strictly controlled conditions, but also risk in human societies as they actually exist, in other words, the actual potential for adverse effects on human health in the real world where people live and work and die.

B. The Interpretation of "Based On"

. . . .

2.Substantive Requirement of Article 5.1 — Rational Relationship Between an SPS Measure and a Risk Assessment

. . . .

We believe that Article 5.1, when contextually read as it should be, in conjunction with and as informed by Article 2.2 of the SPS Agreement, requires that the results of the risk assessment must sufficiently warrant — that is to say, reasonably support — the SPS measure at stake. The requirement that an SPS measure be "based on" a risk assessment is a substantive requirement that there be a rational relationship between the measure and the risk assessment.

. . . The risk assessment could set out both the prevailing view representing the "mainstream" of scientific opinion, as well as the opinions of scientists taking a divergent view. Article 5.1 does not require that the risk assessment must necessarily embody only the view of a majority of the relevant scientific community. In some cases, the very existence of divergent views presented by qualified scientists who have investigated the particular issue at hand may indicate a state of scientific uncertainty. . . .

We turn now to the application by the Panel of the substantive requirements of Article 5.1 to the EC measures at stake in the present case.

. . . .

The Panel states:

> . . . none of the scientific evidence referred to by the European Communities which specifically addresses the safety of some or all of the hormones in dispute when used for growth promotion, indicates that an identifiable risk arises for human health from such use of these hormones if good practice is followed. All of the scientific studies outlined above came to the conclusion that the use of the hormones at issue (all but MGA, for which no evidence was submitted) for growth promotion purposes is safe; most of these studies adding that this conclusion assumes that good practice is followed.

Prescinding from the difficulty raised by the Panel's use of the term "identifiable risk", we agree that the scientific reports listed above do not rationally support the EC import prohibition.

With regard to the scientific opinion expressed by Dr. Lucier at the joint meeting with the experts, and as set out in paragraph 819 of the Annex to the US and Canada Panel Reports, we should note that this opinion by Dr. Lucier does not purport to be the result of scientific studies carried out by him or under his supervision focusing specifically on residues of hormones in meat from cattle fattened with such hormones. Accordingly, it appears that the single divergent opinion expressed by Dr. Lucier is not reasonably sufficient to overturn the contrary conclusions reached in the scientific studies referred to by the European Communities that related specifically to residues of the hormones in meat from cattle to which hormones had been administered for growth promotion.

. . . .

We believe that the above findings of the Panel are justified. . . . Those general studies, are in other words, relevant but do not appear to be sufficiently specific to the case at hand.

. . . .

The European Communities also referred to distinguishable but closely related risks—risks arising from failure to observe the requirements of good veterinary practice, in combination with multiple problems relating to detection and control of such abusive failure, in the administration of hormones to cattle for growth promotion.

The Panel considers this type of risk and examines the arguments made by the European Communities but finds no assessment of such kind of risk. . . .

In the absence of any other relevant documentation, we find that the European Communities did not actually proceed to an assessment, within the meaning of Articles 5.1 and 5.2, of the risks arising from the failure of observance of good veterinary practice combined with problems of control of the use of hormones for growth promotion purposes. . . .

We affirm, therefore, the ultimate conclusion of the Panel that the EC import prohibition is not based on a risk assessment within the meaning of Articles 5.1 and 5.2 of the SPS Agreement and is, therefore, inconsistent with the requirements of Article 5.1.

Since we have concluded above that an SPS measure, to be consistent with Article 3.3, has to comply with, inter alia, the requirements contained in Article 5.1, it follows that the EC measures at issue, by failing to comply with Article 5.1, are also inconsistent with Article 3.3 of the SPS Agreement.

XII. The Reading of Article 5.5 of the SPS Agreement: Consistency of Levels of Protection and Resulting Discrimination or Disguised Restriction on International Trade

. . . .

A. General Considerations: the Elements of Article 5.5

Article 5.5 of the SPS Agreement needs to be quoted in full:

> . . . each Member shall avoid arbitrary or unjustifiable distinctions in the levels it considers to be appropriate in different situations, if such distinctions result in discrimination or a disguised restriction on international trade. . . .

Article 5.5 must be read in context. An important part of that context is Article 2.3 of the SPS Agreement, which provides as follows:

> Members shall ensure that their sanitary and phytosanitary measures do not arbitrarily or unjustifiably discriminate between Members where identical or similar conditions prevail, including between their own territory and that of other Members. Sanitary and phytosanitary measures shall not be applied in a manner which would constitute a disguised restriction on international trade.

When read together with Article 2.3, Article 5.5 may be seen to be marking out and elaborating a particular route leading to the same destination set out in Article 2.3.

. . . .

Close inspection of Article 5.5 indicates that a complaint of violation of this Article must show the presence of three distinct elements. The first element is that the

Member imposing the measure complained of has adopted its own appropriate levels of sanitary protection against risks to human life or health in several different situations. The second element to be shown is that those levels of protection exhibit arbitrary or unjustifiable differences ("distinctions" in the language of Article 5.5) in their treatment of different situations. The last element requires that the arbitrary or unjustifiable differences result in discrimination or a disguised restriction of international trade. . . .

We consider the above three elements of Article 5.5 to be cumulative in nature; all of them must be demonstrated to be present if violation of Article 5.5 is to be found. . . .

B. Different Levels of Protection in Different Situations

. . . .

C. Arbitrary or Unjustifiable Differences in Levels of Protection

. . . .

We do not share the Panel's conclusions that the above differences in levels of protection in respect of added hormones in treated meat and in respect of naturally-occurring hormones in food, are merely arbitrary and unjustifiable. . . .

The conclusion we come to, after consideration of the foregoing factors, is that, on balance, the difference in the levels of protection concerning hormones used for growth promotion purposes, on the one hand, and concerning hormones used for therapeutic and zootechnical purposes, on the other, is not, in itself, "arbitrary or unjustifiable".

We turn to the Panel's comparison between the levels of protection set by the European Communities in respect of natural and synthetic hormones for growth promotion and with respect to carbadox and olaquindox. . . .

Having reviewed the above arguments and counter-arguments, we must agree with the Panel that the difference in the EC levels of protection in respect of the hormones in dispute when used for growth promotion, on the one hand, and carbadox and olaquindox, on the other, is unjustifiable in the sense of Article 5.5.

D. Resulting in Discrimination or a Disguised Restriction on International Trade

. . . .

In the present appeal, it is necessary to address this question only with regard to the difference in the levels of protection established in respect of the hormones in dispute and in respect of carbadox and olaquindox.

. . . .

We are unable to share the inference that the Panel apparently draws that the import ban on treated meat and the Community-wide prohibition of the use of the hormones here in dispute for growth promotion purposes in the beef sector were not really designed to protect its population from the risk of cancer, but rather to keep out US and Canadian hormone-treated beef and thereby to protect the domestic beef producers in the European Communities.

. . . Accordingly, we reverse the conclusion of the Panel that the European Communities has acted inconsistently with the requirements set out in Article 5.5 of the SPS Agreement.

. . . .

XIV. Findings and Conclusions

. . . .

The Appellate Body recommends that the Dispute Settlement Body request the European Communities to bring the SPS measures found in this Report and in the Panel Reports, as modified by this Report, to be inconsistent with the SPS Agreement into conformity with the obligations of the European Communities under that Agreement.

Chapter 10

Customs: The Classification, Valuation and Origin of Imported Goods

A. Overview

1. The International Connection

In the previous chapter, we learned that nations often impose restrictions on imported goods which, even when motivated by legitimate needs, tend to undermine the economic benefits of free trade. Such restrictions are sometimes motivated by domestic economic interests and local politics as governments attempt to provide domestic industry a competitive advantage over imports. Every nation will also have various legitimate concerns that prompt control over and regulation of international trade. The next few chapters of this book address such domestic controls over trade, starting with customs and tariffs. We will focus on U.S. law and institutions (a list of the numerous U.S. federal agencies involved in international trade issues[1] is available on the U.S. Trade Representative website). At almost every turn, these domestic controls and regulations reflect international obligations created by the extensive body of international rules administered by the WTO precisely to curb protectionist impulses.

This chapter is focused on customs—that is, the entry and assessment of tariffs on goods imported into the United States. Tariffs imposed at the national border are among the most common domestic measures that protect local interests from international competition. A 10% tariff obviously adds 10% to the cost of the imported product—a tax that does not apply to similar domestic goods. Historically, the WTO's quasi-institutional predecessor, "the GATT" (1949–1993), focused significant resources on negotiations between nations aimed at reducing tariffs and controlling how such taxes can be imposed.

---

1. https://ustr.gov/about-us/trade-toolbox/us-government-trade-agencies.

The results of the GATT tariff negotiation process are protected by Article II of GATT 47, which generally requires members to honor their tariff reduction commitments in the form of "bindings." GATT 47's "MFN" requirement in Article I "spreads the wealth" by obligating all WTO members to extend all trade benefits to all other members, including tariff reductions. As a result, these internationally sponsored tariff reductions ripple out through the entire WTO membership. The result is a 30,000 page schedule of tariff commitments, the benefits of which ultimately filter down into the domestic system of every WTO member state.

Every member state maintains its own tariff schedule (with the exception of those in custom unions, such as the EU, which share a common schedule). Thus, the actual tariff rates imposed by any particular country for particular goods will correspond to that country's WTO commitments to other members of the WTO for such goods. The United States and Japan will have different tariffs for imported bicycles, and each country's tariff for bicycles will reflect that country's commitment in the WTO negotiations on tariffs. Correspondingly, because of Article I, any reduction in either country's respective tariff on bicycles, even if created strictly as a quid pro quo between the two nations, would have to be extended to the entire WTO membership. Thus, the U.S. tariff on imported bicycles must be the same for all imported "like" bicycles, regardless of the product's origin (among the WTO nations).

The U.S. is not obligated to extend this WTO tariff to bicycles from non-WTO nations that don't fall within the GATT MFN obligation. However, the U.S. typically does so anyway via bi-lateral agreements it has with nearly all non-WTO countries. The U.S. customs law more accurately references MFN status as "normal trade relations" or "NTR." Exceptions to NTR status currently only include Cuba and North Korea. However, temporary trade bans or restrictions may apply to a variety of other countries, including, for example, Iran,[2] Sudan,[3] Myanmar[4] and Syria,[5] among others. These trade restrictions frequently change with events as witnessed in 2012 by increased sanctions on Iran and Syria, and an easing of sanctions on Myanmar.

Domestic tariffs must also be consistent with other WTO rules found in GATT 94 (e.g., Agreements on Rules of Origin, Subsidies, Dumping and Valuation). Similarly, a number of important exceptions to MFN's promise of non-discrimination will also be reflected in the domestic tariff schedule such as special duty free treatment for goods from U.S. free trade agreement partners (e.g., NAFTA). GATT also allows an MFN exception for underdeveloped, poor countries under which both the U.S. and EU have created special tariff preferences.

---

2. https://www.treasury.gov/resource-center/sanctions/Programs/Pages/iran.aspx.
3. https://www.treasury.gov/resource-center/sanctions/Programs/pages/sudan.aspx.
4. https://www.treasury.gov/resource-center/sanctions/Programs/pages/burma.aspx.
5. https://www.treasury.gov/resource-center/sanctions/Programs/pages/burma.aspx.

2. The U.S. Harmonized Tariff Schedule

The primary WTO-based obligations (MFN and tariff concessions) and allowed preferences (free trade agreements, customs unions and reduced tariffs for poor countries) are reflected in the rate columns of the U.S. Harmonized Tariff Schedule.[6] While U.S. Customs and Border Protection (CBP)[7] administers the customs laws and collects the tax due, the International Trade Commission[8] maintains and publishes the Harmonized Tariff Schedule. The general commodity descriptions and most subcategories (out to the sixth digit) in the tariff nomenclature are set through international agreement and cooperation as monitored by the World Customs Organization[9] (and hence a "harmonized" classification system). Review the following example, which includes a section from the Schedule "Table of Contents" and "Chapter Notes." An explanation of how the schedule works is provided later in the chapter. For now, simply note how it is organized with various chapters, notes, descriptions of goods and corresponding tariffs.

U.S. Harmonized Tariff Schedule[10]

SECTION XI: TEXTILE AND TEXTILE ARTICLES

Section Notes[11]

Chapter 50[12]   Silk

Chapter 51[13]   Wool, fine or coarse animal hair; horsehair yarn and woven fabric

Chapter 52[14]   Cotton

Chapter 53[15]   Other vegetable textile fibers; paper yarn and woven fabric of paper yarn

Chapter 54[16]   Man-made filaments

Chapter 55[17]   Man-made staple fibers

Chapter 56[18]   Wadding, felt and nonwovens; special yarns, twine, cordage, ropes and cables and articles thereof

Chapter 57[19]   Carpets and other textile floor coverings

Chapter 58[20]   Special woven fabrics; tufted textile fabrics; lace, tapestries; trimmings; embroidery

6. https://hts.usitc.gov/current.

7. https://www.cbp.gov/trade/basic-import-export.

8. https://dataweb.usitc.gov/scripts/tariff.asp.

9. http://www.wcoomd.org/en/about-us/what-is-the-wco.aspx.

10. https://hts.usitc.gov/current.

11. http://www.wcoomd.org/en/about-us/what-is-the-wco.aspx.

12. https://hts.usitc.gov/view/Chapter%2050?release=basicCorrections2.

13. https://hts.usitc.gov/view/Chapter%2051?release=basicCorrections2.

14. https://hts.usitc.gov/view/Chapter%2052?release=basicCorrections2.

15. https://hts.usitc.gov/view/Chapter%2053?release=basicCorrections2.

16. https://hts.usitc.gov/view/Chapter%2054?release=basicCorrections2.

17. https://hts.usitc.gov/view/Chapter%2055?release=basicCorrections2.

18. https://hts.usitc.gov/view/Chapter%2056?release=basicCorrections2.

19. https://hts.usitc.gov/view/Chapter%2057?release=basicCorrections2.

20. https://hts.usitc.gov/view/Chapter%2058?release=basicCorrections2.

Chapter 59[21]   Impregnated, coated, covered or laminated textile fabrics; textile articles of a kind suitable for industrial use

Chapter 60[22]   Knitted or crocheted fabrics

Chapter 61[23]   Articles of apparel and clothing accessories, knitted or crocheted

Chapter 62[24]   Articles of apparel and clothing accessories, not knitted or crocheted

Chapter 63[25]   Other made up textile articles; sets; worn clothing and worn textile articles; rags

CHAPTER 62 ARTICLES OF APPAREL AND CLOTHING ACCESSORIES, NOT KNITTED OR CROCHETED 1/XI 62-1

Notes

1. This chapter applies only to made up articles of any textile fabric other than wadding, excluding knitted or crocheted articles (other than those of heading 6212).

2. This chapter does not cover:

(a) Worn clothing or other worn articles of heading 6309;

(b) Orthopedic appliances, surgical belts, trusses or the like (heading 9021).

3. For the purposes of headings 6203 and 6204:

(a) The term "suit" means a set of garments composed of two or three pieces made up, in respect of their outer surface, in identical fabric and comprising:

—one suit coat or jacket the outer shell of which, exclusive of sleeves, consists of four or more panels, designed to cover the upper part of the body, possibly with a tailored waistcoat in addition whose front is made from the same fabric as the outer surface of the other components of the set and whose back is made from the same fabric as the lining of the suit coat or jacket; and

—one garment designed to cover the lower part of the body and consisting of trousers, breeches or shorts (other than swimwear), a skirt or a divided skirt, having neither braces nor bibs.

All of the components of a "suit" must be of the same fabric construction, color and composition; they must also be of the same style and of corresponding or compatible size. However, these components may have piping (a strip of fabric sewn into the seam) in a different fabric. If several separate components to cover the lower part of the body area presented together (for example, two pairs of trousers or trousers and shorts, or a skirt or divided

---

21. https://hts.usitc.gov/view/Chapter%2059?release=basicCorrections2.
22. https://hts.usitc.gov/view/Chapter%2060?release=basicCorrections2.
23. https://hts.usitc.gov/view/Chapter%2061?release=basicCorrections2.
24. https://hts.usitc.gov/view/Chapter%2062?release=basicCorrections2.
25. https://hts.usitc.gov/view/Chapter%2063?release=basicCorrections2.

skirt and trousers), the constituent lower part shall be one pair of trousers, or, in the case of women's or girls' suits, the skirt or divided skirt, the other garments being considered separately.

. . . .

Harmonized Tariff Schedule of the United States (2017)
Annotated for Statistical Reporting Purposes

XI
62-5

Heading/ Subheading	Stat. Suf- fix	Article Description	Unit of Quantity	Rates of Duty		
				1		2
				General	Special	
6201		Men's or boys' overcoats, carcoats, capes, cloaks, anoraks (including ski-jackets), windbreakers and similar articles (including padded, sleeveless jackets), other than those of heading 6203:				
		Overcoats, carcoats, capes, cloaks and similar coats:				
6201.11.00		Of wool or fine animal hair.................................	....	41¢/kg + 16.3%	Free (AU, BH, CA, CL, CO, IL, JO, KR, MA, MX, P, PA, PE, SG) 4.1¢/kg + 1.6% (OM)	52.9¢/kg + 58.5%
	10	Men's (434).................................	doz. kg			
	20	Boys' (434).................................	doz. kg			
6201.12		Of cotton:				
6201.12.10	00	Containing 15 percent or more by weight of down and waterfowl plumage and of which down comprises 35 percent or more by weight; containing 10 percent or more by weight of down (353).................................	doz. kg	4.4%	Free (AU, BH, CA, CL, CO, IL, JO, KR, MA, MX, OM, P, PA, PE, SG)	60%
6201.12.20		Other.................................	....	9.4%	Free (AU, BH, CA, CL, CO, IL, JO, KR, MA, MX, OM, P, PA, PE, SG)	90%
		Raincoats:				
	10	Men's (334).................................	doz. kg			
	20	Boys' (334).................................	doz. kg			
		Other: Corduroy:				
	25	Men's (334).................................	doz. kg			
	35	Boys' (334).................................	doz. kg			
		Other:				
	50	Men's (334).................................	doz. kg			
	60	Boys' (334).................................	doz. kg			

3. Determining the Tariff

There are three basic legal issues important in determining what tariff will apply to any particular imported good—Classification, Origin and Valuation. The classification of the good determines which horizontal row of the HTS applies, as illustrated above by Chapter 62 (textiles, apparel, clothing). The categories describe different types of "men's or boy's suits . . . ." Suits made of "wool or fine animal hair" (6203.11) are distinguished from those made of "synthetic fibers" (6203.12). Typically, classifications will identify various types of goods by their name, use or materials (e.g., screwdrivers, metal tool used for driving screws, tools of hardened steel and plastic). Note how the catch-all "other" is often the most specific available classification within a particular category.

"Origin" is essentially the country that the goods are a "product of." Origin determines which of several potentially applicable tariff rates, set out in the right hand columns, will apply to that category of goods. Column 1, which is divided in two sections, sets forth tariffs applicable for that classification of good if imported as a product of a NTR (MFN) country. The "special" subset column references when such goods will receive duty free treatment as the product of either a designated poor, or "free trade agreement," country. Column 2 provides tariff rates that are not set by the WTO system bindings because the producing country is neither a WTO member nor otherwise granted NTR status under U.S. law. Goods from Cuba and North Korea would be subject to such rates, but in fact are generally banned from importation in any event because of foreign policy based embargos.

"Valuation" refers to the value of the goods against which the applicable rate should be calculated (i.e., a 7.5 % tariff on a $100 suit equals a tax of $7.50). How goods are valued and whether various costs such as transportation or packing should be included or excluded is subject to the GATT 94 Agreement on Valuation. Like the other WTO agreements, the basic rules defined in the Valuation Agreement are directly reflected in relevant U.S. federal law—another example of how international legal obligations are incorporated into domestic law.

The importer of goods (directly or through a licensed customs broker) is responsible for the initial determination of the applicable tariff, which requires an assessment of classification, origin and valuation. Under Section 484 of the Tariff Act, as amended (19 U.S.C. § 1484), *the importer of record is responsible for using reasonable care to enter, classify and determine the value of imported merchandise* and to provide any other information necessary to enable the Customs and Border Protection (CBP—now a bureau within in the Department of Homeland Security) to assess duties, collect statistics, and determine whether other applicable legal requirements have been met. According to the CBP:

> The classification and valuation of goods is an important part of the importation and entry process. At a minimum, incorrect classification or valuation may lead to delays and increased duties (plus interest). The failure to use reasonable care in either situation may also lead to detention or seizure of the merchandise, and the imposition of civil or criminal penalties.

The importer's determination is then subject to challenge by the customs service even after the goods have entered the United States. Customs typically inspects a small percentage of imported goods, but the consequences of an importer's error in classification, origin or valuation can prove devastating. Willful transgressions can also lead to serious penalties, fines or jail. When in doubt, or significant sums are at stake, importers can seek advice or binding "letter rulings"[26] from the service on any legal issue,

---

26. https://help.cbp.gov/app/answers/detail/a_id/279/~/binding-ruling-program.

including the applicable tariff (see also CBP summary on "rulings and legal decisions"[27]).
More detail about binding rulings is provided below.

If interested in more detail regarding the traditional process of entry, including documentation, a good summary is provided here.[28] Approximately 96% of the required documentation allowing imports to pay duty and enter the U.S. is filed electronically under the "Automated Broker Interface"[29] (ABI) system. Starting in 2017, Customs & Border Protection (CBP) (and any of the other dozens of federal "partner government agencies"[30] with some trade authority, if applicable) will process almost all U.S. imports and exports using ABI, but through a new "single window" system called the "Automated Commercial Environment"[31] (ACE). The transmission of required data and documentation is accomplished electronically through use of CBP's electronic communication system, which is called "Electronic Data Interchange"[32] (EDI).

CGM Benjamin Franklin, Largest Container Ship to Call at U.S. Port,
Photo by Port of Los Angeles[33]

---

27. https://www.cbp.gov/trade/rulings.

28. https://www.google.com/url?sa=t&rct=j&q=&esrc=s&source=web&cd=2&ved=0ahUKEwiJw9XCmtTPAhWF3YMKHau_DEsQFgguMAE&url=http%3A%2F%2Finternationaltradeattorney.com%3A8008%2FArticles%2FImporter%27s%2520Guide%2520To%2520US%2520Customs%2520Clearance%2520of%2520Imported%2520Goods.pdf&usg=AFQjCNFQ7aLOhOpc0Q2yLdJEgO3WLpVOKQ&sig2=aMTC0rTUXOoNG7qz88tbpA&cad=rja.

29. https://www.cbp.gov/trade/acs/abi/contact-info.

30. https://www.cbp.gov/trade/ace/features#field-content-tab-group-tab-5.

31. https://www.cbp.gov/trade/automated.

32. https://www.cbp.gov/trade/automated/getting-started/transmitting-data-cbp-electronic-data-interchange-edi.

33. https://www.portoflosangeles.org/newsroom/benjaminfranklin.asp.

Port of Los Angeles/Long Beach
By Charles Csavossy (CBP), via <u>Wikimedia Commons</u>[34]

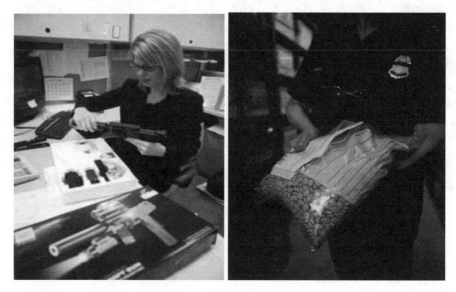

CBP Officers Inspecting "Children's Toy" and Confiscating Counterfeit Viagra,
Photos CBP

The problem and materials that follow focus on these three central legal issues of
classification, origin and valuation.

---

34. https://commons.wikimedia.org/wiki/File:Port_of_Long_Beach,_California_-4.jpg.

B. Problem Ten: Mongolian Designer "Beach & Business" Suits

1. Facts

Your client, the Shiqi department store chain of Poughkeepsie, New York, is considering the importation of a "fresh" new line of men's suits, called "swoots." The subject goods consist of a men's suit jacket with "short pants" designed for "both business and formal beach gatherings." The jacket and short pants are made of 75% nylon and 25% cotton. The shorts are designed to double as a swimsuit with a mesh inner lining so that the entire ensemble may be worn to the beach. The jacket is made of four panels; two front tailored panels and two back panels, which are joined by two side panels. The jacket has a notched collar, a breast pocket, two front pockets, and four interior pockets. The jacket is fully lined. The short pants feature a zippered, placketed fly, two side pockets, two back pockets, and a waistband with belt loops.

The cotton and nylon fabrics used in the suit are both fully formed in the People's Republic of Korea (aka "North Korea"). The suit jacket and shorts are completely cut, sewn and assembled in Mongolia from those fabrics. After assembly, the jacket is finished with buttons, pockets and pressing in China. The jacket and shorts are also packaged together in China and shipped from China to the United States. Retail packaging materials for the suits—hangers, labels and protective coverings—are supplied free of charge to the Chinese exporter by the U.S. based importer of the suits.

The shipment of the suits will carry an invoice price of "$10,000; $100 per suit, CIF Fort Lauderdale." This price does not include a 5% royalty fee that the importer of the short pants suit must pay to its Italian designer for each and every retail sale.

See also Buzz Feed, <u>17 Glorious Photos</u>[35] of Men Walking Around London In Tiny Suit Shorts (or amusing video at: <u>https://vimeo.com/119238710</u>[36])

---

35. https://www.buzzfeed.com/rossalynwarren/british-men-in-shorts-are-so-splendid?utm_term=.ohdLxDpq6p#.uxvkZJ3WP3.
36. https://vimeo.com/119238710.

2. Assignment

Using the resources below, evaluate the likely tariff treatment of the goods described above. First *classify the goods* with as much certainty as possible by referencing the <u>harmonized tariff schedule</u>,[37] General Rules of Interpretation and the *Camelbak* case. Next, use the *Superior Wire* case to evaluate the likely *origin of the goods.* Finally, analyze the proper *value of the shipment* against which the tariff should be assessed, taking into consideration the *Salant* case, as well as the rules on "assists" and royalties. For each set of issues, identify likely problems, uncertainties and arguments.

C. Resources

1. What Is the Proper Classification of the Merchandise?

a. Overview

Classification determines what kind of good is being imported. The U.S. tariff schedule nomenclature is labeled "harmonized" because it follows a uniform international system for classification of goods by categories. This international system is maintained by the <u>World Customs Organization</u>[38] — working in conjunction with the WTO. At the international level, the Harmonized System consists of approximately 5,000 article descriptions which appear as headings and subheadings. These descriptions are arranged into 97 chapters grouped into 21 sections. By using "catch-all" categories such as "other," the system captures virtually all conceivable goods.

The CBP provides this general description of the U.S. classification system on its website:

> Goods in trade generally appear in the Harmonized System in categories or product headings beginning with crude and natural products and continuing in further degrees of complexity through advanced manufactured goods. This progression is found within chapters and among chapters (e.g., live animals are classified in chapter 1, animals hides and skins in chapter 41 and leather footwear in chapter 64). These product headings are designed at the broadest coverage levels with 4-digit numerical codes (or headings) and, where deemed appropriate, are further subdivided into narrower categories assigned two additional digits (which comprise 6-digit numerical codes or subheadings). The first two digits of a 4-digit heading indicate the chapter in which the heading is found (e.g., heading 2106 is in chapter 21).

---

37. https://www.usitc.gov/tata/hts/bychapter/index.htm.
38. http://www.wcoomd.org/.

Harmonized System Convention Obligations

At the essence of the Harmonized System are the headings and subheadings and their related numerical codes; the section, chapter and subheading notes; and the General Rules of Interpretation (for use in the interpretation of the Harmonized System). The basic obligation undertaken by the contracting parties to the Harmonized System Convention is that their customs tariff and foreign-trade statistical nomenclatures be in conformity with the Harmonized System. . . . Each contracting party, however, is permitted to adopt in its national tariff system further detailed subdivisions for classifying goods (that is, for tariff, quota or statistical purposes) so long as any such subdivision is added and coded at a level beyond the 6-digit numerical code provided in the Harmonized System. Coding beyond the 6-digit level is usually at the 8-digit level and is generally referred to as the "national level."

. . . .

Legal Text of the Harmonized System

When classifying merchandise under the Harmonized System, the language of the General Rules of Interpretation, section, chapter and subheading notes, and the terms of the headings and subheadings are to be consulted and applied. They constitute the "legal text" (also known as the "nomenclature") of the Harmonized System. The titles of sections, chapters and subchapters are provided for ease of reference only and have no legal significance.

Heading and Subheading Provisions

Merchandise may be specifically provided for or identified by its common, commercial or technical name in an article or product description (i.e., the text to a heading or subheading) in the Harmonized System. When merchandise is not so specifically provided for in the Harmonized System, the article description covering such merchandise is generally considered to be a "residual provision" (sometimes also referred to as a "basket provision") by use of the phrase "not elsewhere specified or included" or by the use of the term "other."

As evident from the above excerpts, the Harmonized System covers all imported merchandise. In other words, although not all goods are specifically provided for, all goods are *classifiable* and have a place in the Harmonized System. Obviously a product may often appear to be subject to classification under more than one heading. Is frosting simply sugar or is it part of a cake?

What classification applies to "Golden Grains Compost" which consists of "80% dried bat and bird guano, 10% puffed perlite and 10% roasted rice hulls" in a mixture that is "laid down on the wood chips on concrete pads to compost for at least two days before being stuffed into 50 Kg bags for shipment to the United States"? Evaluate this question in light of the following excerpts from the U.S. schedule.

CHAPTER 31 FERTILIZERS

VI

31-1

Notes

1. This chapter does not cover:

(a) Animal blood of heading 0511;

(b) Separate chemically defined compounds (other than those answering to the descriptions in note 2(a), 3(a), 4(a) or 5, below); or

(c) Cultured potassium chloride crystals (other than optical elements) weighing not less than 2.5 g each, of heading 3824; optical elements of potassium chloride (heading 9001).

2. Heading 3102 applies only to the following goods, provided that they are not put up in the forms or packages described in heading 3105:

(a) Goods which answer to one or other of the descriptions given below:

. . . .

3. Heading 3103 applies only to the following goods, provided that they are not put up in the forms or packages described in heading 3105:

(a) Goods which answer to one or other of the descriptions given below:

(i) Basic slag;

(ii) Natural phosphates of heading 2510, calcined or further heat-treated than for the removal of impurities;

(iii) Superphosphates (single, double or triple);

(iv) Calcium hydrogenorthophosphate containing not less than 0.2 percent by weight of fluorine calculated on the dry anhydrous product.

(b) Fertilizers consisting of any of the goods described in (a) above, mixed together, but with no account being taken of the fluorine content limit.

Harmonized Tariff Schedule of the United States (2010)

Chapter 31— Fertilizers
Annotated for Statistical Reporting Purposes

Heading/ SubHeading	Stat Suffix	Article Description	Unit of Quantity	Rates of Duty		
				1		2
				General	Special	
3101.00.00	00	Animal or vegetable fertilizers, whether or not mixed together or chemically treated; fertilizers produced by the mixing or chemical treatment of animal or vegetable products	t	Free		Free
3102		Mineral or chemical fertilizers, nitrogenous:				
3102.10.00	00	Urea, whether or not in aqueous solution	t	Free		Free
		Ammonium sulfate; double salts and mixtures of ammonium sulfate and ammonium nitrate:				
3102.21.00	00	Ammonium sulfate	t	Free		Free
3102.29.00	00	Other	t	Free		Free
3102.30.00	00	Ammonium nitrate, whether or not in aqueous solution	t	Free		Free
3102.40.00	00	Mixtures of ammonium nitrate with calcium carbonate or other inorganic nonfertilizing substances	t	Free		Free
3102.50.00	00	Sodium nitrate	t	Free		Free
3102.60.00	00	Double salts and mixtures of calcium nitrate and ammonium nitrate	t	Free		Free
3102.80.00	00	Mixtures of urea and ammonium nitrate in aqueous or ammoniacal solution	t	Free		Free
3102.90.01	00	Other, including mixtures not specified in the foregoing subheadings	t	Free		Free
3103		Mineral or chemical fertilizers, phosphatic:				
3103.10.00		Superphosphates		Free		Free
	10	Normal and enriched superphosphates, less than 40 percent available phosphorus pentoxide (P_2O_5) equivalent	t			
	20	Concentrated superphosphates, 40 percent or more available phosphorus pentoxide (P_2O_5) equivalent	t			
3103.90.01	00	Other	t	Free		Free
3104		Mineral or chemical fertilizers, potassic:				
3104.20.00	00	Potassium chloride	t	Free		Free
3104.30.00	00	Potassium sulfate	t	Free		Free
3104.90.01	00	Other	t	Free		Free
3105		Mineral or chemical fertilizers containing two or three of the fertilizing elements nitrogen, phosphorus and potassium; other fertilizers; goods of this chapter in tablets or similar forms or in packages of a gross weight not exceeding 10 kg:				
3105.10.00	00	Products of this chapter in tablets or similar forms or in packages of a gross weight not exceeding 10 kg	kg	Free		Free
3105.20.00	00	Mineral or chemical fertilizers containing the three fertilizing elements nitrogen, phosphorus and potassium	t	Free		Free
3105.30.00	00	Diammonium hydrogenorthophosphate (Diammonium phosphate)	t	Free		Free

Accessed from USITC Database.[39]

b. General Rules of Interpretation

In the case of "Golden Grains Compost," classification would be complicated but will have little consequence, since every potential category results in the same (zero) tariff. However, in many cases, the classification can make a considerable difference in the resulting tariff. Review the tariff schedule entries under Chapter 62 in the "Overview" section provided above. Potentially applicable tariffs vary by classification, ranging from 4 to 90% differences that could certainly ruin the importer's day.

---

39. https://www.usitc.gov/tariff_affairs/tariff_databases.htm.

When a product may be classified under more than one heading, the importer must utilize the "Chapter notes" that precede the Chapter descriptions of goods and the "general rules of interpretation." An excerpt from these rules appears below. You will need to consult these rules to understand the case that follows, and to sort out the likely classification of the goods in our problem.

Harmonized Tariff Schedule of the United States
Annotated for Statistical Reporting Purposes

GN p.1

GENERAL RULES OF INTERPRETATION

Classification of goods in the tariff schedule shall be governed by the following principles:

1. The table of contents, alphabetical index, and titles of sections, chapters and sub-chapters are provided for ease of reference only; for legal purposes, classification shall be determined according to the terms of the headings and any relative section or chapter notes and, provided such headings or notes do not otherwise require, according to the following provisions:

2. (a) Any reference in a heading to an article shall be taken to include a reference to that article incomplete or unfinished, provided that, as entered, the incomplete or unfinished article has the essential character of the complete or finished article. It shall also include a reference to that article complete or finished (or falling to be classified as complete or finished by virtue of this rule), entered unassembled or disassembled.

(b) Any reference in a heading to a material or substance shall be taken to include a reference to mixtures or combinations of that material or substance with other materials or substances. Any reference to goods of a given material or substance shall be taken to include a reference to goods consisting wholly or partly of such material or substance. The classification of goods consisting of more than one material or substance shall be according to the principles of rule 3.

3. When, by application of rule 2(b) or for any other reason, goods are, *prima facie*, classifiable under two or more headings, classification shall be effected as follows:

(a) The heading which provides the most specific description shall be preferred to headings providing a more general description. However, when two or more headings each refer to part only of the materials or substances contained in mixed or composite goods or to part only of the items in a set put up for retail sale, those headings are to be regarded as equally specific in relation to those goods, even if one of them gives a more complete or precise description of the goods.

(b) Mixtures, composite goods consisting of different materials or made up of different components, and goods put up in sets for retail sale, which cannot be classified by reference to 3(a), shall be classified as if they consisted of the material or component which gives them their essential character, insofar as this criterion is applicable.

(c) When goods cannot be classified by reference to 3(a) or 3(b), they shall be classified under the heading which occurs last in numerical order among those which equally merit consideration.

4. Goods which cannot be classified in accordance with the above rules shall be classified under the heading appropriate to the goods to which they are most akin.

5. In addition to the foregoing provisions, the following rules shall apply in respect of the goods referred to therein:

(a) Camera cases, musical instrument cases, gun cases, drawing instrument cases, necklace cases and similar containers, specially shaped or fitted to contain a specific article or set of articles, suitable for long-term use and entered with the articles for which they are intended, shall be classified with such articles when of a kind normally sold therewith. This rule does not, however, apply to containers which give the whole its essential character;

(b) Subject to the provisions of rule 5(a) above, packing materials and packing containers entered with the goods therein shall be classified with the goods if they are of a kind normally used for packing such goods. However, this provision is not binding when such packing materials or packing containers are clearly suitable for repetitive use.

6. For legal purposes, the classification of goods in the subheadings of a heading shall be determined according to the terms of those subheadings and any related subheading notes and, *mutatis mutandis*, to the above rules, on the understanding that only subheadings at the same level are comparable. For the purposes of this rule, the relative section, chapter and subchapter notes also apply, unless the context otherwise requires.

ADDITIONAL U.S. RULES OF INTERPRETATION

1. In the absence of special language or context which otherwise requires—

(a) a tariff classification controlled by use (other than actual use) is to be determined in accordance with the use in the United States at, or immediately prior to, the date of importation, of goods of that class or kind to which the imported goods belong, and the controlling use is the principal use . . . .

c. Case Law

The following case is typical of classification disputes. It is important to note the process through which this and other such trade-related disputes are resolved. Once administrative appeals through the customs service are exhausted, the importer sues in the <u>Court of International Trade</u>,[40] a specialized federal court which has exclusive national-wide jurisdiction over international trade and customs issues. A decision by this court may be appealed to the U.S. Court of Appeals for the <u>Federal Circuit</u>.[41] As described on the court's website:

> The Federal Circuit is unique among the thirteen Circuit Courts of Appeals. It has nationwide jurisdiction in a variety of subject areas, including international trade, government contracts, patents, trademarks, certain money claims against the United States government, federal personnel, veterans' benefits, and public safety officers' benefits claims.

i. Camelbak Products, LLC v. United States, 649 F.3d 1361 (Fed. Cir. 2011)

CLEVENGER, Circuit Judge.

This customs case concerns the proper classification of ten styles of CamelBak Products, LLC's ("CamelBak") back-mounted packs ("subject articles"). CamelBak appeals the judgment and decision of the United States Court of International Trade denying CamelBak's motion for summary judgment, granting the United States' (the "government") cross-motion for summary judgment, and holding that the merchandise at issue was properly classified as "travel, sports, and similar bags" under subheading 4202.92.30 of the Harmonized Tariff Schedule of the United States ("HTSUS"). *CamelBak Prods., LLC v. United States,* 704 F.Supp.2d 1335 (Ct. Int'l Trade 2010) (*"CamelBak"*). For the reasons set forth below, we reverse and remand the case for further proceedings.

I

The subject articles are imported back-mounted packs used for outdoor activities and athletics, including cycling, running, hiking and skiing, and are designed to deliver water to the user in a "hands-free" fashion, allowing the user to consume water on-the-go without having to interrupt activity. Each of the subject articles is a textile bag with padded adjustable shoulder straps and features: (a) a polyurethane reservoir or bladder surrounded by a closed-cell polyethylene foam compartment designed to carry and maintain the temperature of water or another beverage; (b) a hydration delivery system composed of flexible tubing attached to the reservoir, a bite valve and a shutoff valve; and (c) a cargo compartment designed to hold food, clothing, gear and supplies. Each reservoir has a capacity of between 35 and 100 ounces of liquid, and each cargo compartment can accommodate between 300 and 1680 cubic inches, depending on the style of pack.

Between August 6, 2004 and August 27, 2004, U.S. Customs and Border Protection ("Customs") liquidated and classified the merchandise at issue under subheading 4202.92.30, HTSUS, as "Trunks, . . . traveling bags, insulated food or beverage bags, . . . knapsacks and backpacks, . . . sports bags . . . and similar containers . . . of

---

40. https://www.cit.uscourts.gov//.
41. http://www.cafc.uscourts.gov/.

textile materials: ... With outer surface of sheeting of plastic or of textile materials: ... travel, sports and similar bags" at a rate of duty of 17.8% ad valorem, based on a prior Customs ruling.[3] After liquidation, CamelBak filed a protest. Customs denied the protest and this action commenced, pursuant to 28 U.S.C. § 1581(a), in the Court of International Trade.

The parties filed cross-motions for summary judgment at the trial court addressing the proper classification of the subject articles. In its motion for summary judgment, CamelBak argued that the subject articles constituted "composite goods" made up of two components—the cargo component, which was prima facie classifiable as a "travel, sports, [or] similar bag[]" and the hydration component, which was prima facie classifiable as an "insulated beverage bag." CamelBak contended that the subject articles had to be classified pursuant to General Rule of Interpretation ("GRI") 3(b)'s essential character test because the two applicable subheadings refer to part only of the subject articles. Specifically, CamelBak argued that the following portions of HTSUS heading 4202 were relevant to the analysis:

4202 Trunks, suitcases, vanity cases, attaché cases, briefcases, school satchels, spectacle cases, binocular cases, camera cases, musical instrument cases, gun cases, holsters and similar containers; traveling bags, insulated food and beverage bags, toiletry bags, knapsacks and backpacks, handbags, shopping bags, wallets, purses, map cases, cigarette cases, tobacco pouches, tool bags, sports bags, bottle cases, jewelry boxes, powder cases, cutlery cases and similar containers, of leather or of composition leather, of sheeting of plastics, of textile materials, of vulcanized fiber or of paperboard, or wholly or mainly covered with such materials or with paper:

Other:

4202.92 With outer surface of sheeting of plastic or of textile materials:

4202.92 Insulated food or beverage bags: With outer surface of textile materials

4202.92.04 Beverage bags whose interior incorporates only a flexible plastic container of a kind for storing and dispensing potable beverages through attached flexible tubing 7%

4292.92.08 Other 7%

4292.92.30 Travel, sports and similar bags: Other 17.8%

---

3. On June 26, 2000, CamelBak filed an Administrative Ruling Request with Customs, seeking a ruling on the classification of eleven of CamelBak's back-mounted packs. On December 18, 2001, Customs issued ruling number HQ964444, classifying three of CamelBak's packs in subheading 4202.92.05 as "Trunks, ... traveling bags, insulated food or beverage bags, ... knapsacks and backpacks, ... sports bags ... and similar containers ... of textile materials: ... With outer surface of sheeting of plastic or of textile materials: ... Insulated food and beverage bags ... With outer surface of textile materials." Customs classified the remaining eight packs (including the Blow Fish, H.A.W.G. and M.U.L.E.) in subheading 4202.92.3020 as "travel, sports, and similar bags ... backpacks."

Applying the essential character test, CamelBak argued that the hydration component (i.e., the insulated beverage bag component) gave the subject articles their essential character and that the subject articles were properly classified as either "insulated food and beverage bags . . . whose interior incorporates only a flexible plastic container of a kind for storing and dispensing potable beverages through attached flexible tubing" under subheading 4202.92.04 or, alternatively, "insulated food and beverage bags . . . other" under subheading 4202.92.08, both dutiable at a rate of 7% ad valorem.

The government argued that the subject articles were not composite goods, but rather that a single tariff provision—the "travel, sports, and similar bags" provision—applied to the articles in their entirety. Thus, the government contended that Customs properly classified the subject articles as a whole as "travel, sports, and similar bags" under subheading 4202.92.30, HTSUS, through a straightforward application of GRI 1.

The Court of International Trade upheld Customs' classification decision concerning the subject articles and granted judgment for the government. CamelBak appeals, and we have jurisdiction pursuant to 28 U.S.C. § 1295(a)(5).

II

We review the grant of summary judgment by the Court of International Trade without deference. *See, e.g., Structural Indus., Inc. v. United States,* 356 F.3d 1366, 1368 (Fed.Cir.2004). We review questions of law de novo, including the interpretation of the terms of the HTSUS, whereas factual findings of the Court of International Trade, including which heading the merchandise falls within, are reviewed for clear error. *Home Depot U.S.A., Inc. v. United States,* 491 F.3d 1334, 1335 (Fed.Cir.2007). "A finding is clearly erroneous when, although there is evidence to support it, the reviewing court is left with a 'definite and firm conviction that a mistake has been committed.'" *Timber Prods. Co. v. United States,* 515 F.3d 1213, 1220 (Fed.Cir.2008) (quoting *United States v. United States Gypsum Co.,* 333 U.S. 364, 395, 68 S. Ct. 525, 92 L. Ed. 746 (1948)).

III

A classification decision involves two underlying steps: (1) ascertaining the proper meaning of the tariff provisions, which is a question of law; and (2) determining which heading the particular merchandise falls within, which is a question of fact. *Cummins Inc. v. United States,* 454 F.3d 1361, 1363 (Fed.Cir.2006). The GRIs govern classifications of imported goods under HTSUS and we apply them in numerical order. *BASF Corp. v. United States,* 482 F.3d 1324, 1325–26 (Fed.Cir.2007).

"Under GRI 1, the court must determine the appropriate classification 'according to the terms of the headings and any relative section of chapter notes' with all terms construed to their common commercial meaning." *Millenium Lumber Distrib., Ltd. v. United States,* 558 F.3d 1326, 1328–29 (Fed.Cir.2009). We apply GRI 1 as a substantive rule of interpretation, such that when an imported article is described in whole by a single classification heading or subheading, then that single classification applies, and the succeeding GRIs are inoperative. *See Mita Copystar Am. v. United States,* 160 F.3d 710, 712 (Fed.Cir.1998). With regard to assessing an imported article pursuant to GRI 1, we consider a HTSUS heading or subheading an *eo nomine* provision when it describes an article by a specific name. *Carl Zeiss, Inc. v. United States,* 195 F.3d 1375, 1379 (Fed.Cir.1999). Absent limitation or contrary legislative intent, an *eo nomine* provision "include[s] all forms of the named article[,]" even improved forms. *Id.*

However, as we held in *Casio, Inc. v. United States,* 73 F.3d 1095 (Fed.Cir.1996), when an article "'is in character or function something other than as described by a specific statutory provision—either more limited or more diversified—and the difference is significant,'" it is not properly classified within an *eo nomine* provision. 73 F.3d at 1097 (quoting *Robert Bosch Corp. v. United States,* 63 Cust.Ct. 96, 103–04, 1969 WL 13787 (1969)). In order to determine whether the subject article is classifiable within an *eo nomine* provision, we look to whether the subject article is merely an improvement over or whether it is, instead, a change in identity of the article described by the statute. *See United Carr Fastener Corp. v. United States,* 54 C.C.P.A. 89, 91, 1967 WL 8910, *2–*3 (CCPA 1967). "The criterion is whether the item possess[es] features *substantially in excess* of those within the common meaning of the term." *Casio,* 73 F.3d at 1098 (quotation marks and citation omitted) (emphasis in original).

When goods are prima facie classifiable under two or more headings or subheadings of HTSUS, we apply GRI 3 to resolve the classification. *Home Depot,* 491 F.3d at 1336. We apply GRI 3(a) when the goods, as a whole, are prima facie classifiable under two or more headings or subheadings to determine which heading provides the most specific description of the goods. *See* GRI 3(a); *Bauer Nike Hockey USA, Inc. v. United States,* 393 F.3d 1246, 1252 (Fed.Cir.2004). When two subheadings "each refer to part only of the materials . . . contained in . . . composite goods," they are "regarded as equally specific" under GRI 3(a) and we apply GRI 3(b) to resolve the classification. GRI 3(a). GRI 3(b) instructs that we classify composite goods made up of different components "as if they consisted of the material or component which gives them their essential character."

IV

In reaching its conclusion that the subject articles are backpacks, the Court of International Trade began its analysis by applying GRI 1 to determine whether the subject articles were classifiable as a whole under a particular heading and subheadings. Turning to heading 4202, which the parties agreed applied to the subject articles, the Court of International Trade defined the terms "traveling bag," "sports bag," "insulated food or beverage bag," and "backpack"[4] and concluded that the

---

4. Specifically, the Court of International Trade defined the terms as follows: (1) a "traveling bag" includes "all forms of flexible containers used by travelers to carry or store items[,]" *Camel-Bak,* 704 F.Supp.2d at 1340–41; (2) a "sports bag" includes "all forms of flexible containers used by individuals to carry or store items while they are engaged in activities involving physical exertion, or active pastime or recreation[,]" *id.* at 1341; (3) an "insulated beverage bag" includes "all forms of flexible reusable containers that are used to maintain the temperature of potable liquids during

subject articles were properly classifiable under heading 4202, HTSUS. *CamelBak,* 704 F.Supp.2d at 1340.

The Court of International Trade next determined that the subject articles were composed of an outer surface of textile materials and properly classifiable under 4202.92, HTSUS. *Id.* at 1342.

Turning to the final set of HTSUS subheadings applicable to the subject articles, the Court of International Trade noted that there were four competing subheadings: " '[i]nsulated food or beverage bags,' '[t]ravel, sports and similar bags,' '[m]usical instrument cases,' and '[o]ther.' " *Id.* The Court of International Trade then looked to Additional U.S. Note 1 to HTSUS Chapter 42 for guidance. Additional U.S. Note 1 explains that the subheading "travel, sports and similar bags" is broad and refers to "goods . . . of a kind designed for carrying clothing and other personal effects during travel, including backpacks and shopping bags of this heading. . . ." *Id.*

The Court of International Trade found as a fact that a portion of each of the subject articles was designed to carry water, while the remainder of the capacity was designed to carry cargo. *Id.* at 1344. Nevertheless, the Court of International Trade reasoned that the articles "fall[ ] within the tariff provision covering 'travel, sports, and similar bags,' and [are] prima facie classifiable thereunder[,]" because they are properly described as "backpacks." *Id.* at 1342. The Court of International Trade further concluded that the subject articles could not be "fairly described as 'beverage bags' " as a whole because "there is simply too much that is designed to carry cargo (rather than beverages)." *Id.* at 1344. The Court of International Trade also determined that "the water-carrying and -dispensing functionalities" of the subject articles "do not remove them from the purview of 'travel, sports and similar bags' " because the tariff provision covering "travel, sports, and similar bags" is an *eo nomine* provision which includes all forms of the named article, even improved forms. *Id.* at 1343.

Having concluded that the "travel, sports and similar bags" subheading encompassed the subject articles as a whole, the Court of International Trade applied GRI 1 and classified the subject articles under subheading 4202.92.30. *Id.* at 1345. In so doing, the Court of International Trade rejected CamelBak's argument that the hydration component of the subject articles removed them from the scope of the *eo nomine* backpack provision, thereby making them new articles of commerce and composite goods. *See id.* Addressing CamelBak's argument, the Court of International Trade explained that "[t]he mere fact that a piece of merchandise may consist of more than one component does not necessarily make that merchandise a 'composite good' subject to classification under GRI 3(b)." *Id.* The Court of International Trade then determined that "[t]here is nothing about incorporating into a backpack a compartment designed to contain (and maintain the temperature of) beverages that

---

their transport or temporary storage[,]" *id.;* and (4) a "backpack" includes all forms of "bags made of sturdy material, which feature padded, adjustable shoulder straps, and which are designed to permit supplies and gear to be carried on the wearer's back[,]" *id.* at 1341–42.

makes the backpack *not* a backpack." *Id.* at 1346 (emphasis in original). That is, "a 'backpack' is a 'backpack,' no matter how . . . elaborate it may be." *Id.* In essence, the Court of International Trade regarded the hydration component of the subject articles as an incidental feature and did not consider its primary design or use as contributing to the classification characteristics of the articles.

V

On appeal, CamelBak concedes that the cargo component of the subject articles is prima facie classifiable as "travel, sports and similar bags" of subheading 4202.92, because it permits a consumer to carry some personal effects, as defined in Additional U.S. Note 1. CamelBak contends, however, that the subject articles cannot be classified under 4202.92.30 by reference to GRI 1 alone, because the "travel, sports and similar bags" provision does not cover the articles as a whole (i.e., the subject articles are not *eo nomine* backpacks). Rather, CamelBak repeats its argument that the subject articles are made up of two major components each of which is prima facie classifiable under a different subheading, i.e., the cargo component, which is prima facie classifiable under 4202.92.30 HTSUS and the hydration component, which is prima facie classifiable under 4202.92.04 HTSUS. Thus CamelBak argues that the Court of International Trade erred when it failed to conduct a GRI 3(b) essential character analysis.

The government, relying on the common meaning of the term "backpack" and Additional U.S. Note 1 to Chapter 42, responds that the Court of International Trade correctly sustained Customs' classification of the subject articles under 4202.92.30 HTSUS as "travel, sports and similar bags" pursuant to GRI 1 because backpacks, as a whole, are designed to carry and organize a multitude of personal effects, including water. . . . Accordingly, the government contends that a GRI 3(b) analysis is not triggered in this case because the Court of International Trade correctly classified the subject articles pursuant to GRI 1.

VI

In this case, we are called upon to determine whether the Court of International Trade correctly classified the subject articles as "backpacks" falling within the "sports, travel, and similar bags" *eo nomine* provision of subheading 4202.92.30, HTSUS. If the subject articles fall within the scope of the *eo nomine* backpack provision then, under *Mita Copystar*, GRI 1 mandates that the subject articles be classified as "travel, sports and similar bags" and GRI 3 is not triggered.[5]

Turning to the classification of the subject articles, we note that although *Casio* sets forth the proposition that a change in identity removes an article from an *eo*

---

5. As a preliminary matter, we note that GRI 3(b), as opposed to GRI 3(a), resolves the proper classification of the subject articles if GRI 3 is triggered. Here, the cargo component of the subject articles is not insulated (i.e., able to maintain the temperature of potable liquids during their transport or temporary storage) and, therefore, does not fall within the "insulated beverage bag" provision of heading 4202, HTSUS. Thus the subject articles are not prima facie classifiable as a whole as insulated beverage bags and GRI 3(a)'s rule of specificity does not apply.

nomine provision, it does not provide the analytical tools or factors for making that determination. The case law of this and our predecessor court, however, provides several analytical tools or factors we can use to assess whether the subject articles are beyond the reach of the *eo nomine* backpack provision. These factors include the design of the subject articles, *see Casio*, 73 F.3d at 1098 (affirming the trial court's finding that the subject articles—synthesizers—were not beyond the scope of the *eo nomine* "electronic musical instrument" tariff provision because the additional features of the articles were "designed primarily to make it easier for a musician to create music"), and the use or function of the subject articles, *see Trans-Atlantic Co. v. United States*, 60 CCPA 100, 471 F.2d 1397, 1399 (1973) ("[W]e think that the primary function of the imported article should govern classification."); *United States v. Quon Co.*, 46 C.C.P.A. 70, 72, 1959 WL 7626, (1959) ("use cannot be ignored in determining whether an article falls within an *eo nomine* tariff provision"); *see also BASF Wyandotte Corp. v. United States*, 855 F.2d 852, 853 (Fed.Cir.1988) (citing *Quon* for the proposition that "the use of a product may be considered in determining the classification of that article"). The design and use/function of the subject articles are important considerations, as our predecessor court observed in *Quon*, when reviewing the classification of certain baskets:

> While unhesitatingly granting the truth of the contention that "baskets" in the tariff act provides for baskets "eo nomine," this does not help us in the least to decide whether the imported articles *are* baskets [and not furniture]. We are not so trusting of our own notions of what things are as to be willing to ignore the purpose for which they were designed and made and the use to which they were actually put. Of all things most likely to help in the determination of the identity of a manufactured article, beyond the appearance factors of size, shape, construction and the like, use is of paramount importance. To hold otherwise would logically require the trial court to rule out evidence of what things actually are every time the [Customs] collector thinks an article, as he sees it, is specifically named in the tariff act.

46 C.C.P.A. at 73 (emphasis in original).

Several commercial factors also guide the court's assessment of whether articles fall within the scope of an *eo nomine* provision, including how the subject articles are regarded in commerce, *see Servo–Tek Prods. Co., Inc. v. United States*, 57 CCPA 13, 416 F.2d 1398, 1400 (1969) (concluding that the subject articles were not regarded in commerce as merely "motors" and should not be classified as such), how the subject articles are described in sales and marketing literature, *see Fairchild Camera & Instrument Corp. v. United States*, 53 C.C.P.A. 122, 124, 1966 WL 8923, (1966) (classifying the subject articles as "cameras" based, in part, on the fact that they were consistently described as "cameras" in sales literature), and whether the additional component is a substantial or incidental part of the whole product, *cf. United States v. N.Y. Merch. Co.*, 58 CCPA 53, 435 F.2d 1315 (1970).

Applying the above factors to the present case, we conclude that the Court of International Trade clearly erred in finding that the subject articles are nothing more than improved backpacks. It is correct that "travel, sports and similar bags" are *eo nomine* and include all forms of backpacks. The subject articles, however, "possess[] features *substantially in excess* of those within the common meaning" of the term backpack as defined by the Court of International Trade, which the court failed to regard. *Casio*, 73 F.3d at 1098 (emphasis in original). Thus, they cannot be classified *eo nomine* as conventional backpacks.

At most, the cargo component is classifiable as a conventional backpack because it is designed and used to carry personal effects. It is undisputed, however, that the hydration component has a different design and primary use: to provide a temperature-maintained, continuous source of hands-free hydration to a user while engaged in a sporting event or recreational activity. When using the subject articles, the user can drink the beverage at will, without removing the article, thereby minimizing any disruption in activity. As Wesley Watson, CamelBak's Vice President of Global Sourcing and Distribution testified, CamelBak's "core product is manufactured around hydration; allowing hydration to be provided to an active user in the best way and the easiest way. Hands-free hydration is a staple or a motto of our organization, and we design products specifically for markets that allow you to drink while you're using, while you're doing an activity." Indeed, the subject articles exist "to provide a hands-free . . . way to drink" and it was error for the Court of International Trade to discount the hydration component and characterize it as a mere feature without considering the subject articles' primary design and use.

That there is a substantial difference in identity of the subject articles from a conventional backpack is further demonstrated by the commercial factors, such as the higher prices CamelBak charges and consumers pay for the subject articles as compared to conventional backpacks, the placement of the subject articles in retail catalogues and stores in a "hydration pack" section rather than a "backpack" section, and CamelBak's reference to the subject articles as "hydration packs" in its literature and marketing materials. These factors demonstrate that subject articles are commercially known, advertised and sold as "hydration packs," as opposed to backpacks, and that consumers purchase them for different reasons than they purchase conventional backpacks.

Finally, the hydration component of the subject articles is not merely incidental to the cargo component but, instead, provides the articles with a unique identity and use that removes them from the scope of the *eo nomine* backpack provision. That is, the subject articles are not merely an improvement over the conventional backpack as the Court of International Trade concluded. Thus, the subject articles are not classifiable as a whole pursuant to GRI 1.

Rather, they are composite goods made up of two components, which lack a single specific classification under HTSUS (i.e., there is no HTSUS provision for combination backpacks and hydration packs). Each component of the subject articles is classifiable under a separate subheading of 4202.92 HTSUS — the cargo component is classifiable as a "travel, sports, or similar bag[]" under 4202.92.30 HTSUS, and the hydration component is classifiable as an "insulated food and beverage bag" under

4202.92.04 (or 4202.92.08) HTSUS. Accordingly, GRI 3(b) controls the classification of the subject articles.

VII

Regarding the application of GRI 3(b), CamelBak contends that there are no factual disputes to resolve with respect to the essential character of the subject articles because the parties agree on the basic nature of the products and the government failed to refute the evidence CamelBak adduced in support of its summary judgment motion. Thus, argues CamelBak, a remand to the Court of International Trade is not necessary and this court can classify the subject articles pursuant to GRI 3(b). We are not persuaded by CamelBak's argument.

First, we note that the essential character of the subject articles is a question of fact. *See Home Depot,* 491 F.3d at 1337 ("the application of this [essential character] test requires a fact-intensive analysis"); *Pillsbury Co. v. United States,* 431 F.3d 1377, 1380 (Fed.Cir.2005) ("Predominance [in the context of GRI 3(b)] is a factual determination. . . ."). Second, contrary to CamelBak's argument, the parties dispute the essential character of the subject articles. Indeed, the government contends that CamelBak cannot prevail on a GRI 3(b) analysis because it failed to demonstrate by competent evidence that any component of the subject articles is classifiable as an insulated beverage bag. Therefore, remand to the Court of International Trade to resolve the GRI 3(b) issue in the first instance is appropriate.

VIII

For the foregoing reasons, we reverse the Court of International Trade's grant of summary judgment to the government and remand the case to the Court of International Trade for further proceedings.

REVERSED AND REMANDED

d. Letter Rulings

Classification is obviously complicated at times. When in doubt, the importer should seek the advice of customs agents in their local port, or a more formal "ruling" from the service. According to the CBP:

> A ruling may be requested under Part 177 of the CBP Regulations (19 C.F.R. Part 177) by any person who, as an importer or exporter of merchandise, or otherwise, has a direct and demonstrable interest in the question or questions presented in the ruling request, or by the authorized agent of such person. A "person" in this context includes an individual, corporation, partnership, association, or other entity or group.

> A request for a valuation or carrier ruling should be in the form of a letter. A request for a ruling regarding tariff classification, certain marking, origin, NAFTA and applicability of Trade Program should be submitted in the form a letter or electronically via the <u>eRulings Template</u>.[42]

---

42. https://apps.cbp.gov/erulings/index.asp.

A more detailed description of the <u>letter ruling process</u>[43] can be found at CBP's website. What about the "Golden Grain Compost" referenced above? Here is a letter ruling relating to its classification.

NY G82229

September 25, 2000

CLA-2-31:RR:NC:SP:236 G82229

CATEGORY: Classification

TARIFF NO.: 3105.90.0050

Mr. Jerry Clay

Golden Grains Co.

P.O. Box 586

Willow, Alaska 99688

RE: The tariff classification of Golden Grains Compost from the Philippines

Dear Mr. Clay:

In your letter dated September 6, 2000, you requested a tariff classification ruling.

You state that the Golden Grains Compost consists of 80% dried bat and bird guano, 10% puffed perlite and 10% roasted rice hulls. The mixture is then laid down on the wood chips on concrete pads to compost for at least two days. The compost will be bagged into 50kg. bags for shipment to the United States.

The applicable subheading for the Golden Grains Compost will be 3105.90.0050, Harmonized Tariff Schedule of the United States (HTS), which provides for Mineral or chemical fertilizers containing two or three of the fertilizing elements nitrogen, phosphorus and potassium; other fertilizers; goods of this chapter in tablets or similar forms or in packages of a gross weight not exceeding 10 kg: Other: Other. The rate of duty will be Free.

Articles classifiable under subheading 3105.90.0050, HTS, which are products of the Philippines, are currently entitled to duty free treatment under the Generalized System of Preferences (GSP) upon compliance with all applicable regulations. The GSP, however, is subject to modification and periodic suspension, which may affect the status of your transaction at the time of entry for consumption or withdrawal from warehouse. To obtain current information on GSP, check the Customs Web site at www.customs.gov. At the Web site, click on "CEBB" and then search for the term "GSP

This ruling is being issued under the provisions of Part 177 of the Customs Regulations (19 C.F.R. 177).

---

43. https://www.cbp.gov/trade/rulings.

A copy of the ruling or the control number indicated above should be provided with the entry documents filed at the time this merchandise is imported. If you have any questions regarding the ruling, contact National Import Specialist Deborah Walsh at 212-637-7062.

>Sincerely,
>Robert B. Swierupski, Director

2. What Is the Origin of the Suits?

a. Overview

Origin refers to the country from which a good comes for customs purposes—not necessarily where it literally originates from physically, but rather where it should be considered "a product of."

In some cases, origin is a simple matter. The good in question is entirely the product of and shipped from a particular country. However, in modern manufacturing, goods often travel to and from different countries, and receive processing in multiple countries prior to entering the U.S. customs territory. For example, a shirt may contain cotton from Brazil, which was turned into cloth in Indonesia, sewn with thread from Egypt, adorned with buttons from the Philippines, and then later processed for sale in Mexico (put into sets, dyed and packaged) before importation. Which country is this shirt a "product of" for purposes of tariff assessment?

Consult one of the tariff schedule samples presented above. The origin of a good will determine whether the applicable tariff comes from Column 1 (general or special) or Column 2 of the schedule. Goods which are the product of a GATT (or bilateral MFN) nation will be subject to Column 1 general tariffs. (The United States calls this MFN status "normal trade relations" or NTR.) If the commodity is a product of a non-NTR country, the goods will be taxed at the much higher rates found in Column 2. Origin is not only relevant to whether the good is entitled to MFN (NTR) treatment, but also as to whether it is entitled to enter the United States duty free under a trade agreement or trade preference program, as indicated in the "special" section of Column 1.

The CBP describes it this way:

> The final three columns appear together under a superior heading entitled "Rates of Duty." The rates of duty in that column apply to goods imported into the customs territory of the United States (which is stated in HTSUS General Note 2 to include "only the States, the District of Columbia and Puerto Rico"). The column designated number 1 is divided into two sub-columns: "General" and "Special." Under the General sub-column are rates of duty for countries qualifying for most-favored-nation, or normal trade relations ("NTR") status. Most goods imported into the United States receive the general rate of duty.

> Under the Special sub-column are found the rates of duty for certain preferential tariff programs (which are designated by alphabetic symbols

and discussed in HTSUS General Note 3). The preferential rates afforded under these programs are generally designed to encourage economic stability and development in certain developing countries (e.g., Caribbean Basin Initiative); to promote trade in a particular industry (e.g., the automotive industry through the United States-Canada Automobile Agreement); or to permit market integration through free trade areas (e.g., North American Free Trade Agreement).

The rates of duty in column 2 apply to products, whether imported directly or indirectly, of certain countries and areas designated in HTSUS General Note 3. The countries and areas listed in General Note 3 are ones to whose goods the United States has decided not to extend NTR status. The rates of duty under column 2 are generally substantially higher than the general or NTR rates of duty . . . .

The consequences of designating origin can be serious not only because it determines the rate of duty that applies but also because U.S. law often prohibits trade with certain countries and severely punishes violators.

The general approach to origin for NTR purposes is described in the following case. We will later discover that there are distinct origin rules for different trade programs, such as free trade agreements like NAFTA and trade preferences for poor nations. These special rules include variations, such as "yarn forward" rules,[44] that apply specifically to textiles.

b. Case Law

i. Superior Wire v. United States, 867 F.2d 1409 (Fed. Cir. 1989)

Before Nies, Bissell and Archer, Circuit Judges.

Archer, Circuit Judge.

Superior Wire (Superior) appeals the judgment of the United States Court of International Trade, that wire drawn in Canada from Spanish wire rod is not "substantially transformed" for purposes of determining the country of origin under a Voluntary Restraint Agreement between the United States and Spain. We affirm.

I

Superior began importing wire rod from Spain into Canada in 1984 following the imposition of preliminary anti-dumping and countervailing duties on wire rod imported from Spain into the United States. In a newly-established wire drawing facility in Canada, Superior drew the wire rod into wire before shipping the wire to its wire mesh operation in Michigan. It claimed Canada as the country of origin instead of Spain.

---

44. http://web.ita.doc.gov/tacgi/fta.nsf/98cd1be34d356ff6852577ae006a6d92/f1edc28e91eeb96 485257375004e6708?OpenDocument.

Superior's practice continued when, pursuant to the Steel Import Stabilization Act of 1984 Pub. L. No. 98-573, 98 Stat. 2948 (1984), *reprinted in* 19 U.S.C. § 2253 note (1982 & Supp. IV 1986), the United States entered into a Voluntary Restraint Agreement (VRA) with Spain covering wire and wire rod. While these products were no longer subject to duties, they were limited by quotas and could not enter the United States without validated export licenses. In March 1987, the Customs Service issued Ruling 075923 JLV, which determined that the drawing of wire from wire rod does not constitute a substantial transformation. Based on this ruling, Superior's imports of drawn wire from Canada were classified as being of Spanish origin.

The Court of International Trade held that Ruling 075923 JLV did not represent a change of "position" on the part of the Customs Service that necessitated publication in the Federal Register and opportunity for public comment. *See* 19 C.F.R. § 177.10(c)(2) (1988). This issue arose because Superior claimed reliance on a ruling letter issued in 1984, Ruling 553052 CW, to a third party, which was available to the public on microfiche but not published in the Customs Bulletin. In that ruling, the Customs Service held that ten-gauge wire drawn in Mexico from wire rod made in the United States would be considered a "substantially transformed constituent material" of concrete reinforcing wire mesh exported to the United States. The ruling permitted the cost or value of the transformed product to be included as part of the Mexican material or processing costs in determining whether not less than thirty-five percent of the appraised value of the imported article (concrete wire mesh) is attributable to a designated beneficiary country (Mexico) and therefore entitled to duty-free entry under the Generalized System of Preferences (GSP). . . . Superior also claimed reliance based on the fact that Customs Service officials had followed Ruling 553052 CW in permitting Superior's Canadian drawn wire to enter the United States as a Canadian product until Ruling 075923 JVL issued.

The Court of International Trade further determined on the merits that the drawing of wire rod into wire does not substantially transform wire rod into a new product for the purpose of determining the country of origin under the VRA.

II

The trial court's findings of fact are reviewed under the clearly erroneous standard of review. . . . Findings of fact may be overturned only when "the reviewing court on the entire evidence is left with the definite and firm conviction that a mistake has been committed." . . . The court is not so restricted with respect to legal conclusions and will reverse those conclusions found to be in error. . . .

III

Preliminarily we must determine whether Superior was entitled to rely on the 1984 ruling letter, and the Customs Service's admittance of its wire imports, as a "position" of the Customs Service which could be changed only after notice in the Federal Register and public comment, or whether the Court of International Trade correctly determined that the Customs Service did not change a prior "position" in issuing Ruling 075923 JLV.

Customs Service regulation 19 C.F.R. § 177.9 (1988) provides in subparagraph (a) that a ruling letter represents the official position of the Customs Service "with respect to the particular transaction or issue described therein." Subparagraph (c) of section 177.9 expressly states, however, that a ruling letter should not be relied on by other persons and they should not "assume that the principles of that ruling will be applied in connection with any transaction other than the one described in the letter." These regulations circumscribe the applicability of a ruling letter and preclude a person other than the recipient from claiming reliance on such a ruling with respect to other transactions. Further, a ruling letter may be modified or revoked if later determined to be erroneous and, except for the person to whom the ruling was addressed, the regulations do not require that notice be given of a revocation or change.

Superior argues that Ruling 553052 CW had become a "position" of the Customs Service . . . because it was available to the public on microfiche and was followed by Customs Service officials in permitting entry of its Canadian drawn wire. That regulation provides generally that any precedential decision of the Customs Service shall be published in the Customs Bulletin or otherwise made available for public inspection and that a precedential decision includes a ruling letter. Section 177.10 (a) reads as follows:

> (a) *Generally.* Within 120 days after issuing any precedential decision under the Tariff Act of 1930, as amended, relating to any Customs transaction (prospective, current, or completed), the Customs Service shall publish the decision in the Customs Bulletin or otherwise make it available for public inspection. For purposes of this paragraph a precedential decision includes any ruling letter, internal advice memorandum, or protest review decision.
>
> . . . .

The Court of International Trade held that ruling letter 553052 CW had not evolved into a position of the Customs Service. . . .

We are convinced that the Court of International Trade correctly held that letter ruling 553052 CW did not represent a position of the Customs Service. The applicable regulations discussed above are not a model of clarity. It is apparent, however, from the language of 19 C.F.R. § 177.9 that ruling letters are not issued by the Customs Service with the expectation that they can generally be relied upon. Rather, they are intended to apply to a specific set of circumstances. If the Customs Service determines that a specific ruling letter is to have broader applicability, then, as provided by 19 C.F.R. § 177.10, it will ordinarily be published in the Customs Bulletin. As the trial court noted, publication in the Customs Bulletin is important in determining whether the Customs Service has established a position.

. . . .

The trial court also appropriately noted that Superior had the option of obtaining its own letter ruling, which would have given it the right to notice before a change. Superior did not choose this approach, but instead relied on a ruling involving different circumstances and different statutory provisions. . . .

With respect to Superior's contention that it should be entitled to rely on the oral advice it received from Customs officials who, in turn, apparently followed Ruling 553052 CW in allowing Superior's wire to be imported until the issuance of Ruling 075923 JLV, the Court of International Trade correctly held that such advice and acquiescence cannot establish a Customs Service position, which would require notice and opportunity for public comment to be changed. . . .

IV

On the country of origin issue, Superior contends that the wire imported into the United States is a product of Canada, not Spain, because the Spanish wire rod was "substantially transformed" in Canada. Substantial transformation requires that "[t]here must be transformation; a new and different article must emerge, 'having a distinctive name, character, or use.'" *Anheuser-Busch Brewing Ass'n v. United States*, 207 U.S. 556, 562, 28 S. Ct. 204, 206 (1908) . . . . Whether such a transformation occurred involves findings of fact by the trial court. These findings may not be set aside unless clearly erroneous. "This standard plainly does not entitle a reviewing court to reverse the finding of the trier of fact simply because it is convinced that it would have decided the case differently. . . . If the district court's account of the evidence is plausible in light of the record viewed in its entirety, the court of appeals may not reverse it." . . .

The Court of International Trade considered the "transformation of wire rod to wire to be minor rather than substantial." The court found that there was no significant change in use or character, but there was a change in name, . . . and concluded that "wire rod and wire may be viewed as different stages of the same product."

Although noting that "[t]he wire emerges stronger and rounder after" drawing the wire rod, the court found "[i]ts strength characteristic . . . is . . . metallurgically predetermined . . . through the fabrication of the wire rod." The court explained that "[t]he chemical content of the rod and the cooling processes used in its manufacture . . . determine the properties that the wire will have after drawing." These findings are "plausible" in light of the record viewed in its entirety and are not clearly erroneous. There was evidence of record to show that the rod producer determines the tensile strength of the drawn wire by the chemistry of the steel, particularly by the mix of carbon and manganese in the molten steel rods, and that the properties desired in the drawn wire dictate the selection of scrap grade.

We are not persuaded by Superior's argument that because wire is "cleaner, smoother . . . and cross-sectionally more uniform" than the wire rod it has a different character. Such changes appear to be primarily cosmetic in the light of the predetermined qualities and specifications of the wire rod.

There was also ample evidence from which the Court of International Trade could determine that there is no change in use between the wire rod and the wire. The end use of wire rod is generally known before the rolling stage and the specifications are frequently determined by reference to the end product for which the drawn wire will be used. Thus, rod used for the production of concrete reinforcing mesh is known as "mesh-grade" or "mesh-quality rod." Moreover, the evidence indicates that if the rod is produced improperly for its intended application, the wire drawing process is incapable of making the product suitable for such use.

With respect to the third of the *Anheuser-Busch* factors, the trial court noted that the two products have different names: wire and wire rod. This is the least persuasive factor and is insufficient by itself to support a holding that there is a substantial transformation. . . .

The Court of International Trade also cited a number of other considerations influencing its decision that a substantial transformation had not occurred in the drawing process, including the fact that there was "no transformation from producers' to consumers' goods . . . no complicated or expensive processing," and "only relatively small value . . . added."

In view of the court's findings and conclusions, we are convinced of the correctness of its decision. The drawing of wire rod into wire is, as the Court of International Trade concluded, not the manufacture of a new and different product as required by *Anheuser-Busch*. Accordingly, Superior's wire products imported via Canada required valid export licenses under the VRA with Spain.

The judgment of the Court of International Trade is

AFFIRMED.

3. What Is the Value of the Problem Merchandise Against Which the Applicable Tariff Will Be Assessed?

a. Overview

You probably noticed that most tariffs consist of a percentage applied to the value of goods imported. "Valuation" refers to the price against which a tariff rate is applied. You can't calculate the actual tax without establishing the value of the imported goods against which the tariff rate will be applied. The value against which customs assesses the applicable tariff can make a substantial difference in the actual tax paid. For example, a 10% tariff on goods valued at $100,000 dollars will generate $10,000 in taxes, while that same 10% tariff will only raise $9,000 if the good is assessed at $90,000 in value.

This obviously provides a great incentive for importers to minimize the value of imported goods. It also explains how the method of valuation can serve as a disguised restriction on trade. For example, the United States formerly used a fictional price to value imported goods based on prices commonly paid for that item in the domestic market. Inevitably, this price was higher than the actual cost of the import (why else would the goods be imported), thus effectively raising the tax and providing domestic producers with added protection against competition.

As with many other potentially protectionist practices, valuation has been subject to international restrictions. Limited rules appeared first in Article VII of the

GATT 47. Finally, a more comprehensive international agreement on the subject of valuation was reached in the Uruguay Round and is now a mandatory part of GATT 94. The methods for valuation established in the <u>Agreement on Implementation of Article VII of the General Agreement on Tariffs and Trade 1994</u>[45] (commonly called the "Valuation Code" or "Valuation Agreement") are now reflected in U.S. law, an excerpt from which appears below. You will need to apply this statute to our problem facts. Read it (and the *Salant* case) carefully in order to resolve the issues of product valuation presented by the problem.

b. U.S. Valuation Statute: 19 U.S.C. § 1401a

(a) Generally

(1) Except as otherwise specifically provided for in this chapter, imported merchandise shall be appraised, for the purposes of this chapter, on the basis of the following:

(A) The transaction value provided for under subsection (b) of this section.

(B) The transaction value of identical merchandise provided for under subsection (c) of this section, if the value referred to in subparagraph (A) cannot be determined, or can be determined but cannot be used by reason of subsection (b)(2) of this section.

(C) The transaction value of similar merchandise provided for under subsection (c) of this section, if the value referred to in subparagraph (B) cannot be determined.

(D) The deductive value provided for under subsection (d) of this section, if the value referred to in subparagraph (C) cannot be determined and if the importer does not request alternative valuation under paragraph (2).

(E) The computed value provided for under subsection (e) of this section, if the value referred to in subparagraph (D) cannot be determined.

(F) The value provided for under subsection (f) of this section, if the value referred to in subparagraph (E) cannot be determined.

. . . .

(b) Transaction value of imported merchandise

(1) The transaction value of imported merchandise is the price actually paid or payable for the merchandise when sold for exportation to the United States, plus amounts equal to—

(A) the packing costs incurred by the buyer with respect to the imported merchandise;

---

45. https://www.wto.org/english/docs_e/legal_e/20-val_01_e.htm.

(B) any selling commission incurred by the buyer with respect to the imported merchandise;

(C) the value, apportioned as appropriate, of any assist;

(D) any royalty or license fee related to the imported merchandise that the buyer is required to pay, directly or indirectly, as a condition of the sale of the imported merchandise for exportation to the United States; and

(E) the proceeds of any subsequent resale, disposal, or use of the imported merchandise that accrue, directly or indirectly, to the seller.

The price actually paid or payable for imported merchandise shall be increased by the amounts attributable to the items (and no others) described in subparagraphs (A) through (E) only to the extent that each such amount (i) is not otherwise included within the price actually paid or payable; and (ii) is based on sufficient information. If sufficient information is not available, for any reason, with respect to any amount referred to in the preceding sentence, the transaction value of the imported merchandise concerned shall be treated, for purposes of this section, as one that cannot be determined.

(2)(A) The transaction value of imported merchandise determined under paragraph (1) shall be the appraised value of that merchandise for the purposes of this chapter only if—

(i) there are no restrictions on the disposition or use of the imported merchandise by the buyer other than restrictions that—

(I) are imposed or required by law,

(II) limit the geographical area in which the merchandise may be resold, or

(III) do not substantially affect the value of the merchandise;

(ii) the sale of, or the price actually paid or payable for, the imported merchandise is not subject to any condition or consideration for which a value cannot be determined with respect to the imported merchandise;

(iii) no part of the proceeds of any subsequent resale, disposal, or use of the imported merchandise by the buyer will accrue directly or indirectly to the seller, unless an appropriate adjustment therefore can be made under paragraph (1)(E); and

(iv) the buyer and seller are not related, or the buyer and seller are related but the transaction value is acceptable, for purposes of this subsection, under subparagraph (B).

(B) The transaction value between a related buyer and seller is acceptable for the purposes of this subsection if an examination of the circumstances of the sale of the imported merchandise indicates that the relationship between such buyer and seller did not influence the price actually paid or payable; or if the transaction value of the imported merchandise closely approximates—

(i) the transaction value of identical merchandise, or of similar merchandise, in sales to unrelated buyers in the United States; or

(ii) the deductive value or computed value for identical merchandise or similar merchandise; but only if each value referred to in clause (i) or (ii) that is used for comparison relates to merchandise that was exported to the United States at or about the same time as the imported merchandise.

(C) In applying the values used for comparison purposes under subparagraph (B), there shall be taken into account differences with respect to the sales involved (if such differences are based on sufficient information whether supplied by the buyer or otherwise available to the customs officer concerned) in—

(i) commercial levels;

(ii) quantity levels;

(iii) the costs, commissions, values, fees, and proceeds described in paragraph (1); and

(iv) the costs incurred by the seller in sales in which he and the buyer are not related that are not incurred by the seller in sales in which he and the buyer are related.

(3) The transaction value of imported merchandise does not include any of the following, if identified separately from the price actually paid or payable and from any cost or other item referred to in paragraph (1):

(A) Any reasonable cost or charge that is incurred for—

(i) the construction, erection, assembly, or maintenance of, or the technical assistance provided with respect to, the merchandise after its importation into the United States; or

(ii) the transportation of the merchandise after such importation.

(B) The customs duties and other Federal taxes currently payable on the imported merchandise by reason of its importation, and any Federal excise tax on, or measured by the value of, such merchandise for which vendors in the United States are ordinarily liable.

(4) For purposes of this subsection—

(A) The term "price actually paid or payable" means the total payment (whether direct or indirect, and exclusive of any costs, charges, or expenses incurred for transportation, insurance, and related services incident to the international shipment of the merchandise from the country of exportation to the place of importation in the United States) made, or to be made, for imported merchandise by the buyer to, or for the benefit of, the seller.

. . . .

(g) Special rules

(1) For purposes of this section, the persons specified in any of the following subparagraphs shall be treated as persons who are related:

(A) Members of the same family, including brothers and sisters (whether by whole or half-blood), spouse, ancestors, and lineal descendants.

(B) Any officer or director of an organization and such organization.

(C) An officer or director of an organization and an officer or director of another organization, if each such individual is also an officer or director in the other organization.

(D) Partners.

(E) Employer and employee.

(F) Any person directly or indirectly owning, controlling, or holding with power to vote, 5 percent or more of the outstanding voting stock or shares of any organization and such organization.

(G) Two or more persons directly or indirectly controlling, controlled by, or under common control with, any person.

. . . .

(h) Definitions. As used in this section—

(1)(A) The term "assist" means any of the following if supplied directly or indirectly, and free of charge or at reduced cost, by the buyer of imported merchandise for use in connection with the production or the sale for export to the United States of the merchandise:

(i) Materials, components, parts, and similar items incorporated in the imported merchandise.

(ii) Tools, dies, molds, and similar items used in the production of the imported merchandise.

(iii) Merchandise consumed in the production of the imported merchandise.

(iv) Engineering, development, artwork, design work, and plans and sketches that are undertaken elsewhere than in the United States and are necessary for the production of the imported merchandise. . . .

Customs maintains a number of guides[46] helpful in determining valuation that you might find helpful.

---

46. www.customs.gov.gd/pdf/BDV.pdf.

c. Case Law on Valuation

Consider the following valuation case decided by the Court of International Trade. Along with its interpretation of "assists," note how the court evaluates the Customs Service's interpretation of the pertinent statute under the *Chevron* standard. Certain costs, such as foreign, domestic and international transportation, may be excluded from the valuation if separately identified and accounted for. Similarly, other items not otherwise included in the price may be added in by customs—packing costs and commissions, royalties, assists and proceeds from subsequent sales, otherwise known as "CRAP." A detailed power point on valuation[47] by the law firm "George R. Tuttle," specializing in customs, may be found on the web.

i. Salant Corporation v. United States, 251 F.3d 166 (CIT 2000)

Opinion

I. Introduction

BARZILAY, JUDGE:

This case was brought by Plaintiff Salant Corporation ("Salant"), to contest the valuation of certain men's shirts by the United States Customs Service ("Customs"). Plaintiff challenges Customs' inclusion of the value of material supplied by Plaintiff but scrapped or wasted during the manufacturing process, within the term assist as used in 19 U.S.C. § 1401a(h)(1)(A) (1994). The parties have cross moved for summary judgment.

For the reasons set out in the following opinion, the Court holds that the fabric waste generated during the manufacturing process of imported shirts is an "assist" under 19 U.S.C. § 1401a(h)(1)(A), and thus its value is properly included in transaction value for appraisement purposes. Therefore, Customs' motion for summary judgment is granted.

II. Background

Salant supplies rolls of fabric free-of-charge to the manufacturers of men's shirts pursuant to contracts for the "cut, make, and trim" ("CMT") of the shirts. *Mem. of Law in Support of Pl.'s Mot. for Summ. J.* at 1 (*"Pl.'s Mem."*). During the manufacturing process, the portion of fabric falling outside the shape of the cut components is scrapped by the manufacturers as waste. *Id.* Following importation of the shirts, Customs appraised them under transaction value, 19 U.S.C. § 1401a(b)(1)(C), which defines that value as "the price actually paid or payable for the merchandise when sold for exportation to the United States, plus amounts equal to . . . the value, apportioned as appropriate, of any assist."

The term "assist" is defined by 19 U.S.C. § 1401a(h)(1)(A) as follows:

> The term "assist" means any of the following if supplied directly or indirectly, and free of charge or at reduced cost, by the buyer of imported mer-

---

47. www.tuttlelaw.com/seminar/2016_summer_series/session3_valuation.pdf.

chandise for use in connection with the production or the sale for export to the United States of the merchandise:

(i) Materials, components, parts, and similar items incorporated in the imported merchandise.

(ii) Tools, dies, molds, and similar items used in the production of the imported merchandise.

(iii) Merchandise consumed in the production of the imported merchandise.

(iv) Engineering, development, artwork, design work, and plans and sketches that are undertaken elsewhere than in the United States and are necessary for the production of the imported merchandise.

Some background on Customs' past practices regarding assists is instructive. From 1984 to 1995, Customs consistently held that scrap or waste in a CMT operation was not considered an assist within the meaning of 19 U.S.C. § 1401a(h)(1)(A). In 1995, after accepting public comment, Customs published notice revoking its earlier rulings and issued Headquarters Ruling Letters ("HRL") 543831 and 545909, which maintained that fabric waste generated in a CMT was part of an assist within the terms of the statute as "merchandise consumed in the production of imported merchandise."

Consistent with its recent inclusion of waste within the definition of an assist, Customs appraised the imported merchandise at its FOB value, and included as assists both the cost of the fabric waste which was scrapped during the CMT process as well as the cost of the fabric incorporated into the shirts in the manufacturing process. Thereafter, Plaintiff brought this suit, contending that it is entitled to summary judgment because fabric waste does not come within the definition of an assist.

In support of its claim, Plaintiff asserts that the waste is neither "material incorporated" nor "merchandise consumed" within the plain meaning of the assist statute, as examined through its legislative history. Plaintiff contends further that even if doubt exists as to whether waste is included within the definition of an assist, that doubt should be resolved in favor of the importer. Defendant responded with a cross-motion for summary judgment, asserting that (1) Customs' decision to reevaluate whether fabric waste should be included as an assist is entitled to deference by the Court as a reasonable interpretation of an ambiguous statute; (2) Salant's interpretation of the plain meaning of the assist statute is simply incorrect; (3) Customs' construction of the plain meaning of the statute is reasonable and should be upheld; and (4) Salant's claim that ambiguity should be resolved in favor of the importer is meritless.

The Court holds in Defendant's favor and hereby grants Defendant's motion for summary judgment because there is no genuine issue of material fact, and because under the plain meaning of the statute read with the facts and circumstances of this case, the definition of assist properly includes fabric waste.

III. Standard of Review

Plaintiff has invoked this Court's jurisdiction under 28 U.S.C. § 1581(a), contesting Customs' appraisal of men's shirts. "Customs' appraisal value is presumed to be correct and the burden of proof is upon the party challenging the decision." *Chrysler Corp. v. United States*, 17 CIT 1049, 1053 (1993) (citing 28 U.S.C. § 2639(a)(1)). Yet, the issue before this Court is one of statutory construction: whether Customs correctly determined that scrap or waste is included within the meaning of "assist" as defined by 19 U.S.C. § 1401a(h)(1)(A). The standard of review for such questions of law is *de novo*. *Intel Singapore, Ltd. v. United States*, 83 F.3d 1416, 1417-18 (Fed. Cir. 1996).

. . . .

The Court's remaining task is to determine, based upon the legislative intent and statutory language, whether or not Customs' interpretation of the assist statute was correct, and whether either party is entitled to judgment as a matter of law. Within the *de novo* standard, Customs asserts that its ruling was reasonable and that it is therefore entitled to deference in accordance with *Chevron U.S.A., Inc. v. Natural Resources Defense Council, Inc.*, 467 U.S. 837 (1984). The Court notes the teaching of the Supreme Court that "[d]eference can be given . . . without impairing the authority of the court to make factual determinations, and to apply those determinations to the law, *de novo*." *United States v. Haggar Apparel Co.*, 526 U.S. 380, —, 119 S.Ct. 1392, 1399 (1999).

The language of *Chevron* sets up a two-pronged test for according deference to an agency's statutory interpretation. In essence, if Congress' intent is clear, no deference is given the agency's construction; however, if Congress' intent is unclear, the court must defer to the agency's interpretation if it is a reasonable construction of the statute. *Chevron* deference has been expanded from statutory directly spoken to the precise question at issue. If the intent of Congress is clear, that is the end of the matter; for the court, as well as the agency, must give effect to the unambiguously expressed intent of Congress. If, however, the court determines Congress has not directly addressed the precise question at issue, the court does not simply impose its own construction of the statute, as would be necessary in the absence of an administrative interpretation. Rather, if the statute is silent or ambiguous with respect to the specific issue, the question for the court is whether the agency's answer is based on a permissible construction of the statute. *Chevron*, 467 U.S. at 842–43.

. . . .

The Court, however, need not decide whether Customs' reinterpretation of the value statute in this case is entitled to *Chevron* deference. Rather, the Court, as the "final authority on issues of statutory construction," employs "the traditional tools of statutory construction," and finds that the fabric waste comes within the plain meaning of the term "assist." *See Chevron*, 467 U.S. at 843 n.9. Therefore, step two of the *Chevron* analysis is unnecessary.

IV. Discussion

A. The plain language of the statute supports Customs' decision to include the entire bolt of fabric as an assist.

"The first and foremost 'tool' to be used is the statute's text, giving it its plain meaning." *Timex V.I., Inc. v. United States*, 157 F.3d 879, 882 (Fed. Cir. 1998). First, the material must be "supplied directly or indirectly, and free of charge or at reduced cost, by the buyer. . . ." 19 U.S.C. § 1401a(h)(1)(A). It is uncontested that Salant does supply entire bolts of fabric free of charge to shirt manufacturers. Second, the fabric must fit within the plain language of subsection (i), "materials . . . incorporated in the imported merchandise," or subsection (iii), "merchandise consumed." Defendant does not contest Plaintiff's assertion that waste fabric is not "material incorporated." Therefore, the Court need only address whether the waste falls within the plain language definition of "merchandise consumed" pursuant to subsection (iii). The Court finds that the plain meaning of the phrase "merchandise consumed" accurately describes the waste or scrap in this case; it thus follows that Customs' determination to include waste fabric within the definition of an assist was correct.

. . . .

Plaintiff claims that because the waste generated during the CMT process in and of itself has no value, it is not a good or commodity that can be bought or sold. *Id.* Hence, it does not fit within the definition of "merchandise," and is more properly characterized as "materials." *Id.* at 8–9.

. . . It is certainly utilized in the process of production, and Defendant's statement that the fabric left over from the manufacture of the shirts "was consumed in the manufacture of those shirts by being rendered worthless" is thus correct.

. . . Considering the statute as a whole, it is neither clear nor evident that Congress' use of the two similar yet distinct terms "material" and "merchandise" requires the conclusion that fabric waste is not part of an assist. Hence, the Court must employ further methods of statutory construction to properly uncover Congress' intent.

B. The structure and history of the statute indicate that waste fabric is properly included as an assist.

"Beyond the statute's text, those 'tools' [of statutory construction] include the statute's structure, canons of statutory construction, and legislative history." *Timex*, 157 F.3d at 882 (citing *Dunn. v. Commodity Futures Trading Comm'n*, 519 U.S. 465, 470–79 (1997)). In this case legislative history includes an examination of the GATT Valuation Code, because "Title II [Customs Valuation] . . . implement[ed] in U.S. law the Agreement on Implementation of Article VII of the General Agreement on Tariffs and Trade (Customs Valuation Agreement). . . ." S. Rep. 96-249 at 108 (1979), *reprinted in* 1979 U.S.C.C.A.N 381, 494. As such, the definition of assist, gleaned from the Customs Valuation Agreement, was codified into law for the first time by the statute. Upon examination of these factors, the Court determines that waste fabric may properly be included as part of an assist.

. . . .

The terms of the statute demonstrate that it is the entire bolt of fabric itself and not merely the scrap that must be considered when determining what is an assist. The statute defines an assist as that which is supplied by the buyer to be used in connection with the production of the imported merchandise. *See* 19 U.S.C. § 1401a(b)(1)(A). Clearly, Salant supplied the entire bolt or bolts of fabric to the manufacturers.

. . . .

V. Conclusion

For the foregoing reasons, the Court holds that Customs properly characterized the fabric waste resulting from the CMT operation in the shirt manufacturing process as an assist. Judgment will be entered accordingly.

D. Specialized Customs Programs & Tariff Exceptions

Congress has created a number of important mechanisms that allow U.S. importers to avoid or delay the payment of tariffs. While some of these mechanisms simply allow for commercial flexibility, they are also clearly designed to create incentives favoring American products. A few of the most important of these mechanisms are briefly described below.

1. Foreign Trade Zones & Bonded Customs Warehouses

On the flexibility side of the ledger, Congress allows for importers to fictionally delay legal "entry" of imported goods (and thus payment of tariffs) by sending those goods into bonded warehousing or designated "foreign trade zones" (often called free trade zones in other countries). Both a designated foreign trade zone and a customs bonded warehouse are not, for tariff purposes, treated as being within the customs territory of the United States. They are similar in function, although foreign trade zones provide greater flexibility.

CBP describes <u>custom bonded warehouses</u>[48] this way:

> A Customs bonded warehouse is a building or other secured area in which imported dutiable merchandise may be stored, manipulated, or undergo manufacturing operations without payment of duty for up to 5 years from the date of importation. . . .

---

48. https://www.google.com/url?sa=t&rct=j&q=&esrc=s&source=web&cd=1&ved =0ahUKEwiI-uT76ezPAhVGwWMKHa_LC00QFggrMAA&url=https%3A%2F%2Fwww.cbp.gov %2Fsites%2Fdefault%2Ffiles%2Fdocuments%2Fbonded_20wh2_2.pdf&usg=AFQ jCNHpf7dZxSu1zJHZlo2hfHsg_9k15g&sig2=aZ3txpyy18CMbAKFWuJm6A&cad=rja.

Duty is not collected until the merchandise is withdrawn for consumption. An importer, therefore, has control over use of his money until the duty is paid upon withdrawal of the merchandise. If no domestic buyer is found for the imported articles, the importer can sell merchandise for exportation, thereby eliminating his obligation to pay.

The agency provides a <u>similar description of foreign trade zones</u>:[49]

Foreign-Trade Zones (FTZ) are secure areas under U.S. Customs and Border Protection (CBP) supervision that are generally considered outside CBP territory upon activation. Located in or near CBP ports of entry, they are the United States' version of what are known internationally as free-trade zones. . . .

Foreign and domestic merchandise may be moved into zones for operations, not otherwise prohibited by law, including storage, exhibition, assembly, manufacturing, and processing . . . . Under zone procedures, the usual formal CBP entry procedures and payments of duties are not required on the foreign merchandise unless and until it enters CBP territory for domestic consumption, at which point the importer generally has the choice of paying duties at the rate of either the original foreign materials or the finished product.

The FTZ program encourages U.S.-based operations by removing certain disincentives associated with manufacturing in the United States. The duty on a product manufactured abroad and imported into the U.S. is assessed on the finished product rather than on its individual parts, materials, or components. The U.S. based manufacturer finds itself at a disadvantage compared with its foreign competitor when it must pay a higher rate on parts, materials, or components imported for use in a manufacturing process. The FTZ program corrects this imbalance by treating products made in the zone, for the purpose of tariff assessment, as if it were manufactured abroad. At the same time, this country benefits because the zone manufacturer uses U.S. labor, services, and inputs.

Additional information and descriptions of free trade zones are provided by <u>Trade.gov</u>.

2. Duty Drawbacks

There are several types of "<u>drawbacks</u>"[50] which essentially provide a refund of tariffs paid on imported goods that are never sold in the domestic U.S. market. The most important of these, manufacturing and "substitution manufacturing" drawbacks, are essentially the refund of tariffs paid on imported "input" products that

---

49. https://www.cbp.gov/border-security/ports-entry/cargo-security/cargo-control/foreign-trade-zones/about.

50. https://www.cbp.gov/trade/programs-administration/entry-summary/drawback.

are subsequently exported out of the United States in the form of finished goods. <u>Substitution manufacturing</u>[51] allows for a drawback of duties paid without the added expense of maintaining distinct inventories of domestic and imported inputs, so long as these are of the same kind and quality. The CBP describes drawbacks as the "most complex commercial program" that it administers.

3. U.S. Made Goods, Returned (<u>Maquiladora</u>[52])

Under Chapter 9802 of the U.S. HTS, American made goods exported for purpose of assembly and limited processing may be eligible for duty free return to the United States under certain conditions. The importer would be required to pay duty on the value added by processing but may not repair, improve or advance the product's value other than through assembly (other provisions of the HTS provide). This provision is typically referred to by the moniker "maquiladora" because of its widespread use to support assembly operations in Mexico, in which cheaper Mexican labor is used to repair, assemble and package (but not "manufacture") U.S. manufactured goods. Maquiladora operations are not limited to Mexico and have been severely criticized for <u>alleged abuse of workers</u>.[53]

4. ATA Carnet

The <u>ATA Carnet</u>[54] ("karnay") allows importers to temporarily bring goods into the U.S. and other participating countries for purposes other than sale, under simplified customs procedures and without paying tariffs. This can be beneficial to companies who want to show products (e.g., trade shows, commercial samples) or temporarily bring in tools of trade. Export.gov describes the benefits of the program on its website:

> What Is An ATA Carnet?
>
> ATA Carnet (aka "Merchandise Passport") is an international customs document accepted by 80 countries and territories. ATA Carnet allows temporary entry of goods, duty-free and tax-free, whether shipped or hand-carried. ATA Carnet system was established by international ATA convention and is governed by World Customs Organization and International Chamber of Commerce and its World Chambers Federation to encourage world trade and reduce trade barriers created by different national customs regulations. The initials "ATA" are from the French and English words "Admission Temporaire/

---

51. https://www.cbp.gov/sites/default/files/assets/documents/2016-Oct/revised%20drawback_refund_2%2810-19-2016%29_0.pdf.

52. http://manufacturinginmexico.org/maquiladora-in-mexico/.

53. http://inthesetimes.com/working/entry/18066/out_of_sight_erik_loomis.

54. https://www.export.gov/article?id=ATA-Carnet.

Temporary Admission." U.S. Customs appointed <u>US Council for International Business</u>[55] as National Guaranteeing Association (NGA).

. . . .

What are the benefits of the ATA Carnet?

- Eliminate duties and value-added taxes (VAT);

- Simplify customs procedures allowing a temporary exporter to use a single document for all customs transactions, make arrangements in advance, and at a predetermined cost;

- Allow for an unlimited entries/departures for up to one year;

- Facilitate reentry into the U.S. by eliminating the need to register the goods with U.S. Customs at the time of departure;

- Eliminate need to file an Electronic Export Information form (former Shipper's Export Declaration) except for those exports that require an export license;

- Eliminate the need for Temporary Importation Under Bond (TIB).

---

55. http://www.uscib.org/ata-carnet-export-service-ud-718/.

Chapter 11

Regulation of Exports

A. Overview

As you might suspect, U.S. government policy strongly promotes export of American goods and services. The government has created many programs designed to facilitate exports, including those designed to gain access[1] to closed foreign markets, assist businesses[2] in the technical aspects of exporting, reduce market and political risks,[3] eliminate barriers[4] and ensure compliance[5] with trade agreements. Government agencies also provide information on potential markets[6] for American goods and services. (*See also* SBA.gov.[7])

Although our government strongly encourages exports, there are competing concerns that cause it to monitor, regulate and sometimes even prohibit exports. Foreign policy objectives, for example, may result in regulations restricting trade with a particular nation. The Treasury Department's "Office of Foreign Assets Control"[8] (OFAC) lists over a dozen country-specific trade sanction programs, as well as programs involving narcotics, terrorism and nuclear proliferation. The OFAC also publishes a list of "specially designated nationals,"[9] which consists of persons and companies subject to trade restrictions or blocked assets in connection with a sanctions program. Similarly, national security concerns may cause the government to restrict exports in certain products or technology with potential military applications.

---

1. http://tcc.export.gov/Report_a_Barrier/how-we-work-with-you.asp.
2. https://www.export.gov/How-to-Export.
3. https://www.google.com/url?sa=t&rct=j&q=&esrc=s&source=web&cd=2&ved=0ahUKE wjL6qHukv7PAhVLslQKHWkwCJcQFggtMAE&url=http%3A%2F%2Ftrade.gov%2Fmedia%2F publications%2Fpdf%2Ftfg2008ch8.pdf&usg=AFQjCNH1wMHxfzpnoQHkJOgKsj36MMppcg& sig2=-kj9stc0f-MtSNtPPIKaFg&bvm=bv.136811127,d.cGw&cad=rja.
4. http://tcc.export.gov/Report_a_Barrier/index.asp.
5. http://tcc.export.gov/trade_agreements_compliance/index.asp.
6. https://www.export.gov/Finding-Foreign-Markets.
7. https://www.sba.gov/managing-business/exporting.
8. https://www.treasury.gov/resource-center/sanctions/Programs/Pages/Programs.aspx.
9. https://www.treasury.gov/resource-center/sanctions/SDN-List/Pages/default.aspx.

Such restrictions may even require that exporters themselves take responsibility for how buyers will use or resell American products and technology.

This chapter focuses on the primary ways in which the United States promotes and regulates exports. Part One reviews the process of export licensing through which policy based restrictions are typically imposed. Part Two reviews export bans and embargos, including federal legislation that prohibits participation in foreign boycotts. Part Three examines government efforts to promote exports, including statutory remedies designed to open foreign markets.

Part One: Export Licensing

A. Overview

The federal government monitors all exports from the United States. For most goods, this simply means that the exporter must file an export declaration (Electronic Export Information[10] or EEI). (See also Census Bureau Guide[11] to "Automated Commercial Environment.") The EEI allows the government to collect data regarding what is being exported and to where. For some destinations and goods, however, government approval in the form of an export license must be secured prior to exportation. In general, this occurs when the goods are either destined for a country considered unfriendly or dangerous, or the goods themselves may be used in ways that potentially threaten national security. Many of these goods are commonly referred to as "dual use" products, since they have both commercial and military applications. Other particularly sensitive types of goods, such as weapons and nuclear materials, are subject to specialized review and licensing, often through several federal agencies and in coordination with other countries under various multilateral non-proliferation regimes[12] (enhanced by the Export Control and Related Border Security Program[13]).[14]

---

10. https://www.export.gov/article?id=Electronic-Export-Information-formerly-known-as -Shipper-s-Export-Declaration.

11. https://www.google.com/url?sa=t&rct=j&q=&esrc=s&source=web&cd=2&cad=rja&uac t=8&ved=0ahUKEwjA7eqC25XSAhVDRiYKHb-KBEcQFgggMAE&url=https%3A%2F%2F www.census.gov%2Fforeign-trade%2Faes%2Faesdirect%2FAESDirect-User-Guide. pdf&usg=AFQjCNHQt-3EY7AN07yYyGMdUmxMkaJ2ZA&sig2=tuu5FNa_FE6DSAYVc5sZig.

12. https://www.state.gov/strategictrade/overview/.

13. https://www.state.gov/t/isn/ecc/.

14. The State Department provides this summary of U.S. multinational export control regimes: The U.S. is a member of various multilateral nonproliferation regimes, including:

- Nuclear Suppliers Group (NSG) — With 39 member states, the NSG is a widely accepted, mature, and effective export-control arrangement which contributes to the nonproliferation of nuclear weapons through implementation of guidelines for control of nuclear and nuclear-related exports.

- Zangger Committee — The purpose of the 35-nation Nuclear Non-proliferation Treaty (NPT) Exporters (Zangger) Committee is to harmonize implementation of the NPT requirements to apply International Atomic Energy Agency (IAEA) safeguards to nuclear ex-

Under the current system, which is under substantial revision, different federal agencies are responsible for export controls over different types of goods. Most exporters will be concerned with three agencies which share primary responsibility— the Department of Commerce, Department of State and Treasury.

For most goods (including software and technology), the Bureau of Industry and Security (BIS) within the Department of Commerce (DOC) implements licensing requirements for exports under the Export Administration Act (EAA), and corresponding administrative regulations (EAR).[15] BIS describes its mission this way:

> Advance U.S. national security, foreign policy, and economic objectives by ensuring an effective export control and treaty compliance system and promoting continued U.S. strategic technology leadership. . . .
>
> The Bureau's mission is to protect the security of the United States, which includes its national security, economic security, cyber security, and homeland security. . . .
>
> For example, in the area of dual-use export controls, the Bureau will vigorously administer and enforce such controls to stem the proliferation of weapons of mass destruction and the means of delivering them, to halt the spread of weapons to terrorists or countries of concern, and to further important U.S. foreign policy objectives. Where there is credible evidence suggesting that the export of a dual-use item threatens U.S. security, the Bureau must act to combat that threat.

---

ports. The Committee maintains and updates a list of equipment and materials that may only be exported if safeguards are applied to the recipient facility (called the "Trigger List" because such exports trigger the requirement for safeguards).

- Missile Technology Control Regime (MTCR)—The 34 MTCR partners have committed to apply a common export policy (MTCR Guidelines) to a common list of controlled items, including all key equipment and technology needed for missile development, production, and operation. MTCR Guidelines restrict transfers of missiles—and technology related to missiles—for the delivery of WMD. The regime places particular focus on missiles capable of delivering a payload of at least 500 kg with a range of at least 300 km—so-called "Category I" or "MTCR-class" missiles.
- Australia Group (AG)—Objective is to ensure that the industries of the thirty-eight participating countries do not assist, either purposefully or inadvertently, states or terrorists seeking to acquire a chemical and/or biological weapons (CBW) capability.
- Wassenaar Arrangement (WA)—The regime with the most extensive set of control lists; it seeks to prevent destabilizing accumulations of arms and dual-use equipment and technologies that may contribute to the development or enhancement of military capabilities that would undermine regional security and stability, and to develop mechanisms for information sharing among the 34 partners as a way to harmonize export control practices and policies.

https://www.state.gov/strategictrade/overview/index.htm.

15. The EAA legislation expired in 2001. In a stunning display of brilliant legislative efficiency, Congress has failed since that time to renew the law, relying instead on Presidential orders under the International Emergency Economic Powers Act to maintain that law's authority through proclamation.

The State Department controls arms exports, through its "Directorate of Defense Trade Controls."[16] The applicable export controls are set out in the "Arms Export Control Act"[17] as implemented by the International Traffic in Arms Regulations (ITAR[18]). The Treasury Department administers most embargos and trade sanctions through its Office of Foreign Assets Control.[19] A number of other federal agencies may also be involved in export control. For example, the Nuclear Regulatory Commission[20] (with the participation of the Department of Energy) controls exportation of goods and technology relating to nuclear materials.

The licensing process, which is reviewed in more detail below, can be complicated. In essence, there are two primary lists of goods, software, and technology that dictate agency jurisdiction and licensing. These lists correspond to various multinational export control regimes. Most goods, under the dual use jurisdiction of BIS, fall within its "commerce control list."[21] For munitions subject to State Department approval, the list is called the "United States Munitions List."[22] If doubt exists about which licensing process the goods or technology is subject to, a "commodity jurisdiction request"[23] may be submitted to the State Department's Directorate. The Directorate has also added new "decision tools"[24] relating to on-going reforms described below:

> DDTC new web-based decision tools for understanding and applying revised regulations:
>
> • Order of Review:[25] Use this tool to help you figure out where your item(s) is controlled.

16. http://www.pmddtc.state.gov/licensing/index.html. The State Department defines goods subject to munitions controls as follows:
An article or service may be designated as a defense article or service if it:
   a. Is specifically designed, developed, configured, adapted or modified for a military application and
   i. Does not have predominant civil applications, and
   ii. Does not have performance equivalent (defined by form, fit, and function) to those of an article or service used for civil applications, or
   b. Is specifically designed, developed, configured, adapted or modified for a military application, and has significant military or intelligence applicability such that control is necessary. https://www.state.gov/strategictrade/overview/.
17. https://www.gpo.gov/fdsys/pkg/USCODE-2010-title22/html/USCODE-2010-title22-chap39.htm.
18. http://www.pmddtc.state.gov/regulations_laws/itar.html.
19. https://www.treasury.gov/resource-center/sanctions/Pages/default.aspx.
20. https://www.nrc.gov/about-nrc/ip/export-import.html.
21. https://www.bis.doc.gov/index.php/regulations/commerce-control-list-ccl.
22. https://www.ecfr.gov/cgi-bin/text-idx?SID=86008bdffd1fb2e79cc5df41a180750a&node=2 2:1.0.1.13.58&rgn=div5.
23. https://www.bis.doc.gov/index.php/licensing/commerce-control-list-classification/commodity-jurisdiction.
24. http://www.pmddtc.state.gov/ECR/index.html.
25. http://www.pmddtc.state.gov/licensing/dt_OrderofReview.htm.

- Specially Designed:[26] Use this tool to help you determine if a particular item is "specially designed" or meets one of the five carve-outs.

Based on these lists, and other factors such as country of destination and end user, exporters submit a license request to the relevant federal agency. The subsequent review process, described further below, may include review by other government agencies, including the intelligence community. In addition to control lists, the system maintains "catch-all" regulations. The State Department provides this description:

> The U.S. export control system also relies on catch-all controls to ensure that problematic dual-use exports—which are not otherwise subject to export controls—are capable of being tracked, discussed with the recipient government, or even denied as an export transaction. Catch-all regulations incident to the dual-use list prohibit the export without a license of any equipment, software, or technology that would contribute to projects of proliferation concern. The Export Administration Regulations provide specific identification of particular foreign entities that the U.S. Government designates as end-users of concern.

B. Pending Export Control Reform

In 2009, the Obama administration launched a major, multi-year Export Control Reform Initiative[27] (ECR) to restructure the export control system with the ultimate goal of unifying the process into "a single control list, single licensing agency, unified information technology system, and enforcement coordination center." As of 2016, phase I & II of the process, involving merger of product lists and modification of the existing regulatory framework, was "nearly complete" (but not set for full implementation until 2018). Export.gov provides this brief status report on the proposed reform:

Current Status

Control Lists and Licensing

> Eighteen of the twenty-one categories of the United States Munitions List have been revised and published for public comment, fifteen of which have been published as final rules. For the items moved to the Commerce Control List, new licensing policies are in effect that allow for streamlined exports of most items to the ultimate government end-use for 36 U.S. allies and most countries that are members of all four multilateral export control regimes. For more information on the status of the rule review process, please

---

26. http://www.pmddtc.state.gov/licensing/dt_SpeciallyDesigned.htm.
27. http://2016.export.gov/ecr/.

refer to <u>Fact Sheet 3 — Rebuilding the Control Lists</u>[28] or the <u>Control List "Tracker" (PDF)</u>[29] (<u>Accessible Version</u>[30]).

Enforcement

Progress has been made in updating the export enforcement system. On November 9, 2010, the President signed Executive Order 13558, establishing an Export Enforcement Coordination Center (E2C2) among the Departments of State, the Treasury, Defense, Justice, Commerce, Energy, and Homeland Security as well as the Intelligence Community. The Department of Homeland Security administers the E2C2 and provides its Director. . . .

Please refer to the <u>E2C2 page</u>[31] or <u>Fact Sheet 5 — Enforcement</u>[32] for additional information on export enforcement.

For additional background information on ECR in general, please visit the <u>ECR Library</u>.[33]

Information Technology

Progress is being made to transition the export licensing agencies to a single secure licensing database administered by the Department of Defense.

In the following materials, we will focus exclusively on the licensing process for general commercial "dual use" goods under EAR, as administered by BIS. Every exporter is legally obligated to determine whether or not their particular export, by virtue of the product's nature or its destination, requires an export license. Exporters may seek classification assistance from BIS and submit license applications by filing a "BIS-748P Multipurpose Application Form," or filing through an online processing system known as "<u>SNAP-R</u>"[34] ("simplified network application process redesign").

The first critical determinates for the license requirement are the nature of the goods and their destination. Thus, the exporter must first classify the exported product, and second. determine whether shipment of that product to particular destinations is prohibited or requires government approval.

---

28. build.export.gov/build/idcplg?IdcService=DOWNLOAD_PUBLIC_FILE&RevisionSelecti onMethod=Latest&dDocName=eg_main_090696.

29. build.export.gov/build/idcplg?IdcService=DOWNLOAD_PUBLIC_FILE&RevisionSelecti onMethod=Latest&dDocName=eg_main_048264.

30. build.export.gov/build/idcplg?IdcService=DOWNLOAD_PUBLIC_FILE&RevisionSelecti onMethod=Latest&dDocName=eg_main_048653.

31. http://2016.export.gov/e2c2/index.asp.

32. build.export.gov/build/idcplg?IdcService=DOWNLOAD_PUBLIC_FILE&RevisionSelecti onMethod=Latest&dDocName=eg_main_090698.

33. http://2016.export.gov/ecr/eg_main_023180.asp.

34. https://www.bis.doc.gov/index.php/licensing/simplified-network-application-process-redesign-snap-r.

The export regulations also place related responsibilities on exporters such as "knowing your buyer," looking for "<u>red flags</u>,"[35] and taking responsibility for actual "end uses" and "re-exportations" of their product. The exporter must also make sure that the buyer is not a restricted end user. The actual end user and end use of a product may prompt the requirement of a license, conditions on a license, or prohibition on export based on "lists" maintained by the various agencies responsible for licensing. Even low technology items not normally subject to licensing may require a license or be prohibited based on the lists.

In essence, the exporter must be concerned with (1) what is being exported; (2) where the export is going; (3) who will get the export; and (4) what will the export be used for? Our goal in this part of the chapter is to understand how the licensing system administered by BIS functions by working through the following problem. The BIS website itself provides the necessary guidance.

C. Problem Eleven: Triggered Spark Gaps

The product pictured above is sold by <u>Information Unlimited</u>[36] next to a caption which reads: "Please note this item may not be sold outside of the United States." Is this true? Read on.

1. Facts

Tariq Ahmed, 47, of Karachi, Pakistan, is the part owner and chief executive officer of a Pakistan based business known as Azam Electronics. His business partner is Mohammed Azam. Sometime in August 2017, he approached Asher Parni, an Israeli national then residing in Cape Town, South Africa. Parni was the owner of a firm in Cape Town, South Africa, known as "Cape Tech Co."

---

35. https://www.bis.doc.gov/index.php/compliance-a-training/export-management-a-compliance/23-compliance-a-training/51-red-flag-indicators.

36. http://www.amazing1.com/pages/hv-parts/spark-gap-switches.html.

Ahmed inquired whether Parni would help him acquire "triggered spark gaps" for a customer in Pakistan. Triggered spark gaps are high speed electrical switches that are often used in medical devices, such as a lithotripter, which treats kidney stones. Triggered spark gaps also have military applications. One such application is as a detonator for nuclear weapons.

The triggered spark gaps that Ahmed sought were manufactured by <u>Perkins Elmer Optoelectronics</u>[37] of Salem, Massachusetts. Parni found a broker named Wilfredo Maralit in Lawrenceville, New York, who was able to obtain 200 Perkins Elmer triggered spark gaps for shipment to South Africa. After the goods were shipped to South Africa, Parni ultimately re-exported the shipment to Azam Electronics in Pakistan.

2. Assignment

Was a license required for this transaction? Have any of the parties associated with the described transaction violated U.S. law? If so, how so, and what kinds of penalties might they face?

D. Resources

1. The Licensing Process Overview

Consult the following concise overviews of the process found at the export.gov and BIS websites. Important parts of these general summaries are described in greater detail in subsequent sections. BIS also provides this brief helpful video, "<u>Can I Export My Product</u>,"[38] outlining licensing basics for exporters.

<u>Export.gov</u>[39]

> To determine whether your item is subject to the EAR, you will need to refer to the EAR's Commerce Control List (CCL) to see if your item has an Export Control Classification Number (ECCN). Every item specifically listed in the EAR has an assigned ECCN. If your item falls under the jurisdiction of the U.S. Department of Commerce and is not listed on the CCL, it is designated as EAR99. Most EAR99 commercial products will not require a license to be exported. Depending on the destination, end user, or end use of the item, even an EAR99 item may require a BIS export license.
>
> Although relatively few items subject to the EAR require export licenses, licenses are required in certain situations involving national security, for-

---

37. https://www.google.com/url?sa=t&rct=j&q=&esrc=s&source=web&cd=3&ved=0ahUKE wjmr6Dzj9bQAhVEySYKHdUrCdMQFggqMAI&url=http%3A%2F%2Fwww.etsc.ru%2Ffiles% 2Ftubes%2Ftriggered_spark_gap.pdf&usg=AFQjCNFmy4_DfSq1Yf2OLttmyTJhZ48DuA&sig2=iv 1DQlm10xaS8jlZcRt1Xw&cad=rja.

38. https://www.youtube.com/watch?v=xOBf2ZM1LxY&feature=youtu.be.

39. https://www.export.gov/article2?id=Export-Administration-Regulations.

eign policy, short supply, nuclear nonproliferation, missile technology, chemical and biological weapons, regional stability, crime control, or anti-terrorism.

BIS[40]

Export Control Classification Number (ECCN)

A key in determining whether an export license is needed from the Department of Commerce is finding out if the item you intend to export has a specific Export Control Classification Number (ECCN). ECCNs are five character alpha-numeric designations used on the Commerce Control List (CCL) to identify dual-use items for export control purposes. An ECCN categorizes items based on the nature of the product, i.e., type of commodity, software, or technology and its respective technical parameters.

An ECCN is different from a Schedule B number, which is used by the Bureau of Census to collect trade statistics. It is also different from the Harmonized Tariff System Nomenclature, which is used to determine import duties.

All ECCNs are listed in the Commerce Control List (CCL) (Supplement No. 1 to Part 774 of the EAR), which is divided into ten broad categories, and each category is further subdivided into five product groups. The first character of the ECCN identifies the broader category to which it belongs and the second character identifies the product group (see example and boxes below).

Commerce Control List Categories
0 = Nuclear materials, facilities and equipment (and miscellaneous items)
1 = Materials, Chemicals, Microorganisms and Toxins
2 = Materials Processing
3 = Electronics
4 = Computers
5 = Telecommunications and Information Security
6 = Sensors and Lasers
7 = Navigation and Avionics
8 = Marine
9 = Propulsion Systems, Space Vehicles, and Related Equipment

Five Product Groups
A. Systems, Equipment and Components
B. Test, Inspection and Production Equipment
C. Material
D. Software
E. Technology

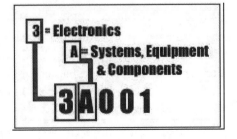

---

40. https://www.bis.doc.gov/index.php/regulations/commerce-control-list-ccl.

If Your Item is Not on the Commerce Control List—EAR99

If your item falls under the jurisdiction of the U.S. Department of Commerce and is not listed on the CCL, it is designated as EAR99. The majority of commercial products are designated EAR99 and generally will not require a license to be exported or reexported. However, if you plan to export an EAR99 item to an embargoed or sanctioned country, to a party of concern, or in support of a prohibited end-use, you may be required to obtain a license.

To obtain further assistance regarding the ECCN of your product, see our or review the "How to Request an ECCN" brochure.[41]

BIS provides the following limited but useful summary of the necessary steps:

US Department of Commerce, <u>Introduction to Commerce Department Export Controls</u>[42]

SUMMARY OF STEPS TO TAKE TO PROCESS YOUR EXPORT

- Ensure that your export is under U.S. Department of Commerce jurisdiction.

- Classify your item by reviewing the Commerce Control List.

- If your item is classified by an Export Control Classification Number (ECCN), identify the Reasons for Control on the Commerce Control List.

- Cross-reference the ECCN Controls against the Commerce Country Chart to see if a license is required. If yes, determine if a License Exception is available before applying for a license.

- Ensure that no prohibited end-users or end-uses are involved with your export transaction. If prohibited end-users or end-uses are involved, determine if you can proceed with the transaction or must apply for a license.

- Export your item using EAR99 or the correct ECCN and the appropriate symbol (e.g., NLR, license exception, or license number and expiration date) on your export documentation (e.g., Automated Export System (AES) record).

2. The Regulations & Specifics: EAR

Now that you have read the general description of the process above, look over the regulatory text (EAR) found at the federal government's "Electronic Federal Code of Regulations" (e-CFR[43]). Follow the links under Title 15 (Commerce and Foreign Trade) for BIS, "Chapters 700–799" and look for provisions relating to export licensing. In particular, Part 732 provides a detailed description of steps to be

---

41. https://www.bis.doc.gov/index.php/forms-documents?task=doc_view&gid=143.

42. https://www.bis.doc.gov/index.php/forms-documents/regulations-docs/142-eccn-pdf.

43. https://www.ecfr.gov/cgi-bin/text-idx?tpl=%2Findex.tpl.

taken in determining if a license is required. There is no need to study the entire guideline, but you should examine the steps provided, in particular reviewing suggested steps 7–10, 12–14, and 18. You will also find it helpful to review "General Prohibitions"[44] set out in Part 736, which essentially correspond to the export licensing requirements stated in the form of prohibitions. The General Prohibitions, which apply to all transactions whether or not a license or license exception is relevant, also reflect the broad reach of the controls and erect certain specific restrictions. For example, General Prohibition 8 forbids transit of goods through Armenia, Azerbaijan, Belarus, Cambodia, Cuba, Georgia, Kazakhstan, Kyrgyzstan, Laos, Mongolia, North Korea, Russia, Tajikistan, Turkmenistan, Ukraine, Uzbekistan, and Vietnam. Finally, Part 738[45] — Commerce Control List and the Country Chart, sets out information and instructions on how to use the ECCN and Country Chart. As set out in greater detail below, cross referencing "reasons for control" in the ECCN entry against destinations listed in the Country Charts indicates, at least initially, whether a license may be required.

3. Classifying Goods for Export: Commerce Control List & ECCNs

BIS provides the following instruction on its website. Read it over and then follow the link provided in the excerpt for the alphabetical "commerce control list index," to find our subject product and then entries for that product under the "Commerce Control List." According to the BIS website:[46]

Commerce Control List Classification

Determination as to whether or not authorization is required to export is determined by the following criteria in the transaction: 1) what is the ECCN of the item; 2) where it is going; 3) who is the end-user; and 4) what is the end-use. While the majority of U.S. commercial exports do not require a license, the first step in this process is determining the correct classification of your item.

If your item is subject to the jurisdiction of the U.S. Department of Commerce, you must then determine if your item has a specific Export Control Classification Number (ECCN)[47] found on the Commerce Control List

---

44. https://www.ecfr.gov/cgi-bin/text-idx?SID=85181ce290c36ebcda3451e59193ba5e&mc=true&node=pt15.2.736&rgn=div5.

45. https://www.ecfr.gov/cgi-bin/text-idx?c=ecfr&SID=9ae4a21068f2bd41d4a5aee843b63ef1&rgn=div5&view=text&node=15:2.1.3.4.24&idno=15.

46. https://www.bis.doc.gov/index.php/licensing/commerce-control-list-classification.

47. https://www.bis.doc.gov/index.php/licensing/commerce-control-list-classification/export-control-classification-number-eccn.

(CCL).[48] Keep in mind that items subject to the Export Administration Regulations (EAR) that are not listed on the CCL are designated EAR99.

There are three ways to determine the Export Control Classification Number (ECCN) for your product.

1. Go to the Source.

Contact the manufacturer, producer, or developer of the item you are exporting to see if they have classified their product and can provide you with the ECCN. If they have exported the item in the past, it is likely they have the ECCN. Keep in mind that ECCNs may change over time, so please review the ECCN to be sure you are in agreement.

2. Self-Classify.

In order to perform a self-classification, you must have a technical understanding of your item, and you need to be familiar with the structure and format of the CCL.[49] . . .

You can also utilize the Commerce Control List Index[50] to navigate the CCL. Begin by searching for your item on the CCL Index. When you find a potential ECCN, you must then read through the ECCN entry on the CCL before determining if your item fits into the parameters of that ECCN. If the ECCN contains a list under the "Items" heading, broken down into subparagraph(s) it is important to read through these subparagraph(s) to determine that your item meets the technical specifications listed in the ECCN category. You may need to review more than one ECCN description before you find the correct ECCN entry.

Read Part 738[51] of the EAR for specific instructions on how to use the CCL. You can also access our Introduction to Commerce Department Export Controls,[52] which is an easy-to-follow guide that walks you through the classification process step-by-step.

3. Request an official classification from the Bureau of Industry and Security (BIS).

Submit a commodity classification request online through the Simplified Network Application Process—Redesign (SNAP-R).[53] You must obtain a Company Identification Number (CIN) before accessing the online SNAP-R system and submitting your request.

---

48. https://www.bis.doc.gov/index.php/licensing/commerce-control-list-classification/commerce-control-list-ccl/17-regulations/139-commerce-control-list-ccl.

49. https://www.bis.doc.gov/index.php/forms-documents?task=doc_download&gid=141.

50. https://www.bis.doc.gov/index.php/forms-documents?task=doc_download&gid=13.

51. https://www.ecfr.gov/cgi-bin/text-idx?c=ecfr&SID=9ae4a21068f2bd41d4a5aee843b63ef1&rgn=div5&view=text&node=15:2.1.3.4.24&idno=15.

52. https://www.bis.doc.gov/index.php/forms-documents?task=doc_download&gid=142

53. https://www.bis.doc.gov/index.php/licensing/simplified-network-application-process-redesign-snap-r.

You can also access our <u>Guidelines to Reexport Publications</u>[54] to gain more insight into what information you should provide at the time of your request.

4. What if my product is not listed?

After careful review of your item against the CCL, if you are convinced your item does not fit into the parameters of any ECCN, your item may be designated as EAR99, keeping in mind it is not controlled by <u>another agency</u>.[55] If this is the case, your item may be exported using the license exception NLR specifying no license is required, as long as all of the following criteria is met:

- The item is not being shipped to a *<u>sanctioned destination</u>*[56]

- The item is not being shipped to a *<u>denied person, sanctioned entity, or prohibited end-user</u>*[57]

- The item will not be used for a specific *<u>end-use</u>*,[58] subject to higher controls.

For further details on these export restrictions, read Parts 736, 742, 744, and 746 of the EAR. If you still need guidance, you may contact the Outreach and Educational Services Division at (202-482-4811) or the Western Regional Office at (949-660-0144). While BIS can provide oral advice and guidance, we cannot give definitive classifications over the phone.

US Department of Commerce, <u>Introduction to Commerce Department Export Controls</u>[59]

Example

Assume that you have polygraph equipment that is used to help law enforcement agencies. What would be your ECCN? Start by looking in the Commerce Control List under the category of electronics (Category 3) and product group which covers equipment (Product Group A). Then read through the list to find whether your item is included in the list. In this example, the item is 3A981 as shown below.

---

54. https://www.bis.doc.gov/index.php/forms-documents?task=doc_download&gid=4.

55. https://www.bis.doc.gov/index.php/about-bis/resource-links.

56. https://www.bis.doc.gov/index.php/policy-guidance/country-guidance/sanctioned-destinations.

57. https://www.bis.doc.gov/index.php/policy-guidance/lists-of-parties-of-concern.

58. https://www.ecfr.gov/cgi-bin/retrieveECFR?gp=1&SID=9ae4a21068f2bd41d4a5aee843b63 ef1&ty=HTML&h=L&n=15y2.1.3.4.28&r=PART.

59. https://www.bis.doc.gov/index.php/forms-documents/regulations-docs/142-eccn-pdf.

3A981 Polygraphs (except biomedical recorders designed for use in medical facilities for monitoring biological and neurophysical responses); fingerprint analyzers, cameras and equipment, n.e.s.; automated fingerprint and identification retrieval systems, n.e.s.; psychological stress analysis equipment; electronic monitoring restraint devices; and specially designed parts and accessories, n.e.s.

License Requirements
Reason for Control: CC

Control(s)	Country Chart
CC applies to entire entry	CC Column 1

License Exceptions
    LVS: N/A
    GBS: N/A
    CIV: N/A

List of Items Controlled
    Unit: Equipment in number
    Related Controls: N/A
    Related Definitions: N/A

The list of items controlled is contained in the ECCN heading.

4. Where Is It Going? The Country Charts

Once the goods are classified, the next step is to cross reference the relevant ECCN and "reasons for control" with the export's destination on the Country Charts.

US Department of Commerce, Introduction to Commerce Department Export Controls[60]

Where are You Exporting?

Exports to embargoed countries and those designated as supporting terrorist activities such as Cuba, Iran, North Korea, Northern Sudan, and Syria are more restricted. However, restrictions vary from country to country.

How to cross-reference the ECCN with the Commerce Country Chart

Once you have classified the item, the next step is to determine whether you need an export license based on the "reasons for control" and the country of ultimate destination. You begin this process by com-

---

60. https://www.bis.doc.gov/index.php/forms-documents/regulations-docs/142-eccn-pdf.

paring the ECCN with the Commerce Country Chart (Supplement No. 1 to Part 738).

Below the main heading for each ECCN entry, you will find "Reason for Control" (e.g., NS for National Security, AT for Anti-Terrorism, CC for Crime Control, etc.). Below this, you will find the "Country Chart" designator which shows the specific export control code(s) for your item (e.g., NS Column 2, AT Column 1, CC Column 1, etc.). These control codes for your ECCN must be cross-referenced against the Commerce Country Chart.

Commerce Country Chart

Reason for Control

Countries	Chemical & Biological Weapons			Nuclear Nonproliferation		National Security		Missile Tech	Regional Stability		Firearms Convention	Crime Control			Anti-Terrorism	
	CB 1	CB 2	CB 3	NP 1	NP 2	NS 1	NS 2	MT 1	RS 1	RS 2	FC 1	CC 1	CC 2	CC 3	AT 1	AT 2
Guyana	X	X		X		X	X	X	X	X	X	X		X		
Haiti	X	X		X		X	X	X	X	X	X	X		X		
Honduras	X	X		X		X	X	X	X	X	X	(X)		X		
Hong Kong	X	X		X		X		X	X	X		X		X		
Hungary	X					X		X	X							
Iceland	X			X		X		X	X			(O)				
India	X	X	X	X	X	X	X	X	X	X		X		X		
Indonesia	X	X		X		X	X	X	X	X		X		X		

If there is an "X" in the box based on the reason(s) for control of your item and the country of destination, a license is required, unless a License Exception is available. Part 742 of the EAR sets forth the license requirements and licensing policy for most reasons for control.

Example

Question: You have polygraph equipment classified as 3A981 for export to Honduras. Would you be required to obtain an export license from the Department of Commerce before selling and shipping it to your purchaser?

Answer: Yes. 3A981 is controlled for Crime Control (CC) reasons under CC Column 1 and the Country Chart shows that such items require a license for Honduras.

If there is no "X" in the control code column(s) specified under your ECCN and country of destination, you will not need an export license unless you are exporting to an end-user or end-use of concern.

> *Example*
>
> Question: You have polygraph equipment classified as 3A981 for ex-port to Iceland. Would you be required to obtain an export license from the Department of Commerce before selling and shipping it to your purchaser?
>
> Answer: No. 3A981 is controlled for Crime Control (CC) reasons under CC Column 1 and the Country Chart shows that such items do not require a license for Iceland unless you are exporting to an end-user or end-use of concern.

Follow the link provided below and **use the Country Charts** to determine if a license is required for exports of triggered spark gaps to South Africa . . . or beyond:

Commerce Country Charts[61]

5. Blacklisted Persons and Entities

Even if a good does not normally require a license for shipment to a particular destination, a license may be required or shipment prohibited to black listed persons and entities.

CBP describes[62] these "black lists" (and provides links) as follows:

Blocked, Denied, Entity and Debarred Persons Lists

Below is a list of links to the Office of Foreign Assets Control's Specially Designated Nationals and Blocked Persons list, the Bureau of Industry and Security's Denied Parties List, the Entry List and the Office of Defense Trade Controls' Debarred Persons Lists.

Each agency is responsible for maintaining and updating their respective lists. Companies, entities, and persons found on the lists are sanctioned by the U.S. government and may not export goods from the United States or receive exported goods from the United States. Exporters are responsible for ensuring that all export transactions are properly authorized.

Exporters are advised to check the Federal Register publication and each agency's web site routinely for changes to the above mentioned lists. Export sanctions, written by the appropriate agency, are published in the Federal

---

61. https://www.bis.doc.gov/index.php/forms-documents/regulations-docs/14-commerce-country-chart.

62. https://www.cbp.gov/trade/trade-community/programs-outreach/blocked-denied-debarred.

Register and are the official source of information about denied persons, Specially Designated Nationals (SDN) or debarred parties.

Look for the participants in our problem transaction on the denied person and entities lists linked below.

The Bureau of Industry and Security — Denied Persons List[63] and Entity List[64]

These lists identify individuals and organizations that are either prohibited from exporting or importing goods subject to EAR (Denied Persons), or will require a license regardless of the product or destination (Entity List). Note that the distinction between these lists does not, contrary to what is suggested by their names, involve the difference between "natural persons" versus "entities." Rather, the Denied List creates a prohibition, whereas the Entity List indicates restrictions, and limitations such as additional license requirements.

The Office of Foreign Assets Control — Special Designated Nationals List[65]

This list is maintained by the Department of Treasury's Office of Foreign Assets Control and involves enforcement of economic and trade sanctions against targeted foreign countries, terrorism sponsoring organizations, and international narcotics traffickers. Note that Treasury also maintains other lists relating to various specific sanction programs such as:

Foreign Sanctions Evaders List:[66] Foreign individuals and entities determined to have violated, attempted to violate, conspired to violate, or caused a violation of U.S. sanctions on Syria or Iran, as well as foreign persons who have facilitated deceptive transactions for or on behalf of persons subject to U.S. Sanctions. Transactions by U.S. persons or within the United States involving Foreign Sanctions Evaders (FSEs) are prohibited.

Sectoral Sanctions Identifications (SSI) List:[67] Individuals operating in sectors of the Russian economy with whom U.S. persons are prohibited from transacting in, providing financing for, or dealing in debt with a maturity of longer than 90 days.

Palestinian Legislative Council (PLC) List:[68] Individuals of the PLC who were elected on the party slate of Hamas, or any other Foreign Terrorist Organization (FTO), Specially Designed Terrorist (SDT), or Specially Designated Global Terrorist (SDGT).

---

63. https://www.bis.doc.gov/index.php/policy-guidance/lists-of-parties-of-concern/denied-persons-list.

64. https://www.bis.doc.gov/index.php/policy-guidance/lists-of-parties-of-concern/entity-list.

65. https://www.treasury.gov/resource-center/sanctions/SDN-List/Pages/default.aspx.

66. https://www.treasury.gov/resource-center/sanctions/SDN-List/Pages/fse_list.aspx.

67. https://www.treasury.gov/resource-center/sanctions/SDN-List/Pages/ssi_list.aspx.

68. https://www.treasury.gov/resource-center/sanctions/SDN-List/Pages/plc_list.aspx.

The List of Foreign Financial Institutions Subject to Part 561 (the Part 561 List):[69] The Part 561 List includes the names of foreign financial Institutions that are subject to sanctions, certain prohibitions, or strict conditions before a U.S. company may do business with them.

Non-SDN Iranian Sanctions Act List (NS-ISA):[70] The ISA List includes persons determined to have made certain investments in Iran's energy sector or to have engaged in certain activities relating to Iran's refined petroleum sector. Their names do not appear on the Specially Designated Nationals or Blocked Persons (SDN) List, and their property and/or interests in property are not blocked, pursuant to this action.

The Treasury offers a sanction lists search tool[71] covering all program lists under its jurisdiction.

The Office of Defense Trade Controls — Debarred Parties List[72]

This is a list of persons who are barred from trade in U.S. munitions based on violations of the Arms Export Control Act (or regulations within ITAR) and is maintained by the U.S. State Department.

The Unverified List[73]

BIS maintains a list of "unverified" firms for which it is unable to "complete an end-use check." According to BIS:

Firms on the unverified list present a "red flag" that exporters have a duty to inquire about before making an export to them.

Parties listed on the Unverified List (UVL) are ineligible to receive items subject to the Export Administration Regulations (EAR) by means of a license exception. In addition, exporters must file an Automated Export System record for all exports to parties listed on the UVL and obtain a statement from such parties prior to exporting, reexporting, or transferring to such parties any item subject to the EAR which is not subject to a license requirement. Restrictions on exports, reexports and transfers (in-country) to persons listed on the UVL are set forth in Section 744.15[74] of the EAR. . . .

Export.gov now offers a consolidated screening list search tool,[75] covering eleven distinct lists, that "may be used as an aid to industry in con-

---

69. https://www.treasury.gov/resource-center/sanctions/programs/pages/iran.aspx#part561.

70. https://www.treasury.gov/resource-center/sanctions/programs/pages/iran.aspx#isa.

71. https://sanctionssearch.ofac.treas.gov/.

72. http://pmddtc.state.gov/compliance/debar.html.

73. https://www.bis.doc.gov/index.php/policy-guidance/lists-of-parties-of-concern/unverified-list.

74. https://www.ecfr.gov/cgi-bin/text-idx?rgn=div5&node=15:2.1.3.4.28#15:2.1.3.4.28.0.1.15.

75. https://www.export.gov/csl-search

ducting electronic screens of potential parties to regulated transactions . . . ." If a transaction party "appears to match," additional due diligence is required: "Prior to taking further action, the user must check the official publication of restricted parties in the Federal Register or the official lists of restricted parties maintained on the web sites of the Departments of Commerce, State and the Treasury to ensure full compliance with all of the terms and conditions of the restrictions placed on the parties on this list."

All lists are regularly updated, requiring the exporter to consult the <u>Federal Register</u>[76] for every transaction.

6. Extraterritorial Application of EAR: Re-Exports & Foreign Goods Containing U.S. Content or Technology

The potential application of U.S. licensing regulations reach far beyond the simple export of a U.S. made product from our territorial boundaries. One important example of this involves the extraterritorial application of EAR to certain goods exported not from American territory but rather from foreign countries. These extraterritorial applications of EAR include goods exported from foreign countries that are *U.S. origin goods,* or contain *U.S. content or technology.* A second important example involves what the regulations describe as "*deemed exports.*" Review the following excerpts from the BIS website to gain a general understanding of the wide net cast by U.S. export controls. Why might this aggressive approach be controversial among our international trading partners?

a. Re-exports of U.S. Origin Goods & Technology

<u>BIS Guidance on Reexports</u>[77]

Guidance on Reexports/Transfers (in-country) of U.S.-Origin Items or Non-U.S.-made Items Subject to the Export Administration Regulations (EAR)

If you are outside the United States and wish to reexport or transfer (in-country) an item (commodity, technology, or software) that is of U.S.-origin or that is subject to the Export Administration Regulations (EAR) (as described in more detail in Parts B-D below), your product may require a license or other authorization from the U.S. Department of Commerce's Bureau of Industry and Security (BIS). Certain additional restrictions are also outlined in part G below.

Determining whether your item is subject to the EAR.

---

76. https://www.federalregister.gov/.
77. https://www.bis.doc.gov/index.php/licensing/reexports-and-offshore-transactions.

Your item is subject to the EAR if it:

1. Was produced in the United States (See <u>Part A</u>[78]);

2. Is a non-U.S.-made product that contains more than a specified percentage of controlled U.S.-origin content (See Part B);

3. Is a non-U.S.-made product based on certain U.S.-origin technology or software and is intended for export (from abroad) to specified destinations (See Part C); or

4. Was made by a plant or major component of a plant located outside the United States, and if that plant or major component of a plant is the direct product of certain U.S. technology or software, and your product is intended for export (from abroad) to specified destinations (See <u>Direct Product Guidance</u>[79]).

A. Determining whether the reexport or transfer (in-country) of a U.S.-origin item or a non-U.S.-made item that is subject to the EAR requires a license from BIS.

You may need to obtain a license or other authorization to "reexport" or transfer (in-country) an item that was produced in the United States. A "reexport" is the shipment or transmission of an item subject to the EAR from one foreign country (i.e., a country other than the United States) to another foreign country. A reexport also occurs when there is "release" of technology or software (source code) subject to the EAR in one foreign country to a national of another foreign country. In-country transfer or transfer (in-country) is a shipment, transmission, or release of items subject to the EAR from one person to another person that occurs outside the United States within a single foreign country. <u>See deemed reexport guidance</u>[80]

. . . .

Also keep in mind . . .

- If the item is a U.S.-origin item and subject to the EAR, it remains subject to the EAR regardless of how many times it is reexported, transferred, or sold.

- Therefore, any subsequent reexports or transfers (in-country) must be done in accordance with the EAR, including any items received prior to their movement from the USML to the CCL.

- When reexporting U.S.-origin items in the form received, use the classification of the U.S.-origin item

B. Determining whether your non-U.S.-made item that incorporates/bundles U.S.-origin content is subject to the EAR (<u>De Minimis Guidelines</u>[81]).

---

78. https://www.bis.doc.gov/index.php/licensing/reexports-and-offshore-transactions#PART-A.
79. https://www.bis.doc.gov/index.php/2011-09-13-13-22-36.
80. https://www.bis.doc.gov/index.php/policy-guidance/deemed-exports/deemed-reexport-guidance1.
81. https://www.bis.doc.gov/index.php/forms-documents/doc_view/1382-de-minimis-guidance.

As noted above, certain foreign-produced items are subject to the EAR because they incorporate or bundle more than a specified percentage value of U.S.-origin controlled content. The following steps are provided as general guidance for determining whether a foreign produced item (commodity, software, or technology) that incorporates/bundles U.S.-origin item(s) is subject to the EAR or is not subject to the EAR pursuant to the de minimis rules in the EAR. This general guidance does not take into account specific U.S.-origin items that are not eligible for de minimis treatment. You should consult Section 734.4 and Supplement 2 to Part 734 for information on such items and guidance on how to calculate the percentage of U.S.-origin controlled content.

1. General guidance regarding incorporation of U.S.-origin controlled commodities into non-U.S.-made items.

If you are a company that incorporates U.S.-origin items into a non-U.S.-made items outside the United States you will need to-

a. Determine the classification (ECCN) of the U.S.-origin commodities exported to you. The U.S. exporter may be able to assist you in determining the ECCN or you may submit a classification request to BIS via SNAP-R (free).

b. Determine if the U.S.-origin commodities are "controlled content." ("U.S. controlled content" is content that would require a U.S. license if it were to be reexported separately to the country of ultimate destination.)

c. Determine if the percentage of U.S.-origin "controlled content" is greater than the percentages outlined in the *de minimis* guidelines

d. If the U.S.-origin controlled content is greater than the *de minimis* percentage, your non-U.S.-made item is subject to the EAR.

If your non-U.S.-made item is subject to the EAR, you need to determine if your non-U.S.-made item requires a license, either because of the ultimate destination or the end-use or end-user. To do this, follow the steps outlined in Part A.[82]

2. Guidance regarding non-U.S.-made software incorporating or bundled with U.S.-origin controlled software and non-U.S.-made technology commingled with or drawn from U.S.-origin controlled technology.

If you incorporate U.S.-origin software into your non-U.S.-made software, or you bundle U.S.-origin software with non-U.S.-made hardware, or if your non-U.S.-made technology is commingled with or drawn from U.S.-origin controlled co-technology, you would follow a process similar to the one outlined above. That process and a related one-time reporting requirement for technology commingling are set forth in Section 734.4 and Supplement 2 to part 734 of the EAR. If there is no fair market value for the technology or software, you may use any reasonable method to determine

---

82. https://www.bis.doc.gov/index.php/licensing/reexports-and-offshore-transactions#PartA2.

the cost of the US-content, e.g., production cost or cost per line of code. You may run your method ideas by us at RPD2@bis.doc.gov.

C. Determining if your non-U.S.-made item is subject to the EAR because it is the <u>direct product</u>[83] of U.S. technology or software.

Non-U.S.-made direct products may be subject to the EAR if they are the direct product of certain types of U.S. technology or software (source code) and are going to specified destinations. See the <u>Direct Product Guidance</u>[84] for specific details.

D. Determining if your non-U.S.-made item that is subject to the EAR requires a license from BIS.

Follow the steps in <u>Section A</u>[85] of this webpage.

b. Deemed Exports

In certain instances, an "export" may take place through the exchange of information or technology, even though no physical goods have been shipped. Such exchanges or releases of information may fall within the category of "deemed" exports.

From the BIS website:

(1) Definition of export. "Export" means an actual shipment or transmission of items subject to the EAR out of the United States, or release of technology or software subject to the EAR to a foreign national in the United States, as described in paragraph (b)(2)(ii) of this section. See paragraph (b)(9) of this section for the definition that applies to exports of encryption source code and object code software subject to the EAR.

(2) Export of technology or software. (See paragraph (b)(9) for provisions that apply to encryption source code and object code software.) "Export" of technology or software, excluding encryption software subject to "EI" controls, includes:

(i) Any release of technology or software subject to the EAR in a foreign country; or

(ii) Any release of technology or source code subject to the EAR to a foreign national. Such release is deemed to be an export to the home country or countries of the foreign national. This deemed export rule does not apply to persons lawfully admitted for permanent residence in the United States and does not apply to persons who are protected individuals under the Immigration and Naturalization Act (8 U.S.C. 1324b(a)(3)). Note that the release of any item to any party with knowledge a violation is about to occur is prohibited by § 736.2(b)(10) of the EAR.

---

83. https://www.bis.doc.gov/index.php/2011-09-13-13-22-36.
84. https://www.bis.doc.gov/index.php/2011-09-13-13-22-36.
85. https://www.bis.doc.gov/index.php/licensing/reexports-and-offshore-transactions#sectionA.

(3) Definition of "release" of technology or software. Technology or software is "released" for export through:

(i) Visual inspection by foreign nationals of U.S.-origin equipment and facilities;

(ii) Oral exchanges of information in the United States or abroad; or

(iii) The application to situations abroad of personal knowledge or technical experience acquired in the United States.

(4) Definition of reexport. "Reexport" means an actual shipment or transmission of items subject to the EAR from one foreign country to another foreign country; or release of technology or software subject to the EAR to a foreign national outside the United States, as described in paragraph (b)(5) of this section.

g. Any release of technology or source code subject to the EAR to a foreign national of another country is a deemed reexport to the home country or countries of the foreign national. However, this deemed reexport definition does not apply to persons lawfully admitted for permanent residence. The term "release" is defined in paragraph (b)(3) of this section. Note that the release of any item to any party with knowledge or reason to know a violation is about to occur is prohibited by § 736.2(b)(10) of the EAR.

. . . .

If you read the above BIS guidance carefully, you will notice that even allowing a foreign national *to view* controlled information technology, while in the United States, may constitute a "deemed" export of that product. Consider these instructions for faculty[86] on export regulations, posted by the Ohio State University. In 2012, former University of Tennessee Professor John Reece Roth[87] began serving his four year prison sentence after being convicted of unlawfully "exporting" restricted technical data, associated with an Air Force project involving advanced plasma technology for drones, to two foreign Chinese students.

c. International Rules on Extraterritoriality

The rules described above make it clear that EAR, and other U.S. export controls, are designed to reach conduct of individuals and entities residing outside of U.S. territorial boundaries. For example, foreign nationals residing outside of the United States, who are normally outside of U.S. legal authority, are explicitly required to comply with licensing limitations such as rules on re-exportation of U.S. origin goods. Even foreign companies that produce products using U.S. based technology or parts are sometimes subjected to EAR. This extension of U.S. export regulations to people

---

86. http://orc.osu.edu/regulations-policies/exportcontrol/.

87. https://archives.fbi.gov/archives/knoxville/press-releases/2012/former-university-of
-tennessee-professor-john-reece-roth-begins-serving-four-year-prison-sentence-on-convictions
-of-illegally-exporting-military-research-data.

and entities outside of U.S. territory, typically described as "extraterritoriality," is extremely controversial and, according to most U.S. trading partners, illegal.

Under generally accepted international legal principles, national legal authority generally only applies within defined limitations which restrict extraterritorial application of national law. The Restatement (Third) of Foreign Relations § 402 provides the following general summary of the internationally accepted rules for exercising national "prescriptive jurisdiction":

§ 402. BASES OF JURISDICTION TO PRESCRIBE

Subject to § 403, a state has jurisdiction to prescribe law with respect to

(1) (a) conduct that, wholly or in substantial part, takes place within its territory;

(b) the status of persons, or interests in things, present within its territory;

(c) conduct outside its territory that has or is intended to have substantial effect within its territory;

(2) the activities, interests, status, or relations of its nationals outside as well as within its territory; and

(3) certain conduct outside its territory by persons not its nationals that is directed against the security of the state or against a limited class of other state interests.

Although nations may obviously extend their national law to all people, things and conduct within territorial boundaries ("territorial jurisdiction"), extraterritorial application of national law is typically allowed only under limited circumstances. These circumstances would include the conduct of citizens overseas ("nationality jurisdiction"), protection of vital governmental interests such as border security ("protective jurisdiction"), and acts outside the territory that have direct, substantial and intended consequences within national boundaries ("territorial effects doctrine").

Do U.S. regulations on export control and licensing violate these principles? Part Two, below, explores this controversial question in greater depth.

7. Enforcement & Penalties

The institutional framework for enforcing U.S. export regulations is perhaps even more complex than the framework governing administration of the licensing process. Our goal, for present purposes, is to identify the primary forms of enforcement, the essential players, and possible penalties. Initially, you must draw the important distinction between civil administrative sanctions and criminal penalties.

Each of the three primary entities involved in the administration of export controls—DOC's BIS (EAR dual use exports), the State Department's DDTC (ITAR munitions), and Treasury's OFAC (trade related foreign policy sanctions)—are also involved in enforcement through administrative sanctions such as civil fines or denial of export privileges. At BIS, for example, the Office of Export Enforcement may issue warning letters for negligent or technical violations. It may also issue "charging letters" potentially leading, after review and recommendations by an administrative law judge (50 U.S.C. § 4615), to very serious penalties. For cases "involving gross negligence, willful blindness to the requirements of the EAR, or knowing or willful violations, BIS is more likely to seek a denial of export privileges or an exclusion from practice, and/or a greater monetary penalty . . . ."(OEE guidelines, 15 C.F.R. Part 766). Even simple negligence or carelessness may lead to such penalties, "if the violation(s) involved harm to national security or other essential interests protected by the export control system, if the violation(s) are of such a nature and extent that a monetary fine alone represents an insufficient penalty or if the nature and extent of the violation(s) indicate that a denial or exclusion order is necessary to prevent future violations of the EAR." Mitigating factors include "voluntary self-disclosure," high quality "export compliance programs," "exceptional cooperation," "substantial assistance" in other investigations, and lack of prior warnings or violations.

Apart from denial of export privileges, civil fines up to the greater of $284,000 per violation (2016), or twice the transaction value, may be imposed.[88] In 2014, 44 administrative cases resulted in 60 million dollars in fines. In 2015, BIS reported[89] 47 cases and 15 million in fines. BIS added over 200 parties to its "Entity List" in these two years. In 2015 and 2016, Treasury's OFAC imposed civil fines of $599,705,997 (15 cases) and $21,609,315 million (9 cases), respectively.

When deemed appropriate, given the egregious or willful nature of the violation, the agencies may also refer cases to the Department of Justice for criminal prosecution. Federal investigative and law enforcement agencies, such as the FBI and CBP, often coordinate and assist in these processes.[90] Criminal violations of the EAA (or while lapsed, the IEEPA), may result in fines up to $1,000,000, and 20 years imprison-

---

88. The Export Administration Act allows for smaller penalties but has been in lapse for many years as described by BIS: "Since August 21, 2001, the EAA has been in lapse and the President, through Executive Order 13222 of August 17, 2001 (3 C.F.R. 2001 Comp. p. 783 (2002)), which has been extended by successive Presidential Notices, has continued the EAR under the International Emergency Economic Powers Act (50 U.S.C. §§ 1701-1706 (2000)) (IEEPA)." https://www.bis.doc .gov/index.php/enforcement/oee/penalties.

89. https://www.bis.doc.gov/index.php/forms-documents/enforcement/1005-don-t-let-this -happen-to-you-1.

90. Executive Order 13558 created the Export Enforcement Coordination Center within the Department of Homeland Security and Immigration and Customs Enforcement. ICE describes it as follows: "The Center strengthens the enforcement of U.S. export laws through the facilitation of partner agency communication and collaboration to keep our nation safe. HSI, as part of the Department of Homeland Security (DHS), manages and operates the Export Enforcement Coordination Center." https://www.ice.gov/eecc#wcm-survey-target-id.

ment, per violation. In 2015, BIS investigations lead to the criminal conviction of 31 individuals and businesses, leading to 156 million dollars in fines, 84 million in forfeitures, and 487 months of prison time.

Here are a few illustrations summarized in a <u>speech by a BIS official</u>:[91]

Weatherford International Ltd.

Our biggest civil penalty in the past year, in fact the biggest ever, was levied against Weatherford International Ltd. in Houston, Texas, and four of its subsidiaries who agreed to pay a combined $100 million for export control violations involving Iran, Syria, Cuba, and other countries. A $50 million civil penalty was imposed for the export of oil and gas equipment to Iran, Syria, and Cuba in violation of the EAR and the Iranian Transactions and Sanctions Regulations (ITSR). BIS also alleged that Weatherford exported items controlled for nuclear non-nonproliferation reasons to Venezuela and Mexico. The Department of Justice imposed a $48 million monetary penalty on Weatherford International Ltd. pursuant to a deferred prosecution agreement entered into on November 26, 2013, and also imposed $2 million in criminal fines pursuant to guilty pleas by two of Weatherford's subsidiaries. Weatherford agreed, as part of the settlement, to hire an unaffiliated third-party expert in U.S. export control laws to audit its compliance with respect to all exports or re-exports to Cuba, Iran, North Korea, Sudan, and Syria for calendar years 2012, 2013, and 2014. The Weatherford investigation was conducted by OEE at BIS, working closely with OFAC and the Department of Justice.

Ming Suan Zhang

On December 10, 2013, as a result of a joint investigation by OEE and HSI at the Department of Homeland Security, Ming Suan Zhang, a citizen of the People's Republic of China, was sentenced to 57 months incarceration and a forfeiture of $1,000 for violating the International Emergency Economic Powers Act by attempting to export high-grade carbon fiber from the United States to China.

More apropos to our chapter problem, consider the case of <u>Asher Karni</u>,[92] an Israeli man working from South Africa, who was convicted of selling triggered stop gaps to a buyer in Pakistan.

---

91. https://www.bis.doc.gov/index.php/component/content/article/148-about-bis/newsroom/speeches/speeches-2014/719-keynote-speech-of-david-w-mills-assistant-secretary-for-export-enforcement-update-conference-july-30-2014.

92. http://articles.latimes.com/2005/aug/05/world/fg-nuke5.

8. Export Compliance Programs

BIS encourages the creation of export compliance programs which, if appropriately instituted, may mitigate penalties when violations occur. Review this linked company description of export compliance at <u>Northrop Grumman</u> Corporation,[93] which <u>paid $15 million in fines</u>[94] in 2008, including a short "<u>test yourself" quiz</u>.[95] The BIS website also provides the following advice:

> Principles of Effective Compliance Programs for Great Weight Mitigation in BIS's Administrative Cases
>
> 1. Whether the company has performed a meaningful risk analysis;
>
> 2. The existence of a formal written compliance program;
>
> 3. Whether appropriate senior organizational officials are responsible for overseeing the export compliance program;
>
> 4. Whether adequate training is provided to employees;
>
> 5. Whether the company adequately screens its customers and transactions;
>
> 6. Whether the company meets record keeping requirements;
>
> 7. The existence and operation of an internal system for reporting export violations;
>
> 8. The existence and result of internal/external review or audits;
>
> 9. Whether remedial activity has been taken in response to export violations.

Compliance programs dovetail with an emphasis on exporter responsibility and self-policing concerning end users and uses. The <u>State Department</u>[96] website summarizes the various warning signs, similar to "<u>red flags</u>"[97] identified by BIS:

> Exporters: Be familiar with your customers
>
> Applying common sense is essential in weeding out potentially problematic transfers. Alarms should sound if:

---

93. https://www.google.com/url?sa=t&rct=j&q=&esrc=s&source=web&cd=7&ved=0ahUKE wjOku3G5abRAhVJyVQKHd3CBZIQFgg7MAY&url=http%3A%2F%2Fwww.corporatecompli ance.org%2FPortals%2F1%2FPDF%2FResources%2Fpast_handouts%2FCEI%2F2010%2F605 _InternationalTradeandExports.pdf&usg=AFQjCNH10DJH2Tz_1PRWkuykncp9xisaVg&sig2=S MICLQ3wzE9IAkGPIOtH8w&bvm=bv.142059868,d.cGw&cad=rja.

94. https://www.pmddtc.state.gov/compliance/consent_agreements/NorthropGrummanCorp. htm.

95. https://www.google.com/url?sa=t&rct=j&q=&esrc=s&source=web&cd=1&ved=0ahUKE wiyqrGf46bRAhXDzlQKHUDBB5YQFggfMAA&url=http%3A%2F%2Fwww.northropgrum man.com%2FCorporateResponsibility%2FEthics%2FDocuments%2Finternational%2Feurope% 2FExport_Control.pdf&usg=AFQjCNF34fQ-V97mWt-dcFXYW6BNZuJorg&sig2=sB524T6mLK DgmeP1wZwDWg&cad=rja.

96. https://www.state.gov/strategictrade/overview/.

97. https://www.bis.doc.gov/index.php/compliance-a-training/export-management-a-compli ance/23-compliance-a-training/51-red-flag-indicators.

A customer or agent —

- Is reluctant to provide end-use/user information
- Is willing to pay cash for high-value shipments
- Has little background or history in the relevant business
- Appears unfamiliar with the product or its use
- Declines normal warranty/service/installation
- Orders products/quantities incompatible with the relevant business
- Provides vague delivery dates or locations

A shipment involves —

- Private intermediary in major weapons sale
- Freight forwarder designated as consignee/end-user
- Intermediate consignee's business or location incompatible with end-user's
- Shipments directed to trading companies, freight forwarders, or companies with no connection to buyer
- Requests for packing inconsistent with normal mode of shipping
- Choice of circuitous or economically illogical routing, or through multiple countries;

The end-user requests —

- Equipment inconsistent with inventory
- Spare parts in excess of projected needs
- Performance/design specs incompatible with resources or environment
- Technical capability/end-use incompatible with consignee's line of business
- End-use at variance with standard practices
- Middleman from third country to place order
- Refuses to state whether goods are for domestic use, export, or re-export

Obviously, export controls impose important additional obligations on U.S. sellers. These obligations include documentation requirements and restrictions on the sale which must be accounted for in the transaction, along with the payment, shipping, and contractual issues we examined earlier in this book. Export.gov's <u>Export Transaction Shipment Checklist</u>[98] provides a nice summary. (*See also* "<u>Documentation for Export Compliance</u>."[99])

Take a look.

---

98. https://www.export.gov/article?id=Export-Transaction-Shipment-Checklist.
99. https://www.export.gov/article?id=U-S-Compliance-related-Documents.

Part Two: Export Bans, Embargos & Anti-Boycott Legislation

A. Trade Embargos & Sanctions

The United States maintains numerous embargos or other trade sanction programs, either unilaterally or in conjunction with the United Nations and other countries. Although some restrictions are long term, others come and go with shifting foreign policy, national security, or trade disputes. Some sanction regimes, such as those imposed against Cuba, Iran and Syria, are comprehensive, while others are "targeted."

Many sanctions are directed at trade with particular countries, but individuals and companies may also be designated for restrictions. For example, in a March 7, 2012, Press Release,[100] the Treasury Department announced the designation of Iranian General Gholamreza Baghbani as a "Specially Designated Narcotics Trafficker." Under the federal "King Pin Act," no U.S. person is allowed to engage in any commercial transaction with General Baghbani or the other 1000 individuals also currently so designated. The Treasury Department's "Office of Foreign Asset Controls" maintains a set of lists for "Specially Designated Nationals"[101] against whom targeted sanctions apply. Many countries are also subject to a wide variety of arms embargos[102] and restrictions maintained by the State Department.

Trade restrictions may arise suddenly and often change. Note for example, the following excerpt from the U.S. Treasury Department website describing immediate sanctions against Russian persons and entities relating to that country's attempt to influence the 2016 U.S. presidential election through computer hacking:

12/29/2016

> Today, the President issued Executive Order 13757, "Taking Additional Steps To Address The National Emergency With Respect To Significant Malicious Cyber-Enabled Activities."[103] This amends Executive Order 13694, "Blocking the Property of Certain Persons Engaging in Significant Malicious Cyber-Enabled Activities." E.O. 13694 authorized the imposition of sanctions on individuals and entities determined to be responsible for or complicit in malicious cyber-enabled activities that result in enumerated harms that are reasonably likely to result in, or have materially contributed to, a significant threat to the national security, foreign policy, or economic health or financial stability of the United States.

---

100. https://www.treasury.gov/press-center/press-releases/Pages/tg1444.aspx.

101. https://www.treasury.gov/resource-center/sanctions/SDN-List/Pages/default.aspx.

102. http://www.pmddtc.state.gov/embargoed_countries/index.html.

103. https://www.treasury.gov/resource-center/sanctions/Programs/Documents/cyber2_eo.pdf.

Sudden changes in export policy may also directly affect already issued licenses. Consider this excerpt from the Federal Register, which appeared soon after civil conflict in Libya broke out during the "Arab Spring" of 2011–2012:

March 3, 2011, Libya Licenses Suspended:

Effective March 3, 2011, all licenses issued by BIS for exports or reexports to Libya under the authority of the Export Administration Regulations (15 C.F.R. 730-774) as kept in force by the International Emergency Economic Powers Act have been suspended indefinitely and all persons currently holding active licenses have been so notified. No further shipments may be made against licenses for exports or reexports to Libya by any person. For further information, please contact the Foreign Policy Division/Bureau of Industry and Security at 202-482-4252.

The dynamic nature of trade sanctions requires exporters to continually keep abreast of both political affairs and the Federal Register. A list of current sanction programs[104] is provided by the U.S. Treasury, which enforces most programs. A summary of country embargos[105] is also presented on the BIS website.

B. Extraterritorial Application of Trade Sanctions

One of most glaring weaknesses of many U.S. trade sanction regimes is that they are imposed unilaterally, or without comprehensive international cooperation. As described above, national legal authority generally only applies within defined international law limitations. These limitations generally restrict extraterritorial application of national law. Since individuals and commercial interests outside of the United States (other than our own citizens) are not legally bound by U.S. trade sanctions, such sanctions are easily circumvented and often do not achieve their intended effect. This problem is compounded by the fact that corporate entities are citizens only of the place of their incorporation. Foreign subsidiaries of U.S. companies are, therefore, not legally citizens of the United States, and generally not subject to U.S. law. A separately incorporated foreign subsidiary is distinct in this regard from "branch" operations that have the same corporate identity as their parent.

Despite these limitations, the United States frequently attempts to extend the reach of its trade sanctions to restrict the activities of traders outside its national territory. This includes persons and entities normally outside the reach of U.S. law, as described above. Sometimes this is done through various definitions of the "United States Person" to whom the sanction rules apply. The 2012 sanctions against Syria provide an example of a relatively modest definition of a "United States Person," consistent with international law, stretching the rules to include "foreign branches" of U.S. companies:

---

104. https://www.treasury.gov/resource-center/sanctions/Programs/Pages/Programs.aspx.
105. https://www.bis.doc.gov/index.php/forms-documents/regulations-docs/420-part-746 -embargoes-and-other-special-controls/file.

Sec. 6. For purposes of this order:

(a) the term "person" means an individual or entity;

(b) the term "entity" means a partnership, association, trust, joint venture, corporation, group, subgroup, or other organization;

(c) the term "United States person" means any United States citizen, permanent resident alien, entity organized under the laws

of the United States or any jurisdiction within the United States (including foreign branches), or any person in the United States . . . .

Under other U.S. trade sanctions, however, the definition of those persons subject to the restrictions (and penalties) is much broader. At various times, U.S. law has defined those who must comply with a particular trade sanction to include foreign entities under the "control" of U.S. persons (defined by, among other criteria, ownership participation) and even foreign persons trading in U.S. based technology or goods. Perhaps the best example of such extraterritorial extensions of trade sanctions is the long-standing U.S. embargo of Cuba.

The Cuban embargo, which was initiated in 1962, has been altered many times over the years. Most recently, it was eased to some extent by the resumption of diplomatic relations with Cuba through President Obama's 2016 executive action.[106] Earlier restrictions still in place include two controversial federal laws enacted in the 90s that were designed to extend the embargo's restrictions extraterritorially.[107] The Cuban Democracy Act of 1992[108] prohibited foreign-based subsidiaries of U.S. companies from trading with Cuba.[109] Prior to the act, such foreign subsidiaries were allowed to do business with Cuba under a licensing system. Since foreign subsidiaries are legal citizens of the place of their incorporation, this provision is highly controversial in that it attempts to enforce U.S. law against the foreign activities of what are essentially foreign corporations. To understand foreign government reaction to the law, one only need to imagine an effort by Saudi Arabia to enforce its boycott of Israel or gender segregation at the offices of a U.S. based subsidiary of a Saudi corporation.

The Cuban Democracy Act was followed, in 1996, by the Cuban Liberty and Democratic Solidarity (Libertad) Act,[110] commonly known as "Helms-Burton." This legislation provided for extension of the embargo to cover foreign corporations doing business with Cuba (by prohibiting U.S. persons from trade with foreign entities en-

---

106. https://obamawhitehouse.archives.gov/the-press-office/2016/10/14/presidential-policy
-directive-united-states-cuba-normalization.

107. Prior to the 1996 Helms-Burton Act, the Cuban embargo was essentially controlled under Presidential discretion through executive orders issued pursuant to delegation under the Trading With the Enemy Act.

108. http://uscode.house.gov/view.xhtml?path=/prelim@title22/chapter69&edition=prelim.

109. The Act also prohibited family remittances, most travel by U.S. citizens to Cuba, access to U.S. ports for vessels previously used in Cuban trade and foreign aid to countries trading with Cuba.

110. https://en.wikipedia.org/wiki/Helms%E2%80%93Burton_Act.

gaged in trade with Cuba), travel restrictions on corporate personnel and their families for doing Cuban business, and treble damages against those allegedly "trafficking" in certain property expropriated from American citizens by the Cuban government.

Helms-Burton evoked outrage by other governments and was roundly condemned by the EU, Britain, Canada and Mexico, among other U.S. trading partners. The EU challenged the Act before the WTO (later withdrawn) and passed a regulation, binding on all member states, which declared Helms-Burton's extraterritorial provisions unenforceable. The EU regulation, followed by similar legislation in other countries like Canada, also provided for a "claw back" action to recover back any U.S. liability created through application of Helms-Burton. The regulation also imposed penalties against U.S. companies and executives who pursued claims under the Act's trafficking provisions. In an interesting irony, paralleling U.S. "anti-boycott" legislation described below, several other countries, including the United Kingdom and Mexico, also passed laws punishing compliance with the Helm-Burton trade boycott.[111] In response, Presidents Clinton, Bush, and Obama have all continuously waived application of Helms-Burton's trafficking provisions under an exception created in the Act. In 2016, President Obama lifted certain trade restrictions[112] previously imposed through executive actions, although most trade is still prohibited by statute.

C. Anti-Boycott Legislation

1. Overview

U.S. law generally prohibits compliance or cooperation with foreign boycotts that are not sanctioned by our government. The primary anti-boycott legislation and resulting regulations (15 C.F.R. Part 760), enforced by BIS, are essentially aimed at the widespread boycott of Israel by a variety of Arab nations. The regulations generally prohibit knowingly refusing to do business with any person for boycott reasons or supplying certain information relating to such boycotts. Regulations applying this anti-boycott law are complex and conduct violating its prohibitions more subtle than blatant agreements not to do business with Israeli concerns. Review the following excerpts from the BIS website on Anti-Boycott Legislation:[113]

Primary Impact:

The Arab League boycott of Israel is the principal foreign economic boycott that U.S. companies must be concerned with today. The antiboycott laws,

---

111. The U.K. legislation, which was called, The Extraterritorial US Legislation (Protection of Trading Interests) Order 1996, also applied to U.S. sanctions against Iran and Libya. http://www.legislation.gov.uk/uksi/1996/3171/introduction/made.

112. http://www.politico.com/story/2016/10/obama-cuba-trade-openings-expanded-229789.

113. https://www.bis.doc.gov/index.php/enforcement/oac.

however, apply to all boycotts imposed by foreign countries that are unsanctioned by the United States.

Who Is Covered by the Laws?

The antiboycott provisions of the Export Administration Regulations (EAR) apply to the activities of U.S. persons in the interstate or foreign commerce of the United States. The term "U.S. person" includes all individuals, corporations and unincorporated associations resident in the United States, including the permanent domestic affiliates of foreign concerns. U.S. persons also include U.S. citizens abroad (except when they reside abroad and are employed by non-U.S. persons) and the controlled in fact affiliates of domestic concerns. The test for "controlled in fact" is the ability to establish the general policies or to control the day to day operations of the foreign affiliate.

The scope of the EAR, as defined by Section 8 of the EAA, is limited to actions taken with intent to comply with, further, or support an unsanctioned foreign boycott.

What do the Laws Prohibit?

Conduct that may be penalized under the TRA [1976 Tax Reform Act] and/or prohibited under the EAR includes:

- Agreements to refuse or actual refusal to do business with or in Israel or with blacklisted companies.
- Agreements to discriminate or actual discrimination against other persons based on race, religion, sex, national origin or nationality.
- Agreements to furnish or actual furnishing of information about business relationships with or in Israel or with blacklisted companies.
- Agreements to furnish or actual furnishing of information about the race, religion, sex, or national origin of another person.
- Implementing letters of credit containing prohibited boycott terms or conditions.

The TRA does not "prohibit" conduct, but denies tax benefits ("penalizes") for certain types of boycott-related agreements.

As noted in the above excerpt, violations of the anti-boycott provisions are triggered by an "intent to comply" with the boycott. Intent to comply, however, does not mean agreement with or desire to further the boycott but rather knowingly engaging in acts or omissions "for boycott reasons." A request for prohibited boycott compliance, even if buried in a boilerplate clause in transaction documents, may trigger application of the regulations and must be reported to BIS. Review the regulatory language and illustrations below regarding "refusals to do business." Precisely what must be shown to establish a violation of this particular restriction?

2. Key Regulatory Provisions Regarding Refusal to Do Business

Title 15, C.F.R. § 760.2

(a) *Refusals to do business.*

Prohibition Against Refusals To Do Business

(1) No United States person may: refuse, knowingly agree to refuse, require any other person to refuse, or knowingly agree to require any other person to refuse, to do business with or in a boycotted country, with any business concern organized under the laws of a boycotted country, with any national or resident of a boycotted country, or with any other person, when such refusal is pursuant to an agreement with the boycotting country, or a requirement of the boycotting country, or a request from or on behalf of the boycotting country.

(2) Generally, a refusal to do business under this section consists of action that excludes a person or country from a transaction for boycott reasons. This includes a situation in which a United States person chooses or selects one person over another on a boycott basis or takes action to carry out another person's boycott-based selection when he knows or has reason to know that the other person's selection is boycott-based.

(3) Refusals to do business which are prohibited by this section include not only specific refusals, but also refusals implied by a course or pattern of conduct. There need not be a specific offer and refusal to constitute a refusal to do business; a refusal may occur when a United States person has a financial or commercial opportunity and declines for boycott reasons to consider or accept it.

(4) A United States person's use of either a boycott-based list of persons with whom he will not deal (a so-called "blacklist") or a boycott-based list of persons with whom he will deal (a so-called "whitelist") constitutes a refusal to do business.

(5) An agreement by a United States person to comply generally with the laws of the boycotting country with which it is doing business or an agreement that local laws of the boycotting country shall apply or govern is not, in and of itself, a refusal to do business. . . .

(6) If, for boycott reasons, a United States general manager chooses one supplier over another, or enters into a contract with one supplier over another, or advises its client to do so, then the general manager's actions constitute a refusal to do business under this section. However, it is not a refusal to do business under this section for a United States person to provide management, procurement, or other pre-award services for another person so long as the provision of such pre-award services is customary for that firm (or industry of which the firm is a part), without regard to the boycotting or non-boycotting character of the countries in which they are performed, and the United States person, in providing such services, does not act to exclude a person or country from the transaction for boycott reasons, or otherwise take actions that are boycott-based. For example, a United States person under contract to provide general management services in connection with a construction project in

a boycotting country may compile lists of qualified bidders for the client if that service is a customary one and if persons who are qualified are not excluded from that list because they are blacklisted.

(7) With respect to post-award services, if a client makes a boycott-based selection, actions taken by the United States general manager or contractor to carry out the client's choice are themselves refusals to do business if the United States contractor knows or has reason to know that the client's choice was boycott-based. . . .

(8) An agreement is not a prerequisite to a violation of this section since the prohibition extends to actions taken pursuant not only to agreements but also to requirements of, and requests from or on behalf of, a boycotting country.

(9) Agreements under this section may be either express or implied by a course or pattern of conduct. There need not be a direct request from a boycotting country for action by a United States person to have been taken pursuant to an agreement with or requirement of a boycotting country.

(10) This prohibition, like all others, applies only with respect to a United States person's activities in the interstate or foreign commerce of the United States and only when such activities are undertaken with intent to comply with, further, or support an unsanctioned foreign boycott. The mere absence of a business relationship with or in the boycotted country, with any business concern organized under the laws of the boycotted country, with national(s) or resident(s) of the boycotted country, or with any other person does not indicate the existence of the required intent.

Examples of Refusals and Agreements to Refuse to Do Business

The following examples are intended to give guidance in determining the circumstances in which, in a boycott situation, a refusal to do business or an agreement to refuse to do business is prohibited. They are illustrative, not comprehensive.

Refusals To Do Business

(i) A, a U.S. manufacturer, receives an order for its products from boycotting country Y. To fill that order, A solicits bids from U.S. companies B and C, manufacturers of components used in A's products. A does not, however, solicit bids from U.S. companies D or E, which also manufacture such components, because it knows that D and E are restricted from doing business in Y and that their products are, therefore, not importable into that country.

Company A may not refuse to solicit bids from D and E for boycott reasons, because to do so would constitute a refusal to do business with those persons.

Definitions

. . . .

(e) "Intent".

(1) This part prohibits a United States person from taking or knowingly agreeing to take certain specified actions with intent to comply with, further, or support an unsanctioned foreign boycott.

(2) A United States person has the intent to comply with, further, or support an unsanctioned foreign boycott when such a boycott is at least one of the reasons for that person's decision whether to take a particular prohibited action. So long as that is at least one of the reasons for that person's action, a violation occurs regardless of whether the prohibited action is also taken for non-boycott reasons. Stated differently, the fact that such action was taken for legitimate business reasons does not remove that action from the scope of this part if compliance with an unsanctioned foreign boycott was also a reason for the action.

(3) Intent is a necessary element of any violation of any of the prohibitions under § 760.2. It is not sufficient that one take action that is specifically prohibited by this part. It is essential that one take such action with intent to comply with, further, or support an unsanctioned foreign boycott. Accordingly, a person who inadvertently, without boycott intent, takes a prohibited action, does not commit any violation of this part.

(4) Intent in this context means the reason or purpose for one's behavior. It does not mean that one has to agree with the boycott in question or desire that it succeed or that it be furthered or supported. But it does mean that the reason why a particular prohibited action was taken must be established.

(5) Reason or purpose can be proved by circumstantial evidence. For example, if a person receives a request to supply certain boycott information, the furnishing of which is prohibited by this part, and he knowingly supplies that information in response, he clearly intends to comply with that boycott request. It is irrelevant that he may disagree with or object to the boycott itself. Information will be deemed to be furnished with the requisite intent if the person furnishing the information knows that it was sought for boycott purposes. On the other hand, if a person refuses to do business with someone who happens to be blacklisted, but the reason is because that person produces an inferior product, the requisite intent does not exist.

(6) Actions will be deemed to be taken with intent to comply with an unsanctioned foreign boycott if the person taking such action knew that such action was required or requested for boycott reasons. On the other hand, the mere absence of a business relationship with a blacklisted person or with or in a boycotted country does not indicate the existence of the requisite intent.

(7) In seeking to determine whether the requisite intent exists, all available evidence will be examined.

3. Enforcement

BIS administers and enforces the anti-boycott regulations through its Office of Anti-Boycott Compliance.[114] Potential penalties are stiff. Here is its summary of enforcement:

---

114. https://www.bis.doc.gov/index.php/enforcement/oac.

Penalties:

The Export Administration Act (EAA) specifies penalties for violations of the Antiboycott Regulations as well as export control violations. These can include:

Criminal:

The penalties imposed for each "knowing" violation can be a fine of up to $50,000 or five times the value of the exports involved, whichever is greater, and imprisonment of up to five years. During periods when the EAR are continued in effect by an Executive Order issued pursuant to the International Emergency Economic Powers Act, the criminal penalties for each "willful" violation can be a fine of up to $50,000 and imprisonment for up to ten years.

Administrative:

For each violation of the EAR any or all of the following may be imposed:

- General denial of export privileges;
- The imposition of fines of up to $11,000 per violation; and/or
- Exclusion from practice.

Boycott agreements under the TRA involve the denial of all or part of the foreign tax benefits discussed above.

When the EAA is in lapse, penalties for violation of the Antiboycott Regulations are governed by the International Emergency Economic Powers Act (IEEPA). The IEEPA Enhancement Act provides for penalties of up to the greater of $250,000 per violation or twice the value of the transaction for administrative violations of Antiboycott Regulations, and up to $1 million and 20 years imprisonment per violation for criminal antiboycott violations.

A BIS Assistant Secretary for Export Enforcement <u>recently summarized</u>[115] an illustrative case:

OAC may impose civil penalties against U.S. businesses for taking actions in furtherance or support of an unsanctioned foreign boycott or for failing to report the receipt of a boycott-related request. In its case against Baker Eastern, SA (Libya), for example, OAC alleged that, Baker Eastern, on twenty-two occasions, furnished to Libyan customs in Libya a Certificate of Origin, each of which contained a statement regarding compliance with the Arab Boycott of Israel, as well as two items of prohibited information: a negative certificate of origin regarding the goods, and a blacklist certification regard-

---

115. https://www.bis.doc.gov/index.php/component/content/article/148-about-bis/newsroom /speeches/speeches-2014/719-keynote-speech-of-david-w-mills-assistant-secretary-for-export -enforcement-update-conference-july-30-2014

ing the producing company. Because Baker Eastern voluntarily disclosed these transactions to OAC and maintains an exceptional multinational compliance program, the company benefited from great weight mitigation in accordance with the Antiboycott Penalty Guidelines.

The Company agreed to pay $182,325 in fines.

Part Three: Export Promotion & Trade Agreement Compliance

The United States government expends enormous resources on export promotion. The two most important illustrations of this effort are 1) programs designed to facilitate, encourage and instruct potential exporters about foreign trade, and 2) trade negotiations and remedies aimed at trade agreement compliance and opening foreign markets.

A. Trade Promotion and Assistance Programs

The website portal "Export.gov," is maintained by the DOC's International Trade Administration (trade.gov) in coordination with 19 federal agencies. As reflected in its self-description below, the portal is perhaps the clearest example of government efforts to promote and facilitate foreign trade.

> Export.gov helps U.S. companies plan, develop and execute international sales strategies necessary to succeed in today's global marketplace. Developed by international trade specialists and economists, here you will find trusted market intelligence, practical advice and business tools to help you understand how to export, connect with foreign buyers, and expand operations in new markets.

Consistent with its mission, Export.gov maintains a series of links providing helpful information about exporting. The pages "Export Basics,"[116] and "Export Education"[117] illustrate this educational approach.

Export Basics Home

Are you ready to make international sales? *Export Basics* helps you assess your export readiness, understand what you need to know and consider before pursuing an international sales strategy, and, when you are ready, develop and implement your export strategy.

---

116. http://2016.export.gov/exportbasics/.
117. https://www.export.gov/Export-Education.

The subsequent sections of *Export Basics* (see navigation to the right) — starting with *Develop Your Export Plan* — will help you develop and implement your export plan. Each section corresponds to the key components of an effective export plan — posing questions you should answer to complete your plan and providing resources to help you answer those questions.

Start here!

- Take our Are you Export Ready?[118] online readiness assessment to find out if you're ready to pursue international sales. (Food and Agricultural Exporters[119])

- Read the ITA Blog on How the Commercial Service Helps Exporters[120]

- The U.S. Commercial Service is pleased to offer you 4 ways to learn exporting.[121]

- Need an introduction to exporting? Browse our step-by-step Basic Guide to Exporting.[122]

- Watch our Are You Ready?[123] and Going Beyond Borders[124] videos to hear a U.S. Commercial Officer talk about issues you should consider before going global and to hear from companies that have worked with the U.S. Commercial Service to make international sales.

- Watch educational videos on how to Take Your Business Global.[125] These videos discuss topics such as getting started, how to connect with your foreign buyer, and they highlight some case studies to show you just how easy it is to get started in exporting.

- Think export success is out of your reach? Read success stories[126] about how companies like yours are succeeding in the international marketplace.

- Learn to sell globally from your e-commerce site with our Preparing Your Business for Global E-Commerce: A Guide for Online Retailers to Manage Operations, Inventory, and Payment Issues[127] manual.

---

118. http://2016.export.gov/begin/assessment.asp.

119. http://www.usda.gov/wps/portal/%21ut/p/_s.7_0_A/7_0_1OB?navid=EXPORTING _GOODS&parentnav=MARKETING_TRADE&navtype=RT.

120. https://blog.trade.gov/2009/05/06/how-commercial-service-helps-exporters/.

121. http://2016.export.gov/exportbasics/eg_main_020141.asp.

122. http://2016.export.gov/basicguide/eg_main_017243.asp.

123. http://www.globalspeak.com/html/export-gov/webcasts.asp.

124. http://www.globalspeak.com/html/export-gov/webcasts.asp.

125. http://www.inc.com/exporting/.

126. http://2016.export.gov/articles/eg_main_021230.asp.

127. http://2016.export.gov/ecommerceguide/index.asp.

Frequently Asked Questions[128]

Go! If you are ready to begin developing your export plan, please proceed onto the next section,

Develop Your Export Plan[129]

Export Education Guide

Check out our comprehensive educational series on exporting . . . click on the links below to navigate between articles or use the drop-down menu to the left of the page.

Guides to Export:

> A Basic Guide To Export[130]

> Trade Finance Guide[131]

> eCommerce Guide[132]

> Export U — Free Webinars for new or novice exporters[133]

> Country Commercial Guides[134]

Export Walkthroughs:

---

128. http://2016.export.gov/exportbasics/eg_main_017462.asp.
129. http://2016.export.gov/exportbasics/eg_main_017448.asp.
130. https://www.export.gov/article2?id=Why-Companies-should-export.
131. https://www.export.gov/article2?id=Introduction.
132. https://www.export.gov/article?id=1-Guide-Overview.
133. http://www.export-u2.com/.
134. http://export.gov/ccg.

> Export Education <u>New</u> Video Series <u>Get Ready to Export!</u>[135] <u>Market Entry Strategy</u>[136] <u>Find Foreign buyers</u>[137] <u>Get Paid & Finance Export</u> <u>Transactions</u>[138] <u>Make the export Sale (New!)</u>[139] <u>You Should Export</u>[140]	**> Product Preparation** <u>Preparing Your Product</u>[141] <u>Product Classification</u>[142] <u>Rules of Origin</u>[143] <u>Foreign Standards & Certifications</u>[144]
> Finding Foreign Markets <u>Choosing a Foreign</u> <u>Representative</u>[145] <u>Evaluating Foreign</u> <u>Representatives</u>[146] <u>Finding Buyers</u>[147] <u>Sales Channels</u>[148] <u>Market Research</u>[149] <u>Free Trade Agreements</u>[150]	**> Logistics** <u>Shipping</u>[151] <u>Documentation</u>[152] <u>Certificates of Origin</u>[153] <u>Trade Problems</u>[154]

---

135. https://www.export.gov/article?id=Get-Ready-to-Export.
136. https://www.export.gov/article?id=Market-Entry-Strategy.
137. https://www.export.gov/article?id=Finding-Foreign-Buyers-Videos.
138. https://www.export.gov/article?id=2-4-Get-Paid-and-Finance-Your-Export-Transaction -Videos.
139. https://www.export.gov/article?id=2-5-Make-the-Export-Sale.
140. https://www.export.gov/article?id=You-Should-Export.
141. https://www.export.gov/article?id=Preparing-your-product-for-export.
142. https://www.export.gov/article?id=Find-HS-Code.
143. https://www.export.gov/article?id=Rules-of-Origin.
144. https://www.export.gov/article?id=Foreign-Standards-and-Certification.
145. https://www.export.gov/article?id=Choosing-a-Foreign-Representative.
146. https://www.export.gov/article?id=Evaluating-foreign-representatives.
147. https://www.export.gov/article?id=Finding-Buyers.
148. https://www.export.gov/article?id=Choosing-a-Sales-Channel.
149. https://www.export.gov/article?id=Getting-Started.
150. https://www.export.gov/article?id=U-S-Free-Trade-Agreements—Introduction.
151. https://www.export.gov/article?id=1-Export-Compliance.
152. https://export.gov/article2?id=U-S-Compliance-related-Documents.
153. https://export.gov/article2?id=Certificates-of-Origin.
154. https://export.gov/article2?id=Advocacy-Center.

>Legal Considerations	>Financial Considerations
Legal Issues[155] Regulations[156] Intellectual Property[157]	Export Financing[158] Pricing[159] Methods of Payment[160] Risk Management[161]
>eCommerce eCommerce[162]	

Prepared by the International Trade Administration. With its network of 108 offices across the United States and in more than 75 countries, the International Trade Administration of the U.S. Department of Commerce utilizes its global presence and international marketing expertise to help U.S. companies sell their products and services worldwide. Locate the trade specialist in the U.S. nearest you by visiting http://export.gov/usoffices.

Links and information provided on the Export.gov and Trade.gov web pages are designed to promote U.S. trade by assisting potential exporters in a multitude of ways. Peruse those sites and the following additional websites which provide good examples of the federal government's effort to promote exports and are important resources for lawyers.

- U.S. Commercial Service[163]

    Described as the "trade promotion arm of the Department of Commerce's International Trade Administration." Among others, follow the link "Services for U.S. Companies,"[164] which includes information on "trade counseling, market intelligence, business matchmaking, and commercial diplomacy."

- United States Trade Representative's "Trade Toolbox."[165]

    Provides linked resources such as Commonly Used Trade Acronyms,[166] Country Profiles,[167] Export Assistance,[168] Free Trade Agreements Tariff

---

155. https://www.export.gov/article?id=Help-Getting-Paid.
156. http://export.gov/article?id=Regulation.
157. https://www.export.gov/article?id=Privacy-Shield-Safe-Harbor.
158. https://export.gov/article2?id=Export-Financing.
159. https://export.gov/article2?id=Tariffs-Taxes.
160. http://www.export.gov/article2?id=How-to-Get-Paid.
161. https://www.export.gov/article?id=Insurance-and-Risk-Mitigation.
162. https://www.export.gov/eCommerce.
163. http://www.trade.gov/cs/.
164. http://www.trade.gov/cs/services.asp.
165. https://ustr.gov/trade-topics/trade-toolbox.
166. https://ustr.gov/about-us/trade-toolbox/commonly-used-trade-acronyms.
167. https://ustr.gov/about-us/trade-toolbox/country-profiles.
168. https://ustr.gov/trade-topics/trade-toolbox/export-assistance.

Tool,[169] Glossary of Trade Terms,[170] Trade Data,[171] Trade Laws,[172] Trade Links,[173] and U.S. Government Trade Agencies.[174]

- U.S. Small Business Association's "US Export Assistance Center"[175]

  Provides lists of regional "Export Assistance Centers" with an emphasis on export financing assistance[176] programs.

Somewhat in contrast to this outward oriented economic policy, the U.S. Government also heavily invests in attracting foreign capital to invest in the United States. If curious, take a look at "SelectUSA"[177] for an illustration.

B. Trade Compliance Remedies & Opening Markets

1. Overview

United States law provides a number of mechanisms which are designed to counter or even retaliate against what Congress considers "unfair trade." These mechanisms, which include actions under §301 of the 1974 Trade Act, and complaints before international trade organizations such as the WTO and NAFTA, are generally administered by the International Trade Administration. The Trade Agreement Compliance Program[178] of the ITA monitors compliance with international trade agreements, as well as identifying market access barriers, and negotiating for improvements. The Trade Compliance Center,[179] as reflected in the following excerpt from its FAQ page, works to eliminate barriers identified by U.S. exporters through negotiation.

Frequently Asked Questions

How does the TCC try to solve trade barrier problems?

If the TCC, in conjunction with other U.S. government trade experts, believes that the trade barrier problem may be the result of a foreign country failing to live up to an obligation under a trade agreement with the United States, the TCC works through senior U.S. government officials and U.S. embassies to get the foreign government to come into compliance with its

---

169. https://ustr.gov/trade-topics/trade-toolbox/free-trade-agreements-tariff-tool.
170. https://ustr.gov/about-us/trade-toolbox/glossary-trade-terms.
171. https://ustr.gov/trade-topics/trade-toolbox/trade-data.
172. https://ustr.gov/about-us/trade-toolbox/trade-laws.
173. https://ustr.gov/trade-topics/trade-toolbox/trade-links.
174. https://ustr.gov/about-us/trade-toolbox/us-government-trade-agencies.
175. https://www.sba.gov/tools/local-assistance/eac.
176. https://www.sba.gov/managing-business/exporting/export-loans/financing-your-small-business-exports.
177. https://www.selectusa.gov/welcome.
178. http://tcc.export.gov/trade_agreements_compliance/index.asp.
179. http://tcc.export.gov/index.asp.

agreement. U.S. government experts will assemble the facts and show officials of the other country why we believe the particular instance is not consistent with their agreement.

The Secretary, Under Secretary of Commerce for International Trade and other high-level officials may contact their counterparts in the other country if necessary.

How does the TCC work?

The TCC works by putting together teams of U.S. government trade experts to focus on the trade problems U.S. companies are facing. The first thing the TCC does when it is informed of a problem is to see if one of the about 250 multilateral or bilateral U.S. trade agreements gives the United States some rights in the particular situation. The TCC then utilizes the existing expertise of the appropriate parts of the U.S. government, and seeks to have this expertise work quickly and efficiently to solve the problems.

What happens if the other country does not remove the barrier?

If the compliance process begun by the TCC does not result in resolving the problem, and if the officials of the foreign country cannot be convinced to act positively, then the U.S. government may examine whether we should turn toward active enforcement of our trade rights.

Agreements such as the WTO and NAFTA provide for enforceable dispute settlement. If the TCC is unable to achieve voluntary compliance on the part of the other country, we then turn to USTR's Enforcement Office and seek to have the problem considered for dispute settlement procedures.

This link provides a list of ITA "success stories"[180] in alleged trade restrictions resolved through active agency intervention (also see "Program Results"[181] and this 6 minute video case study[182]).

The Trade Compliance Center website also offers both a list of problems and barriers as well as a complaint link called "Report a Trade Barrier."[183]

Foreign Trade Barrier Examples[184]

Though there are many different ways that foreign governments can discriminate against U.S. exports and investment, the following are the most common foreign government-imposed trade barriers that U.S. companies encounter abroad:

---

180. http://tcc.export.gov/success_stories/successes_by_industry.asp.
181. http://tcc.export.gov/program_results/index.asp.
182. http://trade.gov/videos/tcc-klinge.mp4.
183. http://tcc.export.gov/Report_a_Barrier/index.asp.
184. http://tcc.export.gov/report_a_barrier/trade_barrier_examples/index.asp.

- High or Unfairly Applied Tariffs[185]

- Classification and Customs Barriers at the Border[186]

- Burdensome Rule of Origin, Certificate of Origin, or Import licensing Requirements[187]

- Technical Barriers to Trade—Unfair Standards, Testing, Labeling, or Certification Requirements[188]

- Unfair Sanitary and Phytosanitary (SPS)—Animal and Plant Welfare—Measures[189]

- Discrimination in Government Procurement[190]

- Intellectual Property Rights Protection Problems[191]

- Excessive or Unfair Government Requirements Related to Investment or Taxation[192]

- Import Licensing[193]

- Concerns about Corruption[194]

- Barriers to Services Provision[195]

- Discriminatory Competition Laws or Unfair Competition from State-Owned Enterprises[196]

If unsure whether you're facing a foreign trade barrier, ask yourself these questions.[197]

If you answered **yes** to any of these questions, you may be facing an unfair trade barrier. Contact us[198] today to report it so that the United States Government can begin working with you to remove the unfair treatment and restore your access to the market.

---

185. http://tcc.export.gov/report_a_barrier/trade_barrier_examples/tariff_barriers.asp.

186. http://tcc.export.gov/report_a_barrier/trade_barrier_examples/customs_barriers.asp.

187. http://tcc.export.gov/report_a_barrier/trade_barrier_examples/rules_of_origin_barriers
.asp.

188. http://tcc.export.gov/report_a_barrier/trade_barrier_examples/certifications_barriers.asp.

189. http://tcc.export.gov/report_a_barrier/trade_barrier_examples/sps_measures.asp.

190. http://tcc.export.gov/report_a_barrier/trade_barrier_examples/government_procure
ment_barriers.asp.

191. http://tcc.export.gov/report_a_barrier/trade_barrier_examples/ipp_problems.asp.

192. http://tcc.export.gov/report_a_barrier/trade_barrier_examples/excessive_unfair_govt
_requirements.asp.

193. http://tcc.export.gov/report_a_barrier/trade_barrier_examples/import_licensing.asp.

194. http://tcc.export.gov/report_a_barrier/trade_barrier_examples/bribery.asp.

195. http://tcc.export.gov/report_a_barrier/trade_barrier_examples/services_barriers.asp.

196. http://tcc.export.gov/report_a_barrier/trade_barrier_examples/competition_laws.asp.

197. http://tcc.export.gov/report_a_barrier/trade_barrier_examples/questions.asp.

198. http://tcc.export.gov/Additional_Info/Contact_TCC/index.asp.

2. Section 301 Investigations

If a reported trade barrier is not resolved through negotiation, more direct legal remedies, such as resort to international dispute settlement or to § 301 investigations under the jurisdiction of the U.S. Trade Representative, may follow. Sections 301-310 of the 1974 Trade Act (19 U.S.C. § 2411) authorize enforcement of U.S. trade agreements and other "international" trade principles through investigation of foreign government practices and retaliation for violations. Originally, § 301 authorized the USTR, after investigation, to recommend unilateral sanctions to be imposed by the President. However, since such unilateral actions are manifestly inconsistent with our obligations under the WTO and other international agreements, U.S. agencies now must first seek recourse before international dispute settlement processes, as the ITA describes in the following excerpt:

U.S. Retaliations[199]

Section 301 is the principal statutory authority under which the United States may impose trade sanctions on foreign countries that either violate trade agreements or otherwise maintain laws or practices that are unjustifiable and restrict U.S. commerce. When an investigation involves an alleged violation of a trade agreement (such as the World Trade Organization (WTO) Agreement or the North American Free Trade Agreement (NAFTA)), United States Trade Representative (USTR) must follow the consultation and dispute settlement procedures set out in that agreement. If the United States finds it necessary to increase duties because of a violation of the WTO, USTR will seek authority from the WTO's Dispute Settlement Body to suspend trade concessions previously granted to the foreign country. Such actions include increasing import duties.

As of January 19, 2017, the USTR website[200] listed the Obama administration's "consistent record of success" in this process, touting 23 successful complaints before the WTO since 2009, including a focus on China (e.g., high-tech steel,[201] rare earths,[202] auto parts subsidies,[203] poultry imports,[204] tires,[205] electronic payment services[206] and, more recently, agricultural subsidies,[207] aircraft[208] and minerals[209]).

---

199. http://www.trade.gov/mas/ian/tradedisputes-enforcement/retaliations/tg_ian_002103.asp.

200. https://ustr.gov/issue-areas/enforcement.

201. https://www.wto.org/english/tratop_e/dispu_e/cases_e/ds252_e.htm.

202. https://ustr.gov/about-us/policy-offices/press-office/press-releases/2015/may/statement-us-trade-representative.

203. https://www.wto.org/english/tratop_e/dispu_e/cases_e/ds340_e.htm.

204. https://www.wto.org/english/tratop_e/dispu_e/cases_e/ds427_e.htm.

205. https://piie.com/publications/policy-briefs/us-tire-tariffs-saving-few-jobs-high-cost.

206. https://www.wto.org/english/tratop_e/dispu_e/cases_e/ds373_e.htm.

207. https://www.bloomberg.com/news/articles/2016-09-13/u-s-files-wto-trade-case-against-chinese-agricultural-subsidies.

208. https://www.wto.org/english/tratop_e/dispu_e/cases_e/ds501_e.htm.

209. thehill.com/policy/finance/trade/288373-us-eu-team-up-on-raw-minerals-trade-case-against-china.

One suspects, perhaps forewarned by a late night "tweet," that this perspective may disappear from the USTR website in 2017.

The following excerpt from <u>China Law Insight</u>[210] provides a good illustration of how the process now works.

Section 301 of the Trade Act of 1974

The United Steelworkers (USW) submitted a Section 301 petition to the United States Trade Representative (USTR) on Sept. 9, 2010 (19 U.S.C. 2411-2420; "Section 301"). The petition alleges that China employs a wide range of World Trade Organization (WTO)-inconsistent policies that protect and unfairly support its domestic producers of wind and solar energy products, advanced batteries, energy-efficient vehicles, and other clean technology industries. Under Section 301, the USTR has 45 days to decide whether to respond to the petition by initiating an investigation or denying it. In this instance, the USTR initiated the investigation on Oct. 15, 2010. The USTR has elected to delay the government to government consultation for the purpose verifying or improving the petition to ensure to prepare for consultation with China. The USTR has published a summary of the petition and is seeking public comment (75 FR 64776-64778 October 20, 2010). During this time the USTR will also be seeking information and advice from petitioner and advisory committees. Public comments and advisory committee advice will be taken into account by the USTR to improve and verify the petition. Section 301 does not require the U.S. government to wait for authorization from the WTO before instituting remedial enforcement actions, but the U.S. has committed to abiding by the WTO dispute settlement mechanism. Failure to obtain approval by the WTO before issuing sanctions would be a violation of the US commitments to the WTO.

3. Special 301

Section 182 of the Trade Act of 1974, 19 U.S.C. § 2242(a)(1)(A) & (B) (creating Section 301 procedures), also specifically addresses alleged violations of intellectual property interests. Commonly known as "Special 301," this provision requires the USTR to identify and monitor countries that fail to adequately protect intellectual property rights or deny market access to businesses reliant on such protections.

In theory, failure to address such concerns could lead to a full blown Section 301 investigation as described above. In practice, the USTR creates an annual "Watch List," "Priority Watch List," and "<u>Notorious Markets List</u>."[211] It also regularly undertakes "Out of Cycle Reviews" (<u>OCRs</u>) of countries and markets. The <u>USTR's press</u>

---

210. http://www.chinalawinsight.com/2010/10/articles/dispute-resolution/china-clean-tech-at-risk-initiation-of-the-recent-section-301-investigation/.

211. https://ustr.gov/sites/default/files/2016-Out-of-Cycle-Review-Notorious-Markets.pdf.

release summary[212] of Special 301 Report for 2016[213] reflects how the United States utilizes this process to pressure our trading partners toward enhanced protection for intellectual property rights, a mainstay of the U.S. economy.

USTR reviewed seventy-three (73) trading partners for this year's Special 301 Report, and placed thirty-four (34) of them on the Priority Watch List or Watch List.

In this year's Report, trading partners on the Priority Watch List present the most significant concerns this year regarding insufficient IPR protection or enforcement or actions that otherwise limited market access for persons relying on intellectual property protection. Eleven (11) countries—Algeria, Argentina, Chile, China, India, Indonesia, Kuwait, Russia, Thailand, Ukraine, and Venezuela—are on the Priority Watch List. These countries will be the subject of particularly intense bilateral engagement during the coming year.

Twenty-three (23) trading partners are on the Watch List, and also merit bilateral attention to address underlying IPR problems: Barbados, Bolivia, Brazil, Bulgaria, Canada, Colombia, Costa Rica, Dominican Republic, Ecuador, Egypt, Greece, Guatemala, Jamaica, Lebanon, Mexico, Pakistan, Peru, Romania, Switzerland, Turkey, Turkmenistan, Uzbekistan, and Vietnam.

USTR also announces that it will launch several OCRs to enhance engagement with trading partners and encourage progress on IPR issues of concern. USTR will conduct an OCR of Watch List countries Colombia and Pakistan, as well as of two countries not currently listed, Spain and Tajikistan. Details appear in Section II of the Report. USTR may conduct additional OCRs of other trading partners as circumstances warrant or as requested by the trading partner.

---

212. https://ustr.gov/about-us/policy-offices/press-office/press-releases/2016/april/ustr-releases-special-301-report.

213. https://ustr.gov/sites/default/files/USTR-2016-Special-301-Report.pdf.

Chapter 12

Free Trade Areas, Customs Unions and Trade Preference Programs for Lesser Developed Countries

A. Overview

One of the cornerstone obligations of the GATT legal regime is to extend most favored nation (MFN) treatment to all WTO members for "like products." This obligation is, essentially, a principle of non-discrimination based on the origin of goods. There are several significant exceptions to this obligation, however. The two most important of these exceptions are the focus of this chapter. First, WTO members are allowed to create and join free trade areas and customs unions, referred to as "regional trade arrangements" (RTAs) by the WTO, without extending the same tariff preferences to the entire WTO membership. Second, members are allowed to create special unilateral trade preference programs for poor, lesser developed countries (called Preferential Trade Agreements or PTAs).

Part One: Free Trade Areas and Customs Unions

A. Overview

Our goal regarding regional trade arrangements, essentially free trade areas and customs unions, is to understand how they generally function and identify some of the common legal issues they create. We will review both NAFTA and the EU as illustrations of free trade areas and customs unions, respectively. The EU is obviously much more than simply a customs union, and the materials will draw some contrasts in this regard to other trade-related institutions. Problem 12 below, loosely based on a real company, is not so much a problem in need of analysis as it is a focal point for discussion about critical attributes and benefits of free trade arrangements and differences between them. Review the materials that follow the problem (or other sources you might find) to answer the questions posed in the assignment below.

B. Problem Twelve: Moving Dirt World-Wide

1. Facts

Doosan Infrastructure[1] is a South Korean company that produces, among other products, heavy construction equipment such as front end loaders, excavators and other earth moving equipment. All of its products are currently manufactured in South Korea. The company has strong overseas sales in some regions, particularly in Asia, but hopes to expand its market significantly throughout both North America and Europe.

Doosan currently has sales dealers and agencies in the U.S., UK, Germany, China, India, Japan and Brazil—all countries where the company has growing

---

sales. It is also considering an investment in manufacturing capacity overseas, including the potential purchase of existing brands such as the Bobcat Company of Fargo, North Dakota.

2. Assignment

Evaluate how a free trade agreement like NAFTA, or a customs union like the European Union Customs Union, might affect Doosan's evaluation of how best to achieve its expansion goals. The following questions will assist you in finding the information you need to evaluate Doosan's options.

General:

- What are the basic GATT rules and limitations on the formation and maintenance of free trade areas and customs unions?
- What are the essential differences between a free trade area and a customs union?
- Why might the differences in tariff practices between free trade areas and customs unions matter to an international business for purposes of sales and business planning?

NAFTA:

- What is the substantive scope of NAFTA?
- How does NAFTA determine the origin of goods and why does this matter?
- What is the institutional structure of NAFTA (including, in particular, dispute settlement arrangements)?

EU:

- What are the primary institutions of the EU and what are their respective roles?
- How is NAFTA different from the EU?
- How is the respective institutional structure of NAFTA and the EU different from the WTO? (Think here not just about the administration of each legal regime but also powers, functions, decision-making authority, constituencies and relationship to domestic law.)

C. Resources

1. Overview

According to the WTO, it's entire membership is involved in at least one "regional trade agreement," which includes both free trade areas and customs unions. The WTO "Maps" page[2] provides a variety of charts illustrating the distribution of such

---

2. https://www.wto.org/english/res_e/maps_e/maps_e.htm#rta.

agreements. The WTO "Regional Trade Agreement Gateway"[3] describes the increasing reliance on RTAs in world trade.

Regional Trade Agreements

As of 1st July 2016, some 635 notifications of RTAs (counting goods, services and accessions separately) had been received by the GATT/WTO. Of these, 435 notifications were made under Article XXIV of the GATT 1947 or GATT 1994; 43 under the Enabling Clause; and 157 under Article V of the GATS. Of these 635 RTAs, 423 were in force.

The overall number of RTAs in force has been increasingly steadily, a trend likely to be strengthened by the many RTAs currently under negotiations. Of these RTAs, Free Trade Agreements (FTAs) and partial scope agreements account for 90%, while customs unions account for 10%.

For up-to-date information on WTO figures on RTAs currently in force, please consult the summary tables contained in the RTA Database.[4]

These WTO figures correspond to 460 physical RTAs (counting goods, services and accessions together), of which 267 are currently in force.

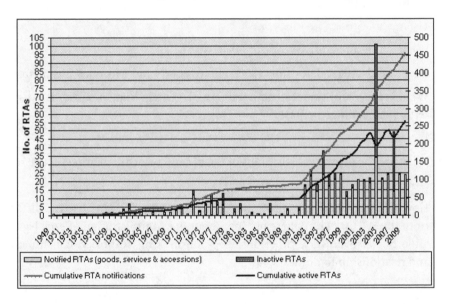

A free trade area, typically created through an international treaty, essentially eliminates tariffs and quotas between the participants for most goods. Other restrictions on trade are sometimes also eliminated, and many agreements extend to services, intellectual property and capital investments. The parties to such agreements continue to maintain their respective prior tariff practices with regard to products originating in all other countries.

---

3. https://www.wto.org/english/tratop_e/region_e/region_e.htm.
4. http://rtais.wto.org/UI/PublicMaintainRTAHome.aspx.

The chart below, with web links following, shows the worldwide distribution of such agreements (<u>from Wikipedia</u>[5]).

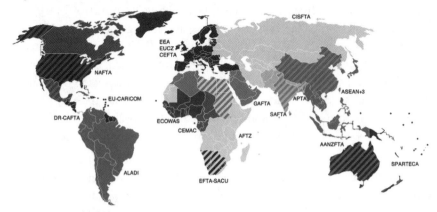

- <u>ASEAN Free Trade Area</u> (AFTA)[6]
- <u>Asia-Pacific Trade Agreement</u> (APTA)[7]
- <u>Central American Integration System</u> (SICA)[8]
- <u>Central European Free Trade Agreement</u> (CEFTA)[9]
- <u>Common Market for Eastern and Southern Africa</u> (COMESA)[10]
- <u>G-3 Free Trade Agreement</u> (G-3)[11]
- <u>Greater Arab Free Trade Area</u> (GAFTA) — June 1957[12]
- <u>Gulf Cooperation Council</u> (GCC)[13]
- <u>North American Free Trade Agreement</u> (NAFTA)[14]
- <u>South Asia Free Trade Agreement</u> (SAFTA)[15]
- <u>Southern African Development Community</u> (SADC)[16]
- <u>Southern Common Market</u> (MERCOSUR)[17]
- <u>Trans-Pacific Strategic Economic Partnership</u> (TPP)[18]

---

5. https://upload.wikimedia.org/wikipedia/commons/6/6a/Free_Trade_Areas.PNG.
6. https://en.wikipedia.org/wiki/ASEAN_Free_Trade_Area.
7. https://en.wikipedia.org/wiki/Asia-Pacific_Trade_Agreement.
8. https://en.wikipedia.org/wiki/Central_American_Integration_System.
9. https://en.wikipedia.org/wiki/Central_European_Free_Trade_Agreement.
10. https://en.wikipedia.org/wiki/Common_Market_for_Eastern_and_Southern_Africa.
11. https://en.wikipedia.org/wiki/G3_Free_Trade_Agreement.
12. https://en.wikipedia.org/wiki/Council_of_Arab_Economic_Unity#Greater_Arab_Free_Trade_Area.
13. https://en.wikipedia.org/wiki/Gulf_Cooperation_Council.
14. https://en.wikipedia.org/wiki/North_American_Free_Trade_Agreement.
15. https://en.wikipedia.org/wiki/South_Asian_Free_Trade_Area.
16. https://en.wikipedia.org/wiki/Southern_African_Development_Community.
17. http://www.mercosur.int/.
18. https://en.wikipedia.org/wiki/Trans-Pacific_Strategic_Economic_Partnership_Agreement.

The United States has been, at least until the 2017 Presidential election, a consistent promoter of free trade agreements. Export.gov[19] asserts that the United States was, as of January 2017, party to 14 free trade agreements involving 20 countries. The USTR web site[20] states that the United States now has free trade arrangements with 20 countries. The latest initiative was the "Trans-Pacific Partnership"[21] involving the United States and 11 other countries (Australia, Brunei Darussalam, Canada, Chile, Malaysia, New Zealand, Peru, Singapore, Japan, and Vietnam) in the Pacific region. Although near completion under the Obama administration, the TPP has an uncertain future[22] in light of Donald Trump's election, and official U.S. withdrawal from the arrangement. In a bit of hyperbole, celebrations in Beijing have been suggested[23] by the media.

A customs union is essentially a free trade area in which participants have also agreed to maintain a common external tariff for all goods entering the union from non-participating countries. An important feature of a customs union is the "free circulation" of goods that have entered the customs territory. Since a common tariff is maintained for all countries within the customs union, imports are subject to tariff only upon first entry and thereafter may move freely within the union territory without additional payments. The Wikipedia chart below,[24] with web links following, illustrates the spread of customs unions around the world.

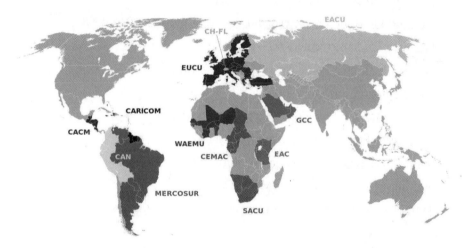

European Union Customs Union[25]

Eurasian Customs Union[26]

---

19. http://2016.export.gov/fta/.

20. https://ustr.gov/trade-agreements/free-trade-agreements.

21. https://ustr.gov/.

22. http://www.abc.net.au/news/2016-11-22/could-the-trans-pacific-partnership-survive-if-the-us-pulls-out/8047834.

23. http://www.bbc.com/news/world-asia-china-38060980.

24. https://en.wikipedia.org/wiki/Customs_union.

25. https://en.wikipedia.org/wiki/European_Union_Customs_Union.

26. https://en.wikipedia.org/wiki/Eurasian_Customs_Union.

Mercosur[27]

Andean Community[28]

East African Community[29]

Southern African Customs Union[30]

Gulf Cooperation Council[31]

Switzerland–Liechtenstein

Caribbean Community[32]

Central American Common Market[33]

West African Economic and Monetary Union[34]

The EU began as, and has continued to maintain, a European customs union[35] (1957 European Economic Community, renamed European Community in 1993, then absorbed into EU in 2009). It has, however, substantially evolved into a European-wide government for many fundamental purposes through the evolution of common economic policy, free circulation of people, a common currency (for the 19 members of the "Euro-Zone"[36]), and fully functional governmental institutions with binding authority.

2. GATT Rules on Regional Trade Agreements

The WTO and the GATT have long recognized that regional trade agreements have both the potential to promote trade and cause detriment to those outside the trade area. Current rules require notification of RTA negotiations ("Transparency Mechanism"[37]) and that the final agreement comport with WTO rules. The WTO excerpt below describes and provides links to these rules, as well as rules governing preferential programs for developing countries. Follow the link to GATT Article XXIV. *What are its essential requirements (pay particular attention to paragraph 5)?*

> When a WTO member enters into a regional integration arrangement through which it grants more favourable conditions to its trade with other parties to that arrangement than to other WTO members' trade, it departs

---

27. https://en.wikipedia.org/wiki/Mercosur.

28. https://en.wikipedia.org/wiki/Andean_Community.

29. https://en.wikipedia.org/wiki/East_African_Community.

30. https://en.wikipedia.org/wiki/Southern_African_Customs_Union.

31. https://en.wikipedia.org/wiki/Gulf_Cooperation_Council.

32. https://en.wikipedia.org/wiki/Caribbean_Community.

33. https://en.wikipedia.org/wiki/Central_American_Integration_System.

34. https://en.wikipedia.org/wiki/Economic_Community_of_West_African_States#West_African_Economic_and_Monetary_Union.

35. https://europa.eu/european-union/topics/customs_en.

36. https://en.wikipedia.org/wiki/Eurozone.

37. https://www.wto.org/english/tratop_e/region_e/trans_mecha_e.htm.

from the guiding principle of non-discrimination defined in Article I of GATT, Article II of GATS, and elsewhere.

WTO Members are however permitted to enter into such arrangements under specific conditions which are spelled out in three sets of rules:

- <u>Paragraphs 4 to 10 of Article XXIV of GATT</u>[38] (as clarified in the Understanding on the Interpretation of Article XXIV of the GATT 1994) provide for the formation and operation of customs unions and free-trade areas covering trade in goods;

- The so-called <u>Enabling Clause</u>[39] (i.e., the 1979 Decision on Differential and More Favorable Treatment, Reciprocity and Fuller Participation of Developing Countries) refers to preferential trade arrangements in trade in goods between developing country Members; and

- <u>Article V of GATS</u>[40] governs the conclusion of RTAs in the area of trade in services, for both developed and developing countries.

Other non-generalized preferential schemes, for example non-reciprocal preferential agreements involving developing and developed countries, require Members to seek a waiver from WTO rules. Such waivers require the approval of three quarters of WTO Members. Examples of such agreements which are currently in force include the US-Caribbean Basin Economic Recovery Act (CBERA), the CARIBCAN agreement whereby Canada offers duty-free non-reciprocal access to most Caribbean countries, Turkey-Preferential treatment for Bosnia-Herzegovina and the EC-ACP Partnership Agreement.

3. Free Trade Areas: The NAFTA Model

Review the following links to answer the questions posed in the assignment and to gain a general understanding of NAFTA and the debate about free trade agreements more generally. Think particularly about the substantive scope of NAFTA (what general trade rules does it provide and over what subjects), its limited institutional framework and its approach to dispute settlement.

i. US Government Overviews: <u>Export.gov</u>[41] and <u>USTR</u>[42]

ii. <u>Substantive Scope</u>:[43] (joint website of the U.S., Canadian and Mexican national governments)

---

38. https://www.wto.org/english/tratop_e/region_e/regatt_e.htm.
39. https://www.wto.org/english/docs_e/legal_e/enabling1979_e.htm.
40. https://www.wto.org/english/docs_e/legal_e/26-gats_01_e.htm#articleV.
41. http://2016.export.gov/fta/NAFTA/.
42. https://ustr.gov/trade-agreements/free-trade-agreements/north-american-free-trade-agreement-nafta.
43. http://www.naftanow.org/agreement/default_en.asp.

iii. The <u>Institution Framework</u>[44] and <u>Dispute Settlement</u>[45]

iv. <u>Rules of Origin</u>[46] (more <u>technical version here</u>[47])

v. Public Citizen, <u>NAFTA's Broken Promises</u>[48]

vi. Illustrative Dispute: <u>Mexican Trucks</u>[49]

4. Customs Union and Beyond: EU and Its Evolution

The EU is both complex and comprehensive—so much so that most law schools offer at least one, and often several, courses devoted to it. Our goal for this class is very limited. The goal is not to study the EU generally but rather simply review its function as a customs union and consider its primary institutional features. Visit the following links to answer the questions posed in the assignment at the begin-

---

44. http://www.naftanow.org/about/default_en.asp.

45. https://www.nafta-sec-alena.org/Home/Dispute-Settlement/Overview-of-the-Dispute-Settlement-Provisions.

46. 2016.export.gov/FTA/nafta/eg_main_017791.asp.

47. https://www.google.com/url?sa=t&rct=j&q=&esrc=s&source=web&cd=2&cad=rja&uact=8&ved=0ahUKEwiY_d2PmLbRAhXl64MKHbrtA7wQFggeMAE&url=https%3A%2F%2Fwww.usitc.gov%2Felearning%2Fhts%2Fmedia%2F2017%2FRulesofOrigina.pdf&usg=AFQjCNFjDVZEhbzvjJk160WStGIEY197gw&sig2=2sc665WsJ1b-2PVTQAb1nQ.

48. https://www.google.com/url?sa=t&rct=j&q=&esrc=s&source=web&cd=4&cad=rja&uact=8&ved=0ahUKEwjWxr2dgrbRAhUL6IMKHU_VDrsQjBAIJTAD&url=http%3A%2F%2Fwww.citizen.org%2Fdocuments%2FNAFTAs-Broken-Promises.pdf&usg=AFQjCNH5KPia0dVpt2V3XncEij1zU27-IA&sig2=IBh5IP1UY7DYBnKwT4Nh9A.

49. http://www.trade.gov/mas/ian/tradedisputes-enforcement/retaliations/tg_ian_002094.asp.

ning of Part One, above. *How is the EU different from NAFTA and other free trade arrangements?*

> i. Generally: About the EU.[50]

> ii. Institutions: (follow links from portal above) and read Wikipedia's overview[51] or Dadalos[52] (UNESCO).

> iii. The EU as Customs Union.[53]

5. The Future of Multi-Lateral Free Trade Agreements

The 2016 U.S. presidential campaign brought into the public spotlight, although void of factual illumination, competing arguments over the relative merits of free trade agreements. Candidate Trump derided NAFTA as "the worst deal ever," claiming that it, and free trade generally, was the source of declining manufacturing jobs in the United States. Whatever the merits of this factually questionable position (*see* Congressional Research Service,[54] CNN Money,[55] New York Times,[56] *but see Trade, Not Productivity*[57]), it has become clear that free trade is beginning to resemble yet another "third rail" of American politics and economic policy.

The Trans-Pacific Partnership[58] agreement, negotiated over a seven year span between 12 Pacific Rim countries—Japan, the United States, Malaysia, Vietnam, Singapore, Brunei, Australia, New Zealand, Canada, Mexico, Chile and Peru (and notably not China)—is DOA in the U.S. Congress. The future for approval of TTIP, the Transatlantic Trade and Investment Partnership,[59] a proposed agreement between the U.S. and European trading partners, looks equally bleak.[60] It is worth noting that some opposition to such agreements is not strictly based on hyper-populist notions of protectionism. Critics, like Professor Tim Canova,[61] have also argued that

---

50. https://europa.eu/european-union/about-eu_en.

51. https://en.wikipedia.org/wiki/Institutions_of_the_European_Union.

52. http://www.dadalos-europe.org/int/grundkurs4/eu-struktur_1.htm.

53. http://ec.europa.eu/taxation_customs/general-information-customs/eu-customs-strategy_en.

54. https://www.fas.org/sgp/crs/row/R42965.pdf.

55. http://money.cnn.com/2016/03/29/news/economy/us-manufacturing-jobs/.

56. https://www.nytimes.com/2016/09/29/business/economy/more-wealth-more-jobs-but-not-for-everyone-what-fuels-the-backlash-on-trade.html?_r=1.

57. www.epi.org/publication/manufacturing-job-loss-trade-not-productivity-is-the-culprit/.

58. https://en.wikipedia.org/wiki/Trans-Pacific_Partnership.

59. https://en.wikipedia.org/wiki/Transatlantic_Trade_and_Investment_Partnership.

60. https://www.nytimes.com/2016/09/29/business/economy/more-wealth-more-jobs-but-not-for-everyone-what-fuels-the-backlash-on-trade.html?_r=0.

61. https://www.abqjournal.com/595628/trade-pacts-vs-national-sovereignty.html.

<u>investor protection</u>[62] provisions, among others, pose <u>significant risks</u>[63] to national regulatory controls over environment and health standards. Despite almost unanimous economic orthodoxy supporting its benefits, is free trade dead, killed by tweet?

Part Two: Trade Preference Programs for Lesser Developed Countries

Among other exceptions to the general MFN obligation, GATT members are permitted to maintain special trade preferences for lesser developed countries without extending those benefits to other GATT members. Both the EU and the United States have taken advantage of this exception to create extensive trade preference programs. The U.S. currently maintains four such programs.

The oldest and most important of these is the Generalized System of Preferences (GSP), under which approximately 4800 products from 131 beneficiary countries enter the U.S. market duty free. Other preference programs, such as the African Growth and Opportunity Act (AGOA), Andean Trade Preferences Act (ATPA) and Caribbean Basin Initiative (CBI), are currently in effect but also subject to periodic renewal.

Our goal in this part of the chapter is to understand how these programs work and how businesses might find them beneficial. Start by reviewing the GSP system, utilizing the information and links provided below.

You should focus on answering basic questions such as:

- *how products and countries qualify for the preferences*

- *how such entitlements are created or modified*

- *how origin is determined*

- *what limitations exist on program benefits (e.g., "graduation" and "competitive need")*

After you have found answers for these basic questions, review the other preference programs for similarities and differences from GSP.

---

62. https://www.google.com/url?sa=t&rct=j&q=&esrc=s&source=web&cd=6&ved=0ahUK EwjLrrvOwrbRAhVH0oMKHTOuCGcQFghAMAU&url=https%3A%2F%2Fstop-ttip.org%2Fwp -content%2Fuploads%2F2016%2F10%2F13.10.16-Legal-Statement-1.pdf&usg=AFQjCNEZrVsXN _LkKD2T3ER6ptYGG3BXbw&sig2=oTEGNj7TRknDPYkI4i98SA&bvm=bv.143423383,d .amc&cad=rja.

63. https://en.wikipedia.org/wiki/Transatlantic_Trade_and_Investment_Partnership.

A. Generalized System of Preferences

1. Excerpt from USTR, <u>GSP Guidebook</u>,[64] 2015

1. GSP-Eligible Articles

Which imports into the United States qualify for duty-free treatment under the GSP?

A GSP-eligible import meets the following requirements (described in more detail below):

   (1) It must be included in the list of GSP-eligible articles;

   (2) It must be imported directly from a designated beneficiary developing country (BDC) or association;

   (3) The BDC or association must be eligible for GSP treatment for that article;

   (4) The article must be the growth, product, or manufacture of a BDC and must meet the value-added requirements;

   (5) The exporter/importer must request duty-free treatment under GSP by placing an "A" before the HTSUS number that identified the imported article on the appropriate shipping documents (form 7501).

Which articles are eligible for duty-free treatment?

Articles classified by CBP under approximately 3,500 eight-digit tariff rate lines are generally eligible for duty-free treatment from all GSP beneficiaries. An additional 1,500 articles are eligible for duty-free treatment when imported from LDBDCs. The combined lists include most dutiable manufactured and semi-manufactured products and also certain agricultural, fishery, and primary industrial products that are not otherwise duty-free. LDBDCs are designated as such pursuant to section 502(a)(2) of the Trade Act of 1974, as amended, and, in practice, are typically GSP beneficiaries that are on the United Nations' list of least developed countries.

   . . . .

Can any article be designated as eligible for GSP?

No. Certain articles are prohibited by law (19 USC 2463) from receiving GSP treatment. These include most textiles and apparel articles, watches, footwear, work gloves, and leather apparel. In addition, the GSP statute precludes eligibility for import-sensitive steel, glass, and electronic articles.

How is an article identified as GSP eligible in the HTSUS?

The letter A in the "Special" tariff column of the HTSUS identifies GSP-eligible articles at an eight-digit level. The following table presents three HTSUS tariff lines to

---

64. https://www.google.com/url?sa=t&rct=j&q=&esrc=s&source=web&cd=1&ved=0ahUKE wiq1c6IxrbRAhVG7IMKHVQNB24QFggcMAA&url=https%3A%2F%2Fustr.gov%2Fsites%2Fde fault%2Ffiles%2FThe%2520GSP%2520Guidebook.pdf&usg=AFQjCNEF8lCgv9LM0De8bSSmgT VtxTx2rw&sig2=lAm3HRZrQa5U3duprrISXg&cad=rja.

illustrate variations in the treatment given to different GSP articles. Under each entry for a GSP eligible article in the HTSUS, the SPI code A, A+, or A* in the "Special" column identifies the article as GSP-eligible under certain conditions. The SPI code A designates articles that are GSP-eligible from any BDC. The SPI code A+ indicates articles that are GSP-eligible only from LDBDCs. The SPI code A* indicates that one or more specific BDCs, listed in General Note 4(d) to the HTSUS, have lost GSP eligibility for that article.

The HTSUS indicates the GSP status of articles as follows:

HTSUS Subheading	Article description	Rate of Duty (%)		Column 2
		Column 1		
		General	Special	
8406.10.10	Steam turbines for marine propulsion	6.70%	Free (A,...)	20%
8413.30.10	Fuel-injection pumps for compression-ignition engines	2.50%	Free (A*, ...)	35%
8708.92.50	Mufflers and exhaust pipes, not for trackers	2.50%	Free (A+,...)	25%

Can the President limit products' GSP eligibility?

Yes. The President may:

(1) remove products from GSP eligibility in response to petitions submitted by interested parties in an annual review;

(2) preclude certain BDCs from GSP eligibility for certain newly designated products when those products are designated;

(3) limit the re-designation of GSP eligibility to certain BDCs when specific articles are re-designated as GSP-eligible; and

(4) remove products for an individual BDC country which has exceeded competitive need limitations (CNLs).

Is the list of eligible articles and countries ever modified?

Yes. The GSP Subcommittee of the Trade Policy Staff Committee (TPSC), chaired by USTR and comprised of representatives of other executive branch agencies, conducts an annual review during which changes are considered to the lists of articles and countries eligible for duty-free treatment under GSP. Modifications made pursuant to the annual review are implemented by executive order, or Presidential Proclamation, and are published in the Federal Register . . . .

How does someone request a modification of the list of articles or countries?

Any person may petition the GSP Subcommittee to request modifications to the list of countries eligible for GSP treatment. However, only an "interested party" may

---

* The Trade Preferences Extension Act of 2015 (Public Law 114-27), allows certain handbags, luggage, and flat goods to be considered for designation for duty-free treatment under GSP. These products were previously prohibited by law (19 USC 2463) from receiving GSP treatment.

petition for modifications to the list of articles eligible for GSP treatment. For purposes of this provision, an interested party is any party who has significant economic interest in the subject matter of the request, or any other party representing a significant economic interest that would be materially affected by the action requested, such as a domestic producer of a like or directly competitive article, a commercial importer or retailer of an article which is eligible for GSP or for which GSP eligibility is requested, or a foreign government. In order to be considered in a particular annual review, petitions must be submitted to the GSP Subcommittee by the deadline for submissions for that review, which is typically announced in the Federal Register in July or August (See suggested outlines of GSP petitions) . . . .

What factors are taken into account in modifying the list of eligible articles or countries?

In modifying the GSP list of articles and countries, the following factors must be considered:

(1) the effect such action will have on furthering the economic expansion of the country's exports;

(2) the extent to which other major developed countries are undertaking a comparable effort to assist a developing country by granting generalized preferences with respect to imports of products of the country;

(3) the anticipated impact of such action on the U.S. producers of like or directly competitive products; and

(4) the extent of the country's competitiveness with respect to eligible products.

In addition, the statute provides mandatory and discretionary factors the President must take into account in designating a country as eligible for GSP. These factors include whether a country has taken or is taking steps to afford to workers in that country internationally recognized worker rights and the extent to which a country is providing adequate and effective protection of intellectual property rights. The full list of factors may be found at 19 USC 2462(b) and (c). Finally, the statute also provides a list of articles that may not be designated as eligible for GSP (19 USC 2463(b)).

Who makes the determinations regarding GSP product and country eligibility?

The President determines which countries and which products are eligible for GSP benefits, based on the recommendations of the U.S. Trade Representative. The GSP Subcommittee conducts the annual reviews of GSP product and country eligibility. These reviews typically involve both public hearings and a public comment period. The GSP Subcommittee reports the findings of these reviews to the TPSC and the U.S. Trade Representative. The Deputy Assistant USTR for GSP oversees the day-to-day operation of the GSP program and chairs the GSP Subcommittee.

Do all beneficiary countries receive duty-free treatment on the entire list of articles?

No. Some otherwise GSP-eligible products from particular BDCs may be ineligible because:

(1) they exceed the CNLs (see below);

(2) the products' GSP eligibility has been removed from one or more particular countries in response to petitions submitted as part of an annual review;

(3) a particular BDC has been found to be sufficiently competitive with respect to that product or products;

(4) the imported articles fail to meet the statutory requirements of GSP; or

(5) the imported articles fail to meet other CBP or other agency requirements.

3. GSP Beneficiary Developing Countries

. . . .

4. Competitive Need Limitations and Requests for Waivers

What are competitive need limitations?

CNLs are quantitative ceilings on GSP benefits for each product and BDC. The GSP statute provides that a BDC is to lose its GSP eligibility with respect to a product if the CNLs are exceeded and if no waiver is granted (see below). There are two different measures for CNLs: when U.S. imports of a particular product from a BDC during any calendar year (1) account for 50 percent or more of the value of total U.S. imports of that product; or (2) exceed a certain dollar value. In accordance with the GSP statute, the dollar-value limit is increased by $5 million annually; the limit was $165 million in 2014 and is $170 million in 2015. Products from a specified beneficiary are considered "sufficiently competitive" when imports exceed one of these limits.

By statute, GSP treatment for an article exceeding either CNL terminates on July 1 of the next calendar year. By statute, CNLs do not apply to LDBDCs and BDCs that are also beneficiaries of the African Growth and Opportunity Act. See Section 503(c)(2)((D).

Are the competitive need limitations ever waived?

Yes. CNLs can be waived under three circumstances:

. . . .

5. Graduation of a Beneficiary Country from GSP

What is graduation and how is it implemented?

Graduation is the removal of a country's GSP eligibility on the basis of factors related to national income or competitiveness. The President may remove a BDC from the GSP program because the country is sufficiently developed or competitive, or may suspend or limit the BDC's access to duty-free treatment with respect to one or more products.

Country graduation occurs:

(1) when the President determines that a beneficiary country is a "high-income country," as defined by the GSP statute (based on World Bank statistics) ("mandatory graduation"); or

(2) as the result of a review of a BDC's advances in economic development and trade competitiveness.

The per capita Gross National Income (GNI) limit for mandatory graduation is set at the lower bound of the World Bank's definition of a "high-income" country (which was $12,736 for 2014). Mandatory graduation takes effect January 1 of the second year after the year in which the President makes the graduation determination, which is announced in the Federal Register.

. . . .

6. Rules-of-Origin Requirements

What are the rules-of-origin requirements?

For an imported article to be GSP-eligible, it must be the growth, product, or manufacture of a BDC, and the sum of the cost or value of materials produced in the BDC plus the direct costs of processing must equal at least 35 percent of the appraised value of the article at the time of entry into the United States. CBP is charged with determining whether an article meets the GSP rules of origin.

An importer, exporter or producer who is uncertain about whether a particular imported article satisfies the rules of origin requirements, may check CROSS, CBP's searchable database, http://rulings.cbp.gov/, to see if CBP has issued a ruling on the same or a similar product, or may contact CBP for a binding ruling. See page eight of this booklet for information on how to obtain a ruling.

Can imported materials be counted toward the 35 percent value-added requirement?

Yes, if the imported material undergoes a double substantial transformation. This means that the imported material must undergo a substantial transformation in the BDC, which means that the imported material is transformed into a new and different constituent material with a new name, character and use. Then the constituent material must be transformed in the BDC into a new and different finished article with a new name, character and use. Inputs from member countries of GSP-eligible regional associations will be treated as single-country inputs for purposes of determining origin.

The calculation of the cost or value of materials produced in the BDC is described in 19 CFR 10.177. A list of the items included in the "direct costs of processing" is provided in 19 CFR 10.178.

CBP's customs value handbook may be found on CBP's web site at: http://www.cbp .gov/document/publications/customs-value. . . .

. . . .

What may be included in the direct costs of processing?

Direct costs of processing include all costs, whether directly incurred in, or which can be reasonably allocated to, the growth, production, manufacture, or assembly of the merchandise. These include the following: actual labor costs, including fringe benefits and on-the-job training costs for production staff and first line supervisors; dies, molds, and tooling costs, as well as depreciation on machinery and equipment; and research, development, design, blue-prints and engineering, quality control, and inspection and testing costs. This list is not exhaustive; further information on valuation can be obtained from Customs.

Which costs may not be included in the direct costs of processing?

Costs that may not be included in the direct costs of processing are those not directly attributable to the merchandise under consideration or are not costs of manufacturing, These costs include profit and general expenses and business overhead (such as administrative salaries, casualty and liability insurance, advertising, and sales representatives' salaries, commissions, or expenses).

. . . .

Does the U.S. GSP contain any special provisions for beneficiary developing countries that are members of a regional association(s)?

Yes. If members of regional associations request and are granted recognition as regional associations under the GSP program, the association's member countries will be considered as one country for purposes of the GSP rules of origin. Articles produced in two or more eligible member countries of an association will be accorded duty-free treatment if the countries collectively meet the rules of origin. In addition, an article produced in an LDBDC may count inputs from LDBDCs and BDCs in its regional association towards the 35 percent domestic content requirement for satisfying the rules of origin for qualifying articles. CBP makes the final determination of rules of origin.

. . . .

2. Government Accountability Office Report on GSP

Please peruse this <u>linked report of the Government Accountability Office</u>[65] regarding the GSP, reading at least the first few pages summarizing its findings.

B. Other Trade Preference Programs

Although the GSP is by far the most extensive U.S. trade preference program, several other initiatives have been created for specific regions. Each operates in ways very similar to the GSP but apply to a much narrower group of countries and some-

---

65. www.gao.gov/new.items/d08443.pdf.

times include special rules on issues such as the origin of goods. These alternative programs include:

African Growth and Opportunity Act, AGOA[66]

Caribbean Basin Initiative, CBI[67]

Andean Trade Preference Act, ATPA[68]

---

66. https://ustr.gov/issue-areas/trade-development/preference-programs/african-growth-and -opportunity-act-agoa.

67. https://ustr.gov/issue-areas/trade-development/preference-programs/caribbean-basin -initiative-cbi.

68. https://ustr.gov/archive/Trade_Development/Preference_Programs/ATPA/Section_Index .html.

Chapter 13

Trade Remedies: Dumping, Government Subsidies & Import Surge "Safeguards"

A. Overview

It is common for countries to provide domestic remedies for industries injured by so-called "unfair trade practices" involving imported products. These remedies most frequently address four specific types of problems: unexpected, harmful "surges" in imports; foreign government subsidies; imports at less than fair value (dumping); and violations of intellectual property rights. In the United States, such remedies are provided by federal law and enforced primarily by administrative agencies. In most cases, the remedies provided involve temporary increases in tariffs or exclusion of the offending imports.

Because governments and domestic industries may easily abuse such remedies in order to protect domestic industries from foreign competition, the GATT rules provide specific limitations on how and when they can be invoked. In essence, the GATT rules control when such remedies may be implemented by providing internationally agreed upon standards, definitions and limitations. Examples of such GATT-based limitations include:

(1) The "Safeguards Agreement" — often called "Escape Clause," this agreement focuses on unexpected and harmful import "surges";

(2) The "Agreement on Subsidies and Countervailing Measures" — the "SCM" provides criteria to distinguish between illegal versus legal government subsidies; and

(3) The "Anti-Dumping Agreement" — technically called the "Agreement on Implementation of Article VI," this agreement defines illegal dumping.

These GATT obligations are directly reflected in corresponding U.S. legislation that authorizes the trade remedies in accordance with GATT standards. This chapter focuses on United States law regarding two of the most commonly invoked trade remedies—those relating to subsidies and dumping. We will also briefly review so-called "Escape Clause" remedies for unexpected, harmful surges in imports. In subsequent chapters, while considering international business aspects of intellectual property, we will examine remedies relating to violations of intellectual property rights by imported products.

Before addressing the chapter problems presented below, review the general explanation of U.S. trade remedy[1] law found at the International Trade Administration's website. Then read the WTO's description of such remedies from an international perspective.[2]

Part One: Dumping & Material Injury

A. Overview

The term "dumping" in trade law generally refers to price discrimination by exporters between their home domestic market and export markets. The legal definition of actionable dumping is phrased in terms of "less than fair value sales," determined by comparing the exporter's home market pricing with its export pricing. Price discrimination between markets might, of course, merely reflect differing market conditions and competition. Similarly, there are arguably few reasons to oppose dumping on economic grounds since such price differentials will eventually work themselves out in a competitive, integrated world market. In the short term, consumers benefit from lower prices and greater competition.

Price discrimination might, however, also reflect predatory practices in the export markets. A producer with excess inventory may want to dump that inventory into a foreign market at a price even below the cost of production. A producer might also choose to export at extremely low prices in order to gain market share or undermine competition. This is arguably unfair competition, particularly if the foreign producer enjoys market power and high profits in its relatively non-competitive home market. Such producers, protected in their home market, arguably use this unfair advantage to target foreign markets and drive out competitors. Anti-dumping remedies, however, are not tied to finding predatory behavior, abusive market power, or efforts to drive out competition. All that is required, essentially, is price discrimination causing material injury. Unfairness is, apparently, in the eyes of the beholder, as long as the beholder is not an economist.

Long before the advent of GATT, the United States and other countries allowed domestic producers to challenge alleged dumping. These legislative remedies often served as significant barriers to trade by protecting domestic producers from foreign price competition. As a result, the WTO system now includes an Anti-Dumping

---

1. http://ia.ita.doc.gov/intro/index.html.
2. https://www.wto.org/english/thewto_e/whatis_e/tif_e/agrm8_e.htm.

Agreement (officially named "Agreement on Implementation of Article VI of GATT 94"). The agreement neither forbids nor endorses dumping, but rather, is agnostic on whether dumping is an unfair trade practice. Instead, the agreement focuses entirely on limiting domestic anti-dumping remedies because of their potential protectionist effects. In particular, the agreement requires a showing of *material injury* to the domestic producers caused by the dumped products. Before analyzing the problem presented below, review the <u>General Explanation of Dumping</u>,[3] and the <u>Anti-Dumping Agreement</u>,[4] provided by the WTO. Also consider a common <u>critique</u>[5] of dumping law, here articulated by the conservative-leaning CATO Institute.

B. Problem Thirteen A: Rocky Mountain Steel

1. Facts

Boashan Iron & Steel is the largest producer of steel in the People's Republic of China. A significant portion of Boashan's products, including 90% of the welded steel rod it produces, is exported. The export of this steel rod to the United States has caused great concern for your largest client, Rocky Mountain Steel of Pueblo Colorado. Rob Simon, Vice President of Rocky Mountain Steel, recently complained to you that: "Underpriced imports of steel rod from China have tripled from 750,000 tons in 2015 to 2.2 million tons in 2016 and have continued increasing in the first quarter 2017. These imports significantly undersold U.S. producers and have created a huge inventory buildup in the U.S. market."

Since the fourth quarter, Rocky Mountain and other domestic steelmakers have been laying off workers and idling plants to bring supply in line with demand for welded steel rod. Rocky Mountain's plants have been operating at about 50% of capacity during the entire year. Steel prices in the U.S. have plummeted by half since last summer along with demand, leaving the world awash in steel and, in particular, steel rod. According to Simon, Boashan has been selling steel rod in the U.S. market for $10 per linear foot even though it sells the same product for $30 per linear foot to countries in the European Union. Boashan's price for steel rod sold within China is set by government regulation at $9 per linear foot.

2. Assignment

Analyze relevant provisions of U.S. law (links provided below) to evaluate trade remedies that Rocky Mountain might pursue. You should be able, at minimum, to advise your client regarding the following:

---

3. https://www.wto.org/english/theWTO_e/whatis_e/tif_e/agrm8_e.htm.
4. https://www.wto.org/english/docs_e/legal_e/legal_e.htm.
5. https://www.cato.org/publications/commentary/antidumping-law-is-discriminatory.

- *how, where and when may an action be brought?*
- *what must be proven in order to prevail (legal requirements/ elements)?*
- *what is the process by which a decision will be reached?*
- *what specific remedies are available if the petitioners prevail?*

C. Resources

1. Anti-Dumping Statutory Provisions

Carefully review federal anti-dumping provisions available at the USITC[6] web-site. Focus first and primarily on § 1673 to determine the essential elements of a dumping claim. You must "parse" the text and also carefully consider relevant definitions found in § 1677. You should also note the pattern in related provisions (§ 1673a-e) that reflects the relevant decision making process and stages in anti-dumping proceedings.

2. Illustrative Case Law

The following case, which involves both dumping and alleged illegal subsidies, is beyond boring. It provides, however, important interpretive detail regarding the essential elements and processes for deciding an unfair trade practice claim, including material injury to the "industry." *What stage in the administrative process does this decision represent? What are the immediate practical consequences?*

> **i. *Certain Circular Welded Carbon Quality Steel Line Pipe from China and Korea, Investigation Nos. 701-TA-455 and 731-TA-1149-1150 (Preliminary), Publication 4003, May 2008*[7]**

> UNITED STATES INTERNATIONAL TRADE COMMISSION
> DETERMINATIONS

On the basis of the record developed in the subject investigations, the United States International Trade Commission (Commission) determines, pursuant to sections 703(a) and 733(a) of the Tariff Act of 1930 (19 U.S.C. § 1671b(a) and 19 U.S.C. § 1673b(a)) (the Act), that there is a reasonable indication that an industry in the United States is materially injured, or threatened with material injury by reason of imports from China and Korea of circular welded carbon quality steel line pipe, provided for in subheading 7306.19 of the Harmonized Tariff Schedule of the United States, that are alleged to be subsidized by the Government of China and sold in the United States at less than fair value (LTFV)....

---

6. https://www.usitc.gov/trade_remedy/USC-Title_19_1671-1677.htm.
7. https://search.usa.gov/search?affiliate=www.usitc.gov&query=Publication%204003.

BACKGROUND

On April 3, 2008, a petition was filed with the Commission and Commerce by Maverick Tube Corp. (Houston, TX), Tex-Tube Co. (Houston, TX), U.S. Steel Corp. (Pittsburgh, PA), and the United Steel, Paper and Forestry, Rubber, Manufacturing, Energy, Allied Industrial and Service Workers International Union, AFL-CIO-CLC (Pittsburgh, PA), alleging that an industry in the United States is materially injured or threatened with material injury by reason of subsidized imports of certain circular welded carbon quality steel line pipe from China and LTFV imports of circular welded carbon quality steel line pipe from China and Korea. . . .

U.S. IMPORTS

. . . China is the largest foreign supplier of line pipe to the United States, accounting for 43.3 percent of the quantity of total imports in 2007, and 38.6 percent of the value. Korea is the second largest foreign supplier of line pipe to the United States, accounting for 27.5 percent of the quantity of total imports in 2007, and 28.3 percent of the value. From 2005 to 2007, the quantity and value of imports of line pipe from China increased by 914.8 percent and 845.0 percent, respectively. At the same time, the unit value of imports of line pipe from China decreased by 6.9 percent. From 2005 to 2007, the quantity and value of imports of line pipe from Korea increased by 102.7 percent and 96.8 percent, respectively. At the same time, the unit value of imports of line pipe from Korea decreased by 2.9 percent. The quantity and value of imports from other countries decreased by 19.0 percent and by 16.5 percent, respectively, from 2005 to 2007. At the same time, the unit value of imports of line pipe from other sources increased by 3.2 percent. . . .

VIEWS OF THE COMMISSION

Based on the record in the preliminary phase of these investigations, we find that there is a reasonable indication that an industry in the United States is materially injured, or threatened with material injury, by reason of imports of certain circular welded carbon quality steel line pipe ("line pipe") from China and Korea that are allegedly sold in the United States at less than fair value ("LTFV") and by reason of imports of such pipe from China that are allegedly subsidized.

I. THE LEGAL STANDARD FOR PRELIMINARY DETERMINATIONS

The legal standard for preliminary antidumping and countervailing duty determinations requires the Commission to determine, based upon the information available at the time of the preliminary determination, whether there is a reasonable indication that a domestic industry is materially injured, threatened with material injury, or whether the establishment of an industry is materially retarded, by reason of the allegedly unfairly traded imports. In applying this standard, the Commission weighs the evidence before it and determines whether "(1) the record as a whole contains clear and convincing evidence that there is no material injury or threat of such injury; and (2) no likelihood exists that contrary evidence will arise in a final investigation." . . .

III. DOMESTIC LIKE PRODUCT AND DOMESTIC INDUSTRY

A. In General

In determining whether there is a reasonable indication that an industry in the United States is materially injured or threatened with material injury by reason of imports of the subject merchandise, the Commission first defines the "domestic like product" and the "industry." Section 771(4)(A) of the Tariff Act of 1930, as amended ("the Act"), defines the relevant domestic industry as the "producers as a [w]hole of a domestic like product, or those producers whose collective output of a domestic like product constitutes a major proportion of the total domestic production of the product." In turn, the Act defines "domestic like product" as "a product which is like, or in the absence of like, most similar in characteristics and uses with, the article subject to an investigation . . . ." . . .[9]

B. Product Description

Commerce defined the imported merchandise within the scope of these investigations as follows: circular welded carbon quality steel pipe of a kind used for oil and gas pipelines ("welded line pipe"), not more than 406.4 mm (16 inches) in outside diameter, regardless of wall thickness, length, surface finish, end finish or stenciling.

The Commission follows the determination of Commerce as to the scope of the imported merchandise alleged to be sold at less than fair value and subsidized in the preliminary phase of these investigations.

Line pipe for use in oil and gas pipelines generally is produced to American Petroleum Institute (API) specifications. The API specifications require higher hydrostatic test pressures and more restrictive weight tolerances for line pipe than for pipe used in low pressure conveyances of water or steam, known as standard pipe. Line pipe has either a black (lacquered) finish or bare surface finish. It is typically marked or "stenciled" with paint on the outside surface by the manufacturer to indicate the specification in conformance with which it has been manufactured. . . .

C. Domestic Like Product

Petitioner proposes that the Commission define one domestic like product, line pipe, coextensive with the scope of the investigation. The Korean Respondents do not disagree. For the reasons discussed below, we define a single domestic like product consisting of line pipe 16 inches and under in diameter, coextensive with the scope of the investigations.

The record in these investigations shows that all line pipe is used for the same general purpose—conveyance of oil and gas—although there is at least some overlap in the uses of line pipe of different sizes. The size range under investigation is gener-

---

9. . . . The Commission generally considers a number of factors including: (1) physical characteristics and uses; (2) interchangeability; (3) channels of distribution; (4) customer and producer perceptions of the products; (5) common manufacturing facilities, production processes, and production employees; and, where appropriate, (6) price. *See Nippon*, 19 CIT at 455 n.4; *Timken Co. v. United States*, 913 F. Supp. 580, 584 (Ct. Int'l Trade 1996).

ally used for gathering oil or gas at the point of extraction or distributing oil and gas to consumers, but it is also used occasionally for large pipeline projects . . . .

Large diameter line pipe, which exceeds 16 inches in diameter, is generally used for transportation of gas and oil over long distances. As large diameter line pipe is generally used for different applications than the size range under investigation, the two size ranges are not generally interchangeable. The Commission has previously determined that large diameter line pipe is a distinct domestic like product from line pipe 16 inches and under in diameter, and we do not find any evidence on the record of these investigations that suggests that we should reconsider that determination.

D. Domestic Industry

The domestic industry is defined as the domestic "producers as a [w]hole of a domestic like product, or those producers whose collective output of a domestic like product constitutes a major proportion of the total domestic production of the product." In defining the domestic industry, the Commission's general practice has been to include in the industry producers of all domestic production of the like product, whether toll-produced, captively consumed, or sold in the domestic merchant market.

Based on our finding that the domestic like product is line pipe, for purposes of the preliminary phase of these investigations we define a single domestic industry consisting of all domestic producers of line pipe.

IV. CUMULATION

A. In General

For purposes of evaluating the volume and price effects for a determination of material injury by reason of the subject imports, section 771(7)(G)(i) of the Act requires the Commission to cumulate subject imports from all countries as to which petitions were filed and/or investigations self-initiated by Commerce on the same day, if such imports compete with each other and with domestic like products in the U.S. market. . . .

B. Views of Commissioners Charlotte R. Lane, Irving A. Williamson, and Dean A. Pinkert Concerning Reasonable Indication of Material Injury

1. Volume of the Subject Imports

Section 771(7)(C) of the Act provides that the "Commission shall consider whether the volume of imports of the merchandise, or any increase in that volume, either in absolute terms or relative to production or consumption in the United States, is significant." The volume of subject imports surged during the period of investigation from 115,596 short tons in 2005 to 410,642 short tons in 2006 and to 458,997 short tons in 2007. . . .

As apparent consumption increased sharply, the increasing subject imports captured substantial market share from both the domestic industry and nonsubject imports. The market share of subject imports measured by quantity rose from 13.2 percent in 2005 to 29.3 percent in 2006 and to 33.4 percent in 2007, while the domestic industry's market share declined from 59.9 percent in 2005 to 52.9 percent in 2007. Nonsubject imports lost even more market share, declining from 26.8 percent in 2005 to 13.8 percent in 2007. The ratio of the quantity of subject imports to U.S. production rose from 20.3 percent in 2005 to 54.8 percent in 2006 and to 59.6 percent in 2007.

Based on the foregoing, for purposes of the preliminary phase of these investigations, we find that the volume of subject imports and the increase in that volume are significant, both in absolute terms and relative to consumption and production in the United States.

2. Price Effects of the Subject Imports

The majority of domestic producers and even a slight majority of importers familiar with the products reported that differences other than price are only sometimes or never a significant factor in sales of line pipe. This suggests that price is an important consideration in purchasing decisions. The record also shows that subject imports from Korea and domestic line pipe are highly substitutable, CR/PR at Tables II-1 and II-2; CR at V-6, PR at V-4.

The Commission's pricing data indicate that prices of imports from China and Korea were lower than domestic prices in all quarters for all four products. . . . Given the consistency and size of the underselling margins and the substitutability of the domestic and imported products, we find underselling by the subject imports to be significant . . . .

We also find that the subject imports have prevented domestic price increases that otherwise would have occurred in the absence of the subject imports. . . .

For the foregoing reasons, we find for purposes of these preliminary determinations that there has been significant underselling by the subject imports and that such imports have suppressed prices to a significant degree.

3. Impact of the Subject Imports on the Domestic Industry

Section 771(7)(C)(iii) of the Act provides that the Commission, in examining the impact of the subject imports on the domestic industry, "shall evaluate all relevant economic factors which have a bearing on the state of the industry."

These factors include output, sales, inventories, ability to raise capital, research and development, and factors affecting domestic prices. No single factor is dispositive and all relevant factors are considered "within the context of the business cycle and conditions of competition that are distinctive to the affected industry."

With demand growing strongly, the domestic industry's production, capacity utilization, shipments, and net sales quantity and value all increased over the period. . . .

With the increase in production and shipment levels, most of the domestic industry's employment indicators also improved over the period of investigation . . . .

There was a decline in productivity, but the industry's capital expenditures increased.

Despite the increase in the output of the domestic industry during a period of strong demand, the industry's profitability suffered. While the industry remained profitable, it experienced a 23.6 percent decline in operating income from 2005 to 2007, and a 49.8 percent decline from 2006 to 2007 alone. The industry lost 7 percentage points of market share as well, despite its unused capacity for production of line pipe. As described above, we attribute this decline in profitability to the presence of low-priced subject imports and their price-suppressing effects. We note the Korean Respondents' argument that disruptive restructuring experienced by several domestic producers is responsible for any lost profitability during the period, but we find significant evidence to the contrary in the record of the preliminary phase of these investigations . . . .

We conclude that subject imports had a significant adverse impact on the condition of the domestic industry during the period of investigation. As discussed above, subject imports gained significant market share from the domestic industry, undersold the domestic product, and suppressed domestic prices for line pipe to a significant degree. As the domestic industry's costs increased and significant volumes of lower-priced subject imports entered the U.S. market, the domestic industry was caught in a cost-price squeeze . . . .

In its notice of initiation, Commerce estimated that the dumping margin for subject line pipe from China ranges from 57.45 to 58.96 percent and that the dumping margin for subject line pipe from Korea ranges from 41.69 percent to 42.75 percent. 73 Fed. Reg. 23188, 23192 (April 29, 2008).

NATURE AND EXTENT OF ALLEGED SUBSIDIES AND SALES AT LTFV

Alleged Subsidies

Commerce initiated on the following types of subsidies: preferential loans, equity infusions and debt-to-equity swaps; tax benefit programs; value-added tax programs; land grants discounts; provision of inputs for less than adequate remuneration; grant programs; and provincial programs.

Alleges Sales at LTFV

The LTFV margins alleged in the petition upon which Commerce based its decision to initiate its investigations, as adjusted by Commerce, are presented in table I-3.

Table I-3 Line pipe: Allegations of LTFV imports

Country	Basis of comparison	Estimated dumping margin (in percent)
China	Export price based on adjusted U.S. price quote and Home market normal value (India surrogate)	57.45 — 58.96
Korea	Constructed export price based on adjusted U.S. price quote and home market normal value	41.69 — 42.75

Source: 73 FR 23192, April 29, 2008.

. . . .

Part Two: Government Subsidies

A. Overview

It is important to recognize initially that not all government subsidies are considered unfair trade practices. Under the GATT rules, beginning with the original 1947 agreement, distinctions are drawn between different types of subsidies in recognition that there may be legitimate reasons for governments to provide such support that outweigh possible trade distortions. Distinctions between "good" and "bad" subsidies also form an essential part of the WTO Agreement on Subsidies and Countervailing Measures ("SCM"). Thus, while some forms of subsidy are always prohibited under the SCM, others are merely labeled "actionable" depending upon circumstances. These distinctions are now reflected in U.S. trade remedy law on subsidies (links provided below).

Apart from defining when subsidies are prohibited and allowed, the SCM also creates corresponding limitations on national remedies that seek to offset subsidies. Just like with dumping, of particular importance is the requirement that such "countervailing duties" only be imposed under national procedures when they cause a domestic industry "material injury."

This means that a WTO member could bring two distinct kinds of claims to a dispute settlement procedure. One kind of claim might allege a violation of the SCM because another government had provided illegal subsidies — a direct challenge to another government's subsidy programs. A second kind of claim would instead allege that another government's national law regulating remedies for subsidies fail to follow SCM requirements. Such claims might contend that the defendant government is applying domestic anti-subsidy laws in a protectionist fashion. For more background on the SCM and WTO approach to subsidies, browse the links provided at the SCM Gateway.[8] You will find easy to follow explanations of the WTO's approach and references to the relevant provisions of the agreement.

Apart from any claims that a government might bring before the WTO regarding a subsidy, a domestic industry can also challenge foreign subsidies under domestic law. Mirroring our international obligations, U.S. subsidy law only condemns, although not with complete precision, those types of subsidies forbidden under the SCM. Such administrative remedies impose countervailing duties on importations of the illegally subsidized import in an amount that would offset the subsidy — hence the label "countervailable." We will focus on these domestic remedies, and how those remedies might be applied to the following problem, working primarily from the relevant statutory text.

---

8. https://www.wto.org/english/tratop_e/scm_e/scm_e.htm.

B. Problem Thirteen B: The Coalition for Fair Lumber Imports

1. Facts

You represent the Coalition for Fair Lumber Imports, an American trade association of softwood lumber producers whose members collectively are responsible for approximately 75% of U.S. softwood production. The Coalition has collected data that indicates a 10% loss of market share for its members during the past two years despite significant price reductions. Nearly all members of the group have been forced to reduce their work force and many have eliminated their second production shifts. The Coalition believes that their primary competition, Canadian softwood producers, are to blame for these economic problems. The group has developed the following information regarding what they believe to be unfair assistance given by the Canadian government to softwood lumber producers in Canada.

1. Forest Access Road Construction and Maintenance Program:

This program was created in 2015 to make available C$75 million to reimburse forest companies for costs incurred for constructing and maintaining primary and secondary forest access roads.

2. Forest Industry Capital Tax credit:

This program provides a 15% tax credit to any company in the forest products industry on investments in manufacturing and processing equipment through 2017.

3. Natural Resources Canada (NRCAN) Research and Development Fund:

Every year since 2002, the Government of Canada has provided a total of C$75 million in research grants to encourage innovation in the forest products sector. NRCAN grants are available to industry employees and forestry academics for research involving harvesting, processing, transportation, resource utilization, tree and wood quality, and wood physics.

4. Stumpage Licensing for Harvesting Government Forests:

In Canada, the vast majority of standing timber used by softwood lumber producers originates from lands owned by the Canadian government. The Canadian provinces of Alberta, British Columbia, Manitoba, Ontario, Quebec, and Saskatchewan have each established programs through which private lumber producers are charged "stumpage" fees for standing timber harvested from government lands at prices significantly below international market prices. As of spring 2016, low quality Lodgepole pine saw timber was commanding the equivalent of C$20-25 per cubic meter in western Montana. This same grade of timber was sold by the Canadian government for roughly C$7.50 per cubic meter during 2016. In January 2017, the government announced a major stumpage fee reduction in the west coast region of British Columbia to aid its lumber industry there.

Canadian news reports confirmed the purpose of the reduction:

- BC Premier Gordon Campbell has "dropped stumpage rates on the B.C. Coast by 50 per cent to $5 a cubic metre . . . as part of a plan to kick-start the moribund forest industry." *Vancouver Sun.*

- "Campbell . . . slashed the stumpage rate on the coast by 70 per cent, to less than $5 per cubic metre, in response to calls from industry." *The Province.*

Photo, by Tony Hisgett,[9] Wikimedia Commons[10]

It's Soft, It's Wood, It's Heading South.

---

9. https://www.flickr.com/people/hisgett/?rb=1.

10. https://commons.wikimedia.org/wiki/File:Log_driving_in_Vancouver.jpg.

2. Assignment

Analyze relevant provisions of U.S. law to evaluate the facts provided above. You should see strong parallels to the anti-dumping statute relevant to Problem 12A. *Just like for that problem, you should be able, at minimum, to explain (a) what procedures must be followed in order to seek and successfully prosecute a countervailing duty claim and (b) what must be shown in order to prevail on such claims. What precisely is a subsidy? Which subsidies are subject to countervailing duties (in WTO terms: "prohibited" versus "actionable")?*

C. Resources

Work through the <u>statutory provisions</u>[11] on countervailable subsidies. Focus primarily on § 1671 and relevant definitions found in § 1677 in order to answer basic questions that your client, the Fair Lumber Coalition, will want answered about the process.

Part Three: Import Surges & Safeguards ("Escape Clause")

The official purpose of a "safeguard" measure is to provide temporary relief to a domestic industry experiencing serious economic injury as the result of an unexpected surge in competing imports. The safeguard, in the form of temporarily higher duties or quotas, should be designed to allow the domestic producers to adjust to increased competition. Please review the following descriptions of "Safeguards" provided by the WTO, and by the U.S. International Trade Commission, which investigates U.S. safeguard petitions. *What would the lumberjacks in Problem 12A, or steel rod folks from Problem 12B, have to show in order to seek a temporary remedy for sudden surges in imports? How are these criteria distinct from those that govern remedies for dumping and subsidies?* You may rely solely on the summaries set out below to answer these basic questions.

A. WTO Summary of Safeguards

<u>Excerpt From WTO, Anti-dumping, subsidies, safeguards: contingencies, etc.</u>:[12]

Safeguards: emergency protection from imports

A WTO member may restrict imports of a product temporarily (take "safeguard" actions) if its domestic industry is injured or threatened with injury caused

---

11. https://www.law.cornell.edu/uscode/text/19/1671.
12. https://www.wto.org/english/thewto_e/whatis_e/tif_e/agrm8_e.htm.

by a surge in imports. Here, the injury has to be serious. Safeguard measures were always available under GATT (Article 19). However, they were infrequently used, some governments preferring to protect their domestic industries through "grey area" measures—using bilateral negotiations outside GATT's auspices, they persuaded exporting countries to restrain exports "voluntarily" or to agree to other means of sharing markets. Agreements of this kind were reached for a wide range of products: automobiles, steel, and semiconductors, for example.

The WTO agreement broke new ground. It prohibits "grey-area" measures, and it sets time limits (a "sunset clause") on all safeguard actions. The agreement says members must not seek, take or maintain any voluntary export restraints, orderly marketing arrangements or any other similar measures on the export or the import side. . . .

An import "surge" justifying safeguard action can be a real increase in imports (an *absolute increase*); or it can be an increase in the imports' share of a shrinking market, even if the import quantity has not increased (*relative increase*).

Industries or companies may request safeguard action by their government. The WTO agreement sets out requirements for safeguard investigations by national authorities. . . .

The agreement sets out criteria for assessing whether "serious injury" is being caused or threatened, and the factors which must be considered in determining the impact of imports on the domestic industry. When imposed, a safeguard measure should be applied only to the extent necessary to prevent or remedy serious injury and to help the industry concerned to adjust. Where quantitative restrictions (quotas) are imposed, they normally should not reduce the quantities of imports below the annual average for the last three representative years for which statistics are available, unless clear justification is given that a different level is necessary to prevent or remedy serious injury.

In principle, safeguard measures cannot be targeted at imports from a particular country. However, the agreement does describe how quotas can be allocated among supplying countries, including in the exceptional circumstance where imports from certain countries have increased disproportionately quickly. A safeguard measure should not last more than four years, although this can be extended up to eight years, subject to a determination by competent national authorities that the measure is needed and that there is evidence the industry is adjusting. Measures imposed for more than a year must be progressively liberalized.

When a country restricts imports in order to safeguard its domestic producers, in principle it must give something in return. The agreement says the exporting country (or exporting countries) can seek compensation through consultations. If no agreement is reached the exporting country can retaliate by taking equivalent action—for instance, it can raise tariffs on exports from the country that is enforcing the safeguard measure. In some circumstances, the exporting country has to wait for three years after the safeguard measure was introduced before it can retaliate in this way—

i.e. if the measure conforms with the provisions of the agreement and if it is taken as a result of an increase in the quantity of imports from the exporting country.

To some extent developing countries' exports are shielded from safeguard actions. An importing country can only apply a safeguard measure to a product from a developing country if the developing country is supplying more than 3% of the imports of that product, or if developing country members with less than 3% import share collectively account for more than 9% of total imports of the product concerned.

The WTO's Safeguards Committee oversees the operation of the agreement and is responsible for the surveillance of members' commitments. Governments have to report each phase of a safeguard investigation and related decision-making, and the committee reviews these reports.

B. International Trade Commission Summary of Safeguards ("Import Relief")

ITC, Understanding Safeguard Investigations[13]

Section 201, Trade Act of 1974 (Global Safeguard Investigations), Import Relief for Domestic Industries

Under section 201, domestic industries seriously injured or threatened with serious injury by increased imports may petition the USITC for import relief. The USITC determines whether an article is being imported in such increased quantities that it is a substantial cause of serious injury, or threat thereof, to the U.S. industry producing an article like or directly competitive with the imported article. If the Commission makes an affirmative determination, it recommends to the President relief that would prevent or remedy the injury and facilitate industry adjustment to import competition. The President makes the final decision whether to provide relief and the amount of relief.

Section 201 does not require a finding of an unfair trade practice, as do the antidumping and countervailing duty laws and section 337 of the Tariff Act of 1930. However, the injury requirement under section 201 is considered to be more difficult than those of the unfair trade statutes. Section 201 requires that the injury or threatened injury be "serious" and that the increased imports must be a "substantial cause" (important and not less than any other cause) of the serious injury or threat of serious injury.

Criteria for import relief under section 201 are based on those in article XIX of the GATT, as further defined in the WTO Agreement on Safeguards. Article XIX of the GATT is sometimes referred to as the escape clause because

---

13. https://www.usitc.gov/press_room/us_safeguard.htm.

it permits a country to "escape" temporarily from its obligations under the GATT with respect to a particular product when increased imports of that product are causing or are threatening to cause serious injury to domestic producers. Section 201 provides the legal framework under U.S. law for the President to invoke U.S. rights under article XIX.

When: The USITC conducts an investigation under section 201 upon receipt of a petition from a trade association, firm, certified or recognized union, or group of workers which is representative of a domestic industry; upon receipt of a request from the President or the USTR; upon receipt of a resolution of the House Committee on Ways and Means or Senate Committee on Finance; or upon its own motion.

Duration: The USITC generally must make its injury finding within 120 days (150 days in more complicated cases) of receipt of the petition, request, resolution, or institution on its own motion and must transmit its report to the President, together with any relief recommendations, within 180 days after receipt of the petition, request, resolution, or institution on its own motion.

Finding: If the USITC finding is affirmative, it must recommend a remedy to the President, who determines what relief, if any, will be imposed. Such relief may be in the form of a tariff increase, quantitative restrictions, or orderly marketing agreements.

The ITC provides links on its website[14] to various safeguard cases that it has decided.

---

14. https://www.usitc.gov/trade_remedy/publications/safeguard_pubs.htm.

Chapter 14

Foreign Corrupt Practices

A. Overview

The Foreign Corrupt Practices Act (FCPA) is a federal anti-bribery statute specifically designed to curb the participation of U.S. businesses in the widespread corruption that infects international business. The Justice Department web site describes the evolution of U.S. anti-bribery law this way:

> As a result of SEC investigations in the mid-1970's, over 400 U.S. companies admitted making questionable or illegal payments in excess of $300 million to foreign government officials, politicians, and political parties. The abuses ran the gamut from bribery of high foreign officials to secure some type of favorable action by a foreign government to so-called facilitating payments that allegedly were made to ensure that government functionaries discharged certain ministerial or clerical duties. Congress enacted the FCPA to bring a halt to the bribery of foreign officials and to restore public confidence in the integrity of the American business system.

> The FCPA was intended to have and has had an enormous impact on the way American firms do business. Several firms that paid bribes to foreign officials have been the subject of criminal and civil enforcement actions, resulting in large fines and suspension and debarment from federal procurement contracting, and their employees and officers have gone to jail. To avoid such consequences, many firms have implemented detailed compliance programs intended to prevent and to detect any improper payments by employees and agents.

> Following the passage of the FCPA, the Congress became concerned that American companies were operating at a disadvantage compared to foreign companies who routinely paid bribes and, in some countries, were permitted to deduct the cost of such bribes as business expenses on their taxes. Accordingly, in 1988, the Congress directed the Executive Branch to commence negotiations in the Organization of Economic Cooperation and Development (OECD) to obtain the agreement of the United States' major trading partners to enact legislation similar to the FCPA. In 1997, almost ten years later, the United States and thirty-three other countries signed the OECD Convention on Combating Bribery of Foreign Public Officials in International Business Transactions. The United States ratified this Convention and

enacted implementing legislation in 1998. *See* Convention and Commentaries on the DOJ web site.

Corruption in international business continues to be a world-wide problem as reported by Transparency International, a non-governmental organization committed to its eradication. Among its many ill effects, bribery of foreign officials by international businesses dramatically undermines economic, social and political development in poor nations. You should visit Transparency's website[1] and the FCPA Data Base[2] to get a sense of the problem's scope and effect.

In 2016, JP Morgan Chase agreed to pay $264 million dollars in fines to the federal government to settle charges of corruption under the FCPA associated with its Chinese "Sons and Daughters" program.[3] The government alleged that the program involved quid pro quo arrangements under which internships and jobs for the children of Chinese officials were linked to business deals. (*See* CNN Money, *JPMorgan fined for hiring kids of China's elite to win business*[4] for the sordid details.)[5] Other recent investigations of large corporations such as Seimans[6] (and Seimans executives[7]) and Wal-Mart[8] have brought significant attention on the FCPA both in the business world and the national press. As the New York Times reported in April, 2012:

> A decade ago, the Foreign Corrupt Practices Act, which bars American companies from bribing officials overseas, was rarely enforced or discussed. Today, it strikes fear throughout the executive offices of companies with overseas operations, generating huge fees for law firms and large fines for the federal government. The transformation of the once-obscure law has been thrown into sharp relief by the allegations that one of the world's largest companies, Wal-Mart,[9] suppressed an internal inquiry into bribery in Mexico in 2005. After details of the case were reported by The New York Times on Sunday, Wal-Mart's stock tumbled.[10]

---

1. https://www.transparency.org/.

2. http://www.fcpablog.com/blog/tag/the-fcpa-database.

3. https://www.nytimes.com/2016/11/17/business/dealbook/jpmorgan-is-said-to-settle -bribery-case-over-hiring-in-china.html?_r=0.

4. http://money.cnn.com/2016/11/17/investing/jpmorgan-china-hiring-bribery-settlement/.

5. In December 2016, United Airlines paid a civil penalty of $2.4 million to the SEC for failing to comply with its own internal compliance procedures designed to prevent corrupt payments domestically. http://www.fcpablog.com/blog/2016/12/8/tom-fox-on-united-sec-uses-new-tool-to -fight-domestic-corrup.html.

6. https://www.sec.gov/news/press/2008/2008-294.htm.

7. https://www.sec.gov/news/press/2011/2011-263.htm.

8. http://www.nytimes.com/2012/11/16/business/wal-mart-expands-foreign-bribery -investigation.html?pagewanted=all.

9. http://www.nytimes.com/2012/04/22/business/at-wal-mart-in-mexico-a-bribe-inquiry -silenced.html.

10. Charlie Savage, *With Wal-Mart Claims, Greater Attention on a Law*, New York Times, April 25, 2012, http://www.nytimes.com/2012/04/26/business/global/with-wal-mart-bribery-case -more-attention-on-a-law.html (citing http://www.nytimes.com/2012/04/24/business/wal-mart -stock-falls-nearly-5-after-report-of-quashed-bribery-inquiry.html).

The Times reported, in some good news for lawyers, that the bribery investigation of Wal-Mart had expanded to its operations in China, India and Brazil and caused the company to institute an extensive "compliance" program:

> Wal-Mart has so far spent $35 million on a compliance program that began in spring 2011, and has more than 300 outside lawyers and accountants working on it, the company said. It has spent $99 million in nine months on the current investigation. Consequences of the expanding investigation could include slower expansion overseas and the identification of even more problems. The company said in the filing on Thursday that new inquiries had begun in countries "including but not limited to" China, India and Brazil.[11]

As of 2017, this enforcement trend had continued unabated, with SEC filings alone revealing 81 companies under investigation[12] for possible violations.

As noted in the Justice Department commentary above, a common early criticism of the FCPA was that it constituted an act of naïve unilateralism that unnecessarily disadvantaged American businesses. Foreign governments either did not prohibit corruption by its nationals doing business in foreign countries, or simply turned a blind eye to the problem. The effort to fight public corruption in international business, however, now has a serious multi-lateral dimension, which includes the creation of several international conventions. Perhaps the most important of these is sponsored by the Organization for Economic Cooperation and Development (OECD[13]), whose member states produce the vast bulk of international trade. The OECD Anti-Bribery Convention[14] requires members to criminalize business-related bribery of foreign public officials and to prosecute or extradite offenders. The OECD has also developed a program to monitor compliance and report on conditions in member states relating to bribery. The significance of the OECD and other conventions lies in their potential for developing a comprehensive, multi-lateral deterrence regime. To the extent that OECD nations fulfill their obligation to implement national foreign anti-bribery laws, the Convention might generate a meaningful response to the problem. Other international conventions relating to international business corruption include:

- The United Nations Convention against Corruption[15] (181 members)

- The Inter-American Convention against Corruption[16] (Organization of American States, 35 members)

- The Civil Law Convention on Corruption[17] (Council of Europe)

---

11. Stephanie Clifford & David Barstow, Wal-Mart Inquiry Reflects Alarm on Corruption, New York Times, November 15, 2012, http://www.nytimes.com/2012/11/16/business/wal-mart-expands -foreign-bribery-investigation.html.

12. http://www.fcpablog.com/blog/2017/1/9/the-corporate-investigations-list-january-2017.html.

13. http://www.oecd.org/about/.

14. http://www.oecd.org/corruption/oecdantibriberyconvention.htm.

15. http://www.unodc.org/unodc/en/treaties/CAC/.

16. http://www.oas.org/juridico/english/fightcur.html.

17. http://www.coe.int/en/web/conventions/full-list/-/conventions/treaty/174.

- The <u>Criminal Law Convention on Corruption</u>[18] (Council of Europe)
- The <u>Convention on Preventing and Combating Corruption</u>[19] (African)

This chapter focuses primarily on the FCPA and its application.

B. Problem Fourteen: Going to the Movies, Gangnam Style

1. Facts

From <u>Wikipedia</u>:[20]

Republic of Korea

<u>Flag</u>   <u>Emblem</u>

Motto: "홍익인간" (<u>Korean</u>) (*de facto*)

"Benefit broadly in the human world/Devotion to the Welfare of Humanity"

Area controlled by the Republic of Korea shown in green

---

18. http://www.coe.int/en/web/conventions/full-list/-/conventions/treaty/173.

19. https://www.au.int/web/en/treaties/african-union-convention-preventing-and-combating -corruption.

20. https://en.wikipedia.org/wiki/South_Korea.

Capital and largest City	<u>Seoul</u>, 37°33′N 126°58′E
Official languages	<u>Korean</u>
<u>Official script</u>	<u>Hangul</u>
<u>Government</u>	<u>Unitary</u> <u>presidential</u> <u>constitutional republic</u>
<u>Population</u>	
• 2016 estimate	50,801,405[4][5] (<u>27th</u>)
• Density	507/km² (1,313.1/sq mi) (<u>23rd</u>)
<u>GDP</u> (<u>PPP</u>)	2016 estimate
• Total	$1.929 trillion[6] (<u>13th</u>)
• Per capita	$37,948[6] (<u>28th</u>)
<u>GDP</u> (nominal)	2016 estimate
• Total	$1.404 trillion[6] (<u>11th</u>)
• Per capita	$27,633[6] (<u>27th</u>)
<u>Drives on the</u>	right

Gerald Pink, owner of the Las Vegas Film Company, was keen to run the Gangnam Korea International Film Festival, a position that could result in nearly U.S. $20 million in related contracting. The contracts include creation of websites, calendars and videos promoting the Republic of Korea (South Korea). He convinced one of his investors, Fred Bornk, to provide $1 million in cash toward what Pink described to Bornk as "promotional activity and sales commissions needed to get the festival."

Pink told Bornk that his investment would be used, among other things, to pay "commissions" to a "well placed" Korean businessman named Jitt Kim. Bornk, a frequent visitor to South Korea, knew that Jitt was the brother-in-law of Jut Kim, a Korean government official in charge of the Tourism Authority of Korea (TAK). TAK was responsible for organizing and awarding contracts for the festival and promoting tourism in Korea.

After consultations with Pink, Jitt Kim created two bank accounts outside of Korea, one in his own name and another in the name of Jut Kim. Pink then sent $700,000 of Bornk's money by wire into Jitt's account. Pink described this payment in an email to Bornk as a "conditional sales commission." Bornk asked no questions about the payment and did not request an accounting. Pink was well aware that Jitt thereafter transferred half of this money into the account held in Jut's name.

Pink next used $150,000 of Bornk's cash, for which no accounts were kept in the records of Las Vegas Film, to bring Korean tourism officials to visit tourist hot-spots in and around Las Vegas on a "training and promotional tour." No training events were actually held. Pink also spent almost $100,000 on expensive presents to various South Korean officials, including $10,000 in French wines to the mayor of Gangnam, the wealthy suburban area of Seoul where the film festival would be held. Pink also provided or offered full time employment with Las Vegas Films in the U.S., including salaries and other benefits, to family members of several Korean public officials working at TAK.

Perhaps not surprisingly, Las Vegas Films was awarded the contract to organize and run the Gangnam Korean film festival. Pink, however, failed to arrange an appropriate visa for travelling to Korea to sign the contract. Rather than waiting the required three weeks for the visa, Pink paid an employee of the Republic of Korea consulate in Las Vegas $1,000 to "expedite" the papers.

2. Assignment

Please analyze whether any of the above actors could be successfully prosecuted under the Foreign Corrupt Practices Act. *Start by developing a list of potentially objectionable conduct under the facts. Then review the FCPA statutory provisions carefully to determine precisely what a federal prosecutor would have to show in order successfully prosecute such conduct.* Pink and friends might want to "lawyer up."

C. Resources

1. Overview

The Department of Justice, which enforces the FCPA, summarizes the Act's central prohibitions this way:

> The Foreign Corrupt Practices Act of 1977, as amended, 15 U.S.C. §§ 78dd-1, et seq. ("FCPA"), was enacted for the purpose of making it unlawful for certain classes of persons and entities to make payments to foreign government officials to assist in obtaining or retaining business. Specifically, the anti-bribery provisions of the FCPA prohibit the willful use of the mails or any means of instrumentality of interstate commerce corruptly in furtherance of any offer, payment, promise to pay, or authorization of the payment of money or anything of value to any person, while knowing that all or a portion of such money or thing of value will be offered, given or promised, directly or indirectly, to a foreign official to influence the foreign official in his or her official capacity, induce the foreign official to do or omit to do an act in violation of his or her lawful duty, or to secure any improper advantage in order to assist in obtaining or retaining business for or with, or directing business to, any person.

The FCPA's central prohibitions apply both to "issuers" of securities regulated by the Securities and Exchange Commission (both domestic and foreign) as well as other "domestic concerns," which includes natural persons. Essentially all U.S. nationals are subject to the Act. As of 1998, the FCPA also applies to "foreign firms and persons who cause, directly or through agents, an act in furtherance of such a corrupt payment to take place within the territory of the United States."[21]

---

21. Federal jurisdiction here is generally predicated on use of the instrumentalities of interstate commerce. However, as stated in the U.S. Attorney <u>Criminal Resource Manual</u>: "For acts

Apart from its anti-bribery provisions, the FCPA also requires issuers of securities listed in the United States to comply with certain accounting procedures to: "(a) make and keep books and records that accurately and fairly reflect the transactions of the corporation and (b) devise and maintain an adequate system of internal accounting controls."

2. Excerpts from the FCPA

§ 78dd-1 [Section 30A of the Securities & Exchange Act of 1934] Prohibited foreign trade practices by issuers

(a) Prohibition

It shall be unlawful for any issuer which has a class of securities registered pursuant to section 78l of this title or which is required to file reports under section 78o(d) of this title, or for any officer, director, employee, or agent of such issuer or any stockholder thereof acting on behalf of such issuer, to make use of the mails or any means or instrumentality of interstate commerce corruptly in furtherance of an offer, payment, promise to pay, or authorization of the payment of any money, or offer, gift, promise to give, or authorization of the giving of anything of value to—

(1) any foreign official for purposes of—

(A) (i) influencing any act or decision of such foreign official in his official capacity,

(ii) inducing such foreign official to do or omit to do any act in violation of the lawful duty of such official, or

(iii) securing any improper advantage; or

(B) inducing such foreign official to use his influence with a foreign government or instrumentality thereof to affect or influence any act or decision of such government or instrumentality,

in order to assist such issuer in obtaining or retaining business for or with, or directing business to, any person;

---

taken *outside* the United States, U.S. issuers and domestic concerns are liable if they take any act in furtherance of a corrupt payment, even if the offer, promise, or payment is accomplished without any conduct within U.S. territory. *See* §§ 78dd-1(g), 78dd-2(i). In addition, U.S. parent corporations may be held liable for the acts of their foreign subsidiaries where they authorized, directed, or controlled the activity in question, as can U.S. citizens or residents, themselves "domestic concerns," who were employed by or acting on behalf of such foreign-incorporated subsidiaries . . . . A foreign company or person is now subject to the FCPA if it takes any act in furtherance of the corrupt payment while within the territory of the United States. There is, however, no requirement that such act make use of the U.S. mails or other means or instrumentalities of interstate commerce. *See* § 78dd-3(a), (f)(1)." https://www.justice.gov/usam/criminal -resource-manual.

(2) any foreign political party or official thereof or any candidate for foreign political office for purposes of—

(A) (i) influencing any act or decision of such party, official, or candidate in its or his official capacity,

(ii) inducing such party, official, or candidate to do or omit to do an act in violation of the lawful duty of such party, official, or candidate, or

(iii) securing any improper advantage; or

(B) inducing such party, official, or candidate to use its or his influence with a foreign government or instrumentality thereof to affect or influence any act or decision of such government or instrumentality.

in order to assist such issuer in obtaining or retaining business for or with, or directing business to, any person; or

(3) any person, while knowing that all or a portion of such money or thing of value will be offered, given, or promised, directly or indirectly, to any foreign official, to any foreign political party or official thereof, or to any candidate for foreign political office, for purposes of—

(A) (i) influencing any act or decision of such foreign official, political party, party official, or candidate in his or its official capacity,

(ii) inducing such foreign official, political party, party official, or candidate to do or omit to do any act in violation of the lawful duty of such foreign official, political party, party official, or candidate, or

(iii) securing any improper advantage; or

(B) inducing such foreign official, political party, party official, or candidate to use his or its influence with a foreign government or instrumentality thereof to affect or influence any act or decision of such government or instrumentality,

in order to assist such issuer in obtaining or retaining business for or with, or directing business to, any person.

(b) Exception for routine governmental action

Subsections (a) and (g) of this section shall not apply to any facilitating or expediting payment to a foreign official, political party, or party official the purpose of which is to expedite or to secure the performance of a routine governmental action by a foreign official, political party, or party official.

(c) Affirmative defenses

It shall be an affirmative defense to actions under subsection (a) or (g) of this section that—

(1) the payment, gift, offer, or promise of anything of value that was made, was lawful under the written laws and regulations of the foreign official's, political party's, party official's, or candidate's country; or

(2) the payment, gift, offer, or promise of anything of value that was made, was a reasonable and bona fide expenditure, such as travel and lodging expenses, incurred by or on behalf of a foreign official, party, party official, or candidate and was directly related to—

(A) the promotion, demonstration, or explanation of products or services; or

(B) the execution or performance of a contract with a foreign government or agency thereof.

. . . .

(f) Definitions

For purposes of this section:

(1) (A) The term "foreign official" means any officer or employee of a foreign government or any department, agency, or instrumentality thereof, or of a public international organization, or any person acting in an official capacity for or on behalf of any such government or department, agency, or instrumentality, or for or on behalf of any such public international organization.

. . . .

(2)(A) A person's state of mind is "knowing" with respect to conduct, a circumstance, or a result if—

(i) such person is aware that such person is engaging in such conduct, that such circumstance exists, or that such result is substantially certain to occur; or

(ii) such person has a firm belief that such circumstance exists or that such result is substantially certain to occur.

(B) When knowledge of the existence of a particular circumstance is required for an offense, such knowledge is established if a person is aware of a high probability of the existence of such circumstance, unless the person actually believes that such circumstance does not exist.

(3)(A) The term "routine governmental action" means only an action which is ordinarily and commonly performed by a foreign official in—

(i) obtaining permits, licenses, or other official documents to qualify a person to do business in a foreign country;

(ii) processing governmental papers, such as visas and work orders;

(iii) providing police protection, mail pick-up and delivery, or scheduling inspections associated with contract performance or inspections related to transit of goods across country;

(iv) providing phone service, power and water supply, loading and unloading cargo, or protecting perishable products or commodities from deterioration; or

(v) actions of a similar nature.

(B) The term "routine governmental action" does not include any decision by a foreign official whether, or on what terms, to award new business to or to continue business with a particular party, or any action taken by a foreign official involved in the decision-making process to encourage a decision to award new business to or continue business with a particular party.

(g) Alternative Jurisdiction

(1) It shall also be unlawful for any issuer organized under the laws of the United States, or a State, territory, possession, or commonwealth of the United States or a political subdivision thereof and which has a class of securities registered pursuant to section 12 of this title or which is required to file reports under section 15(d) of this title, or for any United States person that is an officer, director, employee, or agent of such issuer or a stockholder thereof acting on behalf of such issuer, to corruptly do any act outside the United States in furtherance of an offer, payment, promise to pay, or authorization of the payment of any money, or offer, gift, promise to give, or authorization of the giving of anything of value to any of the persons or entities set forth in paragraphs (1), (2), and (3) of this subsection (a) of this section for the purposes set forth therein, irrespective of whether such issuer or such officer, director, employee, agent, or stockholder makes use of the mails or any means or instrumentality of interstate commerce in furtherance of such offer, gift, payment, promise, or authorization.

(2) As used in this subsection, the term "United States person" means a national of the United States (as defined in section 101 of the Immigration and Nationality Act (8 U.S.C. § 1101)) or any corporation, partnership, association, joint-stock company, business trust, unincorporated organization, or sole proprietorship organized under the laws of the United States or any State, territory, possession, or commonwealth of the United States, or any political subdivision thereof.

§ 78dd-2. Prohibited foreign trade practices by domestic concerns

(a) Prohibition

It shall be unlawful for any domestic concern, other than an issuer which is subject to section 78dd-1 of this title, or for any officer, director, employee, or agent of such domestic concern or any stockholder thereof acting on behalf of such domestic concern, to make use of the mails or any means or instrumentality of interstate commerce corruptly in furtherance of an offer, payment, promise to pay, or authorization of the payment of any money, or offer, gift, promise to give, or authorization of the giving of anything of value to—

[Repeating provisions appearing in 78dd-1 above.]

The full text of the FCPA and unofficial translations into various languages is available here.[22]

---

22. https://www.justice.gov/criminal-fraud/statutes-regulations.

3. How Not to Pay Bribes: DOJ Guide to FCPA

The Justice Department is required by the statute to produce several forms of guidance regarding what conduct may violate the act. It is, if you will, a primer on how not to pay bribes for those who might find that confusing. The first are "guidelines":

> (1) . . . describing specific types of conduct, associated with common types of export sales arrangements and business contracts, which for purposes of the Department of Justice's present enforcement policy, the Attorney General determines would be in conformance with the preceding provisions of this section; and (2) general precautionary procedures which domestic concerns may use on a voluntary basis to conform their conduct to the Department of Justice's present enforcement policy regarding the preceding provisions of this section.

15 U.S.C. § 78dd-1(d).

The DOJ now publishes, with the SEC, *A Resource Guide to the Foreign Corrupt Practices Act*[23] (2012). The guide provides many illustrations. An older useful version was called a *Lay Person's Guide.*[24]

A second important source of DOJ guidance comes in the form of "opinions" under which domestic concerns can receive pre-clearance from the department on the legality of proposed conduct:

> (e) Opinions of Attorney General
>
> (1) The Attorney General . . . shall establish a procedure to provide responses to specific inquiries by domestic concerns concerning conformance of their conduct with the Department of Justice's present enforcement policy regarding the preceding provisions of this section. The Attorney General shall, within 30 days after receiving such a request, issue an opinion in response to that request. The opinion shall state whether or not certain specified prospective conduct would, for purposes of the Department of Justice's present enforcement policy, violate the preceding provisions of this section . . . .

15 U.S.C. § 78dd-1.

"Opinions"[25] issued by the Justice Department create a rebuttable presumption that the pre-cleared conduct "is in conformity with" the FCPA.

---

23. https://www.justice.gov/criminal-fraud/fcpa-guidance.

24. http://globalinvestigationsreview.com/article/1022149/lay-persons-guide-fcpa.

25. https://www.justice.gov/criminal-fraud/opinion-releases-index.

4. Case Law Illustration: Conscious Avoidance & Mens Rea

a. United States v. Kozeny, 667 F.3d 122 (2d Cir. 2011)

Before: POOLER and HALL, Circuit Judges.

Azerbaijan reclaimed its independence in 1991 following the collapse of the Soviet Union, gaining control over its rich stores of oil and natural gas. In the mid-1990s, Azerbaijan began privatizing various state assets. The candidates for privatization included the state-owned oil company, SOCAR. The government alleged that in an attempt to capitalize on this opportunity, Viktor Kozeny and Frederic Bourke Jr. conspired with others in a scheme to illegally purchase SOCAR by bribing the Azerbaijani president and other officials. After a jury trial, Bourke was convicted of conspiring to violate the Foreign Corrupt Practices Act ("FCPA"), 15 U.S.C. § 78dd-1 et seq., 18 U.S.C. § 371, and the Travel Act, 18 U.S.C. § 1953, and of making false statements in violation of 18 U.S.C. § 1001. The district court denied Bourke's motions for new trial and for judgment of acquittal.

On appeal, Bourke vigorously attacks his conviction on several fronts, including (1) the correctness of the jury instructions given, (2) the sufficiency of the evidence, and (3) the propriety of certain evidentiary rulings made by the district court. For the reasons given below, we affirm.

BACKGROUND

Bourke co-founded the accessory company Dooney & Bourke, and considers himself an inventor, investor and philanthropist. In the mid-1990s, Bourke met Viktor Kozeny. Dubbed the "Pirate of Prague" by Fortune magazine, Kozeny is an international entrepreneur known for shady dealings. In a December 1996 article, Fortune detailed how Kozeny and his partner engaged in massive fraud during the privatization of the state-owned industries in the Czech Republic, including engaging in insider trading, purchasing state secrets and participating in various other unsavory business practices. Testimony at trial established that Bourke was aware of Kozeny's "Pirate of Prague" moniker.

In the late 1990s, Azerbaijan began converting state-controlled industries to private ownership through a voucher-based initiative, similar to the one used in the Czech Republic. Among the assets being considered for privatization was SOCAR, the state-owned Azerbaijani oil company. However, observers considered it unlikely that SOCAR would ever actually be privatized, given its economic importance to the country. As part of the privatization process, the Azerbaijani government issued each citizen a voucher book with four coupons. The coupons, which could be freely traded, were used to bid at auction for shares of state-owned enterprises being privatized. Foreigners seeking to participate in the auctions needed to pair their vouchers with options issued by the State Property Committee ("SPC"), the entity charged with administrating the privatization process. Every coupon needed to be matched with an option, so to bid a complete voucher book a foreigner needed to match the four coupons with four options. Voucher books sold for roughly $12.

In May 1997, Kozeny invited Bourke to travel with him to examine potential investments. Their journey included a stop in Azerbaijan. Kozeny created two entities upon returning from the trip: the Minaret Group, an investment bank; and Oily Rock, an entity formed to purchase and own the privatization vouchers issued by the Azerbaijani government. Kozeny recruited Thomas Farrell to work for the entities, and instructed Farrell and other employees to start purchasing vouchers. The vouchers were purchased using U.S. currency flown in on private jets from Zurich or Moscow. Altogether, about $200 million worth of vouchers were purchased.

Kozeny and Farrell were introduced to Ilham Aliyev, the then president's son and vice-president of SOCAR. Aliyev introduced the two to Nadir Nasibov, chair of the SPC, and his deputy, Barat Nuriyev. Kozeny discussed acquiring SOCAR at auction with Nuriyev — an auction that would not be conducted absent a presidential decree. As part of a scheme to purchase SOCAR, Kozeny and Nuriyev agreed that all future purchases of vouchers would be made through Nuriyev and his confederates. Nuriyev told Kozeny purchasing SOCAR would require one million vouchers (four million coupons paired with four million options). Nuriyev also made clear that an "entry fee" would need to be paid to various Azerbaijani officials, including President Aliyev, in the range of $8 to $12 million dollars. The "entry fee" was intended to encourage the president to approve SOCAR's privatization. Kozeny agreed to pay the "fee," with Farrell delivering cash payments to Nuriyev to pass on to the president.

In addition, Nuriyev demanded that two-thirds of Oily Rock's voucher books and options be transferred to Azerbaijani officials. The officials would then be able to receive two-thirds of the profits from SOCAR's eventual privatization without actually investing any money. To make the transfer possible, in September 1997 Kozeny instructed his attorney, Hans Bodmer, to set up a complex corporate structure involving multiple parent and holding companies. In December 1997, Nuriyev told Farrell that Aliyev had doubled the voucher book requirement from one to two million vouchers. At the time Nuriyev had this conversation with Farrell, voucher books had increased in price to approximately $100 each.

This development spurred Kozeny to start seeking out additional investors, an effort he kicked off with a lavish holiday party at his home in Aspen, Colorado. Bourke attended, as did Tom McCloskey, another Aspenite who previously invested in Oily Rock. In January, 1998 Kozeny took a group of potential investors to Azerbaijan, including Bourke and his friend, Robert Evans. The group met with Nuriyev and toured the Minaret Group offices. Carrie Wheeler traveled with the group on behalf of a potential investor. She testified that, "it seemed like the gist of the meeting was to communicate [to] investors that [Kozeny] had a relationship with the government in some way."

Bourke and Evans returned to the Azerbaijani capital, Baku, with Kozeny in February 1998. Bodmer — who traveled separately — testified that Bourke approached him in Baku and questioned him regarding the Azerbaijanis. Bodmer testified that during this so-called "walk-talk," he told Bourke of the nature of the bribery scheme and the corporate structures created to carry it out. Bodmer conveyed the substance of his conversation with Bourke to Rolf Schmid, an associate at Bodmer's law firm.

Schmid memorialized Bodmer's description of the conversation years later in a memorandum:

> Ricky Bourke asked Hans Bodmer about the legal structure of Oily Rock and its subsidiaries, the ownership of vouchers and options by the holding companies, etc. Hans Bodmer remembers that—probably at the beginning of 1998—he left together with Ricky Bourke in Baku and went for a walk together with Ricky Bourke. During this walk he briefed Ricky Bourke in detail about the involvement of the Azeri interests the 2/3:1/3 arrangement.

After traveling to Baku, Bourke set up Blueport, an investment company incorporated in the British Virgin Islands, and invested $7 million in the company. He also recruited other American investors to invest via Blueport, including former Senator George Mitchell. Over time, Blueport would invest roughly $8 million in Oily Rock. In April 1998, Bourke traveled back to Baku for the official opening of the Minaret offices. Mitchell also traveled to Baku for this event, and met with President Aliyev to discuss Oily Rock's investment. Following his conversation, Mitchell told Bourke and Kozeny that the president intended to go forward with SOCAR's privatization. During this same period, Bourke also asked Farrell several times whether "Viktor [was] giving enough" and "[h]as Viktor given them enough money?"

Bourke made another trip to Baku shortly after the Minaret office opening. When he returned home, Bourke contacted his attorneys to discuss ways to limit his potential FCPA liability. During the call, Bourke raised the issue of bribe payments and investor liability. Bourke's attorneys advised him that being linked to corrupt practices could expose the investors to FCPA liability. Bourke and fellow Oily Rock investor Richard Friedman agreed to form a separate company affiliated with Oily Rock and Minaret. This separate company would shield U.S. investors from liability for any corrupt payments made by the companies and Kozeny. To that end, Oily Rock U.S. Advisors and Minaret U.S. Advisors were formed, and Bourke joined the boards of both on July 1, 1998. Directors of the advisory companies each received one percent of Oily Rock for their participation.

In mid-1998, Kozeny and Bodmer told Bourke that an additional 300,000,000 shares of Oily Rock would be authorized and transferred to the Azeri officials. Bourke told a Minaret employee, Amir Farman-Farma, that "Kozeny had claimed that the dilution was a necessary cost of doing business and that he had issued or sold shares to new partners who would maximize the chances of the deal going through, the privatization being a success."

Bodmer set up a Swiss bank account for several Azeri officials—including Nuriyev, his son and another relative, as well as President Aliyev's daughter. From May to September 1998, nearly $7 million in intended bribe payments was wired to these accounts. In addition to the evidence of cash bribes, the government adduced evidence that Bourke and other conspirators arranged and paid for medical care, travel and lodging in the United States for both Nuriyev and his son.

By the end of 1998, Kozeny had abandoned all hope of SOCAR's privatization, and began winding down the investment scheme. The Minaret Group fired most of its employees by the end of January 1999, and drastically reduced the pay of the few who remained. Kozeny told the investors that the vouchers were worthless, good only for "wallpaper." Around the same time, Bourke resigned from the advisory company boards. As time went on, the privatization scheme became an issue in civil litigation by investors in the United Kingdom. Kozeny's attorneys contacted the U.S. Attorney's office in late 2000, and Bourke was subsequently advised he was the subject of an investigation. Bourke entered into a proffer agreement on April 26, 2002. Bourke also waived attorney-client privilege and instructed his attorneys to answer questions from investigators. During his proffer sessions, Bourke was asked specifically about whether Kozeny made corrupt payments, transfers and gifts to Azeri officials, and Bourke denied any such knowledge.

On May 12, 2005, Bourke, Kozeny and David Pinkerton, a managing director for American International Group responsible for its investments in Oily Rock and Minaret, were indicted. Kozeny remains a fugitive in the Bahamas and has never faced trial. The indictment charged Bourke with five counts of violating FCPA, 15 U.S.C. § 78dd-1 et seq.; two counts of violating the Travel Act, 18 U.S.C. § 1952; one count of conspiracy to violate FCPA and the Travel Act, 18 U.S.C. § 371; two counts of money laundering, 18 U.S.C. § 1956; one count of conspiracy to commit money laundering, 18 U.S.C. § 371; and one count of making false statements to FBI agents, 18 U.S.C. § 1001. . . . Bourke ultimately went to trial on three counts: conspiracy to violate FCPA and the Travel Act, conspiracy to launder money, and making false statements to the FBI.

The trial lasted five weeks. At the close of the government's case, Bourke moved pursuant to Federal Rule of Criminal Procedure 29 for a judgment of acquittal, which the district court denied. *United States v. Kozeny*, 638 F.Supp.2d 348 (S.D.N.Y.2009). After three days of deliberations, the jury convicted Bourke on Count One (FCPA conspiracy) and Count Three (false statements) of the indictment, but acquitted on Count Two (conspiracy to commit money laundering). Bourke moved again for a judgment of acquittal or, in the alternative, a new trial. The district court denied the motion. *United States v. Kozeny*, 664 F.Supp.2d 369 (S.D.N.Y.2009). This appeal followed.

DISCUSSION

Bourke raises numerous challenges to his conviction. He primarily argues the district court erred in (1) instructing the jury, (2) allowing his conviction to stand without being supported by sufficient evidence, and (3) certain evidentiary rulings. We address each of his arguments in turn.

I. Jury Instructions.

Bourke challenges the jury instructions on four primary grounds. First, he argues the district court erred in refusing to instruct the jury that it needed to agree unanimously on a single overt act committed in furtherance of the conspiracy. Second, he argues the district court improperly charged the jury on conscious avoidance because (1) there was no factual basis for such a charge; and (2) the government waived its reliance on the conscious avoidance theory. Third, he argues the district court erred by failing to instruct the jury that the government needed to prove Bourke acted "corruptly" and "willfully" to sustain a conviction on FCPA conspiracy. Finally, he argues the district court erred in failing to give the jury Bourke's proposed good-faith instruction.

We review claims of error in jury instructions de novo. *United States v. Wilkerson*, 361 F.3d 717, 732 (2d Cir.2004). . . .

A. Overt acts.

. . . .

We agree with the district court's rationale, and hold that the jury need not agree on a single overt act to sustain a conspiracy conviction. As the district court noted, the overt act taken in furtherance of the conspiracy need not be a crime. . . . We conclude, therefore, that although proof of at least one overt act is necessary to prove an element of the crime, which overt act among multiple such acts supports proof of a conspiracy conviction is a brute fact and not itself element of the crime. The jury need not reach unanimous agreement on which particular overt act was committed in furtherance of the conspiracy.

B. Conscious avoidance.

The district court instructed the jury on conscious avoidance as part of its charge on the substantive FCPA violation (Count One):

> The FCPA provides that a person's state of mind is knowing with respect to conduct, a circumstance, or a result if, and I'm quoting from the statute, the FCPA, if such person is aware that such person is engaging in such conduct; that such circumstance exist [sic] or that such result substantially is certain to occur, or such person has a firm belief that such circumstances exist or that such result is substantially certain to occur. That's the end of the quote.

> When knowledge of existence of a particular fact is an element of the offense, such knowledge may be established when a person is aware of a high probability of its existence, and consciously and intentionally avoided confirming that fact. Knowledge may be proven in this manner if, but only if, the person suspects the fact, realized its high probability, but refrained from obtaining the final confirmation because he wanted to be able to deny knowledge.

> On the other hand, knowledge is not established in this manner if the person merely failed to learn the fact through negligence or if the person actually believed that the transaction was legal.

"A conscious avoidance instruction permits a jury to find that a defendant had culpable knowledge of a fact when the evidence shows that the defendant intentionally avoided confirming the fact." *United States v. Ferrarini*, 219 F.3d 145, 154 (2d Cir.2000). The jury may be instructed on conscious avoidance only where "(1) the defendant asserts the lack of some specific aspect of knowledge required for conviction, and (2) the appropriate factual predicate for the charge exists, i.e., the evidence is such that a rational juror may reach the conclusion beyond a reasonable doubt that the defendant was aware of a high probability of the fact in dispute and consciously avoided confirming that fact." Id. (internal quotation marks, alterations and citation omitted). Without either of those factors, as we explained in Ferrarini:

> [A] jury could be given a conscious avoidance instruction in a case where there was only equivocal evidence that the defendant had actual knowledge and where there was no evidence that the defendant deliberately avoided learning the truth. Under those circumstances, a jury might conclude that no actual knowledge existed but might nonetheless convict, if it believed that the defendant had not tried hard enough to learn the truth.

Id. at 157.

Bourke first argues that the conscious avoidance charge lacks a factual predicate. We disagree. While the government's primary theory at trial was that he had actual knowledge of the bribery scheme, there is ample evidence to support a conviction based on the alternate theory of conscious avoidance. The testimony at trial demonstrated that Bourke was aware of how pervasive corruption was in Azerbaijan generally. Bourke knew of Kozeny's reputation as the "Pirate of Prague." Bourke created the American advisory companies to shield himself and other American investors from potential liability from payments made in violation of FCPA, and joined the boards of the American companies instead of joining the Oily Rock board. In so doing, Bourke enabled himself to participate in the investment without acquiring actual knowledge of Oily Rock's undertakings.

The strongest evidence demonstrating that Bourke willfully avoided learning whether corrupt payments were made came from tape recordings of a May 18, 1999 phone conference with Bourke, fellow investor Friedman and their attorneys, during which Bourke voiced concerns about whether Kozeny and company were paying bribes:

> I mean, they're talking about doing a deal in Iran. Maybe they . . . bribed them, . . . with . . . ten million bucks. I, I mean, I'm not saying that's what they're going to do, but suppose they do that.

Later in the conversation, Bourke remarks:

> I don't know how you conduct business in Kazakhstan or Georgia or Iran, or Azerbaijan, and if they're bribing officials and that comes out. Let's say one of the guys at Minaret says to you, Dick, you know, we know we're going to get this deal. We've taken care of this minister of finance, or this minister of this or that. What are you going to do with that information?

He goes on to say:

> What happens if they break a law in Kazakhstan, or they bribe somebody in Kazakhstan and we're at dinner and one of the guys says, "Well, you know, we paid some guy ten million bucks to get this now." I don't know, you know,

if somebody says that to you, I'm not part of it. I didn't endorse it. But let's say [] they tell you that. You got knowledge of it. What do you do with that? I'm just saying to you in general do you think business is done at arm's length in this part of the world.

Finally, Bourke's attorney testified that he advised Bourke that if Bourke thought there might be bribes paid, Bourke could not just look the other way. Taken together, a rational juror could conclude that Bourke deliberately avoided confirming his suspicions that Kozeny and his cohorts may be paying bribes.

Of course, this same evidence may also be used to infer that Bourke actually knew about the crimes. *See United States v. Svoboda*, 347 F.3d 471, 480 (2d Cir.2003). Relying on *Ferrarini*, 219 F.3d at 157, Bourke argues that the conscious avoidance charge was given in error because the government argued Bourke actually knew of the bribes. We disagree. . . .

Finally, Bourke argues that the conscious avoidance charge improperly allowed the jury to convict him based on negligence, rather than based on evidence that he avoided learning the truth. As detailed above, the record contains ample evidence that Bourke had serious concerns about the legality of Kozeny's business practices and worked to avoid learning exactly what Kozeny was doing. . . .

Finally, the district court specifically charged the jury not to convict based on negligence. There is no reason to suspect that the jury ignored that instruction.

C. Insufficiency of the mens rea charge.

Bourke argues that the district court erred by failing to instruct the jury that it must find he acted "corruptly" and "willfully," because that is the mens rea necessary to sustain a conviction on a substantive FCPA offense. In giving the charge on conspiracy, the district court instructed the jury that:

> [T]he government must prove beyond a reasonable doubt that the defendant knew that he was a member of an operation or a conspiracy that committed or was going to commit a crime, and that his action of joining such an operation or conspiracy was not due to carelessness, negligence or mistake.
>
> Unlawful means simply contrary to the law. The defendant need not have known that he was breaking any particular law or any particular rule. He need only have been aware of the generally unlawful nature of his acts.
>
> An act is done knowingly and willfully if it is done deliberately and voluntarily, that is, the defendant's act or acts must have been the product of his conscious objective, rather than the product of a mistake or accident or mere negligence or some other innocent reason.

Earlier, when charging on the conspiracy FCPA count, the district court instructed the jury as to the elements of a substantive FCPA offense:

> The third element, corruptly and willfully: The third element of a violation of the FCPA is that the person intended to act corruptly and willfully. A person acts corruptly if he acts voluntarily and intentionally, with an im-

proper motive of accomplishing either an unlawful result or a lawful result by some unlawful method or means. The term "corruptly" is intended to connote that the offer, payment, and promise was intended to influence an official to misuse his official position.

A person acts willfully if he acts deliberately and with the intent to do something that the law forbids, that is, with a bad purpose to disobey or disregard the law. The person need not be aware of the specific law and rule that his conduct may be violating, but he must act with the intent to do something that the law forbids.

The district court prefaced its instruction on the substantive elements with:

The substantive offense—that is, the substantive offense of violating the FCPA—has seven elements, which I will define for you. You should note that the government need not prove each of the following elements in order to prove that the defendant engaged in a conspiracy to violate the FCPA. I am instructing you on the elements only that they will aid you in your determination as to whether the government has sustained its proof, burden of proof, with respect to this count.

We need not decide if Bourke properly preserved this issue for appellate review, because we find the charge proper under either a de novo or plain error standard. . . .

Here, the district court instructed the jury to make the necessary findings. The district court instructed the jury that to convict, it must find that he knew of the conspiracy's object, and that Bourke intended for that object to be accomplished. The district court further instructed the jury that one possible object of the conspiracy was to violate FCPA, and to violate FCPA one must act "corruptly" and "willfully." Thus, the district court properly instructed the jury that it must find Bourke knowingly entered a conspiracy that had the object of corruptly and willfully bribing foreign officials and that Bourke intended to aid in achieving this object. Moreover, the jury charge that Bourke urged the district court to adopt would require the jury to find Bourke willfully and corruptly joined a conspiracy to willfully and corruptly bribe foreign government officials—an absurd result unsupported by law. We find no error.

D. Proposed good faith instructions.

. . . .

Bourke argues the district court erred in not giving the jury a separate good faith instruction with respect to FCPA and false statement counts. Even assuming arguendo that Bourke's proposed instruction was legally correct with an adequate basis in the record, his argument fails because the theory was effectively presented elsewhere in the charge. The district court instructed the jury that the government did not meet its burden if the defendant "merely failed to learn the fact through negligence or if the person actually believed that the transaction was legal." It also charged that "the government must prove beyond a reasonable doubt that the defendant knew that he was a member of an operation or conspiracy that committed or was going to commit a crime, and that his action of joining such an operation or conspiracy was not due to carelessness, negligence or mistake." The jury was told that it "must first find that [Bourke] knowingly joined in the unlawful agreement or plan." The jurors were instructed that "knowingly" meant "deliberately and voluntarily," and could not be a "mistake or accident or mere negligence or some other innocent reason."

. . . The failure to give a specific good faith charge does not require a reversal.

. . . .

CONCLUSION

We have examined the remainder of Bourke's arguments and we find them to be without merit. For the reasons given above, we affirm his conviction.

————

In 2013, the 67 year old Burke <u>began serving his sentence</u>.[26]

5. Penalties & Enforcement

Responsibility for enforcement of the FCPA is shared by the Department of Justice and Securities & Exchange Commission. The DOJ is responsible for all criminal enforcement and for civil enforcement against "domestic concerns" other than issuers of listed securities, and foreign companies. The SEC, with a specialized enforcement unit in place since 2010, is responsible for civil enforcement involving issuers of securities. For more detail see the <u>2012 Resource Guide</u>[27] (pages 4-5).

a. Statutory Provisions

15 U.S.C. § 78ff

(a) Willful violations; false and misleading statements

Any person who willfully violates any provision of this chapter (other than section <u>78dd-1</u> of this title), or any rule or regulation thereunder the violation of which is made unlawful or the observance of which is required under the terms of this chapter, or any person who willfully and knowingly makes, or causes to be made, any statement in any application, report, or document required to be filed under this chapter or any rule or regulation thereunder or any undertaking contained in a registration statement as provided in subsection (d) of section <u>78o</u> of this title, or by any self-regulatory organization in connection with an application for membership or participation therein or to become associated with a member thereof which statement was false or misleading with respect to any material fact, shall upon convic-

————

26. https://www.bloomberg.com/news/articles/2013-05-06/bourke-to-report-to-prison-15-yers-after-oil-deal-soured.

27. www.sec.gov/spotlight/fcpa/fcpa-resource-guide.pdf.

tion be fined not more than $5,000,000, or imprisoned not more than 20 years, or both, except that when such person is a person other than a natural person, a fine not exceeding $25,000,000 may be imposed; but no person shall be subject to imprisonment under this section for the violation of any rule or regulation if he proves that he had no knowledge of such rule or regulation.

. . . .

(c) Violations by issuers, officers, directors, stockholders, employees, or agents of issuers

(1) (A) Any issuer that violates subsection (a) or (g) of section 78dd-1 of this title shall be fined not more than $2,000,000.

(B) Any issuer that violates subsection (a) or (g) of section 78dd-1 of this title shall be subject to a civil penalty of not more than $10,000 imposed in an action brought by the Commission.

(2) (A) Any officer, director, employee, or agent of an issuer, or stockholder acting on behalf of such issuer, who willfully violates subsection (a) or (g) of section 78dd-1 of this title shall be fined not more than $100,000, or imprisoned not more than 5 years, or both.

(B) Any officer, director, employee, or agent of an issuer, or stockholder acting on behalf of such issuer, who violates subsection (a) or (g) of section 78dd–1 of this title shall be subject to a civil penalty of not more than $10,000 imposed in an action brought by the Commission.

(3) Whenever a fine is imposed under paragraph (2) upon any officer, director, employee, agent, or stockholder of an issuer, such fine may not be paid, directly or indirectly, by such issuer.

b. Recent Enforcement Actions

The DOJ website provides an alphabetical list of cases[28] that it has prosecuted for criminal violations of the FCPA. Find and review the case of Gerald Green.[29] The SEC website sports an impressive list of successful penalty actions[30] that demonstrates an apparently serious resolve to enforce the FCPA.

From: FCPA Blog[31] (self-described as "The World's Biggest Anti-Corruption Compliance Portal")

---

28. https://www.justice.gov/criminal-fraud/related-enforcement-actions/a.
29. https://www.justice.gov/criminal-fraud/related-enforcement-actions/g.
30. https://www.sec.gov/spotlight/fcpa/fcpa-cases.shtml.
31. http://www.fcpablog.com/blog/2011/1/5/recent-cases-foreign-companies-dominate-new -top-ten.html.

Richard L. Cassin,[32] *The 2016 FCPA Enforcement Index*[33]

Tuesday, January 3, 2017 at 8:08AM

Last year 27 companies paid about $2.48 billion to resolve FCPA cases. It was the biggest enforcement year in FCPA history. Both the number of enforcement actions and the overall amounts paid to resolve them were records.

Four blockbuster FCPA settlements in 2016—Teva Pharmaceutical at $519 million, Odebrecht/Braskem at $419.8 million, Och-Ziff at $412 million, and VimpelCom at $397.6 million—landed on our list of the ten biggest[34] FCPA cases of all time.

For comparison:

In 2015, 11 companies paid $133 million to resolve FCPA cases.

In 2014, 10 companies paid $1.56 billion.

In 2013, 12 companies paid $731.1 million.

In 2012, 12 companies paid $259.4 million.

In 2011, 15 companies paid $508.6 million.

In 2010, 23 companies paid $1.8 billion.

In 2009, 11 companies paid $644 million, and

In 2008, 11 companies paid $890 million.

In 2016, 15 individuals settled civil FCPA charges brought by the SEC.

———

The blog also provides a comprehensive list[35] of other actions and penalties by both DOJ and the SEC.

c. Compliance Programs

A significant number of FCPA investigations involve self-disclosure reflecting a recent government emphasis on compliance programs to mitigate violations. As reported in the Wall Street Journal article "FCPA Inc.: The Business of Bribery,[36] Corruption Probes Become Profit Center for Big Law Firms," this has been a boon to large corporate law firms. There are many useful guides on compliance available on the web including the SEC's "Resource Guide,"[37] and the ABA's "Handbook."[38]

---

32. http://www.fcpablog.com/blog/author/fcpablog.
33. http://www.fcpablog.com/blog/2017/1/3/the-2016-fcpa-enforcement-index.html.
34. http://www.fcpablog.com/blog/2016/12/29/reconsidered-odebrecht-and-braskem-are-on-our-fcpa-top-ten-l.html.
35. www.fcpablog.com/blog/2017/1/3/the-2016-fcpa-enforcement-index.html.
36. https://www.wsj.com/articles/SB10000872396390443862604578028462294611352.
37. https://www.sec.gov/spotlight/fcpa/fcpa-resource-guide.pdf.
38. https://shop.americanbar.org/eBus/Store/ProductDetails.aspx?productId=185949301.

Chapter 15

Intellectual Property Rights in International Business Transactions

A. Overview

Intellectual property plays an essential role in many international business transactions. Even an uncomplicated sale of goods might implicate the patent rights of the inventor, trademark symbols associated with the product and its seller, or copyright interests. Intellectual property itself is often the focus of international transactions, either through direct sale of rights or via licensing. Whatever forms a transaction might involve, the owners of intellectual property must also secure and protect their legal rights from infringement. This vital interest in preserving rights can be both cumbersome and complicated in international business, since intellectual property is generally controlled on a territorial basis by national law.

It is also clear that intellectual property rights play an increasingly vital role in international business transactions and U.S. trade. The International Trade Commission reported in 2016[1] that:

> Intellectual property (IP) has been a vital instrument for achieving such advances throughout our nation's history. A growing number of U.S. and international studies demonstrate the important role of IP in economic activity. This report shows that IP-intensive industries continue to be a major, integral and growing part of the U.S. economy. We find that the 81 industries designated as IP-intensive directly accounted for 27.9 million jobs and indirectly supported an additional 17.6 million jobs in 2014. Together, this represented 29.8 percent of all jobs in the U.S. The total value added by IP-intensive industries amounted to 38.2 percent of U.S. GDP and IP-intensive industries paid 47 percent higher weekly wages compared to other industries. Further,

---

1. https://www.google.com/url?sa=t&rct=j&q=&esrc=s&source=web&cd=&ved=0ahUKEwiTz sTJ2NnRAhWHsVQKHdfwA8sQFgguMAI&url=https%3A%2F%2Fwww.uspto.gov%2Fsites%2Fdef ault%2Ffiles%2Fdocuments%2FIPandtheUSEconomySept2016.pdf&usg=AFQjCNEul1kIFIlK9m 381hKPaKcl-Ofjeg&sig2=3dNWCTdhAIJTDRyJhy_Llg&cad=rja.

at $842 billion the merchandise exports of IP-intensive industries made up 52 percent of total U.S. merchandise exports. Exports of service-providing IP-intensive industries totaled about $81 billion in 2012, accounting for 12.3 percent of total U.S. private exports in services.

This chapter focuses on some basic legal issues regarding the creation, commercialization, and protection of intellectual property rights associated with international transactions. The first section provides a brief primer on the most central IP rights and reviews international efforts to enhance and harmonize their protection. Part Two addresses U.S. domestic customs seizures of imports that allegedly violate trademark and copyright interests, including both counterfeit and "gray" market goods. Part Three examines administrative remedies that patent, copyright and trademark holders may bring against infringing or "unfair" imports.

Part One: Legal Protection for Intellectual Property

A. What Is Intellectual Property?

Before examining some of the common issues involving intellectual property in international business, it is important to understand their essential legal characteristics. Intellectual property is defined by the World Intellectual Property Organization as "creations of the mind: inventions, literary and artistic works, and symbols, names, images, and designs used in commerce." Such "creations of the mind" become property when the law gives to its creator some form of exclusivity of use that can be commercially exploited, commonly through sale or lease. The most common and traditional forms of intellectual property include patents, trademarks, copyrights and trade secrets. The <u>United States Patent and Trademark Office</u>[2] formerly offered the following simple summary:

PATENTS provide rights for up to 20 years for inventions in three broad categories:
Utility patents protect useful processes, machines, articles of manufacture, and compositions of matter. Some examples: fiber optics, computer hardware, medications.

2. https://www.uspto.gov/patents-getting-started/general-information-concerning-patents.

	**Design patents** guard the unauthorized use of new, original, and ornamental designs for articles of manufacture. The look of an athletic shoe, a bicycle helmet, the *Star Wars* characters are all protected by design patents.
	Plant patents are the way we protect invented or discovered, asexually reproduced plant varieties. Hybrid tea roses, Silver Queen corn, Better Boy tomatoes are all types of plant patents.
	TRADEMARKS protect words, names, symbols, sounds, or colors that distinguish goods and services. Trademarks, unlike patents, can be renewed forever as long as they are being used in business. The roar of the *MGM* lion, the pink of the *Owens-Corning* insulation, and the shape of a *Coca-Cola* bottle are familiar trademarks.
	COPYRIGHTS protect works of authorship, such as writings, music, and works of art that have been tangibly expressed. The Library of Congress registers copyrights which last the life of the author plus 50 years. *Gone With The Wind* (the book and the film), Beatles recordings, and video games are all works that are copyrighted.
	TRADE SECRETS are information that companies keep secret to give them an advantage over their competitors. The formula for *Coca-Cola* is the most famous trade secret.

To reinforce these basic conceptions, review the general explanations of patents, copyrights, trademarks and trade secrets provided at one of the following links in order to answer the following basic questions about each of the most common four forms of IP:

- *What does the right protect?*
- *How is the right legally secured?*
- *When and where does it apply?*
- *What interests are enjoyed by the right owner?*
- *What are common forms of infringement?*

1. <u>WIPO</u>[3] (follow links);

2. <u>WTO/TRIPS</u>[4] (general discussion tied into the WTO and TRIPS)

---

3. http://www.wipo.int/about-ip/en/.
4. https://www.wto.org/english/thewto_e/whatis_e/tif_e/agrm7_e.htm.

B. International Regulation and Harmonization of Intellectual Property Law

1. Overview

As the importance of intellectual property in international trade has grown, it has increasing become the subject of international regulation. This part of the chapter reviews the development of international efforts to harmonize and protect intellectual property rights.

One of the most important legal aspects of intellectual property rights is that they are jurisdictionally limited. For example, securing a patent in the United States does not protect your invention from commercial exploitation anywhere in the world other than within the territory of the United States. Similarly, whether your invention can be patented, what precise protection the patent will give you and what remedies are available for its infringement are issues determined by the law of each jurisdiction in which protection is sought. This is particularly important to international transactions, since a seller of a product that depends on IP rights (and most do) must secure those rights in every jurisdiction in which it expects to compete.

Domestic producers will also be concerned with securing such rights in any jurisdiction from which they might expect infringing imports, since it may want to attack counterfeit goods at their source. The governments of developing countries where intellectual property "pirating" is often blatant, however, may not have either the resources or inclination to effectively enforce such rights. In contrast, industrialized nations typically view effective enforcement of intellectual property as a priority given its commercial significance to their developed economies.

The geographic limitations on intellectual property protections and international conflicts over enforcement are inconvenient, expensive and may inhibit international trade. As a result, efforts to internationalize aspects of intellectual property rights began as early as the turn of the 19th century. Although these efforts at international harmonization have not produced impressive results, there are now a number of important treaties regarding intellectual property rights.

The following links from the World Intellectual Property Organization (WIPO) provide useful and brief summaries of three primary treaties. You will find that these treaties provide only limited obligations regarding the substantive rights of the property holder. However, they create several important procedural protections, including the requirement that member states extend national treatment (non-discrimination) to foreign IP applications and establish filing priorities so that the first application filing date in any member state is deemed the filing date in all other member states (for a defined period). The Patent Cooperation Treaty also provides significant benefits by providing not only filing priorities for its international patent application (essentially simultaneous filing in the various member states) but also preliminary determinations of patentability through a centralized search and review process.

Review the following WIPO summaries:

1. 1883 <u>Paris Convention</u>[5] for the Protection of Industrial Property (including trademarks)

2. 1886 <u>Berne Convention</u>[6] for the Protection of Literary and Artistic Works (copyrights)

3. 1970 <u>Patent Cooperation Treaty</u>[7] (harmonization & centralization of some patent processes) (Wikipedia also provides a <u>nice summary</u>[8])

4. <u>Patent Law Treaty of 2000</u>[9]

Corresponding to the evolution of an international legal regime, an international institutional framework with a focus on intellectual property has also developed. The <u>World Intellectual Property Organization</u>[10] ("WIPO"), a "specialized agency"[11] of the United Nations with 184 member states, was created in 1967 by treaty. WIPO describes its mandate as:

> "developing a balanced and accessible international <u>intellectual property</u>[12] (IP) system, which rewards creativity, stimulates innovation and contributes to economic development while safeguarding the public interest . . ." and "promot[ing] the protection of IP throughout the world through cooperation among states and in collaboration with other international organizations . . . ."

The most important recent development regarding international protection of intellectual property is the WTO based "Agreement on Trade Related Aspects of Intellectual Property Rights" (commonly known as "TRIPS"). In addition to increased harmonization, a central purpose for developing TRIPS was to enhance protection for IP rights by creating an international obligation to provide effective domestic remedies for their violations. You should review the description of TRIPS found at the <u>WTO IP gateway</u>.[13]

2. Assignment

Using the WTO gateway links, you should answer the follow simple questions:

- *Precisely what obligations does TRIPS create for WTO members regarding IP?*
- *Does TRIPS provide standards for how and when IP rights must be recognized?*
- *Does TRIPS regulate what rights the holder of IP should be given?*

---

5. http://www.wipo.int/treaties/en/ip/paris/summary_paris.html.

6. http://www.wipo.int/treaties/en/ip/berne/summary_berne.html.

7. http://www.wipo.int/pct/en/treaty/about.html.

8. https://en.wikipedia.org/wiki/Patent_Cooperation_Treaty.

9. http://www.wipo.int/treaties/en/ip/plt/summary_plt.html.

10. http://www.wipo.int/about-wipo/en/.

11. U.N. "specialized agencies" are international organizations that have an agreement with the U.N. to work with the support of, and in cooperation with, the U.N. Many receive U.N. financial support and are subject to some form of U.N. oversight.

12. http://www.wipo.int/about-ip/en/.

13. https://www.wto.org/english/tratop_e/trips_e/trips_e.htm.

- *Does TRIPS provide for protection against infringement of IP rights?*
- *Who can enforce violations of TRIPS and how?*

Part Two: Domestic Remedies for Copyright and Trademark Infringement — Counterfeits, Pirated Goods and the Gray Market

A. Overview

The United States has a comprehensive set of civil, criminal and administrative remedies designed to protect intellectual property. Some of these remedies specifically address infringing imports. This part of the chapter focuses on customs seizures of both pirated and so-called "gray market" imports. Read the introductory section of the Congressional Research Service Report[14] summarizing such remedies generally before addressing the following problem and assignment below.

It's a "Shoupie"!

DangApricot,[15] WikiMedia Commons[16]

---

14. www.fas.org/sgp/crs/misc/RL34109.pdf.
15. https://commons.wikimedia.org/wiki/User:DangApricot.
16. https://commons.wikimedia.org/wiki/File:SharpieVsShoupie.JPG.

B. Problem Fifteen: Shades of Gray and Black

1. Facts

Kid's Rom is a U.S. company which has developed a new software program designed to allow extraordinarily effective internet monitoring. The software allows parents to closely control which web sites their children may access from the family home computer. Kid's Rom has secured a design and utility patent for its program and has registered its trademark with customs. It has recently discovered that Target Department stores around the United States are selling exact copies of this software on disks labeled with the Kid's Rom trademark.

Investigation has revealed that Target has two suppliers of these disks. The first is China Bogusware, a company in the Peoples Republic of China that simply reproduces copies of the Kid's Rom program without permission in a dank, dark back alley warehouse in Shanghai. Bogusware sells the disks to U.S. buyers primarily via the internet through a series of websites. The second source is Euroweb, a British company that purchased the disks from Kid's Rom's wholly owned subsidiary in Amsterdam (which has a license to reproduce the software).

2. Assignment

Describe what legal remedies and courses of action you will pursue on behalf of Kid's Rom based on the references below, and evaluate their potential for success. You should focus on customs seizures, and the distinction between pirated/counterfeit goods and so-called "gray market" imports.

C. Resources

1. Overview

Intellectual property in the United States is primarily controlled by federal law. Among others, the Copyright Act,[17] 17 U.S.C. §§ 101 et seq. (1994),[18] protects copyrights; the Patent Act,[19] 35 U.S.C. §§ 101 et seq. (1994), governs patents; and trademark protection is provided by the Lanham Act[20] (Trademark Act), 15 U.S.C. §§ 1501 et seq. (1994). There are, however, a host of other federal statutes, regulations and treaty obligations related to the creation and protection of intellectual property. WIPO provides links[21] to 168 "texts" of such laws and treaties. In some areas, such as trade

---

17. https://www.copyright.gov/title17/.

18. *See* Digital Millennium Copyright Act (DMCA), Pub. L. No. 105-304, 112 Stat. 2860 (17 U.S.C.A. §§ 101 et seq.), https://www.copyright.gov/reports/studies/dmca/dmca_executive.html, which was designed to address modern copyright problems created by the digital revolution.

19. https://www.uspto.gov/patent/laws-regulations-policies-procedures-guidance-and-training.

20. https://www.uspto.gov/trademark/laws-regulations.

21. http://www.wipo.int/wipolex/en/profile.jsp?code=US.

secrets, state law compliments federal protections. Forty-eight states have adopted the Uniform Trade Secrets Act (Florida version here[22]). In 2016, Congress passed similar federal legislation called the "Defend Trade Secrets Act."[23] The organization "Non-Disclosure Agreements, for free"[24] provides a good summary.[25]

These statutes and related regulations often provide judicial remedies designed to protect against infringement of intellectual property. Typically federal, these remedies may take the form of injunctive relief, civil monetary damages and, for willful violations, even criminal penalties. A U.S. holder of IP rights facing infringing imports may, however, find such judicial remedies frustrating and ineffective in many circumstances. Apart from the inevitable glacial pace of federal civil litigation, personal jurisdiction over likely defendants and enforcement of judgments may be elusive.

Those who have secured intellectual property rights in foreign jurisdictions might similarly seek protection in the courts and administrative processes of those nations. The provision of effective domestic remedies is now an international obligation under the TRIPS regime at the WTO. Nevertheless, the lack of effective enforcement[26] in the places specializing in IP piracy remains a constant and critical problem for U.S. industry.

A third and more effective set of potential remedies lies with customs. Section 42 of the Lanham Act, and 526 of the Tariff Act, both prohibit importation of products that bear a U.S. registered trademark without permission of its owner. Infringing goods may be excluded, seized or forfeited. Consider the following excerpt from a CBP 2016 press release:

> U.S. Customs and Border Protection (CBP) and U.S. Immigration and Customs Enforcement's (ICE) Homeland Security Investigations (HSI) released their annual report[27] stating that the total number of products seized containing Intellectual Property Rights (IPR) infringements increased nearly 25 percent in fiscal year 2015. The collaboration netted 28,865 seizures of shipments, an increase from 23,140 in fiscal year 2014.

> Had these products been genuine, the estimated manufacturer's suggested retail price (MSRP) of the seized goods would have been over $1.35 billion. This is a ten percent increase in the value of seized goods from the previous fiscal year, which were estimated at $1.23 billion MSRP.

Similar authority for customs seizures exists in the EU under Regulation 1383/2003.[28]

---

22. http://www.leg.state.fl.us/statutes/index.cfm?App_mode=Display_Statute&URL=0600-0699/0688/0688.html.
23. https://www.law.cornell.edu/uscode/text/18/1832.
24. http://www.ndasforfree.com/aboutndaagreements.html.
25. http://www.ndasforfree.com/UTSA.html#Uniform_Trade_Secrets_Act_.
26. www.gao.gov/new.items/d05788t.pdf.
27. https://www.cbp.gov/document/stats/ipr-annual-seizure-statistics.
28. http://www.wipo.int/wipolex/en/details.jsp?id=1455.

The remainder of Part Two focuses on the remedy of customs seizures with an emphasis on trademark violations. You will find that the law makes an important distinction between "counterfeit" goods ("black market" goods produced without authority of a license and, thus, "pirated") and "gray market" goods (genuine goods produced under a valid license but imported without permission).

2. Customs Seizure of Counterfeit Goods[29]

a. Section 1526

19 U.S.C. § 1526 Merchandise bearing American trade-mark

(a) Importation prohibited

Except as provided in subsection (d) of this section, it shall be unlawful to import into the United States any merchandise of foreign manufacture if such merchandise, or the label, sign, print, package, wrapper, or receptacle, bears a trademark owned by a citizen of, or by a corporation or association created or organized within, the United States, and registered in the Patent and Trademark Office by a person domiciled in the United States, under the provisions of sections 81 to 109 of title 15, and if a copy of the certificate of registration of such trademark is filed with the Secretary of the Treasury, in the manner provided in section 106 of said title 15, unless written consent of the owner of such trademark is produced at the time of making entry.

(b) Seizure and forfeiture

Any such merchandise imported into the United States in violation of the provisions of this section shall be subject to seizure and forfeiture for violation of the customs laws.

(c) Injunction and damages

Any person dealing in any such merchandise may be enjoined from dealing therein within the United States or may be required to export or destroy such merchandise or to remove or obliterate such trademark and shall be liable for the same damages and profits provided for wrongful use of a trade-mark, under the provisions of sections 81 to 109 of title 15.

(d) Exemptions; publication in Federal Register; forfeitures; rules and regulations

. . . .

(e) Merchandise bearing counterfeit mark; seizure and forfeiture; disposition of seized goods

Any such merchandise bearing a counterfeit mark (within the meaning of section 1127 of title 15) imported into the United States in violation of the provisions of section 1124 of title 15, shall be seized and, in the absence of the written consent of the trademark owner, forfeited for violations of the customs laws. Upon seizure of such

---

29. Customs seizures of goods infringing copyright is authorized under 19 U.S.C. § 1595a(c)(2) (C) for a violation of 17 U.S.C. § 602 (implemented in 19 C.F.R. § 133.42).

merchandise, the Secretary shall notify the owner of the trademark, and shall, after forfeiture, destroy the merchandise. Alternatively, if the merchandise is not unsafe or a hazard to health, and the Secretary has the consent of the trademark owner, the Secretary may obliterate the trademark where feasible and dispose of the goods seized—

(1) by delivery to such Federal, State, and local government agencies as in the opinion of the Secretary have a need for such merchandise,

(2) by gift to such eleemosynary institutions as in the opinion of the Secretary have a need for such merchandise, or

(3) more than 90 days after the date of forfeiture, by sale by the Customs Service at public auction under such regulations as the Secretary prescribes, except that before making any such sale the Secretary shall determine that no Federal, State, or local government agency or eleemosynary institution has established a need for such merchandise under paragraph (1) or (2).

(f) Civil penalties

(1) Any person who directs, assists financially or otherwise, or aids and abets the importation of merchandise for sale or public distribution that is seized under subsection (e) of this section shall be subject to a civil fine.

(2) For the first such seizure, the fine shall be not more than the value that the merchandise would have had if it were genuine, according to the manufacturer's suggested retail price, determined under regulations promulgated by the Secretary.

(3) For the second seizure and thereafter, the fine shall be not more than twice the value that the merchandise would have had if it were genuine, as determined under regulations promulgated by the Secretary.

(4) The imposition of a fine under this subsection shall be within the discretion of the Customs Service, and shall be in addition to any other civil or criminal penalty or other remedy authorized by law.

b. Related Customs Regulations

At minimum examine <u>regulations for Title 19</u>,[30] Part 133: § 133.21; 133.22; 133.23; 133.41–43 (scroll down and follow links).

3. Gray Market Goods

Gray market goods are foreign made imports which bear a genuine U.S. registered trademark whose owner has not consented to their entry into the U.S. market. Their treatment by customs is subject to special rules and exceptions described below. Note the distinct remedies and rules (and exceptions) derived from § 526 of the Tariff Act (codified at 19 U.S.C. § 1526) versus the Lanham Act of 1946, 15 U.S.C. § 1124. Case law interpreting each set of rules is provided below.

---

30. https://www.gpo.gov/fdsys/pkg/CFR-2005-title19-vol1/content-detail.html.

a. General Description and Definition

Consider the following definition of gray market goods provided by the Court in *K-Mart v. Cartier*, 486 U.S. 281 (1988):

> A gray-market good is a foreign-manufactured good, bearing a valid United States trademark, that is imported without the consent of the United States trademark holder. The gray market arises in three general contexts. In case 1, despite a domestic firm's having purchased from an independent foreign firm the rights to register and use the latter's trademark as a United States trademark and to sell its foreign-manufactured products here, the foreign firm imports the trademarked goods and distributes them here, or sells them abroad to a third party who imports them here. In case 2, after the United States trademark for goods manufactured abroad is registered by a domestic firm that is a subsidiary of (case 2a), the parent of (case 2b), or the same as (case 2c), the foreign manufacturer, goods bearing a trademark that is identical to the United States trademark are imported. In case 3, the domestic holder of a United States trademark authorizes an independent foreign manufacturer to use that trademark in a particular foreign location. Again, the foreign manufacturer or a third party imports and distributes the foreign-made goods.

b. Illustrative Case Law

The following two cases are helpful in understanding how § 1526 and the Lanham Act are applied to gray market goods. Each also examines important exceptions.

i. Vittoria North America L.L.C. v. Euro-Asia Imports Inc., 278 F.3d 1076 (10th Cir. 2001)

Exclusive United States distributor, as trademark holder, of bicycle racing tires from foreign manufacturer, brought action against alleged infringer under Tariff Act. The United States District Court for the Western District of Oklahoma, Wayne E. Alley, J., granted partial summary judgment for distributor. Alleged infringer appealed. The Court of Appeals, Ebel, Circuit Judge, held that: (1) assignment agreement between manufacturer and distributor was valid; (2) evidence was sufficient to demonstrate that goodwill was transferred with trademark rights; and (3) common control did not exist between manufacturer and distributor.

Affirmed.

EBEL, Circuit Judge.

In this case we are called upon to interpret provisions of the Tariff Act of 1930 designed to protect domestic owners of trademarks affixed to goods produced overseas by foreign manufacturers. Plaintiff-Appellee Vittoria North America, L.L.C., ("VNA"), an Oklahoma limited liability company, alleges that it is the U.S. owner of the trademark Vittoria, which designates a well-known brand of bicycle tires. VNA alleges that Defendant-Appellant Euro-Asia Imports, a California sole proprietorship, has purchased Vittoria-branded tires overseas and imported them into the United

States in violation of VNA's trademark rights. VNA sued Euro-Asia Imports and its sole proprietor Robert Hansing (collectively "EAI") under § 526 of the Tariff Act (codified at 19 U.S.C. § 1526) ("the Act") seeking damages as well as an injunction to prevent EAI from continuing to import Vittoria bicycle tires into the United States. The Act states:

> Except as provided in subsection (d) of this section, it shall be unlawful to import into the United States any merchandise of foreign manufacture if such merchandise, or the label, sign, print, package, wrapper, or receptacle, bears a trademark owned by a citizen of, or by a corporation or association created or organized within, the United States, and registered in the Patent and Trademark Office by a person domiciled in the United States, under the provisions of sections 81 to 109 of Title 15, and if a copy of the certificate of registration of such trademark is filed with the Secretary of the Treasury, in the manner provided in section 106 of said Title 15, unless written consent of the owner of such trademark is produced at the time of making entry.

In other words, the Act provides so-called "gray market"[2] protection to U.S. owners of trademarks associated with goods of foreign manufacture, prohibiting any other person or entity from importing goods bearing that trademark into the United States without the consent of the trademark owner. *See, e.g., K Mart Corp. v. Cartier, Inc.,* 486 U.S. 281, 288–89 (1988). "The prototypical gray market victim . . . is a domestic firm that purchases from an independent foreign firm the rights to register and use the latter's trademark as a United States trademark and to sell its foreign manufactured products here." *Id.* at 286.

The district court granted VNA partial summary judgment, holding that the evidence showed that VNA owns and has properly registered the Vittoria trademark in the United States, that Vittoria-branded bicycle tires are manufactured overseas, and that EAI has imported Vittoria tires into the United States without VNA's consent. EAI now appeals, arguing that the evidence was insufficient to support summary judgment on the issue of whether VNA is the U.S. owner of the Vittoria trademark. EAI further argues that VNA is not entitled to protection under the Act because VNA is controlled by the foreign manufacturer of Vittoria tires. In addition, EAI argues we should reverse because the district court improperly denied it an opportunity to file a surrebuttal to VNA's reply brief on its motion for summary judgment. We AFFIRM.

I. BACKGROUND

On November 25, 1992, VNA's predecessor Hibdon Tire Center entered into an agreement ("the 1992 Agreement") with Vittoria S.p.A. ("Vittoria Italy"), a company organized under the laws of Italy and with headquarters in Bergamo, Italy. Hibdon

---

2. "Gray market goods" are defined to include "[f]oreign-manufactured goods, bearing a valid United States trademark, that are imported without the consent of the U.S. trademark holder." *Black's Law Dictionary* 701 (6th ed.1990).

Tire Center agreed to form VNA as a North American distributor of Vittoria tires, and Vittoria Italy agreed to designate VNA as its exclusive distributor in the United States, Canada, and Mexico. VNA distributed Vittoria-branded bicycle tires in the United States from that time forward. In February 1999, Vittoria Italy entered into an agreement ("Assignment Agreement") with VNA purporting to assign VNA "all right, title and interest in and to the United States Trademark 'VITTORIA' and the registration therefore . . . , together with the goodwill of the business connected with the use of and symbolized by said Trademark, as well as the right to sue for infringement of the Trademark or injury to said goodwill." The Assignment Agreement stated that "[t]he purpose of this Agreement is to permit Assignee [VNA] to act against infringers and unauthorized importers of Vittoria trademarked products into the United States." Vittoria Italy retained the right to retake title to the Trademark and its associated goodwill upon giving thirty days' written notice to VNA.

Shortly thereafter, VNA filed suit against EAI alleging that it infringed on VNA's trademark rights by importing Vittoria tires into the United States without first gaining VNA's consent. EAI concedes that it has been purchasing Vittoria-branded tires overseas and importing the tires into the United States since the early 1980s. VNA's suit seeks damages, an injunction to prevent further importation by EAI, and confiscation of EAI's inventory of Vittoria-branded products.

The district court granted VNA's motion for partial summary judgment, holding that undisputed facts in the case established VNA's right to protection under 19 U.S.C. § 1526. *Vittoria N. Am., L.L.C. v. Euro Asia Imports,* No. CIV-99-1357 A, slip op. at 1 (W.D.Okla. July 12, 2000). Specifically, the district court found that "Vittoria" is a registered United States Trademark, *id.* at 3, that Vittoria Italy assigned all of its rights, title and interest in the mark to VNA, and that the Assignment Agreement was recorded in the U.S. Patent and Trademark Office, *id.* The district court also found that VNA is not a subsidiary of Vittoria Italy, and has no common officers or directors with Vittoria, *id.* Finally, the district court found that the evidence showed EAI had imported and sold Vittoria-branded products in the United States. *Id.* The district court therefore enjoined EAI from further importation of Vittoria-branded products into the United States, although it did not address the issue of damages in its order. *Id.* at 12.

EAI now appeals the district court's injunction. EAI contends that the evidence relied upon by the district court was insufficient to prove VNA's ownership of the Vittoria trademark in the United States. Further, EAI argues that VNA is not entitled to protection under the Act because it falls under a regulatory exception denying gray market protection to U.S. companies if they are owned by or subject to common control with a foreign manufacturer of the trademarked goods. *See* 19 C.F.R. § 133.23(d)(1). Finally, EAI argues that the district court erred by failing to grant it leave to file a surrebuttal.

II. DISCUSSION

The district court had jurisdiction pursuant to 28 U.S.C. § 1331, and we exercise jurisdiction pursuant to 28 U.S.C. § 1292. "In reviewing [an] injunction, we may also address the summary judgment order that served as the district court's principal legal basis for granting the injunction because the district court's ruling on summary judgment was inextricably intertwined with its ruling granting a permanent injunction."

We review de novo a district court's grant of summary judgment, and affirm only if the "pleadings, depositions, answers to interrogatories, and admissions on file, together with the affidavits, if any, show that there is no genuine issue as to any material fact and that the moving party is entitled to judgment as a matter of law." We draw all inferences and construe the evidence in the light most favorable to the non-moving party.

. . . .

B. *Transfer of Vittoria Trademark to VNA*

We next consider EAI's contention that VNA is not entitled to gray market protection under the Act. In order to prove entitlement to protection under the Act, VNA must show that it is a corporation or association created or organized within the United States, that it owns the Vittoria trademark in the United States, that the trademark is registered in the Patent and Trademark Office of the United States Customs Service, and that EAI is, without VNA's consent, importing Vittoria-branded goods of foreign manufacture. The district court found that undisputed evidence sufficiently established each of these points.

EAI contests whether the evidence demonstrates that VNA owns the Vittoria trademark in the United States. First, EAI asserts that the transfer was invalid for purposes of establishing any rights to gray market protection because the transaction was not at arm's-length and because VNA did not "pay dearly" for the assignment. . . . .[3]

. . . .

C. *The Common Control Exception*

We next consider whether, in spite of a valid transfer of the trademark from Vittoria Italy to VNA, a regulatory exception to the Act removes VNA from the scope of its gray market protections. The regulation in question, 19 C.F.R. § 133.23(d)(1), reads, in relevant part:

---

3. To the extent that EAI's briefs can be construed to argue that the evidence gives rise to an inference that the Assignment Agreement was a sham, we disagree. EAI notes correctly that the evidence is sufficient to show that Vittoria Italy continues to market directly to original equipment manufacturers ("OEMs")—*i.e.,* bicycle manufacturers—in the United States and Canada. Further, EAI points out that the Assignment Agreement contains a clause entitling Vittoria Italy to retake possession of the U.S. rights to the trademark with thirty days written notice. However, Vittoria Italy's continued sales to U.S. OEMs does not show that the transfer lacked validity. Rather, it demonstrates only that VNA has failed to enforce its trademark with respect to that market against Vittoria Italy. Likewise, the thirty-day reassignment clause does not establish that the transfer is a sham, as the district court noted in its summary judgment order.

Gray market goods subject to the restrictions of this section shall be detained for 30 days from the date on which the goods are presented for Customs examination, to permit the importer to establish that any of the following exceptions . . . are applicable:

(1) The trademark or trade name was applied under the authority of a . . . trade name owner who is the same as the U.S. owner, a parent or subsidiary of the U.S. owner, or a party otherwise subject to common ownership or control with the U.S. owner (in an instance covered by § 133.2(d) and 133.12(d) of this part).

EAI does not allege that VNA is the same as Vittoria Italy, is a parent or subsidiary of Vittoria Italy, or that it is subject to common ownership with Vittoria Italy. Rather, EAI argues that the evidence is sufficient to show common control of the two companies or control of VNA by Vittoria Italy.

For the purpose of applying § 133.23, common control is defined as "effective control in policy and operations and is not necessarily synonymous with common ownership." 19 C.F.R. § 133.2(d)(2); *see also United States v. Eighty-Three Rolex Watches*, 992 F.2d 508, 516 (5th Cir. 1993) ("the ties that bind two entities with a profitable business relationship" do not constitute the required "effective control"); *United States v. Eighty Nine Bottles of "Eau de Joy"*, 797 F.2d 767, 772 (9th Cir. 1986) (suggesting that "common control" required "common ownership, operations or management."). "[A] close and profitable business relationship" does not amount to common control. Rather, "[t]he regulatory language makes clear that it contemplates the sort of control that a parent corporation would exercise over a subsidiary or that a common owner might exercise over both organizations."

In this case, EAI asserts genuine questions of material fact exist with respect to the following allegations: (1) VNA and Vittoria Italy work in concert to design, develop and distribute Vittoria products; (2) VNA and Vittoria Italy make joint decisions as to "present and future product ranges"; (3) Vittoria Italy sells Vittoria-branded products directly to original equipment manufacturers in the United States; (4) Vittoria Italy pays a significant percentage of VNA's advertising budget and exercises some measure of control over VNA's marketing of Vittoria products; (5) Vittoria Italy determines which product lines VNA is allowed to market in the United States; (6) Vittoria Italy reimburses VNA for nearly all of its liability for warranty claims on Vittoria products; (7) Vittoria Italy's catalog lists VNA as its "U.S. distributor"; and (8) the president and CEO of Vittoria Italy, Rudie Campagne ("Campagne"), makes decisions about employees of VNA as well as a sister company of VNA called XLM. Although these allegations show a "close and profitable business relationship," they fall short of establishing "common control" as defined in 19 C.F.R. § 133.2(d).

For example, allegations of joint decision making and cooperative efforts to develop and market products for the United States at most give rise to an inference that a close business relationship exists between VNA and Vittoria Italy. Indeed, such cooperative planning is required by the 1992 Agreement. (*Aplt. App.* at 39, ¶ 4.2.)

Similarly, Vittoria Italy's reimbursing VNA for warranty liabilities does not give rise to an inference of control. While Vittoria Italy provides funding to support VNA's advertising, Vittoria Italy has no legal control over how those funds are spent. EAI's evidence that Vittoria Italy controls VNA's employment decisions apparently consists of a single e-mail from Campagne expressing his disapproval with VNA's management team and a "strong request" that it rehire a retired former officer of the company, which it did. Again, this is not evidence of control, but only evidence of VNA's understandable desire to preserve a good business relationship with Vittoria Italy.

VNA is referred to as the U.S. distributor for the "Vittoria Group" in the catalog. However, deposition testimony by VNA executives explains that the term "Vittoria Group" is a collective, descriptive term used to refer to several independent companies, each of which is somehow engaged in the production or sale of Vittoria products. In contrast, EAI has offered no evidence of any legal authority enabling Vittoria Italy or any other party to control VNA's actions.

. . . .

We believe EAI reads too much into Justice Brennan's concurrence by attempting to apply the descriptive word "affiliate" to this context. First, extending the common control exception to companies who merely work together under cooperative contractual arrangements would not advance the two policy considerations for § 526 that Justice Brennan identified in his concurrence. The first of these is that independent U.S. entities which acquire rights to trademarks have significantly greater investment-backed expectations at stake than subsidiaries or other "affiliates" of foreign manufacturers. However, close but independent business allies are also likely to have invested significant financial and human capital into their endeavors, as the record shows to be the case here. Second, Justice Brennan contrasted independent U.S. trademark holders with those covered by the common control exception because, in the latter case, the foreign manufacturer can protect its U.S. marketing efforts simply by restricting who can purchase the product and where those customers can subsequently export it. *Id.* The same cannot be said of U.S. trademark owners associated with foreign manufacturers only by virtue of a contract or other cooperative arrangement rather than by "common control." While close business allies may hope to persuade their partners to adopt such controls, without more they are not able to force an unwilling foreign manufacturer to protect them from gray market importers. Such is the case here.

Finally, we find no evidence that VNA and Vittoria Italy have engaged in fraud or otherwise have attempted to subvert the limits Congress placed on § 526's protections. Although EAI alleges that VNA was created "at the behest" of Vittoria Italy, it points to no evidence that the agreement leading to the creation of VNA was anything but an arm's-length transaction between the Hibdon Tire Center and Vittoria Italy. Further, there is no evidence that Vittoria Italy has any legal authority to control VNA's actions, and no evidence of other connections between them such as interlocking officers or directors.

In sum, we hold that EAI has failed to demonstrate the existence of genuine questions of material fact sufficient to implicate the common control exception to the Act.

. . . .

III. CONCLUSION

For the reasons set forth herein, we AFFIRM the grant of partial summary judgment for VNA.

ii. Lever Brothers Company v. United States, 981 F.2d 1330 (D.C. Cir. 1993)

United States trademark holder brought action seeking to require Customs Service to exclude foreign goods bearing identical trademark. The District Court . . . denied request for preliminary injunction, and trademark holder appealed. The Court of Appeals . . . reversed and remanded. The United States District Court for the District of Columbia, . . . enjoined enforcement of challenged regulation, and government appealed. The Court of Appeals . . . Circuit Judge, held that: (1) "affiliate exception" to prohibition of importation on goods bearing United States trademark was invalid, but (2) injunction was overbroad.

Affirmed in part and vacated and remanded in part.

SENTELLE, Circuit Judge:

The District Court entered a judgment invalidating the "affiliate exception" of 19 C.F.R. § 133.21(c)(1988) as inconsistent with the statutory mandate of the Lanham Act of 1946, 15 U.S.C. § 1124 (1988), prohibiting importation of goods which copy or simulate the mark of a domestic manufacturer, and issued a nationwide injunction barring enforcement of the regulation with respect to *any* foreign goods bearing a valid United States trademark but materially and physically differing from the United States version of the goods. The United States appeals. We conclude that the District Court, obedient to our limited remand in a prior decision in this same cause, properly determined that the regulation is inconsistent with the statute. However, because we conclude that the remedy the District Court provided is overbroad, we vacate the judgment and remand for entry of an injunction against allowing the importation of the foreign-produced Lever Brothers brand products at issue in this case.

I. BACKGROUND

Lever Brothers Company ("Lever US" or "Lever"), an American company, and its British affiliate, Lever Brothers Limited ("Lever UK"), both manufacture deodorant soap under the "Shield" trademark and hand dishwashing liquid under the "Sunlight" trademark. The trademarks are registered in each country. The products have evidently been formulated differently to suit local tastes and circumstances. The U.S. version lathers more, the soaps smell different, the colorants used in American "Shield" have been certified by the FDA whereas the colorants in British "Shield" have not, and the U.S. version contains a bacteriostat that enhances the deodorant properties of the soap. The British version of "Sunlight" dishwashing soap produces less suds, and the American version is formulated to work best in the "soft water" available in most American cities, whereas the British version is designed for "hard water" common in Britain.

The packaging of the U.S. and U.K. products is also somewhat different. The British "Shield" logo is written in script form and is packaged in foil wrapping and contains a wave motif, whereas the American "Shield" logo is written in block form, does not come in foil wrapping and contains a grid pattern. There is small print on the packages indicating where they were manufactured. The British "Sunlight" comes in a cylindrical bottle labeled "Sunlight Washing Up Liquid." The American "Sunlight" comes in a yellow, hour-glass-shaped bottle labeled "Sunlight Dishwashing Liquid."

Lever asserts that the unauthorized influx of these foreign products has created substantial consumer confusion and deception in the United States about the nature and origin of this merchandise, and that it has received numerous consumer complaints from American consumers who unknowingly bought the British products and were disappointed.

Lever argues that the importation of the British products was in violation of section 42 of the Lanham Act, 15 U.S.C. § 1124 which provides that with the exception of goods imported for personal use:

> [N]o article of imported merchandise which shall copy or simulate the name of the [sic] any domestic manufacture, or manufacturer . . . or which shall copy or simulate a trademark registered in accordance with the provisions of this chapter . . . shall be admitted to entry at any customhouse of the United States.

Id. The United States Customs Service ("Customs"), however, was allowing importation of the British goods under the "affiliate exception" created by 19 C.F.R. § 133.21(c)(2), which provides that foreign goods bearing United States trademarks are not forbidden when "[t]he foreign and domestic trademark or trade name owners are parent and subsidiary companies or are otherwise subject to common ownership or control."[3]

In *Lever I,* we concluded that "the natural, virtually inevitable reading of section 42 is that it bars foreign goods bearing a trademark identical to the valid U.S. trademark but physically different," without regard to affiliation between the producing firms or the genuine character of the trademark abroad. 877 F.2d 101, 111 (D.C. Cir. 1989). In so concluding, we applied the teachings of *Chevron U.S.A. Inc. v. NRDC,* 467 U.S. 837 (1984). Under the *Chevron* analysis, if Congress has clearly expressed an intent on a matter, we give that intent full effect (Step One of *Chevron*). If there is any ambiguity, we accept Customs' interpretation, provided only that it is reasonable (Step Two of *Chevron*). The *Lever I* panel found the present controversy to survive barely *Chevron* Step One and "provisional[ly]" concluded that the affiliate

---

3. This case does not involve a dispute between corporate affiliates. Neither Lever US nor Lever UK has authorized the importation which is being conducted by third parties.

exception is inconsistent with section 42 with respect to physically different goods.[4] The "provisional" qualifier on our determination of the invalidity of the exception was a very limited one. Noting that "neither party has briefed the legislative history nor administrative practice in any detail," we adopted the apparently controlling reading of section 42 only "tentatively" and remanded the case to the District Court to allow the parties to "join issue on those points." The panel in *Lever I* thus created a very small window of opportunity for the government to establish that the affiliate exception regulation was consistent with section 42 of the Lanham Act. At that time we said, "[s]ubject to some persuasive evidence running against our tentative conclusion, we must say that Lever's probability of success on its legal argument is quite high." *Id.*

. . . .

After reviewing the submissions of the parties, the District Court found that Customs' administrative practice was "at best inconsistent" and, in any event, had "never addressed the specific question of physically different goods that bear identical trademarks." The District Court concluded that "section 42 . . . prohibits the importation of foreign goods that . . . are physically different, regardless of the validity of the foreign trademark or the existence of an affiliation between the U.S. and foreign markholders." *Id.* The court accordingly concluded that "[n]either the legislative history of the statute nor the administrative practice of the Customs Service clearly contradicts the plain meaning of section 42" and granted summary judgment against the government. *Id.* at 13.

By way of remedy, the District Court enjoined Customs "from enforcing 19 C.F.R. § 133.21(c)(2) as to foreign goods that bear a trademark identical to a valid United States trademark but which are materially, physically different."

II. ANALYSIS

Here the specific question at Step Two of *Chevron* is whether the intended prohibition of section 42 admits of an exception for materially different goods manufactured by foreign affiliates. We apply a very limited Step Two *Chevron* analysis, because we previously concluded that the intent of Congress is virtually plain. *Lever I*, 877 F.2d at 104-05. The government bears a heavy burden in attempting to overcome the apparent meaning of the statute. In *Griffin v. Oceanic Contractors, Inc.*, 458 U.S. 564 (1982), the Supreme Court held that when Congress's "will has been expressed in reasonably plain terms, 'that language must ordinarily be regarded as conclusive.'" A presumption in favor of reasonably clear statutory language will be disrupted only if there is a "'clearly expressed legislative intention' contrary to that language." When we remanded this case, we indicated that the Government could not prevail unless it produced "persuasive evidence" rebutting our tentative reading of the statute,

---

4. In *Lever I*, we expressly recognized that our decision was not in conflict with the Supreme Court's decision in *K Mart Corp. v. Cartier*, . . . which upheld the affiliate exception against a challenge based on section 526 of the Tariff Act of 1930, but "did not reach the question of the exception's validity under section 42 of the Lanham Act."

because the affiliate exception appears to contradict the clear implication of the language of section 42. The legislative history and administrative practice before us, as before the District Court, will not perform that onerous task.

A. *Legislative History and Administrative Practice Prior to Enactment of Lanham Act*

. . . .

The Supreme Court interpreted section 27 more broadly. In *A Bourjois & Co. v. Katzel*, 260 U.S. 244 (1923), the Court held that a third party could not import a face powder manufactured in France when the plaintiff owned the United States trademarks for the product, even though the product sold was "the genuine product of the French concern. . . ." *Id.* at 691. The Supreme Court concluded that even an authentic foreign trademark on "genuine" merchandise may infringe a registered United States trademark.

. . . .

Several conclusions can be drawn from the pre-Lanham Act legislative history and administrative practice. First, at least until 1936, protection from unauthorized importation was consistently based upon ownership of a United States trademark, not upon the nature of the relationship between the trademark owner and the foreign producer. Second, as trademark law became more international, the trend was toward greater protection from foreign importation. Third, although the 1936 regulations implemented the first version of the affiliate exception, the specific question of materially different goods is nowhere addressed.

B. *Legislative History of Section 42 of Lanham Act*

. . . .

It is also noteworthy that the 1944 [Tariff Commission] memorandum does not refer to "affiliates" or "closely affiliated" companies, but only to the importation of one's "own" merchandise. In short, there is nothing in the record concerning the Lanham Act indicating that Congress contemplated — much less intended to allow — an affiliate exception. More to the point, there is no evidence that Congress intended to allow third parties to import physically different trademarked goods that are manufactured and sold abroad by a foreign affiliate of the American trademark holder.

C. *Legislative History and Developments Since Passage of Lanham Act*

The Treasury Department's administrative practice after passage of the Lanham Act has been inconsistent. . . .

After Congress repeatedly considered and failed to enact the affiliate exception, the Treasury Department revived the exception. In 1972 the affiliate exception was adopted in the form at issue here. Under the 1972 regulations, section 42's protections were rendered inapplicable where:

> (1) Both the foreign and the U.S. trademark or trade name are owned by the same person or business entity;

(2) The foreign and domestic trademark or trade name owners are parent and subsidiary companies or are otherwise subject to common ownership or control;

(3) The articles of foreign manufacture bear a recorded trademark or trade name applied under authorization of the U.S. owner.

19 C.F.R. § 133.21(c) (citations omitted).[5]

. . . .

Customs' main argument from the legislative history is that section 42 of the Lanham Act applies only to imports of goods bearing trademarks that "copy or simulate" a registered mark. Customs thus draws a distinction between "genuine" marks and marks that "copy or simulate." A mark applied by a foreign firm subject to ownership and control common to that of the domestic trademark owner is by definition "genuine," Customs urges, regardless of whether or not the goods are identical. Thus, any importation of goods manufactured by an affiliate of a U.S. trademark owner cannot "copy or simulate" a registered mark because those goods are *ipso facto* "genuine."

This argument is fatally flawed. It rests on the false premise that foreign trademarks applied to foreign goods are "genuine" in the United States. Trademarks applied to physically different foreign goods are not genuine from the viewpoint of the American consumer. As we stated in *Lever I:*

> On its face . . . section [42] appears to aim at deceit and consumer confusion; when identical trademarks have acquired different meanings in different countries, one who imports the foreign version to sell it under that trademark will (in the absence of some specially differentiating feature) cause the confusion Congress sought to avoid. The fact of affiliation between the producers in no way reduces the probability of that confusion; it is certainly not a constructive consent to importation.

There is a larger, more fundamental and ultimately fatal weakness in Customs' position in this case. Section 42 on its face appears to forbid importation of goods that "copy or simulate" a United States trademark. Customs has the burden of adducing evidence from the legislative history of section 42 and its administrative practice of an exception for materially different goods whose similar foreign and domestic trademarks are owned by affiliated companies. At a minimum, this requires that the specific question be addressed in the legislative history and administrative practice. The bottom line, however, is that the issue of materially different goods was

---

5. In *Kmart Corp. v. Cartier, Inc.,* 486 U.S. 281 (1988), the Supreme Court struck down 19 C.F.R. § 133.21(c)(3), which allowed the importation of foreign-made goods where the United States trademark owner has authorized the use of the mark, as in conflict with the unequivocal language of section 526 of the Tariff Act. Section 526 prohibits the importation of "any merchandise of foreign manufacture" bearing a trademark "owned by" a citizen of, or by a "corporation . . . organized within, the United States" unless written consent of the trademark owner is produced at the time of entry. By a different majority, the Supreme Court upheld 19 C.F.R. § 133.21(c)(2), the regulation at issue here, as consistent with section 526. As we noted above, the *Kmart* case did not address the validity of these regulations under the Lanham Act. *See supra* n. 4.

not addressed either in the legislative history or the administrative record. It is not enough to posit that silence implies authorization, when the authorization sought runs counter to the evident meaning of the governing statute. Therefore, we conclude that section 42 of the Lanham Act precludes the application of Customs' affiliate exception with respect to physically, materially different goods.

IV. SCOPE OF INJUNCTION

The United States alternatively argues that this Court should vacate the District Court's injunction that applies to materially different goods other than those directly at issue in this case. The District Court's injunction provides that the Customs Service is "enjoined from enforcing [the common ownership or control provision] as to foreign goods that bear a trademark identical to a valid United States trademark but which are materially, physically different."

. . . We therefore conclude that Lever is entitled only to that relief specifically sought in its complaint, namely, that Customs be enjoined from allowing the importation of Lever's "Shield" and "Sunlight" trademarks.

V. CONCLUSION

For the foregoing reasons, we affirm the District Court's ruling that section 42 of the Lanham Act, bars the importation of physically different foreign goods bearing a trademark identical to a valid U.S. trademark, regardless of the trademark's genuine character abroad or affiliation between the producing firms. Injunctive relief, however, is limited to the two products which were the subject of this action. We therefore vacate the District Court's prior order to the extent that it renders global relief and remand for the entry of an injunction consistent with this opinion.

So ordered.

Part Three: Administrative Remedies for Infringing Imports Including Patent Violations

A. Overview

In addition to infringement actions in federal court and customs seizures, federal law provides administrative remedies to combat imports that infringe intellectual property rights. These remedies, contained in 19 U.S.C. § 1337, are administered by the ITC[31] and subject to the Administrative Procedures Act.

Here is how the ITC describes[32] the process:

> **Section 337 investigations** conducted by the U.S. International Trade Commission most often involve claims regarding intellectual property rights, in-

---

31. https://www.usitc.gov/intellectual_property.htm.
32. https://www.usitc.gov/intellectual_property/about_section_337.htm.

cluding allegations of patent infringement and trademark infringement by imported goods. Both utility and design patents, as well as registered and common law trademarks, may be asserted in these investigations. Other forms of unfair competition involving imported products, such as infringement of registered copyrights, mask works or boat hull designs, misappropriation of trade secrets or trade dress, passing off, and false advertising, may also be asserted. Additionally, antitrust claims relating to imported goods may be asserted. The primary remedy available in Section 337 investigations is an exclusion order that directs Customs to stop infringing imports from entering the United States. In addition, the Commission may issue cease and desist orders against named importers and other persons engaged in unfair acts that violate Section 337. Expedited relief in the form of temporary exclusion orders and temporary cease and desist orders may also be available in certain exceptional circumstances. Section 337 investigations, which are conducted pursuant to 19 U.S.C. § 1337 and the Administrative Procedure Act, include trial proceedings before administrative law judges and review by the Commission.

B. Assignment

Please analyze the facts provided in Part One under the relevant <u>provisions of § 337</u>,[33] which appear below. *What advantages does an administrative process under § 337 have over civil litigation in a federal court? Can the remedies offered under § 337 effectively combat counterfeits and patent violating goods that are distributed through internet sales?*

C. Resources

1. Section 1337 Text

§ 1337. Unfair practices in import trade

(a) Unlawful activities; covered industries; definitions

(1) Subject to paragraph (2), the following are unlawful, and when found by the Commission to exist shall be dealt with, in addition to any other provision of law, as provided in this section:

(A) Unfair methods of competition and unfair acts in the importation of articles (other than articles provided for in subparagraphs (B), (C), (D) and (E)) into the United States, or in the sale of such articles by the owner, importer, or consignee, the threat or effect of which is—

---

33. https://www.usitc.gov/intellectual_property/about_section_337.htm.

(i) to destroy or substantially injure an industry in the United States;

(ii) to prevent the establishment of such an industry; or

(iii) to restrain or monopolize trade and commerce in the United States.

(B) The importation into the United States, the sale for importation, or the sale within the United States after importation by the owner, importer, or consignee, of articles that—

(i) infringe a valid and enforceable United States patent or a valid and enforceable United States copyright registered under title 17; or

(ii) are made, produced, processed, or mined under, or by means of, a process covered by the claims of a valid and enforceable United States patent.

(C) The importation into the United States, the sale for importation, or the sale within the United States after importation by the owner, importer, or consignee, of articles that infringe a valid and enforceable United States trademark registered under the Trademark Act of 1946 (15 U.S.C. 1051 et seq.).

(D) The importation into the United States, the sale for importation, or the sale within the United States after importation by the owner, importer, or consignee, of a semiconductor chip product in a manner that constitutes infringement of a mask work registered under chapter 9 of title 17.

(E) The importation into the United States, the sale for importation, or the sale within the United States after importation by the owner, importer, or consigner, of an article that constitutes infringement of the exclusive rights in a design protected under chapter 13 of Title [17 U.S.C.A. § 1301 et seq.]

(2) Subparagraphs (B), (C), and (D) of paragraph (1) apply only if an industry in the United States, relating to the articles protected by the patent, copyright, trademark, mask work or design concerned, exists or is in the process of being established.

(3) For purposes of paragraph (2), an industry in the United States shall be considered to exist if there is in the United States, with respect to the articles protected by the patent, copyright, trademark, mask work or design concerned—

(A) significant investment in plant and equipment;

(B) significant employment of labor or capital; or

(C) substantial investment in its exploitation, including engineering, research and development, or licensing.

(4) For the purposes of this section, the phrase "owner, importer, or consignee" includes any agent of the owner, importer, or consignee.

(b) Investigation of violations by Commission

(1) The Commission shall investigate any alleged violation of this section on complaint under oath or upon its initiative. Upon commencing any such investigation, the Commission shall publish notice thereof in the Federal Register. The Commission shall conclude any such investigation and make its determination under this section

at the earliest practicable time after the date of publication of notice of such investigation. To promote expeditious adjudication, the Commission shall, within 45 days after an investigation is initiated, establish a target date for its final determination.

. . . .

(c) Determinations; review

The Commission shall determine, with respect to each investigation conducted by it under this section, whether or not there is a violation of this section, except that the Commission may, by issuing a consent order or on the basis of an agreement between the private parties to the investigation, including an agreement to present the matter for arbitration, terminate any such investigation, in whole or in part, without making such a determination. Each determination under subsection (d) or (e) of this section shall be made on the record after notice and opportunity for a hearing in conformity with the provisions of subchapter II of chapter 5 of title 5. All legal and equitable defenses may be presented in all cases. A respondent may raise any counterclaim in a manner prescribed by the Commission. Immediately after a counterclaim is received by the Commission, the respondent raising such counterclaim shall file a notice of removal with a United States district court in which venue for any of the counter-claims raised by the party would exist under section 1391 . . . .

. . . .

(d) Exclusion of articles from entry

(1) If the Commission determines, as a result of an investigation under this section, that there is a violation of this section, it shall direct that the articles concerned, imported by any person violating the provision of this section, be excluded from entry into the United States, unless, after considering the effect of such exclusion upon the public health and welfare, competitive conditions in the United States economy, the production of like or directly competitive articles in the United States, and United States consumers, it finds that such articles should not be excluded from entry. The Commission shall notify the Secretary of the Treasury of its action under this subsection directing such exclusion from entry, and upon receipt of such notice, the Secretary shall, through the proper officers refuse such entry.

(2) The authority of the Commission to order an exclusion from entry of articles shall be limited to persons determined by the Commission to be violating this section unless the Commission determines that—

(A) a general exclusion from entry of articles is necessary to prevent circumvention of an exclusion order limited to products of named persons; or

(B) there is a pattern of violation of this section and it is difficult to identify the source of infringing products.

(e) Exclusion of articles from entry during investigation except under bond; procedures applicable; preliminary relief

(1) If, during the course of an investigation under this section, the Commission determines that there is reason to believe that there is a violation of this section, it

may direct that the articles concerned, imported by any person with respect to whom there is reason to believe that such person is violating this section, be excluded from entry into the United States, unless, after considering the effect of such exclusion upon the public health and welfare, competitive conditions in the United States economy, the production of like or directly competitive articles in the United States, and United States consumers, it finds that such articles should not be excluded from entry. The Commission shall notify the Secretary of the Treasury of its action under this subsection directing such exclusion from entry, and upon receipt of such notice, the Secretary shall, through the proper officers, refuse such entry, except that such articles shall be entitled to entry under bond prescribed by the Secretary in an amount determined by the Commission to be sufficient to protect the complainant from any injury. If the Commission later determines that the respondent has violated the provisions of this section, the bond may be forfeited to the complainant.

(2) A complainant may petition the Commission for the issuance of an order under this subsection. The Commission shall make a determination with regard to such petition by no later than the 90th day after the date on which the Commission's notice of investigation is published in the Federal Register. The Commission may extend the 90-day period for an additional 60 days in a case it designates as a more complicated case. The Commission shall publish in the Federal Register its reasons why it designated the case as being more complicated. The Commission may require the complainant to post a bond as a prerequisite to the issuance of an order under this subsection. If the Commission later determines that the respondent has not violated the provisions of this section, the bond may be forfeited to the respondent.

(3) The Commission may grant preliminary relief under this subsection or subsection (f) of this section to the same extent as preliminary injunctions and temporary restraining orders may be granted under the Federal Rules of Civil Procedure.

(4) The Commission shall prescribe the terms and conditions under which bonds may be forfeited under paragraphs (1) and (2).

(f) Cease and desist orders; civil penalty for violation of orders

(1) In addition to, or in lieu of, taking action under subsection (d) or (e) of this section, the Commission may issue and cause to be served on any person violating this section, or believed to be violating this section, as the case may be, an order directing such person to cease and desist from engaging in the unfair methods or acts involved, unless after considering the effect of such order upon the public health and welfare, competitive conditions in the United States economy, the production of like or directly competitive articles in the United States, and United States consumers, it finds that such order should not be issued. The Commission may at any time, upon such notice and in such manner as it deems proper, modify or revoke any such order, and, in the case of a revocation, may take action under subsection (d) or (e) of this section, as the case may be. If a temporary cease and desist order is issued in addition to, or in lieu of, an exclusion order under subsection (e) of this section, the Commission may require the complainant to post a bond, in an amount determined

by the Commission to be sufficient to protect the respondent from any injury, as a prerequisite to the issuance of an order under this subsection. If the Commission later determines that the respondent has not violated the provisions of this section, the bond may be forfeited to the respondent. The Commission shall prescribe the terms and conditions under which the bonds may be forfeited under this paragraph.

(2) Any person who violates an order issued by the Commission under paragraph (1) after it has become final shall forfeit and pay to the United States a civil penalty for each day on which an importation of articles, or their sale, occurs in violation of the order of not more than the greater of $100,000 or twice the domestic value of the articles entered or sold on such day in violation of the order. Such penalty shall accrue to the United States and may be recovered for the United States in a civil action brought by the Commission in the Federal District Court for the District of Columbia or for the district in which the violation occurs. In such actions, the United States district courts may issue mandatory injunctions incorporating the relief sought by the Commission as they deem appropriate in the enforcement of such final orders of the Commission.

(g) Exclusion from entry or cease and desist order; conditions and procedures applicable

(1) If—

(A) a complaint is filed against a person under this section;

(B) the complaint and a notice of investigation are served on the person;

(C) the person fails to respond to the complaint and notice or otherwise fails to appear to answer the complaint and notice;

(D) the person fails to show good cause why the person should not be found in default; and

(E) the complainant seeks relief limited solely to that person; the Commission shall presume the facts alleged in the complaint to be true and shall, upon request, issue an exclusion from entry or a cease and desist order, or both, limited to that person unless, after considering the effect of such exclusion or order upon the public health and welfare, competitive conditions in the United States economy, the production of like or directly competitive articles in the United States, and United States consumers, the Commission finds that such exclusion or order should not be issued.

(2) In addition to the authority of the Commission to issue a general exclusion from entry of articles when a respondent appears to contest an investigation concerning a violation of the provisions of this section, a general exclusion from entry of articles, regardless of the source or importer of the articles, may be issued if—

(A) no person appears to contest an investigation concerning a violation of the provisions of this section,

(B) such a violation is established by substantial, reliable, and probative evidence, and

(C) the requirements of subsection (d)(2) of this section are met.

(h) Sanctions for abuse of discovery and abuse of process

The Commission may by rule prescribe sanctions for abuse of discovery and abuse of process to the extent authorized by Rule 11 and Rule 37 of the Federal Rules of Civil Procedure.

(i) Forfeiture

(1) In addition to taking action under subsection (d) of this section, the Commission may issue an order providing that any article imported in violation of the provisions of this section be seized and forfeited to the United States if—

(A) the owner, importer, or consignee of the article previously attempted to import the article into the United States;

(B) the article was previously denied entry into the United States by reason of an order issued under subsection (d) of this section; and

(C) upon such previous denial of entry, the Secretary of the Treasury provided the owner, importer, or consignee of the article written notice of—

(i) such order, and

(ii) the seizure and forfeiture that would result from any further attempt to import the article into the United States.

(2) The Commission shall notify the Secretary of the Treasury of any order issued under this subsection and, upon receipt of such notice, the Secretary of the Treasury shall enforce such order in accordance with the provisions of this section.

(3) Upon the attempted entry of articles subject to an order issued under this subsection, the Secretary of the Treasury shall immediately notify all ports of entry of the attempted importation and shall identify the persons notified under paragraph (1)(C).

(4) The Secretary of the Treasury shall provide—

(A) the written notice described in paragraph (1)(C) to the owner, importer, or consignee of any article that is denied entry into the United States by reason of an order issued under subsection (d) of this section; and

(B) a copy of such written notice to the Commission.

(j) Referral to President

(1) If the Commission determines that there is a violation of this section, or that, for purposes of subsection (e) of this section, there is reason to believe that there is such a violation, it shall—

(A) publish such determination in the Federal Register, and

(B) transmit to the President a copy of such determination and the action taken under subsection (d), (e), (f), (g), or (i) of this section, with respect thereto, together with the record upon which such determination is based.

(2) If, before the close of the 60-day period beginning on the day after the day on which he receives a copy of such determination, the President, for policy reasons, dis-

approves such determination and notifies the Commission of his disapproval, then, effective on the date of such notice, such determination and the action taken under subsection (d), (e), (f), (g), or (i) of this section with respect thereto shall have no force or effect.

. . . .

2. Other Resources

While you should focus on carefully deciphering the statutory text, a practitioner's summary of § 337 can be found <u>here</u>.[34] The ITC also publishes a useful <u>summary and FAQ</u>[35] document. You can also access pending complaints and a list of outstanding exclusion orders under "intellectual property" "<u>recent 337 complaints</u>"[36] at the ITC website. Good insights regarding § 337 and internet sales are presented in an "<u>Update</u>"[37] entitled *ITC v the Internet: Fighting to Protect IP Rights Against Online Sales of Infringing Imports* by the law firm Sidley Austin.

---

34. http://corporate.findlaw.com/litigation-disputes/a-brief-overview-of-practice-under -section-337.html.

35. www.usitc.gov/intellectual_property/documents/337_faqs.pdf.

36. https://www.usitc.gov/petitions_and_complaints.

37. https://www.sidley.com/en/insights/newsupdates/2010/01/itc-vs-internet-winning-the -fight-to-protect-ip-rights-against-online-sales-of-infringing-imports.

Chapter 16

International Trade in Services

A. Overview

1. International Trade in Services Is a Big Deal

This chapter focuses on international trade in services. From sophisticated international banking to face-painting party clowns, the sale of services comprises an ever-increasing part of many developed economies and forms a critical part of international trade. The <u>2016 Annual Report on Recent Trends in U.S. Service Trade</u>[1] makes clear just how important trade in services is to the U.S. economy:

> Services continue to be a growing and important sector in the U.S. economy, accounting for 79 percent of U.S. gross domestic product (GDP) and 82 percent of employment in 2015. The World Trade Organization (WTO) reports that the U.S. services trade surplus in 2014 was the world's largest at $225.9 billion, followed by that the United Kingdom (UK) at $140.3 billion . . . . As the world's top exporter of services, the United States accounted for $687.6 billion, or 14 percent, of global cross-border commercial services exports in 2014.

The <u>U.S. Trade Representative's website</u>[2] adds this description of trade in services:

> Whether it is telecommunications, financial services, computer services, retail distribution, environmental services, audiovisual services, express delivery, or any other services sector, services trade is interconnecting our world, lowering costs for consumers and businesses, enhancing competition and innovation, improving choice and quality, attracting investment, diffusing knowledge and technology, and allowing for the efficient allocation of resources.

---

1. https://www.google.com/url?sa=t&rct=j&q=&esrc=s&source=web&cd=&ved=0ahUKEwihx syBj97RAhXH4iYKHb3uCp8QFggzMAQ&url=https%3A%2F%2Fwww.usitc.gov%2Fpublications %2F332%2Fpub4643.pdf&usg=AFQjCNEokobRcTEF_v5VeT0WRMDbY99Pnw&sig2=ReX7HbBIC _F3fZHc2uG-TQ&cad=rja.
2. https://ustr.gov/issue-areas/services-investment/services.

Although services are not subject to tariffs, barriers to services trade such as nationality requirements and restrictions on investing generally exceed those for goods. Lowering services barriers will provide a significant payoff for the U.S. and world economy.

The importance of services to the world economy has, not surprisingly, prompted the negotiation of international legal regimes designed to reduce barriers to trade in services. One of the first of these was created within NAFTA, the regional free trade agreement between the United States, Canada and Mexico. A second regime was created with the advent of the WTO and the revamping of GATT and related trade agreements in 1994 (as reviewed in Chapter 9 of this book). The General Agreement on Trade in Services, or GATS, creates a framework for progressively liberalizing trade in services, disciplining national regulations affecting trade in services and resolving disputes through the WTO Dispute Settlement Agreement.

Recently, the United States and other developed economies have also aggressively pursued liberalization of trade in services, e-commerce and telecommunications through bi-lateral (e.g., U.S.-Panama Trade Promotion Agreement[3]) and regional free trade agreements. Services provisions of such agreements are both authorized and coordinated within GATS under Article V. The joint WTO and World Bank portal "ITip"[4] provides a list[5] reporting over 100 regional trade agreements that include services, at least 13 of which involve the United States (also see USTR links to free trade agreement "chapters" on e-commerce and telecommunications[6]).

After many years of negotiations, the Trans-Pacific Partnership Agreement (TPP[7]) was finalized in October 2015. It included, along with controversial provisions[8] on arbitration of government-investor disputes, a chapter on liberalizing "Cross-Border Trade in Services" (full TPP text available here[9]). On January 24, 2017, President Trump officially withdrew U.S. participation in the TPP.

In 2013, the Obama administration launched two new major trade initiatives, to be negotiated since 2015 under so-called "fast track"[10] or "trade promotion authority." Each has a services component. The Transatlantic Trade and Investment Partnership, called T-TIP,[11] contemplates a comprehensive agreement between the U.S. and

---

3. https://ustr.gov/about-us/policy-offices/press-office/fact-sheets/2011/may/services-us-panama-trade-promotion-agreement.

4. http://i-tip.wto.org/services/(S(2skgeab4qh3eibvft2i4ev0y))/default.aspx.

5. rtais.wto.org/UI/PublicMaintainRTAHome.aspx.

6. https://ustr.gov/issue-areas/services-investment/telecom-e-commerce.

7. https://ustr.gov/.

8. https://www.washingtonpost.com/opinions/kill-the-dispute-settlement-language-in-the-trans-pacific-partnership/2015/02/25/ec7705a2-bd1e-11e4-b274-e5209a3bc9a9_story.html?utm_term=.a0c17bdbf6f0.

9. https://ustr.gov/trade-agreements/free-trade-agreements/trans-pacific-partnership/tpp-full-text.

10. https://en.wikipedia.org/wiki/Fast_track_%28trade%29.

11. https://ustr.gov/ttip.

EU aimed at, among many other things, improving market access for international service providers (U.S. view here;[12] EU view here[13]). The second initiative involves trade negotiations with 24 other nations to reach a new Trade in Services Agreement known as "TiSA."[14] According to the USTR:

> Drawing on best practices from around the world, TiSA will encompass state-of-the-art trade rules aimed at promoting fair and open trade across the full spectrum of service sectors—from telecommunications and technology to distribution and delivery services. TiSA will also take on new issues confronting the global marketplace, like restrictions on cross-border data flows that can disrupt the supply of services over the Internet—a rapidly expanding market for U.S. small businesses and entrepreneurs. And TiSA will support the development of strong, transparent, and effective regulatory policies, which are so important to enabling international commerce. Twenty-three economies are presently participating in TiSA,[15] representing 75 percent of the world's $44 trillion services market.

It remains to be seen if these proposed agreements, like the TPP, will fall victim to President Trump's apparent anti-trade positions.

B. Problem Sixteen

1. Facts

The facts of this problem are all about you, the budding international lawyer. Perhaps you are in this class because of the convenient way it fit into your afternoon schedule with no classes on Fridays. Perhaps you have trouble conceiving how international trade law might affect your own career and work as lawyer. What might international trade law have to do with practicing real estate development, estate planning, intellectual property protection, commercial litigation or labor law?

There seems little doubt that the practice of law is increasingly international. You might not realize just how international it is likely to become. The internationalization of practice includes not simply the requirement that lawyers involved in trade must deal with legal regimes from multiple national jurisdictions or international treaties. The reality of modern legal practice is that legal services have increasingly become an international trade commodity in themselves, bought and sold across national boundaries. American lawyers not only counsel foreign clients in the United States about federal and state law but also provide such advice in foreign jurisdictions, opening branch offices, associating with local firms or working for international

---

12. https://ustr.gov/about-us/policy-offices/press-office/fact-sheets/2013/june/wh-ttip.
13. trade.ec.europa.eu/doclib/docs/2015/january/tradoc_152999.2%20Services.pdf.
14. https://ustr.gov/TiSA.
15. https://ustr.gov/tisa/participant-list.

corporations. This legal expertise and skill may be sought not only regarding U.S. law but also foreign and international law as well.

Imagine, for example, that you develop an expertise in estate planning, asset management and taxation. The Latin American clients who seek your advice will not solely be concerned with U.S. law but also how the laws of their home country and perhaps those of other jurisdictions and international treaties may affect their interests. Perhaps it will be convenient and profitable for you to open an affiliate office in Buenos Aires in order to counsel Argentine clients about international asset management. A small U.S. company exporting goods to Spain may need a sales agent or distributor in that country and thereby become subject to Spanish labor and contractual requirements. They may need a lawyer licensed in Spain and they will also need you to guide the way. Where the clients go, so must the lawyers, even if only through a virtual presence.

What does the increasingly international character of legal practice mean for you and other lawyers? What can you do with regard to providing legal services to overseas clients in foreign markets? What can foreign licensed lawyers do on your own home turf in providing such services to your potential clients?

2. Assignment

After completing this chapter, you should be able to provide explanations for the following basic questions, contextualizing each to trade in legal services:

1. *How is international trade in services distinct from trade in tangible goods, and what are the restrictions and obstacles commonly imposed by governments?*

2. *By what methods might a U.S. lawyer deliver legal services to overseas clients in their home jurisdiction? How might foreign lawyers deliver legal services to clients in the United States?*

3. *How do the WTO and GATS attempt to liberalize international trade in services? What specific legal rules ("disciplines") and other obligations does GATS create, particularly regarding market access, national treatment and Article VI: 4 domestic measures?*

4. *How does the approach taken in NAFTA, and within the EU, differ from GATS?*

5. *What is the likely future for international trade in legal services and how might it affect your professional life?*

C. Resources & Materials

1. The Distinct Characteristics of Trade in Services

International trade in services often involves concerns and risks similar to those presented in the sale of goods. Services are by their nature, however, distinct from tangible goods in ways that present unique legal issues. Such distinctions, and governments' legitimate concerns about how international provision of services may affect public health, safety and welfare, have resulted in an international regulatory regime distinct from that governing trade in goods or intellectual property rights. How is trade in services distinct from trade in goods? Consider the following general observations.

a. You Cannot Drop a Service on Your Foot

Perhaps the most common adage concerning the difference between services and goods is that you can't drop a service on your foot. Goods are tangible products, while services involve the performance of defined tasks. Lawyers, doctors, engineers, architects and accountants primarily sell services not goods. Banks, insurance companies, telecommunication providers and transportation carriers are examples of service providers essential to international trade itself. While the production of a tangible good, like a car, may involve the performance of many services, the value of these activities are eventually merged into the final product, a good to be bought and sold. In contrast, if payment is for the performance of a task rather than a tangible object, the transaction is one for services. Such seemingly simple distinctions are central to most legal issues that are unique to trade in services.

b. Services May be Delivered in Distinct Ways Relevant to Trade

There are essentially four principle ways in which a service may be rendered that have legal and practical implications relevant to international trade. These distinct methods of delivering services are incorporated directly into the structure of both NAFTA and GATS, described as "modes of delivery."

First, and most obviously, a service could be delivered from one country into another across international boundaries without the movement of people or capital assets. Referred to in GATS as *cross-border supply*" and "mode 1," this manner of delivering services occurs when the service is provided at a distance, such as the sale of an insurance policy by an American-based insurer to a customer in Barbados. The seller can deliver this service, insuring against risks in Barbados, by entering into a long distance contract that does not require either the buyer or seller to cross international boundaries in order to perform. Other examples of services that may commonly involve cross-border delivery include overseas call centers, accountancy, architectural drawings, banking, computer technical support, and telecommunications. You might also get your fortune told by a Hamatsa <u>Shaman</u> or Greek soothsayer using skype.

Modern technology has greatly expanded the possibilities of such trade, so much so that complicated <u>remote surgery</u>[16] may now be performed with the aid of robotics. Law firms based in the United States now commonly <u>"off-shore" document review</u>[17] and other mundane legal tasks. No doubt advanced communications technology

---

16. http://news.nationalgeographic.com/news/2001/09/0919_robotsurgery_2.html.
17. www.insidecounsel.com/2009/01/01/the-offshore-option?slreturn=1495730289.

Photo Edward Curtis, Public Domain

also makes it easy for a lawyer to provide many types of legal assistance to clients anywhere in the world, if allowed to do so. Sending a brief written in your Miami office via email to a client in Argentina is a clear example of cross-border delivery of legal services using technology.

The second "mode of delivery" recognized by GATS is called "*consumption abroad*" ("mode 2"). Consumption is "abroad," since the purchaser physically travels to another country to receive the service. If you travel to Paris to get an especially stylish haircut, you have engaged in international trade through consumption abroad. Some 750,000 Americans annually travel overseas for "medical tourism"[18] involving services ranging from root canals and "nip & tuck" to major surgeries. Reversing this flow, over 800,000 foreign students[19] currently reside in the United States seeking educational services. Modern technology and the advent of effective long distance learning over the internet suggests that this particular service may eventually develop

---

18. https://www.cdc.gov/features/medicaltourism/.
19. https://www.internationalstudent.com/study_usa/.

significant "mode 1" cross-border delivery forms as well[20]—a potential less likely, one supposes, for haircuts than education.

Perhaps the most traditional manner of delivering services internationally involves the establishment of a physical presence in the place at which the services are rendered. This form of delivery is appropriately, if unimaginatively, dubbed *"commercial presence"* and "mode 3" by GATS. Here, a Swiss bank might, for example, offer financial services to American consumers by opening branch offices in U.S. cities.

Finally, services may sometimes be performed when natural persons providing the service travel overseas to the place of service. The British band, the Rolling Stones, will undoubtedly launch their next world tour before long, all in wheelchairs or walkers, and thus engage in this form of trade in services. GATS labels this "mode 4" type of service trade or *"presence of natural persons."* If a service involves the expertise of individuals applied in person, it obviously requires government permission to enter the jurisdiction and stay for at least some period of time.

c. Trade Restrictions on Services: Market Access, Economic Protectionism and Regulation to Preserve Public Health, Safety and Welfare

Restrictions on the international sale of services take many forms, relying on wide-ranging justifications. Unlike trade in goods, however, such restrictions do not generally involve tariffs. Rather, it is not uncommon for countries to create monopolies for certain services, highly regulate their delivery to protect consumers, engage in restrictive licensing or capital requirements, or require that providers maintain a physical presence in the place of service. Domestic providers may be favored and market access for foreigners denied in myriad ways. The materials below, describing trade in legal services, provide many good illustrations.

Some restrictions on foreign services providers are, of course, simply the product of economic protectionism. It has been reported that Indian lawyers, for example, candidly advocate for restrictions on international legal service providers on grounds

---

20. The International Trade Commission's 2013 Report, *Recent Trends in U.S. Services Trade* notes: After a relatively slow start, MOOCs received a surge of attention in 2012 after the launch of several high-profile websites, namely Coursera,14 edX,15 and Udacity. Student interest in the educational content provided by MOOCs has been substantial, particularly outside the United States. For example, in 2011, Sebastian Thrun and Peter Norvig, both professors at Stanford University, attracted 160,000 students in 209 countries to the online version of their 200-student class on artificial intelligence. Similarly, in the fall of 2012, eight public health classes offered by Johns Hopkins University on Coursera drew more than 170,000 students. However, initial high enrollments for some classes may be deceptive; participation and completion rates are often substantially lower. Coursera, for example, estimates that 40–60 percent of registered students attempt the first assignment, while only 10–15 percent will complete the course.
https://www.google.com/url?sa=t&rct=j&q=&esrc=s&source=web&cd=2&cad=rja&uact=8&ved=0CCYQFjAB&url=http%3A%2F%2Fwww.usitc.gov%2Fpublications%2F332%2Fpub4412.pdf&ei=gW6RVavZGcXutQWGj4DgAg&usg=AFQjCNFX564HYuJAi2KT-cIj_vyAhOUuAg&sig2=0S5uBzKy6bZHl1_-tQGy1w&bvm=bv.96783405,d.b2w.

that they cannot yet compete with the manpower, sophistication and connections of American and British law firms.[21] As with trade in goods, the WTO rules in GATS are often aimed directly at curbing such economically based restrictions, which stifle international competition. Many other restrictions, however, are justified by potentially legitimate concerns over public health, safety and welfare relating to the particular service. Indeed, most services in the United States, from insurance and banking to hairdressing, are highly regulated by state and federal law precisely to protect the public's interests. Just imagine how many elderly men and women would suffer the indignity of blue hair[22] without the detailed licensing rules commonly required for hairdressers in Florida.

Sellers of home insurance policies, for example, are typically required to meet certain criteria which include sufficient capitalization and underwriting standards precisely so that consumers are protected when insured risks actually materialize. Doctors and lawyers are required to demonstrate through licensing that they possess sufficient training, knowledge and skill in their field, because those failing to meet such standards often cause great damage to others. In this regard, the international service provider in cross-border situations often causes especially significant regulatory concerns for governments attempting to ensure public safety, fairness and welfare, since the provider is not physically present in its jurisdiction.

The liberalization of trade in services envisioned by GATS must necessarily account for such concerns and balance the understandable desire of national authorities to provide adequate protections for the public against the goal of increased market access and fair international competition. Governments world-wide are now increasingly at war with smart phone ride-sharing services such as Uber and Lyft over regulatory control.[23] Are these controversies about protecting other vested economic interests (taxi monopolies) from competition or do they arise because of legitimate concern for public safety and quality service — or is it a little bit of both?

2. International Trade in Legal Services: Current Conditions

Export of U.S. legal services is now big business. The International Trade Commission's 2013 Annual Report on Recent Trends[24] in U.S. Services found that, in 2011, the U.S. exported $7.5 billion, imported $1.8 billion and enjoyed a $5.7 billion trade

---

21. *See* Lauren Verbiscusa, *Economic Globalization and the Need for Legal Innovation*, 21 Mich. St. Int'l. L. Rev. 779, 802-05 (2013).

22. http://tvtropes.org/pmwiki/pmwiki.php/Main/ElderlyBlueHairedLady.

23. time.com/3592035/uber-taxi-history/.

24. www.google.com/url?sa=t&rct=j&q=&esrc=s&source=web&cd=4&ved=0CDQQFjAD&url =http%3A%2F%2Fwww.usitc.gov%2Fpublications%2F332%2Fpub4412.pdf&ei =lFeMVZX4MsnboAS-gbr4Bw&usg=AFQjCNFX564HYuJAi2KT-cIj_vyAhOUuAg&sig2 =qaieqyQIt1ZQJ_BizRPN6g&bvm=bv.96782255,d.cGU&cad=rja.

surplus in legal services, primarily through cross-border trade and foreign affiliates. According to Professor Carole Silver:

> Growth in the market for legal services has been substantial in the last twenty-five years, and it has fueled enormous international expansion of elite U.S.-based law firms. Over the twenty years spanning 1988–2008, the number of law firms with overseas offices on the "National Law Journal 250" list of the largest U.S. firms nearly doubled, the number of overseas offices supported by N.L.J. 250 firms nearly quadrupled, and the number of lawyers working in the overseas offices of the firms increased by nearly twelve-fold. This growth has spurred a transformation for many of the largest and most profitable U.S.-based law firms from national to international organizations: in fact, many claim the "global" moniker. They have offices overseas, they serve clients based overseas as well as U.S.-based clients with problems and needs related to their overseas activities, and they advise on foreign law in addition to U.S. law.[25]

She further notes, unsurprisingly, that this rapid growth in the exportation of legal services has been "quite lucrative from the U.S. perspective."

> According to the Bureau's October 2015 report, the United States exported more than nine billion dollars in legal services in 2013, which reflects an increase of almost $800 million over 2012 and substantially outpaces imports of legal services, which amounted to nearly two billion dollars in 2013. Another measure of the vibrancy of the market for global legal services is in cross-border law firm merger activity. According to a recent report, ninety-six global cross-border law firm mergers were announced in 2012 and fifty-six U.S. law firms opened at least one new office outside of the United States in 2012. Relatedly, in the period of 2011–2012, one group of seventy-five U.S.-based law firms supported approximately 530 offices outside of the United States, where approximately 14,000 lawyers worked. And growth post-2008 has occurred in this segment of the market. For example, the American Lawyer's 2014 Global 100 issue reported that more than 25,000 lawyers from the AmLaw 200 practiced in seventy countries.[26]

Trade in legal services is certainly not a one-way street, however. Lawyers licensed in the United State increasingly face competition from foreign licensed attorneys, some of whom sit for state bar exams after earning a U.S. LL.M. degree. There are currently more than 100 U.S. law schools admitting foreign lawyers into LL.M. degree programs, many of them operated exclusively for such students.[27] According to

---

25. Carole Silver, *The Variable Value of U.S. Legal Education in the Global Legal Services Market*, 24 Georgetown J. Legal Ethics 1 (2011).

26. Carole Silver, *What We Know and Need to Know About Global Lawyer Regulation*, 67 S.C. L. Rev. 461(2016).

27. *See* Julie M. Spanbauer, *Lost in Translation in the Law School Classroom: Assessing Required Coursework in LL.M. Programs for International Students*, 35 Int'l J. Legal Info. 396 (2007).

statistics compiled by the National Conference of Bar Examiners,[28] 27 states allow foreign lawyers with U.S. based LL.M. degrees to sit for their bar exam, and, in 2014, 6,372 persons with primary law degrees from outside of the United States took a state bar exam (29% passed). Most U.S. law schools also give foreign lawyers academic credit (one year for civil law degrees and two years for degrees from common law jurisdictions), providing a shorter course of study to earn a J.D. degree.

Apart from obtaining a state license to practice law, there are several other avenues through which foreign lawyers potentially may provide services in the U.S. market, all endorsed by the ABA but not necessarily state law. In January 2015, the Conference of Chief Justices[29] adopted the following resolution encouraging states to liberalize rules on foreign lawyers by method of practice:

> NOW, THEREFORE, BE IT RESOLVED that the Conference of Chief Justices strongly encourages its members to adopt explicit policies that permit the following qualified activities by foreign lawyers as a means to increase available legal services and to facilitate movement of goods and services between the United States and foreign nations:
>
> 1) Temporary practice by foreign lawyers (ABA Model Rule for Temporary Practice by Foreign Lawyers),
>
> 2) Licensing and practice by foreign legal consultants (ABA Model Rule for the Licensing and Practice of Foreign Legal Consultants),
>
> 3) Registration of foreign-licensed in-house counsel (ABA Model Rule of Professional Conduct 5.5),
>
> 4) Pro hac vice appearance in pending litigation in a court or agency by licensed foreign lawyers (ABA Model Rule for Pro Hac Vice Admission),
>
> 5) Foreign lawyer participation in international arbitration or mediation, as counsel, arbitrator, or mediator (ABA Model Rule for Temporary Practice by Foreign Lawyers and ABA Policy Favoring Recognition of Party Freedom to Choose Representatives Not Admitted to Practice Law),
>
> 6) Formal professional association between foreign and United States lawyers who are duly licensed in their home country (ABA Model Rule of Professional Conduct 5.4 and ABA Model Rule for the Licensing and Practice of Foreign Legal Consultants allow such association), and
>
> 7) Foreign lawyer employment of United States lawyers and United States lawyer employment of foreign lawyers who are duly licensed in the United States as a foreign legal consultant or in their home country (ABA Model Rule for the Licensing and Practice of Foreign Legal Consultants provides that locally licensed lawyers may be employed by a law firm based in another country (or lawyer based in another country)).

---

28. http://www.ncbex.org/publications/statistics/.
29. http://ccj.ncsc.org/.

The ABA Model Rules referenced in the above resolution can be accessed <u>here</u>.[30] The Chief Justices' resolution and a wealth of other helpful materials on foreign lawyer access to the U.S. legal services market can be found on the <u>ABA's Task Force on International Trade in Legal Services website</u>.[31]

Professor Laurel Terry, an authority on trade in legal services, created the following <u>charts for the ABA</u>[32] concerning states' regulation of foreign <u>legal service providers</u>.[33] Each are regularly updated on <u>her website</u>.[34]

Jurisdictions with Rules Regarding Foreign Lawyer Practice
by Prof. Laurel Terry (LTerry@psu.edu), April 29, 2015, based on data from the ABA Center for Professional Responsibility and NCBE

LEGEND (see back page for additional information)

Yellow shading = has a foreign legal consultant rule
▬ = rule permits temporary practice by foreign lawyers (also known as FIFO or fly-in, fly-out)
★ = rule permits foreign pro hac vice admission
▲ = rule permits foreign in-house counsel
O = has had at least one foreign-educated applicant sit for a bar exam between 2010 and 2013.

30. https://www.americanbar.org/advocacy/governmental_legislative_work/priorities_policy /promoting_international_rule_law/internationaltradetf/policy.html.

31. https://www.americanbar.org/advocacy/governmental_legislative_work/priorities_policy /promoting_international_rule_law/internationaltradetf.html.

32. https://www.google.com/url?sa=t&rct=j&q=&esrc=s&source=web&cd=1&ved =0CB8QFjAA&url=http%3A%2F%2Fwww.americanbar.org%2Fcontent%2Fdam%2Faba%2Fad ministrative%2Fprofessional_responsibility%2Fmjp_8_9_status_chart.authcheckdam.pdf&ei =1V6UVanTJML6sAXq74eIAg&usg=AFQjCNFxB-2dHKzTSB2DVjRjehZn9uSTBg&sig2 =fkJ4UKsTXXJIXog0pf3luQ&bvm=bv.96952980,d.b2w&cad=rja.

33. https://www.google.com/url?sa=t&rct=j&q=&esrc=s&source=web&cd=2&cad=rja&uact =8&ved=0CCYQFjAB&url=http%3A%2F%2Fwww.personal.psu.edu%2Ffaculty%2Fl%2Fs%2Flst 3%2FTerry_Materials_NCBE-2014.pdf&ei=1V6UVanTJML6sAXq74eIAg&usg=AFQjCNH -1xtgdo38R4qw-_KinD52nVgIHg&sig2=gD8gKnFmX9YV-Owz-vMCpw&bvm=bv.96952980,d.b2w.

34. https://www.google.com/url?sa=t&rct=j&q=&esrc=s&source=web&cd=2&cad=rja&uact =8&ved=0CCYQFjAB&url=http%3A%2F%2Fwww.personal.psu.edu%2Ffaculty%2Fl%2Fs%2Flst 3%2FTerry_Materials_NCBE-2014.pdf&ei=1V6UVanTJML6sAXq74eIAg&usg=AFQjCNH -1xtgdo38R4qw-_KinD52nVgIHg&sig2=gD8gKnFmX9YV-Owz-vMCpw&bvm=bv.96952980,d.b2w.

Jurisdictions with FLC Rules	Explicitly Permit Foreign Lawyer Temporary Practice	Jurisdictions that Permit Foreign Lawyer Pro Hac Vice	Jurisdictions that Permit Foreign In-House Counsel	Since 2010 has had a foreign-educated full-admission applicant
33	10	16	15	32
AK, AZ, CA, CO, CT, DE (Rule 55.2), DC, FL, GA, HI, ID, IL, IN, IA, LA, MA, MI, MN, MO, NH, NJ, NM, NY, NC, ND, OH, OR, PA, SC, TX, UT, VA, WA	CO, DC (Rule 49(c)(13), DE (RPC 5.5(d)), FL, GA, NH, NM (includes transactional matters), OR, PA, VA	CO, DC (Rule 49), GA (Rule 4.4), IL, ME, MI, NM, NY, OH (Rule XII), OK (Art. II(5)), OR, PA, TX (Rule XIX), UT (appellate courts only; see Utah Rule of Appellate Procedure 40; cf. Rule 14-806), VA, WI	AZ, CO (205.5), CT, DC, DE (Rule 55.1), GA, IN (Rule 6(2), KS, NC, OR (allowed on a temporary basis under Rule 5.5(c); further study underway); TX, VA (Part 1A), WA, WI, WV	AL, AK, AZ, CA, CO, CT, DC, FL, GA, HI, IL, IA, LA, ME, MD, MA, MI, MO, NV, NH, NY, OH, OR, PA, RI, TN, TX, UT, VT, VA, WA, WI
ABA Model FLC Rule (2006)	ABA Model Rule for Temporary Practice by Foreign Lawyers	ABA Model Pro Hac Vice Rule	ABA Model Rule re Foreign In-House Counsel and Registration Rule	No ABA policy; Council did not act on Committee Proposal; see state rules
ABA Commission on Multijurisdictional Practice web page	State Rules—Temporary Practice by Foreign Lawyers (ABA chart)	Comparison of ABA Model Rule for Pro Hac Vice Admission with State Versions and Amendments Since August 2002 (ABA chart)	In-House Corporate Counsel Registration Rules (ABA chart); Comparison of ABA Model Rule for Registration of In-House Counsel with State Versions (ABA chart); State-by State Adoption of Selected Ethics 20/20 Commission Policies (ABA chart)	NCBE COMPREHENSIVE GUIDE TO BAR ADMISSIONS

*Note: As the map on the back of this page shows, five jurisdictions—Colorado, the District of Columbia, Georgia, Oregon, and Virginia—have rules for all 5 methods; two jurisdictions have rules on 4 methods (PA and TX); and 12 jurisdictions have rules on 3 methods (AZ, CT, DE, FL, IL, MI, NH, NY, OH, UT, WA, and WI). [Prior editions of the map erroneously included Pennsylvania among the "five method" states.]

Perhaps the most common method of exporting legal services is to gain "Foreign Legal Consultant" status under local law (or "Foreign Legal Practitioner" in EU parlance). Typically, the FLC may advise on the law of their home jurisdiction or, in some jurisdictions, third country and international law. The American Bar Association has adopted a Model Rule[35] for the Licensing and Practice of Foreign Legal Consultants and maintains a compilation[36] of the specific requirements imposed by the 34 states that have authorized such status (similar information may be found in the IBA Report on Trade in Legal Services[37]). In addition to strictly limiting the work of FLCs to advice about the laws of their home jurisdiction,[38] many states impose other, sometimes stringent, requirements. Florida law here is typical. *How many of the requirements and limitations listed in the rule below could be characterized as unjustified restrictions on trade in legal services?*

---

35. http://www.google.com/url?sa=t&rct=j&q=&esrc=s&source=web&cd=4&ved=0CDMQFjAD&url=http%3A%2F%2Fwww.americanbar.org%2Fcontent%2Fdam%2Faba%2Fmigrated%2Fcpr%2Fmjp%2FFLC.authcheckdam.pdf&ei=9UqMVYPjLczHsAWq3IHQCg&usg=AFQjCNGxkZQ-vqqB3bEf9r595nZ1QMk68g&sig2=MK3SQR4InFZHNw4R2blFgw&bvm=bv.96782255,d.b2w&cad=rja.

36. https://www.google.com/url?sa=t&rct=j&q=&esrc=s&source=web&cd=3&ved=0CCsQFjAC&url=http%3A%2F%2Fwww.americanbar.org%2Fcontent%2Fdam%2Faba%2Fadministrative%2Fprofessional_responsibility%2Fforeign_legal_consultants.authcheckdam.pdf&ei=9UqMVYPjLczHsAWq3IHQCg&usg=AFQjCNEtiptmVFGB_cbdJM7qetzJNlr0ZA&sig2=gHg69eif4k3OcAV8r09t-w&bvm=bv.96782255,d.b2w&cad=rja.

37. http://www.ibanet.org/PPID/Constituent/Bar_Issues_Commission/BIC_ITILS_Committee/The_Regulation_of_Interational_Legal_Services.aspx.

38. Ten U.S. states also allow Foreign Legal Consultants to advise clients concerning third country and international law. *See* Carol A. Needham, *Globalization and Eligibility to Deliver Legal Advice: Inbound Legal Services Provided by Corporate Counsel Licensed Only in a Country Outside the United States*, 48 San Diego L. Rev. 379 387–89 (2011).

RULES REGULATING THE FLORIDA BAR

RULE 16-1.2[39] **DEFINITIONS**

A foreign legal consultant is any person who:

(a) has been admitted to practice in a foreign country as an attorney, counselor at law, or the equivalent for a period of not less than 5 of the 7 years immediately preceding the application for certification under this chapter;

(b) has engaged in the practice of law of such foreign country for a period of not less than 5 of the 7 years immediately preceding the application for certification under this chapter and has remained in good standing as an attorney, counselor at law, or the equivalent throughout said period;

(c) is admitted to practice in a foreign country whose professional disciplinary system for attorneys is generally consistent with that of The Florida Bar;

(d) has not been disciplined for professional misconduct by the bar or courts of any jurisdiction within 10 years immediately preceding the application for certification under this chapter and is not the subject of any such disciplinary proceeding or investigation pending at the date of application for certification under this chapter;

(e) has not been denied admission to practice before the courts of any jurisdiction based upon character or fitness during the 15-year period preceding application for certification under this chapter;

(f) has submitted, pursuant to requirements determined by the Supreme Court of Florida, an application for certification under this chapter and the appropriate fees;

(g) agrees to abide by the applicable Rules Regulating The Florida Bar and submit to the jurisdiction of the Supreme Court of Florida for disciplinary purposes;

(h) is over 26 years of age;

(i) maintains an office in the state of Florida for the rendering of services as a foreign legal consultant; and RRTFB — June 1, 2014

(j) has satisfied, in all respects, the provisions of rule 16-1.4.

---

39. https://www.google.com/url?sa=t&rct=j&q=&esrc=s&source=web&cd=1&ved=0ahUKEwj pqava1IvUAhUELMAKHUUzB8sQFggmMAA&url=https%3A%2F%2Fwebprod.floridabar .org%2Fwp-content%2Fuploads%2F2017%2F04%2Frrtfb-chapter-16.pdf&usg=AFQjCNFwKVuO-QNXrI0fIZehX8_xHFWTvlg&cad=rja.

RULE 16-1.3 ACTIVITIES

(a) Rendering Legal Advice. A person certified as a foreign legal consultant under this chapter may render legal services in the state of Florida; provided, however, that such services shall:

(1) be limited to those regarding the laws of the foreign country in which such person is admitted to practice as an attorney, counselor at law, or the equivalent;

(2) not include any activity or any service constituting the practice of the laws of the United States, the state of Florida, or any other state, commonwealth, or territory of the United States or the District of Columbia including, but not limited to, the restrictions that such person shall not:

(A) appear for another person as attorney in any court or before any magistrate or other judicial officer or before any federal, state, county, or municipal governmental agency, quasi-judicial, or quasi-governmental authority in the state of Florida, or prepare pleadings or any other papers in any action or proceedings brought in any such court, or before any such judicial officer, except as authorized in any rule of procedure relating to admission pro hac vice, or pursuant to administrative rule;

(B) prepare any deed, mortgage, assignment, discharge, lease, agreement of sale, or any other instrument affecting title to real property located in the United States, or personal property located in the United States, except where the instrument affecting title to such property is governed by the law of a jurisdiction in which the foreign legal consultant is admitted to practice as an attorney, counselor at law, or the equivalent;

(C) prepare any will or trust instrument affecting the disposition of any property located in the United States and owned by a resident thereof nor prepare any instrument relating to the administration of a decedent's estate in the United States;

(D) prepare any instrument with respect to the marital relations, rights, or duties of a resident of the United States or the custody or care of the children of such a resident;

(E) render professional legal advice on the law of the State of Florida, the United States, or any other state, subdivision, commonwealth, or territory of the United States, or the District of Columbia (whether rendered incident to the preparation of a legal instrument or otherwise); or

(F) render any legal services without utilizing a written retainer agreement that shall specify in bold type that the foreign legal consultant is not admitted to practice law in the state of Florida nor licensed to advise on the laws of the United States or any other state, commonwealth, territory, or the District of Columbia, unless so licensed, and that the practice of the foreign legal consultant is limited to the laws of the foreign country where such person is admitted to practice as an attorney, counselor at law, or the equivalent.

Apart from licensing and certification as a FLC, at least eight states have followed the ABA recommendation of authorizing temporary "fly-in, fly-out" services involving transactions ("temporary presence" delivery), and liberalizing "pro hac vice" policies allowing temporary admission for litigation purposes,[40] conjuring the slightly amusing image of "FIFO Lawyers."[41]

---

40. For example, Florida Rule 4.5-5(d) provides:

(d) Authorized Temporary Practice by Lawyer Admitted in a Non-United States Jurisdiction. A lawyer who is admitted only in a non-United States jurisdiction who is a member in good standing of a recognized legal profession in a foreign jurisdiction whose members are admitted to practice as lawyers or counselors at law or the equivalent and are subject to effective regulation and discipline by a duly constituted professional body or a public authority, and who has been neither disbarred or suspended from practice in any jurisdiction nor disciplined or held in contempt in Florida by reason of misconduct committed while engaged in the practice of law permitted pursuant to this rule does not engage in the unlicensed practice of law in Florida when on a temporary basis the lawyer performs services in Florida that are:

(1) undertaken in association with a lawyer who is admitted to practice in Florida and who actively participates in the matter; or

(2) in or reasonably related to a pending or potential proceeding before a tribunal held or to be held in a jurisdiction outside the United States if the lawyer, or a person the lawyer is assisting, is authorized by law or by order of the tribunal to appear in the proceeding or reasonably expects to be so authorized; or

(3) in or reasonably related to a pending or potential arbitration, mediation, or other alternative dispute resolution proceeding held or to be held in Florida or another jurisdiction and the services are not services for which the forum requires pro hac vice admission:

(A) if the services are performed for a client who resides in or has an office in the jurisdiction in which the lawyer is admitted to practice, or

(B) where the services arise out of or are reasonably related to the lawyer's practice in a jurisdiction in which the lawyer is admitted to practice; or

(4) not within subdivisions (d)(2) or (d)(3), and

(A) are performed for a client who resides or has an office in a jurisdiction in which the lawyer is authorized to practice to the extent of that authorization, or

(B) arise out of or are reasonably related to a matter that has a substantial connection to a jurisdiction in which the lawyer is authorized to practice to the extent of that authorization; or

(5) governed primarily by international law or the law of a non-United States jurisdiction in which the lawyer is a member.

41. http://www.indialegallive.com/constitutional/special-report/the-fifo-lawyers-5872.

Increasingly, U.S. and foreign lawyers also form business "associations," which might include opening overseas offices, partnering with others, and employing foreign counsel.[42]

3. Obstacles & Restrictions on International Trade in Legal Services

The International Bar Association now produces an annual *Global Cross-Border Legal Services Report* that surveys the laws of many national jurisdictions concerning trade in legal services. The IBA presents this information in PDF[43] or a searchable database,[44] by country or theme (such as GATS commitments). *Pick a country that you think might present opportunities for an American lawyer to export her legal talents. Does that country maintain barriers to foreign lawyer services such as citizenship restrictions, local education pre-requisites, onerous certification or licensing rules, restrictions on types of permitted services, local presence requirements or outright prohibitions? Has this country made any international commitments within GATS or other treaties to liberalize trade in legal services?*

Consider the following brief excerpts describing common obstacles to trade in legal services in Japan, India and China. Think back on the Florida rules on FLC status reprinted above and the proposed ABA standards. *Does the U.S. also impose significant obstacles to international legal services? Are these justified?*

a. Barriers to Legal Services Trade: Korea & Japan

Eun Sup Lee, *Trade Barriers in Service/Investment Markets Erected by Korea and Japan*[45]

32 N.C. J. Int'l L. & Com. Reg. 451 (2007)

With regard to professional services, the ability of foreign firms and individuals to provide professional services in Japan has been hampered by a complex network of legal, regulatory, and commercial practice barriers . . . .

---

42. The ABA has indicated that a U.S. lawyer may partner and share legal fees with foreign licensed lawyers without violating the Model Rule of Professional Conduct 5.4. ABA Comm. on Ethics and Professional Responsibility, Formal Op. 01-423 (2001) ("Forming Partnerships with Foreign Lawyers"). This opinion and other policy statements relating to international trade in legal services can be found on the ABA website, https://www.americanbar.org/advocacy/governmental_legislative_work/priorities _policy/promoting_international_rule_law/internationaltradetf/policy.html.

43. https://www.google.com/url?sa=t&rct=j&q=&esrc=s&source=web&cd=3&cad=rja&uact =8&ved=0CC0QFjAC&url=http%3A%2F%2Fwww.ibanet.org%2FDocument%2FDefault .aspx%3FDocumentUid%3D1D3D3E81-472A-40E5-9D9D-68EB5F71A702&ei=S3ORVc2hDsH2s AXCpb8g&usg=AFQjCNEdNW5Pk4rQIaSlNmhRO1Y8u2QgiA&sig2=osfoQexZfpUZLg XC9BzoUA&bvm=bv.96783405,d.b2w.

44. http://www.ibanet.org/PPID/Constituent/Bar_Issues_Commission/BIC_ITILS_Map.aspx.

45. http://www.law.unc.edu/journals/ncilj/issues/volume32/number-3-spring-2007/trade -barriers-in-serviceinvestment-markets-erected-by-korea-and-japan/.

Since 1987, Japan has allowed foreign lawyers to establish offices and advise on matters concerning the law of their home jurisdictions in Japan as foreign legal consultants, subject to certain restrictions. . . . [T]he most critical structural deficiency in Japan's international legal services sector is that severe limitations are imposed on the relationships between Japanese lawyers and registered foreign legal consultants. . . .

Foreign lawyers are required to follow strict accounting guidelines in order to share offices, and the joint enterprise can give only limited advice on Japanese law. Japanese lawyers can form partnerships with individual foreign lawyers, but not with a foreign lawyer's law firm. The "restrictions on foreign lawyers to employ or form partnerships with local lawyers severely handicaps a law firm's ability to serve its clients, and inhibits the growth of international law firms because they force branch offices to farm out work locally." In addition, Japan requires annual residency of 180 days and limits foreign lawyers to only one office in Japan. . . . .

Furthermore, education, language, and cultural differences have worked to keep foreign lawyers from establishing a larger presence in Japan. . . . For example, from the viewpoint of the partner countries, the Japanese excuse for preventing foreign lawyers from participating in any type of litigation is that it is necessary to prevent Japan from becoming a litigious society, which seems to be the same rationale given in Korea. . . . .

Jeanne John, *The KORUS FTA on Foreign Law Firms and Attorneys in South Korea—A Contemporary Analysis on Expansion into East Asia*[46]
33 Nw.J. Int'l L.& Bus. 237 (2012)

The practice of law in Korea was restricted to Korean nationals for forty-seven years, until 1996, when the Korean Attorney-at-Law Act—which governs the practice of law and qualifications of attorneys—was revised for the first time to theoretically allow foreign legal participation in Korea. The actual acknowledged and official legal practice of foreigners in Korea never occurred, however, until recently.

Korea has always prohibited foreign law firms "from opening offices in Korea, forming partnerships with Korean law firms, and recruiting Korean lawyers to provide . . . multijurisdictional services." . . .

. . . [T]he Korean Attorney-at-Law Act has always protected the Korean legal market through extremely rigorous educational requirements. In 1996, while the Act was revised to theoretically allow foreigners to practice in Korea . . . no foreign attorney had been authorized by the Ministry of Justice to practice as a lawyer. Impossible educational requirements included passing an exam offered only in

46. http://scholarlycommons.law.northwestern.edu/njilb/vol33/iss1/5/.

Korean, which, for at least four decades, yielded annual pass rates ranging from less than 5% at best and around 0.25% at worst . . . .

Under the KORUS FTA, lawyers and law firms will enter the Korean legal services market in three stages. . . . In the third stage, estimated to take place around 2017, foreign law firms will be able to enter into joint ventures with Korean law firms, as well as directly employ Korean legal professionals. . . .

The market will not be an open free-for-all for any FLC to establish a practice, however, and foreign attorneys will still be constrained in other ways. . . . Also, as the title "consultant" suggests, no foreign attorney may autonomously represent clients in Korean courtrooms or be self-employed, but must work with some established firm, whether Korean or foreign . . . .

b. China's GATS Commitments & Legal Services

Liyue Huang, *The Legal Service Market in China: Implementation of China's GATS Commitments and Foreign Legal Services in China*[47]

26 N.Y. Int'l L. Rev. 31 (2013)

Potential loss of talent and market share to foreign competitors is a practical concern. Once the Chinese legal service market is accessible, those foreign law firms with strong economic backgrounds will be the front-runners for claiming a market share. . . . In the meantime, China's newly established legal profession is filled with freshly qualified Chinese lawyers who, although legally qualified, may nevertheless lack international practice experience and managerial skills. Moreover, the higher incomes and prestigious profiles offered by foreign law firms will undoubtedly be more attractive than their Chinese counterparts to young Chinese lawyers. Thus, in time, the market will be dominated by large foreign law firms . . . .

Further restrictions are placed on personnel who work in such representative offices. For example, foreign law firms may not employ Chinese practicing lawyers. . . . .

Since legal certification in China is not open to foreign nationals, the possibility of foreign lawyers providing legal service regarding Chinese law virtually does not exist. Moreover, a Chinese lawyer who works in a foreign law firm to provide information on Chinese law must forgo the right to practice law. . . .

As a result of these narrowly drafted Commitment Clauses, the application of Chinese law is almost exclusively within the domain of practicing Chinese lawyers. Since foreign law firms may not employ Chinese practicing lawyers, a foreign client with an issue of substantive Chinese law must engage a Chinese law firm for advice either directly or via a foreign representative office through the

---

47. https://papers.ssrn.com/sol3/papers.cfm?abstract_id=2677593.

Entrustment Clause. Either way, the profit of such services will go to the Chinese law firm . . . .

As such, not only is the market share preserved exclusively for Chinese law firms, but its profitability also will not be compromised by the involvement of foreign law firms.

c. Foreign Legal Consultants in India

Arno L. Eisen, *Legal Services in India: Is There an Obligation Under the GATS or Are There Policy Reasons for India to Open Its Legal Services Market to Foreign Legal Consultants?*[48]
Richmond J. Global L. & Bus. (2012)

The current state of this issue is highlighted by a recent case decided by the Division Bench of the Mumbai High Court; with its decision, the court effectively denied foreign law firms entry into India . . . .

The Indian legal services market is the second largest in the world with somewhere between 600,000 and over 800,000 practicing lawyers . . . . To be enrolled as an advocate, the candidate has to be a citizen of India or a country that allows Indian nationals to practice . . . .

The Mumbai High Court held in its decision in Lawyers' Collective that the words "practicing the profession of law" in section 29 of the Advocates Act of 1961 include advisory legal services provided in non-litigation matters. Thereby, the court made clear that FLCs are barred even from doing transactional or other non-litigation work in India.

Hence, foreign lawyers or law firms effectively cannot establish themselves in India because they will not fulfill the requirements . . . .

[Author's Note: The Indian High Court ruled later in 2012 that foreign lawyers may fly-in and fly-out of India to advise on foreign law but may not maintain offices or "practice" Indian law.]

3. Detriments to be Suffered by India from Opening its Legal Services Market . . .

a. Shrinking Opportunities for Local Indian Lawyers: "Brain Drain" of Top Indian Legal Talent . . . .

c. Indian Firms Being "Pushed" Out of the Legal Services Market

d. Opening the Door to Lawyers from All WTO Member Countries . . . .

Through the MFN clause in Article II of GATS, India would open its door to FLCs from all WTO members with greatly varying backgrounds. This risks undermining the quality control of legal services by the Bar Council of India and domestic authorities.

---

48. http://rjglb.richmond.edu/2012/07/12/legal-services-in-india-is-there-an-obligation-under-the-gats-or-are-there-policy-reasons-for-india-to-open-its-legal-services-market-to-foreign-legal-consultants/.

4. GATS: International Regulation and Liberalization of Trade in Services

The WTO provides this introduction[49] to GATS:

> The GATS was inspired by essentially the same objectives as its counterpart in merchandise trade, the General Agreement on Tariffs and Trade (GATT): creating a credible and reliable system of international trade rules; ensuring fair and equitable treatment of all participants (principle of non-discrimination); stimulating economic activity through guaranteed policy bindings; and promoting trade and development through progressive liberalization.

Membership in GATS (text here[50]) is mandatory for all 161 state parties[51] to the WTO system. GATS goes about achieving the objectives described above in ways similar to but distinct from the approach taken by the WTO in GATT 94. This approach essentially has four distinct but related paths focused on developing a legal framework controlling certain governmental actions and securing state commitments to reduce barriers: (1) create legal "disciplines" to inhibit barriers; (2) secure specific state commitments for different services; (3) sponsor on-going negotiations for further rule development and commitments; and (4) resolve disputes and develop a GATS jurisprudence through the WTO dispute settlement processes.

Creating Legal Disciplines: GATS contemplates the adoption and further development of rules or "disciplines" that are designed to limit economic protectionism and barriers to trade in services and ensure fair competition. Here there are two types of rules—those of general applicability and those that only apply with regard to specific commitments a state party makes concerning particular services or service sectors.

Only a limited number of rules under GATS are generally applicable to all services. These mandatory "general obligations," set out in Part II of the treaty, automatically apply without any specific negotiated commitment by the member state. The most important of these obligations is "Most Favored Nation" treatment (Article II), a nearly ubiquitous feature of all international trade agreements. MFN, a non-discrimination principle that you should be familiar with from studying GATT 94 in Chapter 9, forbids differential treatment of services based on their country of origin—essentially a rule forbidding discrimination between member countries. A U.S. restriction on internet gambling services originating in Barbados would violate MFN if it were not applied equally to such services originating in Germany. It is important to note that GATS allows members to maintain declared exemptions from this MFN obligation (Article II exemptions), which many nations have done for a wide variety of service sectors.

---

49. https://www.wto.org/english/tratop_e/serv_e/gatsqa_e.htm.
50. https://www.wto.org/english/docs_e/legal_e/26-gats_01_e.htm.
51. https://www.wto.org/english/thewto_e/whatis_e/tif_e/org6_e.htm.

"Transparency," outlined in Article III, is a second rule of general application. Transparency requires publication of "all relevant measures of general application which pertain to or affect the operation of this Agreement" and notice of "the introduction of any new, or any changes to existing, laws, regulations or adminis- trative guidelines which significantly affect trade in services covered by its specific commitments . . . ." Other rules designated as generally applicable in the treaty appear to create more vague or "soft" obligations. Of potential future importance to lawyers, Article VII provides the option of recognizing the foreign based cre- dentials of service providers: "a Member may recognize the education or experi- ence obtained, requirements met, or licenses or certifications granted in a particular country." (Panel interpretations of MFN and transparency can be found at the WTO Analytical Index.[52])

The second type of "legal discipline" created under GATS might be described as "specific commitment rules." These rules are not generally applicable to all trade in services but rather only apply regarding specific voluntary commitments of member states about particular services. When a state undertakes a specific commitment regarding, let's say singing barbers,[53] it thereby subjects itself to two types of legal constraints involving "market access" and "national treatment." It is instructive to review the types of prohibited restrictions identified under Article XVI below. Im- portantly, however, both of these types of constraint may be limited by conditions and qualifications imposed by the state when making a commitment for a particu- lar service.

Article XVI on Market Access Provides:

1. With respect to market access through the modes of supply identified in Article I, each Member shall accord services and service suppliers of any other Member treatment no less favourable than that provided for under the terms, limitations and conditions agreed and specified in its Schedule.

2. In sectors where market-access commitments are undertaken, the mea- sures which a Member shall not maintain or adopt either on the basis of a regional subdivision or on the basis of its entire territory, unless otherwise specified in its Schedule, are defined as:

(a) Limitations on the number of service suppliers whether in the form of numerical quotas, monopolies, exclusive service suppliers or the require- ments of an economic needs test;

(b) Limitations on the total value of service transactions or assets in the form of numerical quotas or the requirement of an economic needs test;

---

52. https://www.wto.org/english/res_e/booksp_e/analytic_index_e/gats_01_e.htm#article2B.
53. http://www.irishbarbershop.com/.

(c) Limitations on the total number of service operations or on the total quantity of service output expressed in terms of designated numerical units in the form of quotas or the requirement of an economic needs test;

(d) Limitations on the total number of natural persons that may be employed in a particular service sector or that a service supplier may employ and who are necessary for, and directly related to, the supply of a specific service in the form of numerical quotas or the requirement of an economic needs test;

(e) Measures which restrict or require specific types of legal entity or joint venture through which a service supplier may supply a service; and

(f) Limitations on the participation of foreign capital in terms of maximum percentage limit on foreign shareholding or the total value of individual or aggregate foreign investment.

From Chapter 9 of this book, you should already be familiar with the principle of "national treatment"—the obligation to not discriminate between domestic and foreign providers. In a significant departure from trade in goods under GATT 94, the obligation of national treatment is confined to a state's specific commitments in service sectors and subject to conditions and limitations imposed by the state.

Article XVII provides:

1. In the sectors inscribed in its Schedule, and subject to any conditions and qualifications set out therein, each Member shall accord to services and service suppliers of any other Member, in respect of all measures affecting the supply of services, treatment no less favourable than that it accords to its own like services and service suppliers.

Here a third potential source of rules, not yet developed and adopted, should be noted. Article VI:4, which relates to domestic "measures" that may restrict trade in services, obligates members to develop further "disciplines" relating to "qualification requirements and procedures, technical standards and licensing requirements." Article VI is described further below.

Specific State Commitments or Bindings: The second major prong of GATS' approach rests upon specific negotiated commitments by member states (bindings) to liberalize international trade in particular services or service "sectors"[54] (classification list here[55]). This approach of progressively creating and then expanding binding

---

54. GATS currently utilizes 12 general categories or sectors of service trade: 1. Business; 2. Communication; 3. Construction and Engineering; 4. Distribution; 5. Education; 6. Environment; 7. Financial; 8. Health; 9. Tourism and Travel; 10. Recreation, Cultural, and Sporting; 11. Transport; 12. "Other." Legal services are classified under Business Services, Professional. https://www.wto.org/english/tratop_e/serv_e/mtn_gns_w_120_e.doc.

55. https://www.wto.org/english/tratop_e/serv_e/mtn_gns_w_120_e.doc.

commitments to liberalize trade in services through negotiations is fundamental to GATS. Membership in GATS does not, ipso facto, subject all trade in services in a member state to the obligations of GATS (other than MFN and transparency rules). Rather, each member decides for itself which commitments under the GATS legal regime it is willing to make for which services — reflected in its "Schedule of Specific Commitments."

Vaguely similar to the GATT 94 schedules on tariffs, state commitments regarding services appear as a schedule of bindings that create specific commitments regarding market access and national treatment for a specified service or service sector, under defined terms and conditions. While there are some broad categories or service "sectors" that many states have agreed to include under GATS, every member state's commitments are, in essence, distinct on the issues that really matter. Complicating things further, the specifics of each state's commitment regarding the services it chooses to include may vary by restrictions on modes of delivery and exceptions to MFN treatment. Thus, the specific terms under which trade in a particular service in a particular country is included within GATS depends upon that particular state's schedule of commitments. *Welcome to the matrix.*

The WTO puts it this way:[56]

> It is only by reference to a country's schedule, and (where relevant) its MFN exemption list, that it can be seen to which services sectors and under what conditions the basic principles of the GATS — market access, national treatment and MFN treatment — apply within that country's jurisdiction. The schedules are complex documents in which each country identifies the service sectors to which it will apply the market access and national treatment obligations of the GATS and any exceptions from those obligations it wishes to maintain. The commitments and limitations are in every case entered with respect to each of the four modes of supply which constitute the definition of trade in services in Article I of the GATS: these are cross-border supply; consumption abroad; commercial presence; and presence of natural persons . . . .

> In order to determine the real level of market access represented by a given schedule it is therefore necessary to examine the range of activities covered in each service sector and the limitations on market access and national treatment pertaining to the different modes of supply. In addition, in cases where a country has also tabled a list of MFN exemptions, this must be examined in order to assess the extent to which the country gives preferential treatment to, or discriminate against, one or more of its trading partners.

---

56. https://www.wto.org/english/tratop_e/serv_e/guide1_e.htm.

Country GATS schedules, regional services agreements and related information can be accessed through the WTO-World Bank searchable web-portal, ITIPS.[57] Please visit the portal and look around. *Try searching under "applied regimes" for U.S. commitments relating to the provision of legal services or other topics that suit your interests.* Regarding commitments relating to legal services, Professor Terry notes:

> A 2010 background note on legal services prepared by the WTO Secretariat indicated that seventy-six WTO member states (including the United States) have chosen to assume additional obligations regarding legal services. . . .

> The 2010 background note reported that for at least some modes of supply, almost seventy WTO members had included advisory- consultancy services on home country law as part of their legal services commitments. Approximately sixty WTO member states had "scheduled" legal services for both advisory-consultancy services on home country law and international law but excluding host country (domestic) law. Between twenty-five and thirty countries made commitments for transactional or litigation work in domestic (host country) law.[58]

At first blush this looks promising for liberalization of trade in legal services. On the other hand, consider this (earlier) observation by a different commentator:

> During the initial Uruguay Round negotiations, forty-eight Member States took the decision to submit their legal services sectors to the obligations inherent in Part III of the GATS. Much of the sting of the market access and national treatment obligations was nonetheless removed by the content of Member States' schedules. Most of the Member States that included legal services on their Schedules of Specific Commitments did so by listing their current regulations. The legal effect of listing current laws in a GATS schedule is to effectively exempt those laws from the market access and national treatment obligations.[59]

Negotiating Future Commitments & Rules: The third pillar of GATS' approach to liberalizing trade in services consists of sponsoring on-going negotiations for future progressive liberalization. This obligation for future action not only includes expansion of state commitments regarding more and more services over time ("track one"[60]),

---

57. http://i-tip.wto.org/services/(S(o0rfqj11eg50yz2uqbn1sbpf))/default.aspx.

58. Laurel Terry, *Putting the Legal Profession's Monopoly on the Practice of Law in a Global Context*, 82 Fordham L. Rev. 2903 (2014).

59. Ryan Hopkins, *Liberalizing Trade in Legal Services: The GATS, the Accountancy Disciplines, and the Language of Core Values*, 15 Ind. Int'l & Comp. L. Rev. 427 (2005).

60. https://www.americanbar.org/groups/professional_responsibility/policy/gats _international_agreements/track_one.html.

but also the development of additional legal disciplines ("track two"[61]). As the WTO has candidly recognized:[62]

> In services, the Uruguay Round was only a first step in a longer-term process of multilateral rule-making and trade liberalization. Observers tend to agree that, while the negotiations succeeded in setting up the principle structure of the Agreement, the liberalizing effects have been relatively modest. Barring exceptions in financial and telecommunication services, most schedules have remained confined to confirming status quo market conditions in a relatively limited number of sectors.

Under Article XIX of GATS, member states committed to successive rounds of negotiations toward expanding the scope of services covered and progressive elimination of barriers. In 2001, the WTO's Council on Trade in Services adopted "Guidelines and Procedures"[63] for future negotiations. These negotiations include further development of rules or "disciplines," as well as "request-offer" proposals by states for specific commitments regarding covered services, market access and other restrictive conditions. Legal services are a regular topic in these on-going, perhaps endless, negotiations. It must be very nice in Geneva.[64]

Note that groups or coalitions of states,[65] such as the 11 states forming the "Friends of Fish"[66] coalition, also commonly present joint negotiating positions regarding a wide variety of WTO issues, including services. Proposals by various states can be searched by topic[67] at the WTO GATS website (also see legal services proposals here[68]). Some proposals are broad and general, including "horizontal or multisectorial" proposals. (See, for example, the European Communities proposal[69] for liberalization of professional services, including legal services, focused on limiting broad types of restrictions including residency and nationality requirements.) Often, however, these offers are fairly specific, organized in a schedule by mode of delivery and focused on market access and national treatment. Examine, for example, this

---

61. https://www.americanbar.org/groups/professional_responsibility/policy/gats_international_agreements/track_two.html.

62. https://www.wto.org/english/tratop_e/serv_e/gatsqa_e.htm.

63. https://www.wto.org/english/tratop_e/serv_e/nego_mandates_e.htm.

64. http://www.ville-geneve.ch/welcome-geneva/.

65. https://www.wto.org/english/tratop_e/dda_e/negotiating_groups_e.htm.

66. https://www.wto.org/english/tratop_e/dda_e/negotiating_groups_maps_e.htm?group_selected=GRP024.

67. https://docs.wto.org/dol2fe/Pages/FE_Search/FE_S_S006.aspx?Query=%28+%40Symbol%3d+tn%2fs%2fo%2f*+not+rev.1+%29&Language=ENGLISH&Context=FomerScriptedSearch&languageUIChanged=true.

68. https://docs.wto.org/dol2fe/Pages/FE_Search/FE_S_S006.aspx?Query=%28%20@Symbol=%20s/css/w/*%20or%20tn/s/w/*%29%20and%20%28%20@Title=%20legal%20services%20%29&Language=ENGLISH&Context=FomerScriptedSearch&languageUIChanged=true.

69. http://www.personal.psu.edu/faculty/l/s/lst3/WPDR/W25.doc.

excerpt from the United States' initial offer (<u>2005 Revised Offer here</u>[70]) regarding professional, including legal, services:

UNITED STATES—INITIAL OFFER

Modes of supply: 1) Cross-border supply 2) Consumption abroad 3) Commercial presence 4) Presence of natural persons

Sector or subsector	Limitations on market access	Limitations on national treatment	Additional commitments
I. HORIZONTAL COMMITMENTS			
<u>ALL SECTORS COVERED BY THIS SCHEDULE</u>: For the purpose of this schedule the "United States" is defined as encompassing the 50 states of the United States, plus the District of Columbia.			
All Sectors: Temporary Entry And Stay of Natural Persons	4) Unbound, except for measures concerning temporary entry and stay of nationals of another member who fall into the categories listed below: . . . . <u>Fashion Models and Specialty Occupations</u>—Up to 65,000 persons annually on a worldwide basis in occupations as set out in 8 USC. 1101(a)(15)(H)(i)(b), consisting of (i) fashion models who are of distinguished merit and ability; and (ii) persons engaged in a specialty occupation, requiring (a) theoretical and practical application of a body of highly specialized knowledge; and (b) attainment of a bachelor's or higher degree in the specialty (or its equivalent) as a minimum for entry into the occupation in the United States. Persons seeking admission under (ii) above shall possess the following qualifications: (a) full licensure in a US state to practice in the occupation, if such licensure is required to practice in the occupation in that state; and (b) completion of the required degree, or experience in the specialty equivalent to the completion of the required degree and recognition of expertise in the specialty through progressively responsible positions relating to the specialty. Entry for persons named in this section is limited to three years.	4) Unbound	

. . . .

---

70. https://ustr.gov/sites/default/files/uploads/factsheets/Trade%20Topics/Services%20&%20Investment/Services/US%20Revised%20Offer.pdf.

Modes of supply: 1) Cross-border supply 2) Consumption abroad 3) Commercial presence 4) Presence of natural persons

Sector or subsector	Limitations on market access	Limitations on national treatment	Additional commitments
II. SECTOR-SPECIFIC COMMITMENTS			
1. BUSINESS SERVICES A. PROFESSIONAL SERVICES			
a) 1) Legal Services: practice s or through a qualified US lawyer	For the following jurisdiction, the following commitments apply: in (all states) 1) Services must be supplied by a natural person An in-state office must be maintained for licensure in: District of Columbia, Indiana (or an affiliate with an office and with other attorneys in the state), Michigan, Minnesota (or maintain individual residency in Minnesota), Mississippi, New Jersey, Ohio, South Dakota and Tennessee.	1) In-state or US residency is required for licensure in: Hawaii, Iowa, Kansas, Massachusetts, Michigan, Minnesota (or maintain an office in Minnesota), Mississippi, Nebraska, New Jersey, New Hampshire, Oklahoma, Rhode Island, South Dakota, Vermont, Virginia, Wyoming.	
	2) Services must be supplied by a natural person An in-state office must be maintained for licensure in: District of Columbia, Indiana (or an affiliate with an office and with other attorneys in the state), Michigan, Minnesota (or maintain individual residency in Minnesota), Mississippi, New Jersey, Ohio, South Dakota and Tennessee.	2) In-state or US residency is required for licensure in: Hawaii, Iowa, Kansas, Massachusetts, Michigan, Minnesota (or maintain an office in Minnesota), Mississippi, Nebraska, New Jersey, New Hampshire, Oklahoma, Rhode Island, South Dakota, Vermont, Virginia, Wyoming.	
	3) Services must be supplied by a natural person Partnership in law firms is limited to persons licensed as lawyers US citizenship is required to practice before the US Patent and Trademark Office	3) None	

Sector or subsector	Limitations on market access	Limitations on national treatment	Additional commitments
	4) Services must be supplied by a natural person An in-state office must be maintained for licensure in: District of Columbia, Indiana (or an affiliate with an office and with other attorneys in the state), Michigan, Minnesota (or maintain individual residency in Minnesota), Mississippi, New Jersey, Ohio, South Dakota and Tennessee. US Citizenship is required to practice before the US Patent and Trademark Office	4) In-state or US residency is required for licensure in: Hawaii, Iowa, Kansas, Massachusetts, Michigan, Minnesota (or maintain an office in Minnesota), Mississippi, Nebraska, New Jersey, New Hampshire, Oklahoma, Rhode Island, South Dakota, Vermont, Virginia, Wyoming.	
a) 2) Legal Services: consultancy on law of jurisdiction where service supplier is qualified as a lawyer (such consultancy excludes the following: i) appearing for a person other than himself or herself as attorney in any court, or before any magistrate or other judicial officer, in this state (other than upon admission pro haec vice);	For the following jurisdiction, the following commitments apply: Alaska [2] 1) None 2) None 3) None 4) Unbound, except as indicated in the horizontal section	1) None 2) None 3) None 4) None	a) Practice of international law: permitted, provided foreign legal consultant (FLC) is competent. b) Practice of 3rd-country law: permitted provided that FLC obtains written legal advice from an attorney licensed in that jurisdiction. c) Practice of host-country law: permitted provided that FLC obtains written legal advice from an attorney licensed to practice in that jurisdiction.

Completion of services negotiations have been hampered by the "single undertaking" approach for all WTO negotiations adopted at the Doha Ministerial Conference[71] in 2001, which requires a global agreement concluded at one time. As of 2011, the Council for Trade in Services reported significant gaps and minor progress in the four primary areas of negotiations — market access; domestic regulation; GATS rules; and special accommodation for less developed countries. (Here for news[72] on developments as of July 2015.)

---

71. https://www.wto.org/english/tratop_e/dda_e/dda_e.htm.
72. https://www.wto.org/english/news_e/news15_e/snegs_20apr15_e.htm.

One important area of negotiation involves the general obligations of Article VI to develop additional rules limiting state measures inhibiting trade in services. Article VI:4 contemplates the continuing development of mandatory rules limiting domestic law restrictions through negotiations within the WTO Council on Services:

4. With a view to ensuring that measures relating to qualification requirements and procedures, technical standards and licensing requirements do not constitute unnecessary barriers to trade in services, the Council for Trade in Services shall, through appropriate bodies it may establish, develop any necessary disciplines. Such disciplines shall aim to ensure that such requirements are, inter alia:

(a) based on objective and transparent criteria, such as competence and the ability to supply the service;

(b) not more burdensome than necessary to ensure the quality of the service;

(c) in the case of licensing procedures, not in themselves a restriction on the supply of the service.

Even if negotiations regarding such disciplines, called "Track 2" in GATS parlance, have limited success, Article VI:5 creates a failsafe principle limiting domestic measures by a default:

5. (a) In sectors in which a Member has undertaken specific commitments, pending the entry into force of disciplines developed in these sectors pursuant to paragraph 4, the Member shall not apply licensing and qualification requirements and technical standards that nullify or impair such specific commitments in a manner which:

(i) does not comply with the criteria outlined in subparagraphs 4(a), (b) or (c); and

(ii) could not reasonably have been expected of that Member at the time the specific commitments in those sectors were made.

Dispute Settlement: The fourth pillar of GATS' approach to liberalization authorizes access to the WTO dispute settlement process—the same one that applies to trade in goods under GATT 94. Authorizing recourse to dispute settlement not only allows relatively authoritative resolution of specific disputes but also promotes the development of meaningful interpretations of state obligations. To date, the Dispute Settlement process has been invoked 23 times, including nine cases initiated by the United States. One of the most interesting of these involved claims by Antigua & Barbuda that U.S. prohibitions against on-line gambling services violated GATS. *Please read through the* <u>WTO prepared summary description</u>[73] *of the case and its resolution.*

By now, it should be clear to you that, even though the general approach of GATS is similar to GATT 94, there are fundamental differences between trade in goods versus services which are reflected in the GATS approach to liberalizing trade. Distilled to its essence, GATS functions primarily upon negotiated commitments which may vary

---

73. https://www.wto.org/english/tratop_e/dispu_e/cases_e/ds285_e.htm.

significantly among the various state parties. No member state is required to open up its market to international legal services. If a state choses to do so, it may maintain significant restrictions tied to the distinct ways in which services may be delivered, as described above. Thus, a country might agree to allow market access for foreign legal service providers but only as to mode 4 delivery involving temporary presence of the provider (FIFO). Other states might, in contrast, agree to allow all modes of delivery including cross-border legal services conducted remotely through electronic media.

Further complicating this scenario, most legal rules on state behavior under the "disciplines" of GATS are also the product of on-going negotiation and, thus, variation. Most importantly, market access rules and the traditional obligation of "national treatment"—the promise to not discriminate between foreign and domestic products—are not general obligations under GATS. Rather, state parties have made national treatment commitments only by specific types of services or service "sectors" and may impose exceptions or conditions. Thus, India has begrudgingly allowed foreign lawyers to consult clients but only on a FIFO temporary basis and under restrictions that favor national providers in specified ways. Even the general obligation of MFN is subject to multiple exceptions imposed by the various state parties in the Annex on Article II Exceptions.

To understand how GATS might affect international trade in legal services in a particular country, one must ultimately consider, at minimum, (1) has the state made a commitment regarding legal services (and precisely what kind of legal services), (2) what modes of delivery are included, (3) what exceptions and conditions have been maintained by mode of delivery regarding both market access and national treatment, and (4) has the state maintained relevant MFN exemptions? Eventually, one will also consider whether there are any "horizontal commitments" regarding such services and whether additional disciplines regarding domestic measures (especially licensing) have been adopted under Article VI.

If you just can't get enough GATS, there are several excellent resources available on the web: WTO webpages on GATS;[74] IBA GATS Handbook 2013;[75] and ABA Task Force[76] on International Trade in Legal Services.

5. NAFTA & Services

The North American Free Trade Agreement (NAFTA[77] and text here[78]), which came into legal effect just prior to GATS, created binding commitments to liberalize

---

74. https://www.wto.org/english/tratop_e/serv_e/serv_e.htm.

75. http://www.ibanet.org/PPID/Constituent/Bar_Issues_Commission/BIC_ITILS_Committee/Default.aspx.

76. https://www.americanbar.org/advocacy/governmental_legislative_work/priorities_policy/promoting_international_rule_law/internationaltradetf.html.

77. https://ustr.gov/trade-agreements/free-trade-agreements/north-american-free-trade-agreement-nafta.

78. https://www.nafta-sec-alena.org/Home/Texts-of-the-Agreement/North-American-Free-Trade-Agreement.

trade in services in the NAFTA trade area. In some important ways, NAFTA approached this goal in ways distinct from GATS and with broader reach. Unlike GATS, which operates on what might be described as an "opt-in" approach that requires affirmative action by states to open up particular services, NAFTA took an "opt-out" format—all services not specifically excluded are generally covered, and all non-conforming restrictions not specifically retained are lost. Unlike GATS, essential rules involving national treatment, MFN, licensing, and quantitative restrictions are generally applicable rather than limited to specific commitments. Some services in important sectors were treated separately in their own chapters (e.g., Chapter 13 on Telecommunications, and Chapter 14 on Financial Services).

The U.S. Department of Commerce, International Trade Administration's Trade Compliance Center provides <u>this practical description</u>[79] of Chapter 12:

CHAPTER TWELVE (TRADE IN SERVICES) OF THE NORTH AMERICAN FREE TRADE AGREEMENT (NAFTA)

What is Chapter Twelve of the NAFTA and what does it do?

Chapter Twelve (Trade in Services) of the North American Free Trade Agreement (NAFTA) establishes principles that are designed to ensure that cross-border trade in services among the three Parties to the NAFTA—Canada, Mexico and the United States—is conducted in a non-discriminatory manner. The principles apply to the provision of services from one NAFTA country to another, within a NAFTA country by an individual provider from another NAFTA country, or the consumption of services in one NAFTA country by consumers from another NAFTA partner. Each Party was allowed to maintain measures that do not conform to the principles set forth in the Chapter, which are specified in Annexes to the NAFTA.

. . . .

How can Chapter Twelve of the NAFTA help my company?
Coverage

Chapter Twelve of the NAFTA covers virtually all services except international air transportation and related services. It excludes financial services, which are covered in Chapter Fourteen. It also excludes the procurement of services by governments or state enterprises, which is covered in Chapter Ten. Key sectors covered in Chapter Twelve include: accounting, advertising, architecture, broadcasting, commercial education, construction, consulting, engineering, environmental services, health care management, legal services, land transportation, publishing, telecommunications (also covered in Chapter Thirteen) and tourism.

---

79. http://tcc.export.gov/Trade_Agreements/Exporters_Guides/List_All_Guides/NAFTA_chapter12_guide.asp.

The Three Principles

Canada, Mexico and the United States, the three Parties to the NAFTA, agreed in Chapter Twelve to apply the following principles to their services trade:

National Treatment. Each NAFTA Party agreed to accord the service providers of the other Parties treatment that is no less favorable than the treatment that it provides, in like circumstances, to its own service providers.

Most Favored Nation (MFN) Treatment. Each NAFTA Party agreed to accord the service providers of the other Parties treatment that is no less favorable than the treatment that it accords, in like circumstances, to the service providers of any other country.

Local Presence. No Party may require a service provider of another Party to establish or maintain a representative office or other presence, or to be resident in its territory, as a condition for the provision of a service.

Reservations

In Chapter Twelve, the Parties negotiated to retain certain limited measures that did not conform to the three principles described above. These "non-conforming" measures were specified in Schedules in Annex I to the NAFTA. State and provincial "non-conforming" measures that were in effect when the NAFTA was concluded were also bound and specified in Annex I.

In addition, Annex II specified certain limited sectors, sub-sectors and activities for which Parties may retain or adopt new or more restrictive non-conforming measures.

Quantitative restrictions — defined for the purposes of Chapter Twelve as non-discriminatory measures such as quotas that limit the number of service providers or the operations of a service provider — may also be maintained by the central, state and provincial governments of the Parties. These are specified in Annex V.

Licensing Requirements

Chapter Twelve states that each Party shall endeavor to ensure that its requirements for licensing and certifying nationals of the other Parties do not constitute unnecessary barriers to trade. Requirements should be based on objective and transparent criteria, such as competence and ability to perform a service, and they should not be more burdensome than necessary to ensure the quality of the service. Chapter Twelve describes steps to be taken by the Parties to develop mutually acceptable professional standards, and contains specific provisions relating to legal, engineering and bus and truck transportation services.

Liberalization

In Annex VI to the NAFTA, each Party set forth its commitments to liberalize quantitative restrictions, licensing requirements, performance requirements and other non-discriminatory measures The NAFTA Parties also
committed to consult periodically regarding further liberalization of the
non-conforming measures on which they invoked reservations in Chapter
Twelve.

Can the U.S. Government help me if I have a problem?

Yes. If you believe, in the course of conducting business with Canada or
Mexico, that the Canadian or Mexican government has failed to comply with
the provisions of Chapter Twelve of the NAFTA regarding trade in services,
contact the Office of Trade Agreements Negotiations and Compliance's hotline
at the U.S. Department of Commerce. The Center can help you understand
your rights and the other NAFTA countries' obligations under Chapter Twelve,
and it can alert the relevant U.S. Government officials to help you resolve
your problem. The U.S. Government can, if appropriate, raise the particular facts of your situation with Canadian or Mexican authorities and ask them
to review the matter.

It's 2017. Will NAFTA, and the effort to liberalize trade in services more generally, survive the "great wall of Trump"?[80]

6. European Union Approach to Trade in Professional Services

From its inception as the European Economic Community in 1957, the European
Union has included elimination of barriers to trade in services among its objectives
(*see* Europa History of EU[81] or Wikipedia alternative summary[82]). As everywhere,
liberalization of professional services in the EU poses special problems because of
national sensitivities regarding education, ethics and consumer protection. The excerpt below provides general information from the EU summarizing its approach to
professional services, including law. It is followed by an excerpt from an article focused on how the EU has significantly liberalized trade in legal services.

From the European Commission[83] on Legal Services Trade:

The central principles governing the internal market for services are set
out in the EC Treaty. This guarantees to EU companies the freedom to establish themselves in other Member States, and the freedom to provide ser-

---

80. https://www.washingtonpost.com/blogs/plum-line/wp/2017/01/27/trumps-secret-plan-to
-make-mexico-pay-for-a-border-wall-revealed/?utm_term=.5cba40c06115.

81. https://europa.eu/european-union/about-eu/history/1945-1959_en.

82. https://en.wikipedia.org/wiki/History_of_the_European_Union.

83. http://ec.europa.eu/growth/single-market/services/.

vices on the territory of another EU Member State other than the one in which they are established.

. . . .

The principles of freedom of establishment and free movement of services have been clarified and developed over the years through the case law of the European Court of Justice. In addition, important developments and progress in the field of services have been brought about through specific legislation in fields such as financial services, transport,[84] telecommunications, broadcasting[85] and the recognition of professional qualifications.[86]

. . . .

Free Movement of Professionals[87]

Professionals in the EU can move across borders and practice their occupation or provide services abroad. These webpages provide practical information on EU legislation governing the recognition of professional experience in the EU.

Policy developments

The system of recognition of professional qualifications in the EU is governed by Directive 2005/36/EC, recently amended by Directive 2013/55/EC. The directive provides a modern EU system of recognition of professional experience and promotes automatic recognition of professional experience across the EU.

Learn more about the latest policy developments.[88]

Recognition of professional qualification in practice

In practice, the recognition of professional qualifications laid down in Directive 2005/36/EC enables the free movement of professionals such as doctors or architects within the EU. Other professions, such as lawyers or sailors, fall under the scope of different legislation.

Learn more about the recognition of professional experience in practice.[89]

Transparency and mutual evaluation of regulated professions

To clarify the status of regulated professions in the EU, the European Commission conducted a transparency exercise and a mutual evaluation exercise.

Learn more about transparency and mutual evaluation.[90]

---

84. https://ec.europa.eu/transport/index_en.

85. http://ec.europa.eu/internal_market/media/index_en.htm.

86. http://ec.europa.eu/growth/single-market/services/free-movement-professionals/.

87. http://ec.europa.eu/growth/single-market/services/free-movement-professionals/.

88. http://ec.europa.eu/growth/single-market/services/free-movement-professionals/policy/.

89. http://ec.europa.eu/growth/single-market/services/free-movement-professionals/qualifications-recognition/.

90. http://ec.europa.eu/growth/single-market/services/free-movement-professionals/transparency-mutual-recognition/.

Database of regulated professions

The <u>database of regulated professions</u>[91] contains information on regulated professions, statistics on migrating professionals, contact points and national authorities in EU countries, EEA countries and Switzerland.

a. Commentary on the European Market for Legal Services

Julian Lonbay, <u>Assessing the European Market for Legal Services: Developments in the Free Movement of Lawyers in the European Union</u>[92]

33 Ford. Int'l L. J. 1629, 1638–47 (2010)

The entry barriers and rigorously regulated access to the legal profession in each state have, to a considerable extent, been trumped by European free access rules. Would-be lawyers no longer have to follow the prescribed national routes into the host state professions . . . .

Citizens of EU and EEA Member States who are qualified lawyers have, in principle, a right to migrate. . . .

Lawful residence for a sufficient duration will give rise . . . to the host state professions and now their training regimes. Subsequent access to professions is considerably facilitated by use of the directives on mutual recognition of qualifications, recently revised and consolidated . . . .

There are three key European legislative provisions. . . . Directive 77/249/EC . . . allows lawyers to carry out cross-border legal services and lists the types of lawyers to which it is applicable. However, the list is rather limited . . . .

Directive 98/5 ("Establishment Directive"), allows for . . . . two modes of establishment for lawyers . . . . One is establishment as a home state lawyer . . . . It is important to recognize that, pursuant to the directive, a migrant lawyer can simply establish under his or her home state title, and practice host state law without joining the host state legal profession . . . .

The other mode opened by Directive 98/5 is to transform oneself into a host state lawyer . . . . They can become local lawyers after three years of relevant legal practice in the host state, with no formal examination to complete. . . .

Directive 89/48 . . . , now replaced by a more comprehensive Directive 2005/36 ("Professional Qualifications"), allowed members of regulated professions, including lawyers, to have their qualifications recognized in another Member State in order to enable cross-border practice. Recognition is not automatic, however, and competence may be tested or entry subjected to an "adaptation period," in certain circumstances . . . .

---

91. http://ec.europa.eu/growth/tools-databases/regprof/index.cfm?action=homepage.
92. http://ir.lawnet.fordham.edu/ilj/vol33/iss6/2/.

In the case of lawyers, there is an exception that allows the host state to insist on an aptitude test . . . .

7. The Future of Global Legal Services: Perspectives on TiSA

Until January 2017, both the U.S. government and EU had been quietly promoting the virtues of two new trade initiatives that include services—the Transatlantic Trade and Investment Partnership (T-TIP[93]) and Trade in Services Agreement known as "TiSA."[94] Consider the following promotional blurb from the U.S. Trade Representative, still appearing on its website as of February, 2017. Information on the EU perspective and approach is available on the European Commission's "TiSA Positions Papers" page.[95]

U.S. Trade Representative on TiSA,[96] *Supporting U.S. Jobs Through Services Exports*

Launched in April 2013, the Trade in Services Agreement (TiSA) is a trade initiative focused exclusively on service industries. Drawing on best practices from around the world, TiSA will encompass state-of-the-art trade rules aimed at promoting fair and open trade across the full spectrum of service sectors—from telecommunications and technology to distribution and delivery services. TiSA will also take on new issues confronting the global marketplace, like restrictions on cross-border data flows that can disrupt the supply of services over the Internet—a rapidly expanding market for U.S. small businesses and entrepreneurs. And TiSA will support the development of strong, transparent, and effective regulatory policies, which are so important to enabling international commerce.

Twenty-three economies are presently participating in TiSA,[97] representing 75 percent of the world's $44 trillion services market. TiSA is part of the Obama Administration's ongoing effort to create economic opportunity for U.S. workers and businesses by expanding trade opportunities. Further opening services trade will help grow U.S. services exports and support more American jobs in a sector where we are the world's leader.

Services account for three-quarters of U.S. GDP and 4 out of 5 jobs in the United States. Thanks to our vibrant and open domestic market, the United States is highly competitive in services trade, routinely recording a surplus on the order of $200 billion per year. With every $1 billion in U.S. services exports supporting an estimated 5,900 jobs, expanding services trade globally will unlock new opportunities for Americans.

---

93. http://ir.lawnet.fordham.edu/ilj/vol33/iss6/2/.
94. https://ustr.gov/TiSA.
95. http://trade.ec.europa.eu/doclib/press/index.cfm?id=1133.
96. https://ustr.gov/TiSA.
97. https://ustr.gov/tisa/participant-list.

The New Republic magazine, in contrast, describes TiSA as "the scariest trade deal nobody's talking about,"[98] based on documents from Wikileaks[99] regarding allegedly secret negotiations.

> Though member parties insist that the agreement would simply stop discrimination against foreign service providers, the text shows that TiSA would restrict how governments can manage their public laws through an effective regulatory cap. It could also dismantle and privatize state-owned enterprises, and turn those services over to the private sector. You begin to sound like the guy hanging out in front of the local food co-op passing around leaflets about One World Government when you talk about TiSA, but it really would clear the way for further corporate domination over sovereign countries and their citizens. . . .

> First, they want to limit regulation on service sectors, whether at the national, provincial or local level. The agreement has "standstill" clauses to freeze regulations in place and prevent future rulemaking for professional licensing and qualifications or technical standards. And a companion "ratchet" clause would make any broken trade barrier irreversible.

> It may make sense to some to open service sectors up to competition. But under the agreement, governments may not be able to regulate staff to patient ratios in hospitals, or ban fracking, or tighten safety controls on airlines, or refuse accreditation to schools and universities. . . .

> Corporations would get to comment on any new regulatory attempts, and enforce this regulatory straitjacket through a dispute mechanism similar to the investor-state dispute settlement (ISDS) process in other trade agreements, where they could win money equal to "expected future profits" lost through violations of the regulatory cap.

Representatives from the International Bar Association met with TiSA negotiators in Geneva and reported on the IBA website[100] that the following proposed rules regarding legal services were under consideration:

- A general presumption that all TISA countries should commit themselves to allow cross-border supply (i.e., in the legal services context—the supply of legal services from your home country by e-mail, phone etc.) and consumption overseas (i.e., when a client from abroad comes to you) without limitations.

- The removal of foreign participation limitations, foreign equity caps and joint venture requirements on foreign businesses establishing in TISA countries.

- 'standstill' provisions which would prevent backtracking by signatories to the agreement on the access that they currently permit in service sectors.

---

98. https://newrepublic.com/article/121967/whats-really-going-trade-services-agreement.

99. https://wikileaks.org/tisa/professional/page-3.html.

100. http://www.ibanet.org/Article/NewDetail.aspx?ArticleUid=e74529cf-9784-4000-a482-1377b33fb474.

- The removal of 'economic needs tests' which allow countries to prevent new entrants to their services sectors on the grounds that they cannot prove that their presence would bring economic benefit to the host country.

- A requirement that the rules on the use of business names by foreign firms should be equivalent to those applying to domestic service suppliers.

  Part 2 of the text covers mutual recognition and will seek to facilitate mutual recognition agreements. So far the focus is very much on the role of mutual recognition as an aid to requalification for foreign professionals.

8. U.S. Government Support for Trade in Services

As with many other areas of international trade, the U.S. government provides important support for those engaged in service industries. Take a look at the following website: ITA http://trade.gov/td/services/.

Chapter 17

International Franchising

A. Overview

This chapter focuses on international franchising. Enjoying exponential growth since the 1990s, the franchise business model is now extremely common in the United States and other developed economies. The International Franchise Association's[1] "Economic Outlook Report 2016"[2] estimates that there are over 800,000 franchised businesses in the United States with a gross domestic product of 541 billion dollars. The Report also estimates that, including economic "spillover" effects from these businesses, more than 16 million jobs and $2.1 trillion in economic output is attributable to franchises. Even Hollywood, dramatizing the evolution of McDonald's in *The Founder*,[3] likes the franchise story.

Franchise operations range from enormous fast food companies like McDonald's and Yum! Brands (KFC, Pizza Hut, Taco Bell, and others) to hundreds of low investment business models for individual operators. The web site "Entrepeneur"[4] lists 37 franchise businesses marketed in the United States involving pet care alone. Among others, the site reports franchise opportunities (if this law thing doesn't work out) such as the Geese Police[5] (15 franchises offering dogs trained to chase away Canadian Geese), the Naked Cowboy[6] (yes, 13 franchise owners now play guitar in their underwear in public places for tips), and the Lice Squad[7] (focused on "de-licing" children and homes).

---

1. http://www.franchise.org/about-ifa.
2. www.franchise.org/sites/default/files/Economic%20Impact%20of%20Franchised%20
Businesses_Vol%20IV_20160915.pdf.
3. http://www.historyvshollywood.com/reelfaces/founder/.
4. https://www.entrepreneur.com/franchises/category/pet.
5. https://www.geesepoliceinc.com/about-us.html.
6. https://www.nakedcowboy.com/.
7. https://www.licesquad.com.

Photo attributed to NPR

Increasingly, franchising also forms a major component of international trade, although not currently addressed as such under any existing international trade regime. One author describes this expansion in this way:

> Franchising's explosive growth in the United States proved sufficiently groundbreaking itself. But factor in a new element that was virtually nonexistent back in 1980: the globalization of American franchise networks. The IFA [International Franchise Association] notes that over the past decade, almost half of all units established by US franchisors were situated outside of this country. Approximately 500 US franchise networks have a global presence. McDonald's, now in 119 countries (in 1980 that figure was twenty-eight), features nearly 10,000 foreign franchises; 7-Eleven, nearly 20,000; Yum! Brands, Inc. (Pizza Hut/KFC/Taco Bell/A&W/Long John Silver's) nearly 11,000, adding 1,000 new restaurants a year over the past three years; and InterContinental Hotels Group, the franchisor of Holiday Inns, Crowne Plaza, and InterContinental Hotels (among others), features over 3,650 hotels with 540,000 guest rooms in nearly one hundred countries around the world . . . .[8]

---

8. David Kaufman, *Managing Legal Issues in Franchising, Leading Lawyers on Helping Clients Master the Ownership Process and Avoid Legal Conflicts: An Overview of the Business and Law of Franchising*, 1 Aspatore 2013, 2013 WL 3773409.

A clear sign of the growing importance of franchising to international trade is that Export.gov, a US government agency designed to promote international trade opportunities for American business, now maintains a franchise assistance web site[9] and a "franchise partner service"[10] similar to its "Gold Key Program"[11] (the government's version of "Match.Com for Exporting"[12]). These federal government international trade support services are justified by the assertion that: "61 percent of [survey] respondents currently franchise or operate in international locations, and 16 percent generate between 25 percent and 30 percent of revenue from international activities. Almost three fourths of respondents said they plan to start or accelerate international ventures."

International franchising provides a particularly instructive illustration of the diverse legal issues common to international business transactions. Whether representing a client selling chicken nuggets or sophisticated IT security services, the international franchise lawyer will face a wide range of complex legal issues and tasks — licensing agreements, sale of goods, supply contracts, import/export regulations, antitrust restrictions, on-going business relationships, corporate structure, labor law, diverse foreign regulatory systems, and the preservation of intellectual property — frequently all in addition to franchise-specific laws focused on sale disclosures and protection of franchisees.

Our goals for this chapter are to a) understand franchising as a business model including its advantages and disadvantages for international investors, b) become familiar with the range of legal issues raised by international sale of franchises, including common regulatory requirements and restrictions, and c) identify and survey various contractual provisions that are typically negotiated to address core aspects of the franchise business model. The following problem provides a factual context to work with.

B. Problem Seventeen: Picking Up the Pieces

1. Facts

This problem, the last in the book, is based on an amalgam of actual small business franchise operations involving pet care. Fully endorsed by the Association of Professional Animal Waste Specialists,[13] "Doggies' Doo and Cat's Doo Too" [aka, "Ur Pet Valet"] offers a full complement of pet care services including yard waste clean-up, litterbox maintenance, walking and exercise, mobile grooming, pet sit-

---

9. http://2016.export.gov/industry/franchising/.

10. http://2016.export.gov/Ireland/servicesforu.s.companies/findingirishpartners/franchisepartnerservice/index.asp.

11. http://2016.export.gov/salesandmarketing/eg_main_018195.asp.

12. https://www.mbda.gov/news/blog/2013/03/gold-key-matchcom-exporting?page=1.

13. http://www.apaws.org/.

ting, and behavioral training. It even includes a "<u>pet masseuse</u>"[14] option for canine or feline "sports massage therapy" on the premium package service.

The business model prominently features the use of specially designed cargo vans in which pet grooming services are completed. It also offers an internet based appointment and referral system through which pet owners may, with a phone based app, beckon immediate attention from independent, but fully screened, individuals who arrive within minutes to clean yard waste, walk dogs, or take pets to veterinarian visits. The business website declares, "It's like Pet-Uber, only we're not mean." Doggies Doo currently includes 150 independently owned franchise operations in the United States. The franchise purchase includes 1–4 modified cargo van "groom mobiles," a license to use the brand name, U.S. patent protected web based applications, advertising and promotional support, training, and screening services for the independent "driver-scoopers."

After reading market reports on dramatically increased pet ownership in many newly industrializing countries, the owners of Doggies Doo are keen to explore the possibility of expanding their sale of business franchises to markets outside of the United States.

2. Assignment

Prepare a list of considerations that, exclusive of economic or market conditions, Doggies Doo should take into account as it evaluates potential expansion overseas. What types of franchise arrangements might they consider? *What are the advantages and disadvantages of different structures? What regulatory, disclosure or other legal restrictions might they encounter? How can they protect, through contract and otherwise, their business model, methods and intellectual property from encroachment or theft?*

B. Resources

1. What Is Franchising?

What is a franchise? Franchise lawyer David Kaufmann has provided this helpful description:[15]

> Franchising is a means of establishing a network of independently owned businesses that sells products or services under a common brand name. It is a system of marketing and distribution in which an independent business (the franchisee) is granted—in return for a fee—the right to market the

---

14. http://www.equissage.com/canine-home-study-program.html.
15. Kaufman, *supra*, at 1–3.

goods and services of another (the franchisor) in accordance with the franchisor's established standards and practices, and with its assistance.

The economic underpinnings of franchising center around brand names and the public's perception of quality and uniformity associated with those brand names.

. . . .

Through franchising, the economic burdens of establishing a regional, national, or international chain are shared between the franchisor and its franchisees . . . . [T]he vast majority of regional, national, and international business networks established over the past fifty years have been franchise networks.

In franchising, the various critical functions required to establish a business network — regional, national or international — are parsed between the franchisor and its franchisees. The franchisor develops the business unit model — what products or services will be sold from each unit, where the unit should be situated, how the unit should be built and equipped, how the unit should be operated, and what type of marketing or advertising will be engaged in — along with selecting and adopting for use throughout the network its all-important brand identity. It is the franchisee who, in return for the payment of a fee to the franchisor, acquires the right and assumes the obligation to build and operate a network unit under the franchisor's brand name. Unlike with company-owned units (which franchisors themselves may operate in tandem with their franchised units), the entire expense of developing, opening, and operating a franchised unit . . . and being financially liable for all aspects of that unit — is typically borne solely by the franchisee.

The U.S. Federal Trade Commission,[16] under important disclosure rules considered later in this chapter, provides a simple but broader legal definition:

16 C.F.R. Part 436.1[17]

(h) Franchise means any continuing commercial relationship or arrangement, whatever it may be called, in which the terms of the offer or contract specify, or the franchise seller promises or represents, orally or in writing, that:

(1) The franchisee will obtain the right to operate a business that is identified or associated with the franchisor's trademark, or to offer, sell, or distribute goods, services, or commodities that are identified or associated with the franchisor's trademark;

---

16. https://www.ftc.gov/.

17. https://www.ecfr.gov/cgi-bin/text-idx?SID=2123d4a32a127d5eb3e05e068e8970c9&mc=true&node=sp16.1.436.a&rgn=div6.

(2) The franchisor will exert or has authority to exert a significant degree of control over the franchisee's method of operation, or provide significant assistance in the franchisee's method of operation; and

(3) As a condition of obtaining or commencing operation of the franchise, the franchisee makes a required payment or commits to make a required payment to the franchisor or its affiliate.[18]

What then are the essential elements that characterize the typical franchise model? First, and most centrally, there is a license to utilize the trademarked brand, know-how, methods and systems of the franchisor (brand/IP element). Second, franchising contemplates a continuing business relationship between the independently owned franchise and the franchisor which includes both on-going assistance and the right of the franchisor to control aspects of the franchise essential to the brand and business model (operations element). Third, the franchisee and franchisor are independent business entities with the franchisee being responsible for the capital investment, economic risks, liabilities and daily operations of the franchised business (business relationship element). Fourth, all of the above, as well as the initial purchase of the franchise and on-going royalties, are controlled by a franchise agreement, largely dictated by the franchisor (contractual rights and obligations element). All of these essential characteristics of a franchise have some influence on how the franchise network will be structured, particularly in the international context.

2. Franchise Types, Forms & Business Models

a. Generally

There are several distinct franchise forms and structures common in the United States and internationally. A more traditional and limited form involves "product franchising," which focuses on the sale and distribution of the franchisor's products rather than a branded service or method of doing business (e.g., product distribution franchises such as "Shell" gasoline stations, and "Ford" dealerships). A now more

---

18. The European Union "Block Exemption Regulation," which involves potential anti-competitive aspects of franchising, provides a more detailed and technical definition of "franchise" and "franchise agreement" now commonly used in the European Union:

... (a) "franchise" means a package of industrial or intellectual property rights relating to trademarks, trade names, shop signs, utility models, designs, copyrights, know-how or patents, to be exploited for the resale of goods or the provision of services to end users;

(b) "franchise agreement" means an agreement whereby one undertaking, the franchisor, grants the other, the franchisee, in exchange for direct or indirect financial consideration, the right to exploit a franchise for the purposes of marketing specified goods and/or services; it includes at least obligations relating to:

—the use of a common name or shop sign and a uniform presentation of contract premises and/or means of transport,

—the communication by the franchisor to the franchisee of know-how,

—the continuing provision by the franchisor to the franchisee of commercial or technical assistance during the life of the agreement [...]

common variety of franchising, almost synonymous with the term, focuses on a "business format" that includes uniform methods, services, customer practices and products. Perhaps the most famous business format franchise of them all is McDonald's. According to Business Insider,[19] a McDonald's franchisee pays an initial franchise fee of $45,000, must purchase an existing or new restaurant facility (investment averaging between $955,708 and $2.3 million), pay 8–12% of sales as rent, and ongoing royalties of 4% of gross sales—in exchange for use of the brand and all that comes with it, including support and training. For McDonald's franchisees, this might include attendance at Hamburger University,[20] described this way at a McDonald's corporate website:

> Today, Hamburger University is situated on an 80 acres campus with 19 full-time resident instructors. The facility comprises 13 teaching rooms, a 300 seat auditorium, 12 interactive education team rooms, and 3 kitchen labs. Hamburger University interpreters can provide simultaneous interpretation, and the faculty has the ability to teach in 28 different languages.

Hamburger University[21]

The franchisee operates under the franchise brand as an independent business (neither an agent, nor employee of the franchisor) with all that typically entails, owning or leasing physical space, maintaining a labor force, financing, accounting and cost management. While independently owned and operated, franchises must nevertheless comply with a host of requirements that preserve the value of the brand as a part of their contractual agreements. To varying degrees depending on the franchise arrangement, many mundane aspects of the business, ranging from physical

---

19. http://www.businessinsider.com/what-it-costs-to-open-a-mcdonalds-2014-11.

20. mcdonalds.wikia.com/wiki/Hamburger_University.

21. http://mcdonalds.wikia.com/wiki/Hamburger_University; https://creativecommons.org/licenses/by-sa/3.0/.

layout and signage, to the temperature of coffee, may be controlled by the franchisor, which also frequently provides various types of assistance and marketing. Consider again the approach of McDonald's, whose franchise agreement provides:

> The McDonald's System is a comprehensive restaurant system for the retailing of a limited menu of uniform and quality food products, emphasizing prompt and courteous service in a clean, wholesome atmosphere .... The foundation of the McDonald's System and *the essence of this License is adherence by Licensee to standards and policies of Licensor providing for the uniform operation of all McDonald's restaurants ... including, but not limited to, serving only designated food and beverage products; the use of only prescribed equipment and building layout and designs; strict adherence to designated food and beverage specifications and to Licensor's prescribed standards of Quality, Service, and Cleanliness ....*[22]

These basic features of franchising reveal some of the model's fundamental advantages and disadvantages. Since the franchisee invests its own capital and is responsible for the entire expense of opening and operating the franchise, the franchisor is able to expand its business operations without such burdens, engaging fewer costs and economic risks while significantly expanding the distribution of its brand into new markets. Franchising, in one sense, is essentially a relatively low cost method of expanding the delivery of products and services without the usual risks associated with direct ownership and management of retail distribution outlets. Considering the enormous costs and risks of expansion into foreign markets through direct operations, these benefits are particularly pronounced with international franchising. Local ownership of the foreign franchise unit also comes with the critical benefits of local knowledge of market conditions, legal requirements, and culturally sensitive practices. However, since the franchise units are independently owned and operated, the franchisor correspondingly loses some degree of control, creates certain risks for the brand (if things go badly) and enjoys far less income than would be possible through its own direct operations. The franchisee also enjoys significant advantages from the arrangement, gaining the economic value of the established brand, a proven business model and methods, and the support, marketing, customer base and business sophistication of the larger enterprise. The franchisee, however, loses some independence and control over his investment (from rules and restrictions imposed to protect the brand) and bears the ultimate risk of termination.

b. Franchise Network Structures and Organization — The International Context

There are, of course, many ways to structure the organization of a franchise network. The most common include (1) direct, single unit franchising — franchisor directly sells and manages the franchise units (including through a foreign branch or corporate subsidiary); (2) area representative franchising — the franchisor operates

---

22. Quoted in *Husain v. McDonald's Corp.*, 205 Cal. App. 4th 860, 869; 140 Cal. Rptr. 3d 370 (2012).

through an area representative who sells and manages franchise units on the franchisor's behalf; (3) multiple unit, area development franchising—the franchisor contracts with a franchisee/developer who is granted the right to operate multiple franchise units within a defined geographic area and time period, under direct control of the franchisor; (4) master franchising (or "regional sub-franchising")—the franchisor grants another party, the "sub-franchisor," the exclusive right to sell and operate franchises in a defined geographic region, in essence becoming the franchisor in that area; and (5) joint venture franchising—the franchiser joins forces with another entity to sell and operate a franchise network.

The following excerpt from a speech by a franchise expert at <u>UNIDROIT</u>[23] discusses some of the advantages and disadvantages of these approaches in the context of international franchising.

Address by Lena Peters, Research Officer

Unidroit, February 17–18, 1995[24]

Direct franchising

In direct franchising it is the franchisor itself which grants franchises to individual franchisees in the foreign country. In this case there is an international contract to which the franchisor and the franchisee are parties.

The main problems associated with this type of franchising at international level are the difficulty of franchisors to control the performance of the franchisees as these are located in another country which is often at a great distance, and the difficulty for franchisors to provide franchisees with the assistance they need not only before they open the outlet (e.g. site selection and the feasibility studies which precede this selection, contacts with local suppliers, etc.), but also for the whole duration of the contract.

The question of intellectual and industrial property rights in the foreign country needs to be considered. Franchisors should when they are contemplating expanding their activities abroad examine the possibility of registering their trademarks in the country or countries they are considering entering even several years in advance, as they need to protect their trademarks from speculators: it does happen that speculators register foreign trademarks and then require high sums as payment from the real owners of those trademarks when the latter later try to enter the country.

. . . .

It should be observed that direct franchising is not used extensively internationally.

---

23. http://www.unidroit.org/about-unidroit/overview.

24. ¶ 7313 Unidroit Official Surveys Global Franchising, Describes Organization's Franchising Study, 2015 CCH INCORPORATED, A Wolters Kluwer business. All rights reserved.

Subsidiary or branch office

Franchising through a subsidiary or through a branch office are two methods which are often treated together, although there are differences which derive from the fact that a subsidiary, albeit controlled by the franchisor, is a separate legal entity whereas a branch is not. Whether the franchisor decides to set up a branch office or a subsidiary will often depend upon tax and general management considerations. Whatever the differences, both the subsidiary and the branch office act as franchisor for the purpose of granting franchises. An advantage of this approach is that the franchisor is present in the foreign country as a corporate body. The contract will in this case be a domestic contract subject to the local legislation.

The problems associated with this method of franchising internationally are similar to those associated with direct franchising. In addition the franchisor will have to rely on local personnel to a very great extent, also to avoid having to transfer too many of the staff members employed in its home country to the foreign subsidiary. The franchisor will not be able to avoid sending staff from its own company, as it is necessary when starting a business to have people in place that know the business and that can help solve any problems that might arise. In fact, the franchisor is likely to have to send more people than first anticipated. This situation involves a series of practical problems, such as the obtaining of work and residence permits for those members of staff who are foreigners. It should also be noted that these employees will be subject to the local labour laws.

Area Development Agreements

Area development agreements traditionally involve an arrangement whereby the developer is given the right to open a multiple number of outlets to a predetermined schedule and within a given area, in which case there will be a unit franchise agreement between the franchisor and the area developer for every outlet, or unit, that the developer opens. . . .

Area development agreements have in the past been used mostly in domestic franchising, but are now being used increasingly also in international franchising.

. . . .

In an arrangement such as a development agreement the developer will need to have available, or to be able to generate, substantial financial resources so as to be able to open the required number of outlets. A consequence of this is that if the franchisor at a later stage wishes to take over this network it will be very expensive for it to do so. It is therefore essential that the right person is chosen as developer and that good relations are established between the developer and the franchisor.

Master Franchise Agreements

The master franchise agreement is the most common type of agreement in international franchising. In master franchise agreements the franchisor grants a person in another country, the sub-franchisor, the exclusive right within a certain territory (such as a country) to open franchise outlets itself and/or to grant franchises to sub-franchisees. In other words, the sub-franchisor acts as franchisor in the foreign country.

In this case there are two agreements involved: an international agreement between the franchisor and the sub-franchisor (the master franchise agreement), and a national franchise agreement between the sub-franchisor and each of the sub-franchisees (the sub-franchise agreements). There is no direct relationship between the franchisor and the sub-franchisees. The franchisor transmits all its rights and duties to the sub-franchisor, who will be in charge of the enforcement of the sub-franchise agreements and of the general development and working of the network in that country. If a sub-franchisee does not fulfil its obligations it is the duty of the sub-franchisor to intervene, the franchisor will normally not be able to do so. All the franchisor will be able to do is to sue the sub-franchisor for breach if it did not fulfil its obligation to enforce the sub-franchise agreements as laid down in the master franchise agreement.

The advantages of a system such as this include that the local sub-franchisor will be familiar with the habits, tastes, culture and laws of its country, and that it will know its way about the local bureaucracy and will therefore know where to turn for all the necessary permits.

The disadvantages instead include that the financial return of the franchisor will be reduced by the amount due to the sub-franchisor, and that the franchisor will have to rely on the sub-franchisor to control the performance of the sub-franchisees, as the franchisor has no direct relationship with them. Clearly, this is true also in reverse, in that the sub-franchisees will have to rely on the sub-franchisor for anything which concerns the franchise and will not be able to apply directly to the franchisor.

There are a number of issues which may be problematic in master franchise arrangements. Perhaps the most problematic of all are the consequences of the agreement coming to an end. A distinction should here be made between the situation where the agreement expires and where it is terminated for breach of the sub-franchisor.

Master franchise agreements are typically concluded for a very long term. It is very expensive to set up an international network and it would be even more expensive to withdraw from it. Consequently contracts are concluded for twenty years or more, renewable, and unless the enterprise is a complete failure the contract will normally be renewed. If, however, despite this the contract were to end, a whole series of problems could ensue, including the fate of the sub-franchise agreements. . . .

Often contracts will provide for the assignment of the rights under the master franchise agreement to the franchisor, or for an option on the part of the franchisor to take over the rights and duties of the sub-franchisor with respect to the sub-franchisees.

. . . .

As indicated above, franchise formulas often have to be adapted when they are transplanted into another country, and unless the countries are culturally, and perhaps geographically, close to each other, franchisors may have problems bridging the cultural gap between the two countries, which involves differences in language, habits, tastes and laws. This holds true also for master franchise arrangements.

Joint ventures

In the case of joint ventures the franchisor and a local partner create a joint venture; this joint venture then enters into a master franchise agreement with the franchisor, and proceeds to open franchise outlets and to grant sub-franchises just as a normal sub-franchisor would do.

An arrangement such as this will have to consider legislation on joint ventures in addition to all the other legislation which needs to be taken into account.

To the possible areas where problems might arise which were described above must be added the fact that the double link may create conflicts of interest for the franchisor.

To the advantages of an arrangement such as this must be included that it could be one way of solving the problem of financing franchise operations in countries where financial means are scarce.

Ms. Peters is also one of the primary authors of a "Guide to Master Franchise Agreements"[25] published by UNIDROIT. The guide is an excellent resource—detailed and comprehensive. Another useful, but less comprehensive guide, is published by WIPO.[26]

In light of these tips concerning franchise contracting (extended to operating manuals and other documentation), what essential terms would you counsel Doggies Doo to include in their franchise agreements?

Other helpful and practical advice regarding a host of issue involving international franchising, including the advantages and disadvantages of various franchise structures, can be found at the ABA Forum on Franchising[27] (which includes an "International Division").

---

25. www.unidroit.org/english/guides/2007franchising/franchising2007-guide-2nd-e.pdf.
26. ftp://ftp.wipo.int/pub/library/ebooks/wipopublications/wipo_pub_480(e).pdf.
27. https://www.americanbar.org/groups/franchising.html.

3. Regulation of Franchising

Perhaps not surprisingly, as the sale of franchised operations has expanded, particularly in and from the United States, opportunities for fraud, deception, opportunism and abusive business practices have also grown. For recent varieties of abuse, *see Franchise Fraud: Wake Up and Smell the Fine Print*,[28] Mother Jones, 2009; *True Story, Quiznos Lawsuits Start with a Bang, Unfold Like a Crime Novel*,[29] Franchise Times, 2013; and generally "The Unhappy Franchisee."[30] The Federal Government and many states have responded by enacting laws or regulations specifically focused on franchising. A number of other countries have followed suit. In general, there are three common types of franchise regulations—those simply requiring presale disclosures, those expanding upon disclosures to include registration and review by government authorities, and those focused upon protecting franchisees in their on-going business relationship with the franchisor.

a. Federal Law: FTC Franchise Disclosures Rule

The U.S. federal government's approach rests solely upon pre-sale disclosures, which are required under the Federal Trade Commission's so-called "Franchise Rule." Under this regulation, most franchisors must provide a "Franchise Disclosure Document"[31] (FDD) at least 14 days prior to any payment or binding agreement. According to the FTC:

> The Franchise Rule gives prospective purchasers of franchises the material information they need in order to weigh the risks and benefits of such an investment. The Rule requires franchisors to provide all potential franchi-

---

28. http://www.motherjones.com/politics/2009/02/franchise-fraud-wake-and-smell-fine-print.

29. http://www.franchisetimes.com/October-2013/True-Story/.

30. http://www.unhappyfranchisee.com/.

31. Since a number of states also require disclosures, the FTC for some time has accepted state disclosure guidelines developed by the North American Securities Administrators Association called the Uniform Franchise Offering Circular (UFOC). In 2008, the FTC amended its disclosure rule, separating out business opportunity regulation, and now requires the more extensive FDD. According to the FTC:

> The Rule amendments bring the FTC's Rule into much closer alignment with state franchise disclosure laws, which are based upon the UFOC Guidelines, developed and administered by the North American Securities Administrators Association ("NASAA"). Although the amended Rule closely tracks the UFOC Guidelines, in some instances it requires more extensive disclosures—mostly with respect to certain aspects of the franchisee-franchisor relationship. For example, the amended Rule requires more extensive disclosures on: lawsuits the franchisor has filed against franchisees; the franchisor's use of so-called "confidentiality clauses" in lawsuit settlements; a warning when there is no exclusive territory; an explanation of what the term "renewal" means for each franchise system; and trademark-specific franchisee associations. In a few instances, the amended Rule requires less than the UFOC guidelines—for example, it does not require disclosure of so-called "risk factors," franchise broker information, or extensive information about every component of any computer system that a franchisee must purchase.

https://www.ftc.gov/news-events/press-releases/2007/01/ftc-issues-updated-franchise-rule.

sees with a disclosure document containing 23 specific items of information about the offered franchise, its officers, and other franchisees.

The Agency does not, however, require registration or filing of disclosures. Nor does it review or otherwise monitor disclosure documents or any resulting franchise relationship. Only the FTC may seek remedies for violations of the disclosure rules (as a violation of Section 5 of the Federal Trade Commission Act). There is no private right of action, and the disclosure requirements do not apply to franchises sold outside of U.S. territories.[32] The text of the FTC Franchise Rule may be found in 16 C.F.R. § 436.2   Obligation to furnish documents.[33] The required contents of a FTC compliant disclosure are set out at 16 C.F.R. Subpart C — Contents of a Disclosure Document.[34]

Two ABA commentators conveniently provided the following abbreviated summary of disclosure topics covered by the rule:[35]

> *FDD Disclosure Format.* Franchisors must present information on 23 different disclosure topics in their FDDs: the franchisor and its parents, predecessors, and affiliates; the business experience of its principal officers, directors, and managers; litigation; bankruptcy; initial fees that the franchisee must pay; other fees; an estimate of the franchisee's initial investment;

---

32. Issues sometimes arise over whether a particular business arrangement, perhaps designated as a distributorship, dealership or license, qualifies as a franchise. According to the FTC's Franchise Rule Compliance Guide: this amended FTC disclosure rule applies whenever a "commercial business arrangement," whether nominated a franchise, distributorship or otherwise, includes three elements: "(1) promise to provide a trademark or other commercial symbol; (2) promise to exercise significant control or provide significant assistance in the operation of the business; and (3) require a minimum payment of at least $500 during the first six months of operations." The amended rule "covers relationships that are represented either orally or in writing as having the characteristics specified in the amended Rule's definition of 'franchise,' regardless of whether the representations are, in fact, true or can be fulfilled." The Compliance Guide adds: "Business Opportunities: Disclosure requirements and prohibitions pertaining to business opportunities are now set forth in a separate Rule — 16 C.F.R. Part 437. At present, Part 437 is substantively identical to the disclosure requirements and prohibitions set forth in the original Franchise Rule. The Commission, however, is contemplating amending Part 437, and there is an ongoing rulemaking on that issue." FTC Franchise Rule Compliance Guide, page 6, https://www.ftc.gov/tips-advice/business-center/guidance /franchise-rule-compliance-guide. The Business Opportunity Rule is found at: 16 C.F.R. Part 437. Regarding the potential overlap with distribution arrangements *See* Andres Jaglom, *The Broad Scope of the Franchise Laws: Traps for the Distribution Contract Drafter*, SV045 ALI-CLE 199, American Law Institute Continuing Legal Education, ALI-CLE Course Materials, June 18-20, 2014, http://www.thsh.com/Publications/Other-Publications/The-Broad-Scope-of-Franchise-Laws -Traps-for-the-.aspx.

33. https://www.ecfr.gov/cgi-bin/text-idx?SID=2123d4a32a127d5eb3e05e068e8970c9&mc =true&node=sp16.1.436.b&rgn=div6.

34. https://www.ecfr.gov/cgi-bin/text-idx?SID=2123d4a32a127d5eb3e05e068e8970c9&mc =true&node=se16.1.436_15&rgn=div8.

35. Susan A. Grueneberg & Jonathan C. Solish, *Franchising 101: Key Issues in the Law of Franchising*, ABA Business Law Today (2010), https://www.americanbar.org/publications/blt/2010/03/01_solish. html.

restrictions that the franchisor imposes on products and services; the franchisee's obligations during the relationship; financing that might be available through the franchisor; the franchisor's obligations to provide assistance and information about advertising, computer systems, and training; the territorial rights that the franchisee will receive; the franchisor's trademarks; its patents, copyrights, and proprietary information; the franchisee's obligation to participate in the actual operation of the franchise business; restrictions on what the franchisee may sell; information about renewal, termination, transfer, and dispute resolution; any public figures who endorse the franchise; optional financial performance representations; information about outlets and franchisees; the franchisor's financial statements; a list of contracts required of the franchisee; and a receipt form.

A more detailed summary of required disclosures can be found on the FTC website under A Consumer's Guide to Buying a Franchise.[36] Comprehensive guidance can be found in the FTC's Franchise Rule Compliance Guide.[37]

b. State Regulation of Franchise Sales

The FTC Franchise Rule does not preempt state franchise laws, which are often more extensive and may involve both registration requirements and regulation of the on-going franchise relationship. The following excerpt, again from David Kaufman, summarizes common state approaches.[38]

> So today there are three distinct bodies of law governing franchising in the United States: federal and state franchise registration/disclosure laws, state franchise relationship laws, and federal and state business opportunity laws.
>
> The federal government and fifteen states have laws, rules, or regulations requiring franchisors—prior to offering or selling a franchise—to prepare and disseminate to prospective franchisees a prospectus-type disclosure document containing all information necessary for such prospects to make informed investment decisions.
>
> . . . Under eleven of the fifteen state franchise registration/disclosure statutes, a franchisor must first register itself and its franchise disclosure document, a daunting task for the uninitiated, before any franchise advertising appears, any franchise offers are made, or any franchise sale is effected. . . .
>
> *State Franchise Relationship Laws*
>
> Twenty states, the US Virgin Islands, and Puerto Rico have enacted what are commonly referred to as franchise "relationship" laws.

---

36. https://www.ftc.gov/tips-advice/business-center/guidance/consumers-guide-buying-franchise.
37. https://www.ftc.gov/tips-advice/business-center/guidance/franchise-rule-compliance-guide.
38. David Kaufman, *supra*.

The reason for this nomenclature is simple. These statutes typically address the substance of the franchisor-franchisee relationship by governing when and under what circumstances a franchisor may terminate a franchise agreement or refuse to renew a franchise, the minimum advance notice of franchise termination or expiration that must be given to franchisees, and, in some (but not all) relationship laws, certain other aspects of the franchisor-franchisee relationship are addressed, such as fair dealing, discriminatory treatment, market protection, and "encroachment."

Another franchise lawyer, Philip Zeidman, provides the following more detailed description of state "franchise relationship" laws.

> . . . .
>
> [W]hile there is no "relationship" regulation at the federal level, an even larger number of states regulate this relationship between the parties. A typical provision of state law prohibits termination of the relationship, without regard to what the contract provides, except for "good cause," a standard that varies in different states. Other typical "relationship" provisions prohibit a refusal to renew the relationship or a refusal to permit the dealership or distributorship to be transferred to others or impose some occasionally vague requirements, such as the obligation to treat the buyer "fairly."
>
> Other aspects of the state relationship laws worth noting: They often require minimum standards of notice. Some prohibit discrimination among franchises. Some also address encroaching on a franchisee's territory or interfering with association among franchisees. They generally apply to all franchisees, regardless of industry, and the definition of "franchise" may be broader than that in the state's disclosure law.
>
> . . . State registration or disclosure laws do provide a private right of action for franchisees. These laws also authorize the state administrator directly, or through the state attorney general, to bring an action on behalf of the people of the state to enjoin an unlawful act or practice or to enforce compliance with the franchise laws.
>
> . . . The individual "relationship" state statutes must be examined with care to identify the precise remedies available to an injured franchisee. One of the most significant is the obligation of repurchase, based typically on compensation to the franchisee for certain assets of the franchised business upon termination or non-renewal without good cause . . . .[39]

---

39. Philip Zeidman, *With the Best of Intentions: Observations on the International Regulation of Franchising*, 19 Stan. J.L., Bus. & Fin. 237 (2014), https://www.questia.com/library/journal/1P3-354774330l/with-the-best-of-intentions-observations-on-the-international.

c. Franchise Regulation in Foreign Nations

Although the FTC Rule does not apply to U.S. franchises sold outside of U.S. territory, the spread of franchising internationally has prompted a number of countries to enact rules and regulations governing both the franchise sale and the ongoing franchise relationship.[40] The International Franchise Association (IFA) website maintains a list of countries that regulate franchises and links to summaries published by the organization, Getting the Deal Through.[41] It also provides a handy visual aid in the form of a map[42] of countries with either disclosure laws, relationship laws or both.

The following brief excerpts from several practice oriented publications survey a variety of specific legal issues raised by international franchising (an excellent source of such material is the ABA Forum on Franchising [43]). The authors not only describe examples of many of the regulatory issues an international franchise sale might encounter, but also provide useful insights regarding contractual objectives and concerns. As you read, start compiling a list of issues that ought to be addressed in franchise agreements.

i. Mark Abell, The Regulation of International Franchising,[44] Who's Who Legal, ABA Section of International Law, November 2010

Twenty-nine different nations have franchise-specific laws, and the lack of any common approach . . . . In addition, general commercial law can have a substantial impact on franchising.

Anti-trust regulations are aimed at preventing restraint of trade and generally focus upon classical competition law issues such as tying, full line forcing, retail price maintenance, exclusivity and so on . . . .

Pure franchise regulations focus upon areas of potential abuse in franchising, namely pre-contractual disclosure and the in-term relationship between the franchisor and its franchisees . . . .

A number of themes can be identified:

Piloting concepts. . . . [P]rohibiting franchising by a franchisor that has not piloted the operation. In China, franchisors are required to establish and operate two company-owned units for more than one year before granting franchises to third parties . . . .

Cooling-off period . . . . [i]n addition to the period between service of the disclosure document and closing, a further period during which the franchisee can withdraw is appropriate. Malaysia, Mexico and Taiwan require a cooling-off period . . . during which the franchisee can withdraw from the relationship without penalty . . . .

---

40. In 2002, UNIDROIT (Institute for the Unification of Private Law) publicized a model disclosure law similar to the FTC Franchise Rule. For an overview of the UNIDROIT approach *see* Lena Peters, *The UNIDROIT Model Franchise Disclosure Law: An International Instrument Vis-à-vis National Legislation*, 39 UCC L.J. 3, Winter 2007.

41. https://gettingthedealthrough.com/area/14/franchise/.

42. http://www.franchise.org/international-franchising-laws.

43. https://www.americanbar.org/groups/franchising.html.

44. http://whoswholegal.com/news/features/article/28705/regulation-international-franchising.

A general duty of good faith

The Canadian provinces, China, Korea and Malaysia impose a duty of good faith on both the franchisor and the franchisee, which impacts upon what the franchisor is permitted to do during the relationship . . . .

Registration requirements

Some jurisdictions require the franchisor to register relevant details and the documentation with a government agency . . . .

Compulsory contents of franchise agreements

A number of countries insist that a franchise agreement should contain certain standard clauses.

Non-Franchise Specific Legislation

Franchising is, of course, also regulated by general commercial law. The laws that are of most relevance tend to be good faith, anti-trust, misrepresentation, breach of contract, employment law, commercial agency law, consumer law and unfair competition law . . . .

ii. Other Limitations on International Franchising

Ward, Plave & Nowak, _Unique and Often Overlooked Issues and Limitations on Doing Business in International Franchising_

37th Annual Forum on Franchising[45]

In Indonesia, the Ministry of Industry regulates the places at which some franchised units may be operated (whether in a traditional market or in a modern shopping mall) . . . [and] Foreign entities may not carry out retail businesses, except through large scale hypermarket businesses . . . .

Unique Pre-contract Disclosure Obligations . . .

Market Study

. . . [T]here are some countries that take the additional step of requiring the franchisor to provide a market study as part of its disclosure . . . .

Anticipated Revenue

. . . Some countries do, unfortunately, require franchisors to confront this task. One example of this is Malaysia, which requires a "financial forecast for three years" to be included in the franchise disclosure document. . . .

Local Industry Development Considerations

. . . In Nigeria, the NOTAP Act prohibits the registration of any agreement for technology transfer where there is an obligation to acquire equipment, tools, parts

---

45. www.americanbar.org/content/dam/aba/administrative/franchising/materials2014/w22 .pdf. Available among a host of other instructional materials on franchising at ABA Forum on Franchising, Materials.

or raw materials exclusively from the transferor (in this case the franchisor) or any other person or given source . . . .

Specifying suppliers

. . . In Australia, requiring a franchisee to purchase only from a specified third party supplier, or a from a list of specified suppliers is prohibited, unless . . . .

Restricting customers

For certain franchise systems, franchisors may try to limit a franchisee's ability to sell goods or render services only to a defined territory or to particular types of customers . . . . However, certain countries prohibit or limit this behavior . . . . The Russian Civil Code bans franchise agreement clauses that would limit a franchisee's ability to sell goods or render services to customers outside of the protected territory.

Continuous Disclosure Obligations

U.S. franchisors . . . may be unaware of an obligation, imposed in certain countries, to provide ongoing disclosure post execution of the franchise agreement . . . .

C. Contracting Issues in the Franchise Relationship

Franchise arrangements are complex and may require a number of carefully drafted documents. At the heart of such arrangements is a franchise agreement and license under which the franchisor's intellectual and industrial property, know-how, business methods, and operational system is protected, controlled and granted to the franchisee. Ongoing operational requirements, central to protection of the franchise and brand (system compliance), are often set out in a detailed Operations Manual which the franchisee is contractually obligated to follow. While it is well beyond the scope of this chapter to attempt a detailed review of such contractual provisions, it is instructive to identify the range of issues that should be addressed in the documents. Excerpts in the previous section on legal regulation of international franchising provide a good starting point. You might also review a sample agreement[46] or two[47] including a McDonald's Master Franchise Agreement.[48] (A few other samples can be found here.[49]) The excerpts below provide additional practical insights regarding franchise contracting. *Use these materials and what you have learned so far to make a list of the most important issues that you think ought to be addressed in a franchise agreement for Doggies Doo.*

---

46. https://www.google.com/url?sa=t&rct=j&q=&esrc=s&source=web&cd=8&ved=0CGkQ
FjAHahUKEwj0pYOFwNnIAhVT1GMKHcqiDqQ&url=https%3A%2F%2Fsiegler.files.wordpress
.com%2F2008%2F03%2Fsample-franchise-agreement.doc&usg=AFQjCNE7lbGhdXw9Wgz46p
HGj4GOOmkUIQ&sig2=4RzPIpZ_ktCVPzcW3Z1wIQ&cad=rja.

47. http://contracts.onecle.com/type/79.shtml.

48. https://www.sec.gov/Archives/edgar/data/1508478/000119312511077213/dex101.htm.

49. http://www.freefranchisedocs.com/.

1. Managing Issues in the Franchise Agreement

Alan Greenfield, *The Basics of Franchising and Helpful Tips for Those New to Franchising,*

1 Aspatore 2013, *available at* 2013 WL 3773415 (2013)

What Are Essential Elements of the Franchise Agreement from a Franchisor's Perspective?

Franchise companies have increasingly become an attractive investment for private equity companies or other multi-system owners. Consequently, franchise agreements should anticipate a potential acquisition by a third party that may also own a competing franchise system, or a potential acquisition by the franchise company of a competing system. Also, as previously noted, franchise agreements should allow the franchisor to make modifications to its system and trademarks to continue to develop (or modernize) the system and adapt to trends in the market.

Protecting the brand is imperative, so in preparing its franchise agreement, a franchise company should carefully consider which defaults may be cured by the franchisee and which defaults rise to a level where immediate termination of the franchise agreement without an opportunity to cure is appropriate.

Carefully drafted non-competition and non-solicitation covenants are important to help ensure the covenants' enforceability and should be reviewed regularly to address any changes in the law.

Finally, franchisees often form a business entity for purposes of entering into the franchise agreement. It is also common for franchisees to sign the franchise agreement in their individual capacity and form a business entity at a later point in time. Franchise agreements should address both situations and (unless perhaps the franchisee entity is a publicly traded entity) should require the franchisee owner(s) to sign a personal guaranty whenever a business entity is utilized.

. . . .

If a franchise company is considering international expansion, it is also important for the company to register its marks in the foreign jurisdictions to protect its brand in those countries . . . .

2. Some Essential Elements of the Franchise Agreement

Address by Lena Peters, Research Officer, Unidroit, February 17–18, 1995[50]

The basic elements of a franchise are therefore that:

— the franchisee in exchange undertakes to follow the method elaborated by the franchisor and to pay an entrance fee and/or royalties . . . .

---

50. ¶ 7313 Unidroit Official Surveys Global Franchising, Describes Organization's Franchising Study, 2015 CCH INCORPORATED, A Wolters Kluwer business.

— the franchisor retains rights of control over the performance of the franchisee; and

— the franchisor undertakes to provide the franchisee with training and on-going assistance.

Examples of such arrangements or undertakings are:

— an undertaking by the franchisor not to grant other franchises or itself to engage in the franchised business within a certain specified area . . . ("territorial exclusivity");

— an obligation on the part of the franchisee to sell only the products of the franchisor ("product exclusivity");

— an obligation on the part of the franchisee to buy the products it sells or uses in the franchise business only from the franchisor or from suppliers approved and/or indicated by the franchisor; . . .

. . . Restrictive covenants. . . . The franchisee will in this case be prevented from engaging in an activity competing with that of the franchise . . . .

. . . As can be seen from the above, there are a number of issues which should be considered as regards franchise agreements.

These include:

— the licensing of intellectual and industrial property;

— the ownership of improvements to the intellectual/industrial property and to the know-how . . . ;

— questions arising out of leasing arrangements, particularly when the franchisee leases equipment and/or premises from the franchisor . . . ;

— the investments to be made and the financing of the franchise outlet;

— product liability and the general liability of the parties to the franchise agreement for acts or omissions of the other party and in connection therewith the question of insurance;

— the possibility of resolving disputes through a mediation procedure before having recourse to either a court or arbitration;

— the consequences of the termination of the agreement.

In light of these tips concerning franchise contracting (extended to operating manuals and other documentation), what essential terms would you counsel Doggies Doo to include in their franchise agreements?

Index